CROCHET

JACKETS, WRAPS & MORE™

EDITED BY
CAROL ALEXANDER

HOUSE of
WHITE
BIRCHES
PUBLISHERS
SINCE 1947

JACKETS, WRAPS & MORE™

Copyright © 2007 DRG, 306 East Parr Road, Berne, IN 46711. All rights reserved. This publication may not be reproduced in part or in whole without written permission from the publisher.

EDITOR Carol Alexander
ART DIRECTOR Brad Snow
PUBLISHING SERVICES DIRECTOR Brenda Gallmeyer

ASSOCIATE EDITORS Kristine M. Frye, Lisa M. Fosnaugh
ASSISTANT ART DIRECTOR Nick Pierce
COPY SUPERVISOR Michelle Beck
COPY EDITORS Nicki Lehman, Mary O'Donnell, Susanna Tobias
TECHNICAL EDITOR Agnes Russell

GRAPHIC ARTS SUPERVISOR Ronda Bechinski
GRAPHIC ARTISTS Jessi Butler, Minette Collins Smith
PRODUCTION ASSISTANTS Marj Morgan, Judy Neuenschwander

PHOTOGRAPHY Tammy Christian, Don Clark, Matthew Owen, Jackie Schaffel
PHOTO STYLISTS Tammy Smith, Tammy Steiner

PUBLISHING DIRECTOR David McKee
BOOK MARKETING DIRECTOR Dwight Seward

Printed in China
First Printing 2007

Library of Congress Control Number: 2007921288
Hardcover ISBN: 978-1-59217-153-8
Softcover ISBN: 978-1-59217-190-3

Every effort has been made to ensure the accuracy and completeness of the instructions in this book. However, we cannot be responsible for human error or for the results when using materials other than those specified in the instructions, or for variations in individual work.

1 2 3 4 5 6 7 8 9

DRGbooks.com

A Note From the Editor

Today's fashionable woman wants it all when it comes to style and versatility in her wardrobe.

From classic, traditional pieces to chic, contemporary designs, the variety of fashions and accessories in *Jackets, Wraps & More* will create a look that's just right for any occasion to go from the boardwalk or bistro to the boardroom or ballet in perfect style.

Whether your taste caters to bold, colorful expression or sleek, sophisticated flair, our impressive array of jackets, wraps, tops, hats, purses, scarves and more will take you from sporty and playful to dazzling and elegant.

This enticing collection includes styles for women of all ages and features a tantalizing mix of yarns and threads in a delicious blend of colors, textures and weights.

With these sensational wardrobe essentials, more is never too much!

Warm regards,

Carol Alexander

CONTENTS

JACKETS 6

Cut-Away Cardi	8
Very Victorian	12
Loopy Jacket	16
Tabbard Jacket	20
Granny Square Dress & Jacket	24
Shawl-Collared Cardigan	30
Cropped Bomber Jacket	34
Ruby Goes to Town	38
Perfect in Plum Coat	40
Confetti Cover-Up	42

WRAPS 50

Gold Nugget Cocktail Cover-Up	52
Enchanted Evening	54
Butterflies & Roses Filet Shawl	56
Sunset Poncho	60
Cozy Café Au Lait Shrug	62
Ruffled Shoulder Wrap	64
Triangles Shawl	67
Peekaboo Poncho	70
Cool Class Dress & Shoulder Cover	72
Lilac Shawl	76

& MORE 82

Sleeveless Shorty Vest	84
Hot Pants Set	88
Kiwi Vest & Headband	92
Ladder-Stitch Cloche	94
Starlight Scarf	96
Moonlight Magic	98
Earth Child	100
Granny Square Shrink Vest	102
Sweater For a Special Evening	104
Cowl-Neck Sweater	108
Clam Shell Purse	111
Hidden Treasures Scarf	114
Ladybug & Victorian Boot Pins	117
Lacy Pineapples Shell	120
Earthy Glow Tunic Vest	124
Short & Sexy Tank	128
Classy Continental Hat	132
Beaded Mesh Scarf	134
Bead-dazzling Purse	136
Wrap-Tie Top	138
Hot Summer Nights	141
City Lights Vest	144
Suede Fringed Vest	146
Glam Gal Hat & Purse	149
Canyon Colors Hat & Scarf	152
Flower Purse	154
Seaside Scallops Reversible Bag	156
Fashion Flower Pins	159
Foiled Heart Necklace	162

General Instructions 174 ■ Stitch Guide 175
Special Thanks 176 ■ Buyer's Guide 176

JACKETS, WRAPS & MORE 5

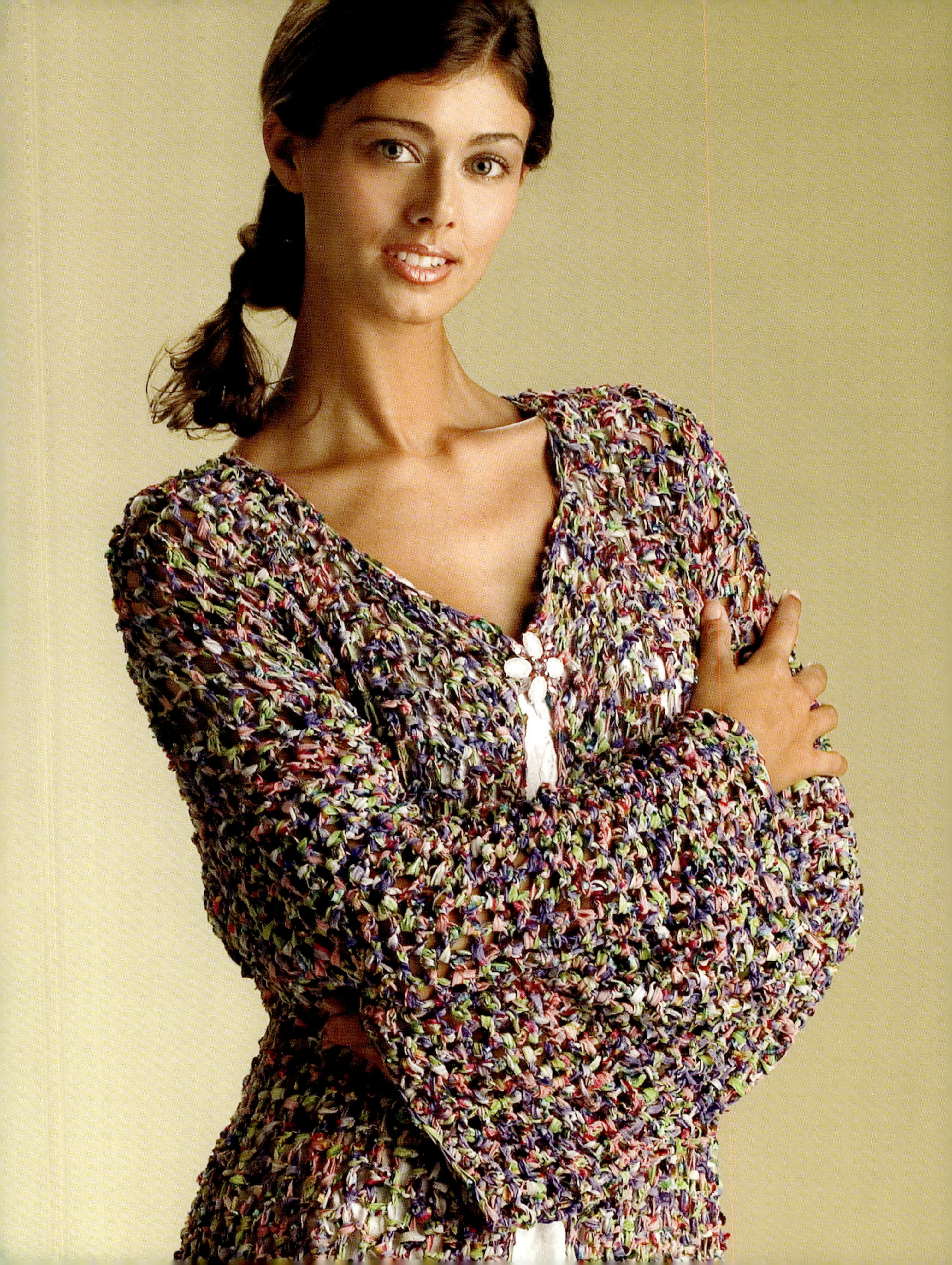

JACKETS

Jackets are the must-have essential for any wardrobe. Our beautiful array of flattering jackets will take you from classic to contemporary for daytime or evening with a variety of designs, weights and colors for perfect year-round style and comfortable wear.

JACKETS

CUT-AWAY CARDI

DESIGN BY LISA GONZALEZ

INTERMEDIATE

Finished Sizes
Instructions given fit 28–30-inch bust *(X-small)*; changes for 32–34-inch bust *(small)*, 36–38-inch bust *(medium)*, 40–42-inch bust *(large)*, 44–46-inch bust *(X-large)* and 48–50-inch bust *(2X-large)* are in [ ].

Finished Garment Measurements
Bust: 27–29 inches *(X-small)* [30–32 inches *(small)*, 34–36 inches *(medium)*, 38–40 inches *(large)*, 42–44 inches *(X-large)*, 46–48-inches *(2X-large)*]

Materials
- Classic Elite Premiere light (light worsted) weight yarn (1¾ oz/108 yds/50g per hank): 8 [8, 9, 10, 10, 12] hanks #5291 robin's egg
- Size G/6/4mm crochet hook or size needed to obtain gauge
- Yarn needle
- 12 x 15mm decorative shank button

3 LIGHT

Gauge
[Sc, ch 5] 4 times = 4 inches; 9 rows = 4 inches

Pattern Notes
Weave in loose ends as work progresses.
Cardigan should be very close fitting.
Cardigan uses net stitch throughout but varies number of chains per stitch to create subtle shaping effect. There is no right or wrong side due to the nature of the net stitch.

Special Stitch
Net Stitch (net st): Ch 5, [sc in next ch-5 sp, sk next sc, ch 5] across, ending with sc in turning ch, turn.

CARDIGAN

Back
Row 1: Loosely ch 63 [71, 79, 87, 95, 103], ch 5, sk first 2 chs of foundation ch, [sc in next ch, sk next 3 chs, ch 5] across, ending with sc in last ch, turn. *(16 [18, 20, 22, 24, 26] sc, 15 [17, 19, 21, 23, 25] ch-5 sps) (St count does not include turning ch here and throughout.)*
Row 2: Work in **net st** *(see Special Stitch)* across.
Rows 3–6: Rep row 2.
Row 7: Ch 4, [sc in next ch sp, ch 4] across, ending with sc in turning ch, turn.
Rows 8–15: Rep row 7.
Row 16: Ch 3, [sc in next ch sp, ch 3] across, ending with sc in turning ch, turn.
Rows 17–20: Rep row 16.
Rows 21–31: Rep row 7.
Rows 32–44: Rep row 2.

Armhole Shaping
Row 45: Ch 1, sc in first sc, 4 sc in next ch-5 sp, ch 5, [sc in next ch-5 sp, sk next sc, ch 5] across omitting last ch-5 sp and sc in turning ch, turn.
Row 46: Ch 5, [sc in next ch-5 sp, sk next sc, ch 5] across, ending with sc in last ch-5 sp, leaving group of last 5 sc unworked, turn. *(14 [16, 18, 20, 22, 24] sc, 14 [16, 18, 20, 22, 24] ch-5 sps)*
Row 47: Rep row 2.
Row 48: Rep row 45.
Row 49: Rep row 46. *(12 [14, 16, 18, 20, 22] sc, 12 [14, 16, 18, 20, 22] ch-5 sps)*
Row 50: Rep row 2.

8 JACKETS, WRAPS & MORE

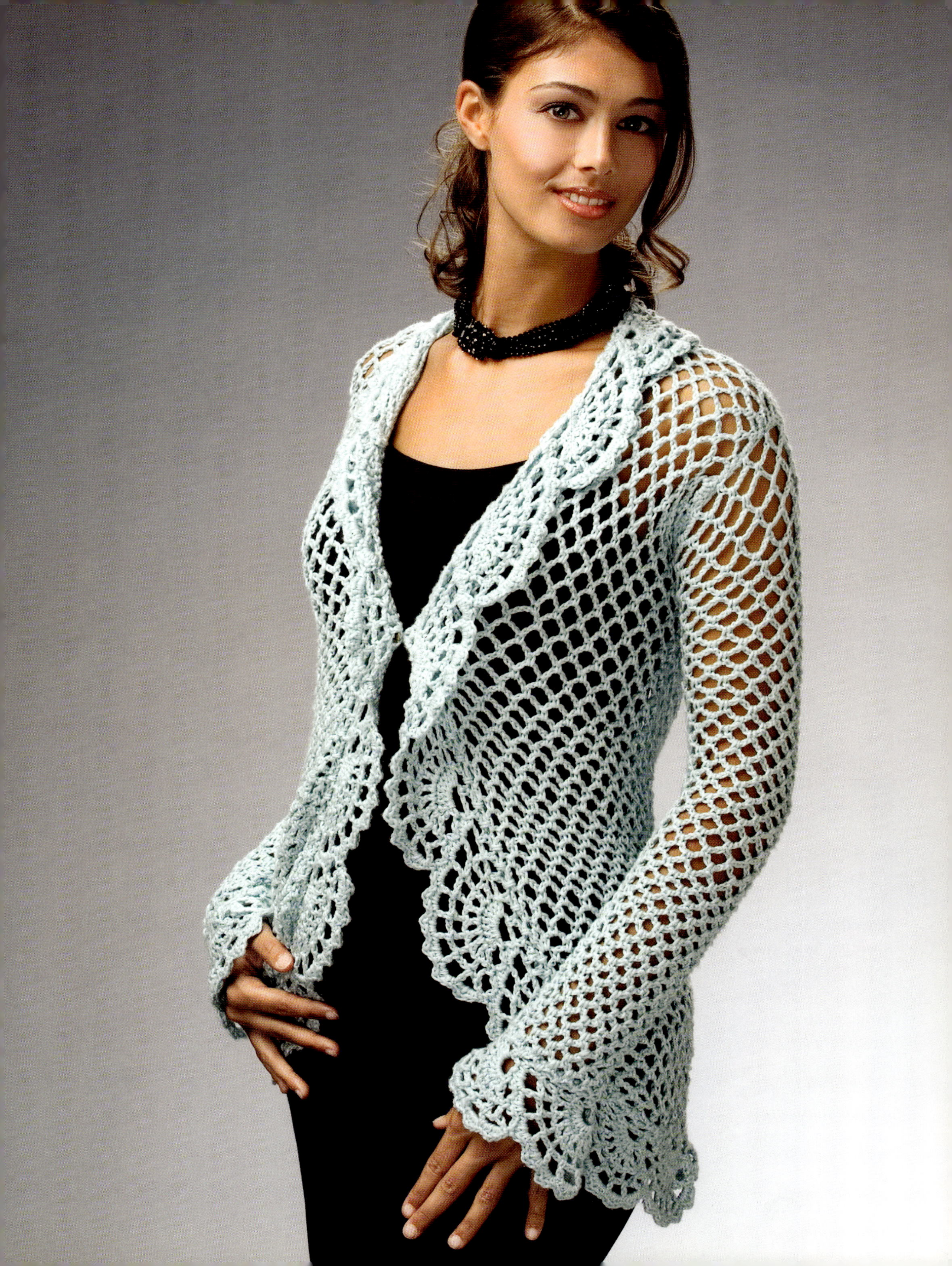

JACKETS

Rows 51–58: Rep row 7. At the end of row 58 for sizes X-small, small, medium and large, fasten off.

For Size X-Large Only
Rows 59 & 60: Rep row 7. At the end of Row 60, fasten off.

For Size 2X-Large Only
Rows 59–62: Rep row 7. At the end of Row 62, fasten off.

Front
Make 2.
Row 1: Loosely ch 19 [23, 27, 31, 35, 39], ch 5, sk first 2 chs of foundation ch, [sc in next ch, sk next 3 chs, ch 5] across, ending with sc in last ch, turn. *(5 [6, 7, 8, 9, 10] sc, 4 [5, 6, 7, 8, 9] ch-5 sps)*
Row 2: Ch 5, [sc in next ch-5 sp, sk next sc, ch 5] across, ending with sc in turning ch, ch 5 and sc again in turning ch, turn. *(6 [7, 8, 9, 10, 11] sc, 5 [6, 7, 8, 9, 10] ch-5 sps)*
Row 3: Work in net st across.
Rows 4 & 5: Rep row 3.
Row 6: Rep row 2. *(7 [8, 9, 10, 11, 12] sc, 6 [7, 8, 9, 10, 11] ch-5 sps)*
Row 7: Ch 4, [sc in next ch sp, sk next sc, ch 4] across, ending with sc in turning ch, turn.
Rows 8 & 9: Rep row 7.
Row 10: Rep row 7, working (sc, ch 4, sc) in last ch-4 sp, turn. *(8 [9, 10, 11, 12, 13] sc, 7 [8, 9, 10, 11, 12] ch-4 sps)*
Rows 11–13: Rep row 7.
Row 14: Rep row 10. *(9 [10, 11, 12, 13, 14] sc, 8 [9, 10, 11, 12, 13] ch-4 sps)*
Rows 15–18: Rep row 7.
Row 19: Ch 3, [sc in next ch sp, sk next sc, ch 3] across, ending with sc in turning ch, turn.
Rows 20–23: Rep row 19.
Rows 24–31: Rep row 7.
Rows 32–44: Rep row 3.

Armhole Shaping
Row 45: Ch 1, sc in first sc, 4 sc in next ch-5 sp *(armhole edge)*, ch 5, [sc in next ch sp, sk next sc, ch 5] across, ending with sc in last ch-5 sp, leaving turning ch unworked, turn.
Row 46: Ch 5, [sc in next ch sp, sk next sc, ch 5] across, ending with sc in 2nd sc of 4-sc group, turn. *(8 [9, 10, 11, 12, 13] sc, 7 [8, 9, 10, 11, 12] ch-5 sps)*
Row 47: Rep row 3.
Row 48: Rep row 45.
Row 49: Rep row 46, ending with sc in last ch-5 sp and leaving turning ch unworked, turn. *(6 [7, 8, 9, 10, 11] sc, 5 [6, 7, 8, 9, 10] ch-5 sps)*

10   JACKETS, WRAPS & MORE

Row 50: Rep row 3.
Rows 51–58: Rep row 7. At the end of row 58 for sizes X-small, small, medium and large, fasten off.

For Size X-Large Only
Rows 59 & 60: Rep row 7. At the end of row 60, fasten off.

For Size 2X-Large Only
Rows 59–62: Rep row 7. At the end of row 62, fasten off. Holding Back to Front and working through both thicknesses, sc shoulders tog. Matching sts, sc side seams tog.

Sleeve
Make 2.
Row 1: Loosely ch 47 [51, 51, 55, 59, 67], ch 5, sk first 2 chs of foundation ch, [sc in next ch, sk next 3 chs, ch 5] across, ending with sc in last ch, turn. *(12, [13, 13, 14, 15, 17] sc, 11 [12, 12, 13, 14, 16] ch-5 sps)*
Row 2: Work in net st across.
Rows 3–5: Rep row 2.
Row 6: Ch 4, [sc in next ch sp, sk next sc, ch 4] across, ending with sc in turning ch, turn.
Rows 7–30: Rep row 6.
Row 31: Ch 3, [sc in next ch sp, sk next sc, ch 3] across, ending with sc in turning ch, turn.
Rows 32–44: Rep row 31. At the end of row 44, for size X-small only, fasten off.

For Sizes Small, Medium Only
Rows 45–48: Rep row 31. At the end of row 48, fasten off.

For Size Large Only
Rows 45–52: Rep row 31. At the end of row 52, fasten off.

For Size X-Large Only
Rows 45–54: Rep Row 31. At the end of row 54, fasten off.

For Size 2X-Large Only
Rows 45–58: Rep row 31. At the end of row 58, fasten off.

Edging
Note: *For each Sleeve, work 3 [3, 3, 4, 4, 5] rep of Edging.*
For Body, work 22 [22, 22, 23, 24, 25] rep of Edging. After completing, check to be sure each section of Edging is long enough.

First Edging Repeat
Row 1: Ch 8, sl st to join in first ch, ch 3, 9 dc in ring, turn.
Row 2: Ch 4 *(counts as first dc, ch-1)*, dc in next dc, [ch 1, dc in next dc] 8 times, turn.
Row 3: Ch 5 *(counts as first dc, ch-2)*, dc in next dc, [ch 2, dc in next dc] 8 times, turn.
Row 4: Ch 6 *(counts as first dc, ch-3)*, dc in next dc, [ch 3, dc in next dc] 8 times, turn.
Row 5: Ch 1, [(sc, hdc, dc, hdc, sc) in next ch-3 sp] 9 times, turn.

Additional Edging Repeat
Row 6: Ch 8, sk next sc, sk next hdc, sl st in next dc, turn.
Rows 7–10: Rep rows 2–5 of First Rep of Edging. Continue to rep Additional Edging. Repeat until Edging, as indicated in note, is completed, ending last rep with row 5.

Edging
Row 1: Working along edge that will be attached to Cardigan, ch 5, *sc in top of last dc of row 3, ch 2, sc in 3rd ch of row 2, ch 2, sc in top of last dc of row 1, ch 2, sc in ring, ch 2, sc in last dc of row 4 of previous rep, rep from * along Edging, ending with (sc, ch 2, sc) in beg ch-8 ring of row 1 of First Edging Repeat, fasten off.

Attaching Edging
With RS facing, working through both thicknesses, ch 3, working in ch-3 sps, *insert hook through Edging ch sp and through Sleeve ch sp and complete sc, ch 3, sk next sc on Sleeve and Edging, rep from * until Edging is attached.

Finishing
Sew button to inside edge at junction of joining of Front and Edging about level with beg of armhole. For buttonhole, use natural ch sp on opposite edge. ■

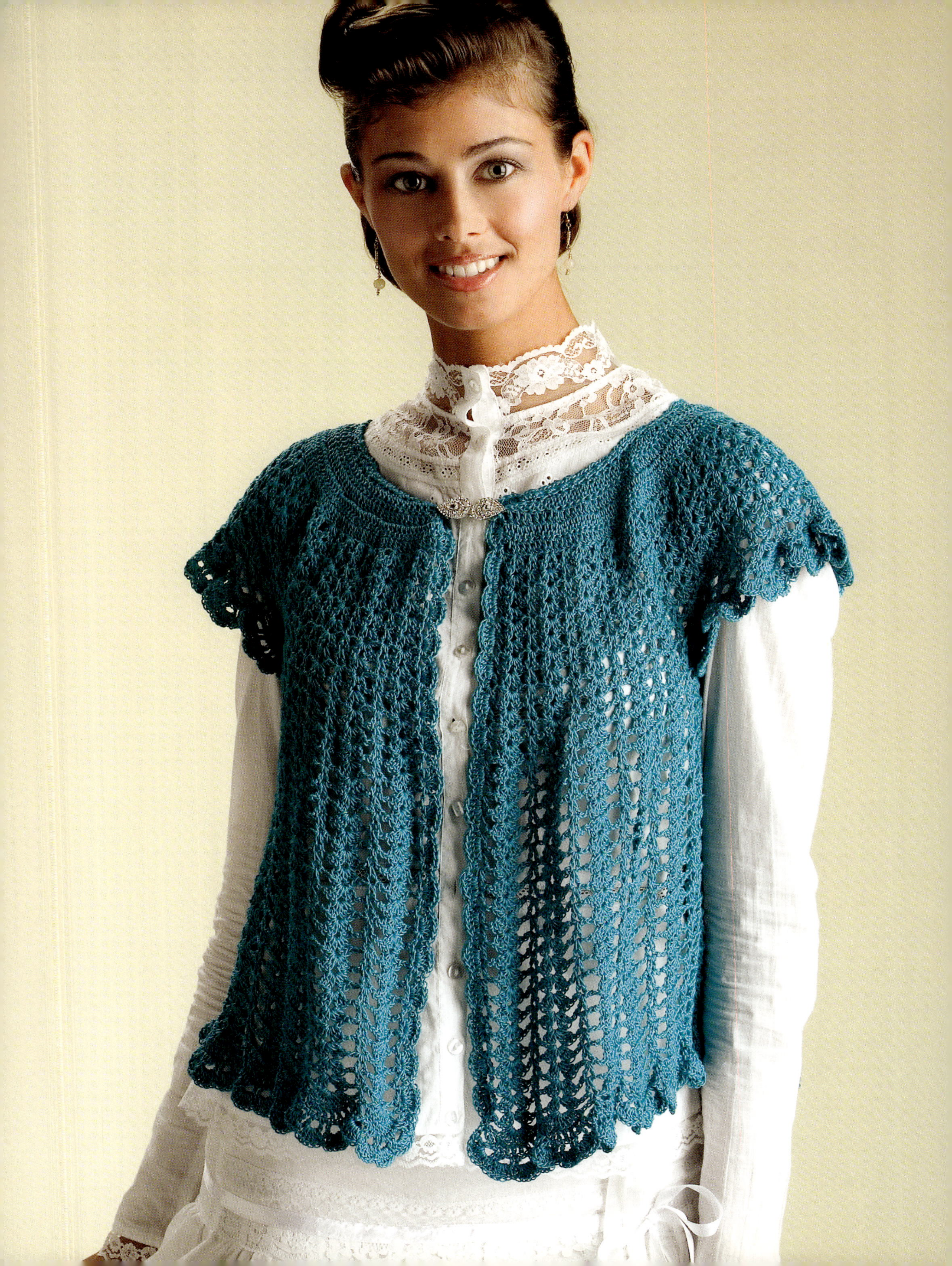

VERY VICTORIAN

DESIGN BY SUE CHILDRESS

INTERMEDIATE

Finished Size
Instructions given fit most women sizes small–large.

Finished Garment Measurements
Chest: 40 inches
Back neck length: 17 inches
Neck to armhole: 7 inches
Neck to bottom of sleeve: 7 inches

Materials
- Grignasco Cotton 5 medium (worsted) weight cotton yarn (1¾ oz/202 yds/50g per ball): 6 balls #082 light jade
- Size D/3/3.25mm crochet hook or size needed to obtain gauge
- Tapestry needle
- ¾ x 2-inch rhinestone clasp closure
- Stitch marker

Gauge
6 dc = 1 inch; 3 dc rows = 1 inch; 4 shell rows = 2 inches

Pattern Notes
Weave in loose ends as work progresses.
Join rounds with a slip stitch unless otherwise stated.

Special Stitches
Shell: (2 dc, ch 2, 2 dc) in indicated st.
V-stitch (V-st): (Dc, ch 1, dc) in indicated st.
Beginning V-stitch (beg V-st): Ch 4 *(counts as first dc, ch-1)*, dc in same st as beg ch-4.
Double shell: (2 dc, ch 2) twice, 2 dc indicated st.
Large shell: (3 dc, ch 2, 3 dc) in indicated st.
Scallop: 9 dc in indicated st.

JACKET

Body
Row 1: Beg at neckline, ch 140, dc in 3rd ch from hook, dc in each rem ch across, turn. *(138 dc)*
Row 2: Ch 3 *(counts as first dc)*, dc in each of next 2 dc, [2 dc in next dc, dc in each of next 3 dc] 33 times, dc in each of next 2 dc, turn. *(170 dc)*
Row 3: Ch 3, dc in next 4 dc, [2 dc in next dc, dc in each of next 5 dc] 27 times, dc in each of next 3 dc, turn. *(197 dc)*
Row 4: Ch 3, dc in each of next 7 dc, [2 dc in next dc, dc in each of next 6 dc] 26 times, dc in next 7 dc, turn. *(223 dc)*
Row 5: Beg V-st *(see Special Stitches)* in first dc, [ch 1, sk next 2 dc, **shell** *(see Special Stitches)* in next dc, ch 1, sk next 2 dc, **V-st** *(see Special Stitches)* in next dc] across, turn. *(37 shells, 38 V-sts)*
Row 6: Sl st into ch-1 sp of beg V-st, beg V-st in same ch-1 sp, [ch 1, shell in ch-2 sp of next shell, ch 1, V-st in ch-1 sp of next V-st] across, turn.
Rows 7–12: Rep row 6.
Row 13: Sl st into ch-1 sp of beg V-st, beg V-st in same ch-1 sp, [ch 1, shell in ch-2 sp of next shell, ch 1, V-st in ch-1 sp of next V-st] 5 times, ch 1 *(front)*, **double shell** *(see Special Stitches)* in ch-2 sp of next shell, [ch 1, V-st in ch-1 sp of next V-st, ch 1, shell in ch-2 sp of next shell] 6 times, ch 1, V-st in ch-1 sp of next V-st, ch 1 *(sleeve)*, double shell in ch-2 sp of next shell, [ch 1, V-st in ch-1 sp of next V-st, ch 1, shell in ch-2 sp of next shell] 11 times, ch 1, V-st in ch-1 sp of next V-st, ch 1 *(back)*, double shell in ch-2 sp of next shell, [ch 1, V-st in ch-1 sp of next V-st, ch 1, shell in ch-2 sp of next shell] 6 times,

JACKETS

ch 1, V-st in ch-1 sp of next V-st, ch 1 *(sleeve)*, double shell in ch-2 sp of next shell, [ch 1, V-st in ch-1 sp of next V-st, ch 1, shell in ch-2 sp of next shell] 5 times, ch 1, V-st in ch-1 sp of next V-st *(front)*, turn.

Row 14: Sl st into ch-1 sp of beg V-st, beg V-st in same ch-1 sp, [ch 1, shell in ch-2 sp of next shell, ch 1, V-st in ch-1 sp of next V-st] 5 times, *ch 1, shell in first ch-2 sp of next double shell, ch 1, V-st between next 2 dc, ch 1, shell in ch-2 sp of next ch-2 sp of same double shell*, [ch 1, V-st in ch-1 sp of next V-st, ch 1, shell in ch-2 sp of next shell] 6 times, ch 1, V-st in ch-1 sp of next V-st, rep between *, [ch 1, V-st in ch-1 sp of next V-st, ch 1, shell in ch-2 sp of next shell] 11 times, ch 1, V-st in ch-1 sp of next V-st, rep from * to *, [ch 1, V-st in ch-1 sp of next V-st, ch 1, shell in ch-2 sp of next shell] 6 times, ch 1, V-st in ch-1 sp of next V-st, rep from * to *, [ch 1, V-st in ch-1 sp of next V-st, ch 1, shell in ch-2 sp of next shell] 5 times, ch 1, V-st in ch-1 sp of next V-st, turn.

Row 15: Sl st into ch-1 sp of beg V-st, beg V-st in same ch-1 sp, [ch 1, shell in ch-2 sp of next shell, ch 1, V-st in ch-1 sp of next V-st] 6 times, ch 1, **scallop** *(see Special Stitches)* in ch-2 sp of next shell, [ch 1, sc in ch-1 sp of next V-st, ch 1, scallop in ch-2 sp of next shell] 7 times, [ch 1, V-st in ch-2 sp of next shell, ch 1, shell in ch-2 sp of next shell] 13 times, ch 1, V-st in ch-1 sp of next V-st, [ch 1, scallop in ch-2 sp of next shell, ch 1, sc in ch-1 sp of next V-st] 7 times, ch 1, scallop in ch-2 sp of next shell, [ch 1, V-st in ch-1 sp of next V-st, ch 1, shell in ch-2 sp of next shell] 6 times, ch 1, V-st in ch-1 sp of next V-st, turn.

Row 16: Sl st into ch-1 sp of beg V-st, beg V-st in same ch-1 sp, [ch 1, shell in ch-2 sp of next shell, ch 1, V-st in ch-1 sp of next V-st] 6 times, *ch 1, [dc in next dc of 9-dc scallop, ch 1] 9 times, sc in next sc*, rep from * to * across next 7 scallops, [ch 1, V-st in ch-1 sp of next V-st, ch 1, shell in ch-2 sp of next shell] 13 times, ch 1, V-st in ch-1 sp of next V-st, rep from * to * across next 8 scallops, [ch 1, V-st in ch-1 sp of next V-st, ch 1, shell in ch-2 sp of next shell] 6 times, ch 1, V-st in ch-1 sp of next V-st, turn.

Row 17: Sl st into ch-1 sp of beg V-st, beg V-st in same ch-1 sp, [ch 2, **large shell** *(see Special Stitches)* in ch-2 sp of next shell, ch 2, V-st in ch-1 sp of next V-st] 6 times, *ch 2, sk next dc, [5 dc in next ch-1 sp, sc in next ch-1

JACKETS, WRAPS & MORE

sp] 4 times, ch 2, sc in next sc*, rep from * to * across next 8 scallops, [ch 2, V-st in next ch-1 sp of next V-st, ch 2, large shell in ch-2 sp of next shell] 13 times, ch 2, V-st in ch-1 sp of next V-st, turn.

Row 18: Sl st into ch-1 sp of beg V-st, beg V-st in same ch-1 sp, [ch 2, large shell in ch-2 sp of next large shell, ch 2, V-st in ch-1 sp of next V-st] 6 times, ch 5 *(underarm)*, sk next 8 scallops of sleeve, V-st in ch-1 sp of next V-st, [ch 2, large shell in ch-2 sp of next large shell, ch 1, V-st in ch-1 sp of next V-st] 13 times, ch 5 *(underarm)*, sk next 8 scallops of sleeve, V-st in ch-1 sp of next V-st, [ch 2, large shell in ch-2 sp of next large shell, ch 2, V-st in ch-1 sp of next V-st] 6 times, turn.

Row 19 (RS): Place marker on RS, sl st into ch-1 sp of beg V-st, beg V-st in same ch-1 sp, [ch 2, large shell in ch-2 sp of next large shell, ch 2, V-st in ch-1 sp of next V-st] 6 times, *ch 2, sk next 2 chs of ch-5, large shell in 3rd ch of ch-5, ch 2, sk rem 2 chs of ch-5*, [V-st in ch-1 sp of next V-st, ch 2, large shell in ch-2 sp of next large shell, ch 2] 13 times, V-st in ch-1 sp of next V-st, rep from * to *, V-st in ch-1 sp of next V-st, [ch 2, large shell in ch-2 sp of next large shell, ch 2, V-st in ch-1 sp of next V-st] 6 times, turn.

Row 20: Sl st into ch-1 sp of beg V-st, beg V-st in same ch-1 sp, [ch 2, large shell in ch-2 sp of next large shell, ch 2, V-st in ch-1 sp of next V-st] across, turn.

Rows 21–37: Rep row 20.

Row 38: Sl st into ch-1 sp of V-st, ch 1, sc in ch-1 sp of next V-st, [ch 2, 9 dc in ch-2 sp of next large shell, ch 2, sc in ch-1 sp of next V-st] across, turn.

Row 39: Ch 1, sc in first sc, [ch 3, dc in each of next 9 dc, ch 3, sc in next sc] across, turn.

Row 40: Ch 1, sc in first sc, *ch 3, dc in first dc of 9-dc group, [ch 2, dc in next dc] 8 times, ch 3, sc in next sc, rep from * across, turn.

Rnd 41 (RS): Now working in rounds, ch 1, sc in next sc, *[5 dc in next ch-2 sp, sc in next ch-2 sp] 4 times**, sk next 2 ch-3 sps*, rep from * to * across bottom, ending last rep at **, sk last ch-3 sp, sc in next sc, working up right front of Vest in side edge of V-sts, [5 dc in side edge of next row, sc in side edge of next row] across to neckline edge, working across opposite side of foundation ch, sc in first ch, [**sc dec** *(see Stitch Guide)* in next 2 chs, sc in next ch] across neckline, turn, working back across neckline, ch 1, sc in first sc, [sc dec in next 2 sc, sc in next sc] across neckline, turn, working across neckline, ch 1, sc in first sc, [ch 2, sc in next sc] across to end of neckline, working down left front, sc in side edge of first row, [5 dc in side edge of next row, sc in side edge of next row] across to bottom edge, join in beg sc, fasten off.

Finishing
Sew rhinestone clasp to each side of row 1 of Vest. Press Vest. ■

JACKETS

LOOPY JACKET
DESIGN BY MARTY MILLER

INTERMEDIATE

Finished Sizes
Instructions given fit 32–34-inch bust *(small)*; changes for 36–38-inch bust *(medium)*, 40–42-inch bust *(large)*, 44–46-inch bust *(X-large)* and 48–50-inch bust *(2X-large)* are in [ ].

Finished Garment Measurements
Bust: 37 inches *(small)* [42 inches *(medium)*, 47 inches *(large)*, 52 inches *(X-large)*, 58 inches *(2X-large)*]
Length: 17½ inches *(small)* [18 inches *(medium)*, 18½ *(large)*, 19 inches *(X-large)*, 21 inches *(2X-large)*]
Sleeve length: 18 inches *(small)* [18 inches *(medium)*, 18 inches *(large)*, 18½ inches *(X-large)*, 18½ inches *(2X-large)*]

GAUGE
11 sts = 4 inches; 15 rows = 4 inches

PATTERN NOTES
Weave in loose ends as work progresses.
Join rounds with a slip stitch unless otherwise stated.

Materials
- Red Heart Plush medium (worsted) weight yarn (6 oz/278 yds/170g per skein):
    5 [6, 7, 7, 8] skeins #9103 cream
- Size I/9/5.5mm crochet hook or size needed to obtain gauge
- Tapestry needle
- Stitch markers
- ⅞-inch shell button

4 MEDIUM

Loop stitch is worked with wrong side facing, but loops will be on right side when jacket is completed.

SPECIAL STITCHES
Loop stitch (lp st): Insert hook in next st, wrap yarn around index finger twice, insert hook catching the 2 strands of yarn on index finger and draw through st onto hook, drop lps from index finger, yo, draw through all 3 lps on hook.

Foundation chain (foundation ch): Ch 2, insert hook in first ch of ch-2, yo, draw up a lp, yo, draw through first lp on hook *(this is the foundation ch)*, yo, draw through both lps on hook, *insert hook in foundation ch, yo, draw up a lp, yo, draw through first lp on hook, yo, draw through both lps on hook, rep from * until indicated number of foundation chs are completed.

JACKET

Body
Row 1: Starting at bottom edge, work **foundation ch** *(see Special Stitches)* 96 [116, 128, 144, 160] sts, turn. *(96 [116, 128, 144, 160] foundation chs)*
Row 2 (RS): Ch 1, sc in each st across, turn.
Row 3 (WS): Ch 1, sc in first st, **lp st** *(see Special Stitches)* in each st across to last st, sc in last st, turn.
Rows 4–37 [4–39, 4–41, 4–41, 4–43]: [Rep rows 2 and 3 alternately] 17 [18, 19, 19, 20] times.

Right Front
Row 38 [40, 42, 42, 44]: Ch 1, sc in each of next 23 [28, 31, 35, 39] sts, turn.

16 JACKETS, WRAPS & MORE

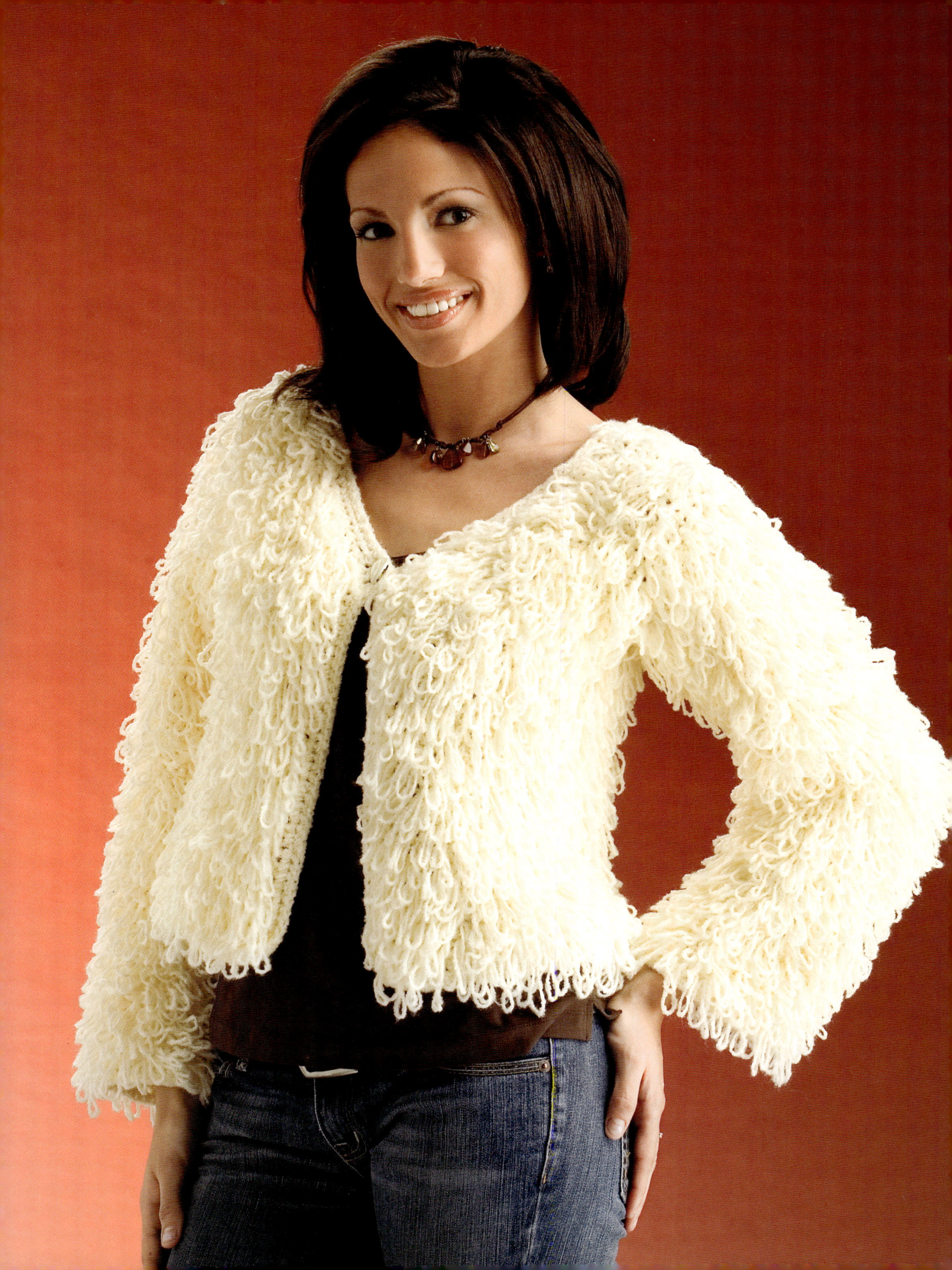

JACKETS

Row 39 [41, 43, 43, 45]: Ch 1, lp st in each st across to last st, sc in last st *(center front st)*, turn. *(23 [28, 31, 35, 39] sts)*

Row 40 [42, 44, 44, 46]: Ch 1, sc in each st across, turn.

Row 41 [43, 45, 45, 47]: Ch 1, lp st in each st across to last st, sc in last st, turn.

Row 42 [44, 46, 46, 48]: Ch 1, **sc dec** *(see Stitch Guide)* in next 2 sts, sc in each rem st across, turn. *(22 [27, 30, 34, 38] sc)*

Row 43 [45, 47, 47, 49]: Ch 1, lp st in each st across to last st, sc in last st, turn.

Rows 44–63 [46–67, 48–69, 48–69, 50–75]: [Rep rows 42 and 43 {44 and 45, 46 and 47, 46 and 47, 48 and 49} alternately] 10 [12, 12, 12, 13] times. *(12 [16, 19, 23, 23] sts at end of last rep)*

For Sizes Small, Medium, Large & X-large Only
Row 64 [68, 70, 70]: Ch 1, sc in each st across, turn. *(12 [16, 19, 23] sc)*

Row 65 [69, 71, 71]: Ch 1, lp st in each st across to last st, sc in last st, turn.

Row 66 [70, 72, 72]: Ch 1, sc in each st across, fasten off.

For Size 2X-large Only
Row 76: Rep row 46, fasten off. *([23] sc)*

Back

For All Sizes
Row 38 [40, 42, 42, 44]: Sk 2 sts on last row of Body next to Right Front, attach yarn in next st, ch 1, sc in same st as beg ch-1, sc in each of next 45 [55, 61, 69, 77] sts, turn. *(46 [56, 62, 70, 78] sc)*

Row 39 [41, 43, 43, 45]: Ch 1, lp st in each st across, turn.

Row 40 [42, 44, 44, 46]: Ch 1, sc in each st across, turn.

Rows 41–60 [43–64, 45–66, 45–66, 47–70]: [Rep rows 39 and 40 {41 and 42, 43 and 44, 43 and 44, 45 and 46} alternately] 10 [11, 11, 11, 12] times.

Row 61 [65, 67, 67, 71]: Rep row 39 [41, 43, 43, 45].

Right Shoulder

Row 62 [66, 68, 68, 72]: Ch 1, sc in each of next 12 [16, 19, 23, 23] sts, turn. *(12 [16, 19, 23, 23] sc)*

Row 63 [67, 69, 69, 73]: Ch 1, lp st in each st across, turn.

Rows 64 & 65 [68 & 69, 70 & 71, 70 & 71, 74 & 75]: Rep rows 62 and 63 [66 and 67, 68 and 69, 68 and 69, 72 and 73].

Row 66 [70, 72, 72, 76]: Ch 1, sc in each st across, fasten off.

Left Shoulder

Rows 62–66 [66–70, 68–72, 68–72, 72–76]: Sk next 24 [24, 24, 24, 32] sts on row 61 [65, 67, 67, 71], attach yarn in next st, rep Right Shoulder rows 62–66 [66–70, 68–72, 68–72, 72–76].

Left Front

Row 38 [40, 42, 42, 44]: With last row of Body facing, from Back, sk next 2 sts, attach yarn in next st, ch 1, sc in same st as beg ch-1, sc in each of next 22 [27, 30, 34,

18 JACKETS, WRAPS & MORE

JACKETS

38] sc, turn. *(23 [28, 31, 35, 39] sc)*

Row 39 [41, 43, 43, 45]: Ch 1, sc in first st *(front edge)*, lp st in each rem st across, turn. *(23 [28, 31, 35, 39] sts)*

Row 40 [42, 44, 44, 46]: Ch 1, sc in each st across, turn.

Row 41 [43, 45, 45, 47]: Ch 1, sc in first st, lp st in each rem st across, turn.

Row 42 [44, 46, 46, 48]: Ch 1, sc in each st across to last 3 sts, sc dec in next 2 sts, sc in last st, turn. *(22 [27, 30, 34, 38] sc)*

Row 43 [45, 47, 47, 49]: Ch 1, sc in first st, lp st in each rem st across, turn.

Rows 44–63 [46–67, 48–69, 48–69, 50–75]: [Rep rows 42 and 43 {44 and 45, 46 and 47, 46 and 47, 48 and 49} alternately] 10 [11, 11, 11, 13] times.

For Sizes Small, Medium, Large & X-large Only

Row 64 [68, 70, 70]: Ch 1, sc in each st across, turn.

Row 65 [69, 71, 71]: Ch 1, sc in first st, lp st in each rem st across, turn.

Row 66 [70, 72, 72]: Ch 1, sc in each st across, fasten off.

For Size 2X-large Only

Row 76: Rep row 46, fasten off.

Sleeve

Make 2.

Note: *Sleeve is started at wrist area, start increase with one st on row 6, placing away from beginning of row. Work the next 3 rows even, increase on row 10, placing increase 1 st away from end of row. Work in this pattern, 3 rows even, 1 row increase, alternating the end of the row where the increase is until sleeve has 44 [48, 52, 54, 56] sts then work remainder of the rows even.*

Row 1: Work 38 [42, 46, 48, 50] foundation chs, turn.

Row 2: Ch 1, sc in each st across, turn. *(38 [42, 46, 48, 50] sc)*

Row 3: Ch 1, lp st in each st across, turn.

Rows 4 & 5: Rep rows 2 and 3.

Row 6: Ch 1, sc in first st, 2 sc in next st, sc in each rem st across, turn. *(39 [43, 47, 49, 51] sc)*

Row 7: Rep row 3.

Rows 8 & 9: Rep rows 2 and 3.

Row 10: Ch 1, sc in each st across to last 2 sts, 2 sc in next st, sc in last st, turn. *(40 [44, 48, 50, 52] sc)*

Rows 11–13: Rep rows 7–9.

Row 14: Rep row 6. *(41 [45, 49, 51, 53] sts)*

Rows 15–17: Rep rows 7–9.

Row 18: Rep row 10. *(42 [46, 50, 52, 54] sts)*

Rows 22–25: Rep rows 11–14. *(43 [47, 51, 53, 55] sts)*

Row 26: Rep row 10. *(44 [48, 52, 54, 56] sts)*

Row 27: Rep row 3.

Rows 28–70 [28–72, 28–72, 28–74, 28–74]: Rep rows 2 and 3. At the end of last rep, fasten off.

Finishing

With RS tog, whipstitch shoulder seams, sl st Sleeve into armhole smoothly, sl st Sleeve seam closed.

Jacket Trim

Rnd 1: Attach yarn at bottom edge, ch 1, sc evenly spaced around Jacket, working 3 sc in each front lower corner and 2 chs in top right corner where the dec for the neck edge starts *(for the button lp)* and **sc dec** *(see Stitch Guide)* in next 3 sts at back of shoulder, join in beg sc, do not turn.

Rnd 2: Ch 1, sc in each sc around, inc at each front corner and sc dec at the dec of shoulders, work 2 sc in the button lp ch-2 sp, join in beg sc, fasten off.

Sew shell button opposite button lp.

Sleeve Trim

Rnd 1: Attach yarn at Sleeve seam, ch 1, sc in each st around, join in beg sc, fasten off.

Rep on opposite Sleeve. ■

JACKETS, WRAPS & MORE

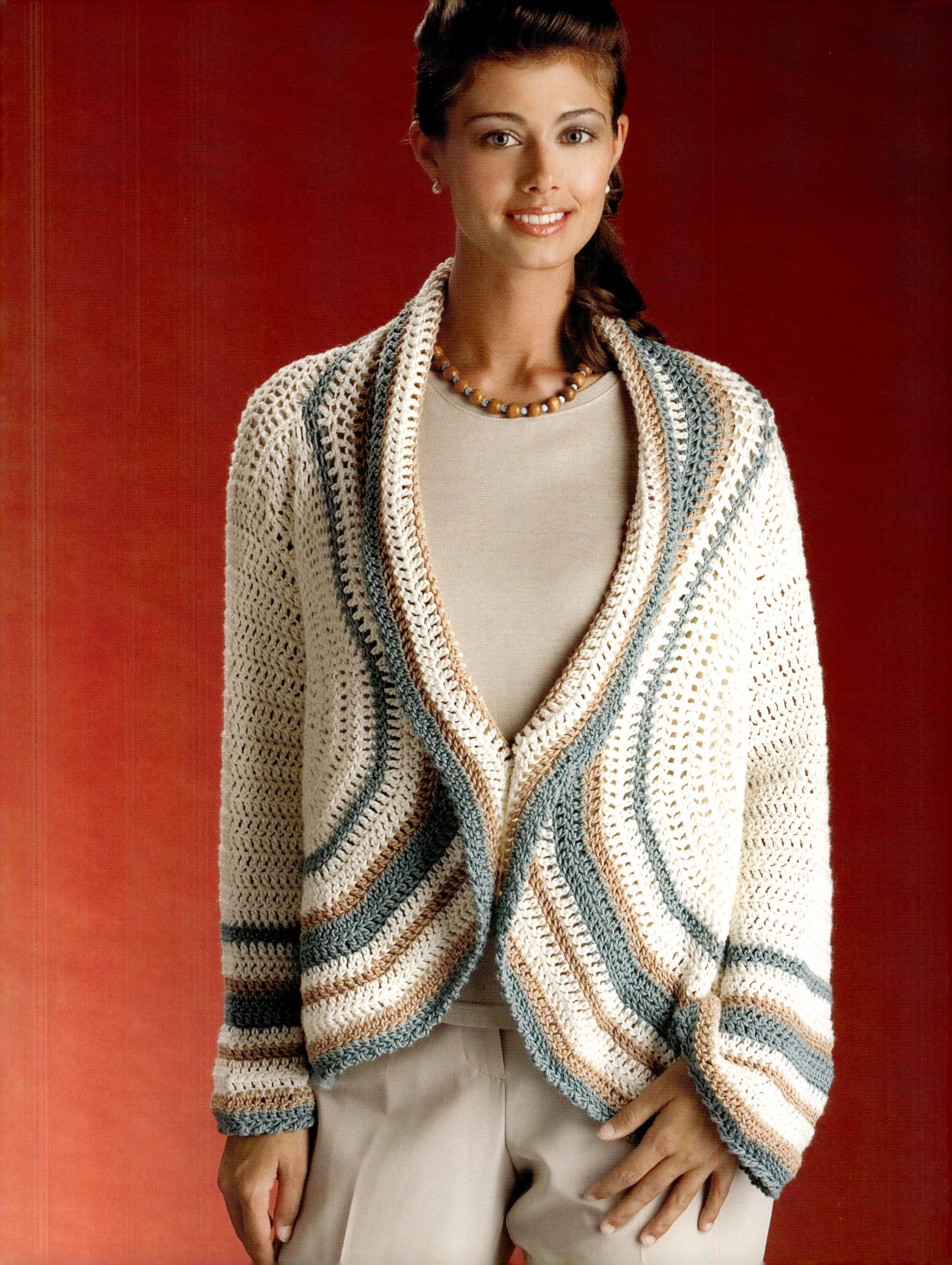

TABARD JACKET

DESIGN BY MARTY MILLER

INTERMEDIATE

Finished Sizes
Instructions given fit 32–34-inch bust *(small)*; changes for 36–38-inch bust *(medium)*, 40–42-inch bust *(large)*, 44–46-inch bust *(X-large)*, 48–50-inch bust *(2X-large)* and 52–54-inch bust *(3X-large)* are in [ ].

Finished Garment Measurements
Bust: 40 inches *(small)* [43 inches *(medium)*, 46 inches *(large)*, 49 inches *(X-large)*, 51 inches *(2X-large)*, 54 inches *(3X-large)*]
Length: 22½ inches *(small)* [23½ inches *(medium)*, 4½ *(large)*, 25½ inches *(X-large)*, 25½ inches *(2X-large)*, 26½ inches *(3X-large)*]
Sleeve length: 18½ inches *(small)* [18½ inches *(medium)*, 19½ inches *(large)*, 19½ inches *(X-large)*, 19½ inches *(2X-large)*, 19½ inches *(3X-large)*]

Gauge
Size H hook: 3 dc = 1 inch; 2 dc rows or rnds = 1 inch

Materials
- TLC Cotton Plus medium (worsted) weight yarn (3½ oz/178 yds/100g per ball):
    5 [6, 7, 8, 9, 10] balls #3100 cream *(A)*
    2 [2, 3, 3, 4, 4] balls each #3303 tan *(B)* and #3503 spruce *(C)*
- Sizes H/8/5mm and I/9/5.5mm crochet hooks or size needed to obtain gauge
- Tapestry needle
- Stitch markers

Pattern Notes
Weave in loose ends as work progresses.
Join rounds with a slip stitch unless otherwise stated.
Size I hook is used only for beginning chain of Jacket Back.
Start the Jacket with Back, then work oval Fronts and connect them to the Back leaving space for the armholes. Then work around these 3 pieces to form the Collar and front and bottom edges.
Place markers at designated stitches and move markers each row or rnd.

JACKET

Back
Row 1: With size I hook and A, ch 63 [66, 69, 72, 75, 78], with size H hook *(beg sk 3 chs count as first dc)*, dc in 4th ch from hook *(beg sk 3 chs count as first dc)*, dc in each rem ch across, turn. *(61 [64, 67, 70, 73, 76] dc)*
Row 2 (RS): Ch 3 *(counts as first dc)*, dc in each dc across, turn.
Rows 3–18 [3–20, 3–22, 3–24, 3–24, 3–26]: Rep row 2. At the end of last rep, fasten off.

Front
Make 2.
Row 1: With size H hook and A, ch 21 [24, 27, 30, 33, 36], dc in 4th ch from hook *(beg sk 3 chs count as first dc)*, dc in each rem ch across to last ch, 6 dc in last ch, place marker in first and last dc of 6-dc group, working on the opposite side of foundation ch, dc in each ch across, turn. *(42 [48, 54, 60, 66, 72] dc)*

JACKETS

do not remove markers. *(90 [102, 114, 126, 132, 144] dc)*
With WS of Back and first Front facing out, place the straight edge of Front (ends of rows) and side edge of Back with foundation chs tog at top. From bottom upward toward armhole, sew through both thicknesses for 4 [5, 6, 7, 7, 9] rows. Fasten off. Sew shoulder seam from armhole edge through both thicknesses of 9 [12, 15, 18, 21, 24] sts or approximately 3 [4, 5, 6, 7, 8] inches. Sew 2nd Front on opposite side edge of Back in same manner.

Border

Note: Border is worked in rnds around entire Jacket. Collar shaping begins at top edge of Jacket after dc dec in 2nd st of shoulder seam by working around the posts of dc sts at the top edge of Jacket Back.

Rnd 1: With WS of Jacket facing, starting at the bottom, attach C 1 st to the right of bottom left seam on back, ch 3, dc in each st to first marker, [2 dc in next dc, dc in each of next 8 dc] 6 times, dc in each dc to 1 st before shoulder seam, **dc dec** (see Stitch Guide) in last st before seam and in first st of seam, dc dec in 2nd st of shoulder seam and in post of next dc, dc in the post of each dc to 1 st before next shoulder seam, dc dec in last post and shoulder seam, dc dec in shoulder seam and next dc, dc in each dc to next marker, [2 dc in next dc, dc in each of next 8 dc] 6 times, dc in each st to end of rnd, join in 3rd ch of beg ch-3, fasten off, turn.

Note: At the end of rnd 1, there is a 6-st inc at rounded end of each Front and a 4-st dec at the collar. Count the number of sts rem and write this number down.

Rnd 2: Attach A, ch 3, dc in each dc to first marker, [2 dc in next dc, dc in each of next 9 dc] 6 times between markers, dc in each dc to first collar dec, dc dec in dec of rnd 1, dc to next dec of rnd 1, dc dec in next dec of rnd 1, dc in each dc to next marker, [2 dc in next dc, dc in each of next 9 dc] 6 times, dc in each st to end of rnd, join in 3rd ch of beg ch-3, turn. *(10-st inc)*

Rnd 3: Ch 3, dc in each dc to first marker, [2 dc in next dc, dc in each of next 10 dc] 6 times, dc in each dc to next marker on 2nd Front, [2 dc in next dc, dc in each

Row 2 (RS): Ch 3, dc in each dc to first marker, 2 dc in each of next 6 dc, dc in each rem dc, turn. *(48 [54, 60, 66, 72, 78] dc)*

Row 3: Ch 3, dc in each dc to first marker, [2 dc in next dc, dc in next dc] 6 times, sc in each rem dc across, turn. *(54 [60, 66, 72, 78, 84] dc)*

Row 4: Ch 3, dc in each dc to first marker, [2 dc in next dc, dc in each of next 2 dc] 6 times, dc in each rem dc across, turn. *(60 [66, 72, 78, 84, 90] dc)*

Row 5: Ch 3, dc in each dc to first marker, [2 dc in next dc, dc in each of next 3 dc] 6 times, dc in each rem dc across, turn. *(66 [72, 78, 84, 90, 96] dc)*

Rows 6–9 [6–10, 6–11, 6–12, 6–12, 6–13]: [Rep row 5] 4 [5, 6, 7, 7, 8] times working inc of 6 dc between markers on each row, turn. At the end of last row, fasten off,

22 JACKETS, WRAPS & MORE

of next 10 dc] 6 times, dc in each rem dc around, join in 3rd ch of beg ch-3, fasten off, turn. *(12-st inc)*

Rnd 4: Attach B, rep rnd 3, inc 6 dc between each marker on each front evenly spaced across, dc in each rem dc, join in 3rd ch of beg ch-3, fasten off, turn. *(12-dc inc)*

Rnds 5 & 6: With C, rep rnd 4.

Rnd 7: Attach A, rep rnd 4.

Rnd 8: Attach B, rep rnd 4.

Rnds 9 & 10: Attach A, rep rnd 4.

Rnd 11: Attach B, rep rnd 4.

Rnd 12: Attach C, rep rnd 4.

Rnd 13: Attach B, ch 1, **reverse sc** *(see Fig. 1)* in each st around, join in first sc, fasten off.

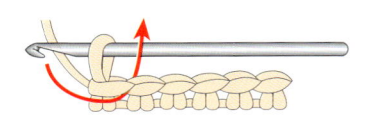

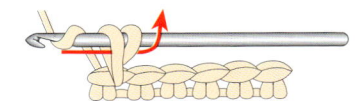

Reverse Single Crochet
Fig. 1

Sleeve

Rnd 1: With WS facing, attach A at underarm, ch 3 *(counts as first dc)*, work 47 [51, 55, 59, 63, 63] dc evenly spaced around armhole opening, join in 3rd ch of beg ch-3, turn. *(48 [52, 56, 60, 64, 64] dc)*

Rnd 2: Ch 3, dc dec in next 2 sts, dc in each rem st around, join in 3rd ch of beg ch-3, turn. *(47 [51, 55, 59, 63, 63] dc)*

Rnds 3–6: Rep rnd 2. *(43 [47, 51, 55, 59, 59] dc at end of last rnd)*

Rnd 7: Ch 3, dc in each dc around, join in 3rd ch of beg ch-3, turn.

Rnd 8: Rep rnd 2. *(42 [46, 50, 54, 58, 58] dc)*

Rnds 9–18: [Rep rnds 7 and 8 alternately] 5 times. *(37 [41, 45, 49, 53, 53] dc)*

Rnds 19–22 [19–22, 19–24, 19–24, 19–24, 19–24]: Rep rnd 7. At the end of last rep, fasten off, turn.

Rnd 23 [23, 25, 25, 25, 25]: Attach C, rep rnd 7, fasten off, turn.

Rnds 24 & 25 [24 & 25, 26 & 27, 26 & 27, 26 & 27, 26 & 27]: Attach A, rep rnd 7. At the end of last rep, fasten off, turn.

Rnd 26 [26, 28, 28, 28, 28]: Attach B, rep rnd 7, fasten off, turn.

Rnds 27 & 28 [27 & 28, 29 & 30, 29 & 30, 29 & 30, 29 & 30]: Attach C, rep rnd 7. At the end of last rep, fasten off, turn.

Rnd 29 [29, 31, 31, 31, 31]: Attach A, ch 3, dc around, inc 6 [6, 6, 6, 6, 10] dc evenly spaced around, join in 3rd ch of beg ch-3, fasten off, turn. *(43 [47, 51, 55, 59, 63] dc)*

Rnd 30 [30, 32, 32, 32, 32]: Attach B, rep rnd 7, fasten off, turn.

Rnd 31 [31, 33, 33, 33, 33]: Attach A, ch 3, dc around, inc 6 dc evenly spaced around, join in 3rd ch of beg ch-3, turn. *(49 [53, 57, 61, 65, 69] dc)*

Rnd 32 [32, 34, 34, 34, 34]: Rep rnd 7, fasten off, turn.

Rnd 33 [33, 35, 35, 35, 35]: Attach B, rep rnd 31 [31, 33, 33, 33, 33], fasten off, turn. *(55 [59, 63, 67, 71, 75] dc)*

Rnd 34 [34, 36, 36, 36, 36]: Rep rnd 7, do not turn.

Rnd 35 [35, 37, 37, 37, 37]: Ch 1, reverse sc in each st around, join in beg sc, fasten off. Rep on opposite armhole opening. ∎

JACKETS

GRANNY SQUARE DRESS & JACKET

DESIGNS BY TAMMY HILDEBRAND

INTERMEDIATE

Finished Sizes
Instructions given fit 32–34-inch bust *(small)*; changes for 36–38-inch bust *(medium)*, 40–42-inch bust *(large)* and 44–46-inch bust *(X-large)* are in [ ].

Finished Garment Measurements
Bust: 36 inches *(small)* [40½ inches *(medium)*, 43 inches *(large)*, 48 inches *(X-large)*]

Materials
- DMC Senso size 3 crochet cotton (150 yds per ball):
  Dress: 7 [7, 8, 8] balls #N1005 terra cotta
  5 [5, 6, 6] balls #N1002 ecru
  3 [3, 4, 4] balls each #N1012 black and #N1004 burnt orange
  Jacket: 4 [5, 6, 6] balls #N1005 terra cotta
  2 [2, 3, 3] balls #N1002 ecru
  1 [1, 2, 2] balls each #N1012 black and #N1004 burnt orange
- Sizes E/4/3.5mm, F/5/3.75mm and G/6/4mm crochet hooks or sizes needed to obtain gauge
- Tapestry needle

Gauge
Size E hook: Large Motif = 5 inches square
Size F hook: Large Motif = 6 inches square
Size G hook: Large Motif = 7 inches square

Pattern Notes
Weave in loose ends as work progresses.

Join rounds with a slip stitch unless otherwise stated. For shorter length, omit one motif on each strip. For size small, use size E hook; size medium, use size F hook; size large, use size F hook on rounds 1–3 of Large Motifs and size G hook on all other rounds; size X-large, use size G hook.
Alternate colors on Large Motif, round 1 black (ecru), round 2 ecru (burnt orange), round 3 terra cotta (black), round 4 ecru (terra cotta), rounds 5 and 6 burnt orange (ecru). Always alternate placement of Large Motifs, never place 2 of the same color sequence next to one another.

Special Stitches
Chain-3 join (ch-3 join): Ch 1, drop lp, insert hook in center ch of corresponding ch-3 on previous motif, pick up dropped lp and draw through, ch 1.
Chain-5 join (ch-5 join): Ch 2, drop lp, insert hook in center ch of corresponding ch-5 on previous motif, pick up dropped lp and draw through, ch 2.
V-Stitch (V-st): (Dc, ch 1, dc) in indicated st.

DRESS

Large Motif
Rnd 1: Ch 3, join in 3rd ch from hook to form ring, ch 3 *(counts as first dc)*, 15 dc in ring, join in 3rd ch of beg ch-3, fasten off. *(16 dc)*
Rnd 2: Join with sc in any st, 3 dc in next st, [sc in next st, 3 dc in next st] 7 times, join in beg sc, fasten off. *(8 sc, 24 dc)*

JACKETS, WRAPS & MORE

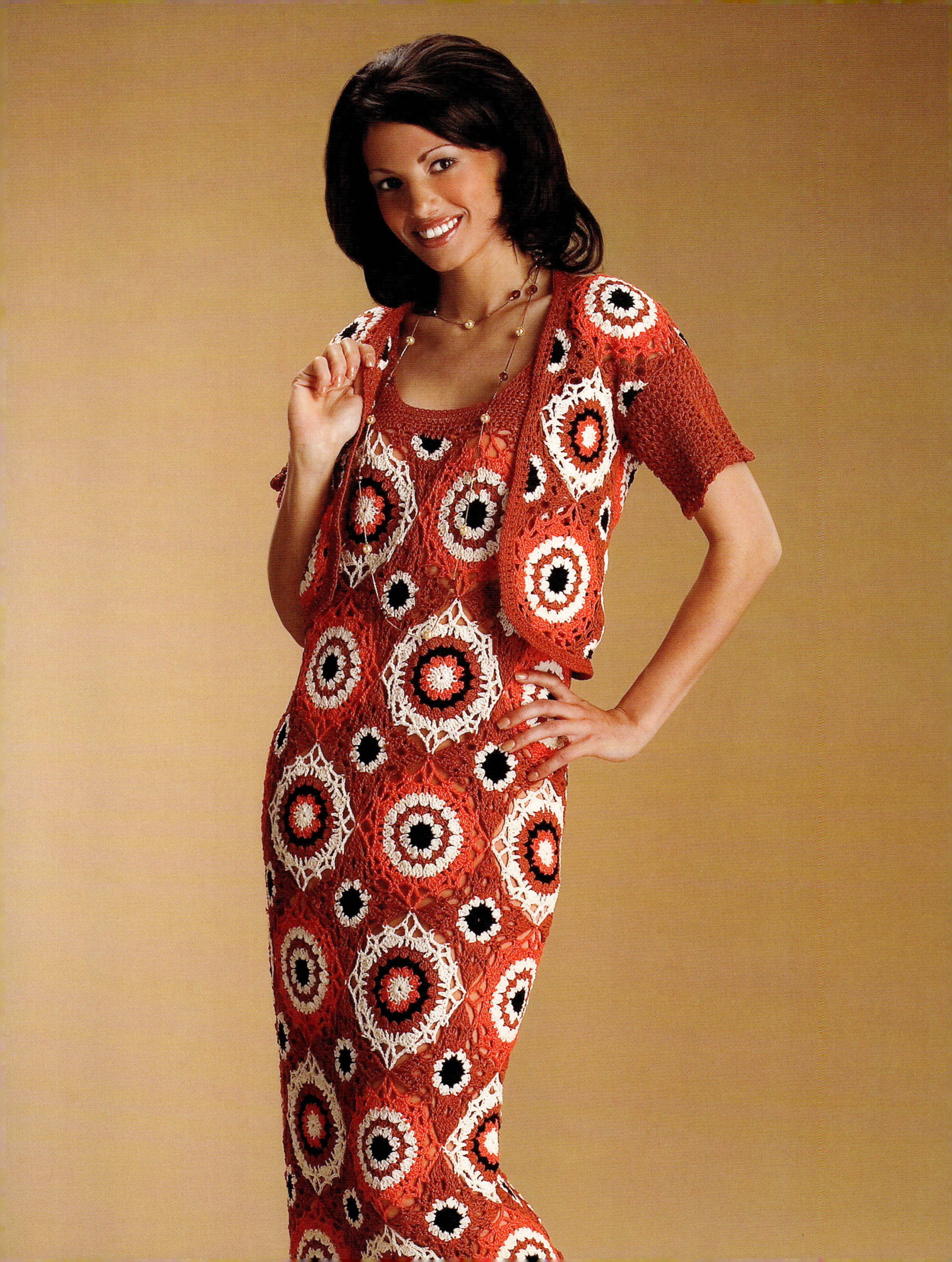

JACKETS

Rnd 3: Join in center st of any 3-st group, ch 3, 3 dc in next sc, [dc in center st of next 3-st group, 3 dc in next sc] 7 times, join, fasten off. *(32 dc)*

Rnd 4: Join in center st of any 3-st group, ch 3, 2 dc in same sp, sk next st, 5 dc in next st, [sk next st, 3 dc in next st, sk next st, 5 dc in next st] 7 times, join in 3rd ch of beg ch-3, fasten off. *(64 dc)*

Rnd 5: Join in center st of any 3-st group, ch 4, sk next st, dc in next st, sk next st, 5 dc in next st, sk next st, dc in next st, ch 1, sk next st, [dc in next st, ch 1, sk next st, sk next st, 5 dc in next st, sk next st, dc in next st, ch 1] 7 times, join in 3rd ch of beg ch-4. *(64 dc)*

Joining Rnd

First Strip
First Motif Only
Rnd 6: Ch 6 *(counts as first dc, ch-3)*, dc in same sp as joining, ch 2, (sc, ch 3, sc) in center st of next 5-st group, ch 2, sk next 3 sts, (tr, ch 5, tr) in next st, ch 2, (sc, ch 3, sc) in center st of next 5-st group, ch 2, sk next 3 sts, [(dc, ch 3, dc) in next st, ch 2, (sc, ch 3, sc) in center st of next 5-st group, ch 2, sk next 3 sts, (tr, ch 5, tr) in next st, ch 2, (sc, ch 3, sc) in center st of next 5-st group, ch 2, sk next 3 sts] 3 times, join in 3rd ch of beg ch-6, fasten off. *(16 sc, 8 dc, 8 tr)*

Motifs 2–7
Rnd 6: Ch 6 *(counts as first dc, ch-3)*, dc in same sp as joining, ch 2, (sc, ch 3, sc) in center st of next 5-st group, ch 2, sk next 3 sts, (tr, **ch-5 join**—*see Special Stitches*, tr) in next st, ch 2, (sc, ch 3, sc) in center st of next 5-st group, ch 2, sk next 3 sts, [(dc, ch 3, dc) in next st, ch 2, (sc, ch 3, sc) in center st of next 5-st group, ch 2, sk next 3 sts, (tr, ch 5, tr) in next st, ch 2, (sc, ch 3, sc) in center st of next 5-st group, ch 2, sk next 3 sts] 3 times, join in 3rd ch of beg ch-6, fasten off.

Strips 2–5
First Motif Only
Rnd 6: Rep rnd 6 of Motif 2.

Motifs 2–7
Rnd 6: Ch 6, dc in same sp as joining, ch 2, (sc, ch 3, sc) in center st of next 5-st group, ch 2, sk next 3 sts,

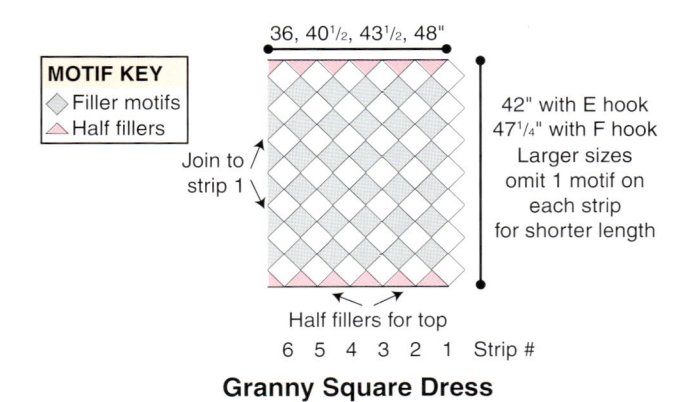

MOTIF KEY
◇ Filler motifs
△ Half fillers

36, 40½, 43½, 48"

42" with E hook
47¼" with F hook
Larger sizes
omit 1 motif on
each strip
for shorter length

Join to strip 1

Half fillers for top
6 5 4 3 2 1   Strip #

**Granny Square Dress
Joining Diagram**

(tr, ch-5 join, tr) in next st, ch 2, (sc, ch 3, sc) in center st of next 5-st group, ch 2, sk next 3 sts, (dc, ch 3, dc) in next st, ch 2, (sc, ch 3, sc) in center st of next 5-st group, ch 2, sk next 3 sts, (tr, ch-5 join, tr) in next st, ch 2 (sc, ch 3, sc) in center st of next 5-st group, ch 2, sk next 3 sts, [(dc, ch 3, dc) in next st, ch 2, (sc, ch 3, sc) in center st of next 5-st group, ch 2, sk next 3 sts, (tr, ch 5, tr) in next st, ch 2, (sc, ch 3, sc) in center st of next 5-st group, ch 2, sk next 3 sts] twice, join in 3rd ch of beg ch-6, fasten off.

Strip 6
First Motif Only
Rnd 6: Joining this strip to corresponding Motif of both Strip 1 and Strip 5, ch 6, dc in same sp as joining, ch 2, (sc, ch 3, sc) in center st of next 5-st group, ch 2, sk next 3 sts, [(tr, ch-5 join, tr) in next st, ch 2, (sc, ch 3, sc) in center st of next 5-st group, ch 2, sk next 3 sts, (dc, ch 3, dc) in next st, ch 2, (sc, ch 3, sc) in center st of next 5-st group, ch 2, sk next 3 sts, (tr, ch 5, tr) in next st, ch 2, (sc, ch 3, sc) in center st of next 5-st group, ch 2, sk next 3 sts, (dc, ch 3, dc) in next st, ch 2, (sc, ch 3, sc) in center st of next 5-st group, ch 2, sk next 3 sts] twice, ch 2, (sc, ch 3, sc) in center st of next 5-st group, ch 2, sk next 3 sts, (dc, ch 3, dc) in next st, ch 2, (sc, ch 3, sc) in center st of next 5-st group, ch 2, join in 3rd ch of beg ch-6, fasten off.

Motifs 2–7
Rnd 6: Joining this strip to corresponding Motif of both Strip 1 and Strip 5, ch 6, dc in same sp as joining,

JACKETS, WRAPS & MORE

JACKETS

ch 2, (sc, ch 3, sc) in center st of next 5-st group, ch 2, sk next 3 sts, [(tr, ch-5 join, tr) in next st, ch 2, (sc, ch 3, sc) in center st of next 5-st group, ch 2, sk next 3 sts, (dc, ch 3, dc) in next st, ch 2, (sc, ch 3, sc) in center st of next 5-st group, ch 2, sk next 3 sts] 3 times, ch 2, (sc, ch 3, sc) in center st of next 5-st group, ch 2, sk next 3 sts, (dc, ch 3, dc) in next st, ch 2, (sc, ch 3, sc) in center st of next 5-st group, ch 2, join in 3rd ch of beg ch-6, fasten off.

Filler Motif

Rnd 1: With black, rep rnd 1 of Large Motif. *(16 dc)*
Rnd 2: Attach ecru with sc in any st, 3 dc in next st, [sc in next st, 3 dc in next st] 7 times, join in beg sc, fasten off. *(8 sc, 24 dc)*
Rnd 3: Attach terra cotta with sc in any sc, 2 sc in same st, sk next st, sc in next st, sk next st, (3 tr, ch 3, 3 tr) in next st, sk next st, sc in next st, sk next st, [3 sc in next st, sk next st, sc in next st, sk next st, (3 tr, ch 3, 3 tr) in next st, sk next st, sc in next st, sk next st] 3 times, join in beg sc. *(20 sc, 24 tr)*

Joining Rnd

Rnd 4: Working in openings between flower motifs, ch 3, drop lp, insert hook in center ch of corresponding ch-3 on flower motif, pick up dropped lp and draw through, ch 1, hdc in same st on filler motif, ch 2, sk next 3 sts, (hdc, **ch-3 join**—*see Special Stitches*, hdc) in next st, sk next st, (3 tr, ch-5 join, 3 tr) in next ch-3 sp, sk next st, (hdc, ch-3 join, hdc) in next st, ch 2, sk next 3 sts, [(hdc, ch-3 join, hdc) in next st, ch 2, sk next 3 sts, (hdc, ch-3 join, hdc) in next st, (3 tr, ch-5 join, 3 tr) in next ch-3 sp, sk next st, (hdc, ch-3 join, hdc) in next st, ch 2, sk next 3 sts] 3 times, join in 2nd ch of beg ch-3, fasten off. *(24 hdc, 24 tr)*

Half Filler For Top of Dress

Rnd 1: With black, ch 3, join in 3rd ch from hook to form a ring, ch 3, 8 dc in ring, fasten off. *(9 dc)*
Rnd 2: Join ecru with sc in first st, [3 dc in next st, sc in next st] 4 times, fasten off. *(5 sc, 12 dc)*
Rnd 3: Join terra cotta in first st, ch 3, 2 dc in same st, sk next st, sc in next st, sk next st, 3 sc in next st, sk next st, sc in next st, sk next st, (3 tr, ch 3, 3 tr) in next st, sk next st, sc in next st, sk next st, 3 sc in next st, sk next st, sc in next st, sk next st, 3 dc in last st, turn. *(10 sc, 6 dc, 6 tr)*

Joining Rnd

Rnd 4: Working in openings along top and bottom, ch 5, drop lp, insert hook in center ch of corresponding ch-5 on Large Motif, pick up dropped lp and draw through, ch 2, dc in same sp on Half Filler, (hdc, ch-3 join, hdc) in next st, [ch 2, sk next 3 sts, (hdc, ch-3 join, hdc) in next st] twice, (3 tr, ch-5 join, 3 tr) in next ch-3 sp, sk next st, [(hdc, ch-3 join, hdc) in next st, ch 2, sk next 3 sts] twice, (hdc, ch-3 join, hdc) in next st, (dc, ch-5 join, dc) in last st, fasten off. *(12 hdc, 4 dc, 6 tr)*

Half Filler For Bottom of Dress

Rnds 1–3: Rep rnds 1–3 of Half Filler For Top of Dress.

Joining Rnd
Rnd 4: Working in openings along top and bottom, ch 6, drop lp, insert hook in center ch of corresponding ch-5 on Large Motif, pick up dropped lp and draw through, ch 2, tr in same sp on Half Filler, (hdc, ch-3 join, hdc) in next st, [ch 2, sk next 3 sts, (hdc, ch-3 join, hdc) in next st] twice, (3 tr, ch-5 join, 3 tr) in next ch-3 sp, sk next st, [(hdc, ch-3 join, hdc) in next st, ch 2, sk next 3 sts] twice, (hdc, ch-3 join, hdc) in next st, (tr, ch-5 join, tr) in last st, fasten off. *(12 hdc, 10 tr)*

Bottom Trim
Rnd 1: Join terra cotta in center ring of any Half Filler along bottom of Dress, ch 5, dc in same sp, working in row ends of Half Filler, [sk next row, (dc, ch 2, dc) in each of next 3 rows, (dc, ch 2, dc) in ch-5 sp on next Large Motif, (dc, ch 2, dc) in next 3 rows of next Half Filler, (dc, ch 2, dc) in center ring] around, omitting last (dc, ch 2, dc), join in 3rd ch of beg ch-5.
Rnds 2 & 3: Sl st in next ch-2 sp, ch 5, dc in same sp, (dc, ch 2, dc) in next ch-2 sp and each ch-2 sp to end, join in 3rd ch of beg ch-5.
Rnd 4: Sl st in next ch-2 sp, ch 1, (2 sc, ch 2, 2 sc) in same sp and each ch-2 sp to end, join in beg sc, fasten off.

Top Edging
Rnd 1: Join terra cotta in ch-5 sp of any Large Motif along top of dress, ch 3, 2 dc in same sp, working in row ends of Half Filler, [3 hdc in each of next 2 rows, hdc in each of next 2 rows, hdc in center of ring, hdc in each of next 2 rows, 3 hdc in each of next 2 rows, 3 dc in ch-5 sp on Large Motif] around, omitting last 3 dc, join in 3rd ch of beg ch-3. *(102 hdc, 18 dc)*

Front Panel
Row 1: Now working in rows, sl st in next st, ch 2 *(counts as first hdc)*, hdc in each of next 59 sts, turn. *(60 hdc)*
Row 2 & 3: Sl st in next st, ch 2, hdc in each st up to last st, leaving last st unworked, turn. *(56 hdc)*
Row 4: Sl st in next st, ch 2, hdc in each of next 18 sts, sc in each of next 18 sts, sc in each of next 18 sts, hdc in each of next 19 sts, turn. *(18 sc, 38 hdc)*

First Strap
Row 1: Ch 2, hdc in each of next 18 sts, turn. *(19 hdc)*
Row 2: Sl st in next st, ch 2, hdc in each st to end, turn. *(18 hdc)*
Row 3: Ch 2, hdc in each st to last st, leaving last st unworked, turn. *(17 hdc)*
Rows 4–11: [Rep rows 2 and 3 alternately] 4 times. *(9 hdc)*
Rows 12–22: Ch 2, hdc in each st to end, turn. At the end of last rep, fasten off.

2nd Strap
Row 1: Sk next 18 sts on Row 4 of Front Panel, join terra cotta in next st, ch 2, hdc in each of next 18 sts, turn.
Row 2: Ch 2, hdc in each st to last st, leaving last st unworked, turn.
Row 3: Sl st in next st, ch 2, hdc in each st to end, turn.
Rows 4–11: [Rep rows 2 and 3 alternately] 4 times.
Rows 12–22: Ch 2, hdc in each st to end, turn. At the end of last rep, fasten off.

Back Panel
Row 1: Join terra cotta in next st of Top Edging, ch 2, hdc in each of next 59 sts, turn. *(60 hdc)*
Rows 2–4: Rep rows 2–4 of Front Panel.

Straps
Rep pattern for Front Panel Straps.
Stitch last row of each Front Strap and Back Strap tog.

Collar Edging
Rnd 1: Join terra cotta with sc in first st of row 4 on Front Panel, sc in each of next 17 sts, working in row ends of First Strap, sc in each row, sc in each st across Back Panel, sc in each row end of 2nd Strap, join in beg sc, fasten off.

Armhole Trim
Rnd 1: Working in row ends of straps, around armhole opening, join terra cotta with sc in any row, sc in each row, join in beg sc.
Rnd 2: Ch 5, dc in same st, [sk next st, (dc, ch 2, dc) in

CONTINUED ON PAGE 46

JACKETS

SHAWL-COLLARED CARDIGAN

DESIGN BY MELISSA LEAPMAN

EASY

Finished Sizes
Instructions given fit 32–34-inch bust *(small)*; changes for 36–38-inch bust *(medium)*, 40–42-inch bust *(large)* and 44–46-inch bust *(X-large)* are in [ ].

Finished Garment Measurements
Bust: 37¾ inches *(small)* [40 inches *(medium)*, 43½ inches *(large)*, 46¾ inches *(X-large)*]
Length: 23½ inches *(small)* [24 inches *(medium)*, 24½ inches *(large)*, 25 inches *(X-large)*]

Gauge
14 sts = 4 inches; 12 rows = 4 inches
Take time to check gauge.

Special Stitches
Beginning increase (beg inc): (Ch 1, sc, dc) in sc or work (ch 3, sc) in dc.
End increase (end inc): (Sc, dc) in sc or (dc, sc) in dc.

MATERIALS
- Medium (worsted) weight yarn: 28 [32, 36, 40] oz/1,400 [1,600, 1,800, 2,000] yds/794 [907, 1,021, 1,134]g sapphire variegated
- Size H/8/5mm crochet hook or size needed to obtain gauge
- Tapestry needle
- Sewing needle
- Sewing thread
- 7 matching ¾-inch shank buttons
- Stitch markers

4 MEDIUM

CARDIGAN

Back
Row 1 (RS): Beg at bottom, ch 66 [70, 76, 82], sc in 2nd ch from hook, [dc in next ch, sc in next ch] across, turn. *(65 [69, 75, 81] sts)*
Row 2: Ch 3 *(counts as first dc)*, [sc in next dc, dc in next sc] across, turn.
Row 3: Ch 1, [sc in next dc, dc in next sc] across, turn.
Rows 4–47: [Rep rows 2 and 3 alternately] 22 times.

Armhole Shaping
Row 48: Sl st in each of next 4 [6, 6, 8] sts, (sl st, ch 3) in next st, [sc in next dc, dc in next sc] across, leaving last 4 [6, 6, 8] sts unworked, turn. *(57 [57, 63, 65] sts)*
Row 49: Rep row 3.
Rows 50–71 [50–75, 50–75, 50–77]: [Rep rows 2 and 3 alternately] 11 [13, 13, 14] times.
Row 72 [76, 76, 78]: Rep row 2. Fasten off.

Pocket Lining
Make 2.
Row 1: Ch 18, sc in 2nd ch from hook, [dc in next ch, sc in next ch] across, turn. *(17 sts)*
Rows 2–17: [Rep rows 2 and 3 of Back] 8 times. At the end of last row, fasten off.

Left Front
Row 1 (RS): Ch 36 [38, 42, 44], sc in 2nd ch from hook, [dc in next ch, sc in next ch] across, turn. *(35 [37, 41, 43] sts)*

30 JACKETS, WRAPS & MORE

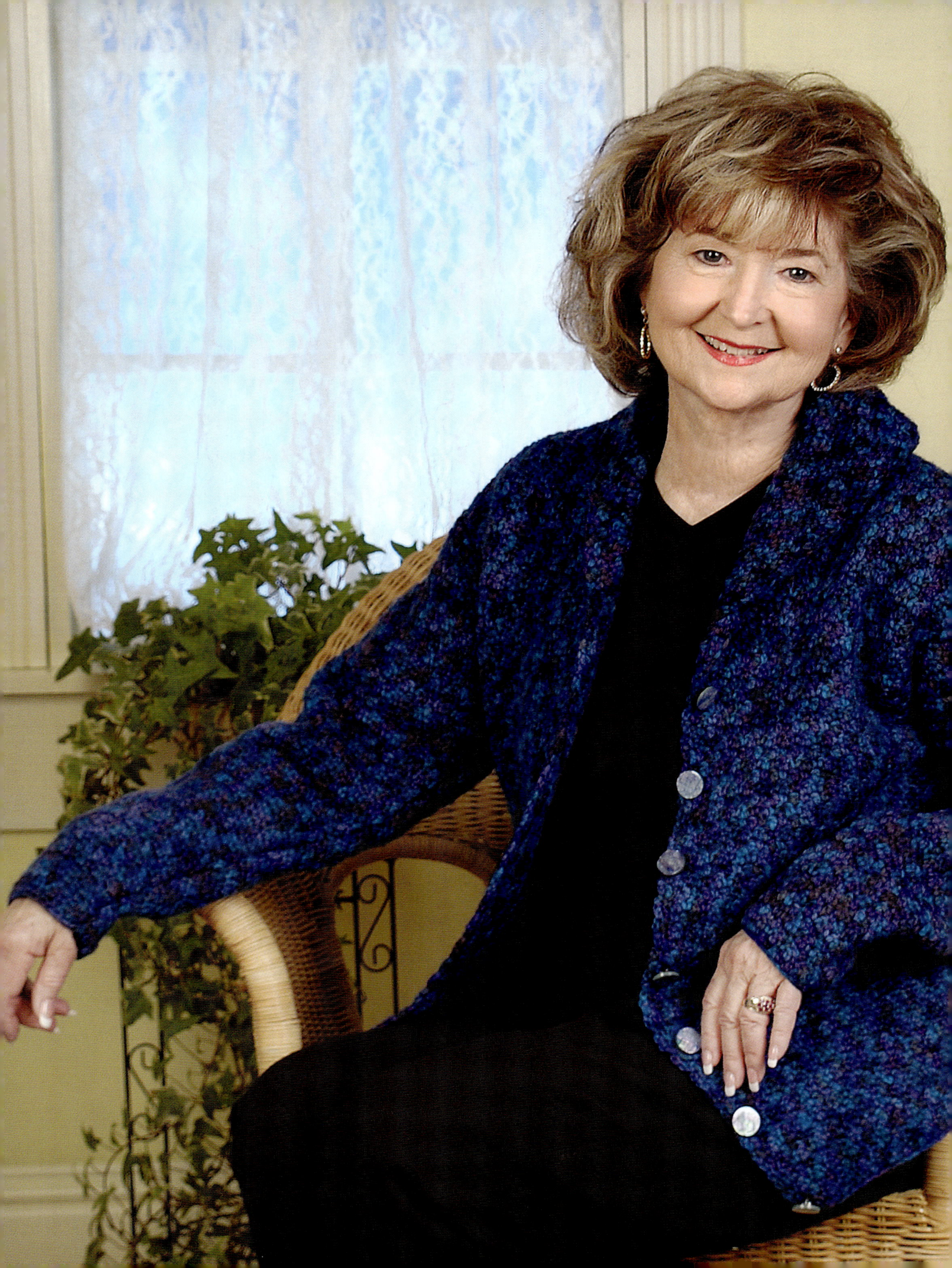

JACKETS

Rows 2–19: [Rep rows 2 and 3 of back alternately] 9 times.
Row 20 (WS): Ch 3, work as established across 7 [9, 11, 11] sts, pick up Pocket Lining and holding in place, work in pattern across 17 sts of Pocket Lining, sk next 17 sts of Left Front, work in pattern across rem 10 [10, 12, 14] sts, turn.
Row 21: Rep row 3 of Back.
Rows 22–47: [Rep rows 2 and 3 alternately of Back] 13 times.

Armhole Shaping
Row 48 (WS): Ch 3, work in pattern across leaving last 4 [6, 6, 8] sts unworked, turn. *(31 [31, 35, 35] sts)*
Rows 49 & 50 [49–52, 49–52, 49–54]: Rep rows 3 and 2 of Back alternately] 1 [2, 2, 3] times.
Note: *Place a marker at neckline edge, this will be the ending point of collar.*

Neck Shaping
Row 1 (RS): Ch 1, work in pattern across to last 2 sts, **dc dec** *(see Stitch Guide)* in last 2 sts, turn. *(30 [30, 34, 34] sts)*
Row 2: Ch 1, sk first st, work in pattern across, turn. *(29 [29, 33, 33] sts)*
Rows 3–8: [Rep rows 1 and 2 of Neck Shaping] 3 times. *(23 [23, 27, 27] sts)*
Row 9: Ch 1, work in pattern across, turn.
Row 10: Ch 1, sk first st, work in pattern across row, turn. *(22 [22, 26, 26] sts)*
Rows 11–18 [11–18, 11–22, 11–22]: [Rep rows 9 and 10 alternately] 4 [4, 6, 6] times. *(18 [18, 20, 20] sts at end of last row)*
Rows 19–22 (19–24, 23 & 24, 23 & 24): Work in pattern across each row, turn. At the end of last row, fasten off.

Right Front
Rows 1 & 2: Rep rows 1 and 2 of Left Front.
Row 3: Ch 1, work first 2 sts in pattern, ch 2, sk next 2 sts *(buttonhole)*, work in pattern across, turn.
Row 4: Ch 3, work in pattern across, turn.
Row 5: Ch 1, work in pattern across, turn.
Rows 6–9: [Rep rows 4 and 5 alternately] twice.
Row 10: Rep row 4.
Rows 11–18: Rep rows 3–10.
Row 19: Rep row 3.
Row 20 (WS): Ch 3, work in pattern across 9 [9, 11, 13] sts, pick up Pocket Lining and holding in place, working in pattern across 17 sts of Pocket Lining, sk next 17 sts of Right Front, work in pattern across last 8 [10, 12, 12] sts, turn.
Rows 21–26: [Rep rows 5 and 4 alternately] 3 times.
Rows 27–42: [Rep rows 3–10 consecutively] twice.
Rows 43–47: Rep rows 3–7.

Armhole Shaping
Row 48: Sl st in each of first 4 [6, 6, 8] sts, [sl st, ch 3] in next st, work in pattern across, turn. *(31 [31, 35, 35] sts)*

Medium, Large & X-Large Sizes Only
Rows [49 & 50, 49 & 50, 49 & 50]: Rep rows 5 and 4.

All Sizes
Row 49 [51, 51, 51]: Rep row 3.
Row 50 [52, 52, 52]: Rep row 4.

X-Large Size Only
Rows 53 & 54: Rep rows 5 and 4.
Note: *Place a marker at neckline edge, this will be the starting point of Collar.*

Neck Shaping
Row 1: Ch 1, sk first st, work in pattern across, turn. *(30 [30, 34, 34] sts)*
Row 2: Ch 1, work in pattern across to last 2 sts, dc dec in last 2 sts, turn. *(29 [29, 33, 33] sts)*
Rows 3–8: Rep rows 1 and 2 alternately of Neck Shaping] twice. *(23 [23, 27, 27] sts at end of last row)*
Row 9: Ch 1, work in pattern across, turn.
Row 10: Ch 1, work in pattern across to last 2 sts, dc dec in last 2 sts, turn. *(22 [22, 26, 26] sts)*
Rows 11–18 [11–18, 11–22, 11–22]: [Rep rows 9 and 10 alternately] 4 [4, 6, 6] times. *(18 [18, 20, 20] sts at end of last row)*
Rows 19–22 [19–24, 23 & 24, 23 & 24]: Ch 1, work in pattern across row, turn. At the end of last row, fasten off.

Sleeve
Make 2.
Row 1 (RS): Ch 32 [32, 34, 36], rep row 1 of Back. *(31 [31, 33, 35] sts)*
Row 2: Ch 3, work in pattern across, turn.
Row 3: Ch 1, work in pattern across, turn.
Row 4 (WS): Beg inc *(see Special Stitches)*, work in pattern across row to last st, **end inc** *(see Special Stitches)* in last st, turn. *(33 [33, 35, 37] sts)*
Row 5: Ch 1, work in pattern across row, turn.
Rows 6 & 7 [6–9, 6–15, 6–19]: [Rep rows 4 and 5 alternately] 1 [2, 5, 7] times. *(35 [37, 45, 51] sts at end of last row)*
Rows 8–10 [10–12, 16–18, 20–22]: Rep rows 2, 3 and 2.
Row 11 [13, 19, 23]: Beg inc, work in pattern across row to last st, end inc in last st, turn. *(37 [39, 47, 53] sts)*
Next rows: Rep rows 8–11 [10–13, 16–19, 20–23] until there are 57 [63, 63, 69] sts.
Next rows: Rep rows 2 and 3 until Sleeve measures 20 inches or until Sleeve is desired length. At end of last row, fasten off.

Assembly
Sew each Pocket Lining to WS of Sweater.
Matching ends of rows of Back and Fronts tog, leaving center 21 [21, 23, 25] sts of Back unworked, sew each Front to Back across 18 [18, 20, 20] sts at each edge.
Matching center of last row of Sleeve to shoulder seam, sew last row of Sleeve to ends of rows on Front and Back to underarm, sew ends of rows at top of Sleeve to underarm on Front and Back. Sew Sleeve and side seams.
With sewing needle and thread, sew buttons on Left Front opposite buttonholes on Right Front.

Collar
Row 1: With RS facing, working around neckline edge, join with sl st at marker on Right Front, ch 1, sc in same st, evenly sp 30 [30, 32, 43] sc across to shoulder seam, sc in each of next 21 [21, 23, 25] sts across Back to next shoulder seam, evenly sp 31 [31, 33, 35] sc across to marked row on Left Front, turn. *(83 [83, 89, 95] sts)*
Row 2: Ch 1, sc dec in first 2 sts, dc in next st, [sc in next st, dc in next st] across to last 2 sts, sc dec in last 2 sts, turn. *(81 [81, 87, 93] sts)*
Rows 3–16: Ch 1, sc dec in first 2 sts, work in pattern across to last 2 sts, sc dec in last 2 sts, turn. *(53 [53, 59, 65] sts at end of last row)*
Rows 17–24: Ch 1, sc dec in first 3 sts, work in pattern across to last 3 sts, sc dec in last 3 sts, turn. At the end of last row, fasten off. *(21 [21, 27, 33] sts at end of last row)* ∎

JACKETS

CROPPED BOMBER JACKET

DESIGN BY DARLA SIMS

INTERMEDIATE

Finished Sizes
Instructions given fit 32-34-inch bust *(small)*; changes for 36-38-inch bust *(medium)*, and 40-42-inch bust *(large)* are in [ ].

Finished Garment Measurements
Bust: 38½ inches *(small)* [44 inches *(medium)*, 49 inches *(large)*]

Gauge
Size G hook: 5 sc = 1 inch; 9 sc back lp rows = 2 inches
Size H hook: 10 hdc = 3 inches; 6 pattern rows = 2 inches
Take time to check gauge.

Pattern Note
Pattern is established in rows 4–9.

Special Stitches
Bobble: Hdc in each of next 5 sts, drop lp from hook, insert hook in first st of 5-hdc group, pull dropped lp through, push bobble to right side of work.
Cross-stitch (cross-st): Sk next 2 sts 3 rows below, working around last 2 rows, yo, insert hook in next st, yo, pull up long lp, yo, pull through all 3 lps on hook, sk next st on last row behind st just made, hdc in next st on last row; working around last 2 rows, yo, insert hook in sk st 3 rows below, yo, pull up long lp, yo, pull through all 3 lps on hook, sk next st on last row behind st just made.

Materials
- Lion Brand Wool-Ease medium (worsted) weight yarn (3 oz/197 yds/85g per skein): 7 [8, 9] skeins #099 fisherman
- Sizes G/6/4mm and H/8/5mm crochet hooks or sizes needed to obtain gauge
- Tapestry needle
- Ornate hook and eyes: 5 sets

JACKET

Body
Row 1: With size H hook, ch 126 [142, 158], hdc in 3rd ch from hook *(2 sk chs count as first hdc)*, hdc in each ch across, turn. *(125 [141, 157] hdc)*
Row 2 (RS): Ch 2 *(counts as first hdc)*, hdc in each st across, turn.
Row 3: Ch 2, hdc in each st across, turn.
Row 4: Ch 2, hdc in each of next 3 sts, 5 hdc in next st, [hdc in each of next 3 sts, 5 hdc in next st] across to last 4 sts, hdc in each of last 4 sts, turn.
Row 5: Ch 2, hdc in each of next 3 sts, **bobble** *(see Special Stitches)*, [hdc in each of next 3 sts, bobble] across to last 4 sts, hdc in each of last 4 sts, turn.
Row 6: Ch 1, hdc in first st, **cross-st** *(see Special Stitches)*, [hdc in next bobble, cross-st] across to last st, hdc in last st, turn.
Rows 7–9: Ch 2, hdc in each st across, turn.
Rows 10–27: Work in pattern *(see Pattern Note)*.

Right Front
Row 28: Work in pattern across first 29 [33, 37] sts, hdc in next st, leave rem sts unworked, turn.
Rows 29–42: Work in pattern.

34 JACKETS, WRAPS & MORE

Neck Shaping
Row 43: Ch 2, hdc in each of next 23 [25, 28] sts, leave rem sts unworked, turn. *(24 [26, 29] hdc)*
Row 44: Ch 2, **hdc dec** *(see Stitch Guide)* in next 2 sts, work in pattern across, turn. *(23 [25, 28] hdc)*
Row 45: Work in pattern.
Rows 46–49: [Rep rows 44 and 45 alternately] twice. *(19, [21, 24] hdc at end of last row)*
Row 50: Rep row 44. *(20, [22, 25] hdc)*
Rows 51 [51, 51–53]: Ch 2, hdc in each st across, turn. At end of last row, fasten off.

Back

Row 28: Sk next st on row 27 *(armhole)*, join with sl st in next st, ch 2, 5 hdc in next st, [hdc in each of next 3 sts, 5 hdc in next st] 15 [17, 19] times, hdc in next st, leave rem sts unworked, turn. *(47 [53, 59] hdc, 16 [18, 20] hdc groups)*
Rows 29–48: Work in pattern.
Rows 49–51 [49–51, 49–53]: Ch 2, hdc in each st across, turn. At end of last row, fasten off.

Left Front

Row 28: Sk next st on row 27 *(armhole)*, join with sl st in next st, ch 2, 5 hdc in next st, [hdc in each of next 3 sts, 5 hdc in next st] 6 [7, 8] times, hdc in each of last 4 sts, turn.

JACKETS

Rows 29–42: Work in pattern. At end of last row, fasten off.

Neck Shaping
Rows 43: Sk first 6 [8, 9] sts, join with sl st in next st, ch 2, hdc in each st across, turn. *(24 [26, 29] hdc)*
Row 44: Work in pattern across to last 3 sts, hdc dec in next 2 sts, hdc in last st, turn. *(23 [25, 28] hdc)*
Row 45: Work in pattern.
Rows 46–49: [Rep rows 44 and 45 alternately] twice.
Row 50: Rep row 44. *(20 [22, 25] hdc)*
Rows 51 [51, 51–53]: Ch 2, hdc in each st across, turn. At end of last row, fasten off.
Sew shoulder seams.

Waist Ribbing
Row 1: Working in starting ch on opposite side of row 1 on Body, with size G hook, join with sc in first ch, sc in each of next 7 [3, 5] chs, **sc dec** *(see Stitch Guide)* in next 2 sts, [sc in each of next 4 chs, sc dec in next 2 sts] across to last 7 [3, 5] sts, sc in each of last 7 [3, 5] chs, turn. *(106 [118, 132] sc)*
Row 2: Ch 9, sc in 2nd ch from hook, sc in each ch across, sl st in each of first 2 sts on row 1, turn. *(8 sc)*
Row 3: Ch 1, sk sl sts, sc in **back lp** *(see Stitch Guide)* of each st across, turn.
Row 4: Ch 1, sc in back lp of each st across, sl st in both lps of each of next 2 sts on row 1, turn.
Rows 5–106 [5–118, 5–132]: [Rep rows 3 and 4 alternately] 51 [57, 64] times.
Row 107 [119, 133]: Rep row 3. Fasten off.

Right Front Placket
Row 1: Working in sts and in ends of rows across Right Front, with size G hook, join with sc in first st on Waist Ribbing, evenly sp 72 sc across to row 42 on Body, turn. *(73 sc)*
Row 2: Ch 6, sc in 2nd ch from hook, sc in each ch across, sl st in each of first 2 sts on row 1, turn. *(5 sc)*
Row 3: Working the following rows in back lps only, ch 1, sk sl sts, sc in each st across, turn.
Row 4: Ch 1, sc in back lp of each st across, sl st in each of next 2 sts on row 1, turn.

Rows 5–72: [Rep rows 3 and 4 alternately] 34 times.
Row 73: Rep row 3.
Row 74: Ch 1, sc in each st across, sl st in last st on row 1. Fasten off.

Left Front Placket
Row 1: Working in sts and in ends of rows across Left Front, with size G hook, join with sc in row 42, evenly sp 72 sc across, turn. *(73 sc)*
Rows 2–74: Rep same rows of Right Front Placket.

Neck Ribbing
Row 1: Working in sts and in ends of rows across neck edge, with size G hook, join with sc in first unworked st on row 42, evenly sp 69 sc across to last unworked st on row 42 on opposite side, turn. *(70 sc)*
Row 2: Ch 1, sl st in first st on row 1, ch 2, sc in 2nd ch from hook, sl st in each of next 2 sts on row 1, turn. *(1 sc)*
Row 3: Ch 1, sk sl sts, sc in back lp of next st, turn.
Row 4: Ch 2, sc in 2nd ch from hook, sc in back lp of next st, sl st in both lps of each of next 2 sts on row 1, turn. *(2 sc)*
Row 5: Ch 1, sk sl sts, sc in back lp of each st across, turn.
Row 6: Ch 2, sc in 2nd ch from hook, sc in back lp of

each st across, sl st in both lps of next 2 sts on row 1, turn. *(3 sc)*

Rows 7–10: Rep rows 5 and 6 alternately. *(5 sc at end of last row)*

Row 11: Ch 1, sk sl sts, sc in back lp of each st across, turn.

Row 12: Ch 1, sc in back lp of each st across, sl st in both lps of each of next 2 sts on row 1, turn.

Rows 13–62: [Rep rows 11 and 12 alternately] 25 times.

Row 63: Rep row 11.

Row 64: Ch 1, working in back lps, sc dec in first 2 sts, sc in each st across, sl st in both lps of each of next 2 sts on row 1, turn. *(4 sc)*

Row 65: Ch 1, sk sl sts, sc in back lp of each st across, turn.

Rows 66–69: [Rep rows 64 and 65 alternately] twice. *(2 sc at end of last row)*

Row 70: Ch 1, working in back lps, sc dec in first 2 sts, sl st in both lps of each of next 2 sts on row 1, turn. *(1 sc)*

Row 71: Ch 1, sk sl sts, sc in back lp of next st. Fasten off.

Sleeve

Make 2.

Row 1: With size H hook, ch 42, hdc in 3rd ch from hook, hdc in each ch across, turn. *(41 hdc)*

Rows 2 & 3: Ch 2, hdc in each st across, turn.

Row 4: Ch 2, hdc in each of next 3 sts, 5 hdc in next st, [hdc in each of next 3 sts, 5 hdc in next st] across to last 4 sts, hdc in each of last 4 sts, turn. *(32 hdc, 9 hdc groups)*

Row 5: For inc row, ch 2, hdc in same st, work in pattern across to last st, 2 hdc in last st, turn.

Note: After working inc row, work next sts as needed to maintain pattern.

Rows 6–8: Work in pattern.

Rows 9–36 [9–36, 9–44]: [Rep rows 5–8 consecutively] 14 [14, 18] times.

Row 37 [37, 45]: Rep row 5. *(59 [59, 63] hdc)*

Large Size Only

Fasten off.

Small & Medium Sizes Only

Rows 38–43 [38–45]: Work in pattern. At end of last row, fasten off.

For All Sizes

Matching center of last row on Sleeves to shoulder seams, sew Sleeves to armholes.

Sew hooks and eyes evenly spaced down Front Plackets as shown in photo. ∎

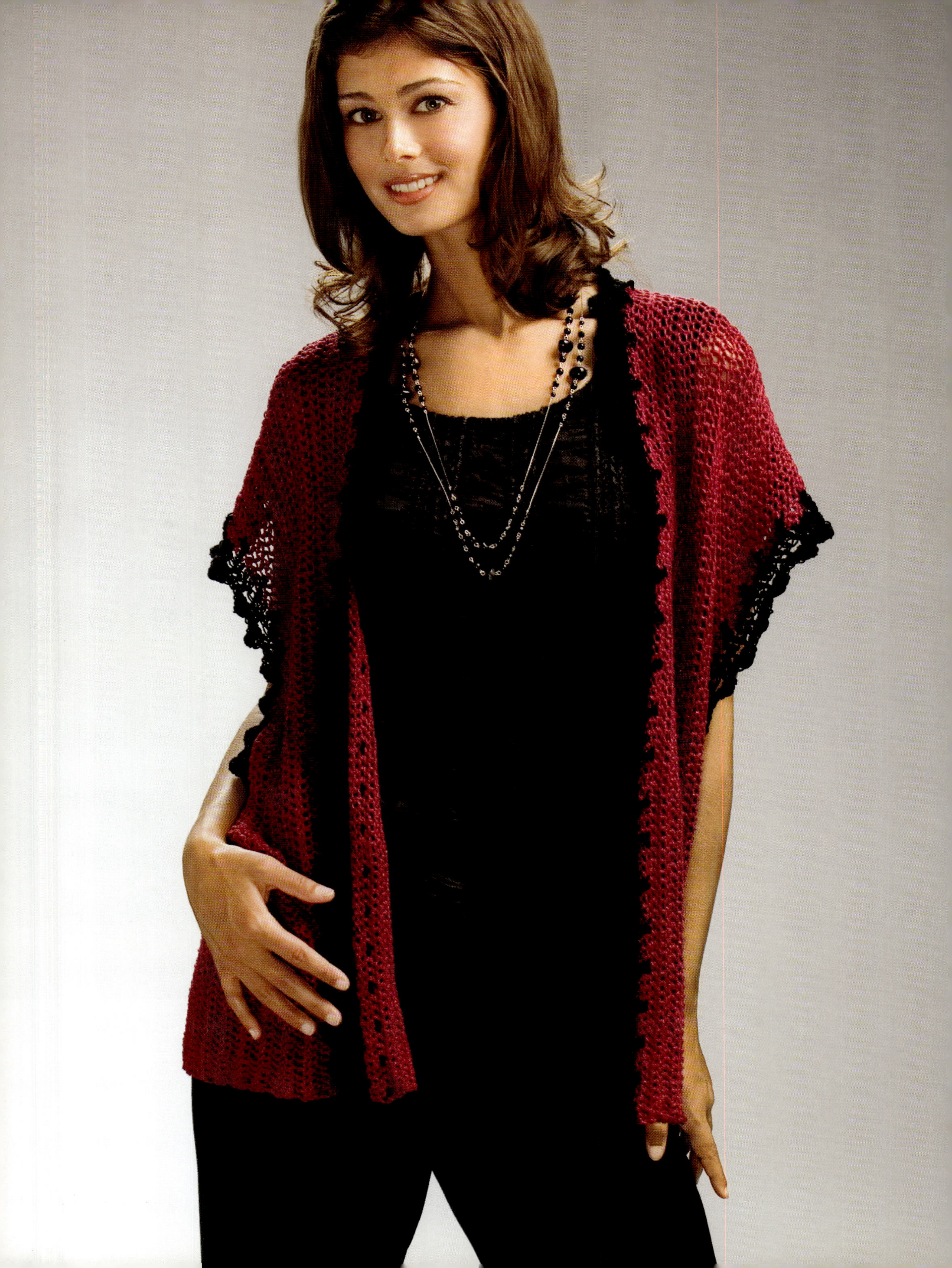

JACKETS

RUBY GOES TO TOWN

DESIGN BY MARY BETH TEMPLE

INTERMEDIATE

Finished Sizes
Instructions given fit 32–34-inch bust *(small)*; changes for 36–38-inch bust *(medium)*, 40–42-inch bust *(large)*, 44–46-inch bust *(X-large)*, 48-50-inch bust *(2X-large)* and 52-54-inch bust *(3X-large)* are in [ ].

Finished Garment Measurements
Bust: 44 inches *(small)* [47 inches *(medium)*, 52 inches *(large)*, 55 inches *(X-large)*, 60 inches *(2X-large)*, 64 inches *(3X-large)*]

Gauge
16 dc = 4 inches; 4 rows = 2 inches

Pattern Notes
Weave in loose ends as work progresses. Garment is sized for a loose fit. For a closer fitting garment, go down one size.

Materials
- Bernat Cool Crochet light (DK) weight yarn (1¾ oz/200 yds/50g per ball):
  5 balls #74435 velveteen *(A)*
- Patons Grace light (DK) weight yarn (1¾ oz/136 yds/50g per ball):
  2 balls #60040 night *(B)*
- Size H/8/5mm crochet hook or size needed to obtain gauge
- Tapestry needle
- Straight pins

WRAP

Back
Row 1 (RS): With A, ch 45 [47, 47, 47, 49, 49], dc in 4th ch from hook and in each rem ch across, turn. *(42 [44, 44, 44, 46, 46] dc)*
Row 2: Ch 3 *(counts as first dc)*, dc in each st across, turn.
Row 3: Ch 3, dc in each st across, ch 41 [43, 43, 43, 45, 45], turn.
Row 4: Dc in 4th ch from hook, dc in each ch and each dc across, turn. *(80 [84, 84, 84, 88, 88] dc)*
Row 5: Ch 3, dc in each st across, turn.
Rep row 5 until Back measures 21 [21½, 25, 26½, 29, 31] inches, ending with a RS row.
Row 6: Ch 3 *(counts as first dc)*, dc in each of next 41 [43, 43, 43, 45, 45] dc, turn. *(42 [44, 44, 44, 46, 46] dc)*
Rows 7 & 8: Rep row 6. At the end of row 8, fasten off.

Front
Make 2.
Row 1: With A, ch 83 [87, 87, 87, 91, 91], dc in 4th ch from hook, dc in each rem ch across, turn. *(80 [84, 84, 84, 88, 88] dc)*
Row 2: Ch 3, dc in each st across, turn.
Rep row 2 until Front measures 19 [20½, 23, 24½, 27, 29] inches.
Rows 3–5: Ch 3, dc in each dc across, turn. At the end of last rep, fasten off.
With RS facing, pin Fronts and Back tog and join shoulder seams with sc. Sc side seams tog, turn garment RS out.

Front Trim
Row 1: With RS facing, attach B at bottom of right front, ch 3, **fpdtr** *(see Stitch Guide)* around dc 2 rows below, sk dc directly behind fpdtr, [dc in each of next 3 dc, fpdtr around dc 2 rows below, sk dc directly behind fpdtr] up front, around neckline and down left front, ending with dc in last st, turn.

CONTINUED ON PAGE 47

JACKETS

PERFECT IN PLUM COAT

DESIGN PROVIDED COURTESY OF DMC CORPORATION

EXPERIENCED

Finished Size
Instructions given fit medium 36–38-inch bust *(medium)*

Finished Garment Measurements
Bust: 43½ inches
Back Waist Length: 59 inches

Materials
- DMC Senso Wool Cotton size 3 crochet cotton (100 yds per ball):
    - 69 balls #1308 plum
- Size H/8/5mm crochet hook or size needed to obtain gauge
- Tapestry needle
- Stitch markers
- 1¼-inch wooden buttons: 6

Gauge
Motif: 6½ inches square; **Pattern Stitches 1, 2 and 3:** 19 sts = 5 inches; **Pattern Stitch 1:** 9 rows = 4 inches; **Pattern Stitch 2:** 9 rows = 4 inches; **Pattern Stitch 3:** 14 rows = 6 inches; **Pattern Stitch 4:** 4 rows = 3 inches

Pattern Notes
Weave in loose ends as work progresses.
Hold 2 strands of crochet cotton together as 1 throughout unless otherwise stated.
Join rounds with slip stitch unless otherwise stated.

Special Stitches
Bobble: [Yo, insert hook in indicated st, yo, draw up a lp, yo, draw through 2 lps on hook] 5 times in indicated st, yo, draw through all 6 lps on hook, ch 1 to lock.
Shell: 3 dc in indicated st.

Pattern Stitch 1
Row 1 (WS): Ch 3 *(counts as first dc)*, **bpdc** *(see Stitch Guide)* around next st, [**fpdc**—*see Stitch Guide)* around each of next 2 sts, bpdc around each of next 2 sts] across, ending with bpdc around next st, dc in last st, turn.
Row 2: Ch 3, fpdc around next st, [bpdc around each of next 2 sts, fpdc around each of next 2 sts] across, ending with fpdc around next st, dc in last st, turn.

Pattern Stitch 2
Row 1 (WS): Ch 1, sc in each st across, turn.
Row 2: Ch 3, dc in each of next 2 sts, [**bobble** *(see Special Stitches)* in next st, dc in each of next 3 sts] across, turn.
Row 3: Rep row 1.
Row 4: Ch 3, dc in next st, [ch 2, sk next 2 sts, dc in each of next 2 sts] across, turn.
Row 5: Ch 3, fpdc around next st, [dc in each of next 2 chs, fpdc around each of next 2 sts] across, turn.
Row 6: Rep row 4.
Row 7: Rep row 1.
Row 8: Rep row 2.
Row 9: Rep row 1.

Pattern Stitch 3
Row 1 (WS): Ch 3, bpdc around next st, [fpdc around each of next 6 sts, bpdc around each of next 2 sts] across, ending with bpdc around next st, dc in last st, turn.
Row 2: Ch 3, fpdc around next st, [bpdc around each of next 2 sts, fpdc around each of next 2 sts] across, ending with fpdc around next st, dc in last st, turn.
Row 3: Ch 3, bpdc around next st, [fpdc around each of next 2 sts, bpdc around each of next 2 sts] across, ending with bpdc in next st, dc in last st, turn.
Row 4: Ch 3, fpdc around next st, [bpdc around each of

CONTINUED ON PAGE 48

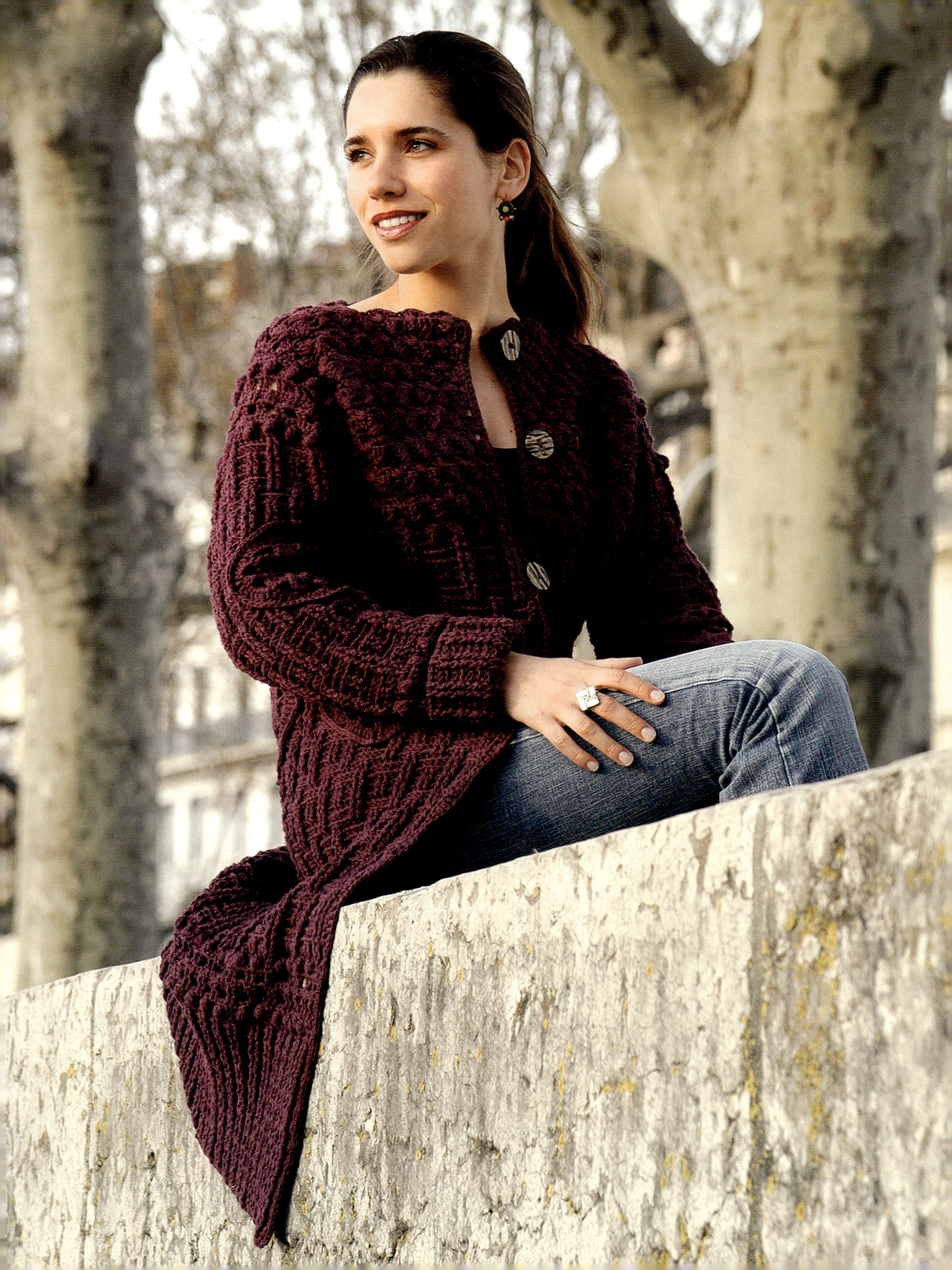

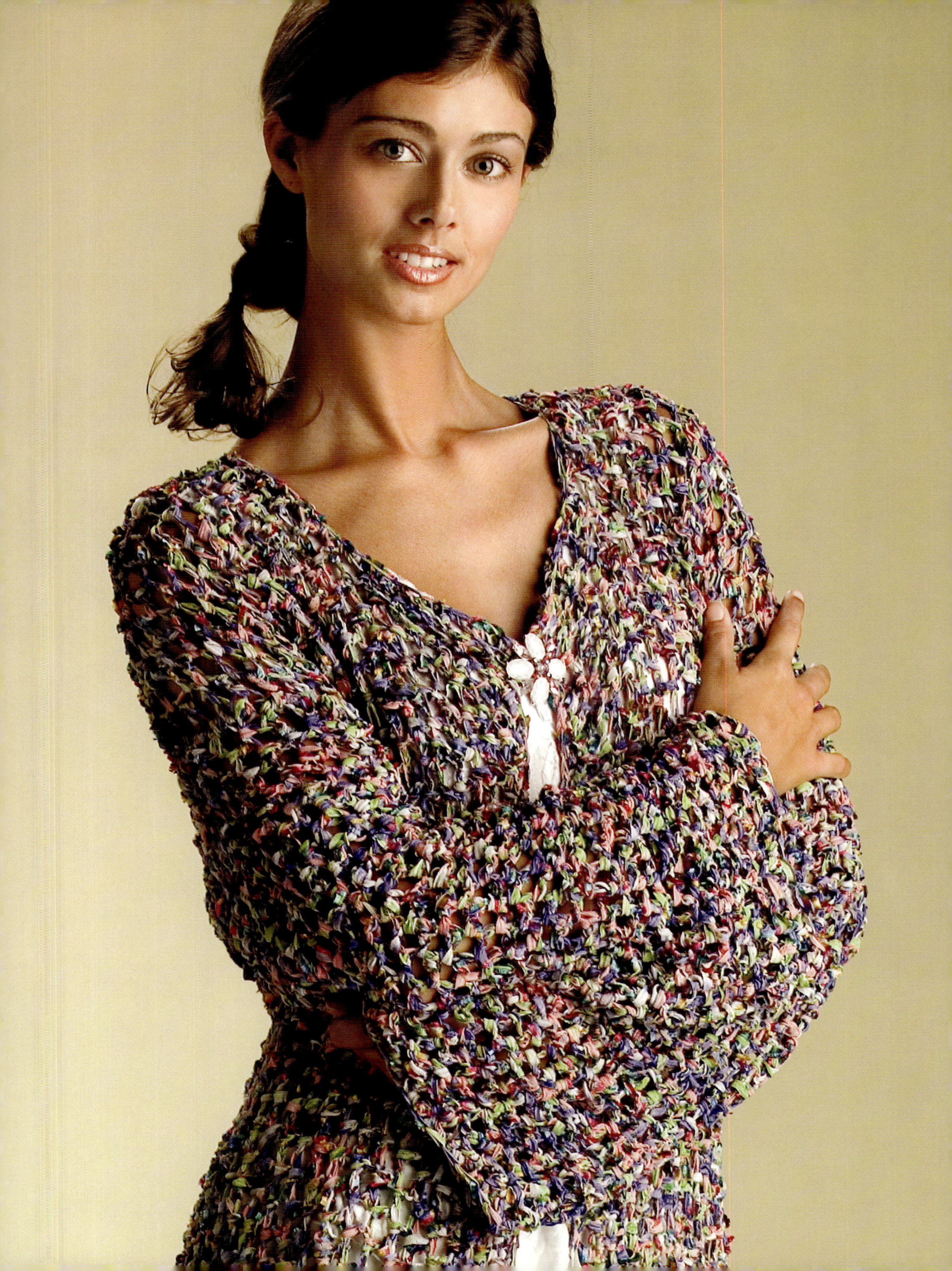

CONFETTI COVER-UP

DESIGN BY LISA GONZALEZ

EASY

Finished Sizes
Instructions given fit woman's small/medium; changes for medium/large, large/X-large, 2X-large and 3X-large are in [ ].

Finished Garment Measurements
Bust: 34–36 inches *(small/medium)* [38–40-inches *(medium/large)*, 42–46 inches *(large/X-large)*, 48–50 inches *(2X-large)*, 52–54 inches *(3X-large)*]

Materials
- Classic Elite Bangles bulky (chunky) weight yarn (1¾ oz/83 yds/50g per ball): 24 [25, 25, 26, 27] balls #6704 heliotrope
- Size K/10½/6.5mm crochet hook or size needed to obtain gauge
- Blunt-end yarn needle
- Stitch markers

Gauge
[Dc, ch 1] 6 times = 4 inches; 6 rows = 4 inches

Pattern Notes
Weave in loose ends as work progresses.
Join rounds with a slip stitch unless otherwise stated.
Cover-up is crocheted vertically in several pieces then assembled.
Pattern also includes a cropped version of the Cover-up following each piece.

COVER-UP

Back
Row 1: Loosely ch 117 [123, 129, 135, 135], dc in 5th ch from hook, [ch 1, sk 1 ch, dc in next ch] across, ending with dc in last ch, turn.

JACKETS, WRAPS & MORE 43

JACKETS

Row 2: Ch 4 *(counts as first dc, ch-1)*, sk first dc, [dc in next ch-1 sp, ch 1, sk next dc] across, ending with dc in last ch sp, turn. *(113 [119, 125, 131, 131] sts)*
Rep row 2 until Back measures 20 [23, 25, 27, 29] inches wide when placed on a flat surface, fasten off.

Cropped Back
Row 1: Ch 54 [59, 65, 71, 71], rep row 1 of Back.
Row 2: Rep row 2 of Back. *(49 [55, 61, 67, 67] sts)*
Rep row 2 until Cropped Back measures the same width as Back.

Front
Make 2.
Row 1: Rep row 1 of Back.
Row 2: Rep row 2 of Back.
Rep row 2 until Front measures 8 [9, 10, 11, 12] inches wide when placed on a flat surface.

Cropped Front
Make 2.
Row 1: Ch 54 [59, 65, 71, 71], rep row 1 of Front.
Row 2: Rep row 2 of Front.
Rep row 2 until Cropped Front measures the same width as Front.

Neckline Shaping
Row 3: Ch 4, sk first dc, *dc in ch-1 sp, sk next dc, ch 1, rep from * for 93 [99, 105, 109, 109] sts, leaving rem sts unworked, turn.
Row 4: Ch 4, sk first dc, [dc in next ch-1 sp, ch 1, sk next dc] across, ending with dc in last ch sp, turn.
Rep row 4 until Front measures 10 [11½, 12½, 13½, 14½] inches wide when placed on a flat surface, fasten off.

Cropped Neckline Shaping
Row 3: Ch 4, sk next dc, *dc in ch-1 sp, sk next dc, ch 1, rep from * for 29 [35, 41, 45, 45] sts, leaving rem sts unworked, turn.
Row 4: Ch 4, sk first dc, [dc in next ch-1 sp, ch 1, sk next dc] across, ending with dc in last ch sp, turn.
Rep row 4 until Cropped Neckline Shaping measures the same width as Neckline Shaping. Fasten off.

JACKETS

Sleeve
Make 2.
Row 1: Ch 61 [63, 63, 65, 65], dc in 5th ch from hook, [ch 1, sk 1 ch, dc in next ch] across, turn.
Row 2: Ch 4, sk first dc, [dc in next ch-1 sp, ch 1, sk next dc] across, ending with dc in last ch sp, turn.
Rep row 2 until Sleeve measures 14½ [15, 16, 17, 18] inches when placed on a flat surface, fasten off. Holding sides of Sleeve tog, sew or crochet tog.

Cropped Sleeve
Make 2.
Row 1: Ch 23 [25, 25, 27, 27], rep row 1 of Sleeve starting with dc in 5th ch.
Row 2: Rep row 2 of Sleeve.
Rep row 2 until cropped Sleeve measures the same width as Sleeve. Holding sides of Sleeve tog, sew or crochet tog.

Assembly
Sew or crochet Fronts and Back tog at shoulders. Center Sleeve at shoulder seam, sew or crochet Sleeve into armhole opening. Sew or crochet side seams tog, leaving approximately 5 inches unattached at each bottom side seam.

Cover-up Edging
Rnd 1: Beg at back neck, loosely sc around, taking care to sc in ch-1 sps only. Work 3 sc in each front neckline corner, bottom front and side corners, join in beg sc, fasten off.

Sleeve Edging
Rnd 1: Beg at Sleeve seam, sc around taking care to sc in ch-1 sps only, join in beg sc, fasten off.

Finishing
Taking care not to twist ribbon, weave ribbon through ch-1 sps on row just below bust, tie ends in a bow. ■

JACKETS continued

GRANNY SQUARE DRESS & JACKET CONTINUED FROM PAGE 29

next st] around, join in 3rd ch of beg ch-5, fasten off. Rep on other armhole.

JACKET

Strip 1
First Motif
Rnds 1–6: Rep Large Motif for Dress.

Motifs 2–5
Rep Large Motif for Dress.

Motif 6
Rnds 1–5: Rep rnds 1-5 of Large Motif for Dress.
Rnd 6: Folding strip in half and joining to First Motif to create side seam, ch 6, dc in same sp as joining, ch 2, (sc, ch 3, sc) in center st of next 5-st group, ch 2, sk next 3 sts, (tr, ch-5 join, tr) in next st, joining to First Motif, ch 2, (sc, ch 3, sc) in center st of next 5-st group, ch 2, sk next 3 sts, (tr, ch-5 join, tr) in next st, joining to Motif 5 of current strip, ch 2, (sc, ch 3, sc) in center st of next 5-st group, ch 2, sk next 3 sts, (dc, ch 3, dc) in next st, ch 2, (sc, ch 3, sc) in center st of next 5-st group, ch 2, sk next 3 sts, (tr, ch 5, tr) in next st, ch 2, (sc, ch 3, sc) in center st of next 5-st group, ch 2, sk next 3 sts, (dc, ch 3, dc) in next st, ch 2, (sc, ch 3, sc) in center of next 5-st group, ch 2, sk next 3 sts, (tr, ch 5, tr) in next st, ch 2, (sc, ch 3, sc) in center of next 5-st group, ch 2, join in 3rd ch of beg ch-6, fasten off.

Strip 2
First Motif
Rnds 1–6: Rep Large Motif for Dress.

Motifs 2 & 3
Rep Large Motif for Dress.

Strip 3
First Motif
Rnds 1–6: Rep Large Motif for Dress.

Motifs 2–5
Rep Large Motif for Dress.

Motif 6
Rnds 1–5: Rep rnds 1-5 of Large Motif for Dress.
Rnd 6: Rep rnd 6 of Motif 6 of Jacket.

Filler Motif
Using diagram as a guide, rep rnds 1-4 of Filler Motif for Dress.

Half Filler Motif
Using diagram as a guide, rep rnds 1-4 of Half Filler Motif for Top of Dress.

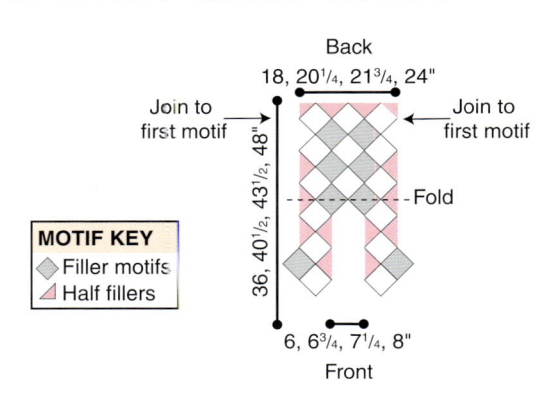

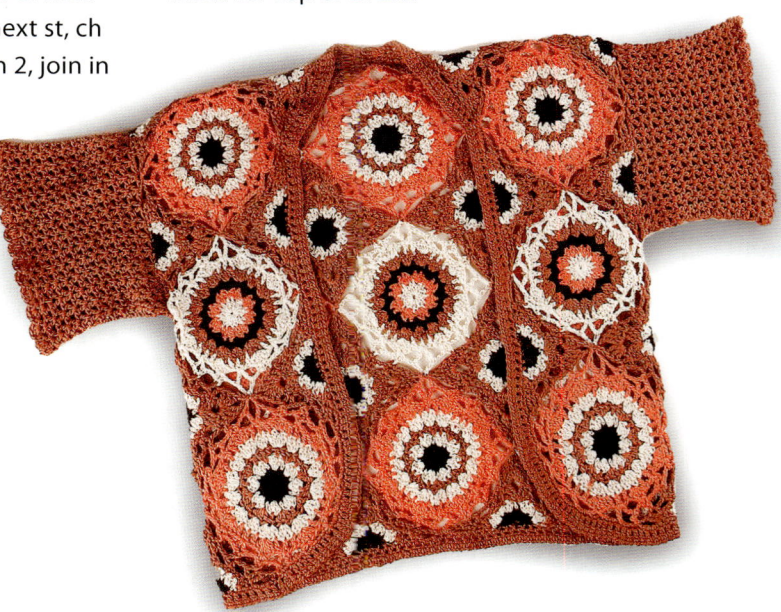

Granny Square Jacket Joining Diagram

Back: 18, 20¼, 21¾, 24"
36, 40½, 43½, 48"
Front: 6, 6¾, 7¼, 8"

MOTIF KEY
- Filler motifs
- Half fillers

JACKETS continued

Sleeve

Rnd 1: Working in row ends of Half Fillers around armhole opening, join terra cotta in center of side seam, [3 sc in next row, 2 sc in next row, sc in next row, 2 sc in next row, sc in bottom of ring, 2 sc in next row, sc in next row, 2 sc in next row, 3 sc in next row, sc in ch-5 sp on next Large Motif] 3 times, omitting last sc, sk sl st, join in first sc. *(54 sc)*

Rnd 2: Ch 4, dc in same st, sk next st, [**V-st** *(see Special Stitches)* in next st, sk next st] around, join in 3rd ch of beg ch-4. *(27 V-sts)*

Rep on opposite Armhole.

Rnds 3–12: Sl st into first ch-1 sp, ch 4, dc in same ch-1 sp, V-st in ch-1 sp of each V-st around, join in 3rd ch of beg ch-4.

Rnd 13: Sl st into first ch-1 sp, ch 3, 2 dc in same sp, sl st in sp before next V-st, [3 dc in next V-st, sl st in sp before next V-st] around, join in 3rd ch of beg ch-3, fasten off.

Front Panel & Neck Edging

Rnd 1: Starting at bottom of right front panel, join terra cotta with sc in center ch-5 sp on Large Motif, 3 sc in same sp, 3 sc in next ch-2 sp, 2 sc in next ch-3 sp, 3 sc in next ch-2 sp, 4 sc in next ch-3 sp, 3 sc in next ch-2 sp, 2 sc in next ch-3 sp, 3 sc in next ch-2 sp, 3 sc in next ch-5 sp, working in row ends of Half Fillers, *3 sc in next row, 2 sc in next row, sc in next row, 2 sc in next row, sc in bottom of ring, 2 sc in next row, sc in next row, 2 sc in next row, 3 sc in next row, sc in ch-5 sp on next Large Motif*, rep between * twice, working in sps and sts of Filler Motifs along back of neck, 3 sc in next ch-3 sp, [sc in each of next 4 sts, (sc in next ch-3 sp, sc in next st, 2 sc in next ch-2 sp, sc in next st) twice, sc in next ch-3 sp, sc in each of next 4 sts, sc in ch-5 sp on next Large Motif] twice, rep between * twice, 3 sc in next ch-5 sp, 3 sc in next ch-2 sp, 2 sc in next ch-3 sp, 3 sc in next ch-2 sp, 4 sc in next ch-3 sp, 3 sc in next ch-2 sp, 2 sc in next ch-3 sp, 3 sc in next ch-2 sp, 4 sc in next ch-5 sp, working along bottom of back, rep between * 3 times, 3 sc in next row, 2 sc in next row, sc in next row, 3 sc in next row, join in beg sc.

Rnd 2: Ch 3, dc in each st around, join in 3rd ch of beg ch-3.

Rnd 3: Ch 1, sc in first st, ch 1, [sc in next st, ch 1] around, join in beg sc, fasten off. ■

RUBY GOES TO TOWN CONTINUED FROM PAGE 39

Row 2: Ch 4, sk fpdtr, [dc in each of next 3 dc, ch 1, sk fpdtr] across, ending with dc in last dc, turn.

Row 3: Ch 1, sc in first dc, (hdc, dc, tr, dc, hdc) in ch-1 sp, [sc in each of next 3 dc, (hdc, dc, tr, dc, hdc) in next ch-1 sp] across, ending with sc in last dc, fasten off.

Arm Trim

Row 1: With RS facing, attach B at back of armhole for right Arm Trim *(at front of armhole for left Arm Trim) (do not work row 1 in ends of rows at underarm)*, ch 3, *fpdtr around vertical post of dc 2 rows below, sk dc directly behind fpdtr**, dc in each of next 3 dc, rep from * around armhole to opposite edge, ending last rep at **, dc in next dc, turn.

Row 2: Ch 3, sk 1 unworked row to the left toward underarm, sl st in side edge of 2nd dc row at underarm, ch 1, *dc in each of next 3 dc, ch 1, sk next fpdtr**, rep from * around armhole, ending last rep at **, sk next row of underarm, sl st in next row, turn.

Row 3: Ch 1, sc in first dc, (hdc, dc, tr, dc, hdc) in ch-1 sp, [sc in each of next 3 dc, (hdc, dc, tr, dc, hdc) in next ch-1 sp] across, ending with sc in last dc, fasten off. Rep on opposite armhole. ■

JACKETS continued

PERFECT IN PLUM COAT CONTINUED FROM PAGE 40

next 6 sts, fpdc around each of next 2 sts] across, ending with fpdc around next st, dc in last st, turn.
Row 5: Rep row 3.
Row 6: Rep row 2.
Row 7: Rep row 1.
Row 8: Ch 3, bpdc around each of next 3 sts, [fpdc around each of next 2 sts, bpdc around each of next 6 sts] across, ending with bpdc around each of next 3 sts, dc in last st, turn.
Row 9: Rep row 3.
Row 10: Rep row 2.
Row 11: Ch 3, fpdc around each of next 3 sts, [bpdc around each of next 2 sts, fpdc around each of next 6 sts] across, ending with fpdc around each of next 3 sts, dc in last st, turn.
Row 12: Rep row 2.
Row 13: Rep row 3.
Row 14: Rep row 8.

Pattern Stitch 4
Row 1 (WS): Ch 3, [sk next 2 sts, **shell** *(see Special Stitches)* in next st, shell in previous st] across, ending with sk 2 dc in last st where applicable, turn.
Row 2: Ch 4, shell in same st, [sk next shell, shell in first dc of next shell, shell in last dc of previous shell] across, 4 dc in last st turn.
Row 3: Ch 3, [shell in first dc of next shell, shell in last dc of previous shell] across, dc in last st, turn.

COAT

Back
Row 1: Ch 84, dc in 4th ch from hook *(first 3 chs count as first dc)*, dc in each rem ch across, turn. *(82 dc)*
Row 2: Working Pattern Stitch 1, work row 1.
Rows 3–19: Working Pattern Stitch 1, rep row 2.
Rows 20–28: Work Pattern Stitch 2.
Row 29: Ch 3, dc in each st across, turn.
Rows 30–92: Work Pattern Stitch 3 [rows 1–14] 4 times, rep rows 1–7.

Armhole
Row 93: Sl st in each of first 12 sts, ch 4, work row 1 of Pattern Stitch 4 in next 60 sts, leaving rem sts unworked, turn.
Row 94: Work row 1 of Pattern Stitch 4.
Row 95: Work row 2 of Pattern Stitch 4.
Row 96: Work row 3 of Pattern Stitch 4.
Rows 97–104: Rep rows 2 and 3 of Pattern Stitch 4. At end of last row, fasten off.

Front
Make 2.
Row 1: Ch 44, dc in 4th ch from hook *(3 sk chs count as first dc)*, dc in each rem ch across, turn. *(42 dc)*
Rows 2–92: Rep rows 2–92 of Back.

Left Armhole
Row 93: Sl st in each of first 12 sts, ch 3, work row 1 of Pattern Stitch 4 in each st across, turn.

Right Armhole
Row 93: Ch 3, work row 1 of Pattern Stitch 4 in each st across, leaving last 11 sts unworked, turn.

Left & Right Front
Rows 94–104: Rep rows 94–104 of Back.

Sleeve
Make 2.
Row 1: Ch 48, dc in 4th ch from hook *(3 sk chs count as first dc)*, dc in each rem ch across, turn. *(46 dc)*
Rows 2–43: Rep rows 2–43 of Back, inc 1 st at beg and end of every 4th row. *(66 sts)*
Rows 44–50: Work rows 1–7 of Pattern Stitch 2. At the end of last row, fasten off.

Motif
Make 7.
Rnd 1: Ch 10, sl st in first ch to form ring, ch 1, 16 sc in ring, join in beg sc. *(16 sc)*
Rnd 2: Ch 7 *(counts as first dc, ch-4)*, sk next st, [dc in next st, ch 4, sk next st] around, join in 3rd ch of beg ch-7.
Rnd 3: Sl st in next ch sp, ch 1, (sc, dc, tr, ch 1, tr, dc, sc) in same ch sp, (sc, dc, tr, ch 1, tr, dc, sc) in each ch sp around, join in beg sc.
Rnd 4: Ch 9 *(counts as first tr, ch-5)*, *[sc in next ch-1 sp, ch 5] twice, tr in sp between next 2 sts, ch 5, rep from * around, ending with ch 5, sl st in 4th ch of beg ch-9.
Rnd 5: Ch 4, *[dc in each of next 5 chs, sk next st] twice, dc in each of next 5 chs, (tr, ch 3, tr) in next tr, rep from * around, ending with ch 3, sl st in 4th ch of beg ch-4.
Rnd 6: Ch 1, *sc in each of first 15 dc, sc in next tr, sc in next ch, ch 1, sk next ch, sc in next ch, sc in next tr, rep from * around, ending with last sc in 4th ch of beg ch-4 of previous rnd, fasten off.

Border
Working in ends of rows, join with sc in bottom corner of 1 Front, evenly sp sc across, fasten off. Rep Border on rem front.

Right Front Only
Join with sc at the end of Pattern Stitch 2, *sc in next st, hdc in each of next 2 sts, dc in each of next 2 sts, tr in next st, ch 1 *(buttonhole)*, tr in next st, dc in each of next 2 sts, hdc in each of next 2 sts, sc in next st, rep from * across to end of Pattern Stitch 3, fasten off.

Assembly
With RS tog, sc shoulder seams tog across 4½ inches. Fold first Sleeve in half, place fold at shoulder seam, sc in place, fasten off. Attach 2nd Sleeve in same manner. With RS tog, sc Sleeve and side seams closed.
Sew buttons to Left Front opposite ch-1 buttonhole sps of Right Front.
Sew 3 Motifs in diamond shape to Back and 1 to each Front and each Sleeve. ■

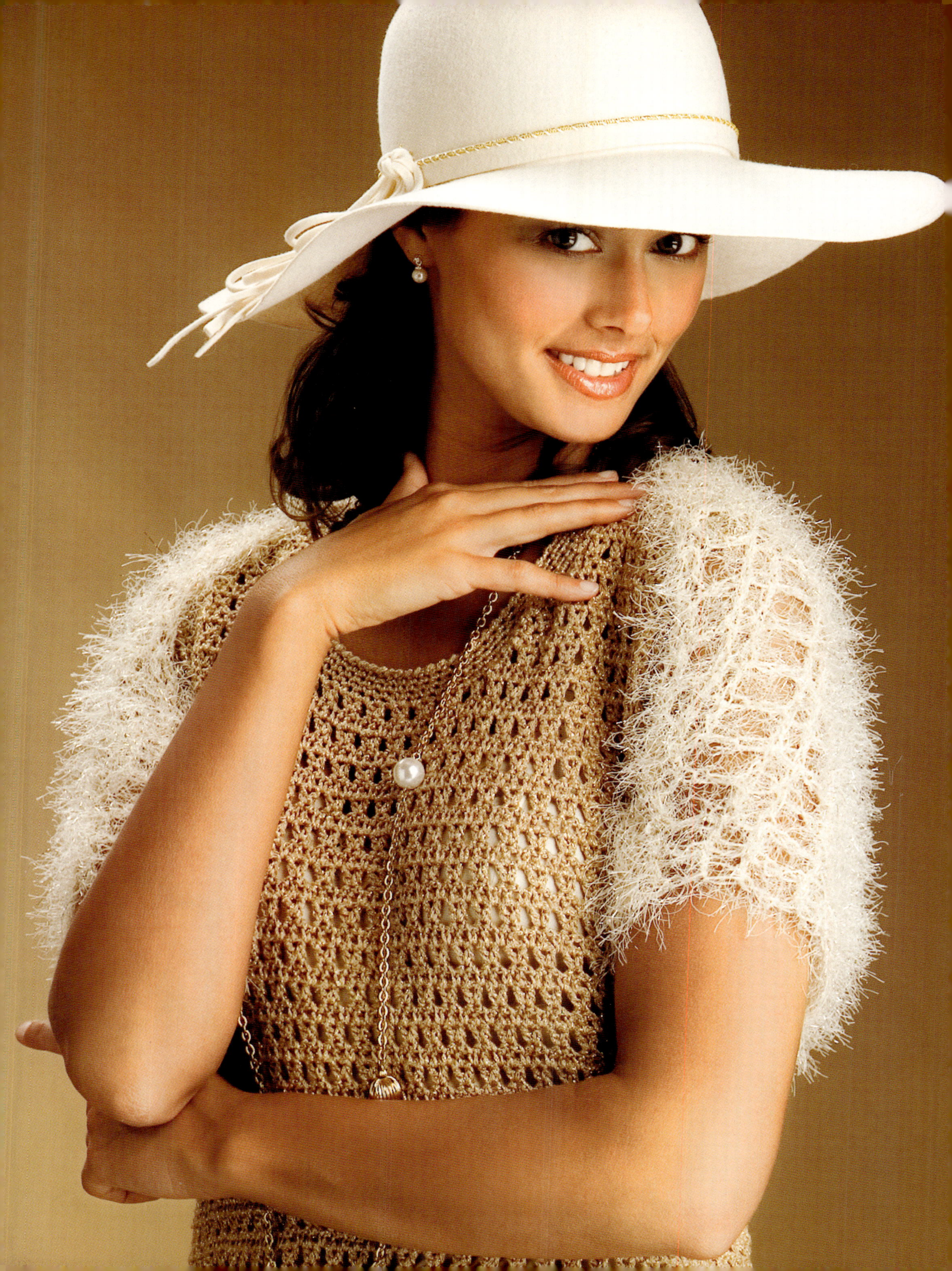

WRAPS

Wraps add the perfect finishing touch to a variety of styles from daytime chic to nighttime glamour. From simple to sophisticated, our charming collection of shawls, shrugs and ponchos will have you covered for any occasion.

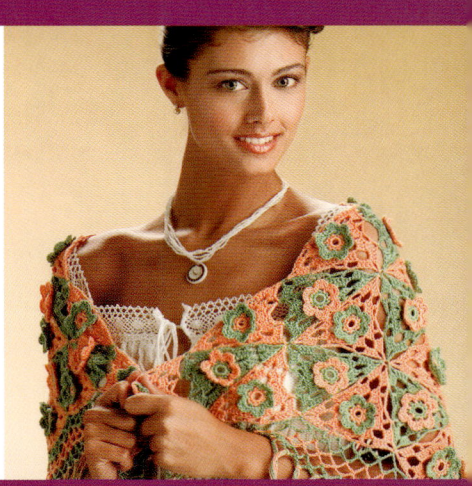

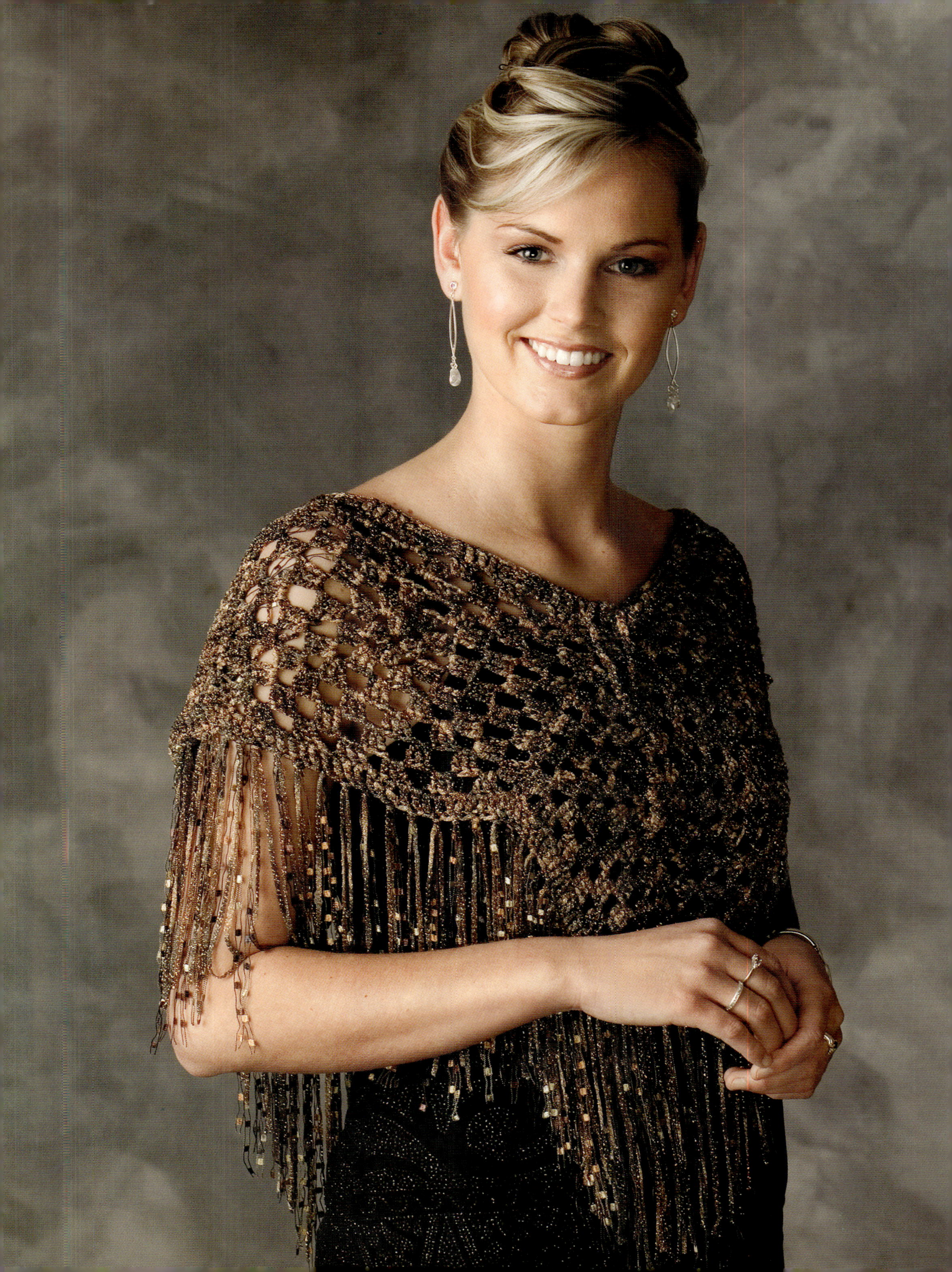

GOLD NUGGET COCKTAIL COVER-UP

DESIGN BY LAINIE HERING

INTERMEDIATE

Finished Size
One size fits most

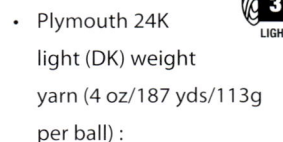

Materials
- Plymouth 24K light (DK) weight yarn (4 oz/187 yds/113g per ball):
    3 balls #61 gold
- Plymouth Eros novelty weight nylon ladder yarn (2 oz/165 yds/57g per ball):
    1 ball #3253 gold
- Size H/8/5mm crochet hook or size needed to obtain gauge
- Tapestry needle

Gauge
Squares = 8 inches square

Special Stitches
Beginning Popcorn (beg pc): Ch 4 *(counts as first tr)*, 3 tr in same ch sp, drop lp from hook, insert hook in top of beg ch-4, pull dropped lp through.

Popcorn (pc): 4 tr in ch sp indicated, drop lp from hook, insert hook in first tr of group, pull dropped lp through.

COVER-UP

Square
Make 6.

Rnd 1: With 24K, ch 5, sl st in first ch to form ring, **beg pc** *(see Special Stitches)* in ring, ch 3, [**pc** *(see Special Stitches)* in ring, ch 3] 3 times, join with sl st in top of beg pc. *(4 pc, 4 ch sps)*

Rnd 2: Sl st in first ch sp, ch 4 *(counts as first tr)*, 2 tr, ch 3, 3 tr) in same ch sp, ch 1, *(3 tr, ch 3, 3 tr) in next ch sp, ch 1, rep from * around, join with sl st in top of ch-4. *(24 tr, 4 ch-1 sps, 4 ch-3 sps)*

Rnd 3: Sl st in each of next 2 sts, sl st in next ch-3 sp, ch 4, (2 tr, ch 3, 3 tr) in same ch-3 sp, ch 2, 3 tr in next ch-1 sp, ch 2, *(3 tr, ch 3, 3 tr) in next ch-3 sp, ch 2, 3 tr in next ch-1 sp, ch 2, rep from * around, join with sl st in 4th ch of beg ch-4. *(36 tr, 8 ch-2 sps, 4 ch-3 sps)*

Rnds 4–6: Sl st in each of next 2 sts, sl st in next ch-3 sp, ch 4, (2 tr, ch 3, 3 tr) in same ch-3 sp, ch 2, [3 tr in next ch-2 sp, ch 2] across to next corner ch-3 sp, *(3 tr, ch 3, 3 tr) in next ch-3 sp, ch 2, [3 tr in next ch-2 sp, ch 2] across to next corner ch-3 sp, rep from * around, join with sl st in 4th ch of beg ch-4. At end of last rnd, fasten off. *(72 tr, 20 ch-2 sps, 4 ch-3 sps)*

Shoulder Piece
Make 4.

Join 24K with sl st in any corner ch sp, ch 4, evenly sp 24 tr across to next corner ch sp. Fasten off.

CONTINUED ON PAGE 79

WRAPS

ENCHANTED EVENING

DESIGN BY LAURA GEBHARDT

EASY

Finished Sizes
Instructions given fit small; changes medium, large, X-large and 2X-large are in [ ].

Materials
- SRK Collection Sari bulky (chunky) weight nylon ribbon (1¾ oz/104 yds/50g per ball): 5 [6, 7, 8, 8] balls #58 pink
- Size K/10½/6.5mm crochet hook or size needed to obtain gauge
- Tapestry needle

Gauge
12 sc = 4 inches; 13 sc rows = 4 inches

Pattern Note
Weave in loose ends as work progresses.

Special Stitches
Paris stitch (Paris st): (2 dc, ch 2, sc) in indicated st or sp.
Beginning Paris stitch (beg Paris st): Ch 3 *(counts as first dc)*, (dc, ch 2, sc) in same st as beg ch-3.

CAPELET

Collar
Row 1: Ch 98 [102, 106, 110, 114], sc in 2nd ch from hook, sc in each rem ch across, turn. *(97 [101, 105, 109, 113] sc)*
Row 2: Ch 1, sc in each sc across, turn.
Rows 3–12 [3–12, 3–14, 3–15, 3–15]: Rep row 2.

54   JACKETS, WRAPS & MORE

For Sizes X-Large & 2X-Large Only
Row 16: Ch 1, 2 sc in first sc, sc in each sc to approximate halfway point of row, 2 sc in each of next 2 sc, sc in each rem sc to last sc, 2 sc in last sc, turn. *([113, 117] sc)*

Body
For All Sizes
Row 13 [13, 15, 17, 17]: Beg Paris st *(see Special Stitches)* in first st, [sk next st, **Paris st** *(see Special Stitches)* in next st] across, turn. *(49 [51, 53, 57, 59] Paris sts)*
Rows 14–37 [14–37, 16–43, 18–49, 18–49]: Beg Paris st in first ch-2 sp, [Paris st in each rem ch-2 sp] across, turn.

Ties
Row 1: With RS facing, attach yarn with sl st in sc at end of row 12 [12, 14, 16, 16], ch 80, sl st in 2nd ch from hook, sl st in each rem ch across, fasten off.
Rep row 1 of Ties on opposite side of row 12 [12, 14, 16, 16].

Collar Edging
Row 1: With RS facing, working in opposite side of foundation ch, attach yarn, ch 1, **reverse sc** *(see Fig. 1)* in each ch across, leaving a length, fasten off.
Thread rem length into tapestry needle, fold Collar in half and tack beg and end of Collar and loose edge of Collar as desired. ■

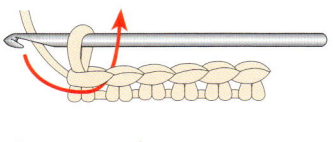

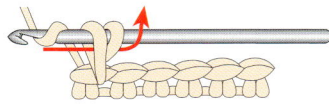

Reverse Single Crochet Fig. 1

WRAPS

BUTTERFLIES & ROSES FILET SHAWL

DESIGN BY KATHRYN WHITE

INTERMEDIATE

Finished Size
30 x 84 inches

Materials
- Grandma's Best size 10 crochet cotton (350 yds per ball):
    7 balls cream
- Sewing thread (1,000 yds per spool):
    3 spools gold
- Size 5/1.90mm steel crochet hook or size needed to obtain gauge
- Big-eye beading needle
- Size 8 gold seed beads: 85g

Gauge
9 extended dc = 1 inch; 7 extended dc rows = 2 inches

Pattern Notes
Weave in loose ends as work progresses.
It is recommended to check design after every row for accuracy to avoid missing or adding blocks or mesh and having to redo sections
Chart shows half the Shawl. Follow chart to center, then from center back out to edge.

Special Stitches
Extended double crochet (extended dc): Yo, insert hook in indicated st, yo, draw up lp, [yo, draw through 2 lps on hook] twice.
Mesh: (Extended dc in next st, ch 2, sk next 2 sts, extended dc in next st) for 1 mesh. When 1 or more mesh are side by side, they share the center st between them, so 2 meshes will be (extended dc in next st, ch 2, sk next 2 sts) twice and extended dc in next st.
Block: 4 extended dc make up 1 block. When one or more blocks are side by side, they share the center st between them, so 2 blocks will be 7 extended dc, 3 blocks will be 10 extended dc and 4 blocks will be 13 extended dc.
Increase a block at beginning of row (inc a block at beg of row): Ch 5, extended dc in 4th ch from hook, extended dc in next ch, extended dc in next extended dc.
Increase multiple blocks at beginning of row (inc multiple blocks at beg of row): Ch 5 for first inc and add 3 more chs for each block required. For 2 block inc, ch 8; 3 block inc, ch 11; 4 block inc, ch 14; 5 block inc, ch 17; 6 block inc, ch 20; extended dc in 4th ch from hook and in each rem ch.
Increase a block or blocks at end of row (inc a block or blocks at end of row): For first extended dc, tr in the base of the last extended dc where it joins the row, work a tr in the base of the previous tr just completed, continue adding sts in this manner until the required number of blocks is completed. For each block, add 3 sts as the last extended dc of the row counts as the shared st. For 2 blocks, 6 tr; 3 blocks, 9 tr; 4 blocks, 12 tr; 5 blocks, 15 tr; 6 blocks, 18 tr.
Decrease at beginning of row (dec at beg of row): Sl st across the top of the number of meshes or blocks required to complete the next extended dc, then (ch

56 JACKETS, WRAPS & MORE

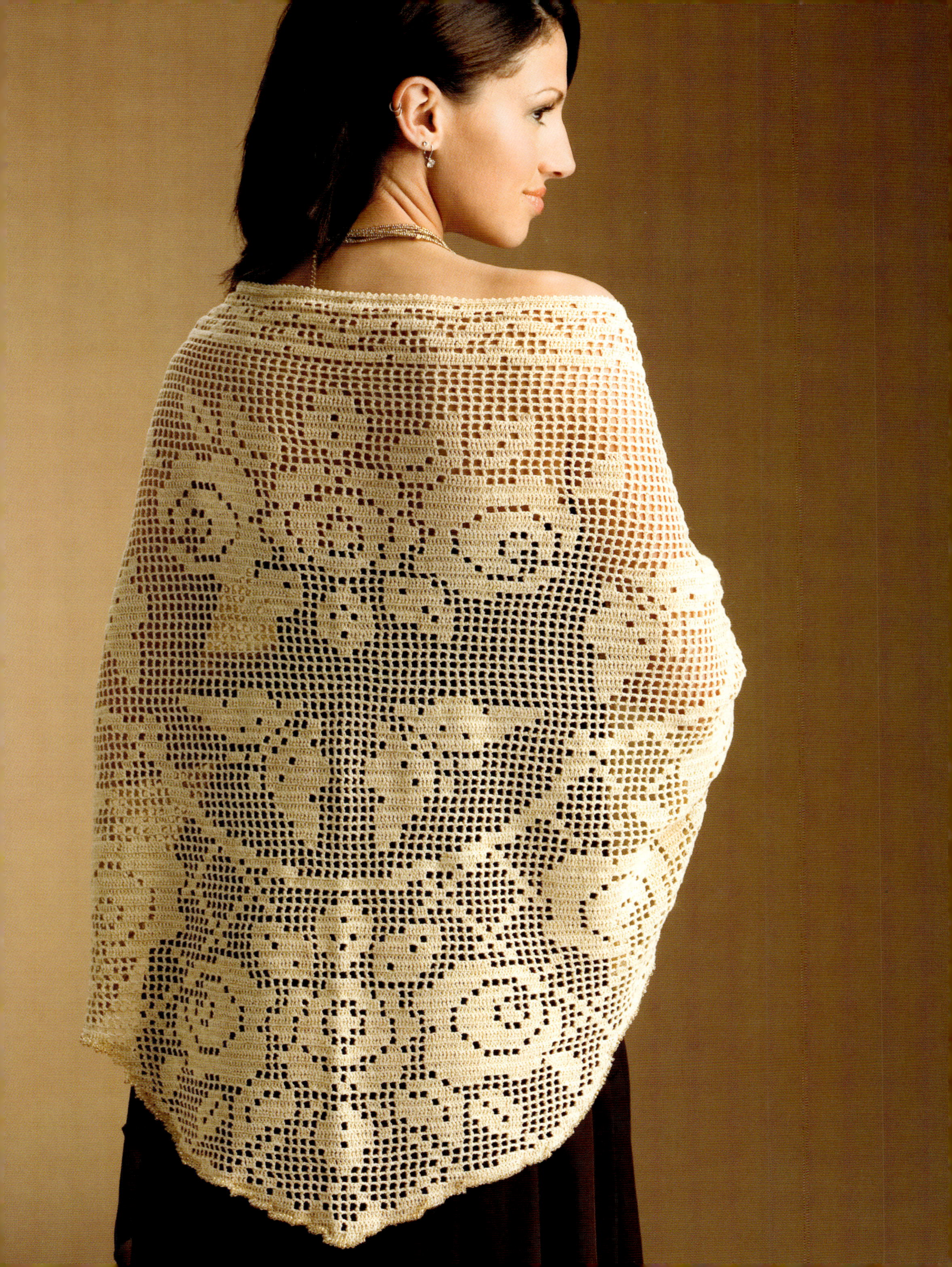

WRAPS

5, sk next 2 sts, extended dc in next extended dc) for mesh st or (ch 3, extended dc in next 3 sts) for block.

Decrease at end of row (dec at end of row): Work indicated number of blocks or mesh required as indicated by chart.

Bead single crochet (bead sc): Insert hook in indicated st, yo, draw up a lp, move 1 bead up next to work, yo, draw through 2 lps on hook.

3-bead single crochet (3-bead sc): Insert hook in indicated st, yo, draw up a lp, move 3 beads up next to work, yo, draw through 2 lps on hook.

4-bead single crochet (4-bead sc): Insert hook in indicated st, yo, draw up a lp, move 4 beads up next to work, yo, draw through 2 lps on hook.

5-bead single crochet (5-bead sc): Insert hook in indicated st, yo, draw up a lp, move 5 beads up next to work, yo, draw through 2 lps on hook.

SHAWL

Row 1: With 1 strand each cream and gold, ch 12, **extended dc** (see Special Stitches) in 4th ch from hook, extended dc in each rem ch across, turn. (3 blocks)

Rows 2–105: Follow Chart (see Fig. 1), working blocks and mesh as indicated, using Special Stitches as a guide, turn at end of each row.

Top edging

Row 106: Ch 1, sc in first extended dc, [ch 1, sk 1 extended dc, sc in next extended dc] across, turn.

Row 107: Sl st into ch-1 sp, ch 1, (sc, ch 2, sc) in same ch-1 sp as beg ch-1, [(sc, ch 2, sc) in next ch-1 sp] across, fasten off.

Beaded Edging

Note: String 2,875 beads onto cream crochet cotton. This is approximately 35 extra beads.

With WS facing, attach cream to upper corner of Shawl and, working in side edge of rows, ch 1, **bead sc** (see Special Stitches) in same st as beg ch-1, Beaded Edging is worked in this manner, **3-bead sc** (see Special Stitches) in the side post of each extended dc going down (vertical), 3-bead sc in each st of each block exposed on row (horizontal). Continue across the Shawl in this manner to the center 3 blocks at the beg of the Shawl (row 1), work across these 10 sts, 3-bead sc twice, **4-bead sc**

JACKETS, WRAPS & MORE

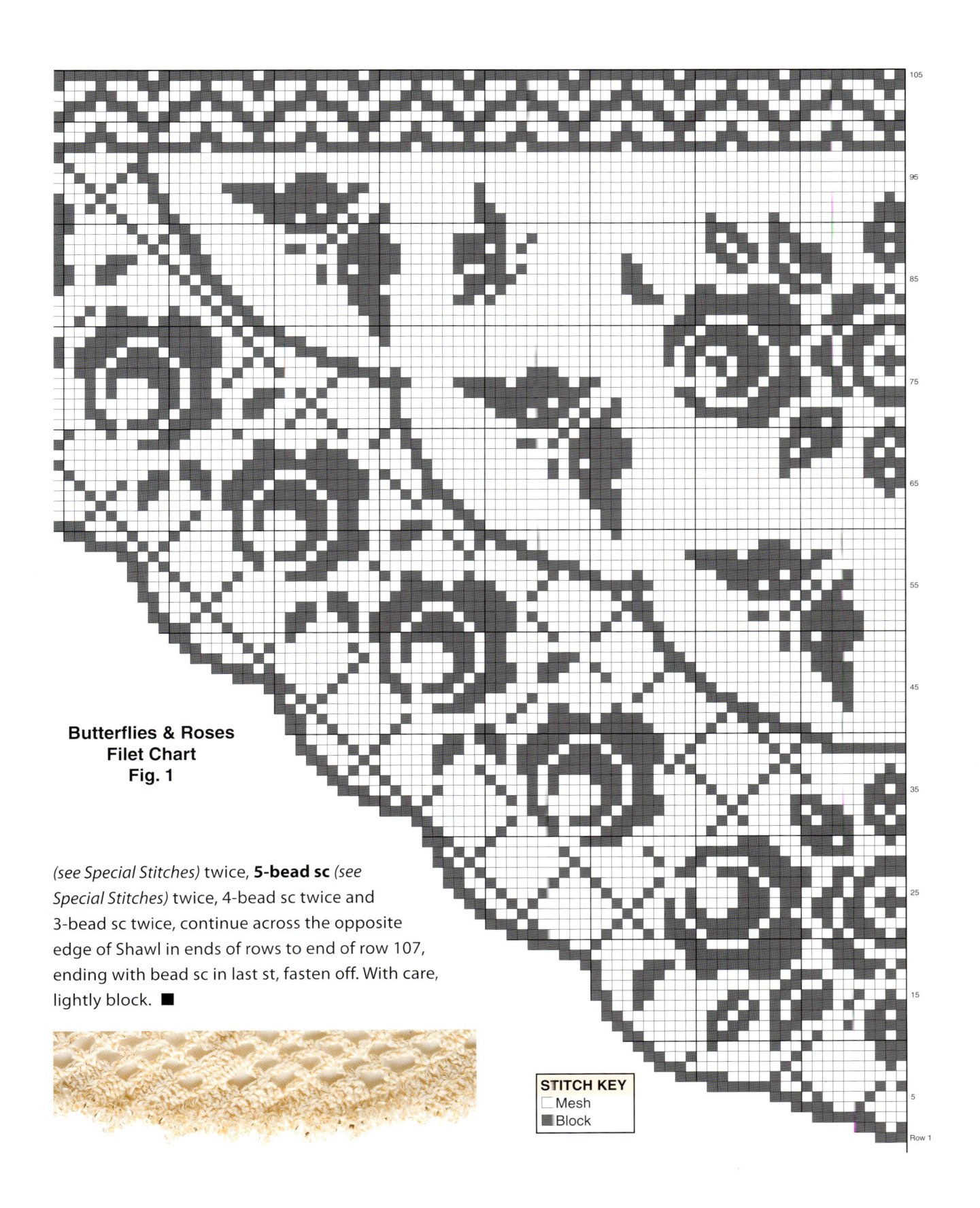

WRAPS

**Butterflies & Roses
Filet Chart
Fig. 1**

(see Special Stitches) twice, **5-bead sc** *(see Special Stitches)* twice, 4-bead sc twice and 3-bead sc twice, continue across the opposite edge of Shawl in ends of rows to end of row 107, ending with bead sc in last st, fasten off. With care, lightly block. ∎

STITCH KEY
☐ Mesh
■ Block

JACKETS, WRAPS & MORE 59

WRAPS

SUNSET PONCHO
DESIGN BY MARY JANE PROTUS FOR COATS & CLARK

EASY

Finished Size
One size fits most women

Finished Garment Measurement
21 inches long x 60-inch circumference

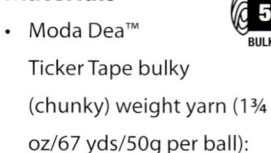

Materials
- Moda Dea™ Ticker Tape bulky (chunky) weight yarn (1¾ oz/67 yds/50g per ball): 10 balls #9273 sunset
- Size N/15/10mm crochet hook or size needed to obtain gauge
- Tapestry needle
- Stitch markers

Gauge
[Sk next 3 tr, 4 tr in next sc, ch 4, sc in next tr] = 3½ inches; 4 rows = 3¼ inches

Pattern Notes
Weave in loose ends as work progresses.
Join rounds with a slip stitch unless otherwise stated.

PONCHO

Body
Row 1 (WS): Ch 54, sc in 2nd ch from hook, [sk next 3 chs, 4 tr in next ch, ch 4, sk next 3 chs, sc in next ch] 6 times, sk next 3 chs, 4 tr in last ch, turn.
Row 2: Ch 1, sc in first tr, [sk next 3 tr, 4 tr in next sc, ch 4, sc in next tr] 6 times, sk next 3 tr, 4 tr in last sc, turn.
Rep row 2 until Body measures 60 inches, ending on WS.

60 JACKETS, WRAPS & MORE

Last row: Ch 1, sc in first tr, [ch 3, sk next 3 tr, sc in next sc, ch 3, sc in next tr] 6 times, ch 3, sk next 3 tr, sc in last sc, fasten off.

Place st marker on right edge at 16 inches *(side seam)*, then measure 28 inches and place another st marker *(neck opening)*, then measure 16 inches and place the last st marker *(side seam)*. Fold fabric in half, and, working through both thicknesses, sew seam from beg to first st marker, remove marker, fasten off, sk 28 inches, sew seam from st marker to end.

Neckline Trim

Rnd 1 (RS): Attach yarn at seam, ch 1, sc evenly spaced around neckline opening, join in beg sc, fasten off.

Edging

Rnd 1 (RS): Attach yarn at seam, ch 1, sc evenly spaced across to corner, (sc, ch 1, sc) in corner, ch 4, *sk tr row end, sc in sc row end, ch 4, rep from * to next corner, (sc, ch 1, sc) in corner, sc evenly spaced across to first sc, join in beg sc, fasten off.

Fringe

Cut 22-inch lengths of sunset, holding 2 strands tog, fold in half forming a lp, insert hook into any sc along long edge, or into the ch-1 sp at corner, working from WS of the body and into the lp, draw the lp through, draw yarn ends through lp on hook, pull gently to secure. Trim ends. ■

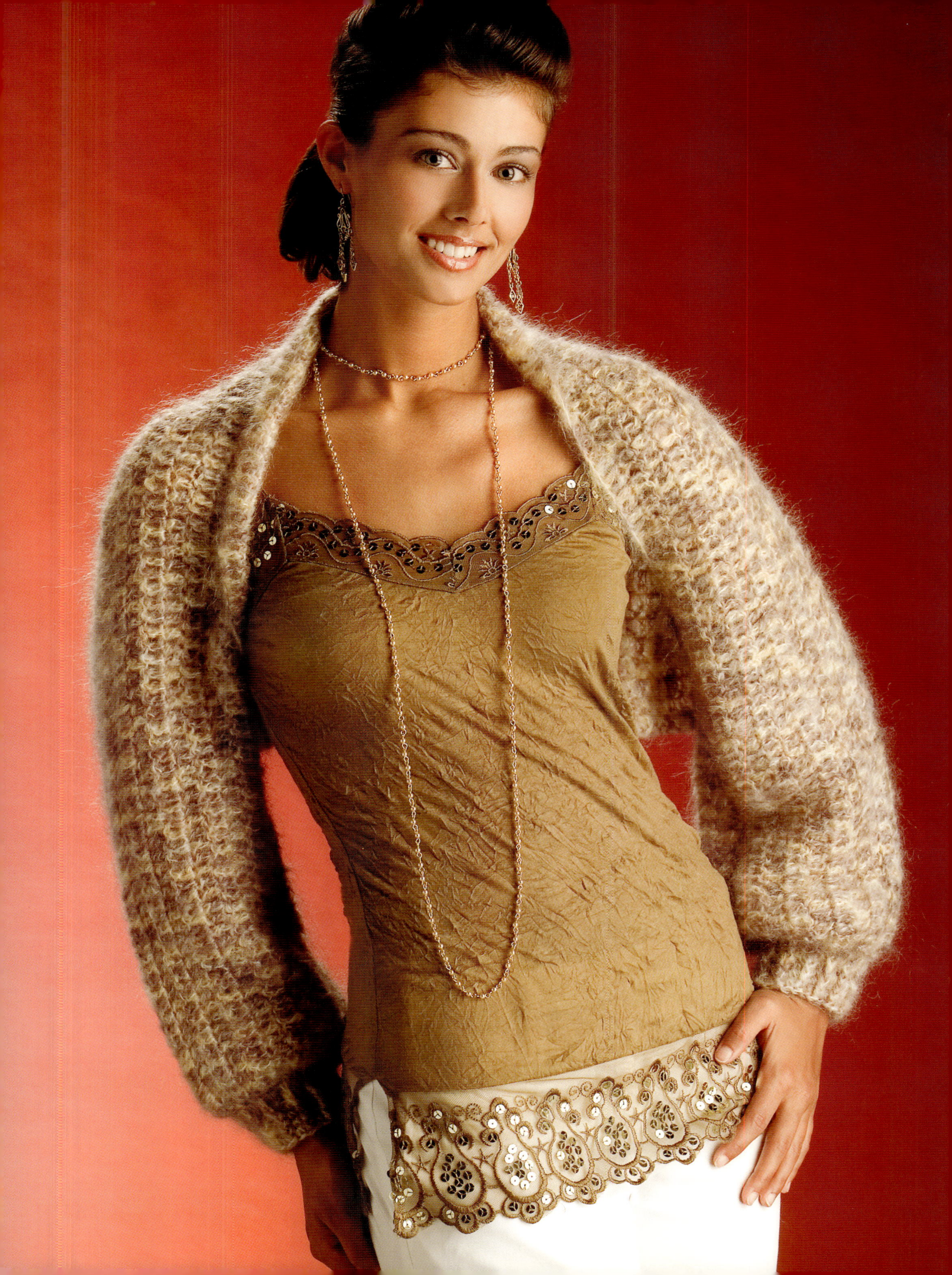

COZY CAFÉ AU LAIT SHRUG

DESIGN BY JEWDY LAMBERT

EASY

Finished Size
Shrug measures 18 x 60 inches, excluding Cuffs. Each Cuff measures 2 inches.

Materials
- King Cole Luxury Mohair bulky (chunky) weight yarn (1¾ oz/110 yds/50g per ball): 4 balls #261 Vienna
- Size K/10½/6.5mm crochet hook or size needed to obtain gauge
- Tapestry needle

5 BULKY

Gauge
8 dc = 3 inches; 6 dc rows = 4 inches

Pattern Notes
Weave in loose ends as work progresses.
Join rounds with a slip stitch unless otherwise stated. For individual sizing, measure from wrist of outstretched arm across shoulders behind nape of neck to wrist of opposite outstretched arm. Make a chain the length of this measured distance; if working pattern for larger sizes, add several rows as desired to the Body. Work Sleeve Shaping and Cuffs as indicated working 1 additional st into each row on each Cuff.

SHRUG

Body
Row 1: Ch 149, dc in 4th ch from hook, dc in each rem ch across, turn. *(146 dc)*

Row 2: Ch 3 *(counts as first dc)*, dc in each dc across, turn.
Rows 3–25: Rep row 2. At the end of row 25, do not fasten off.

CONTINUED ON PAGE 80

JACKETS, WRAPS & MORE

RUFFLED SHOULDER WRAP

DESIGN BY JOYCE BRAGG

INTERMEDIATE

Finished Sizes

Instructions given fit 28–30-inch bust *(X-small)*; changes for 32–34-inch bust *(small)*, 36–38-inch bust *(medium)*, 40–42-inch bust *(large)*, 44–46-inch bust *(X-large)*, 48–50-inch bust *(2X-large)* and 52–54-inch bust *(3X-large)* are in [ ].

Gauge

3 dc = 1 inch; 2 dc rnds = 1 inch

Pattern Notes

Weave in loose ends as work progresses.
Join rounds with a slip stitch unless otherwise stated.

WRAP

Materials

- Patons Glittallic bulky (chunky) weight yarn (1¾ oz/61 yds/50g per skein):
  7 [7, 8, 9, 9, 10, 10] skeins #66008 cream gleam
- Size K/10½/6.5mm crochet hook or size needed to obtain gauge
- Tapestry needle
- 1½-inch shank button

Body

Rnd 1: Starting at center back, ch 10, join in first ch to form a ring, ch 2 *(counts as first hdc)*, 19 hdc in ring, join in 2nd ch of beg ch-2. *(20 hdc)*

Rnd 2: Ch 2, 2 hdc in next hdc, [hdc in next hdc, 2 hdc in next hdc] around, join in 2nd ch of beg ch-2. *(30 hdc)*

Rnd 3: Ch 2, hdc in each of next 5 hdc, ch 3, [hdc in each of next 6 hdc, ch 3] 4 times, join in 2nd ch of beg ch-2. *(30 hdc, 5 ch-3 sps)*

Rnd 4: Ch 2, hdc in each of next 5 hdc, ch 3, dc in next ch-3 sp, ch 3, [hdc in each of next 6 hdc, ch 3, dc in next ch-3 sp, ch 3] around, join in 2nd ch of beg ch-2. *(30 hdc, 10 ch-3 sps, 5 dc)*

Rnd 5: Ch 2, hdc in each of next 5 hdc, *ch 3, dc in next ch-3 sp, ch 3, dc in next ch-3 sp, ch 3**, hdc in each of next 6 hdc, rep from * around, ending last rep at **, join in 2nd ch of beg ch-2. *(30 hdc, 15 ch-3 sps, 10 dc)*

Rnd 6: Ch 3 *(counts as first dc)*, dc in each hdc, 3 dc in each ch-3 sp, dc in each dc around, join in 3rd ch of beg ch-3. *(85 dc)*

For Sizes Medium, Large, X-Large, 2X-Large & 3X-Large Only

Rnd 7: Ch 3, dc in each st around, join in 3rd ch of beg ch-3.

For All Sizes

Rnd 7 [7, 8, 8, 8, 8, 8]: Ch 6 *(counts as first dc, ch-3)*, sk next dc, dc in next dc, [ch 3, sk next dc, dc in next dc] around, join in 3rd ch of beg ch-6. *(43 dc, 43 ch-3 sps)*

Rnd 8 [8, 9, 9, 9, 9, 9]: Ch 6, [dc in center ch of ch-3 sp, ch 3] around, join in 3rd ch of beg ch-3. *(43 dc)*

For Sizes Small, Medium, Large, X-Large, 2X-Large & 3X-Large Only

Rnd 9 [10, 10, 10, 10, 10]: Rep rnd 8 [9, 9, 9, 9, 9].

64   JACKETS, WRAPS & MORE

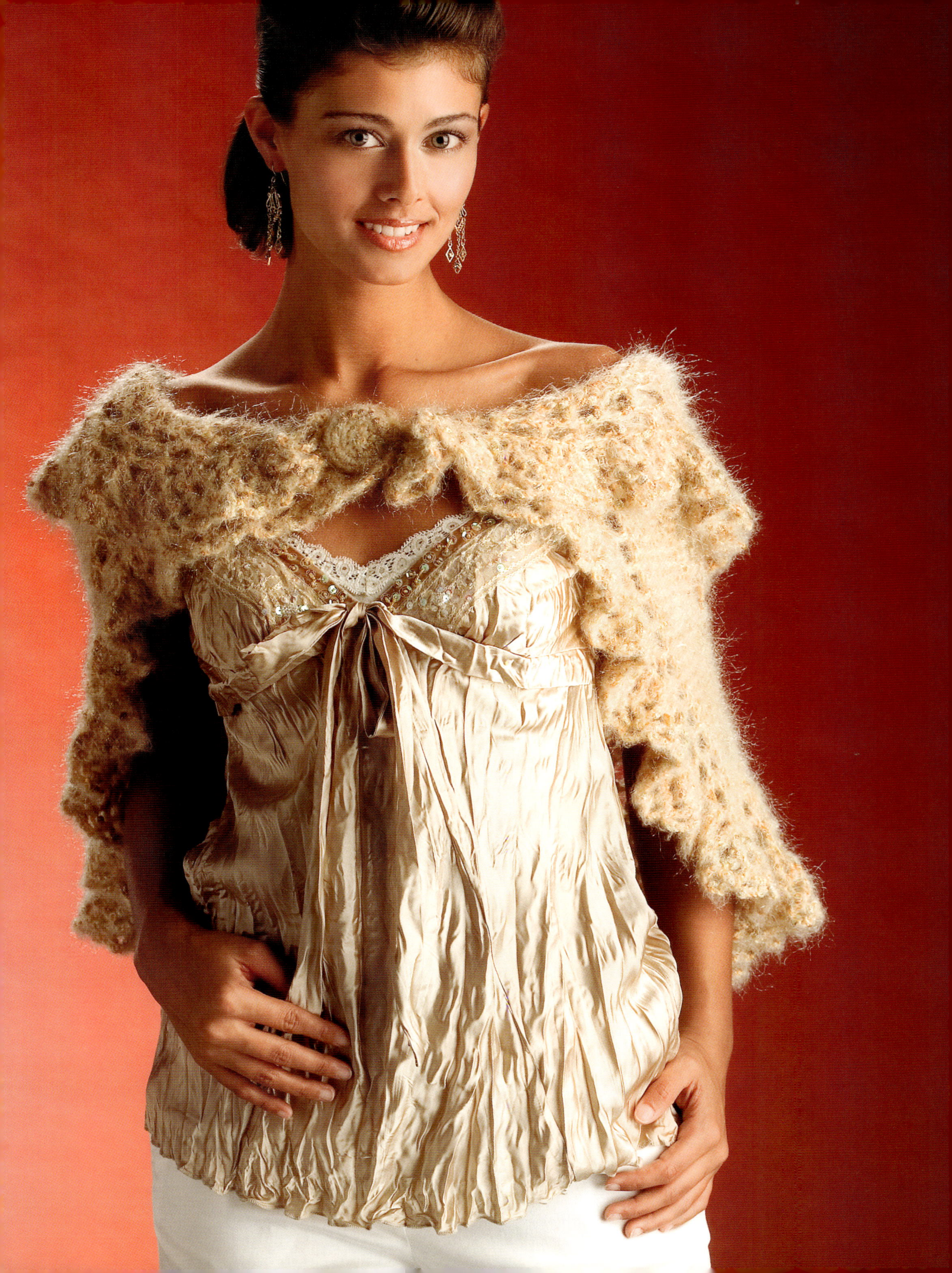

WRAPS

For Sizes Medium, Large, X-Large, 2X-Large & 3X-Large Only
Rnd 11 [12, 13, 14, 14]: [Rep rnd 9 [9, 9, 9, 9] 1 [2, 3, 4, 4] times.

For All Sizes
Rnd 9 [10, 12, 13, 14, 15, 15]: Sl st in center ch of ch-3 sp, ch 3, dc in same ch, ch 3, [2 dc in center ch of next ch-3 sp, ch 3] around, join in 3rd ch of beg ch-3. *(86 dc, 43 ch-3 sps)*

Rnd 10 [11, 13, 14, 15, 16, 16]: Rep rnd 9 [10, 12, 13, 14, 15, 15].

Rnd 11 [12, 14, 15, 16, 17, 17]: Sl st in center ch of ch-3 sp, ch 3, dc in same ch, [ch 3, 2 dc in center ch of next ch-3 sp] around, ending with 2 dc in center ch of last ch-3 sp, do not ch-3, join in 3rd ch of beg ch-3. *(86 dc, 42 ch-3 sps)*

Rnd 12 [13, 15, 16, 17, 18, 18]: Sl st in center ch of ch-3 sp, ch 5 *(counts as first dc, ch-2)*, 4 dc in each of next 7 ch-3 sps, [ch 2, 4 dc in each of next 7 ch-3 sps] 4 times, ch 2, 4 dc in each of next 6 ch-3 sps, 3 dc in same ch sp as beg ch-5, join in 3rd ch of beg ch-5. *(168 dc, 6 ch-2 sps)*

Rnd 13 [14, 16, 17, 18, 19, 19]: Sl st into ch-2 sp, ch 4 *(counts as first hdc, ch-2)*, hdc in each of next 28 dc, [ch 2, hdc in next ch-2 sp, ch 2, hdc in each of next 28 dc] around, ending with ch 2, join in 2nd ch of beg ch-4.

Rnd 14 [15, 17, 18, 19, 20, 20]: Sl st into ch-2 sp, ch 4, *hdc in each of next 28 hdc**, [ch 2, hdc in next ch-2 sp] twice, ch 2, rep from * around, ending last rep at **, ch 2, hdc in next ch-2 sp, ch 2, join in 2nd ch of beg ch-4.

Rnd 15 [16, 18, 19, 20, 21, 21]: Sl st into ch-2 sp, ch 4, *hdc in each of next 28 hdc**, [ch 2, hdc in next ch-2 sp] 3 times, ch 2, rep from * around, ending last rep at **, [ch 2, hdc in next ch-2 sp] twice, ch 2, join in 2nd ch of beg ch-4.

Rnd 16 [17, 19, 20, 21, 22, 22]: Ch 3, [3 dc in each ch-2 sp, dc in each hdc] around, join in 3rd ch of beg ch-3.

Rnd 17 [18, 20, 21, 22, 23, 23]: Ch 6, sk next dc, [dc in next dc, ch 3, sk next dc] around, join in 3rd ch of beg ch-6.

Rnd 18 [19, 21, 22, 23, 24, 24]: Sl st in center ch of ch-3 sp, ch 6, [dc in center ch of next ch-3 sp, ch 3] around, join in 3rd ch of beg ch-6.

CONTINUED ON PAGE 80

JACKETS, WRAPS & MORE

TRIANGLES SHAWL

DESIGN BY NAZANIN FARD

EASY

Finished Size
48 inches across top x 44 inches each side, excluding Tassels

Materials
- Aunt Lydia's Fashion Crochet size 3 crochet cotton (150 yds per ball):
    5 balls each #325 tangerine *(A)* and #625 sage *(B)*
- Size E/4/3.5mm crochet hook or size needed to obtain gauge
- Tapestry needle

Gauge
6 sc = 1 inch

Pattern Notes
Weave in loose ends as work progresses.
Join rounds with a slip stitch unless otherwise stated.
Shawl switches between A and B for each triangle. There is a total of 81 motifs, 36 motifs with rnds 1–4 crocheted with B and rnds 5 and 6 crocheted with A and 45 motifs with rnds 1–4 crocheted with A and rnds 5 and 6 crocheted with B.

SHAWL

First Motif
Rnd 1: With A, ch 6, join in first ch to form a ring, ch 1, 12 sc in ring, join in beg sc. *(12 sc)*

Rnd 2: Ch 10 *(counts as first dc, ch-7)*, *sk next sc, dc in next sc, ch 3**, sk next sc, dc in next sc, ch 7, rep from * around, ending last rep at **, join in 3rd ch of beg ch-10. *(3 ch-7 sps, 3 ch-3 sps)*

WRAPS

Rnd 3: Ch 3 (counts as first dc), 3 dc in next ch sp, *ch 6, 4 dc in same ch sp, 3 dc in next ch sp**, 4 dc in next ch sp, rep from * around, ending last rep at **, join in 3rd ch of beg ch-3.

Rnd 4: Sl st in next dc, ch 6 (counts as first dc, ch-3), *(4 dc, ch 5, 4 dc) in next ch sp, ch 3, sk next 2 dc, dc in next dc, ch 3, sk next 2 dc, sc in next dc, ch 3**, sk next 2 dc, dc in next dc, ch 3, rep from * around, ending last rep at **, join in 3rd ch of beg ch-3, fasten off.

Rnd 5: Join B to any unused sc of rnd 1, ch 1, sc in same sc as beg ch-1, ch 3, [sc in next sc of rnd 1, ch 3] around, join in beg sc. (6 ch-3 sps)

Rnd 6: Ch 1, (sc, hdc, 3 dc, hdc, sc) in each ch-3 sp around, join in beg sc, fasten off.

2nd Motif

Rnds 1–3: With B, rep rnds 1–3 of First Motif.

Rnd 4: Sl st into next dc, ch 6, *4 dc in next ch sp, ch 2, sl st in corresponding ch-5 sp of previous motif, ch 2, 4 dc in same ch sp, ch 1, sl st in corresponding ch-3 sp of previous motif, ch 1, sk next 2 dc, dc in next dc, ch 3, sk next 2 dc, sc in next dc, ch 3, sk next 2 dc, dc in next dc, ch 1, sl st in corresponding ch-3 sp of previous motif, ch 1, rep from * to join to adjacent motifs, otherwise work the same as rnd 4 for First Motif, fasten off.

Rnds 5 & 6: Join A, rep rnds 5 and 6 of First Motif.

Rem Motifs

Rep as for 2nd Motif alternating A and B as indicated in Motif Assembly Diagram (Fig. 1).

Border

Row 1: Join B to left side of top corner of Shawl, ch 7, sc in same ch sp, *[ch 7, sc in next ch sp] 4 times, ch 7, sc in the joining of the chs of next 2 Motifs, rep from * to point of Shawl, ch 7, sc in same ch sp, rep from * to next corner, ending with ch 7, sc in same ch sp, turn.

Row 2: [Ch 7, sc in next ch sp] across to bottom point, ch 7, sc in same ch sp, [ch 7, sc in next ch sp] across to next point, fasten off.

Row 3: Join A in first ch sp of previous row, ch 7, sc in same ch sp, [ch 7, sc in next ch sp] across to bottom point, ch 7, sc in same ch sp, [ch 7, sc in next ch sp] across to next point, turn.

Row 4: Rep row 2.

Row 5: Join B, rep row 3.

Row 6: Rep row 2.

Fringe

Cut 2-12-inch strands of both A and B. Hold strands tog, fold in half, insert hook in ch sp of row 6, draw strands through at fold to form a lp on hook, draw cut ends through lp on hook, pull gently to secure. ∎

Triangles Shawl Motif Assembly Diagram Fig. 1

MOTIF KEY
A
B

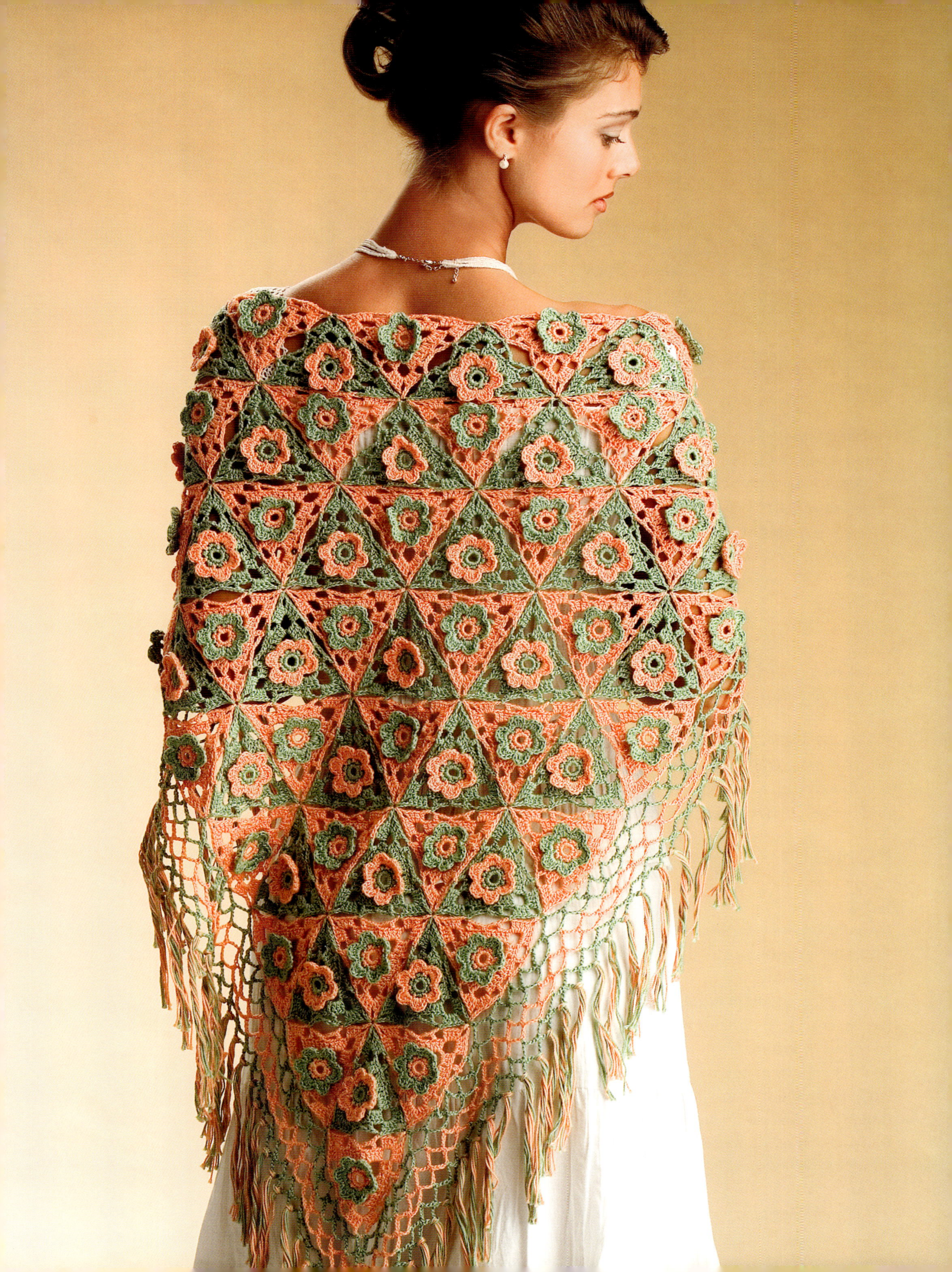

WRAPS

PEEKABOO PONCHO
DESIGN BY JEWDY LAMBERT

EASY

Finished Sizes
Instructions given fit 32–36-inch bust *(small/medium)*; changes for 38–42-inch bust *(medium/large)* and 44–50-inch bust *(X-large/2X-large)* are in [ ].

Materials
- Moda Dea™ Beadnik medium (worsted) weight yarn (1¾ oz/103 yds/50g per ball): 5 [6, 6] balls #2914 blue beat
- Size I/9/5.5mm crochet hook or size needed to obtain gauge
- Tapestry needle

Gauge
6 tr = 2 inches; 2 tr rnds = 1¾ inches

Pattern Notes
Weave in loose ends as work progresses.
Join rounds with a slip stitch unless otherwise stated.
Additional yarn is required for longer Ponchos.

PONCHO

Body
Foundation rnd (RS): Beg at neckline, ch 100 [108, 116], taking care not to twist, join in first ch to form a ring, ch 3 *(counts as first dc)*, dc in each of next 23 [25, 27] chs, (dc, ch 5, dc) in next ch, [dc in each of next 24 {26, 28} chs, (dc, ch 5, dc) in next ch] around, join in 3rd ch of beg ch-3, turn.

Rnd 1: Ch 4 *(counts as first tr)*, tr in each dc around and 7 tr in each ch-5 sp, join in 4th ch of beg ch-4, turn.

Rnd 2: Ch 4, tr in each tr around, work (tr, ch 5, tr) in 4th tr of each 7-tr group, join in 4th ch of beg ch-4, turn.

Rnd 3: Ch 4, tr in each tr around, working 7 tr in each ch-5 sp around, join in 4th ch of beg ch-4, turn.

Rnds 4–13: [Rep rnds 2 and 3 alternately] 5 times. At the end of rnd 13, fasten off or for longer Poncho continue to rep rnds 2 and 3 alternately to desired length. ■

JACKETS, WRAPS & MORE

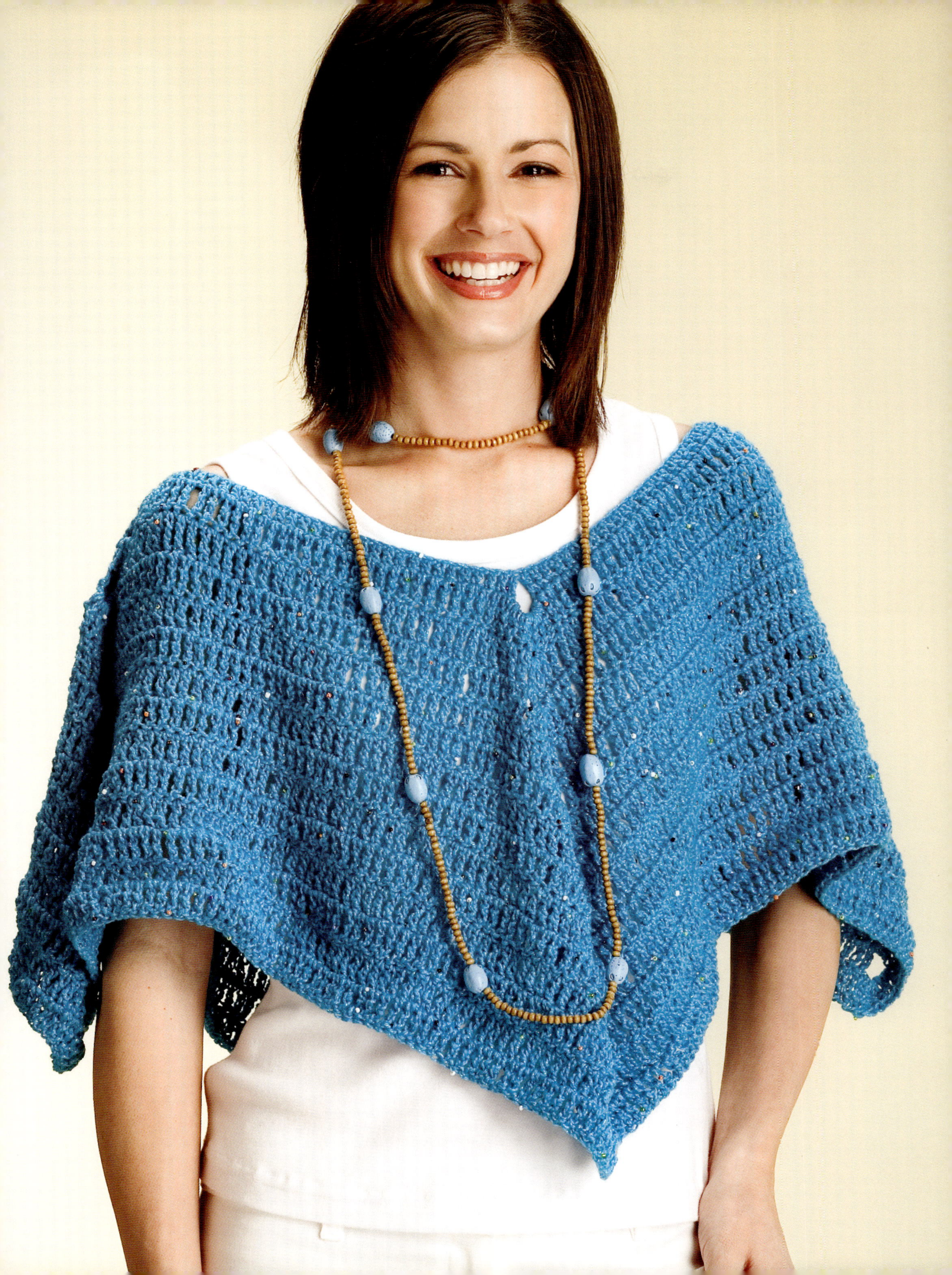

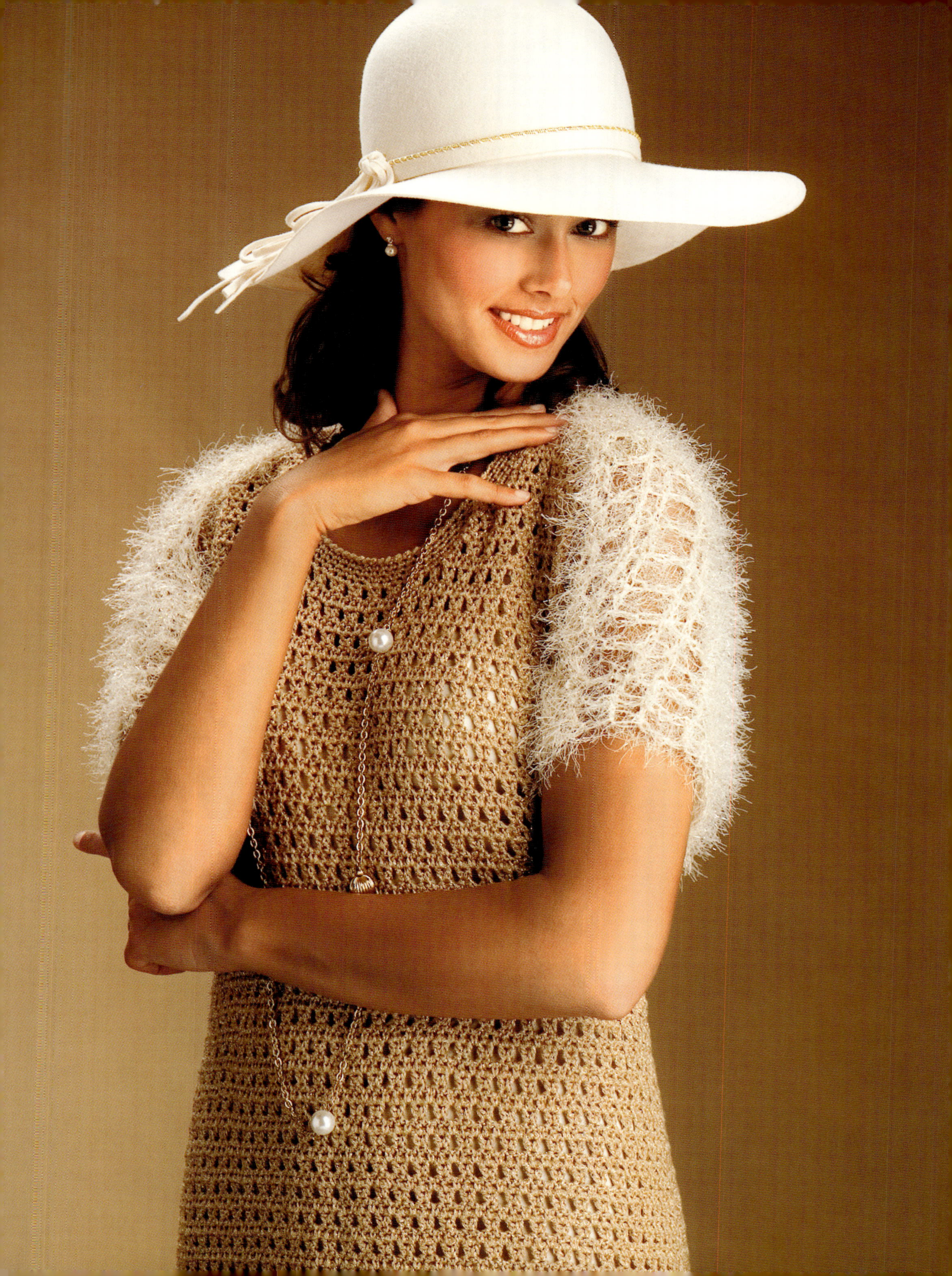

WRAPS

COOL CLASS DRESS & SHOULDER COVER

DESIGNS BY SVETLANA AVRAKH

INTERMEDIATE

Finished Sizes

Dress: Instructions given fit 28–34-inch bust (X-small/small); changes for 36–38-inch bust (medium), 40–42-inch bust (large) and 44–46-inch bust (X-large) are in [ ].

Shoulder Cover: Instructions given fit X-small/small; changes for medium and large/X-large are in [ ].

Finished Garment Measurements

Dress Bust: 37 inches (X-small/small) [41 inches (medium), 45 inches (large), 49½ inches (X-large)]

Shoulder Cover Cuff to Cuff: 18 inches (X-small/small) [19 inches (medium), 20 inches (large/X-large)]

Width of Back: 16 inches (X-small/small) [16 inches (medium), 17 inches (large/X-large)]

Materials

- Patons Brilliant light (light worsted) weight yarn (1¾ oz/166 yds/50g per skein): 9 [10, 11, 12] skeins #03023 gold glow
- Patons Silverlash medium (worsted) weight yarn (1¾ oz/164 yds/50g per skein): 2 skeins #81008 crystallite cream
- Sizes F/5/3.75mm and N/15/10mm crochet hooks or sizes needed to obtain gauge
- Tapestry needle
- Stitch markers
- Straight pins

Gauge

Size F hook: 9 sc = 2 inches; 21 rows = 4 inches
Size N hook: 6 sts = 2 inches; 2 rows = 2 inches

Pattern Notes

Weave in loose ends as work progresses.
Join rounds with a slip stitch unless otherwise stated.

Special Stitches

V-stitch (V-st): (Hdc, ch 1, hdc) in indicated st.
Beginning V-stitch (beg V-st): Ch 3 (counts as first hdc, ch-1), hdc in same st as beg ch-3.
Beginning decrease (beg dec): Ch 2 (counts as first dc), yo, insert hook in next sc, yo, draw up a lp, [yo, draw through 2 lps on hook] twice.
Ending decrease (ending dec): Yo, insert hook in indicated st, yo, draw up a lp, yo, draw through 2 lps on hook, yo, insert hook in next st, yo, draw up a lp, yo, draw through 2 lps on hook, yo, draw through all lps on hook.

DRESS

Back

Row 1 (RS): With size F hook and gold glow, ch 100 [109, 118, 130], hdc in 4th ch from hook (counts as first V-st), *ch 1, sk next 2 chs, **V-st** (see Special Stitches) in next ch, rep from * across, turn. (33 [36, 39, 43] V-sts)
Row 2: Sl st in ch-1 sp of first V-st, ch 4 (counts as first dc, ch-1), *sc in next ch-1 sp, ch 1, dc in next V-st, ch 1, rep from * across, ending with dc in last V-st, turn.

JACKETS, WRAPS & MORE 73

WRAPS

Row 3: Beg V-st (see Special Stitches) in first dc, *ch 1, sk next sc, V-st in next dc, rep from * across, ending with V-st in 3rd ch of beg ch-4, turn.

Rep rows 2 and 3 until piece measures 14 inches.

Row 4 (RS): Beg dec (see Special Stitches), ch 1, V-st in next dc, *ch 1, sk next sc, V-st in next dc, rep from * to last sc and dc, **ending dec** (see Special Stitches) in last sc and dc, turn. (31 [34, 37, 41] V-sts)

Row 5 (WS): Ch 1, sc in first st, *ch 1, dc in next V-st, ch 1, sc in next ch-1 sp, rep from * across, ending with dc in last V-st, sc in last st, turn.

Row 6 (RS): Ch 4, *V-st in next dc, sk next sc, ch 1, rep from * across, ending with dc in last sc, turn.

Rep rows 5 and 6 until piece measures 21 inches, ending with a RS row, turn.

Row 7 (WS): Beg dec in first V-st and dc, *ch 1, sc in next ch-1 sp, ch 1, dc in next V-st, rep from * to last V-st, ch 1, ending dec in V-st and dc, turn.

Row 8: Beg V-st, *ch 1, sk next sc, V-st in next dc, rep from * across, ending with V-st in last st, turn. (31 [34, 37, 41] V-sts)

Row 9: Sl st in ch-1 sp of first V-st, ch 4, *sc in next ch-1 sp, ch 1, dc in next V-st, ch 1, rep from * across, ending with dc in last V-st, turn.

Rep rows 8 and 9 alternately until piece measures 28 inches, ending with a RS row, turn.

Armhole Shaping

Row 1: Sl st in each st to 3rd V-st, ch 4, *sc in next ch-1 sp, ch 1, dc in next V-st, ch 1, rep from * to last 3 V-sts, dc in next V-st, leaving rem 2 V-sts unworked, turn.

Row 2: Beg dec in first st and next sc, V-st in next dc, *ch 1, sk next sc, V-st in next dc, rep from * to last sc and dc, ending dec in sc and dc, turn. (25 [28, 31, 35] V-sts)

Row 3: Beg dec in first st and next V-st, *ch 1, sc in next ch-1 sp, ch 1, dc in next V-st, ch 1, rep from * to last V-st, ending dec in V-st and last st, turn.

[Rep rows 2 and 3 of Armhole Shaping alternately] 1 [2, 3, 4] times. (23 [24, 25, 27] V-sts)

Row 4: Beg V-st, *ch 1, sk next sc, V-st in next dc, rep from * across, ending with V-st in last st, turn.

Row 5: Sl st in ch-1 sp of first V-st, ch 4, *sc in next ch-1

74 JACKETS, WRAPS & MORE

sp, ch 1, dc in next V-st, ch 1, rep from * across, ending with dc in last V-st, turn.
Rep rows 4 and 5 alternately until Armhole measures 7 [7, 8, 8] inches, ending with a RS row, turn.

First Neck Shaping
Row 1: Sl st in ch-1 sp of first V-st, ch 4, [sc in next ch-1 sp, ch 1, dc in next V-st, ch 1] 4 [4, 5, 5] times, omitting ch-1 at end of last rep, ending dec in next ch-1 sp and V-st, leaving rem sts unworked, turn.
Row 2: Sl st in next dc, beg V-st, *ch 1, sk next sc, V-st in next dc, rep from * across, fasten off.

2nd Neck Shaping
Row 1: With WS facing, sk next 11 [12, 11, 13] V-sts, attach gold glow with sl st in next V-st, beg dec, *ch 1, sc in next ch-1 sp, ch 1, dc in next V-st, rep from * across, turn.
Row 2: Beg V-st, *ch 1, sk next sc, V-st in next dc, rep from * to last 2 sts, V-st in next dc, fasten off.

Front
Rep Back to Armhole Shaping.

Armhole Shaping
Row 1: Rep row 1 of Armhole Shaping.
Rep rows 2 and 3 of Armhole Shaping alternately until Armhole measures 3 [3, 4, 4] inches.

First Neck Shaping
Row 1: Sl st in ch-1 sp of first V-st, ch 4, [sc in next ch-1 sp, ch 1, dc in next V-st, ch 1] 7 [7, 8, 8] times, omitting ch-1 at end of last rep, ending dec in next ch-1 sp and V-st, leaving rem sts unworked, turn.
Row 2: Sl st in next dc, beg V-st, *ch 1, sk next sc, V-st in next dc, rep from * across, ending with V-st in 3rd ch of ch-4.
Row 3: Sl st in ch-1 sp of first V-st, ch 4, *sc in next ch-1 sp, ch 1, dc in next V-st, ch 1, rep from * to last V-st, omitting last ch-1 at end of last rep, ending dec in next ch-1 sp and V-st, turn
[Rep rows 2 and 3] 3 times for each size. *(5 [5, 6, 6] V-sts)*
Work even until Front Neck Shaping is same length as Back Neck Shaping, fasten off.

2nd Neck Shaping
Row 1: With WS facing, sk next 7 [8, 7, 9] V-sts, attach gold glow with sl st in next V-st, beg dec in next 2 sts, *ch 1, sc in next ch-1 sp, ch 1, dc in next V-st, rep from * across, turn.
Row 2: Beg V-st, *ch 1, sk next sc, V-st in next dc, rep from * to last 2 sts, V-st in next dc, turn.
Row 3: Beg dec in first V-st and next ch-1 sp, *dc in next V-st, ch 1, sc in next ch-1 sp, ch 1, rep from * to end of row, ending with 1 dc in last V-st, turn.
Work even until Front Neck Shaping is same length as Back Neck Shaping, fasten off.

Finishing
Pin garment pieces to measurements. Cover with a damp cloth, leave cloth to dry. Sew side and shoulder seams.

Neckline Trim
Rnd 1 (RS): Attach gold glow with sl st at left shoulder seam, ch 1, sc evenly spaced around neckline opening, join in beg sc.
Rnds 2–4: Ch 1, sc in each sc around, join in beg sc.
Rnd 5: Ch 1, **reverse sc** *(see Fig. 1)* in each st around, join in beg sc, fasten off.

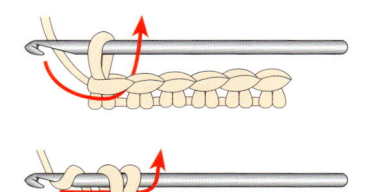

Reverse Single Crochet Fig. 1

Armhole Trim
Rnd 1 (RS): Attach gold glow with sl st in side seam, ch 1, sc evenly sp around Armhole opening, join in beg sc.
Rnds 2–4: Ch 1, **sc dec** *(see Stitch Guide)* in next 2 sc, sc in each sc to last 2 sc, sc dec in next 2 sc, join in beg sc.

CONTINUED ON PAGE 81

WRAPS

LILAC SHAWL

DESIGN BY JOSIE RABIER

INTERMEDIATE

Finished Size
60 inches across x 32 inches deep, excluding Fringe

Materials
- Bernat Softee Baby fine (sport) weight yarn (5 oz/455 yds/140g per ball):
    3 balls #30185 soft lilac
- G/6/4mm crochet hook or size needed to obtain gauge

3 LIGHT

Gauge
4 dc = 1 inch, 2 dc rows = 1 inch

Special Stitches
Joining: Ch 2, sl st in 3rd ch of corresponding or next ch-5 sp of other Motif, ch 2.

Split popcorn (split pc): 4 dc in each of next 2 ch sps, drop lp from hook, insert hook in first st of 8 dc group, pull dropped lp through, ch 1.

Picot: Ch 9, sl st in 9th ch from hook.

SHAWL

First Row

First Motif

Rnd 1: Ch 4, sl st in first ch to form ring, ch 3 *(counts as first dc)*, 19 dc in ring, join with sl st in 3rd ch of beg ch-3. *(20 dc)*

Rnd 2: Ch 3 *(counts as first dc)*, dc in same st, 2 dc in each st around, join with sl st in 3rd ch of beg ch-3. *(40 dc)*

Rnd 3: Ch 3, dc in each of next 4 sts, ch 7, [dc in each of next 5 sts, ch 7] around, join with sl st in 3rd ch of beg ch-3. *(40 dc, 8 ch sps)*

Rnd 4: Ch 3, dc in each of next 4 sts, *ch 3, sl st in center ch of next ch-7, ch 3**, dc in each of next 5 sts, rep from * around, ending last rep at **, join with sl st in 3rd ch of beg ch-3. *(40 dc, 16 ch sps)*

Rnd 5: Ch 2 *(ch-2 is not used or counted as st)*, **dc dec** *(see Stitch Guide)* in next 4 sts, *ch 5, sl st in next sl st between ch-3 sps, ch 5**, dc dec in next 5 sts, rep from * around, ending last rep at **, join with sl st in top of beg dc. *(8 dc, 16 ch sps)*

Rnd 6: Ch 8 *(counts as first dc, ch-5)*, dc in same st, *sl st in next ch sp, ({dc, ch 5} twice, dc) in next sl st *(corner)*, sl st in next ch sp, (dc, ch 5, dc) in next dc, sl st in next ch sp, (dc, ch 5, dc) in next sl st, sl st in next ch sp**, (dc, ch 5, dc) in next dc, rep from * around ending last rep at **, join with sl st in 3rd ch of beg ch-8. Fasten off.

2nd Motif

Rnds 1–5: Rep rnds 1–5 of First Motif.

Rnd 6: Ch 8, dc in same st, sl st in next ch sp, (dc, ch 5, dc) in next sl st, joining to side of last Motif, work **joining** *(see Special Stitches)*, dc in same sl st in this Motif, sl st in next ch sp, dc in next dc, work joining, dc in same dc on this Motif, sl st in next ch sp, dc in next sl st, work joining, dc in same sl st on this Motif, sl st in next ch sp, dc in next dc, work joining, dc in same dc on this Motif, sl st in next ch sp, dc in next sl st, work joining, dc in same sl st on this Motif, (ch 5, dc) in same sl st, *sl st in next ch sp, (dc, ch 5, dc) in next dc, sl st in next ch sp, (dc, ch 5, dc) in next sl st, sl st in next ch sp**, (dc, ch 5, dc) in next dc, sl st in next ch sp, ({dc, ch 5} twice, dc) in next sl st, rep from * around ending last rep at **, join with sl st in 3rd ch of beg ch-8. Fasten off.

Rep 2nd Motif 5 times for total of 7 Motifs on this row.

JACKETS, WRAPS & MORE

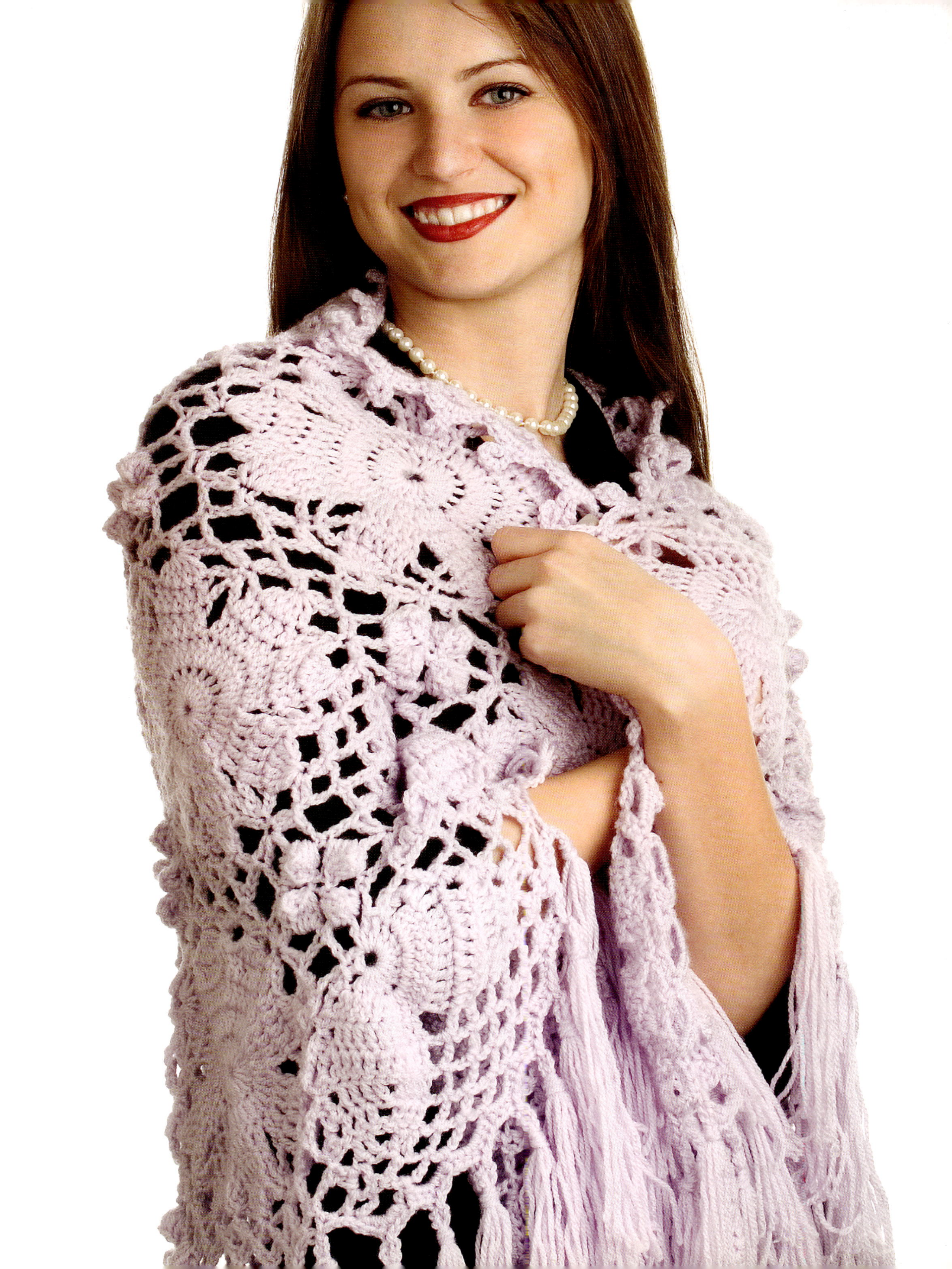

WRAPS

2nd Row

First Motif

Joining to bottom of 2nd Motif on last row, work same as First Row 2nd Motif.

2nd Motif

Rnds 1–5: Rep rnds 1–5 of First Row First Motif.

Rnd 6: Ch 8, dc in same st, sl st in next ch sp, (dc, ch 5, dc) in next sl st, joining to bottom of next Motif on last row, work joining, dc in same sl st in this Motif, *sl st in next ch sp, dc in next dc, work joining, dc in same dc on this Motif, sl st in next ch sp, dc in next sl st, work joining, dc in same sl st on this Motif, sl st in next ch sp, dc in next dc, work joining, dc in same dc on this Motif, sl st in next ch sp, dc in next sl st, work joining, dc in same sl st on this Motif*, joining to side of last Motif on this row, work joining, dc in same sl st on this Motif, rep between *, (ch 5, dc) in same sl st, sl st in next ch sp, (dc, ch 5, dc) in next dc, sl st in next ch sp, (dc, ch 5, dc) in next sl st, sl st in next ch sp, (dc, ch 5, dc) in next dc, sl st in next ch sp, ({dc, ch 5} twice, dc) in next sl st, sl st in next ch sp, (dc, ch 5, dc) in next dc, sl st in next ch sp, (dc, ch 5, dc) in next sl st, sl st in next ch sp, join with sl st in 3rd ch of beg ch-8. Fasten off.

Rep 2nd Motif 3 times for total of 5 Motifs.

3rd Row

First Motif

Joining to bottom of 2nd Motif on last row, work same as First Row 2nd Motif.

2nd Motif

Work same as 2nd Row 2nd Motif.
Rep 2nd Motif once for total of 3 Motifs on this row.

4th Row

First Motif

Joining to bottom of 2nd Motif on last row, work same as First Row 2nd Motif.

Border Motif

Row 1: Ch 4, sl st in first ch to form ring, ch 4 *(counts as first tr)*, 10 dc in ring, tr in ring, turn. *(10 dc, 2 tr)*

Row 2: Ch 4, 2 dc in each dc across, tr in last tr, turn. *(20 dc, 2 tr)*

Row 3: Ch 4, dc in each of next 10 sts, ch 5, dc in each of next 10 sts, tr in last st, turn.

Row 4: Ch 4, dc in each of next 10 sts, ch 5, sl st in next ch sp, ch 5, dc in each of next 10 sts, tr in last st, turn.

Row 5: Ch 4, dc in each of next 4 sts, sk next 2 sts, dc in each of next 4 sts, [ch 5, sl st in next ch sp] twice, ch 5, dc in each of next 4 sts, sk next 2 sts, dc in each of next 4 sts, tr in last st, turn.

Row 6: Ch 4, dc in each of next 3 sts, sk next 2 sts, dc in each of next 3 sts, [ch 5, sl st in next ch sp] 3 times, ch 5, dc in each of next 3 sts, sk next 2 sts, dc in each of next 3 sts, tr in last st, turn.

Row 7: Ch 4, dc in each of next 2 sts, sk next 2 sts, dc in each of next 2 sts, [ch 5, sl st in next ch sp] 4 times, ch 5, dc in each of next 2 sts, sk next 2 sts, dc in each of next 2 sts, tr in last st, turn.

Row 8: Ch 4, dc in next dc, sk next 2 sts, dc in next st, [ch 5, sl st in next ch sp] 5 times, ch 5, dc in next dc, sk next 2 sts, dc in next st, tr in last st, turn.

Rnd 9: Now working in rnds, ch 9 *(counts as first tr, ch-5)*, sk next 2 dc, sl st in next ch sp, [ch 5, sl st in next ch sp] 5 times, ch 5, tr in last st, working in ends of rows, dc in end of next row, ch 2, working on last Motifs at end of first 2 rows, sl st in center ch of 5th ch sp from joining on First Motif, ch 2, dc in same row on this Motif, *sl st in next row, dc in end of next row, ch 2, sl st in center ch of next ch sp on other Motif, ch 2, dc in same row on this Motif*, rep between * twice, dc in next beg ring, ch 2, dc in center ch of next ch sp on other Motif, dc in same ring on this Motif, ch 2, working on next Motif at end of row, sl st in center ch sp of next ch sp after joining on other Motif, ch 2, dc in same ring on this Motif, rep between * 4 times, join with sl st in 3rd ch of beg ch-9.

Rep in each indentation between rows on each side of Shawl, ending with 3 Border Motifs on each side.

Filler Motif

Working in sps between joined Motifs *(there are 8 ch-2 sps at center)*, join in any ch sp, ch 3, 3 dc in same sp, 4 dc in next ch sp, drop lp from hook, insert hook in top

78   JACKETS, WRAPS & MORE

WRAPS continued

of ch-3, pull dropped lp through, [**split pc** (see Special Stitches)] 3 times, join with sl st in sp between first and 2nd pc. Fasten off.
Work a Filler Motif in each sp between Motifs.

Edging
Note: In the following rnd, sl st in dc between ch-5 sps.
With RS facing, join with sl st in center corner dc of top right-hand corner Motif before long straight edge, work the Edging in the following steps:
A. *(3 hdc, **picot**—see Special Stitches, 3 hdc) in each of next 5 ch-5 sps, 2 hdc in next ch-2 sp, picot, 2 hdc in next ch-2 sp, rep from * 5 times, (3 hdc, picot, 3 hdc) in each of next 10 ch-5 sps, 2 hdc in next ch-2 sp, picot, 2 hdc in next ch-2 sp;
B. *(3 hdc, picot, 3 hdc) in each of next 7 ch-5 sps, 2 hdc in next ch-2 sp, picot, 2 hdc in each of next 2 ch-2 sps, picot, 2 hdc in next ch-2 sp, rep from *, (3 hdc, picot, 3 hdc) in each of next 7 ch-5 sps;
C. 2 hdc in next ch-2 sp, picot, 2 hdc in next ch-2 sp, (3 hdc, picot, 3 hdc) in each of next 5 ch-5 sps, 2 hdc in next ch-2 sp, picot, 2 hdc in next ch-2 sp;
D. Rep step B;
E. 2 hdc in next ch-2 sp, picot, 2 hdc in next ch-2 sp, (3 hdc, picot, 3 hdc) in each of last 5 ch-5 sps, join with sl st in beg sl st. Fasten off.

Fringe
For each Fringe, cut 7 strands each 13 inches in length. With all strands held tog, fold in half, insert hook in each picot st of E, pull fold through, pull all loose ends through fold, tighten. Trim.
Attach Fringe in each picot on sides and bottom edge of Shawl. ■

GOLD NUGGET COCKTAIL COVER-UP CONTINUED FROM PAGE 53

With RS tog, sew 3 Squares tog according to diagram (see Fig. 1). Sew Shoulder Pieces as indicated on diagram.

Trim
Working around bottom edge, join 24K with sl st in any tr, ch 4 (counts as first tr), tr in each tr and in each ch sp around with 2 tr in each joining, join with sl st in top of ch-4. Fasten off.
Rep around neck edge, working **tr dec** (see Stitch Guide) in 3 sts at each V.

Drawstring
With 24K, leaving 5-inch length at beg and end, make ch 55 inches in length. Fasten off.
Weave drawstring through sts around neck edge beg and ending in front.

Fringe
Cut one strand Eros, 18 inches long, fold strand in half, insert hook in st, draw fold through st on hook to form a lp, draw ends through lp on hook. Pull to tighten. Pull to tighten.
Fringe in every other st around bottom edge. ■

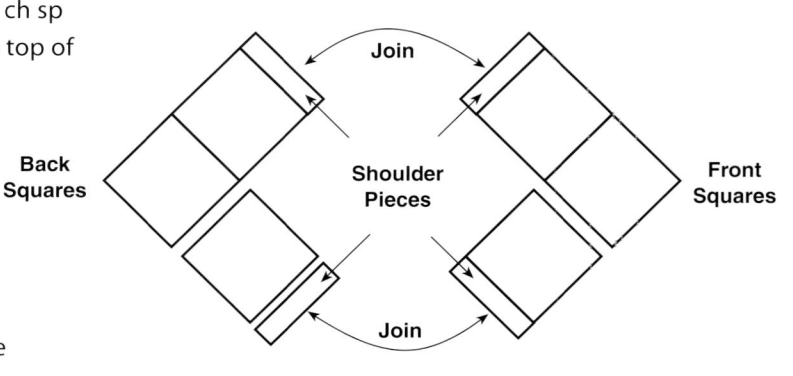

Fig. 1
Gold Nugget Cocktail Cover-Up Diagram

WRAPS continued

COZY CAFÉ AU LAIT SHRUG CONTINUED FROM PAGE 63

First Sleeve Shaping
Row 26 (WS): Holding row 25 to opposite side of foundation ch of row 1, working through both thicknesses, ch 1, sc in each of next 36 sts across edge, fasten off. *(36 sc)*

2nd Sleeve Shaping
Row 26 (WS): Working on opposite end of Shrug Body, holding row 25 to opposite side of foundation ch of row 1, join yarn in first st, ch 1, sc in same st as beg ch-1, sc in each of next 35 sts, fasten off, turn Shrug RS out. *(36 sc)*

Cuff
Rnd 1 (RS): Attach yarn in row 26 of Sleeve Shaping, ch 1, sc in side edge of row 26, work 1 sc in side edge of each row, join in beg sc, turn. *(26 sc)*
Rnd 2 (WS): Ch 3, dc in each sc around, join in 3rd ch of beg ch-3, turn.
Rnd 3 (RS): Ch 1, sc in same st as beg ch-1, **fpdc** *(see Stitch Guide)* around next sc, [sc in next sc, fpdc around next sc] around, join in beg sc, do not turn.
Rnds 4–6 (RS): Ch 1, [sc in sc, fpdc around fpdc directly below] around, join in beg sc.
At the end of rnd 6, fasten off. Rep on opposite Sleeve Shaping. ■

RUFFLED SHOULDER WRAP CONTINUED FROM PAGE 66

For Sizes Large, X-Large, 2X-Large & 3X-Large Only
Rnd [23, 24, 25, 25]: [Rep rnd 22 [23, 24, 24] 1 [1, 2, 2] times or as many rnds as needed for desired length.

For All Sizes
Rnds 19–23 [20–23, 22–25, 24–27, 25–28, 27–30, 27–30]: Sl st in center of next ch sp, ch 1, sc in same ch sp, ch 6, [sc in center of next ch sp, ch 6] around, join in beg sc. At the end of last rep, fasten off.

Button
Rnd 1: Ch 2, 8 sc in 2nd ch from hook, do not join, work in continuous rnds. *(6 sc)*
Rnd 2: 2 sc in each sc around. *(16 sc)*
Rnd 3: Rep rnd 2. *(32 sc)*
Rnds 4–8: Sc in each sc around. At the end of last rep,

80 JACKETS, WRAPS & MORE

sl st in next st, leaving a length of yarn, fasten off. Weave rem length through rnd 8, insert button into opening and draw opening closed, knot to secure, sew Button to left edge.

Fold ¼ of top edge of Wrap backwards and use natural sp on opposite edge for buttonhole.
Leave Wrap buttoned and pull over your head or unbutton and button as desired. ■

COOL CLASS DRESS AND SHOULDER COVER CONTINUED FROM PAGE 75

Rnd 5: Ch 1, reverse sc in each st around, join in beg sc, fasten off.
Rep on other Armhole.

SHOULDER COVER

First Half
Row 1: Beg at center back with size N hook and crystallite cream, ch 36 [36, 40], dc in 4th ch from hook, [ch 2, sk next 2 chs, dc in each of next 2 chs] 8 [8, 9] times, turn. *(18 [18, 20] dc)*
Row 2: Ch 3 *(counts as first dc)*, dc in next dc, [ch 2, dc in each of next 2 dc] across, turn.
Rep row 2 until First Half is 8 [9, 10] inches long, ending with a RS row, place a marker at each end of last row, turn.

Shaping
Row 1: Ch 3, dc in next dc, ch 1, dc in each of next 2 dc, [ch 2, dc in each of next 2 dc] 6 [6, 7] times, ch 1, dc in next 2 dc, turn.
Row 2: Ch 3, dc in next dc, sk next ch-1 sp, dc in each of next 2 dc, ch 2, [dc in each of next 2 dc, ch 2] 5 [5, 6] times, dc in each of next 2 dc, sk next ch-1 sp, dc in each of next 2 dc, turn. *(18 [18, 20] dc)*
Row 3: Ch 3, dc in each of next 2 dc, sk next dc, ch 2, [dc in each of next 2 dc, ch 2] 5 [5, 6] times, turn. *(16 [16, 18] dc)*
Row 4: Ch 3, dc in next dc, sk next dc, ch 2, [dc in each of next 2 dc, ch 2] 5 [5, 6] times, turn. *(14 [14, 16] dc)*
Row 5: Ch 3, dc in next dc, ch 1, dc in each of next 2 dc, [ch 2, dc in each of next 2 dc] 4 [4, 5] times, turn. *(14 [14, 16] dc)*
Row 6: Ch 3, dc in next dc, sk next ch-1 sp, dc in each of next 2 dc, ch 2, [dc in each of next 2 dc, ch 2] 3 [3, 4] times, dc in each of next 2 dc, sk next ch-1 sp, dc in each of next 2 dc, fasten off. *(14 [14, 16] dc)*

2nd Half
Row 1: Beg at center back in opposite side of foundation ch of First Half, with size N hook, attach crystallite cream in first ch, ch 3, dc in next ch, [ch 2, sk next 2 chs, dc in each of next 2 chs] 8 [8, 9] times, turn. *(18 [18, 20] dc)*
Rep row 2 until 2nd Half is 8 [9, 10] inches long, ending with a RS row, place a marker at each end of last row, turn.

Shaping
Rows 1–6: Rep rows 1–6 of First Half Shaping.

Finishing
Sew rows 1–5 of Shaping tog at each end of Shoulder Cover. ■

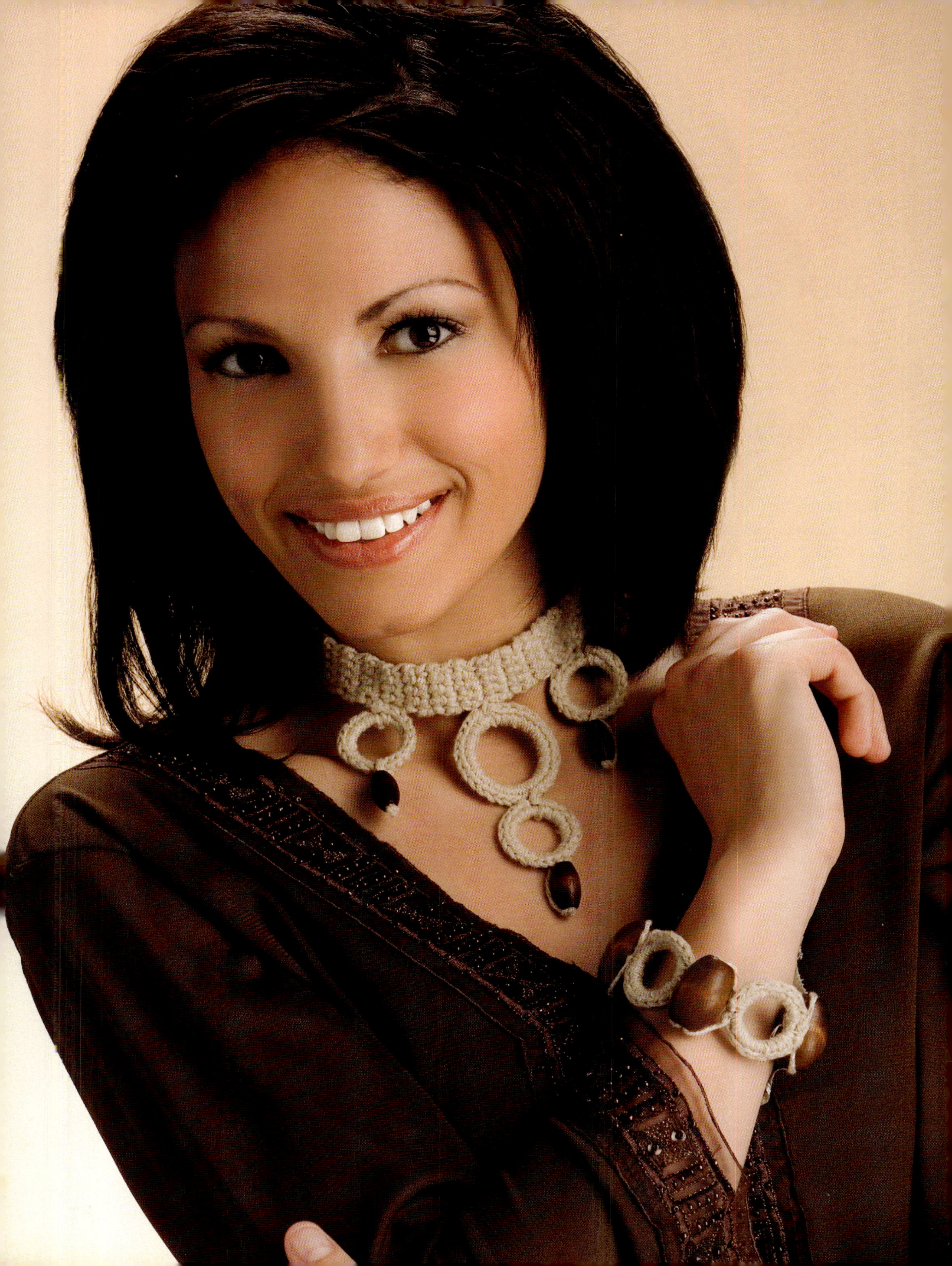

& MORE

More is never too much when dressing up your wardrobe with stylish fashions and chic accessories. From fun jewelry, sparkling scarves and head-turning hats to dazzling purses, jazzy vests and classic tops, you'll want to make them all to maximize your style!

SLEEVELESS SHORTY VEST

DESIGN BY DARLA SIMS

INTERMEDIATE

Finished Sizes
Instructions given fit 32–34-inch bust *(small)*; changes for 36–38-inch bust *(medium)*, 40–42-inch bust *(large)* and 44–46-inch bust *(X-large)* are in [ ].

Finished Garment Measurements
Bust: 36½ inches *(small)* [40 inches *(medium)*, 44½ inches *(large)*, 50 inches *(X-large)*]

Gauge
Size H hook: 4 sc = 1 inch; 4 rows = 1 inch
Size I hook: 6 dc = 2 inches
Size K hook: 5 dc = 2 inches; 4 dc rows = 3 inches

Pattern Note
Weave in loose ends as work progresses.

VEST

BACK
Ribbing
Row 1: With size H hook, ch 8, sc in 2nd ch from hook,

Materials
- Red Heart Bijou super bulky (super chunky) weight yarn (1¾ oz/84 yds/50g per ball): 6 [7, 8, 9] balls #3638 peridot
- Sizes H/8/5mm, I/9/5.5mm and K/10½/6.5mm crochet hooks or sizes needed to obtain gauge
- Yarn needle
- 1⅝-inch pendants: 2

SUPER BULKY 6

sc in each rem ch across, turn. *(7 sc)*
Row 2: Ch 1, working in **back lp** *(see Stitch Guide)* of each st, sc in each st across, turn. *(7 sc)*
Rows 3–46 [3–50, 3–56, 3–60]: Rep row 2.

Body
Row 1: With size I hook, working across side edge of Ribbing rows, ch 3 *(counts as first dc)*, work 45 [49, 55, 59] dc across, turn. *(46 [50, 56, 60] dc)*
Row 2: With size K hook, ch 3, dc in each dc across, turn.
Rows 3–9: Ch 3, dc in each dc across, turn. At the end of row 9, fasten off.

Armhole Shaping
Row 10: Sk first 5 [5, 7, 8] sts, attach yarn to next st, ch 3, dc in each dc across to last 5 [5, 7, 8] sts, leaving these sts unworked, turn. *(36 [40, 42, 44] dc)*
Row 11: Ch 3, dc in each dc across, turn.
Rows 12–20 [12–20, 12–22, 12–22]: Rep row 11. At the end of last rep, fasten off.

Left Front
Ribbing
Row 1: Rep row 1 of Back Ribbing. *(7 sc)*
Rows 2–22 [2–24, 2–28, 2–30]: Rep row 2 of Back Ribbing.

Body
Row 1: With size I hook, working across side edge of Ribbing rows, ch 3, work 22 [24, 27, 29] dc across, turn. *(23 [25, 28, 30] dc)*

JACKETS, WRAPS & MORE

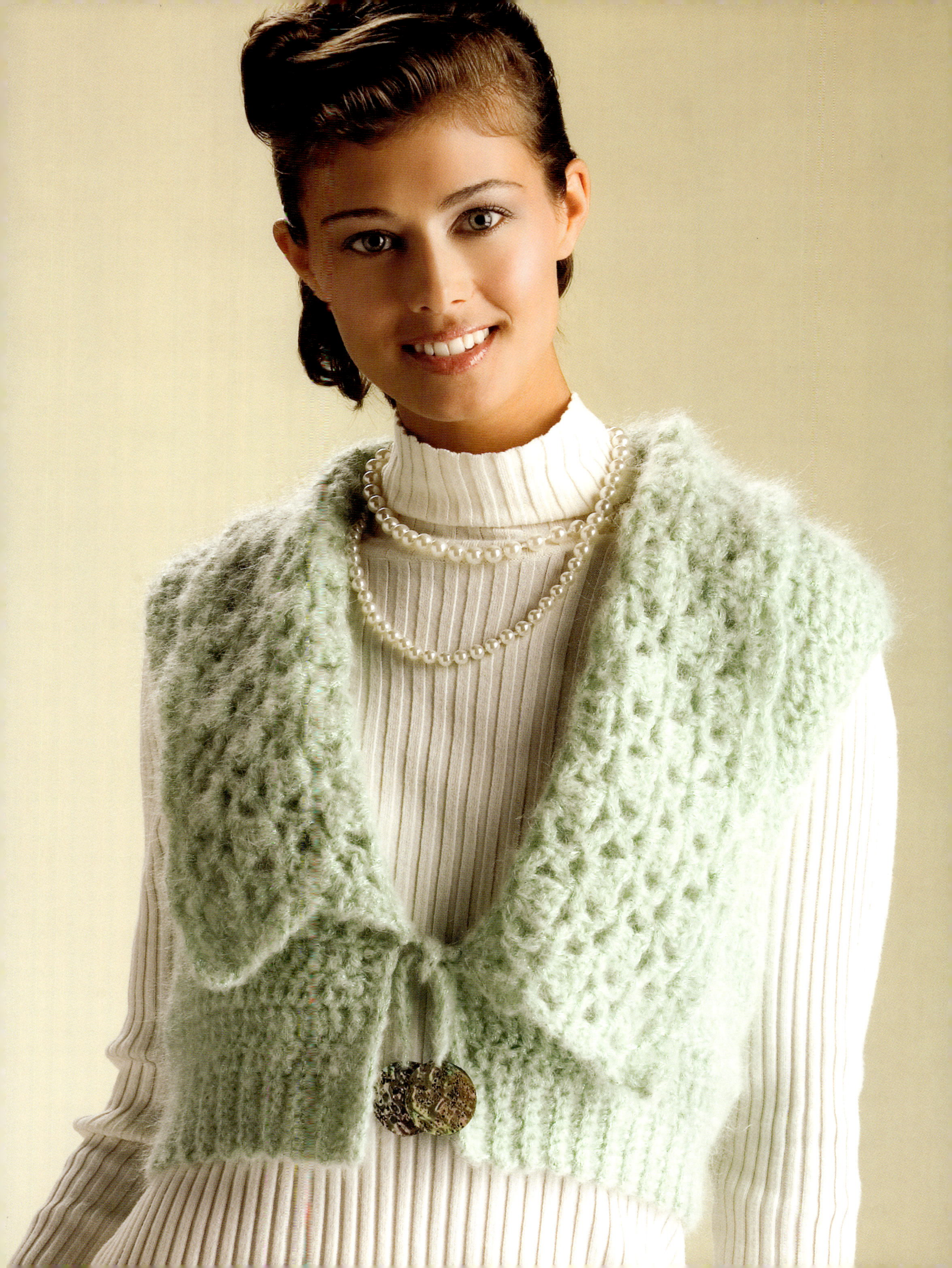

Row 2: With size K hook, ch 3, dc in each dc across, turn.
Row 3: Ch 3, dc in each dc across to last 2 dc, **dc dec** (see Stitch Guide) in next 2 dc, turn. *(22 [24, 27, 29] dc)*
Row 4: Ch 3, dc in each dc across, turn.
Rows 5–8: [Rep rows 3 and 4 alternately] twice. *(20 [22, 25, 27] dc)*
Row 9: Rep row 3. *(19 [21, 24, 26] dc)*

Armhole Shaping
Row 10: Ch 3, dc in each dc across to last 5 [5, 7, 8] dc, leaving rem sts unworked, turn. *(14 [16, 17, 18] dc)*
Row 11: Ch 3, dc across to last 2 dc, dc dec in next 2 dc, turn. *(13 [15, 16, 17] dc)*
Row 12: Ch 3, dc in each dc across, turn.
Rows 13–16: [Rep rows 11 and 12 alternately] twice. *(11 [13, 14, 15] dc)*
Row 17: Rep row 11. *(10 [12, 13, 14] dc)*

For Sizes Small & Medium Only
Rows 18–20: Rep row 12. At the end of last rep, fasten off.

For Sizes Large & X-Large Only
Row 18: Rep row 12.
Row 19: Rep row 11. *([12, 13] dc)*
Rows 20–22: Rep row 12. At the end of last rep, fasten off.

Right Front
Ribbing
Rows 1–22 [1–24, 1–28, 1–30]: Rep rows 1–22 [1–24, 1–28, 1–30] of Back Ribbing rows.

Body
Row 1: With size I hook, working across side edge of Ribbing rows, ch 3, work 22 [24, 27, 29] dc across, turn. *(23 [25, 28, 30] dc)*
Row 2: With size K hook, ch 3, dc in each dc across, turn.
Row 3: Ch 3, dc dec in next 2 sts, dc in each rem dc across, turn. *(22 [24, 27, 29] dc)*
Row 4: Ch 3, dc in each dc across, turn.
Rows 5–8: [Rep rows 3 and 4 alternately] twice. *(20 [22, 25, 27] dc)*
Row 9: Rep row 3, fasten off. *(19 [21, 24, 26] dc)*

Shape Armhole
Row 10: Sk first 5 [5, 7, 8] dc, attach yarn in next dc, ch 3, dc in each rem dc across, turn. *(14 [16, 17, 18] dc)*
Row 11: Ch 3, dc dec in next 2 sts, dc in each rem dc across, turn. *(13 [15, 16, 17] dc)*
Row 12: Ch 3, dc in each dc across, turn.
Rows 13–16: [Rep rows 11 and 12 alternately] twice. *(11 [13, 14, 15] dc)*
Row 17: Rep row 11. *(10 [12, 13, 14] dc)*

For Sizes Small & Medium Only
Rows 18–20: Rep row 12. At the end of last rep, fasten off.

For Sizes Large & X-Large Only
Row 18: Rep row 12.
Row 19: Rep row 11. *([12, 13] dc)*
Rows 20–22: Rep row 12. At the end of last rep, fasten off.

Assembly
Sew shoulder and side seams.

Collar
Row 1: With size I hook, attach yarn at lower Right Front, ch 1, work 44 [44, 46, 46] sc to shoulder seam, 16 [16, 18, 18] sc across Back, 44 [44, 46, 46] sc from shoulder seam to lower Left Front, turn, fasten off. *(104 [104, 110, 110] sc)*
Row 2: Sk first 12 sc, attach yarn with sc in next sc, sc in each of next 31 [31, 33, 33] sc, 2 sc in next st at shoulder seam, sc across Back neck, 2 sc in next st at shoulder seam, sc in each of next 32 [32, 34, 34] sc down Left Front, leaving last 12 sts unworked, turn. *(82 [82, 87, 87] sc)*
Row 3: With size K hook, ch 1, sc in each of next 2 sc, ch 3, sk next 2 sc, sc in next sc, [ch 2, sk next sc, sc in next sc, ch 3, sk next 2 sc, sc in next sc] across, ending with sc in next sc, turn.
Row 4: Ch 3, dc in first st, ch 2, sc in next ch-3 sp, ch 2, [3 dc in next ch-2 sp, ch 2, sc in next ch-3 sp, ch 2] across, ending with 2 dc in last st, turn.
Row 5: Ch 3, sc in next ch-2 sp, [ch 2, sc in next ch-2 sp, ch 3, sc in next ch-2 sp] across, ending with ch 1, hdc in last st, turn.
Row 6: Ch 3, 3 dc in next ch-2 sp, [ch 2, sc in next ch-3 sp, ch 2, 3 dc in next ch-2 sp] across, ending with ch 2, sc in last st, turn.
Row 7: Ch 2, sc in next ch-2 sp, [ch 3, sc in next ch-2 sp, ch 2, sc in next ch-2 sp] across, ending with hdc in last st, turn.
Row 8: Ch 3, dc in same st as beg ch-3, ch 2 [sc in next ch-3 sp, ch 2, 3 dc in next ch-2 sp, ch 2] across, ending with 2 dc in last st, turn.
Rows 9–12: Rep rows 5–8. Fasten off.

Tie
Make 2.
For each tie, cut 1 length 2 yds long and thread through pendant, with pendant at center, fold yarn in half lengthwise. Form a slip knot close to pendant, ch 12, fasten off.
Sew a tie to first sc of row 2 of Collar at each side of front opening. ■

HOT PANTS SET

DESIGNS BY JOYCE BRAGG

INTERMEDIATE

Finished Sizes
Instructions given fit woman's X-small; changes for small, medium, large and X-large are in [ ].

Finished Garment Measurements
Top: Empire waist: 27 inches (X-small) [28 inches (small), 29 inches (medium), 30 inches (large), 31 inches (X-large)]

Shorts: Hip (unstretched): 27 inches (X-small) [29 inches (small), 31 inches (medium), 32 inches (large), 33 inches (X-large)]

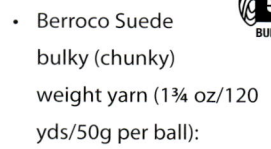

Gauge
Size G hook: 5 sc = 1 inch; 5 sc rows = 1 inch

Pattern Notes
Weave in loose ends as work progresses.
Join rounds with a slip stitch unless otherwise stated.
Top is loose fitting, designed to wear over a tank or t-shirt.

Special Stitch
Block stitch (block st): At the beg of a row, ch 3 *(counts as first dc)*, within a row or rnd replace ch-3 with a dc, *dc in next st, [insert hook over vertical post of last dc, yo, draw up a lp] 3 times, yo, draw through all 4 lps on hook, dc in next st, rep from * as indicated.

Materials
- Berroco Suede bulky (chunky) weight yarn (1¾ oz/120 yds/50g per ball):
    6 balls #3753 Belle Star
    1 ball #3737 Roy Rodgers
- Sizes F/5/3.75mm and G/6/4mm crochet hooks or size needed to obtain gauge
- Tapestry needle
- Stitch markers

5 BULKY

SHORTS

First Leg
Rnd 1: With size G hook and pink, ch 73 [78, 83, 88, 91], sc in 2nd ch from hook, sc in each rem ch across, taking care not to twist, join in first sc. *(72 [77, 82, 87, 90] sc)*

Rnd 2: Work **block st** *(see Special Stitch)*, place marker on first block st, block st around, join in 3rd ch of beg ch-3.

Rnd 3: Ch 1, working in **back lps** *(see Stitch Guide)*, sc in each st around, join in beg sc, fasten off. *(72 [77, 82, 87, 90] sts)*

2nd Leg
Rnds 1–3: Rep rnds 1–3 of First Leg, do not fasten off at the end of rnd 3.

Joining
Rnd 4: Ch 1, working in back lps, sc in each of next 34 [36, 38, 40, 42] sts, sc in 3rd st on first leg and in each of next 67 [71, 75, 79, 83] sts, leaving 4 [5, 5, 6, 6] sc free for crotch, sk next 4 [5, 5, 6, 6] sts on 2nd leg for crotch, sc in next sc and in each of next 33 [35, 37, 39, 41] sts, join in beg sc, place marker. *(136 [144, 153, 161, 165] sts)*

Upper Shorts
Rnds 1 & 2: Ch 1, working in back lps only, sc in each st around, join in beg sc.

Rnd 3: Work block st in next 3 sts *(hip area)*, sc in each of next 66 [70, 74, 78, 82] sts, block st in next 3 sts *(hip area)*,

88 JACKETS, WRAPS & MORE

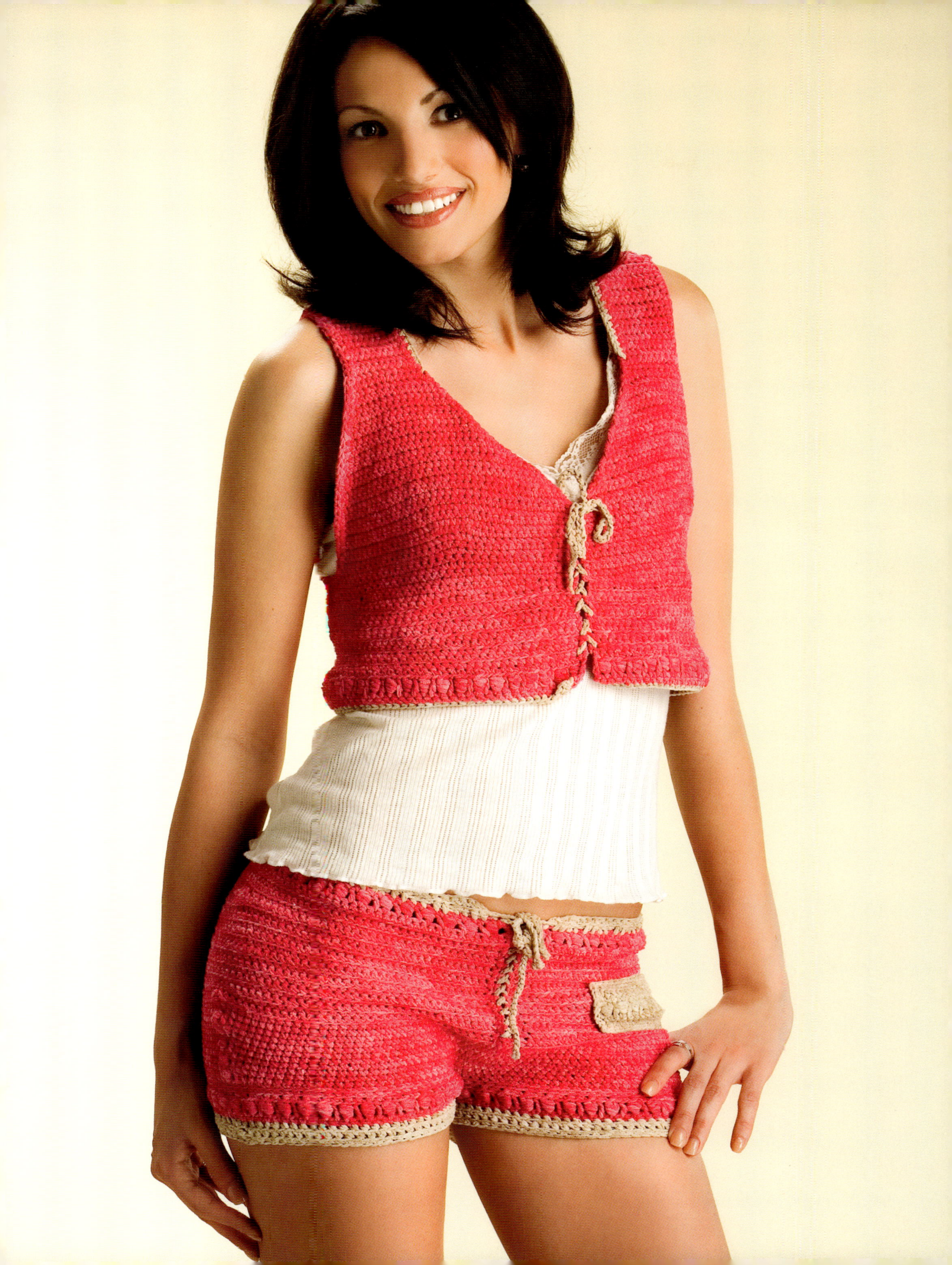

sc in each rem st around, join in 3rd ch of beg ch-3.
Rnd 4: Ch 1, sc in each st around, join in beg sc.
Short row: With a separate ball of pink, attach in 8th st from block st, sc in each of next 53 [57, 61, 74, 78] sts, sl st in next st, turn, sl st in first sc, sc in each of next 51 [55, 59, 72, 76] sts, fasten off.
Rnd 5: Block st in same 3 sts as block st below, sc in each of next 67 [71, 75, 79, 83] sts, block st in same 3 sts as block st below, sc in each rem st around, join in 3rd ch of beg ch-3.
Rep rnds 4 and 6 alternately until piece measures 3 [3½, 4, 4, 4½] inches from crotch, fasten off.

Front Opening

Row 1: With WS facing, attach pink in **front lp** (see Stitch Guide) of 41st [43rd, 45th, 47th, 49th] st from center of block st of hip area, ch 1, sc in front lp of same st as beg ch-1, sc in front lp of each st to last 4 sts, turn.
Row 2: Ch 1, working in front lps, sc in each st, turn.
Rep row 2 until piece measures 7 [7½, 8, 8½, 9] inches from crotch, ending on WS, fasten off.
Row 3: Working another short row, with RS facing, attach pink in 36th [38th, 40th, 42nd, 44th] st, working in front lps only, ch 1, sc in each of next 75 [77, 79, 81, 83] sts across back of shorts, turn.
Row 4: Sl st in first st, sc in front lp of each of next 75 [77, 79, 81, 83] sts, sl st in next st, fasten off.
Row 5: Attach pink in first sc st before previous short rows, ch 1, working in front lps only, sc in each st across, turn.
Rows 6–8: Ch 1, working in front lps only, sc in each st across, turn.
Row 9: Ch 3, work block st, [sk next st, block st] across, turn.
Row 10: Ch 1, sc in each st across, working around front opening, sc evenly spaced down front opening and up opposite edge, join in beg sc, fasten off.

Waistline Trim

Row 11: With RS facing, attach beige, ch 2 (counts as first hdc), hdc in each sc of row 10, turn.
Row 12: Ch 1, working in front lps only, sc in each st across, fasten off.

Lower Leg Border

Rnd 1: With RS facing, attach beige in opposite side of foundation ch of Leg, ch 2, hdc in each st around, join in 2nd ch of beg ch-2.
Rnd 2: Ch 2, hdc in each st around, join in 2nd ch of beg ch-2.
Rnd 3: Ch 1, working in back lps only, sc in each st around, join in beg sc, fasten off.
Rep on opposite Leg.

Front Closure

With size F hook and beige, crochet a ch 15 [15, 16, 17, 17] inches, fasten off and lace ch through the sc on each side of opening. Beg at bottom corners, sk 2 sts between each lacing, ending at last sc row of pink color, tie ends in a bow.

Drawstring

With size F hook and beige, crochet a ch approximately 30 inches or to length desired to fit Shorts size. Starting at center back, weave ch through hdc sts of row 11 of Waistline Trim, draw ends up, tie in a bow and let it fall over bow of Front Closure.

Pocket

Row 1: Beg at bottom, with size F hook and beige, ch 16, sc in 2nd ch from hook, sc in each rem ch across, turn. (15 sc)
Row 2: Ch 2, hdc in each st across, turn.

90 JACKETS, WRAPS & MORE

& MORE

Short Front Rows

Row 1: With size G hook, attach a separate ball of pink with sl st in 6th sc from beg, working in both lps, sc in each of next 20 [25, 25, 25, 30] sts, sl st in next st, turn, sc in each of next 20 [20, 30, 35, 35] sts, draw up a lp, drop yarn.

Row 1: With size G hook, attach a separate ball of pink with sl st in 6th sc of opposite side, sc in both lps of each of next 20 [25, 25, 25, 30] sts, sl st in next st, turn, sc in each of next 20 [20, 30, 35, 35] sts, fasten off.

Row 2: With RS facing, attach pink in first st, ch 1, sc in each st across, turn.

Rows 3 & 4: Ch 1, sc in each st across, turn.

Left Front Armhole

Row 1: Ch 1, sk first st, sc in each of next 15 [15, 20, 25, 25] sts, 2 sc in next st, sc in each of next 18 [18, 23, 28, 28] sts, turn.

For Sizes X-Small, Small & Medium Only

Row 2: Ch 1, sc in each of next 18 [18, 23] sts, 2 sc in next sc, sc in each rem sc across, turn.

Row 3: Ch 1, sc in each of next 15 [15, 20] sts, 2 sc in next st, sc in next st, 2 sc in next st, sc across to armhole, turn.

For Sizes Large & X-Large Only

Row 2: Ch 1, sc in each of next 28 [28] sts, 2 sc in next st, sc in each rem st across, turn.

Row 3: Ch 1, sc in each st to within 1 st before inc on previous row, 2 sc in next st, sc in next st, 2 sc in next st, sc in each rem sc across to armhole, turn.

For All Sizes

Row 4: Sk first sc at armhole, sc in each st to within 1 st before inc of previous row, inc 1 st in sc on each side of inc sts on previous row, sc in rem sc sts across, turn.

Row 5: Ch 1, sc in each st to within 1 st before inc on previous row, inc 1 st on each side of inc on previous row, sc in each rem sc across, turn.

Rows 6–10: Ch 1, sc in each sc across, turn. Ending with last rep at front edge, turn.

CONTINUED ON PAGE 164

Row 3: Block st across row, turn.
Row 4: Ch 1, sc in each st across, turn.
Row 5: Rep row 2.
Row 6: Ch 2, working in back lps only, hdc in each st across, turn.

Note: For larger Pocket, continue to rep row 6 to desired width.

Row 7: Ch 1, working down side edge of rows, sc evenly spaced in opposite side of foundation ch, 2 sc in corner, sc in each ch across, 2 sc in corner, sc in each st up opposite edge, sl st in next st, leaving a length of yarn, fasten off.

Sew Pocket to front left side of Pants.

TOP

Body

Foundation row: With size G hook and pink, ch 137 [142, 147, 152, 157] sc in 2nd ch from hook, sc in each rem ch across, turn. *(136 [141, 146, 151, 156] sts)*

Row 1: With size F hook, work block st across, turn.
Row 2: With size G hook, working in front lps only, ch 1, sc in each st across, turn. *(136 [141, 146, 151, 156] sts)*
Row 3: Ch 1, sc in each st across, turn.
Row 4: Ch 1, working in front lps only, sc in each st across, turn.
Rows 5–12: [Rep rows 3 and 4 alternately] 4 times. At the end of last rep, fasten off.

JACKETS, WRAPS & MORE

KIWI VEST & HEADBAND

DESIGNS BY JOYCE BRAGG

INTERMEDIATE

Finished Sizes
Vest: Bust: Instructions given fit 32–34-inch bust (small); changes for 36–38-inch bust (medium) and 40–42-inch bust (large) are in [ ].
Headband: 18½ inches, excluding ties

Finished Garment Measurements
Bust: 32 inches (small) [36 inches (medium), 40 inches (large)]

Gauge
Size F hook (small): 14 sts = 5 inches; 4 rows = 1 inch
Size G hook (medium): 18 sts = 4 inches; 5 rows = 1 inch
Size H hook (large): 20 sts = 4 inches; 6 rows = 1 inch

Pattern Notes
Weave in loose ends as work progresses.
Join rounds with a slip stitch unless otherwise stated.
Row 3 establishes the Vest pattern.

VEST

Right Front
Foundation row: Beg at shoulder, with size F [G, H] hook, ch 16, sl st in 2nd ch from hook, sl st in each rem ch across, turn.
Row 1: Ch 1, [hdc in next st, sl st loosely in next st] across, turn. *(15 sts)*
Row 2: Ch 2 *(counts as first hdc)*, sk first sl st, working in

Materials
- TLC Cotton Plus medium (worsted) weight yarn (3½ oz/178 yds/100g per ball): 3 balls #3643 kiwi
- Sizes F/5/3.75mm, G/6/4mm and H/8/5mm crochet hooks or sizes needed to obtain gauge
- Tapestry needle

MEDIUM 4

back lp *(see Stitch Guide)* of each st across, [sl st loosely in next hdc, hdc in next sl st] across, turn. *(15 sts)*
Row 3: Ch 1, working in back lps only, [hdc in sl st, sl st loosely in hdc] across, turn.
Rows 4–11: [Rep rows 2 and 3] 4 times.
Row 12: Rep row 2.

Neck & Armhole Shaping
Row 13: Maintaining pattern of row 3 in back lps only, hdc in sl st and sl st loosely in hdc, work 2 sts in first st, work in pattern across, turn. *(16 sts)*
Rep row 13 until Front measures 6½ inches from first inc, ending at armhole edge, turn. *(31 sts)*
Row 14: At armhole edge, ch 13, sl st in 2nd ch from hook, sl st in each ch, sl st loosely in last st made before ch-13, continue in pattern across, to last 2 sts, **dec 1 st** *(see Stitch Guide)* in last 2 sts, turn.
Row 15: Work in pattern of row 3 across, turn.
Row 16: Work in pattern of row 3 across, dec 1 st in last 2 sts, turn.
Rep rows 15 and 16 until armhole measures 3 inches, ending at armhole edge, do not work last st and turning ch, turn.
Row 17: Maintaining pattern of row 3, dec 1 st at beg and end of row, turn.
Row 18: Work even in pattern of row 3 across, turn.
Rep rows 17 and 18 until 3 sts rem.
Row 19: Ch 2, sk 1 st, hdc in last st, fasten off.

Left Front
Work Left Front same as Right Front, pattern is reversed.

Back
Make 2.
Foundation row: Beg at shoulder, with size F [G, H]

CONTINUED ON PAGE 165

92 JACKETS, WRAPS & MORE

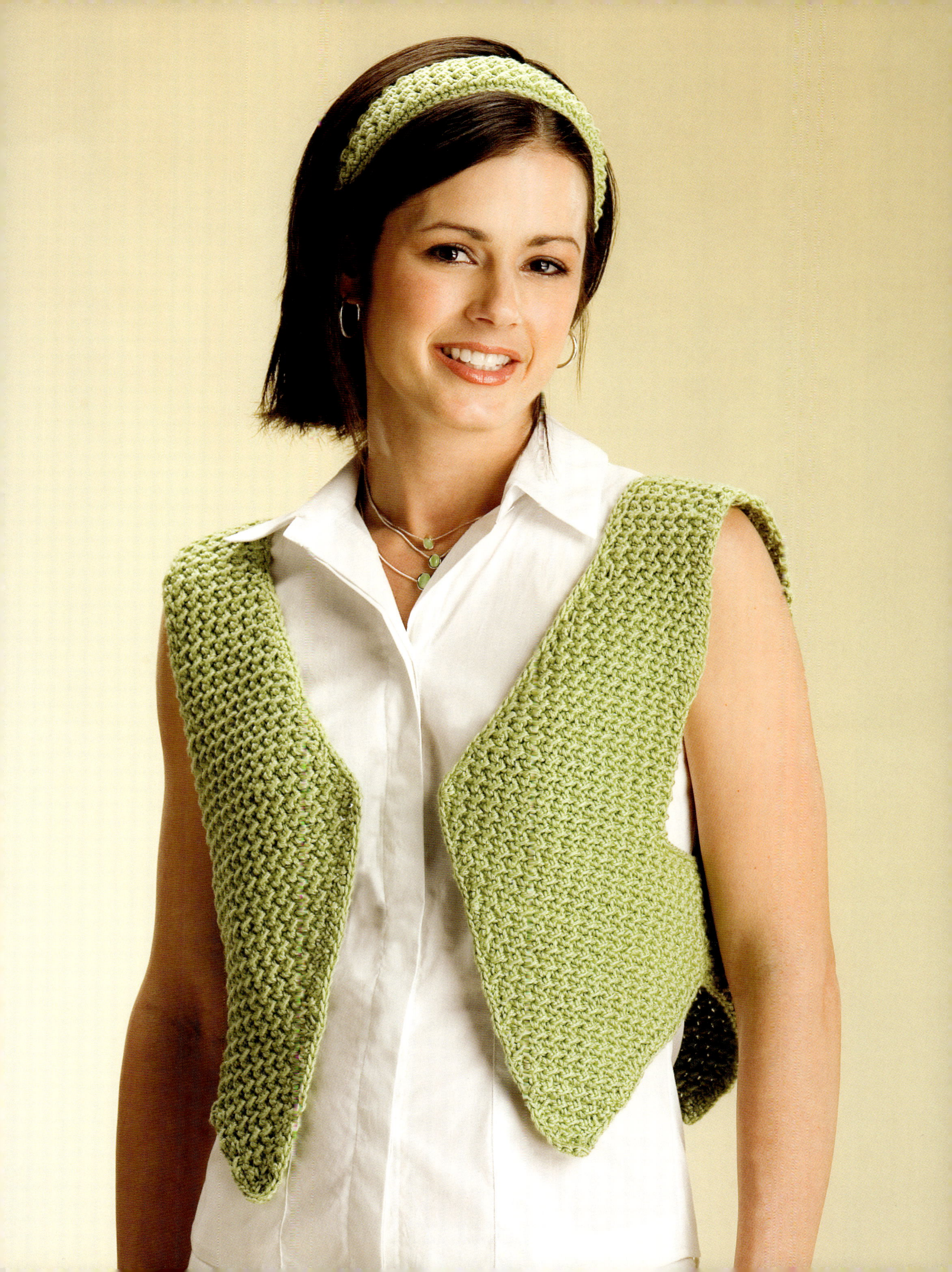

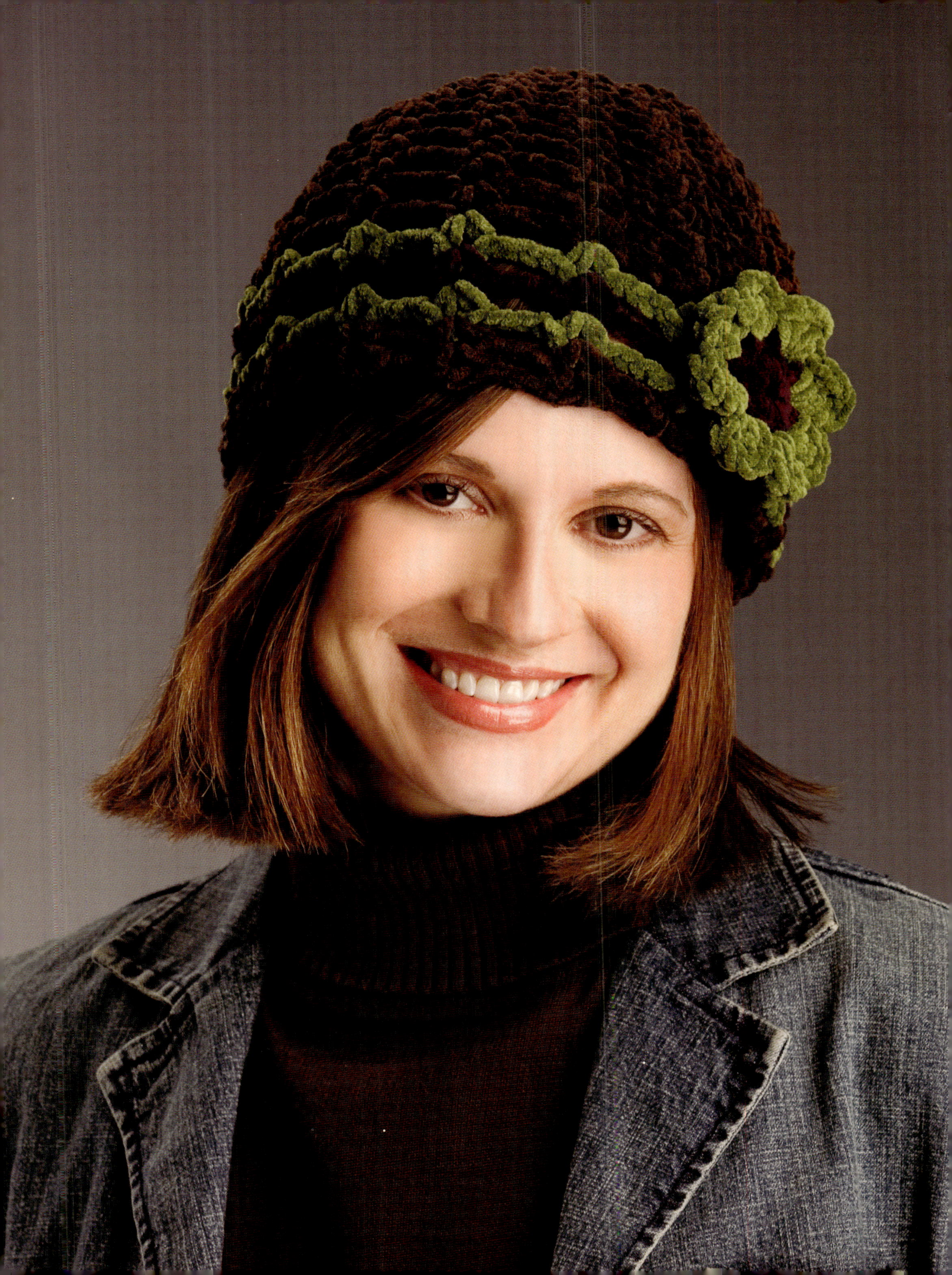

LADDER-STITCH CLOCHE

DESIGN BY KATHERINE ENG

BEGINNER

Finished Size
Adult

Finished Garment Measurements
Bottom circumference = 22 inches

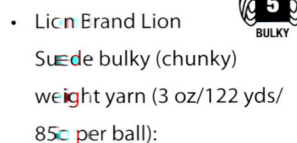

Materials
- Lion Brand Lion Suede bulky (chunky) weight yarn (3 oz/122 yds/85g per ball):
  - 1½ oz/61 yds/43g #126 coffee
  - ½ oz/20 yds/14g each #132 olive and #147 eggplant
- Size H/8/5mm crochet hook or size needed to obtain gauge
- Tapestry needle

Gauge
First 2 rnds = 1½ inches

Pattern Notes
Weave in loose ends as work progresses.
Join rounds with a slip stitch unless otherwise stated.
For smaller size, use size G hook.

CLOCHE

Rnd 1: With coffee, ch 4, join in first ch to form a ring, ch 1, 8 sc in ring, join in beg sc. *(8 sc)*

Rnd 2: Ch 1, (sc, ch 2, sc) in each sc around, join in beg sc. *(8 ch-2 sps)*

Rnd 3: Sl st into ch-2 sp, ch 1, (sc, ch 2, sc) in same ch-2 sp, ch 1, [(sc, ch 2, sc) in next ch-2 sp, ch 1] around, join in beg sc.

Rnd 4: Sl st into ch-2 sp, ch 1, (sc, ch 2, sc) in same ch-2 sp, (sc, ch 2, sc) in next ch-1 sp, [(sc, ch 2, sc) in next ch-2 sp, (sc, ch 2, sc) in next ch-1 sp] around, join in beg sc. *(16 ch-2 sps)*

Rnd 5: Sl st into ch-2 sp, ch 1, (sc, ch 2, sc) in same ch-2 sp and in each rem ch-2 sp around, join in beg sc.

Rnd 6: Rep rnd 3.

Rnd 7: Sl st into ch-2 sp, ch 1, (sc, ch 2, sc) in same ch-2 sp, ch 2, [(sc, ch 2, sc) in next ch-2 sp, ch 2] around, join in beg sc.

Rnd 8: Sl st into ch-2 sp, ch 1, (sc, ch 2, sc) in same ch-2 sp, ch 2, sk next ch-2 sp, [(sc, ch 2, sc) in next ch-2 sp, ch 2, sk next ch-2 sp] around, join in beg sc.

Rnd 9: Sl st into ch-2 sp, ch 1, (sc, ch 2, sc) in same ch-2 sp, ch 3, sk next ch-2 sp, [(sc, ch 2, sc) in next ch-2 sp, ch 3, sk next ch-2 sp] around, join in beg sc.

Rnd 10: Sl st into next ch-2 sp, ch 1, (sc, ch 2, sc) in same ch-2 sp, ch 3, sk next ch-3 sp, [(sc, ch 2, sc) in next ch-2 sp, ch 3, sk next ch-3 sp] around, join in beg sc.

Rnds 11 & 12: Rep rnd 10. At the end of rnd 12, fasten off.

Rnd 13: Draw up a lp of olive in first ch-2 sp of previous rnd, ch 1, rep rnd 10, fasten off.

Rnd 14: Draw up a lp of eggplant in first ch-2 sp of previous rnd, ch 1, rep rnd 10, fasten off.

Rnd 15: Rep rnd 13.

Rnd 16: Draw up a lp of coffee in first ch-2 sp of previous rnd, ch 1, (sc, ch 2, sc) in same ch-2 sp, ch 2, sk next ch-3 sp, [(sc, ch 2, sc) in next ch-2 sp, ch 2, sk next ch-3 sp] around, join in beg sc.

CONTINUED ON PAGE 166

STARLIGHT SCARF

DESIGN BY SUE CHILDRESS

EASY

Finished Size
2¼ x 42 inches

Materials
- Tahki Star light (DK) weight yarn (163 yds/20g ball):
    1 ball #19 Sagittarius
- Berroco Softwist medium (worsted) weight yarn (1¾ oz/100 yds/50g per hank):
    1 hank #9443 smoothie
- Size I/9/5.5mm crochet hook or size needed to obtain gauge
- Tapestry needle
- Ornamental pin (optional)

Gauge
With 1 strand of each held tog: 2 dc and ch-2 = 1 inch

SCARF

Row 1: With 1 strand each held tog, ch 156, dc in 4th ch from hook, [ch 2, sk next 2 chs, dc in each of next 2 chs] across, turn. *(39 groups 2-dc, 38 ch-2 sps)*

Row 2: Ch 3 *(counts as first dc)*, 2 sc in next ch-2 sp, [ch 2, 2 sc in next ch-2 sp] across, ending with dc in last dc, turn.

Row 3: Ch 3, dc in same dc as beg ch-3, [ch 2, 2 dc in next ch-2 sp] across, ending with 2 dc in last dc, turn.

Row 4: Ch 6, working in dc of row 1, [sk 2 sc of row 2, sc in first dc of next 2-dc group of row 1, ch 6] across, ending with sc in top of first dc of row 3, turn.

Row 5: Rep row 2.

Row 6: Rep row 3.

Row 7: Ch 6, working in dc of row 3, [sk 2 sc of row 5, sc in first dc of next 2-dc group of row 3, ch 6] across, ending with sc in top of first dc of row 6, **do not turn.**

Row 8: Working in ends of Scarf rows, [ch 6, sc in end of next row] 5 times, fasten off.

Row 9: Working in opposite end of Scarf rows, attach 1 strand each in row end, ch 1, sc in same row, [ch 6, sc in next row] 5 times, fasten off.

Finishing

Pass end of Scarf through ch-2 sp of row 3 approximately 6 inches up from opposite end of scarf, secure with pin. ■

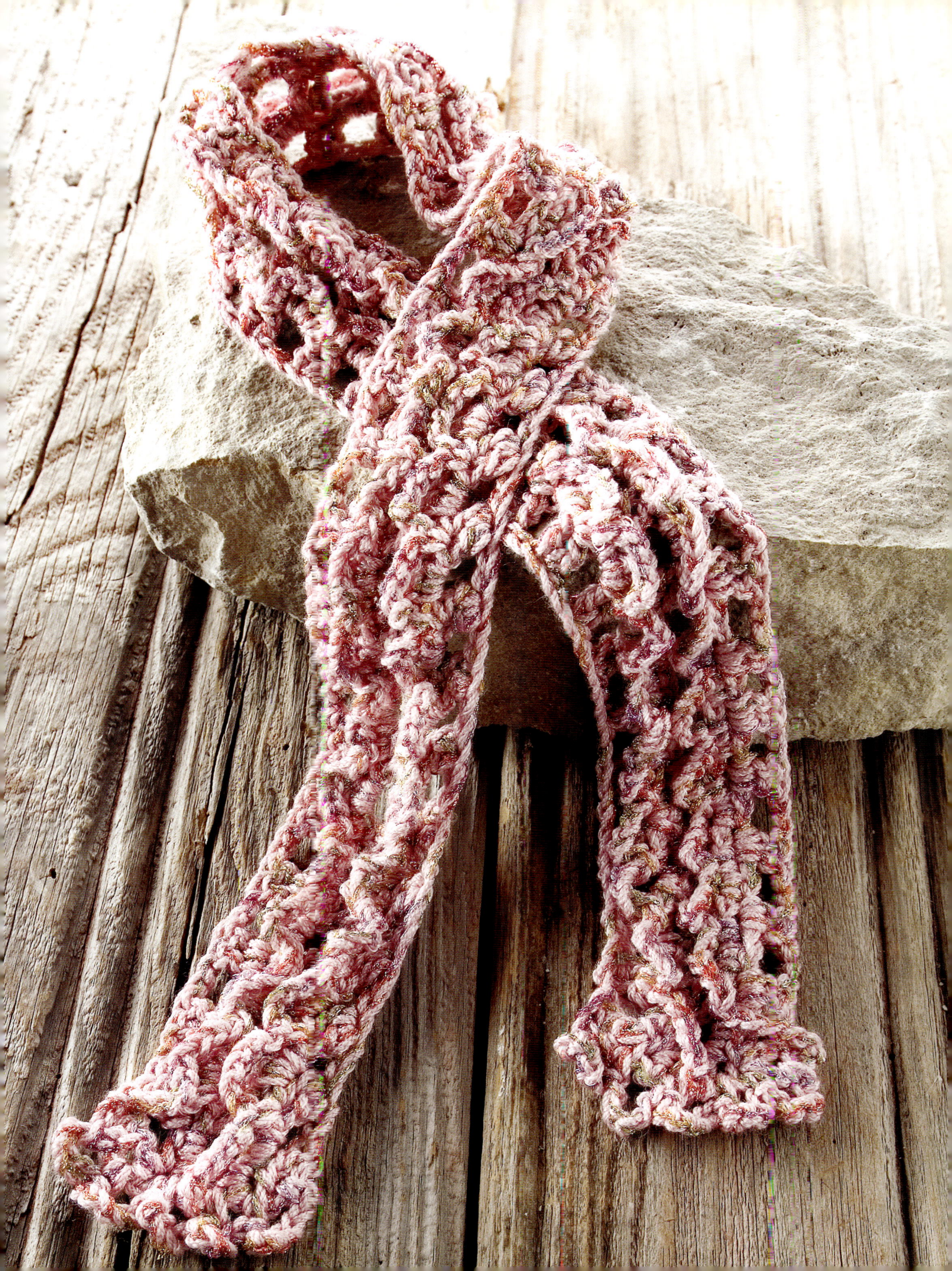

MOONLIGHT MAGIC

DESIGN BY JOHANNA DZIKOWSKI

Finished Size

7 inches square, excluding Shoulder Strap

Materials

- Lion Brand Moonlight Mohair bulky (chunky) weight yarn (1¾ oz/82 yds/50g per skein):
    1 skein #205 glacier bay
- Lion Brand Chenille Thick & Quick super bulky (super chunky) weight yarn (3 oz/100 yds/80g per skein):
    20 yds #111 midnight blue
- Size I/9/5.5mm crochet hooks or size needed to obtain gauge
- Tapestry needle

Gauge

5 dc = 2 inches

Pattern Notes

Weave in loose ends as work progresses.
Join rounds with a slip stitch unless otherwise stated.

EVENING BAG

Flap

Rnd 1: With glacier bay, ch 6, join in first ch to form a ring, ch 1, [sc in ring, ch 3] 12 times, join in beg sc. *(12 ch-3 sps)*

Rnd 2: Sl st into ch-3 sp, ch 1, sc in same ch-3 sp as beg ch-1, ch 3, [sc in next ch-3 sp, ch 3] around, join in beg sc.

Rnd 3: Sl st into ch-3 sp, ch 1, sc in same ch-3 sp, ch 4, [sc in next ch-3 sp, ch 4] around, join in beg sc, fasten off. *(12 ch-4 sps)*

Rnd 4: Attach dark blue in any ch-4 sp, ch 1, sc in same ch-4 sp, ch 5, [sc in next ch-4 sp, ch 5] around, join in beg sc. *(12 ch-5 sps)*

Rnd 5: Ch 1, [8 hdc in next ch-5 sp, sc in next ch-5 sp] around, join in first hdc, fasten off. *(48 hdc, 6 sc)*

Body

Row 1: With glacier bay, ch 19, sc in 2nd ch from hook, sc in each rem ch across, turn. *(18 sc)*

Row 2: Ch 1, dc in each sc across, turn.

Row 3: Ch 1, dc in each dc across, turn.

Rows 4–18: Rep row 3.

Row 19: Ch 1, sc in each dc across, leaving a length of yarn, fasten off.

Holding row 1 and row 19 of Body tog for top opening, with rem length of yarn, sew each side seam.

Shoulder Strap

Note: Roll remainder of glacier bay into 2 equal balls.

Row 1: Attach first ball of glacier bay in sewn side seam, ch 1, 3 sc in same st, turn. *(3 sc)*

Row 2: Ch 1, hdc in each sc across, turn. *(3 hdc)*

Row 3: Ch 1, hdc in each hdc across, turn.

Rows 4–17: Rep row 3. At the end of row 17, fasten off.

Row 18: Attach midnight blue in first hdc, ch 1, hdc in

each hdc across, turn.
Row 19: Ch 1, hdc in each hdc across, turn.
Rep row 19 until Strap reaches desired length or until dark blue is gone.

Row 20: Attach glacier bay to last row of dark blue, ch 1, hdc in each of next 3 hdc, turn.
Rows 21–35: Rep row 3.
Row 36: Ch 1, work 3 sc in opposite side seam, fasten off. ∎

JACKETS, WRAPS & MORE 99

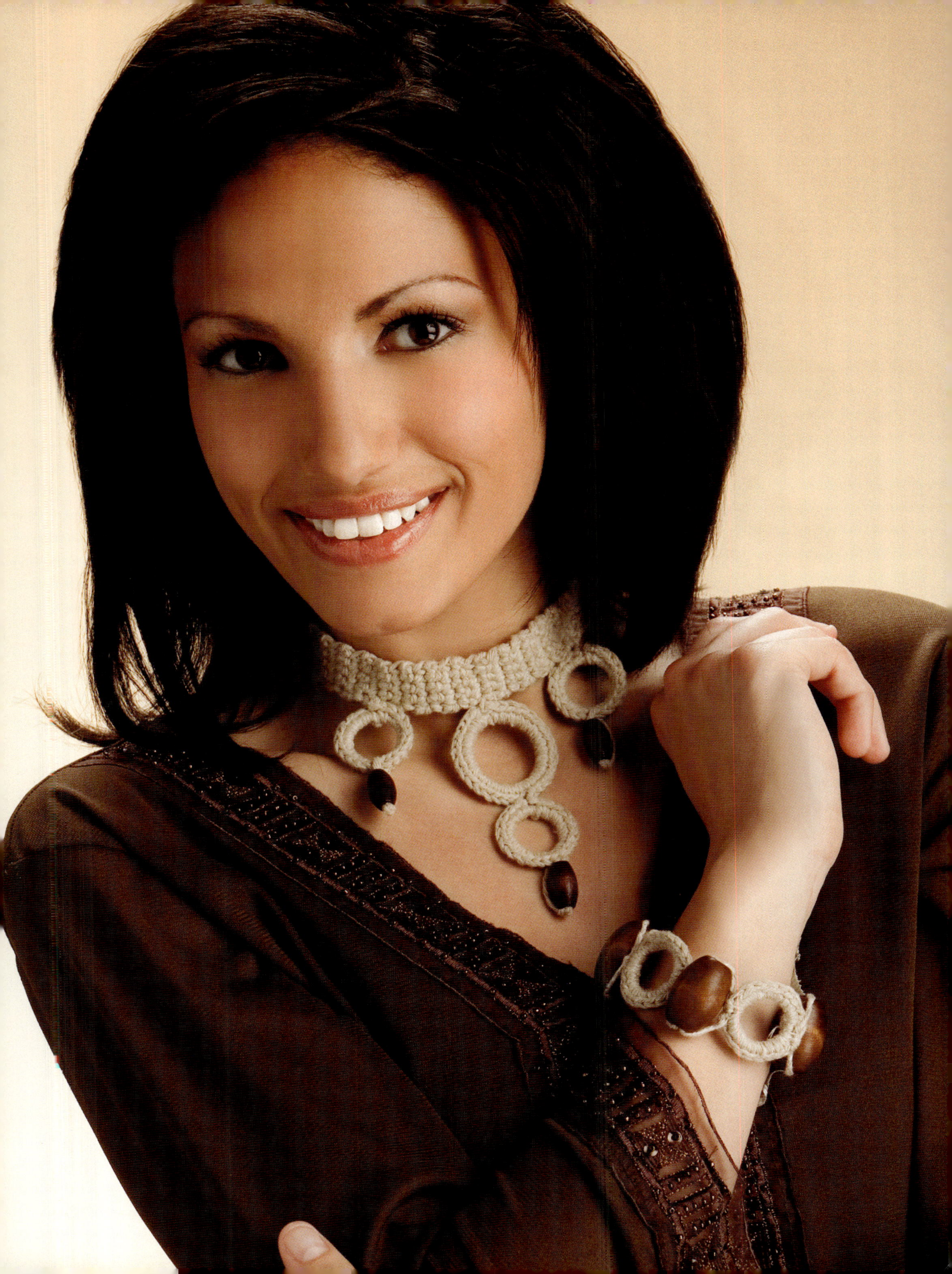

& MORE

EARTH CHILD

DESIGNS BY MARY JANE HALL

EASY

Finished Sizes
Choker: 7/8 x 13¼ inches
Bracelet: 7 inches in diameter

Materials
- Aunt Lydia's "Denim" Quick 8-ply crochet medium (worsted) weight thread (400 yds per ball): 300 yds #1021 linen
- Size E/4/3.5mm crochet hook or size needed to obtain gauge
- Yarn needle
- ¾-inch metal rings: 7
- 1¼-inch metal ring: 1
- 18mm wooden oval beads: 3
- 28mm wooden oval beads: 4
- 15mm button: 1

4 MEDIUM

Gauge
3 sc = 1 inch

Pattern Notes
Weave in loose ends as work progresses.
Join rounds with a slip stitch unless otherwise stated.
If larger Bracelet is desired add one 1¼-inch metal ring and one 28mm wooden bead for a 2-inch increase in diameter.

CHOKER

Neckband
Row 1: Ch 5, sc in 2nd ch from hook, sc in each rem ch across, turn. *(4 sc)*
Row 2: Ch 1, sc in each sc across, turn.
Rows 3–69: Rep row 2. If longer choker is desired, add needed number of rows.

Buttonhole
Row 70: Ch 5, sk first 3 sc, sl st in 4th sc, turn.
Row 71: Work 7 sc over ch-5 sp, sl st in side edge of row 69, fasten off.

Large Ring
Rnd 1: Attach linen to 1¼-inch metal ring, ch 1, work 30 sc over metal ring, join in beg sc, leaving a length of cotton, fasten off. *(30 sc)*

CONTINUED ON PAGE 167

JACKETS, WRAPS & MORE **101**

GRANNY SQUARE SHRINK VEST

DESIGN BY MARTY MILLER

EASY

Finished Sizes

Instructions given fit 28–30-inch bust *(X-small)*; changes for 32–34-inch bust *(small)*, 36–38-inch bust *(medium)*, 40–42-inch bust *(large)* and 44–46-inch bust *(X-large)* are in [ ].

Finished Garment Measurements

Bust: 27 inches *(X-small)* [31 inches *(small)*, 35 inches *(medium)*, 49 inches *(large)*, 43 inches *(X-large)*]

Length: 14½ inches *(X-small)* [16½ inches *(small)*, 18 inches *(medium)*, 19½ inches *(large)*, 20½ inches *(X-large)*]

Gauge

Rnds 1 and 2 = 4 inches; 5 dc = 2 inches

Pattern Notes

Weave in loose ends as work progresses.
Join rounds with a slip stitch unless otherwise stated.

Materials

- Lion Brand Lion Suede bulky (chunky) weight yarn (3 oz/122 yds/85g per skein): 2 [3, 3, 4, 5] skeins #110 denim
- Size J/10/6mm crochet hook or size needed to obtain gauge
- Tapestry needle
- Stitch markers

5 BULKY

VEST

Body

Make 2.

Rnd 1: Ch 6, join in first ch of ch-6, ch 3 *(counts as first dc)*, 15 dc in ring, join in 3rd ch of beg ch-3. *(16 dc)*

Rnd 2: Ch 3, dc in same st as beg ch-3, 2 dc in each dc around, join in 3rd ch of beg ch-3. *(32 dc)*

Rnd 3: Ch 5 *(counts as first dc, ch-2)*, sk next dc, [dc in next dc, ch 2, sk next dc] around, join in 3rd ch of beg ch-5. *(16 dc, 16 ch-2 sps)*

CONTINUED ON PAGE 167

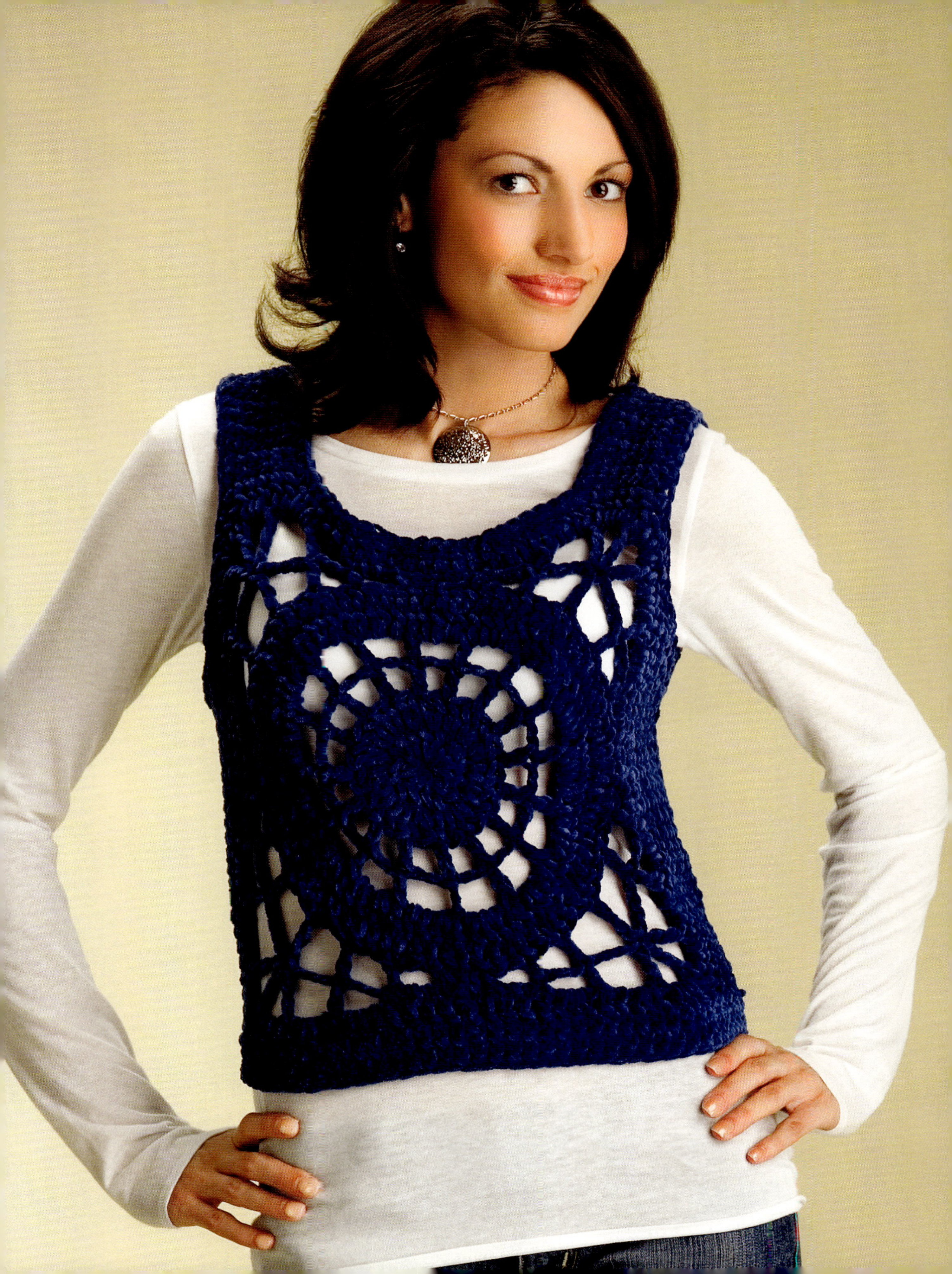

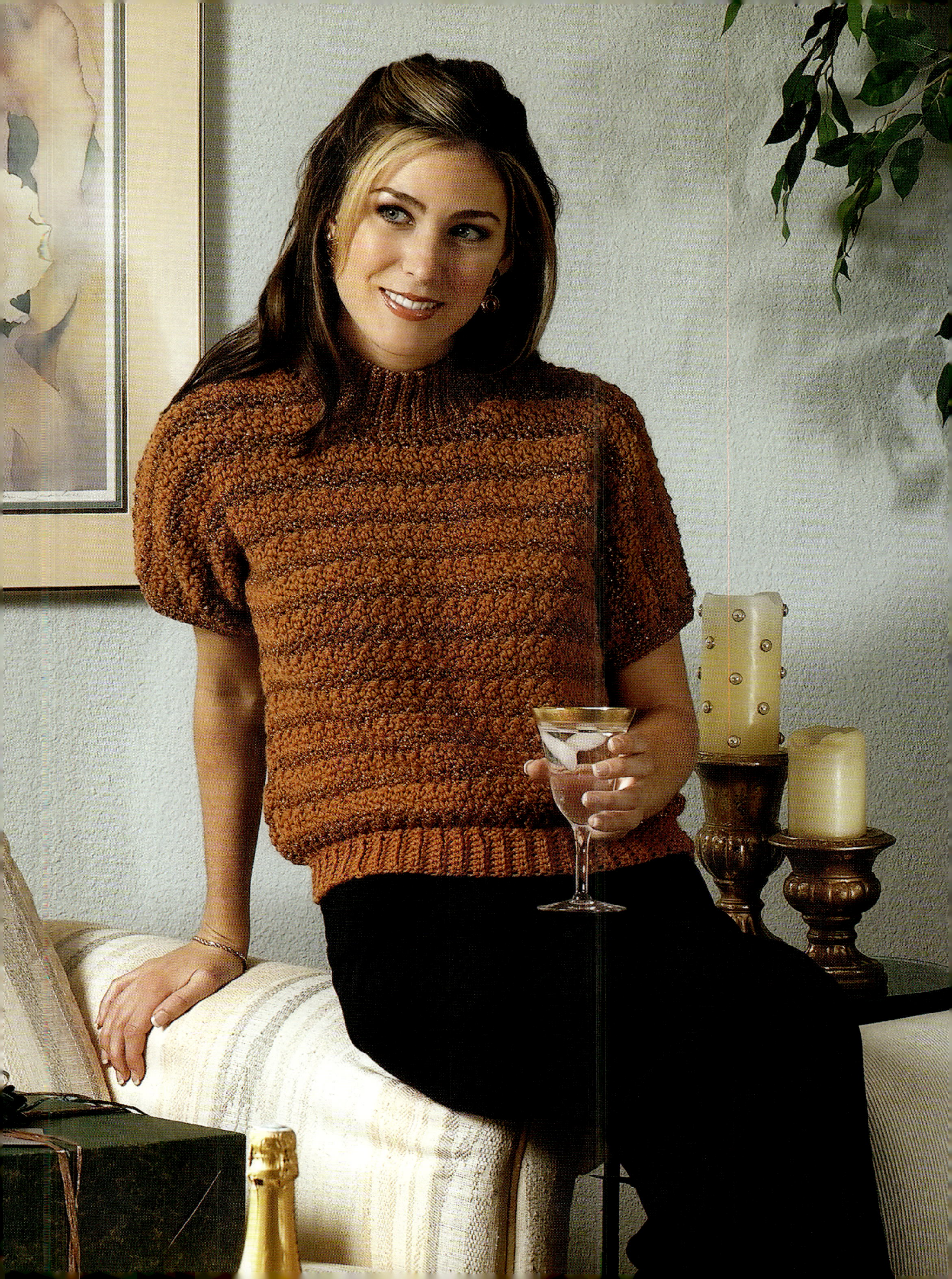

SWEATER FOR A SPECIAL EVENING

DESIGN BY DARLA SIMS

INTERMEDIATE

Finished Sizes
Instructions given fit 32-24-inch bust *(small)*; changes for 36-38-inch bust *(medium)*, 40-42-inch bust *(large)*, 44-46-inch bust *(X-large)*, 48-50-inch bust *(2X-large)* and 52-54-inch bust *(3X-large)* are in [ ].

Finished Garment Measurements
Bust: 36 inches *(small)* [40 inches *(medium)*, 44 inches *(large)*, 48 inches, *(X-large)*, 50 inches *(2X-large)*, 55 inches *(3X-large)*]

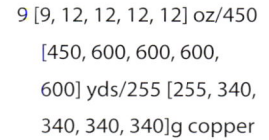

Gauge
Size G hook: 5 sc = 1 inch; 5 sc back lp rows = 1 inch
Size I hook: 12 pattern sts = 4 inches; 12 pattern rows = 4 inches
Take time to check gauge.

Pattern Note
To work in pattern, repeat rows 2–5 consecutively.

Materials
- Medium (worsted) weight yarn:
  9 [9, 12, 12, 12, 12] oz/450 [450, 600, 600, 600, 600] yds/255 [255, 340, 340, 340, 340]g copper
- Lion Brand Glitterspun medium (worsted) weight yarn (1¾ oz/115yds/50g per ball):
  5 [5, 6, 6, 7, 7] balls #135 bronze
- Sizes G/6/4mm and I/9/5.5mm crochet hooks or sizes needed to obtain gauge
- Tapestry needle

SWEATER

Back
Row 1: With size I hook and copper, ch 55 [61, 67, 73, 79, 85], sc in 2nd ch from hook, dc in next ch, [sc in next ch, dc in next ch] across, turn. *(54 [60, 66, 72, 78, 84] sts)*
Row 2: Ch 1, sc in each dc and dc in each sc across **changing colors** *(see Stitch Guide)* to bronze in last st made, turn. Drop copper. Pick up again when needed.
Row 3: Ch 1, sc in each dc and dc in each sc across, turn.
Row 4: Ch 1, sc in each dc and dc in each sc across changing to copper in last st, turn. Drop bronze. Pick up again when needed.
Row 5: Ch 1, sc in each dc and dc in each sc across, turn.
Rows 6–30: Work in pattern *(see Pattern Note)* until piece measures about 11 inches from beg, ending with row 4. At end of last row, do not change to copper. Fasten off both yarns.

Sleeves
Row 31: Join copper with sl st in last st of row 30, ch 12. Fasten off. Join copper with sl st in first st of row 30, for sleeve, ch 13, sc in 2nd ch from hook, dc in next ch, [sc in next ch, dc in next ch] across to row 30, work in pattern across to ch-12, [sc in next ch, dc in next ch] across, turn. *(78 [84, 90, 96, 102, 108] sts)*
Next rows: Work in pattern until piece measures 19 [19½, 20, 20½, 21, 21½] inches from beg. At end of last row, fasten off.

JACKETS, WRAPS & MORE **105**

& MORE

JACKETS, WRAPS & MORE

Front

Work same as back until piece measures 16 [16½, 17, 17½, 18, 18½] from beg.

First Shoulder

Row 1: Work in pattern across first 34 [36, 39, 42, 44, 46] sts, leaving rem sts unworked, turn.
Row 2: Work in pattern.
Row 3: Work in pattern across to last 2 sts, **dc dec** *(see Stitch Guide)* in last 2 sts, turn. *(33 [35, 38, 41, 43, 45] sts)*
Rows 4–9: [Rep rows 2 and 3 alternately] 3 times. *(30 [32, 35, 38, 40, 42] sts at end of last row)*
Row 10: Work in pattern. Fasten off.

2nd Shoulder

Row 1: Sk next 10 [12, 12, 12, 14, 16] sts at center front neck edge, using yarn color to maintain pattern, join with sl st in next st, ch 1, work in pattern across, turn. *(34 [36, 39, 42, 44, 46] sts)*
Row 2: Work in pattern.
Row 3: Ch 2 *(ch-2 is not used or counted as st)*, sk first st, work in pattern across, turn. *(33 [35, 38, 41, 43, 45] sts)*
Row 4: Work in pattern across leaving ch-2 unworked.
Rows 5–10: [Rep rows 3 and 4 alternately] 3 times. At end of last row, fasten off. *(30 [32, 35, 38, 40, 42] sts at end of last row)*

For shoulder seams, sew last row on each Front shoulder to 30 [32, 35, 38, 40, 42] sts to each end of last row on Back leaving center 18 [20, 20, 20, 22, 24] sts on Back open for neck edge.

Neck Ribbing

Rnd 1: With size G hook, join bronze with sc in first st after left shoulder seam, evenly sp 11 sc in ends of rows across to center front sts, sc in each of next 10 [12, 12, 12, 14, 16] sts at center front, evenly sp 12 sts in ends of row across to right shoulder seam, sc in each of next 18 [20, 20, 20, 22, 24] sts across Back neck edge, join with sl st in beg sc. *(52 [56, 56, 56, 60, 64] sc)*
Row 2: Ch 12, sc in 2nd ch from hook, sc in each ch across, sk first st on rnd 1, sl st in each of next 2 sts, turn. *(11 sc)*

Note: *Sl sts are not worked into or counted as sts.*
Row 3: Working in **back lps** *(see Stitch Guide)*, ch 1, sk sl sts, sc in each sc across, turn.
Row 4: Ch 1, sc in back lps of each sc across, sl st in both lps of each of next 2 sts on rnd 1, turn.
Rows 5 & 6: Rep rows 3 and 4.
Row 7: Rep row 3. Leaving 10-inch end for sewing, fasten off.

Matching sts, sew back lps of last row and starting ch at beg of row 2 tog to form rib.

Arm Band

Row 1: Working in ends of rows on 1 Sleeve, with size G hook and bronze, join with sc in end of first row, sc in next row, [**sc dec** *(see Stitch Guide)* in next 2 rows, sc in each of next 2 rows] across Sleeve *(last rep may not end evenly)*, turn.
Rows 2–5: Ch 1, sc in each st across, turn. At end of last row, fasten off.

Rep on other Sleeve.

Sew Sleeve and side seams.

Bottom Ribbing

Rnd 1: With RS of work facing, working on opposite side of starting ch on row 1 at bottom edge, with size G hook and copper, join with sc in first st after 1 side seam, sc in each of next 3 chs, sc dec in next 2 chs, [sc in each of next 4 chs, sc dec in next 2 chs] around Front and Back, join with sl st in beg sc, **do not turn**. *(90 [100, 110, 120, 130, 140] sts)*
Row 2: Ch 8, sc in 2nd ch from hook, sc in each ch across, sk first st on rnd 1, sl st in each of next 2 sts, turn. *(7 sc)*

Note: *Sl sts are not worked into or counted as sts.*
Row 3: Ch 1, sk sl sts, sc in back lps of each sc across, turn.
Row 4: Ch 1, sc in back lps of each sc across, sl st in both lps in each of next 2 sts on rnd 1, turn.
Next rows: Rep rows 3 and 4 alternately around rnd 1, ending with row 3. Leaving 10-inch end for sewing, fasten off.

Matching sts, sew back lps of last row and starting ch at beg of row 2 tog to form rib. ■

COWL-NECK SWEATER

DESIGN BY CAROLYN CHRISTMAS AND DARLA HASSELL

INTERMEDIATE

Finished Sizes
Instructions given fit 32–34-inch bust *(small)*; changes for 36–38-inch bust *(medium)*, 40–42-inch bust *(large)* and 44–46-inch bust *(X-large)* are in [ ].

Finished Garment Measurements
Bust: 32½ inches *(small)* [37 inches *(medium)*, 41 inches *(large)*, 44 inches *(X-large)*].

Gauge
11 sc = 3¼ inches; 5 pattern rows = 2 inches
Take time to check gauge.

Pattern Note
Pattern is established in rows 2 and 3.

Materials
- Fine (sport) weight chenille yarn:
  13 [14, 15, 16] oz/1,170 [1,260, 1,350, 1,440] yds/369 [397, 425, 454]g raspberry
- Size I/9/5.5mm crochet hook or size needed to obtain gauge
- Tapestry needle

SWEATER

Back
Row 1: Beg at bottom edge, ch 56 [64, 70, 76], sc in 2nd ch from hook, [ch 1, sk next ch, sc in next ch] across, turn. *(55 [63, 69, 75] sts and ch sps)*
Row 2: Ch 1, sc in first st, sc in next ch-1 sp, [ch 1, sk next st, sc in next ch-1 sp] across to last st, sc in last st, turn.
Row 3: Ch 1, sc in first st, [ch 1, sk next st, sc in next ch-1 sp] across to last 2 sts, ch 1, sk next st, sc in last st, turn.
Next rows: Rep rows 2 and 3 alternately until piece measures 15 [15, 15½, 15½] inches from beg ending with row 3.

Armhole Shaping
Next row: Sl st in first st, sl st in next ch-1 sp, sl st in next st, (sl st, ch 1, sc) in next ch-1 sp, [ch 1, sk next st, sc in next ch-1 sp] across to last 2 sts and last ch sp, leave last 2 sts and last ch sp unworked, turn.
Next 2 rows: Ch 1, sk first st, sc in next ch-1 sp, [ch 1, sk next st, sc in next ch-1 sp] across to last st, leaving last st unworked, turn.
Next rows: Rep rows 2 and 3 alternately until piece measures 19 [19½, 20, 21] inches from beg ending with row 3.

First Shoulder Shaping
Last row: Ch 1, sc in first st, sc in next ch-1 sp, [ch 1, sk next st, sc in next ch-1 sp] 4 times, leaving rem ch sps unworked. Fasten off.

2nd Shoulder Shaping
Last row: Sk across to last 5 ch sps and last 5 sts, join with sc in next ch-1 sp, [ch 1, sk next st, sc in next ch-1 sp] 4 times, sc in last st. Fasten off.

Front
Work same as Back to armholes.

Armhole Shaping
Next row: Sl st in first st, sl st in next ch-1 sp, sl st in

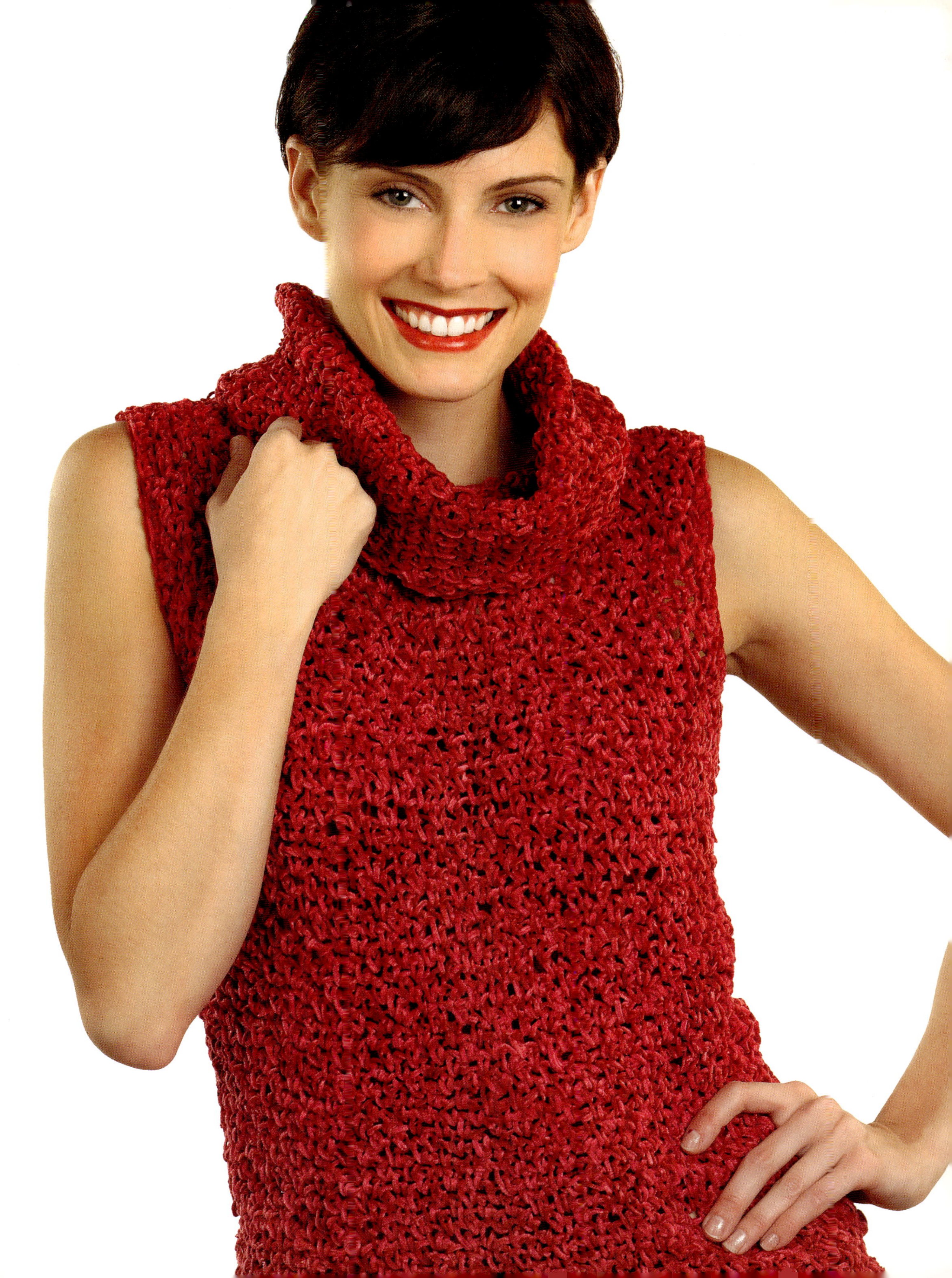

next st, (sl st, ch 1, sc) in next ch-1 sp, [ch 1, sk next st, sc in next ch-1 sp] across to last 2 sts and last ch sp, leave last 2 sts and last ch sp unworked, turn.
Next 3 rows: Ch 1, sk first st, sc in next ch-1 sp, [ch 1, sk next st, sc in next ch-1 sp] across to last st, leaving last st unworked, turn.
Next rows: Rep rows 2 and 3 of Back alternately until length of piece measures 19 [19½, 20, 21] inches from beg ending with row 2.

First Shoulder Shaping
Next row: Ch 1, sc in first st, [ch 1, sk next st, sc in next ch-1 sp] 7 times, leaving rem ch sps unworked, turn.
Next row: Sl st in first st, sl st in next ch-1 sp, sl st in next st, [sc in next ch-1 sp, ch 1, sk next st] 5 times, sc in next ch-1 sp, sc in last st, turn.
Next row: Ch 1, sc in first st, [ch 1, sk next st, sc in next st] 5 times, leaving rem sts unworked, turn.
Next row: Ch 1, sk first st, sc in next ch-1 sp, [ch 1, sk next st, sc in next ch-1 sp] 4 times, sc in last st. Fasten off.

2nd Shoulder
Next row: Sk across to last 7 ch sps and last 8 sts, join with sc in next ch-1 sp, [ch 1, sk next st, sc in next ch-1 sp] 6 times, ch 1, sk next st, sc in last st, turn.
Next row: Ch 1, sc in first st, sc in next ch-1 sp, [ch 1, sk next st, sc in next ch-1 sp] 5 times, leave rem sts and ch sps unworked, turn.
Next row: Ch 1, sk first st, sc in next ch-1 sp, [ch 1, sk next st, sc in next ch-1 sp] 4 times, ch 1, sk next st, sc in last st, turn.
Next row: Ch 1, sc in first st, sc in next ch-1 sp, [ch 1, sk next st, sc in next ch-1 sp] 4 times, leaving last st unworked. Fasten off.
Sew shoulders seams.
Sew side seams.

Neck Edging
Working on neckline, join with sc in center back ch sp, sc in each ch-1 sp and in end of each row around, with sc in end of each shoulder seam, join with sl st in beg sc. Fasten off.

Armhole Edging
Working in sts and in ends of rows around 1 armhole, join with sc in end of side seam at center bottom, evenly sp 120 sc around armhole, join with sl st in beg sc. Fasten off.
Rep on other armhole.

Bottom Scalloped Edging
Rnd 1: Working in starting ch on opposite side of row 1, join with sc in end of 1 side seam, sc in each ch around with sc in end of other side seam, join with sl st in beg sc.
Rnd 2: Ch 1, sc in first st, sk next st, 5 dc in next st, sk next st, [sc in next st, sk next st, 5 dc in next st, sk next st] around, join with sl st in beg sc. Fasten off.

Cowl Collar
Row 1: Ch 30, sc in 2nd ch from hook, [ch 1, sk next ch, sc in next ch] across, turn. *(29 sts and ch sps)*
Row 2: Ch 1, sc in first st, sc in next ch-1 sp, [ch 1, sk next st, sc in next ch-1 sp] across to last st, sc in last st, turn.
Row 3: Ch 1, sc in first st, [ch 1, sk next st, sc in next ch-1 sp] across to last 2 sts, ch 1, sk next st, sc in last st, turn.
Next rows: Rep rows 2 and 3 alternately until piece fits around Neck Edging, ending with row 3.
At end of last row, fasten off. Matching sts and chs, sew first and last row of piece tog. Sew 1 edge of Cowl Collar to Neck Edging. ■

CLAM SHELL PURSE

DESIGN BY JOYCE BRAGG

INTERMEDIATE

Finished Size
9 x 10 inches, excluding Handle

Materials
- J&P Coats Crochet Nylon size 18 thread (150 yds per tube):
  2 tubes #19 black
- Berroco Crystal FX light (light worsted) weight yarn (1¾ oz/146 yds/50g per ball):
  1 ball #4701 titanium
- Size G/6/4mm crochet hook or size needed to obtain gauge
- Tapestry needle
- Sewing needle
- Black thread
- 12 x 24-inch black lining material
- 18mm magnetic fastener
- ¼-inch diameter x 10 inches long multi temp glue stick
- Stitch marker

Gauge
5 sc = 1 inch

Pattern Note
Weave in loose ends as work progresses.

PURSE

Body
Make 2.

Row 1: With black, ch 14, sc in 2nd ch from hook, sc in each of next 11 chs, 3 sc in last ch, working on opposite side of foundation ch, sc in each of next 12 chs, turn. *(27 sc)*

Row 2: Ch 1, working in **back lp** *(see Stitch Guide)* of each st of Body unless otherwise stated, sc in each of next 12 sts, 3 sc in next st, sc in next st *(center top of Body)*, 3 sc in next st, sc in each of next 12 sts, turn. *(31 sc)*

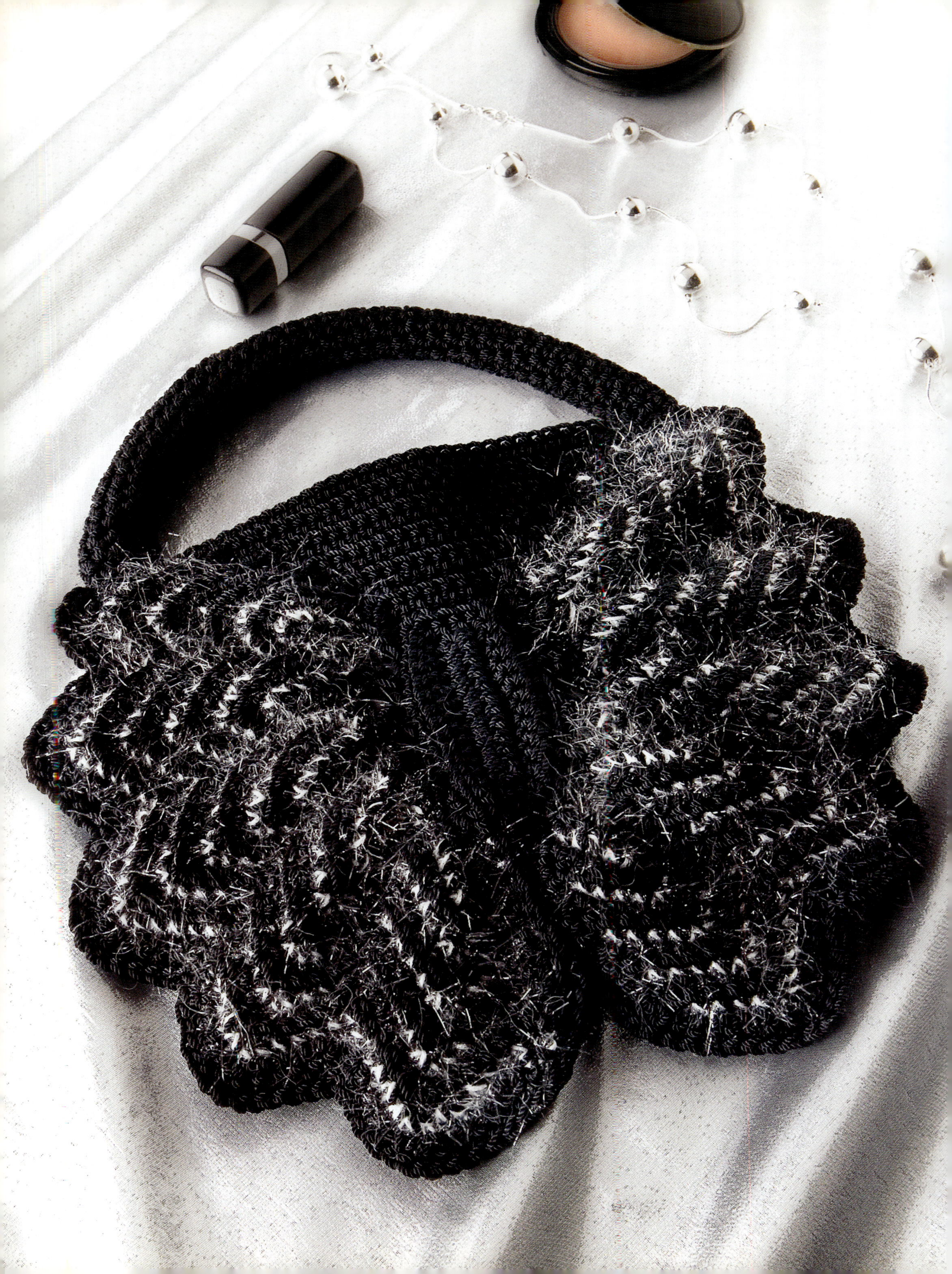

Row 3: Ch 1, sc in each of next 13 sts, 3 sc in next st, sc in each of next 3 sts, 3 sc in next st, sc in each of next 13 sts, turn. *(35 sc)*

Row 4: Sl st in each of next 3 sts, ch 1, sc in same st as last sl st, *[ch 11, sk next st, sc in next st] 5 times*, sk next st, 3 sc in next st, sc in each of next 5 sts *(center top of Body)*, 3 sc in next st, sk 1 st, sc in next st, rep from * to *, turn.

Row 5: Draw up a lp of titanium, working with both black and titanium, ch 1, *[sk next st, sc in each of next 5 chs, 3 sc in next ch, 5 sc in each of next 5 chs] 5 times*, sk next 2 sc of previous row, with black only, 3 sc in next st, sc in each of next 7 sts *(center top of Body)*, 3 sc in next st, sk next 2 sc of previous row, with both strands, [sc in each of next 5 chs, 3 sc in next ch, sc in each of next 5 chs, sk next st] 5 times, turn.

Row 6: With black only, ch 1, sk first st, *[sc in each of next 5 sts, 3 sc in next st, sc in each of next 5 sts, sk next 2 sts of previous row] 5 times*, 3 sc in next st, sc in each of next 9 sts *(center top of Body)*, 3 sc in next st, sk next 2 sts of previous row, rep between *, turn.

Row 7: Working with both strands, ch 1, sk first st, *[sc in each of next 5 sts, 3 sc in next st, sc in each of next 5 sts, sk next 2 sts of previous row] 5 times*, with black only, 3 sc in next st, sc in each of next 11 sts *(center top of Body)*, 3 sc in next st, sk next 2 sts of previous row, with both strands, rep between *, turn.

Row 8: With black only, ch 1, sk first st, *[sc in each of next 5 sts, 3 sc in next st, sc in each of next 5 sts, sk next 2 sts of previous row] 5 times*, 3 sc in next st, sc in each of next 13 sts *(center top of Body)*, 3 sc in next st, sk next 2 sts of previous row, rep between *, turn.

Rows 9–14: Rep rows 7 and 8, inc 2 sts in each row at center top Body. At the end of row 14 across center top of Body, 3 sc, 25 sc, 3 sc, fasten off first Body section. Do not fasten off black on 2nd Body section.

Handle

Rnd 1: With a separate strand of black, ch 6, sl st in first ch to form a ring, sc in each of next 6 chs, do not join, place stitch marker to mark rnds. *(6 sc)*

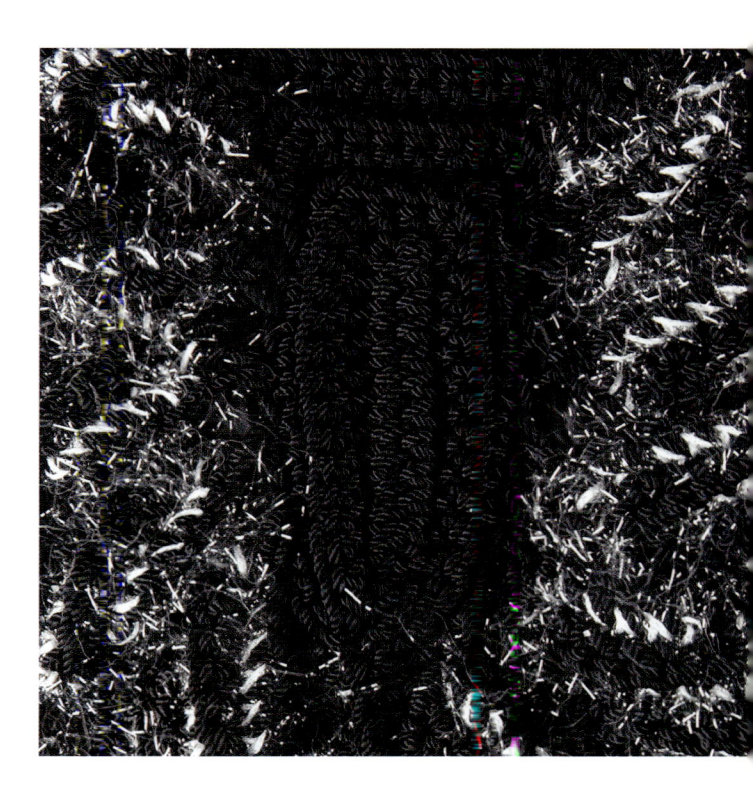

Rnd 2: Sc in each sc around.
Rep rnd 2 until Handle is 10 inches long and glue stick is covered when inserted, sl st in next st, fasten off.

Lining

Using Body as a pattern, cut 2 pieces of black lining material. Leaving top open, sew sides and bottom of seams closed. Allowing ¼-inch seam allowance, attach magnetic fastener at center top of lining. Set lining aside.

Finishing

Pick up Body section that has black still attached, sl st in each of next 4 sts *(placement for end of Handle)*, ch 1, holding WS of Body sections tog and matching sts, sc in each st around to opposite side working 3 sc in each center sc of each 3-sc group to within last 4 sts *(placement for end of Handle)*, fasten off.

Insert lining into Purse, fold raw top edge under and sew to top edge of Purse.

Sew each end of Handle to sk sts at top edge of each Body section. ■

HIDDEN TREASURES SCARF

DESIGN BY BRENDA STRATTON

INTERMEDIATE

Finished Size
5½ x 60 inches

Materials
- Medium (worsted) weight acrylic yarn:
    8 oz/400 yds/227g blue
    5 oz/250 yds/142g white
- Sizes G/6/4mm and I/9/5.5mm crochet hooks or size needed to obtain gauge
- Sewing needle
- Sewing thread
- Star flower beads:
    2 pink pearl
    2 green pearl
- White 6mm pearls: 2
- White sewing thread

Gauge
Size I hook: Working in pattern: 2 star sts = 1 inch; 2 star st rows = 1 inch

Special Stitches
Beginning foundation star stitch (beg foundation star st): Yo, insert hook in 2nd ch from hook, yo, pull up lp, yo, insert hook in same ch, yo, pull up lp, sk next ch, insert hook in next ch, yo, pull up lp, yo, pull through all lps on hook, ch 1 to secure *(eye)*.
Foundation star stitch (foundation star st): [Yo, insert hook in same ch as last leg of last star st made, yo, pull up lp] twice, sk next ch, insert hook in next ch, yo, pull up lp, yo, pull through all lps on hook, ch 1 to secure *(eye)*.
Beginning star stitch (beg star st): [Yo, insert hook in eye of last star st made on previous row, yo, pull up lp] twice, insert hook in eye of next star st, yo, pull up lp, yo, pull through all lps on hook, ch 1 to secure *(eye)*.
Star stitch (star st): [Yo, insert hook in same st as last leg of last star st made, yo, pull up lp] twice, insert hook in eye of next star st, yo, pull up lp, yo, pull through all lps on hook, ch 1 to secure *(eye)*.
End star stitch (end star st): [Yo, insert hook in same st as last leg of last star st made, yo, pull up lp] twice, insert hook in ch-1 at end of row, yo, pull up lp, yo, pull through all lps on hook, ch 1 to secure *(eye)*.
Cluster (cl): Holding back last lp of each st on hook, work 2 tr in indicated st, yo, pull through all lps on hook.

SCARF

Foundation row (RS): With size I hook and blue, ch 20, **beg foundation star st** *(see Special Stitches)*, work in **foundation star st** *(see Special Stitches)* across, turn. *(9 star sts)*
Row 1: Ch 1, **beg star st** *(see Special Stitches)*, 7 **star sts** *(see Special Stitches)*, **end star st** *(see Special Stitches)*, turn.
Rows 2–7: Rep row 1 for pattern. At end of last row, fasten off.

114   JACKETS, WRAPS & MORE

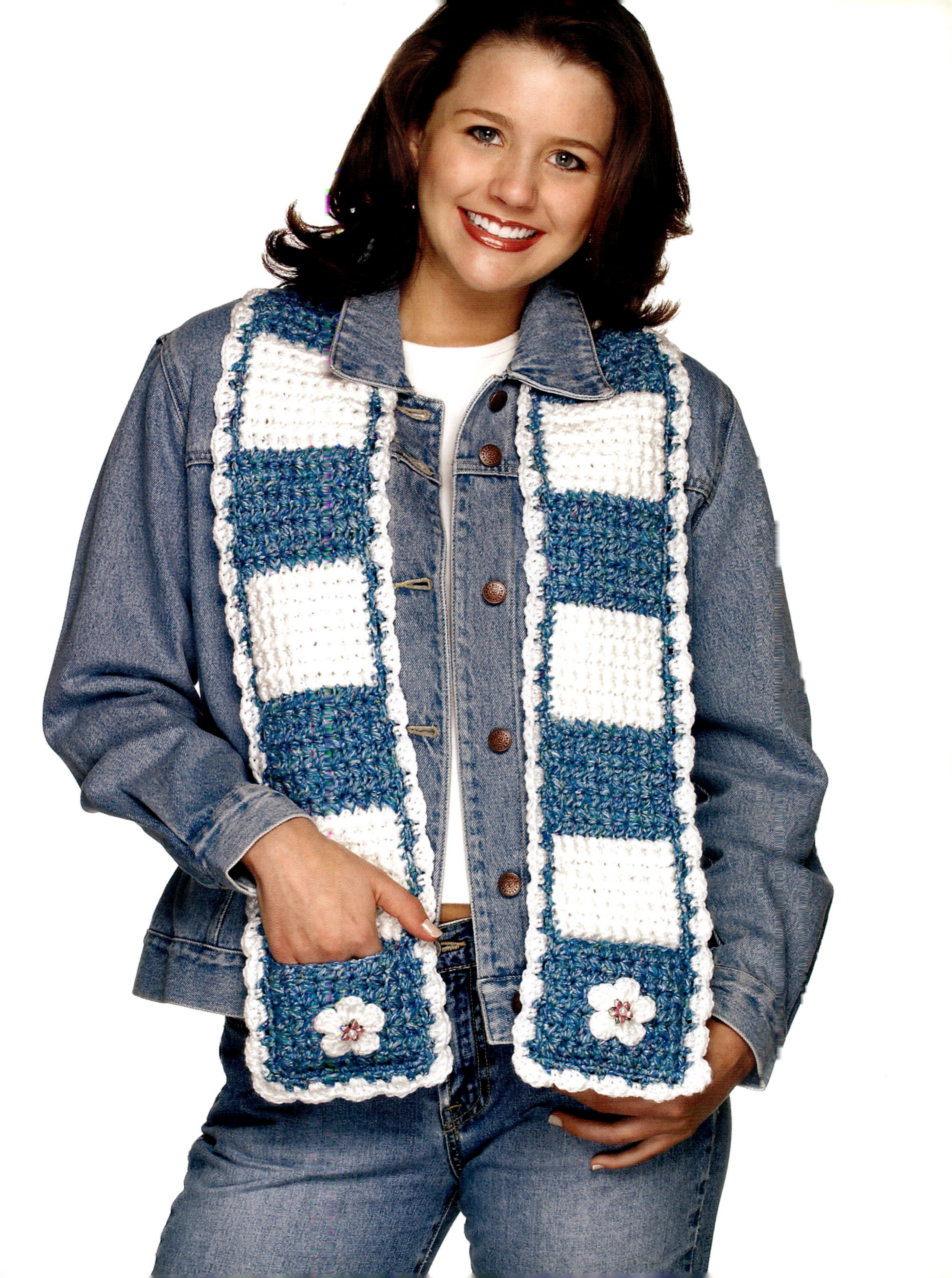

Row 8: With size I hook, RS facing, join white with sl st in last eye of last star st worked in previous row, rep row 1.
Rows 9–15: Rep row 1. At end of last row, fasten off.
Row 16: With blue, rep row 8.
Rows 17–23: Rep rows 9–15.
Rows 24–135: [Rep rows 8–23 consecutively] 7 times. At end of last row, fasten off.

Pocket
Make 2.
Foundation row: Rep Foundation row of Scarf.
Rows 1–7: Rep rows 1–7 of Scarf.
Attaching Pockets
Pin Pockets in place at each end of Scarf.

With size I hook, working through both thicknesses, join blue with sl st at upper left corner of either Pocket, ch 1, sc in same st, *evenly sp sc across to corner, 3 sc in corner st, evenly sp sc across to next corner, 3 sc in corner, evenly sp sc across to top of same Pocket*, working through Scarf only, evenly sp sc across to top corner of next Pocket, working through both thicknesses, rep between * once, working through Scarf only, evenly sp sc across to first sc, join with sl st in beg sc. **Do not fasten off.**

Edging
Rnd 1: Ch 1, sc in same sc as joining, *ch 2, [sk next sc, sc in next sc, ch 2] across to next corner, (sc, ch 2, sc) in corner sc, rep from * around, join with sl st in beg sc. Fasten off.
Rnd 2: With size I hook and RS facing, join white with sl st in last ch-2 sp before any corner, ch 1, sc in same ch sp, *5 dc in corner ch sp, sc in next ch sp, [3 dc in next ch sp, sc in next ch sp] across to next corner, rep from * around, ending with 3 dc in last ch sp, join with sl st in beg sc. Fasten off.

Flower
Make 2.
With size G hook and white, ch 4, sl st in first ch to form ring, [(ch 4, **cl**—see Special Stitches, ch 4, sl st) in ring] 5 times. Fasten off.

Finishing
Place green star flower bead at center of Flower, then place pink pearl star flower bead on top of the green bead, staggering points. Sew beads in place, starting from the WS of the Flower.
Place 6mm pearl at center of star flowers. Push the needle up through the center of the 2 star flower beads, and through center of pearl, then down through the star flower beads and the Flower in the opposite direction. Rep several times to secure. Fasten off.
Sew 1 Flower to front of each Pocket. ■

LADYBUG & VICTORIAN BOOT PINS

DESIGNS BY TERRY DAY

EASY

Finished Sizes
Ladybug: 3 inches tall
Victorian boot: 3¼ inches tall

Materials
- Size 10 crochet cotton:
    12 yds peach
    10 yds red
    7 yds black
    1 yd gold metallic
- Size 5/1.90mm steel crochet hook or size needed to obtain gauge
- 1¼-inch pin backs: 2
- 4-inch square black felt
- Stitch markers
- Scrap of fiberfill
- Red fabric paint
- Craft glue
- Hot-glue gun
- Wax paper
- Fabric stiffener
- 4mm pre-strung pearl beads: 11
- 12mm gold ribbon rosette with gold leaves: 1

Gauge
8 sc = 1 inch

Pattern Notes
Weave in loose ends as work progresses.
Do not join rounds unless otherwise stated.
Mark first stitch of each round with stitch marker.

JACKETS, WRAPS & MORE **117**

LADYBUG

Body
Rnd 1: With black, ch 5, 2 sc in 2nd ch from hook, sc in each of next 2 chs, 4 sc in last ch, working on opposite side of foundation ch, sc in each of next 2 chs, 2 sc in next ch. *(12 sc)*
Rnd 2: Sc in each sc around.
Rnd 3: Rep rnd 2.
Rnd 4: Sc in next sc, 2 sc in next sc, sc in each of next 3 sc, 2 sc in next sc, sc in next sc, 2 sc in next sc, sc in each of next 3 sc, 2 sc in last sc. *(16 sc)*
Rnd 5: 2 sc in each sc around. *(32 sc)*
Rnd 6: 2 hdc in first sc, hdc in each of next 3 sc, 2 hdc in next sc, sc in each of next 11 sc, 2 hdc in next sc, hdc in each of next 3 sc, 2 hdc in next sc, sc in each of next 11 sc, sl st to join in top of first hdc, fasten off. *(36 sts)*

Head
Rnd 1: With black, ch 2, 6 sc in 2nd ch from hook. *(6 sc)*
Rnd 2: 2 sc in each sc around. *(12 sc)*
Rnd 3: [Sc in next sc, 2 sc in next sc] around, sl st in next sc, leaving a 6-inch length for sewing, fasten off. *(18 sc)*
Sew Head to end of Body across 6 sts.

Antenna
Make 2.
With 2 strands black, ch 13, leaving a 2-inch length, fasten off. Sew Antenna to center front underside of rnd 3 of Head far enough apart so that when stiffened they can form a heart shape.

Wing
Make 2.
Row 1: With red, ch 3, sc in 2nd ch from hook, sc in next ch, turn. *(2 sc)*
Rows 2–8: Ch 1, 2 sc in first sc, sc in each rem sc across, turn. *(9 sc)*
Rows 9–11: Ch 1, sc in each sc across, turn.
Row 12: Ch 1, **sc dec** *(see Stitch Guide)* in next 2 sc, sc in each sc across to last 2 sc, turn. *(7 sc)*
Row 13: Rep row 12, do not turn. *(5 sc)*
Rnd 14: Ch 1, evenly sp sc in each st around outer edge, sl st to join in beg sc, fasten off.

Finishing
Following manufacturer's directions, stiffen all pieces. Crumple piece of wax paper into a small ball and place underneath Body and each Wing to give rounded dome shape. Using photo as a guide, shape top of Antennas into heart shape, touching at center. Dry completely.
Cut 6 small hearts from black felt, glue 3 to each Wing. Position Head and Body on black felt, trace around outer edge, cut out piece of felt, place fiberfill between Body and felt and glue felt to bottom of Body and Head.
Glue Wings to Body with hot-glue gun.
With red fabric paint, paint red eyes on Head.
To strengthen Antenna, making sure glue does not show on front, place a small bead of glue just where Antenna touch at center back of heart.
Vertically center pin back on back of Ladybug and attach with hot-glue gun.

VICTORIAN BOOT

Toe
Row 1 (RS): With peach, ch 2, sc in 2nd ch from hook, turn. *(1 sc)*
Row 2: Ch 1, 2 sc in first sc, turn. *(2 sc)*
Row 3: Ch 1, 2 sc in first sc, sc in next sc, turn. *(3 sc)*
Row 4: Ch 1, 2 sc in first sc, sc in each rem sc across, turn. *(4 sc)*
Row 5: Ch 1, sc in each of next 3 sc, 2 sc in next sc, turn. *(5 sc)*
Row 6: Rep row 4. *(6 sc)*
Row 7: Ch 1, sc in each sc across, turn.
Row 8: Ch 1, 3 sc in first sc, sc in each rem sc across, turn. *(8 sc)*
Row 9 (RS): Rep row 7, fasten off.

Shaft
Row 1: With peach, ch 8, sc in 2nd ch from hook, sc in each rem ch across, turn. *(7 sc)*
Row 2: Ch 1, sc in each sc across, turn.
Rows 3–11: Rep row 2.
Row 12: Ch 1, 2 sc in first sc, sc in each sc across to last sc, 2 sc in last sc, turn. *(9 sc)*
Row 13: Rep row 12. *(11 sc)*
Rows 14–16: Rep row 2.
Row 17: Rep row 12, fasten off. *(13 sc)*
Row 18: Attach gold metallic with sl st in first sc, ch 1, sc in same sc as beg ch-1, [ch 3, sc in next sc] across, fasten off. *(12 ch-3 sps)*

Sew RS of row 9 of Toe piece to side of Shaft with Toe pointing to left and bottom edges even. With Toe still pointing left, attach peach with sc in side of row 17 of Shaft, sc around outside edge of Boot working 2 sc in very tip of Toe, ending on opposite side of row 17, fasten off.

Heel
Row 1: With top of Shaft facing and Toe pointing to the left, attach peach with sc in first st of Shaft bottom, sc in each of next 3 sts, turn. *(4 sc)*
Row 2: Ch 1, [**sc dec** *(see Stitch Guide)* in next 2 sc] twice, turn. *(2 sc)*
Row 3: Ch 1, 2 sc in first sc, 2 sc in next sc, turn. *(4 sc)*
Row 4: Ch 1, 2 sc in first sc, sc in each of next 2 sc, 2 sc in last sc, fasten off. *(6 sc)*

Sole
Row 1: With Toe facing, attach peach with sc at very tip of Toe, sc in next 5 sc, turn. *(6 sc)*
Row 2: Ch 1, sc in each sc across, turn.
Row 3: Rep row 2, do not turn.
Row 4: Sc in side edge of row 3, sc in each side edge of rows 2 and 1, sl st in next st on bottom of Boot, fasten off.

Finishing
Following manufacturer's directions, stiffen Boot, shape and place on wax paper to dry.
Using photo as a guide, position pearl beads from row 17 to instep of Boot, glue in place with craft glue. Glue ribbon rosette to instep with hot-glue gun. Vertically center pin back on back of Boot and attach with hot-glue gun. ■

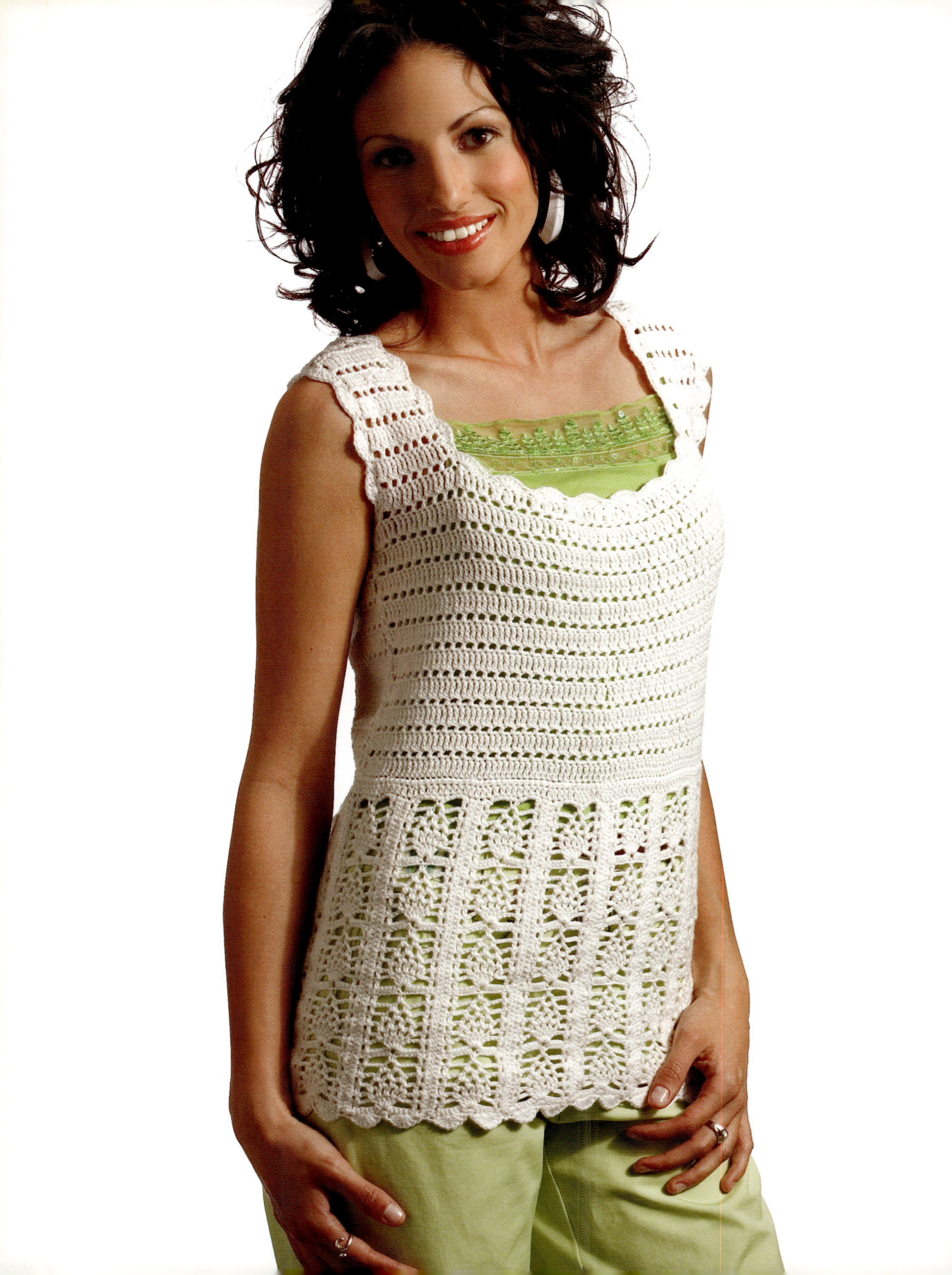

LACY PINEAPPLES SHELL

DESIGN BY TAMMY HILDEBRAND

INTERMEDIATE

Finished Sizes
Instructions given fit 32–34-inch bust *(small)*; changes for 36–38-inch bust *(medium)*, 40–42-inch bust *(large)* and 44–46-inch bust *(X-large)* are in [ ].

Finished Garment Measurements
Bust: 36 inches *(small)* [40 inches *(medium)*, 44 inches *(large)*, 48 inches *(X-large)*]
Length: Shoulder to bottom edge of Panels: 13¼ inches *(small)*, 14¼ inches *(medium)*, 15¼ inches *(large)*, 16¼ inches *(X-large)*

Gauge
Size 4 steel hook: Strip = 2¼ inches wide
Size 3 steel hook: Strip = 2½ inches wide
Size 2 steel hook: Strip = 2¾ inches wide
Size 1 steel hook: Strip = 3 inches wide
Size C hook: 22 tr = 4 inches
Size D hook: 20 tr = 4 inches
Size E hook: 18 tr = 4 inches
Size F hook: 16 tr = 4 inches

Materials
- DMC Senso Microfiber light (worsted) weight yarn (1½ oz/150 yds per ball): 9 [11, 13, 15] balls #1101 white
- Sizes 4/2.00mm, 3/2.10mm, 2/2.20mm and 1/2.25mm steel crochet hooks or sizes needed to obtain gauge
- Sizes C/2/2.75mm, D/3/3.25mm, E/4/3.5mm and F/5/3.75mm crochet hooks or sizes needed to obtain gauge
- Tapestry needle
- Stitch markers

Pattern Notes
Weave in loose ends as work progresses.
Join rounds with a slip stitch unless otherwise stated.

Special Stitch
Shell: 7 dc in indicated st.

SHELL

Strip 1
Row 1: With size 4 [3, 2, 1] steel hook, ch 16, sc in 2nd ch from hook, sc in each of next 6 chs, ch 2, sk next ch, sc in each of next 7 chs, turn. *(14 sc,*
Row 2: Ch 3 *(counts as first dc)*, dc in next st, ch 3, 5 dc in next ch-2 sp, ch 3, sk next 4 sts, dc in each of next 2 sts, turn. *(9 dc)*
Row 3: Ch 3, dc in next st, ch 2, sc in next dc, [ch 3, sc in next dc] 4 times, ch 2, dc in each of next 2 dc, turn. *(4 dc, 5 sc, 4 ch-3 sps)*
Row 4: Ch 3, dc in next st, ch 2, sc in next ch-3 sp, [ch 3, sc in next ch-3 sp] 3 times, ch 2, dc in each of next 2 dc, turn. *(4 dc, 4 sc, 3 ch-3 sps)*
Row 5: Ch 3, dc in next dc, [ch 3, sc in next ch-3 sp] 3 times, ch 3, dc in each of next 2 dc, turn. *(4 dc, 3 sc, 4 ch-3 sps)*
Row 6: Ch 3, dc in next dc, ch 4, sk next ch-3 sp, sc in next ch-3 sp, ch 3, sc in next ch-3 sp, ch 4, sk next ch-3 sp, dc in each of next 2 dc, turn. *(4 dc, 2 sc, 2 ch-4 sps, 1 ch-3 sp)*

JACKETS, WRAPS & MORE

Row 7: Ch 3, dc in next dc, ch 5, sc in rem ch-3 sp, ch 5, dc in each of next 2 dc, turn. *(4 dc, 1 sc, 2 ch-5 sps)*
Row 8: Ch 1, sc in each of next 2 dc, sc in each of next 5 chs, ch 2, sk next sc, sc in each of next 5 chs, sc in each of next 2 dc, turn. *(14 sc, ch-2 sp)*
Rows 9–36: [Rep rows 2–8 consecutively] 4 times.
Rows 37–42: Rep rows 2–7. At the end of last rep, fasten off.

Strip 2

Rows 1–42: Rep rows 1–42 of Strip 1.

Strips 3 & 4

Rows 1–36: Rep rows 1–36 of Strip 1.
Rows 37–40: Rep rows 2–5 of Strip 1.
Row 41: Ch 3, dc in next st, [ch 3, sc in next ch-3 sp] twice, fasten off.

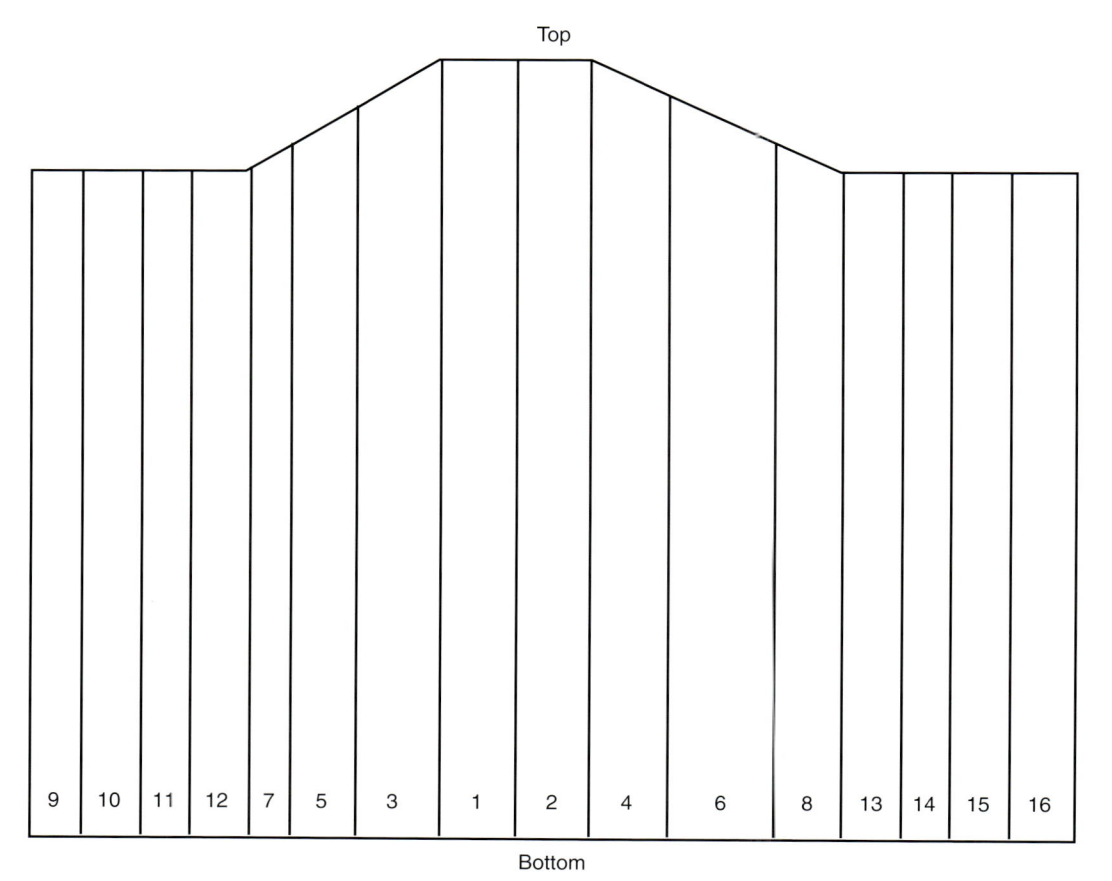

Top

9 | 10 | 11 | 12 | 7 | 5 | 3 | 1 | 2 | 4 | 6 | 8 | 13 | 14 | 15 | 16

Bottom

Lacy Pineapples Shell Strip Assembly

Strips 5 & 6

Rows 1–36: Rep rows 1–36 of Strip 1.
Rows 37 & 38: Rep rows 2 and 3 of Strip 1.
Row 39: Ch 3, dc in next st, ch 2, sc in next ch-3 sp, ch 3, sc in next ch-3 sp, fasten off.

Strips 7 & 8

Rows 1–36: Rep rows 1–36 of Strip 1.
Row 37: Rep row 2 of Strip 1.
Row 38: Ch 3, dc in next st, ch 2, sc in next st, [ch 3, sc in next st] twice, fasten off.

Strips 9–16

Rows 1–29: Rep rows 1–29 of Strip 1.
Rows 30–35: Rep rows 2–7 of Strip 1. At the end of row 35, fasten off.

Strip Edging

Row 1: Working in ends of rows, join white in side edge of first row with sc, [2 sc in side edge of each dc row, sc in side edge of each sc row] across, fasten off.
Row 2: Working in side edge of rows on opposite side of same Strip, rep row 1.

Strip Assembly

Using diagram as a guide, sew strips tog as indicated.

Strip Bottom Trim

Rnd 1: With size C [D, E, F] hook, working in bottom edge of row 1 of Strips, join white with sc in center of any strip joining, *sk 3 chs of foundation ch, **shell** (see Special Stitch) in 4th ch, sk next 3 chs of foundation ch, sc in next ch, sk next 3 chs of foundation ch, shell in next ch, sk next 3 chs of foundation ch, sc in joining of strips, rep from * around, join in beg sc, fasten off.

Strip Top Edging

Rnd 1: With size C [D, E, F] hook, working in sts and chs of last row of Strips, join white with sc in center of Strips 1 and 2 of joining, sc in same sp and work 11 sc evenly spaced across top of same strip *(12 sc)*, work 12 sc evenly spaced across next 6 strips, 13 sc across next strip, 12 sc across each of next 9 strips, join in beg sc. *(194 sc)*

Rnd 2: Ch 3, dc in each st around, join in 3rd ch of beg ch-3, fasten off. *(194 dc)*

Back Panel

Row 1: With size C [D, E, F] hook, ch 100, tr in 5th ch from hook *(first 4 chs count as first tr)*, tr in each rem ch across, turn. *(97 tr)*
Row 2: Ch 3 *(counts as first hdc, ch-1)*, sk next st, hdc in next st, [ch 1, sk next st, hdc in next st] across, turn *(49 hdc)*

CONTINUED ON PAGE 169

EARTHY GLOW TUNIC VEST

DESIGN BY ZENA LOW

INTERMEDIATE

Finished Sizes

Instructions given fit 32–34-inch bust *(small)*; changes for 36–38-inch bust *(medium)*, 40–42-inch bust *(large)*, 44–46-inch bust *(X-large)*, 48–50-inch bust *(2X-large)* and 52–54-inch bust *(3X-large)* are in [ ].

Finished Garment Measurements

Bust: 36 inches *(small)* [39 inches *(medium)*, 46 inches *(large)*, 49 inches *(X-large)*, 52 inches *(2X-large)*, 56 inches *(3X-large)*]

Gauge

21 sc = 4 inches; 22 rows = 4 inches

Pattern Notes

Weave in loose ends as work progresses.
Join rounds with a slip stitch unless otherwise stated.
For ease in counting beginning foundation chain, attach a safety pin every 50 chains.

Materials

- Patons Brilliant light (light worsted) weight yarn (1¾ oz/166 yds/50g per ball): 5 [6, 7, 7, 8, 9] balls #03012 earthy glow
- Size H/8/5mm crochet hook or size needed to obtain gauge
- Tapestry needle
- Safety pins

VEST

Body

Foundation row (WS): Beg at bottom edge of Vest, ch 188 [206, 242, 260, 278, 296], dc in 4th ch from hook *(first 3 chs count as first dc)*, [ch 2, sk next 2 ch, dc in next ch] across to last ch, dc in last ch, turn. *(64 [70, 82, 88, 94, 100] dc)*

Row 1: Ch 3 *(counts as first dc)*, dc in next dc, ch 2, dc in next dc, [ch 4, tr in each of next 4 dc, dc in next dc, ch 2, dc in next dc] across to last dc, dc in top of turning ch, turn.

Row 2: Ch 3, dc in next dc, ch 2, dc in next dc, [ch 4, sc in each of next 4 tr, ch 4, dc in next dc, ch 2, dc in next dc] across to last dc, dc in top of turning ch, turn.

Row 3: Ch 3, dc in next dc, ch 2, dc in next dc, [ch 4, sc in each of next 4 sc, ch 4, dc in next dc, ch 2, dc in next dc] across to last dc, dc in top of turning ch, turn.

Row 4: Rep row 3.

Row 5: Ch 3, dc in next dc, ch 2, dc in next dc, *ch 2, [tr in next sc, ch 2] 4 times, dc in next dc, ch 2, dc in next dc, rep from * to last dc, dc in top of turning ch, turn.

Row 6: Ch 3, dc in next dc, ch 2, dc in next dc, *[ch 2, dc in next tr] 4 times, [ch 2, dc in next dc] twice, rep from * to last dc, dc in top of turning ch, turn.

Note: Rows 1–6 form pattern and Block pattern.
Rep Block pattern 7 [7, 7, 8, 8, 8] times, ending last rep with a WS row, turn.

Right Front

For Sizes Small, 2X-Large & 3X-Large Only

Row 1: Ch 3, dc in next dc, [ch 2, dc in next dc, ch 4,

124 JACKETS, WRAPS & MORE

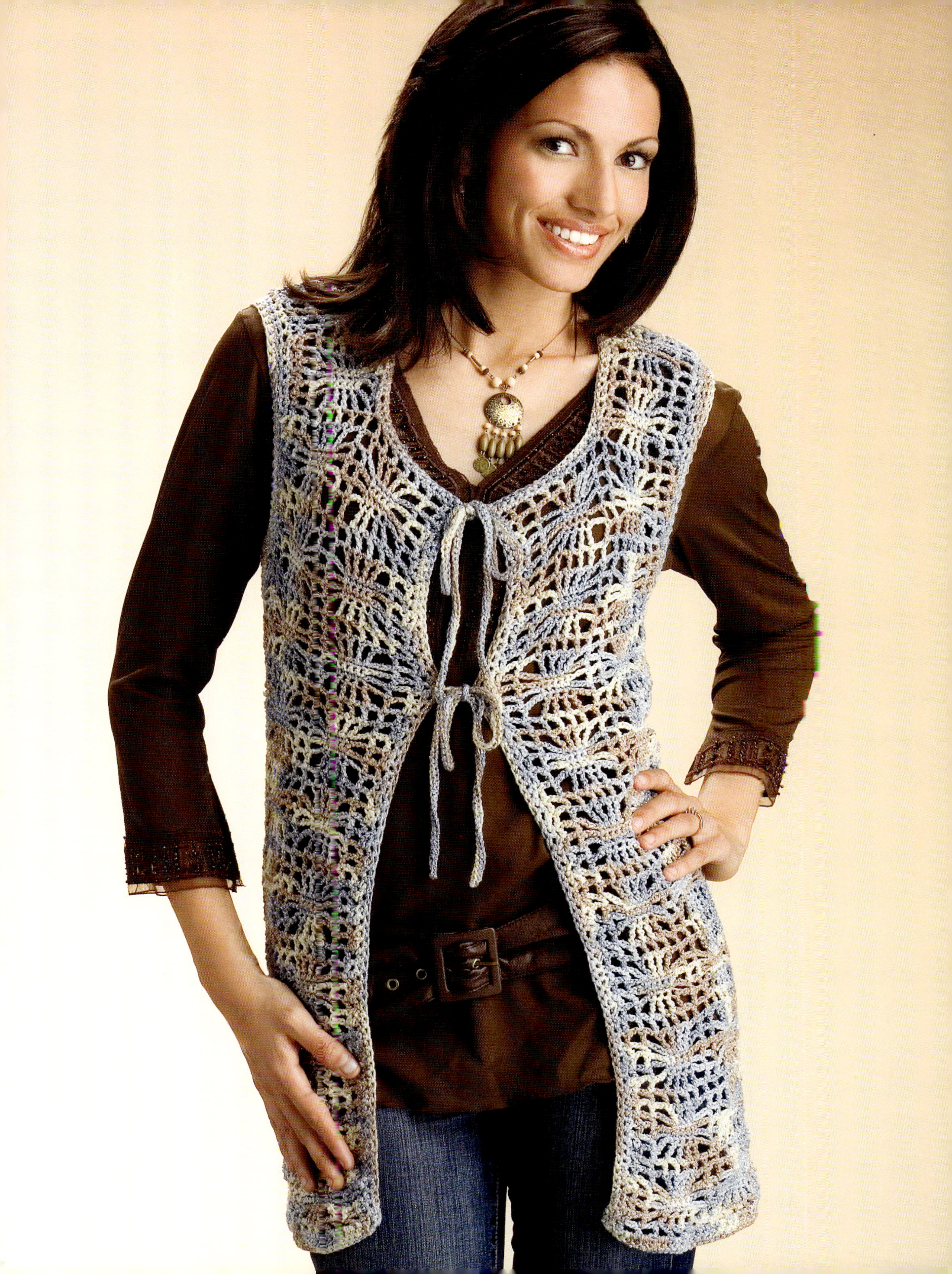

tr in each of next 4 dc, ch 4, dc in next dc] 2 [2, 3] times, dc in next ch-2 sp, turn, leaving rem sts unworked.
Row 2: Ch 3, dc in next dc, ch 2, pattern across to end of row, turn.

For Sizes Medium, Large & X-Large Only
Row 1: Ch 3, dc in next dc, [ch 2, dc in next dc, ch 4, tr in each of next 4 dc, ch 4, dc in next dc] twice, [ch 2, dc in next dc] 1 [3, 4] time(s), dc in next ch-2 sp, turn.
Row 2: Ch 3, dc in next dc, ch 2, pattern across to end of row, turn.

For All Sizes
Continue even in pattern until Block pattern has been completed twice, ending with a WS row, fasten off, turn.

Neck Shaping
Row 1: Sk first 8 [8, 9, 10, 11, 11] dc at neckline edge, attach yarn with sl st in next ch-2 sp, ch 3, work in pattern across to end of row, turn.
Row 2: Ch 3, work in pattern across to end of row, turn. Continue in pattern until Block pattern has been completed twice, ending with a WS row, fasten off, turn.

Back
With RS facing, sk next 6 [7, 9, 10, 10, 12] dc, attach yarn with sl st in next ch-2 sp and proceed as follows:

For Sizes Small, Large, & 3X-Large Only
Row 1: Ch 3, [dc in next dc, ch 4, tr in each of next 4 dc, ch 4, dc in next dc, ch 2] 3 [4, 5] times, dc in next dc, ch 4, tr in each of next 4 dc, ch 4, dc in next dc, dc in next ch-2 sp, leaving rem sts unworked, turn.
Row 2: Ch 3, dc in next dc, work in pattern across to last 2 dc, dc in next dc, dc in top of turning ch, turn.

For Sizes Medium, X-Large & 2X-Large Only
Row 1: Ch 3, [dc in next dc, ch 2] 4 [4, 2] times, [dc in next dc, ch 4, tr in each of next 4 dc, ch 4, dc in next dc, ch 2] 3 [4, 5] times, [dc in next dc, ch 2] 3 [3, 1] time(s), dc in next dc, dc in next ch-2 sp, leaving rem sts unworked, turn.

Row 2: Ch 3, [dc in next dc, ch 2] 3 [2, 1] time(s), work in pattern across to last 5 [5, 3] dc, [ch 2, dc in next dc] 4 [4, 2] times, dc in top of turning ch, turn.

For All Sizes
Continue even in pattern until Block pattern has been completed 4 times, ending with a WS row, fasten off, turn.

Left Front
With RS facing, sk next 6 [7, 9, 10, 10, 12] dc, attach yarn with sl st in next ch-2 sp and proceed as follows:

For Sizes Small, 2X-Large & 3X-Large Only
Row 1: Ch 3, [dc in next dc, ch 4, tr in each of next 4 dc, ch 4, dc in next dc, ch 2] 2 [3, 3] times, dc in next dc, dc in top of turning ch, turn.
Row 2: Ch 3, work in pattern across to end of row, turn.

For Sizes Medium, Large & X-Large Only
Row 1: Ch 3, [dc in next dc, ch 2] 1 [3, 4] time(s), [dc in next dc, ch 4, tr in each of next 4 dc, ch 4, dc in next dc, ch 2] twice, dc in next dc, dc in top of turning ch, turn.
Row 2: Ch 3, work in pattern across to end of row, turn.

For All Sizes
Continue even in pattern until Block pattern has been completed twice, ending with a WS row, turn.

Neck Shaping
Row 1: Work in pattern across to last 8 [8, 9, 10, 11, 11] dc, dc in next ch-2 sp at neck edge, leaving rem sts unworked, turn.

Row 2: Ch 3, work in pattern across to end of row, turn. Continue working even in pattern until Block pattern has been completed twice, ending with a WS row, fasten off. Matching sts, sew Fronts to Back across shoulders.

Armhole Edging

Rnd 1: With RS facing, attach yarn with sl st in any st of armhole opening, ch 1, work 60 [60, 80, 80, 80, 80] sc evenly spaced around armhole opening, join in beg sc.
Rnd 2: Ch 1 sc in each sc around, join in beg sc.
Rnd 3: Rep rnd 2, fasten off.
Rep on opposite armhole.

Vest Edging

Rnd 1: With RS facing, attach yarn with sl st in lower Left Front, ch 3, dc in each of next 2 sts, [2 dc in next ch-2 sp, sk next st, 2 dc in next ch-2 sp, dc in next dc] across to last 2 sts, dc in each of next 2 sts, working up Right Front, ch 1, sc evenly spaced up front, working 3 sc at corner points and **sc dec** (see Stitch Guide) in next 2 sts at each corner of neck edge, sc in each sc down Left Front, join in top of beg ch-3, do not turn.
Rnd 2: Ch 1, sc in each dc across bottom edge, sc in each sc up Right Front, around neckline and down Left Front, working 3 sc at each point and sc dec in each neckline corner, join in beg sc.
Rnd 3: Ch 1, sc in each sc and in each ch-2 sp and 3 sc in 2nd sc of each corner, 3 sc in 2nd sc of each corner, join in beg sc.
Fasten off and weave in ends.

Ties

Make 4.

Make a ch 15 inches in length, turn ch sideways, sl st in back of 2nd ch from hook, sl st in **back bar** (see Fig. 1) of each chain to end of ch, fasten off. Sew first set of Ties to fronts at beg of Neck Shaping and sew 2nd set 4 inches below first set.
Tie each set of Ties in a bow. ■

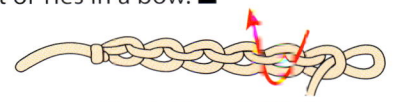

Back Bar of Chain
Fig. 1

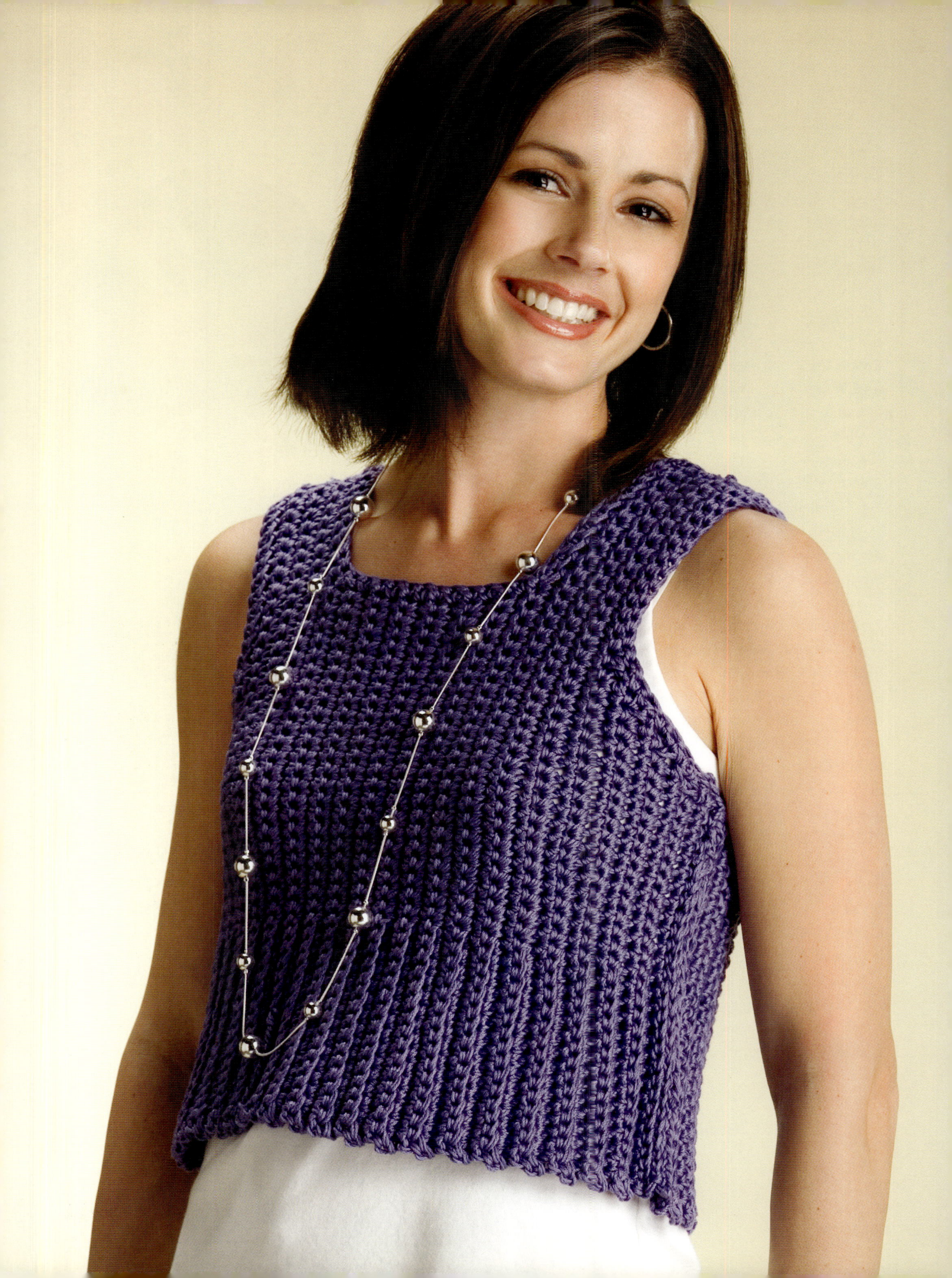

SHORT & SEXY TANK

DESIGN BY MARTY MILLER

INTERMEDIATE

Finished Sizes
Instructions given fit 32–34-inch bust *(small)*; changes for 36–38-inch bust *(medium)*, 40–42-inch bust *(large)* and 44–46-inch bust *(X-large)* are in [ ].

Finished Garment Measurements
Bust: 32 inches *(small)* [36 inches *(medium)*, 40 inches *(large)*, 44 inches *(X-large)*]
Length: 17 inches *(small)* [19 inches *(medium)*, 21 inches *(large)*, 23 inches *(X-large)*]

Gauge
11 sc = 4 inches; 12 sc rows = 4 inches

Pattern Notes
Weave in loose ends as work progresses.
Join rounds with a slip stitch unless otherwise stated.
Top is crocheted vertically with 2 strands held together throughout.

Special Stitch
Foundation single crochet (foundation sc): Ch 2, insert hook in first ch of ch-2, yo, draw up a lp, yo, draw through first lp on hook *(making next foundation chain)*, yo, draw through 2 lps on hook, [insert hook in foundation ch just made, yo, draw up a lp, yo, draw through first lp on hook *(making the next foundation chain)*, yo, draw through 2 lps on hook] rep indicated number of times.

Materials
- Tahki Cotton Classic medium (worsted) weight yarn (1¾ oz/108 yds/50g per skein): 7 [9, 11, 13] skeins #3924 dark lavender
- Size K/10½/6.5mm crochet hook or size needed to obtain gauge
- Tapestry needle

TANK

Body
Row 1: Work 27 [30, 33, 36] **foundation sc** *(see Special Stitch)* sts, turn. *(27 [30, 33, 36] sc)*
Row 2 (RS): Ch 1, 2 sc in first sc, sc in each of next 11 [14, 14, 17] sc, working in **back lp** *(see Stitch Guide)* of each st, sc in each of next 15 [15, 18, 18] sc *(bottom ribbing)*, turn. *(28 [31, 34, 37] sc)*
Row 3: Ch 1, working in back lps only, sc in each of next 15 [15, 18, 18] sts, sc in each of next 11 [14, 14, 17] sc, 2 sc in next sc, hdc in last sc, turn. *(29 [32, 35, 38] sts)*
Row 4: Ch 1, 2 sc in first st, sc in each of next 13 [16, 16, 19] sts, working in back lp sc in each of each of next 15 [15, 18, 18] sts, turn. *(30 [33, 36, 39] sts)*
Row 5: Ch 1, working in back lps only, sc in each of next 15 [15, 18, 18] sts, sc in each of next 13 [16, 16, 19] sts, 2 sc in next st, hdc in last st, turn. *(31 [34, 37, 40] sts)*
Row 6: Ch 1, 2 sc in first st, sc in each of next 15 [15, 18, 18] sts, sc in back lp of each of next 15 [15, 18, 18] sts, turn. *(32 [35, 38, 41] sts)*
Row 7: Ch 1, working in back lps only, sc in each of next 15 [15, 18, 18] sts, sc in each of next 15 [18, 18, 21] sts, 2 sc in next sc, hdc in last st, turn. *(33 [36, 39, 42] sts)*
Row 8: Ch 1, 2 sc in first st, sc in each of next 17 [20, 20, 23] sts, working in back lps only, sc in each of next 15 [15, 18, 18] sts, turn. *(34 [37, 40, 43] sts)*

JACKETS, WRAPS & MORE 129

For Sizes Medium, Large & X-Large Only
Row 9: Ch 1, working in back lps only, sc in each of next 15 [18, 18] sts, sc in each of next 20 [20, 23] sts, 2 sc in next st, hdc in last st, turn. ([38, 41, 44 sts])
Row 10: Ch 1, 2 sc in first st, sc in each of next 22 [22, 25] sts, working in back lps only, sc in each of next 15 [18, 18] sts, turn. ([39, 42, 45 sts])

For Sizes Large & X-Large Only
Row 11: Ch 1, working in back lps only, sc in each of next 18 [18], sc in each of next 22 [25] sc, 2 sc in next sc, hdc in last sc, turn. ([43, 46 sts])
Row 12: Ch 1, 2 sc in first st, sc in each of next 24 [27] sts, working in back lps only, sc in each of next 18 [18] sts, turn. ([44, 47 sts])

For Size X-Large Only
Row 13: Ch 1, working in back lps only, sc in each of next 18 sts, sc in each of next 27 sc, 2 sc in next st, hdc in last st, turn ([48 sts])
Row 14: Ch 1 2 sc in first st, sc in each of next 29 sts, working in back lps only, sc in each of next 18 sts, turn. ([49 sts])

First Strap
For All Sizes
Row 9 [11, 13, 15]: Ch 1, working in back lps only, sc in each of next 15 [15, 18, 18] sts, sc in each of next 19 [24, 26, 31] sts, work 1 foundation sc in same st as last sc, work 13 [13, 13, 13] more foundation sc, turn. (48 [53, 58, 63] sts)
Row 10 [12, 14, 16]: Ch 1, sc in each of next 33 [38, 40, 45] sts, working in sc in back lp of each of next 15 [15, 18, 18] sts, turn. (48 [53, 58, 63] sts)
Row 11 [13, 15, 17]: Ch 1, working in back lps only, sc in each of next 15 [15, 18, 18] sts, sc in each of next 33 [38, 40, 45] sts, turn. (48 [53, 58, 63] sts)
Row 12 [14, 16, 18]: Rep row 10 [12, 14, 16].
Rows 13–15 [15–18, 17–20, 19–22]: [Rep rows 11 and 12 {13 and 14, 15 and 16, 17 and 18}] alternately twice.
Row 17 [19, 21, 23]: Ch 1, working in back lps only, sc in each of next 15 [15, 18, 18] sts, sc in each of next

23 [28, 30, 35] sts, turn. *(38 [43, 48, 53] sts)*

Row 18 [20, 22, 24]: Ch 1, sc in each of next 22 [27, 29, 34] sts, working in back lps only, sc in each of next 15 [15, 18, 18] sts, turn. *(38 [42, 47, 52] sts)*

Rows 19–30 [21–34, 23–38, 25–42]: [Rep rows 17 and 18 {19 and 20, 21 and 22, 23 and 24} alternately] 6 [7, 8, 9] times.

2nd Strap

Row 31 [35, 39, 43]: Ch 1, working in back lps only, sc in each of next 15 [15, 18, 18] sts, sc in each of next 23 [28, 30, 31] sts, work 1 foundation sc in same st as last sc, work 9 [9, 9, 13] more foundation sts, turn. *(48 [53, 58, 63] sts)*

Rows 32–38 [36–42, 40–46, 44–50]: Rep rows 10–16 [12–18, 14–20, 16–22].

Row 39 [43, 47, 51]: Ch 1, working in back lps only, sc in each of next 15 [15, 18, 18] sts, sc in each of next 18 [23, 25, 30] sts, **sc dec** (see Stitch Guide) in next 2 sts, turn. *(34 [39, 44, 49] sts)*

Row 40 [44, 48, 52]: Ch 1, sc dec in next 2 sts, sc in each of next 17 [22, 24, 29] sts, working in back lps only, sc in each of next 15 [15, 18, 18] sts, turn. *(33 [38, 43, 48] sts)*

Row 41 [45, 49, 53]: Ch 1, working in back lps only, sc in each of next 15 [15, 18, 18] sts, sc in each of next 16 [21, 23, 28] sts, sc dec in next 2 sts, turn. *(32 [37, 42, 47] sts)*

Row 42 [46, 50, 54]: Ch 1, sc dec in next 2 sts, sc in each of next 15 [20, 22, 27] sts, working in back lps only, sc in each of next 15 [15, 18, 18] sts, turn. *(31 [36, 41, 46] sts)*

Row 43 [47, 51, 55]: Ch 1, working in back lps only, sc in each of next 15 [15, 18, 18] sts, sc in each of next 14 [19, 21, 26] sts, sc dec in next 2 sts, turn. *(30 [35, 40, 45] sts)*

Row 44 [48, 52, 56]: Ch 1, sc dec in next 2 sts, sc in each of next 13 [18, 20, 25] sts, working in back lps only, sc in each of next 15 [15, 18, 18] sts, turn. *(29 [34, 39, 44] sts)*

Row 45 [49, 53, 57]: Ch 1, working in back lps only, sc in each of next 15 [15, 18, 18] sts, sc in each of next 12 [17, 19, 24] sts, sc dec in next 2 sts, turn. *(28 [33, 38, 43] sts)*

Row 46 [50, 54, 58]: Ch 1, sc dec in next 2 sts, sc in each of next 11 [16, 18, 23] sts, working in back lps only, sc in each of next 15 [15, 18, 18] sts, turn. *(27 [32, 37, 42] sts)*

For Size Small Only

Row 47: Ch 1, working in back lps only, sc in each of next 15 sts, sc in each of next 12 sts, turn. *(27 sts)*

Rows 48–92: Rep rows 2–46. At the end of row 92, turn.

For Sizes Medium, Large & X-Large Only

Row 51 [55, 59]: Ch 1, working in back lps only, sc in each of next 15 [18, 18] sts, sc in each of next 15 [17, 22] sc, sc dec in next 2 sc, turn. *([31, 36, 41] sts)*

Row 52 [56, 60]: Ch 1, sc dec in next 2 sc, sc in each of next 14 [16, 21] sts, working in back lps only sc in each of next [15, 18, 18] sts, turn. *([30, 35, 40] sts)*

Row 53 [57, 61]: Ch 1, working in back lps only, sc in each of next 15 [18, 18] sts, sc in each of next 15 [17, 22] sts, turn. *([30, 35, 40] sts)*

For Size Medium Only

Rows 54–104: Rep rows 2–52. At the end of row 104, turn.

CONTINUED ON PAGE 171

CLASSY CONTINENTAL HAT

DESIGN BY SHIRLEY PATTERSON

EASY

Finished Sizes
Instructions given fit 24¾-inch head circumference; changes for 27-inch head circumference are in [ ].

Materials
- Red Heart Grandé super bulky (super chunky) weight yarn (6 oz/143 yds/170g per skein):
    1 skein #2368 dark brown
- Bernat Soft Bouclé bulky (chunky) weight yarn (5 oz/255 yds/140g per ball):
    1 ball #22927 misty shades
- Size H/8/5mm crochet hook or size needed to obtain gauge
- Stitch markers

Gauge
With super bulky yarn: 4 sc = 1½ inches; 3 rows = 1 inch
Take time to check gauge.

Pattern Notes
Work in continuous rounds.
Mark first stitch of each round to keep count of stitches.
Do not join or turn unless otherwise stated.

HAT

Top
Rnd 1: With dark brown, ch 2, 6 sc in 2nd ch from hook, **do not join or turn** (see Pattern Note). *(6 sc)*
Rnd 2: 2 sc in each st around. *(12 sc)*
Rnd 3: [Sc in next st, 2 sc in next st] around. *(18 sc)*
Rnd 4: [Sc in each of next 2 sts, 2 sc in next st] around. *(24 sc)*
Rnd 5: [Sc in each of next 3 sts, 2 sc in next st] around. *(30 sc)*
Rnd 6: [Sc in each of next 4 sts, 2 sc in next st] around. *(36 sc)*
Rnd 7: [Sc in each of next 5 sts, 2 sc in next st] around. *(42 sc)*
Rnd 8: [Sc in each of next 6 sts, 2 sc in next st] around. *(48 sc)*
Rnd 9: [Sc in each of next 7 sts, 2 sc in next st] around. *(54 sc)*
Rnd 10: [Sc in each of next 8 sts, 2 sc in next st] around. *(60 sc)*

Side
Rnd 11: Working in **back lps** (see Stitch Guide), [sc in each of next 9 sts, 2 sc in next st] around. *(66 sc)*
Rnd 12: Sc in each st around.

Larger Size Only
Rnd 13: [Sc in each of next 10 sts, 2 sc in next st] around. *(72 sc)*

132 JACKETS, WRAPS & MORE

Both Sizes

Rnds 13–22 [14–23]: Sc in each st around. At end of last rnd, join with sl st in next sc.

Brim

Rnd 23 [24]: Ch 3 *(counts as first dc)*, 2 dc in next st, [dc in next st, 2 dc in next st] around, join with sl st in 3rd ch of beg ch-3. *(99 [108] dc)*

Rnd 24 [25]: Ch 3, dc in each st around, join with sl st in 3rd ch of beg ch-3. Fasten off.

Rnd 25 [26]: Join misty shades, with sc in any st, sc in each st around, join with sl st in beg sc. Fasten off.

Finishing

1. Join dark brown with sl st in rem lp on rnd 10 of top, sl st in each st around, join with sl st in beg sl st. Fasten off.
2. Join misty shades with sl st around any st on rnd 21, sl st around each st around, join with sl st in beg sl st. Fasten off.
3. Rep step 2 on rnd 22 [23]. ∎

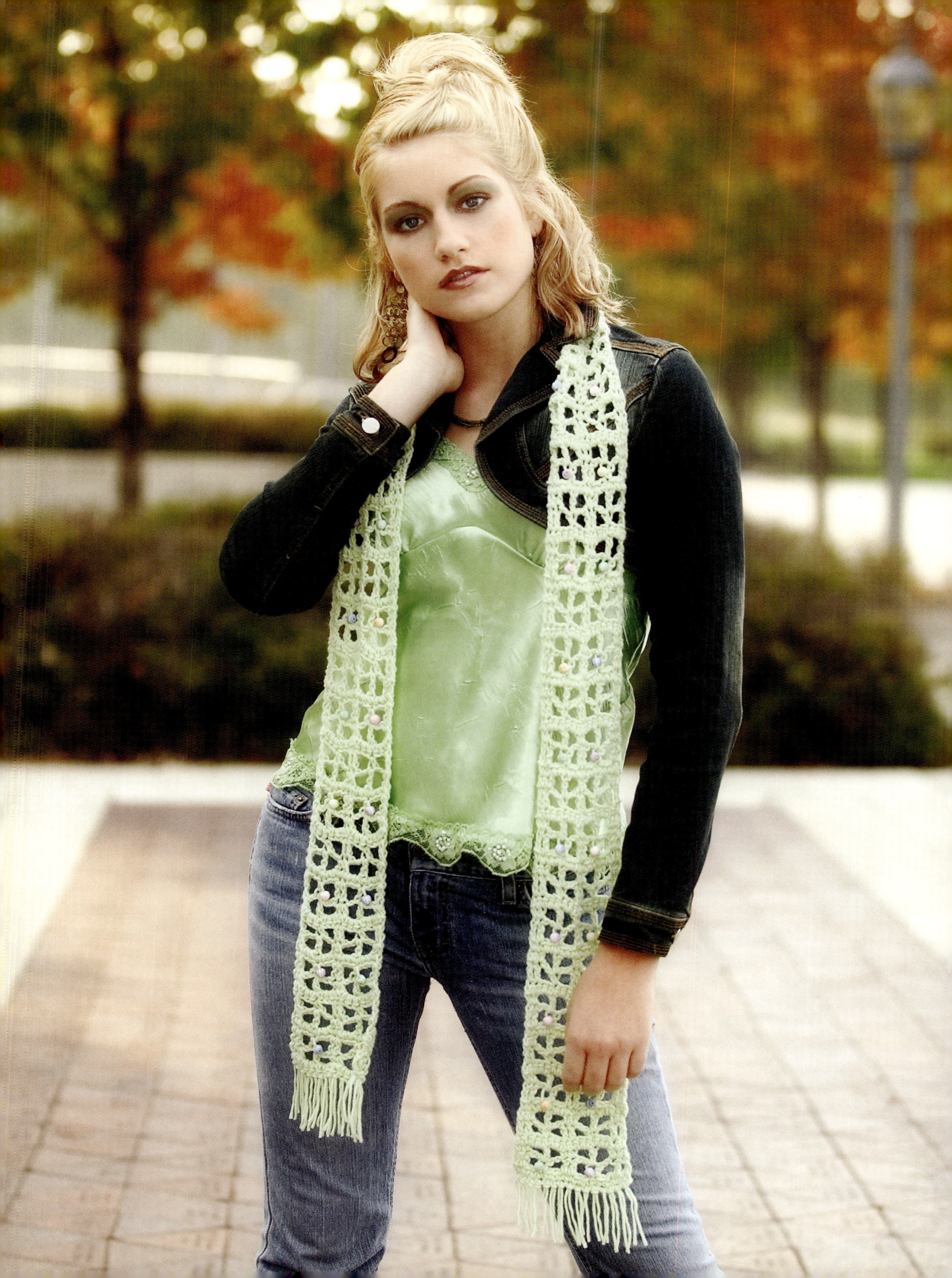

BEADED MESH SCARF

DESIGN BY BELINDA "BENDY" CARTER

EASY

Finished Sizes
4¼ x 65 inches, excluding Fringe

Materials
- Medium (worsted) weight yarn: 3½ oz/175 yds/99g light green
- Size H/3/5mm crochet hook or size needed to obtain gauge
- Assorted color of 10mm round opaque beads
- Beading needle

Gauge
15 sts = 4 inches; 6 rows = 3 inches

Special Stitch
Bead single crochet (bead sc): Push bead up to hook, then sc, bead will appear on back side of sts.

SCARF

Row 1 (RS): String 44 beads onto yarn, ch 17, sc in 2nd ch from hook and in each ch across, turn. *(16 sc)*

Row 2: Ch 3 *(counts as first dc)*, dc in next st, [ch 2, sk next 2 sts, **bead sc** *(see Special Stitch)* in next st, ch 2, sk next 2 sts, dc in each of next 2 sts] across, turn.

Row 3: Ch 1, sc in each of first 2 sts, [ch 2, sk next ch sp, dc in next st, ch 2, sk next ch sp, sc in each of next 2 sts] across, turn.

Row 4: Ch 1, sc in each st and ch across, turn. *(16 sc)*

Row 5: Ch 3, dc in next st, [ch 2, sk next 2 sts, sc in next st, ch 2, sk next 2 sts, dc in each of next 2 sts] across, turn.

Row 6: Ch 1, sc in each of first 2 sts, [ch 2, sk next ch sp, dc in next st, ch 2, sk next ch sp, sc in each of next 2 sts] across, turn.

Row 7: Ch 1, sc in each st and ch across, turn. *(16 sc)*

Rows 8–127: [Rep rows 2–7 consecutively] 20 times.

Rows 128–130: Rep rows 2–4. At end of last row, fasten off.

Fringe
Cut 1 strand 5 inches in length, fold strand in half. With WS facing, pull fold through st, pull ends through fold. Pull ends to tighten. Attach Fringe across both short ends of Scarf. Trim ends. ■

BEAD-DAZZLING PURSE

DESIGN BY GLENDA WINKLEMAN

BEGINNER

Finished Size

9½ x 11 inches, excluding Handles

Materials
- Moda Dea Orbit super bulky (super chunky) weight yarn (1¾ oz/36 yds/50g per ball):
    3 balls #3934 moonbeam
- Moda Dea Frivolous medium (worsted) weight yarn (1¾ oz/83 yds/50g per ball):
    1 ball #9563 ultra violet
- Size L/11/8mm crochet hook or size needed to obtain gauge
- Sewing needle and thread
- 1-inch-wide hook-and-loop tape: 4 inches
- 1 pair beaded purse handles by Handle Connection
- 12 x 19-inch piece of fabric
- Decorative pin

Gauge

7 sc = 3 inches; 7 sc rows = 3 inches

Pattern Notes

Weave in loose ends as work progresses.
Join rounds with a slip stitch unless otherwise stated.

PURSE

Rnd 1: Beg at bottom of Purse, with moonbeam, ch 21, 3 sc in 2nd ch from hook, sc in each rem ch across to last ch, 3 sc in last ch, working on opposite side of foundation ch, sc in each ch across, join in beg sc. *(42 sc)*

Rnd 2: Ch 1, [2 sc in each of next 3 sts, sc in each of next 18 sts] twice, join. *(48 sc)*

Rnds 3–21: Ch 1, sc in each st around, join in beg sc. At the end of rnd 21, fasten off.

Rnd 22: Holding 2 strands of ultra violet tog, join with sc in first st of previous rnd, sc in each st around, join in beg sc, fasten off.

Assembly

With moonbeam, sew handles to center of top edge of Purse.

For lining, with RS tog, fold fabric in half matching 12-inch ends at top edge. Sew ¼-inch seam along each end. Turn top edge down to WS ¼-inch and press. Place lining in Purse and sew in place along top inside edge. Center hook-and-loop tape near top inside of Purse and sew in place. Attach decorative pin to center front of Purse. ■

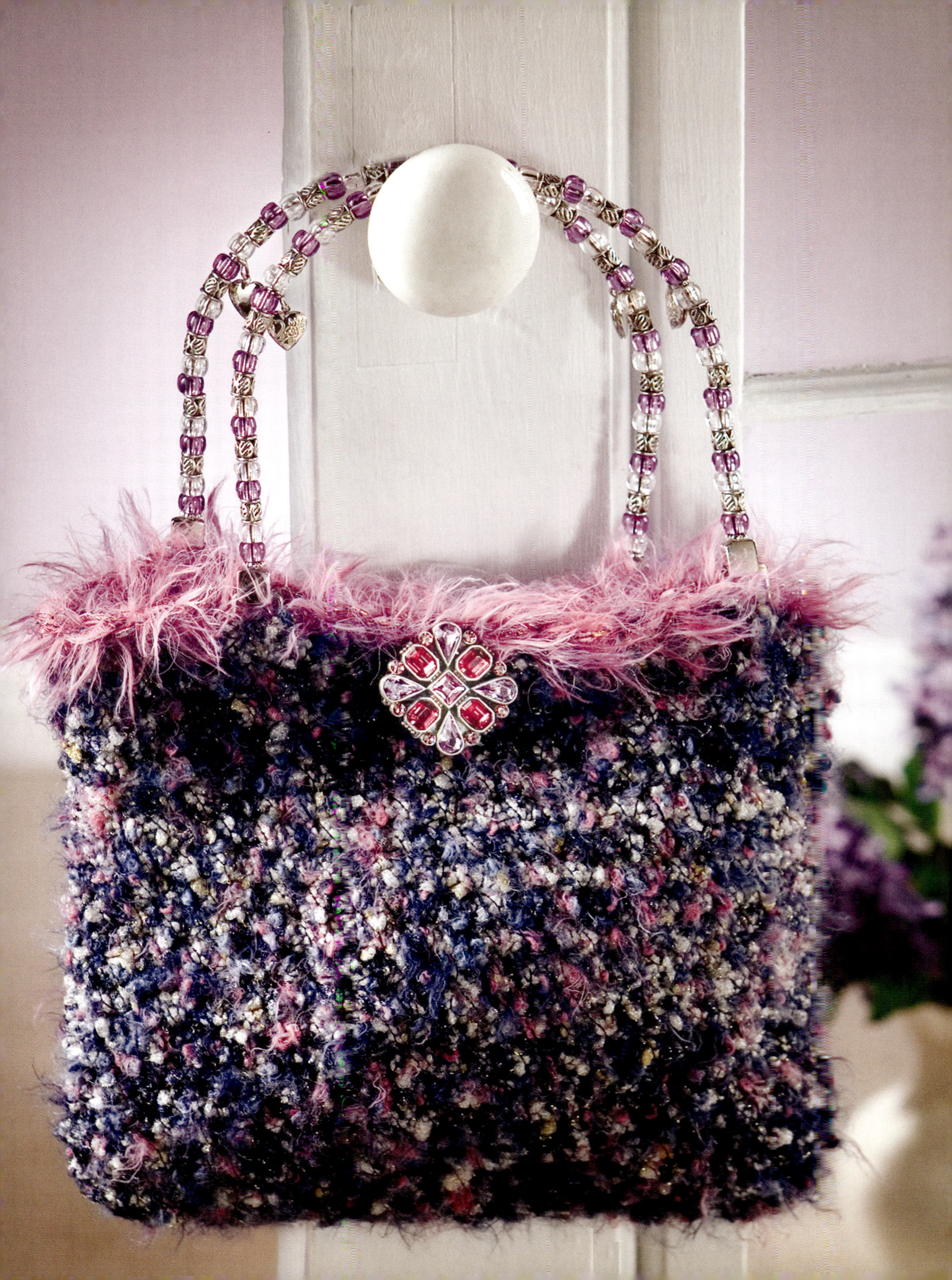

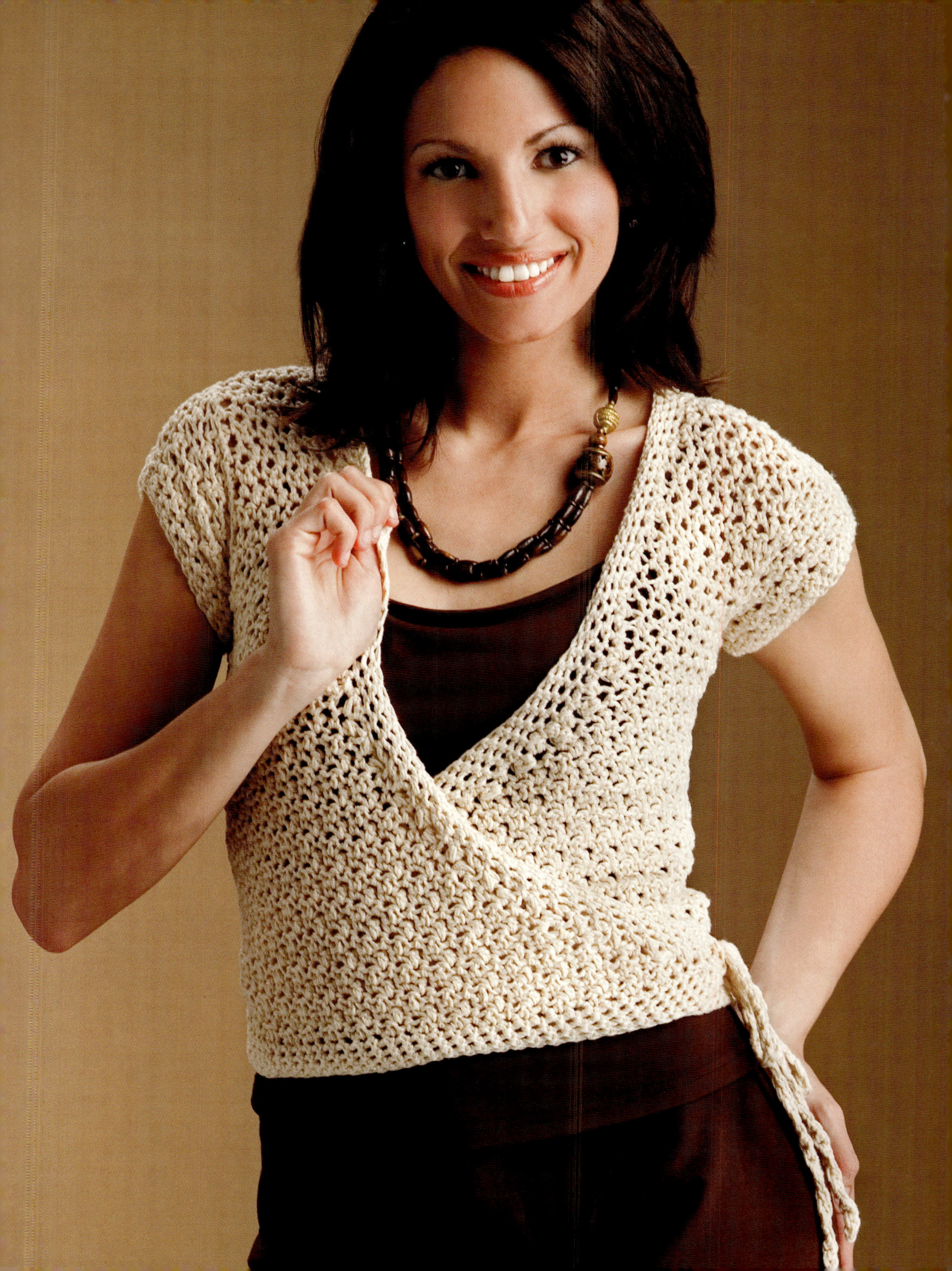

WRAP-TIE TOP

DESIGN BY MARTY MILLER

INTERMEDIATE

Finished Sizes
Instructions given fit 32–34-inch bust *(small)*; changes for 36–38-inch bust *(medium)*, 40–42-inch bust *(large)* and 44–46-inch bust *(X-large)* are in [ ].

Finished Garment Measurements
Bust: 32 inches *(small)* [36 inches *(medium)*, 41 inches *(large)*, 47½ inches *(X-large)*]

Gauge
5 sts = 2 inches; 6 rows = 2 inches

Pattern Notes
Weave in loose ends as work progresses.
Join rounds with a slip stitch unless otherwise stated.
Top is crocheted with 2 strands held together throughout.

Special Stitch
Foundation single crochet (foundation sc): Ch 2, insert hook in first ch, yo, draw up a lp, yo, draw through first lp on hook to create a ch, yo, draw through 2 lps on hook, [insert hook in the ch created by drawing through first lp on hook, yo, draw up a lp, yo, draw through first lp on hook, yo, draw through both lps on hook] across indicated number of times.

Materials
- Bernat Cool Crochet light (light worsted) weight yarn (1¾ oz/200 yds/50g per ball):
  6 [8, 10, 12] balls #74008 summer cream
- Size K/10½/6.5mm crochet hook or size needed to obtain gauge
- Tapestry needle
- Stitch markers

Pattern Stitch
Row 1: [Sc in next st, dc in next st] across, turn.
Row 2: Ch 2 *(does not count as a stitch)*, [sc in each dc, dc in each sc] across, turn.

TOP

Body
Row 1: Starting at bottom edge, with 2 strands of summer cream held tog, work 113 [129, 145, 161] foundation sc *(see Special Stitch)*, turn. *(113 [129, 145, 161] foundation sc)*
Row 2: Ch 2 *(does not count as a st)*, **hdc dec** *(see Stitch Guide)* in next 2 sts, rep row 1 of Pattern Stitch to last 2 sts, hdc dec in last 2 sts, turn. *(111 [127, 143, 159] sts)*
Rows 3–24: Rep row 2. *(67 [83, 99, 115] sts)*

For Size Small Only
Place st marker at beg and end of last row, turn.

For Sizes Medium, Large & X-Large Only
Rows 25–28: Rep row 2 of Body 4 times. *([75, 91, 107] sts)*

For Size Medium Only
Place st marker at beg and end of last row, turn.

For Sizes Large & X-Large Only
Rows 29–32: Rep row 2 of Body 4 times. *([83, 99] sts)*

For Size Large Only
Place st marker at beg and end of last row, turn.

For Size X-Large Only
Rows 33–36: Rep Row 2 of Body 4 times. *([91] sts)*
Place st marker at beg and end of last row, turn.

Left Front

Row 25 [29, 33, 37]: Ch 2, hdc dec in next 2 sts, rep row 2 of Pattern Stitch in next 14 [16, 18, 20] sts, turn. *(15 [17, 19, 21] sts)*

Row 26 [30, 34, 38]: Rep row 2 of Pattern Stitch across, ending with sc in last st, turn.

Row 27 [31, 35, 39]: Ch 2, hdc dec in next 2 sts, rep row 2 of Pattern Stitch across, turn. *(14 [16, 18, 20] sts)*

Row 28 [32, 36, 40]: Rep row 2 of Pattern Stitch across, turn.

Row 29 [33, 37, 41]: Ch 2, hdc dec in next 2 sts, rep row 2 of Pattern Stitch across rem sts, turn. *(13 [15, 18, 19] sts)*

Row 30 [34, 38, 42]: Rep row 2 of Pattern Stitch across, turn.

Rows 31–36 [35–40, 39–44, 43–48]: [Rep rows 29 and 30 {33 and 34, 37 and 38, 41 and 42} alternately] 3 times. *(10 [12, 14, 16] sts)*

Rows 37–40 [41–44, 45–48, 49–52]: Rep row 30 [34, 38, 42]. At the end of last rep, fasten off.

Back

Row 25 [29, 33, 37]: Attach yarn in next unworked st after row 24 [28, 32, 36] of Left Front, ch 2, work in Pattern Stitch across 34 [38, 42, 46] sts, sc in next st, turn. *(35 [39, 43, 47] sts)*

Row 26 [30, 34, 38]: Ch 2, dc in first sc, work in Pattern Stitch across, ending with dc in last st, turn.

Rows 27–38 [31–42, 35–46, 39–50]: [Rep rows 25 and 26 {29 and 30, 33 and 34, 37 and 38} alternately] 6 times.

First Shoulder Shaping

Row 39 [43, 47, 51]: Ch 2, work in Pattern Stitch across 10 [12, 14, 16] sts, turn.

Row 40 [44, 48, 52]: Ch 2, work in Pattern Stitch across 10 [12, 14, 16] sts, fasten off.

CONTINUED ON PAGE 172

HOT SUMMER NIGHTS

DESIGN BY COLETTE BLAIR

EXPERIENCED

Finished Sizes
Instructions given fit 32–34-inch bust *(small)*; changes for 36–38-inch bust *(medium)* and 40–42-inch bust *(large)* are in [ ].

Finished Garment Measurements
Bust: 32 inches *(small)* [36 inches *(medium)*, 40 inches *(large)*]

Materials
- J&P Coats Royale Classic size 10 crochet cotton (350 yds per ball)
    - 2 balls #12 black
    - 1 ball #494 victory red
- Size 8/1.50mm steel crochet hook or size needed to obtain gauge
- Tapestry needle
- Sewing needle and thread
- Size 3 hook and eye fasteners: 2
- ¼-inch-wide black elastic: 30 inches

Gauge
4 rows = 1 inch

Pattern Notes
Weave in loose ends as work progresses.
Cut black elastic in half, set aside.

TOP

Front
Row 1: With black, ch 105 [110, 113], 2 dc in 4th ch from hook, *sk next 2 chs, (sl st, ch 3, 2 dc) in next ch, rep from * across, turn. *(35 [37, 39] dc groups)*
Row 2: Ch 2, sl st in ch-3 sp, ch 3, 2 dc in same ch-3 sp, [sl st in next ch-3 sp, ch 3, 2 dc in same ch-3 sp] across, turn.
Rows 3–9: Rep row 2.

Row 11: Ch 2, sk first sp, [sl st in next ch-3 sp, ch 3, 2 dc in same ch-3 sp] 7 [9, 11] times, turn.
Row 12: Ch 2, sk first sp, [sl st in next ch-3 sp, ch 3, 2 dc in same ch-3 sp] 5 [7, 9] times, sk last sp, turn.
Row 13: Ch 2, sk first sp, sl st in next sp, [sl st in next ch-3 sp, ch 3, 2 dc in same ch-3 sp] 3 [5, 7] times, fasten off, turn.
Row 14: Attach black in row 9 and working across rows 10–13 of Left Front, [ch 4, sl st in next ch-3 sp] across, turn. *(22 [24, 26] ch-4 sps)*
Rows 15–19: [Ch 4, sl st in next ch sp] across, turn.
Row 20: Ch 2, sl st in next ch-4 sp, ch 3, 2 dc in same ch-4 sp, [sl st, ch 3, 2 dc] 21 [23, 25] times, turn. *(22 [24, 26] dc groups)*
Row 21: Sl st in next ch sp, [ch 6, sl st in next ch sp] 13 [14, 16] times, leaving rem lps unworked, turn.
Row 22: Ch 2, sl st in first sp, [ch 6, sl st in next sp] 13 [14, 16] times, turn.
Row 23: Ch 2, sl st in first ch sp, ch 3, 2 dc in same ch sp, [sl st in next ch sp, ch 3, 2 dc in same ch sp] across, fasten off.

Right Front

Row 10: Working from opposite edge of Front, attach black in 4th ch-3 sp, rep row 10 of Left Front.
Rows 11–23: Rep rows 11–23 of Left Front.

Bottom Front

Row 1: With opposite side of row 1 of Front facing, attach black in first st, ch 3, 2 dc in same ch sp, [sk next 2 sts, sl st in next st, ch 3, 2 dc in same st] across, turn.
Row 2: Ch 2, sl st into ch-3 sp, ch 3, 2 dc in same ch-3 sp, [sl st in next ch-3 sp, ch 3, 2 dc in same ch-3 sp] across, turn.
Row 3: Ch 2, sl st into first sp, [ch 6, sl st in next sp] 31 [33, 35] times, turn.
Row 4: Rep row 3.
Row 5: Ch 2, sl st into first ch sp, ch 3, 2 dc in same ch sp, [sl st in next ch sp, ch 3, 2 dc in same ch sp] across, turn. *(31 [33, 35] dc groups)*
Row 6: Ch 2, sk first ch sp, [sl st in next ch sp, ch 3, 2 dc in same ch sp] across to last ch sp, sk last ch sp, turn. *(29 [31, 33] dc groups)*

Left Front

Row 10: Sk first 3 ch-3 sps, sl st in next ch-3 sp, ch 3, 2 dc in same ch-3 sp, [sl st in next ch-3 sp, ch 3, 2 dc in same ch-3 sp] 8 [10, 12] times, turn. *(9 [11, 13] dc groups)*

Rows 7–15: Rep row 6. At the end of last rep, fasten off. *(11 [12, 14] dc groups)*
Row 16: Attach victory red at beg of V-shape angle, [ch 6, sl st in next ch sp] 34 [36, 38] times, turn.
Rows 17 & 18: Ch 2, sc in next ch sp, [ch 6, sl st in next ch sp] across, turn. At the end of row 18, fasten off.
Rows 19–28: Attach black in first victory red ch sp, *ch 3, 2 dc in same ch sp, sl st in next sp*, rep in next 2 victory red sps, ch 2, turn, rep from * to * (4 ch sps at end of rep), ch 2, turn, rep from * to * across 4 ch sps and 2 more victory red ch sps, ch 2, turn, continue toward middle, rep from * to * across ch sps, adding 2 victory ch sps before ch 2, turn. At middle fasten off, rep rows 19-28 on opposite edge.
Rows 29–33: With black, sl st in ch sp, ch 3, 2 dc in same ch sp, [sl st in next ch sp, ch 3, 2 dc in same ch sp] across, turn.

Ruffle
Row 34: [Sl st in ch sp, ch 3, 2 dc in same ch-3 sp, sl st in next ch, ch 3, 2 dc in same ch] in each ch sp across, doubling the dc groups across, turn.
Rows 35–41: Ch 2, [sl st in next ch sp, ch 3, 2 dc in same ch sp] across, turn. At the end of row 41, fasten off.

Back
Make 2.
Row 1: With black, ch 37, 2 dc in 4th ch from hook, [sk 2 chs, sl st in next ch, ch 3, 2 dc in same ch] across, turn. *(12 [12, 12] dc groups)*
Rows 2–24: Ch 2, [sl st into next ch sp, ch 3, 2 dc in same ch sp] across, turn. At the end of row 24 on first back, fasten off. Do not fasten off 2nd piece, turn.

Back Bottom Joining
Row 25: Ch 2, *[sl st in next ch sp, ch 3, 2 dc in same ch sp] across 2nd back section, pick up first back section and rep from * across first section, turn.
Rows 26–33: Ch 2, [sl st in next ch sp, ch 3, 2 dc in same ch sp] across, turn.

Ruffle
Rows 34–41: Rep rows 34–41 of Front Ruffle. Fasten off.

Joining
With RS of Front and Back tog, sew side seams.

Bodice Trim
Row 1: Attach victory red with sl st in first ch sp at back left top, ch 3, 2 dc in same ch sp, [sl st in next ch sp, ch 3, 2 dc in same ch sp] across left back, front and right back, fasten off.

Shoulder Strap
Make 2.
Row 1: With black, ch 133, dc in 4th ch from hook, dc in each rem ch across, turn.
Row 3: Ch 3, dc in each st across, turn.
Row 4: Ch 1, sc in each st across, fasten off.
Row 5: Holding row 4 of shoulder strap to opposite side of foundation ch, place 15-inch length of elastic between layers, attach victory red, and working through both thicknesses, ch 1, sc in each st across, fasten off.

Sew one end of first Strap to center of left side of Back and opposite end of strap to center of left side of Front. Repeat on right side with 2nd Strap. ■

& MORE

CITY LIGHTS VEST

DESIGN BY JEWDY LAMBERT

INTERMEDIATE

Finished Sizes
Instructions given fit 40–42-inch bust *(large)*

Finished Garment Measurement
Bust: 42 inches *(large)*

Materials
- Lion Brand Moonlight Mohair bulky (chunky) weight yarn (1¾ oz/82 yds/50g per ball): 5 balls #201 rain forest
- Sizes M/13/9mm and P/15/10mm crochet hooks or sizes needed to obtain gauge
- Yarn needle

Gauge
Size M hook: 6 dc = 2½ inches; 3 dc rows = 2½ inches
Size P hook: 3 dc = 1½ inches

Pattern Notes
Weave in loose ends as work progresses.
Join rounds with a slip stitch unless otherwise stated.

VEST

Body
Row 1: With size P hook, ch 100, 2 dc in 3rd ch from hook, *dc in each of next 3 chs, [**dc dec** *(see Stitch Guide)* in next 3 chs] twice, dc in each of next 3 chs**, [3 dc in next ch] twice, rep from * across, ending last rep at **, 3 dc in last ch, turn. *(98 sts)*
Row 2: Ch 3 *(counts as first dc)*, 2 dc in same st as beg ch-3, *dc in each of next 3 dc, [dc dec in next 3 dc] twice, dc in each of next 3 dc**, [3 dc in next dc] twice, rep from * across, ending last rep at **, 3 dc in last dc, turn.
Rows 3–11: Rep row 2.

144 JACKETS, WRAPS & MORE

First Front

Row 12: With size M hook, ch 3, dc in each of next 21 dc, turn. *(22 dc)*

Row 13: Ch 3, dc in each dc across to last dc, leaving last dc unworked, turn. *(21 dc)*

Rows 14–16: Rep row 13. *(18 dc)*

Row 17: Ch 3, dc in each dc across, turn.

Rows 18–21: Rep row 17. At the end of last rep, fasten off.

2nd Front

Row 12: With size M hook, attach yarn in first dc of row 11, ch 3, dc in each of next 21 dc, turn. *(22 dc)*

Rows 13–21: Rep rows 13–21 of First Front.

Back

Row 12: With size M hook, sk next 5 dc of row 11 of Body, attach yarn in next dc, ch 3, dc in each of next 43 dc, leaving rem 5 dc unworked, turn. *(44 dc)*

Row 13: Sl st in next st, ch 3, dc in each dc across to last dc, leaving last dc unworked, turn. *(42 dc)*

Rows 14–19: Ch 3, dc in each dc across, turn.

First Shoulder Shaping

Row 20: With size M hook, ch 3, dc in each of next 17 dc, turn. *(18 dc)*

Row 21: Ch 3, dc in each of next 17 dc, turn.

Row 22: With WS facing, holding Front to Back shoulder, matching sts and working through both thicknesses, sl st in each st across, fasten off.

2nd Shoulder Shaping

Row 20: With size M hook, sk next 6 dc of row 19 for back neck opening, attach yarn in next dc, ch 3, dc in each of next 17 dc, turn.

Rows 21 & 22: Rep rows 21 and 22 of First Shoulder Shaping.

Trim

Rnd 1: With size M hook, attach yarn at shoulder seam, ch 1, sc in each sc evenly spaced around outer edge of Vest, join in beg sc, fasten off.

Armhole Trim

Rnd 1: With size M hook, attach yarn at underarm, ch 1, sc evenly spaced around armhole opening, join in beg sc, fasten off.

Rep on opposite armhole opening. ■

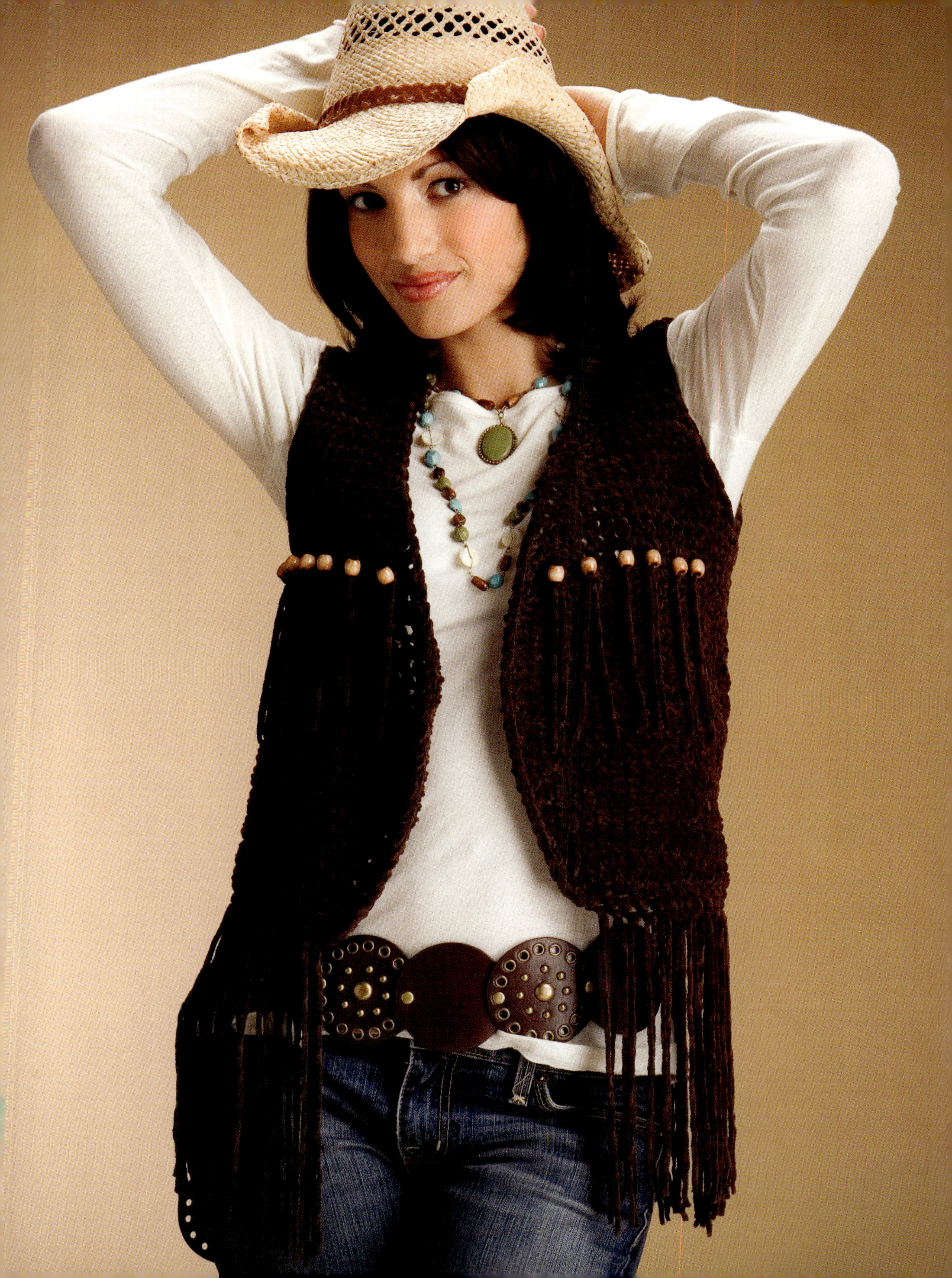

SUEDE FRINGED VEST

DESIGN BY TAMMY HILDEBRAND

INTERMEDIATE

Finished Sizes
Instructions given fit 32–34-inch bust *(small)*; changes for 36–38-inch bust *(medium)*, 40–42-inch bust *(large)* and 44–46-inch bust *(X-large)* are in [ ].

Finished Garment Measurement
Bust: 35 inches *(small)* [39 inches *(medium)*, 43 inches *(large)*, 47 inches *(X-large)*]

Gauge
9 sc = 4 inches; 8 rows = 4 inches

Pattern Notes
Weave in loose ends as work progresses.
Join rounds with a slip stitch unless otherwise stated.

Materials
- Lion Brand Lion Suede bulky (chunky) weight yarn (3 oz/122 yds/85g per skein): 3 [4, 4, 5] skeins #126 coffee
- Size J/10/6mm crochet hook or size needed to obtain gauge
- Tapestry needle
- 12 [14, 6, 18] wooden pony beads

VEST

Front Panel
Make 2.
Row 1: Ch 14 [16, 18, 20], sc in 2nd ch from hook, sc in each rem ch across, turn. *(13 [15, 17, 19] sc)*
Row 2: Ch 1, sc in each st across, turn.
Row 3: Ch 1, 2 sc in first st, sc in each rem st across, turn. *(14 [16, 18, 20] sc)*
Rows 4–9: [Rep rows 2 and 3 alternately] 3 times. *(17 [19, 21, 23] sc at end of last row)*
Rows 10–21: Rep row 2.
Row 22: Ch 1, sc in first st, sc in each st to last st, leaving last st unworked, turn. *(16 [18, 20, 22] sc)*
Row 23: Rep row 2.
Rows 24–29: [Rep rows 22 and 23 alternately] 3 times. *(13 [15, 17, 19] sc)*
Row 30: Sl st in next st, ch 1, sc in same st, sc in each st up to last st, leaving last st unworked, turn. *(11 [13, 15, 17] sc)*
Row 31: Rep row 2.
Rows 32–35 [32–37, 32–39, 32–41]: [Rep rows 30 and 31 alternately] twice [3, 4, 5] times. *(7 [9, 11, 13] sc,*
Rows 36–44 [38–46, 40–48, 42–50]: Rep row 2. At the end of last rep, fasten off.

Back Panel
Row 1: Ch 41 [46, 51, 56], sc in 2nd ch from hook, sc in each rem ch across, turn. *(40 [45, 50, 55] sc)*
Row 2: Ch 1, sc in each st across, turn.
Rows 3–29: Rep row 2.
Row 30: Sl st in next st, ch 1, sc in same st, sc in each st across to last st, leaving last st unworked, turn. *(38 [43, 48, 53] sc)*
Row 31: Rep row 2.
Rows 32–35: [Rep rows 30 and 31 alternately] twice. *(34 [39, 44, 49] sc)*
Rows 36–41 [36–43, 36–45, 36–47]: Rep row 2.

First Shoulder
Row 42 [44, 46, 48]: Ch 1, sc in first st, sc in each of next 5 [7, 9, 11] sts, leaving rem sts unworked, turn. *(6 [8, 10, 12] sc)*

JACKETS, WRAPS & MORE **147**

14 [16, 18, 20] rows open for armhole. Sew side seam on opposite edge.

Edging
Rnd 1: Working in row ends, join with sc in first row of right Front Panel, sc in each row, working in sts across Back, sc in each of next 1 [2, 2, 2] sts, [{**sc dec** *(see Stitch Guide)* in next 2 sts} twice, sc in each of next 4 sts, {sc dec in next 2 sts} twice] twice, sc in each of next 1 [3, 2, 3] sts, working in row ends of left Front Panel, sc in each row, working in opposite side of foundation ch of row 1, sc in each ch, join in beg sc. *(170 [185, 198, 212] sc)*

Front Trim
Row 1: Ch 2, hdc in each of next 43 [45, 47, 49] sts, sc in each of next 1 [2, 2, 3] sts, [sc dec in next 2 sts] twice, [sc in each of next 2 sts, sc dec in next 2 sts] twice, sc dec in next 2 sts, sc in each of next 1 [2, 2, 2] sts, hdc in each rem st down front, fasten off. *(11 [13, 13, 14] sc, 88 [92, 96, 100] hdc)*

Armhole Edging
Rnd 1: Working in row ends around armhole opening, join with sc in any row, sc in each row around, join in beg sc, fasten off. *(28 [32, 36, 40] sc)*
Rep on opposite armhole opening.

Bottom Fringe
Cut 66 [75, 84, 93] yarn lengths each 18 inches long. Fold 1 strand in half, working in sc across bottom, insert hook in st, draw strand through at fold to form a lp on hook, draw cut strands through lp on hook, pull to tighten ends. Trim ends even.

Bead Fringe
Cut 12 [14, 16, 18] yarn lengths each 11 inches long. Place 1 bead on each strand, with bead at center, fold strand in half. With front facing, working around post of sts of row 21 on right Front Panel, [insert hook around post of next st, draw fold through to form a lp, pushing bead close to front of Vest, draw cut ends through lp on hook, tighten, sk next st] 6 [7, 8, 9] times. Rep Bead Fringe on opposite Front Panel. ∎

Rows 43 & 44 [45 & 46, 47 & 48, 49 & 50]: Rep row 2. At the end of last rep, fasten off.

2nd Shoulder
Row 42 [44, 46, 48]: Sk next 22 [23, 24, 25] sts on row 41 [43, 45, 47], attach yarn with sc in next st, sc in each of next 5 [7, 9, 11] sts, turn. *(6 [8, 10, 12] sc)*
Rows 43 & 44 [45 & 46, 47 & 48, 49 & 50]: Rep row 2. At the end of last rep, fasten off.

Assembly
Matching sts on last row of Back Panel with sts on last row of Front Panel, sew shoulder seam tog. Rep for 2nd Front Panel.
Starting at row 1, matching row ends of rows 1–30 of Front and Back Panels, sew side seam tog, leaving last

GLAM GAL HAT & PURSE

DESIGNS BY SUE CHILDRESS

INTERMEDIATE

Finished Sizes
Hat: 22 inches in diameter
Purse: 6-inch base x 7 inches high, excluding Drawstrings

Materials
- Araucania Nature Wool medium (worsted) weight yarn (3 oz/240 yds/100g per skein):
  - 1 skein #RO17 *pink* (A)
  - 2 skeins #RO29 *shaded pinks variegated* (B)
- Sirdar Ava bulky (chunky) weight yarn (1¾ oz/102 yds/50g per skein):
  - 1 skein #024 *damask rose* (C)
- Tahki Flower bulky (chunky) weight yarn (1 oz/38 yds/25g per skein):
  - 1 skein #16 *azalea* (D)
- Sizes G/6/4mm and K/10½/6.5mm crochet hooks or sizes needed to obtain gauge
- Tapestry needle
- Stitch marker
- 2½-inch square cardboard

Gauge
Size G hook: 5 sc = 1 inch; 5 sc rnds = 1 inch
Size K hook: 3 hdc = 1 inch; 3 hdc rnds = 1½ inches

JACKETS, WRAPS & MORE 149

Pattern Notes

Weave in loose ends as work progresses.
Join rounds with a slip stitch unless otherwise stated.

HAT

Rnd 1: With size G hook and B, ch 4, join in first ch to form a ring, ch 1, 6 sc in ring, do not join rnds, use st marker to mark rnds. *(6 sc)*
Rnd 2: 2 sc in each sc around. *(12 sc)*
Rnd 3: [2 sc in next sc, sc in next sc] around. *(18 sc)*
Rnd 4: [2 sc in next sc, sc in each of next 2 sc] around. *(24 sc)*
Rnd 5: [2 sc in next sc, sc in each of next 3 sc] around. *(30 sc)*
Rnd 6: [2 sc in next sc, sc in each of next 4 sc] around. *(36 sc)*
Rnd 7: [2 sc in next sc, sc in each of next 5 sc] around. *(42 sc)*
Rnd 8: [2 sc in next sc, sc in each of next 6 sc] around. *(48 sc)*
Rnd 9: [2 sc in next sc, sc in each of next 7 sc] around. *(54 sc)*
Rnd 10: [2 sc in next sc, sc in each of next 8 s] around. *(60 sc)*
Rnd 11: [2 sc in next sc, sc in each of next 9 sc] around. *(66 sc)*
Rnd 12: [2 sc in next sc, sc in each of next 10 sc] around. *(72 sc)*
Rnd 13: [2 sc in next sc, sc in each of next 11 sc] around. *(78 sc)*
Rnd 14: [2 sc in next sc, sc in each of next 12 sc] around. *(84 sc)*
Rnd 15: [2 sc in next sc, sc in each of next 13 sc] around. *(90 sc)*
Rnd 16: Ch 2 *(counts as first hdc)*, **bphdc** *(see Stitch Guide)* around each sc around, join in 2nd ch of beg ch-2. *(90 hdc)*
Rnd 17: Ch 2, hdc in each st around, join in 2nd ch of beg ch-2.
Rnds 18–20: Rep rnd 17. Turn at the end of rnd 20.
Rnd 21 (WS): Drop B, draw up a lp of D, sc in each st around, join in beg sc.
Rnd 22: Ch 1, sc in each st around, join in beg sc, fasten off, turn.
Rnd 23 (RS): Draw up a lp of B, ch 2, hdc in each st around, join in 2nd ch of beg ch-2. *(90 hdc)*
Rnds 24–27: Rep rnd 17. At the end of rnd 27, fasten off.
Rnd 28: With size K hook, attach 2 strands of C in any hdc, ch 2, hdc in each hdc around, join in 2nd ch of beg ch-2, fasten off.

PURSE

Body

Rnd 1: With size K hook and 2 strands of B, leaving 2-inch length at beg, ch 3, 8 hdc in first ch of ch-3, join in 3rd ch of beg ch-3. Draw end of beg tail to close opening, knot ends to secure. *(9 hdc)*

Rnd 2: Ch 2 *(counts as first hdc)*, hdc in same st as beg ch-2, 2 hdc in each rem hdc around, join in 2nd ch of beg ch-2. *(18 hdc)*

Rnd 3: Ch 2, hdc in next hdc, [2 hdc in next hdc, hdc in next hdc] around, join in 2nd ch of beg ch-2. *(26 hdc)*

Rnd 4: Rep rnd 3. *(38 hdc)*

Rnd 5: Ch 2, hdc in same st as beg ch-2, hdc in next hdc, [2 hdc in next hdc, hdc in each of next 2 hdc] 11 times, 2 hdc in next hdc, hdc in next hdc, 2 hdc in next hdc, join in 2nd ch of beg ch-2. *(52 hdc)*

Rnd 6: Ch 2, [hdc in each of next 2 hdc, 2 hdc in next hdc] 16 times, hdc in each of next 3 hdc, join in 2nd ch of beg ch-2. *(68 hdc)*

Rnd 7: Ch 2, bphdc around each hdc around, join in top of beg ch-2.

Rnd 8: Ch 2, hdc in each st around, join in 2nd ch of beg ch-2.

Rnds 9–14: Rep rnd 8. **Turn** at the end of rnd 14.

Rnd 15 (WS): Draw up a lp of D, ch 2, hdc in each hdc around, join in 2nd ch of beg ch-2.

Rnd 16: Ch 2, hdc in each hdc around, join in 2nd ch of beg ch-2, fasten off, turn.

Rnd 17 (RS): Attach 2 strands of A in any hdc, ch 2, hdc in each hdc around, join in 2nd ch of beg ch-2.

Rnds 18–21: Rep rnd 8. At the end of rnd 21, fasten off.

Rnd 22: Attach 2 strands of C in any hdc, ch 2, hdc in each hdc around, join in 2nd ch of beg ch-2, fasten off.

Drawstring

Make 2.

With size K hook and 2 strands of A, ch 100, fasten off. Weave each Drawstring through rnd 19 in opposite directions. Knot first Drawstring ends tog approximately 2 inches from end, rep at opposite edge.

Tassel

Make 4.

Holding 2 strands of A and 1 strand of D tog, wrap 15 times around cardboard. With a 6-inch length of A, pass through top edge and knot, remove from cardboard, tie another length of A approximately 1 inch down from top of Tassel, trim bottom edge of strands evenly. Attach 1 Tassel to each end of Drawstring. ■

CANYON COLORS HAT & SCARF

DESIGNS BY ALINE SUPLINSKAS

BEGINNER

Finished Sizes
Scarf: 5½ x 64 inches
Hat: 22 inches in circumference

Materials
- Lion Brand Color Waves bulky (chunky) weight yarn (3 oz/125 yds/85g per skein): 2 skeins #398 pebble beach
- Lion Brand Fun Fur bulky (chunky) weight yarn (1¾ oz/60 yds/50g per ball): 2 balls #124 champagne
- Size K/10½/6.5mm crochet hook or size needed to obtain gauge
- Tapestry needle
- Elastic thread: 3 yds
- Stitch marker

Gauge
Scarf: (Ch 1, sc) = 1 inch; 3 rows = 1 inch
Hat: 5 dc = 2 inches; 3 rows = 1¾ inches

Pattern Notes
Weave in loose ends as work progresses.
Join rounds with a slip stitch unless otherwise stated.

SCARF

Row 1: With pebble beach, ch 183 loosely, sc in 3rd ch from hook, [ch 1, sk 1 ch, sc in next ch] across, turn. *(91 ch-1 sps)*

Row 2: Ch 2 *(counts as a ch sp)*, sc in first sp, [ch 1, sc in next ch sp] across, turn.

Rows 3–16: Rep row 2. At the end of row 16, fasten off.

HAT

Rnd 1 (RS): With pebble beach, ch 3, sl st in first ch to form a ring, ch 3 *(counts as first dc)*, 13 dc in ring, join in 3rd ch of beg ch-3. *(14 dc)*

Rnd 2: Working in sps between sts, sl st in next sp, ch 3, dc in same sp, 2 dc in each rem sp around, join in 3rd ch of beg ch-3. *(28 dc)*

Rnd 3: Sl st in sp between dc sts, ch 3, [dc in next sp between dc sts] around, join in 3rd ch of beg ch-3.

Rnd 4: Ch 3, [dc in each of next 3 dc, 2 dc in next dc] 6 times, dc in each of next 3 dc, join in 3rd ch of beg ch-3. *(34 dc)*

Rnd 5: Ch 3, [dc in each of next 4 dc, 2 dc in next dc] 6 times, dc in each of next 3 dc, join in 3rd ch of beg ch-3. *(40 dc)*

Rnd 6: Ch 3, [dc in each of next 5 dc, 2 dc in next dc] 6 times, dc in each of next 3 dc, join in 3rd ch of beg ch-3. *(46 dc)*

CONTINUED ON PAGE 173

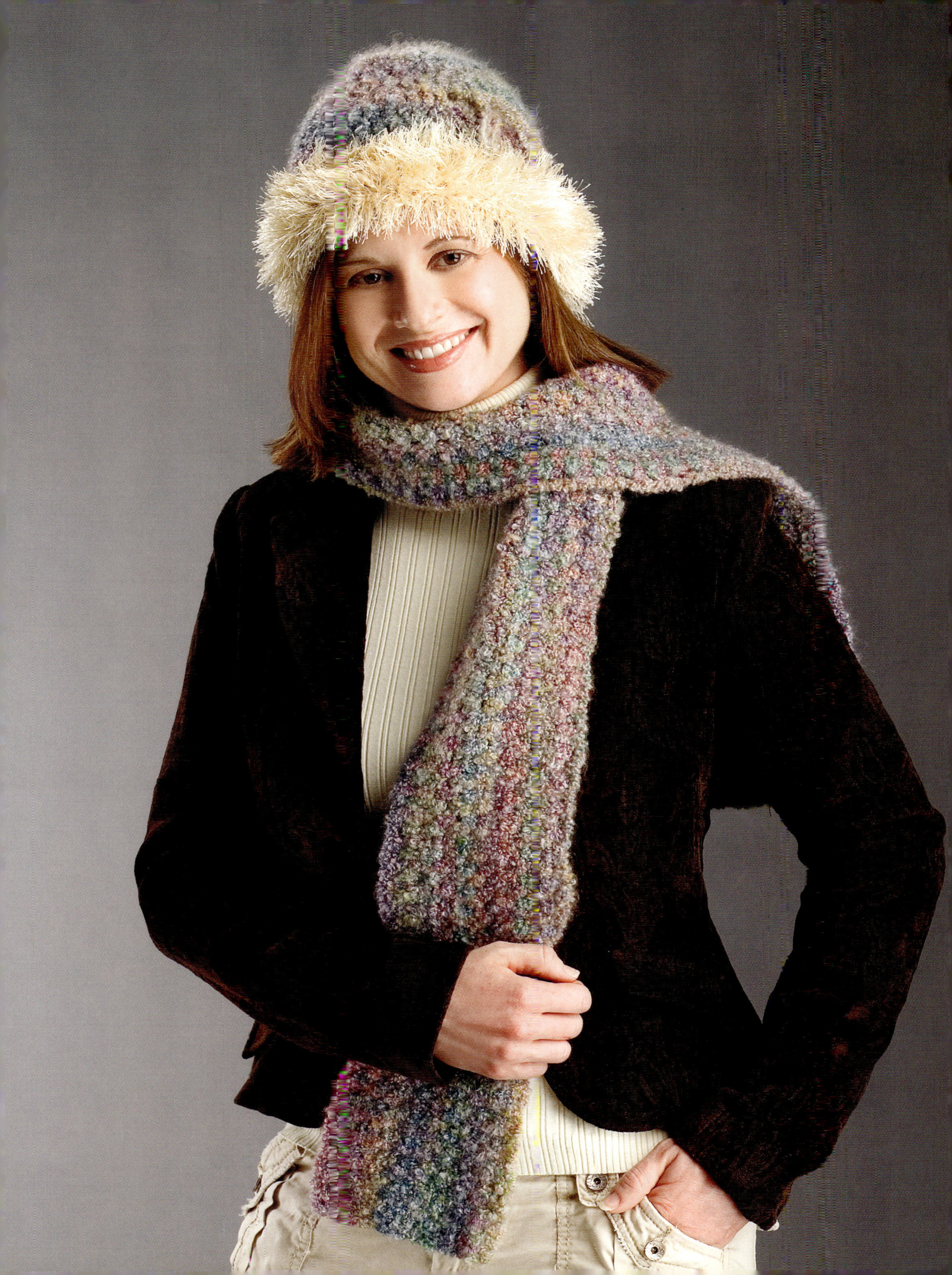

FLOWER PURSE

DESIGNS BY JULENE WATSON

EASY

Finished Size
3¼ x 3¾ inches, excluding Neck Loop

Materials
- Fine (sport) weight yarn: ½ oz/50 yds/14g each white, pink and green
- Size E/4/3.5mm crochet hook or size needed to obtain gauge
- Tapestry needle
- Stitch marker
- ½-inch pearl shank button

2 FINE

Gauge
Rose = 3 inches in diameter; [sc, ch 1] 4 times = 1 inch

Pattern Notes
Weave in loose ends as work progresses.
Join rounds with a slip stitch unless otherwise stated.
This design can be made larger using light or medium weight yarn or smaller by using size 10 crochet cotton.

Special Stitches
3-treble crochet cluster (3-tr cl): *Yo hook twice, insert hook in indicated st, yo, draw up lp, [yo, draw through 2 lps on hook] twice, rep from * twice, yo, draw through all 4 lps on hook.

Beginning 3-treble crochet cluster (beg 3-tr cl): Ch 3 *(counts as first tr)*, *yo hook twice, insert hook in indicated st, yo, draw up lp, [yo, draw through 2 lps on hook] twice, rep from * once, yo, draw through all 3 lps on hook.

PURSE

Purse Front
Rnd 1: With white, ch 4, join in first ch to form a ring, **beg 3-tr cl** *(see Special Stitches)* in ring, ch 2, (**3-tr cl**—*see Special Stitches*, ch 2) 5 times in ring, join in top of beg 3-tr cl. *(6 tr cls, 6 ch-2 sps)*

Rnd 2: Sl st into ch-2 sp, (beg 3-tr cl, ch 2, 3-tr cl, ch 2) in same ch-2 sp, (3-tr cl, ch 2) twice in each ch-2 sp around, join in top of beg 3-tr cl. *(12 tr cls, 12 ch-2 sps)*

Rnd 3: Rep rnd 2. At the end of rnd 2, fasten off. *(24 tr cls, 24 ch-2 sps)*

Purse Back

Rnds 1–3: Rep rnds 1–3 of Purse Front. At the end of rnd 3, do not fasten off.

Row 4: Now working in rows, sl st in next ch-2 sp, beg 3-tr cl in same ch-2 sp, [ch 1, 3-tr cl in next ch-2 sp] 5 times, leaving a 6-inch length of yarn, fasten off. *(6 tr cl, 5 ch-2 sps)*

Leaf

Row 1: With green, ch 15, sc in 2nd ch from hook, sc in each rem ch across to last ch, 5 sc in last ch *(tip of leaf)*, working on opposite side of foundation ch, sc in each ch across, 3 sc in last ch *(bottom tip)*.

Row 2: Ch 1, working in **back lp** *(see Stitch Guide)* of each st, sc in each st ending 4 sc from the center sc of tip, turn.

Row 3: Ch 1, working in **front lp** *(see Stitch Guide)* of each st, sc in each st down side with 3 sc in center sc at bottom tip, then sc up other side, ending 3 sc from tip of leaf, turn.

Row 4: Ch 1, working in back lp of each st, sc in each st down side with 3 sc in center sc at bottom tip, then sc up other side, ending 3 sc from tip of leaf, turn.

Row 5: Rep row 3, fasten off.

Carefully sew the Leaf across Purse Front with bottom tip near center of the Purse Front and tip of Leaf slightly out over the edge of the Purse Front.

Rose

Rnd 1: With pink, ch 6, join in first ch to form a ring, ch 1, [sc in ring, ch 3] 6 times, join in beg sc. *(6 ch-3 sps)*

Rnd 2: Ch 1, (sc, hdc, 3 dc, hdc, sc) in each ch-3 sp around, join in beg sc. *(6 petals)*

Rnd 3: Working behind petals, sl st around **back post** *(see Stitch Guide)* of sc post of rnd 1, ch 5, [sl st around post of next sc of rnd 1, ch 5] 5 times, join in beg sl st. *(6 ch-5 sps)*

Rnd 4: Ch 1, (sc, hdc, 5 dc, hdc, sc) in each ch-5 sp around, join in beg sc. *(6 petals)*

Rnd 5: Working behind petals, sl st around sl st of rnd 3, ch 7, [sl st around next sl st of rnd 3, ch 7] 5 times, join in beg sl st. *(6 ch-7 sps)*

Rnd 6: Ch 1, (sc, hdc, 7 dc, hdc, sc) in each ch-7 sp around, join in beg sc. *(6 petals)*

Rnd 7: Working behind petals, sl st around sl st of rnd 5, ch 9 [sl st around next sl st of rnd 5, ch 9] 5 times, join in beg sl st. *(6 ch-9 sps)*

Rnd 8: Ch 1, (sc, hdc, 9 dc, hdc, sc) in each ch-9 sp around, join in beg sc, fasten off. *(6 petals)*

Finishing

Rnd 1: With WS of Purse Front and Back together Front facing, matching tr cl sts and working through both thicknesses, attach white with sl st in center bottom cl, ch 1, sc in same tr cl, [2 sc in next ch-2 sp, sc in next tr cl] 3 times, ch 150 *(Neck Loop)*, sk the next tr cl of row 4 of Purse Back, sk next tr cl, working through both thicknesses, [sc in next tr cl, 2 sc in next ch-2 sp] around to beg of rnd, join in beg sc, fasten off.

With rem length of white yarn, position the Rose so that 2 outer petals of Rose are centered across the 6 tr cl of row 4 of purse back, sew petals to tr cl and ch-2 sps across row 4.

Position pearl shank button on front at center of Rose, sew button to Purse Front. To close Purse, pass button through center of Rose. ■

JACKETS, WRAPS & MORE 155

SEASIDE SCALLOPS REVERSIBLE BAG

DESIGN BY JEWDY LAMBERT

INTERMEDIATE

Finished Size
12 x 13 inches, excluding Shoulder Strap

Materials
- Fine (sport) weight cotton yarn (1¾ oz/166 yds/50g per ball):
    3 balls light sage
- Size C/2/2.75mm crochet hook or size needed to obtain gauge
- Tapestry needle
- Stitch markers

Gauge
5 dc = ¾ inch; 3 dc rows = ¾ inch

Pattern Note
Weave in loose ends as work progresses.

BAG

Body
Row 1: Ch 207, dc in 6th ch from hook, sk next 2 chs, 5 dc in next ch, sk next 2 chs, dc in next ch, place marker *(side panel)*, sc in next ch, *ch 3, sk next 2 chs, sc in next ch, [ch 5, sk next 3 chs, sc in next ch] 3 times, ch 3, sk next 2 chs, sc in next ch*, rep between * 4 times, place marker *(front panel)*, dc in next ch, ch 1, sk next ch, dc in next ch, sk next 2 chs, 5 dc in next ch, sk next 2 chs, dc in next ch, ch 1, sk next ch, dc in next ch, place marker *(side panel)*, sc in next ch, rep between * 5 times *(back panel)*, turn.

Row 2: Ch 4 *(counts as first dc, ch-1)*, dc in next dc, sk next 2 dc of 5-dc group, 5 dc in next dc, sk next 2 dc of same 5-dc group, dc in next dc, ch 1, dc in next dc, place marker, dc in next st, *ch 3, sk next ch-3 sp, sc in next ch sp, 9 dc in next ch sp, sc in next ch sp, ch 3, sk next ch-3 sp**, 3 dc in next sc*, rep between * 4 times, ending last rep at **, dc in next sc, place marker, dc in next dc, ch 1, dc in next dc, sk next 2 dc of 5-dc group, 5 dc in next dc, sk next 2 dc of same 5-dc group, dc in next dc, ch 1, dc in next dc, place marker, rep between * 5 times, turn.

Row 3: Ch 4, dc in next dc, sk next 2 dc of 5-dc group, 5 dc in next dc, sk next 2 dc of same 5-dc group, dc in next dc, ch 1, dc in next dc, place marker, sc in next st, *ch 1, sk next 3 chs and next sc, dc in next dc, [ch 1, dc in next dc] 8 times, ch 1, sk next sc and next ch-3 sp**, sc in each of next 3 sts*, rep between * 4 times, ending last rep at **, sc in next st, place marker, dc in next dc, ch 1, dc in next dc, sk next 2 dc of 5-dc group, 5 dc in next dc, sk next 2 dc of same 5-dc group, dc in next dc, ch 1, dc in next dc, place marker, rep between * 5 times, turn.

Row 4: Ch 4, dc in next dc, sk next 2 dc of 5-dc group, 5 dc in next dc, sk next 2 dc of same 5-dc group, dc in next dc, ch 1, dc in next dc, place marker, dc in next dc, [ch 1, sk next ch-1 sp, dc in next dc] 3 times, ch 1, sk next ch-1 sp, (dc, ch 1, dc) in next dc, ch 1, sk next ch-1 sp, dc in next dc] 4 times *(dc-crescent completed)*, sk next ch-1 sp and next sc, sc in next sc**, sk next sc and next ch-1 sp*, rep from * 4 times, ending last rep at **, place marker, dc in next dc, ch 1, dc in next dc, sk next

156   JACKETS, WRAPS & MORE

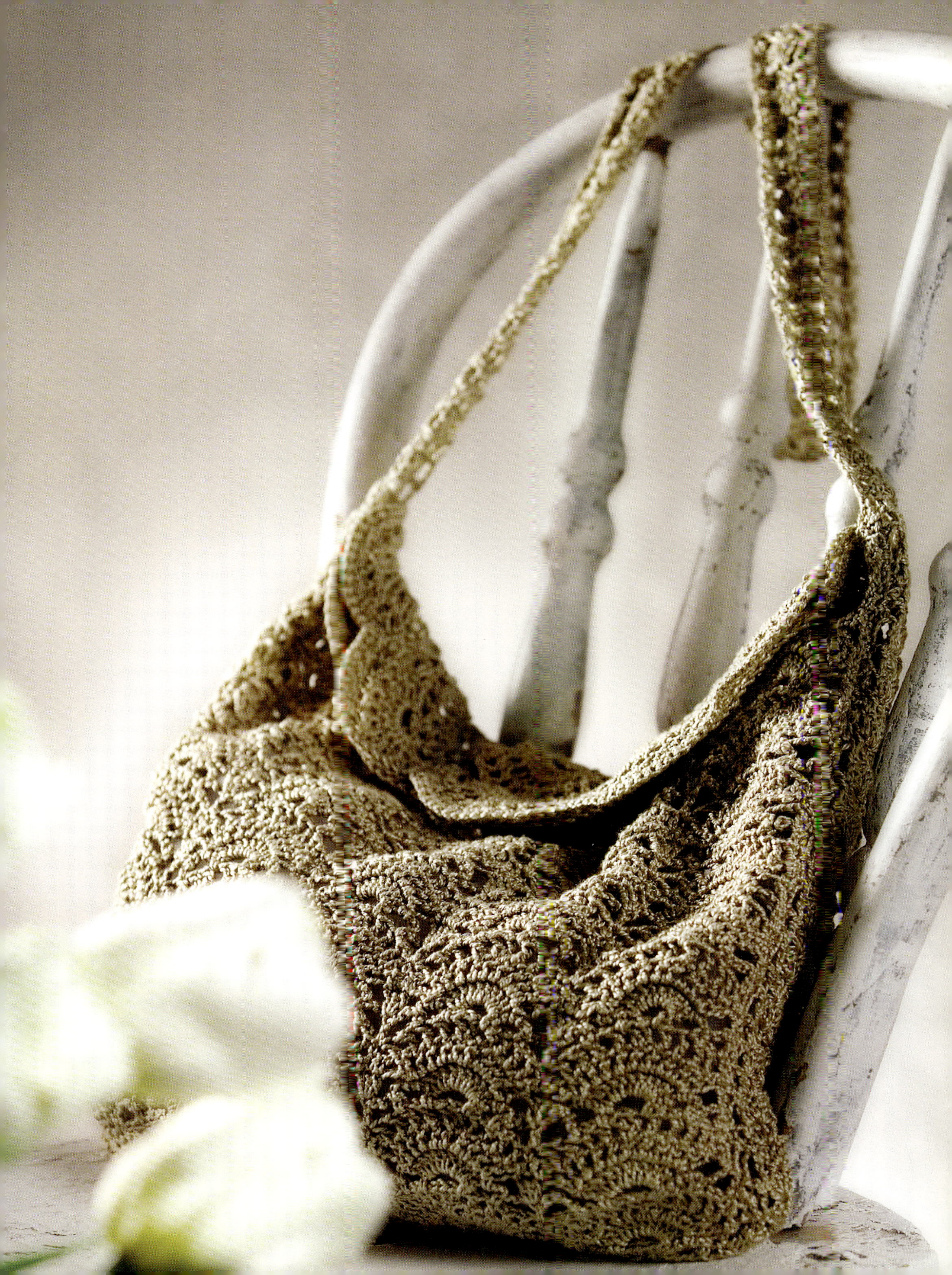

group, 5 dc in next dc, sk next 2 dc of same 5-dc group, dc in next dc, ch 1, dc in next dc *(side panel)*, sc in each st across main Body of Bag**, dc in next dc, rep from *, ending last rep at **, turn.

Row 42: *Ch 4, dc in next dc, sk next 2 dc of 5-dc group, 5 dc in next dc, sk next 2 dc of same 5-dc group, dc in next dc, ch 4, sc in next dc, sc in each sc across Body of Bag**, sc in next dc, rep from * across, ending last rep at **, fasten off.

First Shoulder Strap

Row 1: Attach light sage in 3rd ch of ch-4 of side panel, ch 4, dc in next dc, sk next 2 dc of 5-dc group, 5 dc in next dc, sk next 2 dc of same 5-dc group, dc in next dc, ch 1, dc in next dc, turn.
Row 2: Ch 4, dc in next dc, sk next 2 dc of 5-dc group, 5 dc in next dc, sk next 2 dc of same 5-dc group, dc in next dc, ch 1, dc in next dc, turn.
Rows 3–40: Rep row 2. At the end of last rep, fasten off.

2nd Shoulder Strap

Rows 1–39: Rep rows 1–39 of First Shoulder Strap.
Row 40: Rep row 2 of First Shoulder Strap, do not turn, using care that straps are not twisted, matching sts and working through both thicknesses, sl st across, fasten off.

Bottom

Row 1: Ch 12, dc in 4th ch from hook, dc in each of next 8 chs, turn. *(10 dc)*
Row 2: Ch 3 *(counts as first dc)*, dc in each dc across, turn. *(10 dc)*
Rows 3–35: Rep row 2. At the end of row 35, fasten off.

Edging

Row 1: Working down side edge of Bag, attach light sage in side edge of last row of Body, working in first dc of side panel, ch 1, sc evenly sp to bottom edge, working in foundation ch and side edge of Bottom, sc evenly spaced across, working up opposite side edge, sc evenly spaced in dc of side panel to top edge of Body, fasten off.
Rep row 1 of Edging on opposite side edge of Body. ■

2 dc of 5-dc group, 5 dc in next dc, sk next 2 dc of same 5-dc group, dc in next dc, ch 1, dc in next dc, place marker, rep between * 5 times, turn.
Row 5: Ch 4, dc in next dc, sk next 2 dc of 5-dc group, 5 dc in next dc, sk next 2 dc of same 5-dc group, dc in next dc, ch 1, dc in next dc, place marker, dc in next st, ch 3, *sc in 3rd dc of dc-crescent, ch 5, sk next ch-1 sp, sk next dc, sc in next ch, ch 5, sk next dc, ch-1 sp and next dc, sc in next ch-1 sp, ch 5, sk next dc and next ch-1 sp, sc in next dc, ch 3, sk rem sts of dc-crescent, 1 dc in next st**, ch 3*, rep between * 4 times, ending last rep at **, place marker, dc in next dc, ch 1, dc in next dc, sk next 2 dc of 5-dc group, 5 dc in next dc, sk next 2 dc of same 5-dc group, dc in next dc, ch 1, dc in next dc, place marker, rep between * 5 times, turn.
Row 6–37: [Rep rows 2–5 consecutively] 8 times.
Rows 38–40: Rep rows 2–4.
Row 41: Ch 4, *dc in next dc, sk next 2 dc of 5-dc

FASHION FLOWER PINS

DESIGNS BY DARLA SIMS

RAINBOW BRIGHT

EASY

Finished Size
3½ inches in diameter

Materials
- Lion Brand Incredible Ribbon bulky (chunky) weight yarn (1¾ oz, 110 yds/50g per ball):
   1 ball #201 rainbow
- Lion Brand Fun Fur bulky (chunky) weight yarn (1¾ oz, 60 yds/50g per ball):
   1 ball #194 lime
- Lion Brand Microspun light (DK) weight yarn (2½ oz/168 yds/70g per ball):
   1 ball #194 lime
- Sizes G/6/4mm and P/15mm crochet hooks or size needed to obtain gauge
- Tapestry needle
- 1-inch pin back

Gauge
Size P hook: Rnds 1 & 2 = 3½ inches

Special Stitch
Picot: Ch 3, sl st in 3rd ch from hook.

Flower
Rnd 1: With size P hook and rainbow, ch 4, 13 sc in 4th ch from hook, join with sl st in beg sc. *(13 sc)*
Rnd 2: Picot *(see Special Stitch)*, [sl st in next st, picot] around, join with sl st in joining sl st on last rnd. Fasten off.

Center
With size G hook, holding 1 strand of Fun Fur and 1 strand of Microspun tog, ch 4, 5 dc in 4th ch from hook, drop lp from hook, insert hook in top of 4th ch of beg ch-4, pull dropped lp through, ch 1. Fasten off.
Sew to center of Flower.
Sew pin back to back of Flower.

& MORE

KATHY

EASY

Finished Size
3½ inches in diameter

Materials
- Bernat Satin medium (worsted) weight yarn (3½ oz/163 yds/100g per skein):
  ¼ oz/12 yds/7g each
  #04317 star dust,
  #04732 mai tai and
  #04236 evergreen
- Size G/6/4mm crochet hook or size needed to obtain gauge
- Tapestry needle
- Sewing needle
- Sewing thread
- Raspberry glass beads: 5
- 1-inch pin back

4 MEDIUM

Gauge
Rnds 1 & 2 = 2 inches

Special Stitches
Beginning cluster (beg cl): Ch 3 (counts as first dc), holding back last lp of each st on hook, 3 dc in same st, yo, pull through all lps on hook, ch 3, sl st in same st.
Cluster (cl): Holding back last lp of each st on hook, 4 dc in next st, yo, pull through all lps on hook.

Flower
Rnd 1: With star dust, ch 2, 9 sc in 2nd ch from hook, join with sl st in **front lp** (see Stitch Guide) of beg sc. (9 sc)
Rnd 2: Beg cl (see Special Stitches) in front lp of first st (petal), (sl st, ch 3, **cl**–see Special Stitches, ch 3, sl st) in front lp of each st around, join with sl st in joining sl st of last rnd. Fasten off. (9 petals)
Rnd 3: Working in **back lp** (see Stitch Guide) of sts on rnd 1, join mai tai with sl st in first sc, ch 9, sl st in same st (petal), [(sl st, ch 9, sl st) in next sc] around, join with sl st in beg sl st. Fasten off. (9 petals)
Rnd 4: Join evergreen with sl st between any 2 petals, [ch 5, sl st in 2nd ch from hook, sc in next ch, hdc in next ch, dc in next ch, sl st between same petal and next petal] 8 times, ch 5, sl st in 2nd ch from hook, sc in next ch, hdc in next ch, dc in next ch, join with sl st in beg sl st. Fasten off.

Finishing
Thread beads onto sewing thread. Tie ends of thread tog, pulling beads into circle.
Sew circle of beads to center of Flower.
Sew pin back to back of Flower.

160 JACKETS, WRAPS & MORE

SAHEYO

EASY

Finished Size
5½ inches in diameter

Materials
- Lion Brand Homespun bulky (chunky) weight yarn (6 oz/185 yds/170g per skein):
  - ¼ oz/8 yds/7g #311 cocoa
- Size C/E/4mm crochet hook or size needed to obtain gauge
- Tapestry needle
- Sewing needle
- Sewing thread
- 1 large wooden bead
- 9 small wooden beads
- 6-inch piece faux leather fringe

BULKY 5

Gauge
Rnd 1 = 1 inch

Flower

Center
Ch 2, 10 sc in 2nd ch from hook, join with sl st in beg sc. *(10 sc)*

First Petal
Row 1: Ch 1, hdc in first st, 2 hdc in next st, leaving rem sts unworked, turn. *(3 hdc)*
Row 2: Ch 1, 2 hdc in each st across, turn. *(6 hdc)*
Row 3: Ch 1, **hdc dec** *(see Stitch Guide)* in first 2 sts, hdc in each of next 2 sts, hdc dec in last 2 sts, turn. *(4 hdc)*
Row 4: Ch 1, [hdc dec in next 2 sts] twice, turn. *(2 hdc)*
Row 5: Ch 1, hdc dec in 2 sts. Fasten off.

Next Petal
Row 1: Join with sl st in next unworked sc on Center, ch 1, hdc in same st, 2 hdc in next st, leaving rem sts unworked, turn. *(3 hdc)*
Rows 2–5: Rep rows 2–5 of First Petal.
Rep Next Petal 3 times for total of 5 Petals.

Beaded Trim
Cut 20-inch length of yarn and tie knot in end. [Thread small bead on yarn, tie knot in yarn at top of bead] 9 times. Trim ends.

Finishing
1. Sew center of Beaded Trim between any 2 petals as shown in photo.
2. Roll leather fringe tightly and insert in center of Flower. Using sewing needle and sewing thread, sew to back of Flower.
3. Sew large bead to center of Flower. ■

FOILED HEART NECKLACE

DESIGN BY MARY LAYFIELD

EASY

Finished Size
One size fits most

Materials
- Red Heart Lustersheen fine (sport) weight yarn (4 oz/335 yds/113g per skein):
    1 skein #2 black
- Size B/1/2.25mm crochet hook or size needed to obtain gauge
- Sewing needle
- Sewing thread
- Accessories from Blue Moon Bead Co.:
    14 clear E-beads with 8mm foil beads
    1 large #65406 red/black foil heart
    1 package #64116 matching red/black foil 8mm beads
    Silver hook and eye

3 LIGHT

Special Stitch
Cross-stitch (cross-st): Sk next st, dc in next st, dc in st just sk.

NECKLACE

Row 1: Ch 97, sc in 2nd ch from hook and in each ch across, turn.

Row 2: Ch 3 *(counts as first dc)*, dc in next st, **cross-st** *(see Special Stitch)*, [dc in next st, cross-st, dc in next st, cross-st, 2 dc in next st, cross-st] 4 times, [dc in next st, cross-st] 5 times, [2 dc in next st, cross-st, dc in next st, cross-st, dc in next st, cross-st] 4 times, 2 dc in next st, cross-st, dc in each of last 2 sts, **do not turn**. Fasten off. Attach hook and eye to ends of row 1.

Row 3: Sk first 31 sts, join with sc in next st, ch 10, sk next 3 sts, sc in next st, ch 16, sk next 13 sts, sc in next st, (dc, ch 2, dc) in next st *(center)*, ch 16, sk next 13 sts, sc in next st, ch 10, sk next 3 sts, sc in each of next 2 sts leaving rem sts unworked, turn.

Row 4: Sc in each of next 10 chs, sc in each of first 2 chs of ch-16, ch 8, sk next 3 chs, sc in next ch, ch 9, sk next 4 chs, sc in next ch, ch 14, sc in 6th ch of next ch-16, ch 9, sk next 4 chs, sc in next ch, ch 8, sk next 3 chs, sc in each of last 2 chs, sc in each of next 10 chs, sc in next st on row 2. Fasten off.

Row 5: Working across chs of ch-14, join with sc in first ch, sc in each of next 5 chs, ch 9, sk next 2 chs, sc in each of last 6 chs. Fasten off.

Sew beads to Necklace as shown in photo or as desired. ■

JACKETS, WRAPS & MORE

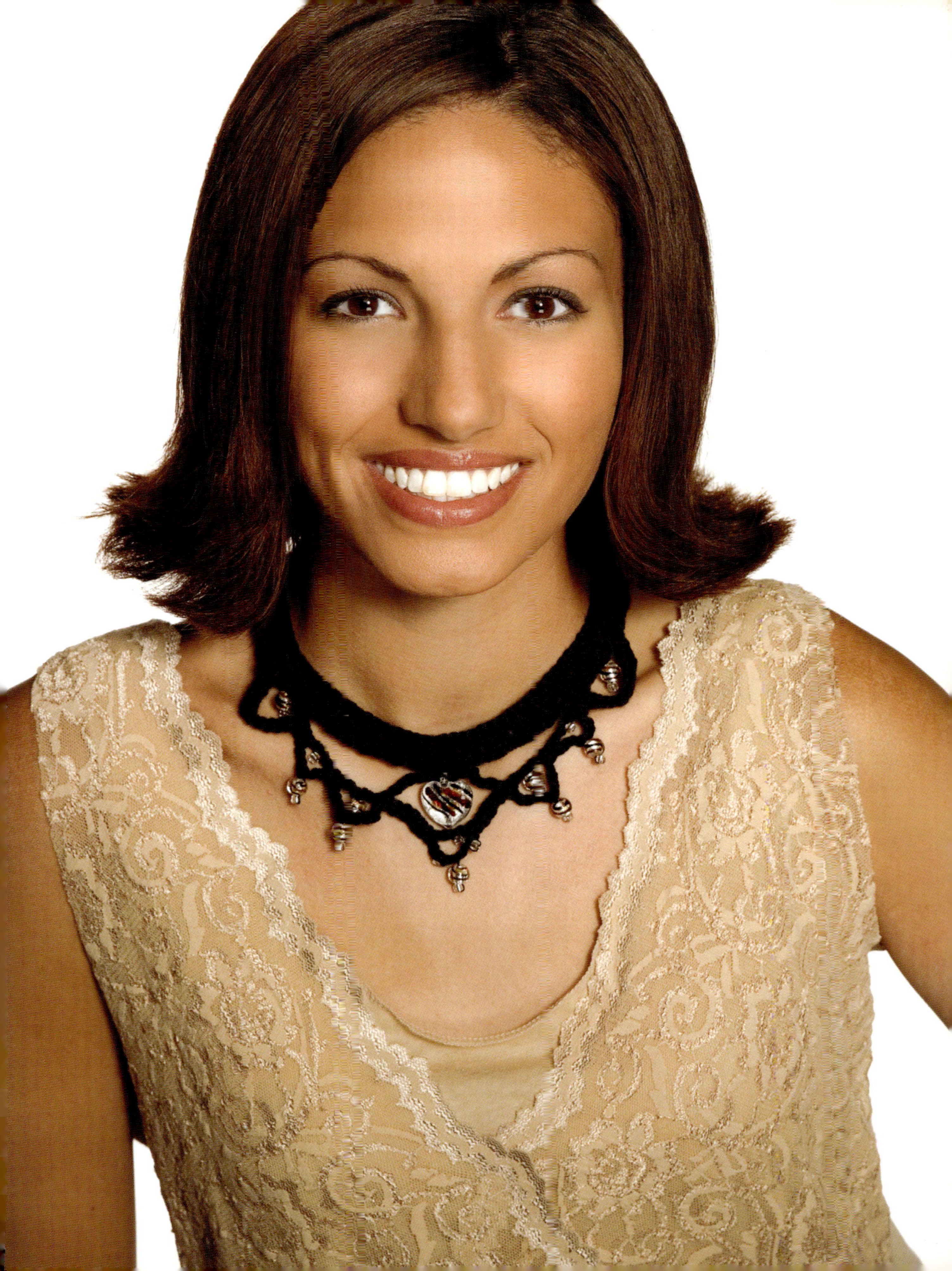

& MORE continued

HOT PANTS SET CONTINUED FROM PAGE 91

Neck & Shoulder Shaping
Row 1: Sl st in first sc, sc in each rem sc across, sc in beg ch-1 of previous row, turn.
Row 2: Ch 1, sk first sc, sc in each st across, turn, do not work in ch-1 sp of previous row at neck edge.
Rep rows 1 and 2 alternately until 10 [10, 11, 12, 13] sts rem.
Rows 3–14: Ch 1, sc in each st across, turn. At the end of last rep, fasten off.

Right Front Armhole
Row 1: Attach pink in 33rd st from Right Front edge, ch 1, sc in each of next 17 [17, 22, 27, 27] sts, inc in next st, sc in each rem st across, turn.

For Sizes X-Small, Small & Medium Only
Row 2: Ch 1, sc in each of next 15 [15, 20] sts, 2 sc in next sc, sc in each rem sc across, turn.
Row 3: Ch 1, sc in each of next 18 [18, 23] sts, 2 sc in next st, sc in next st, 2 sc in next st, sc in each rem st across, turn.

For Sizes Large & X-Large Only
Row 2: Ch 1, sc in each of next 28 [28] sts, 2 sc in next st, sc in each rem st across, turn.
Row 3: Ch 1, sc in each st to within 1 st before inc on previous row, 2 sc in next st, sc in next st, 2 sc in next st, sc in each rem sc across to armhole, turn.

For All Sizes
Rows 4–10: Rep rows 4–10 of Left Front Armhole, working inc and dec sts.

Neck & Shoulder Shaping
Row 1: Ch 1, sc across, turn, do not work in ch-1 of previous row at neck edge.
Row 2: Sk first st, sc in each st across, sc in beg ch-1 of previous row, turn.
Rep rows 1 and 2 alternately until 10 [10, 11, 12, 13] sts rem.
Rows 3–14: Ch 1, sc in each st across, turn. At the end of last rep, fasten off.

Back
Row 1: With RS facing, attach pink in the 8th st from beg of armhole edge of Right Front, ch 1, sc in each st across to last 8 sts of Left Front, turn.
Row 2: Ch 1, sc in each st across, turn, do not work in turning ch-1 of previous row.
Rep row 2 until back measures 10 inches from beg.

First Back Neck
Note: Place marker at center Back stitch.
Row 1: Ch 1, sc in same st as beg ch-1, sc in each st to marked st, turn.
Row 2: Ch 1, do not work in same st with beg ch-1 at neck edge, sc in each rem st across, turn.
Row 3: Ch 1, sc in each st across, turn.
Rep rows 2 and 3 alternately until Back measures 10 inches.
Row 4: With size F hook, work block st across row, turn.
Row 5: With size G hook, ch 1, sc in each st across.
Row 6: Holding WS of Front and Back Shoulders tog and working through both thicknesses, sl st in front lps only across, fasten off.

2nd Back Neck
Row 1: Attach pink in next st after marked st at center Back, ch 1, sc in same st as beg ch-1, sc in each st across, turn.
Row 2: Ch 1, sc in each st across, do not work in same st as beg ch-1 at neck edge, turn.
Row 3: Ch 1, sc in each st across, turn.

164 JACKETS, WRAPS & MORE

& MORE continued

Rep rows 2 and 3 alternately until Back measures 10 inches.
Row 4: With size F hook, work block st across, turn.
Row 5: With size G hook, ch 1, sc in each st across. Fasten off.
Row 6: Holding WS of Front and Back Shoulders tog and working through both thicknesses, sl st in front lps only across, fasten off.

Armhole Trim
Rnd 1: With size G hook, attach pink at underarm, ch 1, sc evenly spaced around armhole opening, join in beg sc, fasten off.
Rep on opposite armhole.

Neckline Trim
Row 1: With size G hook, attach pink in Right Front neck edge in first row without an inc sc evenly spaced up neckline across Back Neckline and to opposite side of Left Front, ending in last row of neckline without inc st, fasten off.
Row 2: With size G hook, attach beige with sl st 1 st before previous row, sc in each sc of previous row, sl st in next st, fasten off.

Bottom Trim
Row 1: With size G hook, attach beige in Left Front bottom edge and working across opposite side of foundation ch, ch 1, sc in each st across bottom edge of Top, fasten off.

Drawstring
With size F hook and beige, make a ch to desired length and lace through ends of every other row beg at lower edge just above block st row, up to first dec row of center front, tie ends in a bow. ∎

KIWI VEST & HEADBAND CONTINUED FROM PAGE 92

hook, ch 16, sl st in 2nd ch from hook, sl st in each rem ch across, turn.
Rows 1–12: Rep rows 1–12 of Right Front.

Neck & Armhole Shaping
Row 13: Rep row 13 of Neck and Armhole Shaping. Rep row 13 until Back measures 6½ inches from first inc, ending at armhole edge, turn. (3 sts)
Row 14: At armhole edge, ch 13, sl st in 2nd ch from hook, sl st in each ch, sl st loosely in last st made before ch-13, continue in pattern across to last 2 sts, turn.
Row 15: Work even in pattern across, turn.
Rep row 15 until Back measures 4 inches from armhole.
Row 16: Rep row 17 of Right Front.
Row 17: Rep row 18 of Right Front.
Rep rows 16 and 17 until 3 sts rem.
Row 18: Ch 2, sk 1 st, hdc in next st, fasten off.

Assembly
Holding RS of Backs tog and working through both thicknesses, sc Backs tog across the 4-inch section worked straight at center back.
Holding RS of Front and Back tog at shoulders sc through both thicknesses. Holding sides tog, sc through both thicknesses of each side seam.

& MORE continued

Outer Trim
Rnd 1: With RS facing and size F [G, H] hook, attach yarn at side seam, ch 1, sc evenly spaced around entire outer edge, working 2 sc in each outer point of Vest, join in beg sc, fasten off.

Tie
With size F [G, H] hook, ch 100, fasten off.
Insert 1 end of ch from from front to back through right front center point, insert same end from back to front through left front center point, pull ends even, tie ends in a bow.

HEADBAND
Row 1: With size G hook, ch 101, sl st loosely in 2nd ch from hook, hdc in next ch, [sl st loosely in next ch, hdc in next ch] across, turn.
Row 2: Ch 1, working in back lps only, [sl st loosely in hdc, hdc in next sl st] across, turn.
Rep row 2 until Headband is 1¾ inches wide. At the end of last rep, do not fasten off.

Trim & Ties
Rnd 1: Ch 1, sc in each st across last row, *ch 35, sl st in 2nd ch from hook, sl st in each rem ch across *(Tie)*, sc in same st as last sc, sc evenly spaced across ends of rows, ch 35, sl st in 2nd ch from hook, sl st in each rem ch across *(Tie)*, sc in same st as last sc, sc evenly spaced across opposite side of foundation ch, rep between *, join in beg sc, fasten off.
When wearing Headband, tie strands tog in a bow at back neckline. ∎

LADDER-STITCH CLOCHE CONTINUED FROM PAGE 95

Rnd 17: Sl st into ch-2 sp, ch 1, (sc, ch 2, sc) in same ch-2 sp, ch 1, sk next ch-2 sp, [(sc, ch 2, sc) in next ch-2 sp, ch 1, sk next ch-2 sp] around, join in beg sc, fasten off.

FLOWER
Rnd 1: With eggplant, ch 4, join in first ch to form a ring, ch 1, 8 sc in ring, join in beg sc. *(8 sc)*
Rnd 2: [Ch 3, sl st in next sc] 8 times, fasten off. *(8 ch-3 sps)*
Rnd 3: Draw up a lp of olive in any ch-3 sp, ch 1, (sc, 3 dc, sc) in same ch-3 sp and in each rem ch-3 sp around, join in beg sc, leaving an 8-inch length, fasten off.
Position Flower at joining seam of rnd 14 of Cloche and sew in place using tapestry needle and 8-inch length. ∎

& MORE continued

EARTH CHILD CONTINUED FROM PAGE 101

Small Ring

Make 3.
Rnd 1: Attach linen to ¾-inch metal ring, ch 1, work 20 sc over ring, join in beg sc, leaving a length for sewing, fasten off. *(20 sc)*

Finishing

Using rem lengths and yarn needle, sew Large Ring to row 33 of Neckband and 1 Small Ring to row 24 and row 42. Sew a Small Ring to the center bottom of the Large Ring.

Cut a 16-inch length of linen, fold length in half and with yarn needle pass the linen length through an 18mm bead. Tie a double knot in ends to keep bead from slipping off. With yarn needle attach loose ends to center bottom of Small Ring, tie at back to secure, fasten off. Attach one 18mm bead to each rem Small Ring. Weave in all loose ends.

BRACELET

Small Ring

Make 4.
Rnd 1: Attach linen to rem ¾-inch metal rings, ch 1, 20 sc over ring, join in first sc, fasten off. *(20 sc)*

Finishing

With yarn needle and a long length of linen, pass through a 28mm bead and sew each loose end of linen passed through bead to Small Ring. Continue to sew beads and Small Rings alternately tog forming a strip, ending with sewing last Small Ring to first bead to form a closed circle. Weave in all loose ends. ∎

GRANNY SQUARE SHRINK VEST CONTINUED FROM PAGE 102

Rnd 4: Ch 6 *(counts as first dc, ch-3)*, sk next dc, [dc in next dc, ch 3, sk next dc] around, join in 3rd ch of beg ch-6. *(16 dc, 16 ch-3 sps)*
Rnd 5: Ch 3, 4 dc in next ch-3 sp, [dc in next dc, 4 dc in next ch-3 sp] around, join in 3rd ch of beg ch-3. *(80 dc)*

For Size X-Small Only

Rnd 6: Ch 1, sc in joining, sc in next dc, ch 3, sk next 2 dc, hdc in next dc, ch 3, sk next 2 dc, dc in next dc, ch 3, sk next 2 dc, (dc, ch 2, tr, ch 2, dc) in next dc, ch 3, sk next 2 dc, dc in next dc, ch 3, sk next 2 dc, hdc in next dc, ch 3, sk next 2 dc, sc in each of next 3 dc, rep from * around, ending with sc in last dc, join in beg sc.
Rnd 7: Ch 3, sk first sc, dc in next sc, *2 dc in next ch-3 sp, dc in next hdc, [2 dc in next ch-3 sp, dc in next dc] twice, 2 dc in next ch-3 sp, tr in next tr, [2 dc in next ch-3 sp, dc in next dc] twice, 2 dc in next ch-3 sp, dc in next hdc, 2 dc in next ch-3 sp, dc in each of next 3 sc, rep from * around, ending with dc in last sc, join in top of beg ch-3, fasten off.

JACKETS, WRAPS & MORE **167**

& MORE continued

around, ending last rep at **, sc in last sc, join in beg sc.
Rnd 9: Ch 3, dc in each of next 4 sc, *3 dc in next ch-3 sp, dc in next dc, 4 dc in next ch-3 sp, dc in next tr, 3 dc in next ch-2 sp, tr in next tr, 3 dc in next ch-2 sp, dc in next tr, 4 dc in next ch-3 sp, dc in next dc, 3 dc in next ch-3 sp, dc in each of next 9 sc, rep from * around, ending with dc in each of next 4 sc, join in 3rd ch of beg ch-3, fasten off sizes small and medium only. *(136 dc)*

For Size Large Only
Rnd 10: Ch 3, dc in each dc around, working (dc, tr, dc) in each corner tr, join in 3rd ch of beg ch-3, fasten off.

For Size X-Large Only
Rnds 10 & 11: Ch 3, dc in each dc around, working (dc, tr, dc) in each corner tr, join in 3rd ch of beg ch-3, fasten off.

First Front Side Panel
For All Sizes
Row 1: With RS facing, attach yarn on bottom right in corner tr, ch 1, sc in same st as joining, sc in each of next 20 [25, 28, 31, 34] sts, turn. *(21 [26, 29, 32, 35] sc)*
Row 2: Ch 1, sc in first sc, **sc dec** *(see Stitch Guide)* in next 2 sts, sc in each rem st across, turn. *(20 [25, 28, 31, 34] sc)*
Row 3: Ch 1, sc in each st across to last 3 sts, sc dec in next 2 sts, sc in last st, turn. *(19 [24, 27, 30, 34] sc)*

For Size X-Small Only
Row 4: Rep row 2, fasten off. *(18 sc)*

For Size Small Only
Rows 4 & 5: Rep rows 2 and 3. *([22] sc)*
Row 6: Rep row 2, fasten off. *([21] sc)*

For Size Medium Only
Rows 4–7: [Rep rows 2 and 3 alternately] twice. At the end of last rep, fasten off. *([23] sc)*

For Size Large Only
Rows 4–7: [Rep rows 2 and 3 alternately] twice. *([26] sc)*
Rows 8–10: Ch 1, sc in each st across, turn. At the end of last rep, fasten off.

For Sizes Small, Medium, Large & X-Large Only
Rnd 6: Ch 3, dc in each dc around, join in 3rd ch of beg ch-3.
Rnd 7: Ch 1, sc in joining, sc in next dc, *ch 3, sk next 2 dc, hdc in next dc, ch 3, sk next 2 dc, dc in next dc, ch 4, sk next 2 dc, tr in next dc, ch 4, sk next 2 dc, dc in next dc, ch 3, sk next 2 dc, hdc in next dc, ch 3, sk next 2 dc, sc in each of next 3 dc, rep from * around, ending with sk next 2 dc, sc in last dc, join in beg sc.
Rnd 8: Ch 1, sc in joining, sc in next sc, *2 sc in next ch-3 sp, sc in next hdc, ch 3, dc in next dc, ch 3, (tr, {ch 2, tr} twice) in next tr, ch 3, dc in next dc, ch 3, sc in next hdc, 2 sc in next ch-3 sp**, sc in each of next 3 sc, rep from *

168 JACKETS, WRAPS & MORE

& MORE continued

For Size X-Large Only
Rows 4–9: [Rep rows 2 and 3 alternately] 3 times. ([28] sc)
Rows 10–14: Ch 1, sc in each st across, turn. At the end of last rep, fasten off.

2nd Front Side Panel
Rows 1–4 [1–6, 1–7, 1–10, 1–14]: Rep rows 1–4 [1–6, 1–7, 1–10, 1–14] of First Front Side Panel.

First & 2nd Back Side Panels
Rep First and 2nd Front Side Panels.

Strap
Make 2 each front & back.
Row 1: With RS facing, join yarn at upper right tr, ch 1, sc in same st as joining and in each of next 4 [5, 5, 6, 6] sts, turn. *(5 [6, 6, 7, 7] sc)*
Row 2: Ch 1, sc in each sc across, turn.
Rows 3–9 [3–9, 3–10, 3–12, 3–14]: Rep Row 2. At the end of last rep, fasten off.
With RS facing, join yarn in 5th [6th, 6th, 7th, 7th] st from left corner tr, rep rows 1–9 [1–9, 1–10, 1–12, 1–14].

With RS tog, matching sts and sewing through top lps only, sew shoulders tog. With RS tog, sew side seams.

Bottom Edging
Rnd 1 (WS): Attach yarn at side seam, ch 1, sc evenly spaced around, join in beg sc, turn.
Rnds 2–4: Ch 1, sc in each sc around, join in beg sc. At the end of last rep, fasten off.

Armhole Trim
Rnd 1 (RS): Attach yarn at underarm, ch 1, sc evenly spaced around, working sc dec where the strap joins each Front and Back to keep piece flat, join in beg sc, fasten off.
Rep on opposite armhole opening.

Neckline Trim
Rnd 1 (RS): Attach yarn at shoulder seam, ch 1, sc evenly spaced around, working sc dec at 4 corners where the strap joins each Front and Back to keep piece flat, join in beg sc, fasten off. ■

LACY PINEAPPLES SHELL CONTINUED FROM PAGE 123

Row 3: Ch 4, tr in each ch-1 sp and each hdc across, turn.
Rows 4–19: [Rep rows 2 and 3 alternately] 8 times.
Row 20: Sl st in each of next 6 sts, ch 3, sk next st, hdc in next st, [ch 1, sk next st, hdc in next st] 42 times, leaving last 6 sts unworked, turn. *(43 hdc)*
Row 21: Rep row 3. *(85 tr)*

First Strap
Row 1: Ch 3, sk next st, hdc in next st, [ch 1, sk next st, hdc in next st] 6 times, turn. *(8 hdc)*
Row 2: Ch 4, tr in each ch-1 sp and each hdc across, turn.
Rows 3–10: [Rep rows 1 and 2 alternately] 4 times. At the end of last rep, fasten off.

2nd Strap
Row 1: Sk next 55 sts of row 21 of back panel, join with

JACKETS, WRAPS & MORE 169

& MORE continued

sl st in next st, ch 3, sk next st, hdc in next st, [ch 1, sk next st, hdc in next st] 6 times, turn. *(8 hdc)*
Row 2: Rep row 2 of First Strap.
Rows 3–10: [Rep rows 1 and 2 of First Strap alternately] 4 times.

Front Panel

Row 1: With size C [D, E, F] hook, ch 100, tr in 5th ch from hook, tr in each of next 13 chs, dc in each of next 15 chs, hdc in each of next 16 chs, sc in each of next 5 chs, hdc in each of next 16 chs, dc in each of next 15 chs, tr in each of next 15 chs, turn. *(5 sc, 32 hdc, 30 dc, 30 tr)*
Row 2: Ch 3, sk next st, [hdc in next st, ch 1, sk next st] 22 times, hdc in each of next 5 sts, [ch 1, sk next st, hdc in next st] across, turn. *(51 hdc)*
Row 3: Ch 4, [tr in next ch-1 sp, tr in next st] 7 times, dc in next ch-1 sp, [dc in next st, dc in next ch-1 sp] 7 times, [hdc in next st, hdc in next ch-1 sp] 8 times, sc in each of next 5 sts, [hdc in next ch-11 sp, hdc in next st] 8 times, dc in next ch-1 sp, [dc in next st, dc in next ch-1 sp] 7 times, tr in next st, [tr in next ch-1 sp, tr in next st] across, turn.
Row 4: Rep row 2.
Row 5: Ch 4, tr in each of next 45 sts, sc in each of next 5 sts, tr in each rem st across, turn. *(5 sc, 92 tr)*
Row 6: Rep row 2.
Rows 7–18: [Rep rows 3–6 consecutively] 3 times.
Row 19: Rep row 3.
Row 20: Sl st in each of next 6 sts, ch 3, sk next st, [hdc in next st, ch 1, sk next st] 19 times, ch 1, sk next st, hdc in each of next 5 sts, [ch 1, sk next st, hdc in next st] across to last 6 sts, leaving rem 6 sts unworked, turn. *(45 hdc)*
Row 21: Rep row 5.
Row 22: Ch 3, sk next st, [hdc in next st, ch 1, sk next st] 19 times, hdc in each of next 5 sts, [ch 1, sk next st, hdc in next st] across, turn. *(45 hdc)*
Row 23: Ch 4, [tr in next ch-1 sp, tr in next st] 6 times, [dc in next ch-1 sp, dc in next st] 6 times, [hdc in next ch-1 sp, hdc in next st] 4 times, [sk next ch-1 sp, hdc in next st] 3 times, hdc in next ch-1 sp, sc in each of next 5 sts, hdc in next ch-1 sp, [hdc in next st, sk next ch-1 sp] 3 times, [hdc in next st, hdc in next ch-1 sp] 4 times, [dc in next st, dc in next ch-1 sp] 6 times, [tr in next st, tr in next ch-1 sp] 6 times, tr in last st, turn. *(5 sc, 24 hdc, 24 dc, 25 tr)*
Row 24: Ch 3, sk next st, [hdc in next st, ch 1, sk next st] 17 times, hdc in each of next 5 sts, [ch 1, sk next st, hdc in next st] across, turn. *(43 hdc)*
Row 25: Ch 4, tr in next ch-1 sp, [tr in next st, tr in next ch-1 sp] 17 times, sc in each of next 5 sts, [tr in next ch-1 sp, tr in next st] across, turn. *(5 sc, 74 tr)*
Row 26: Rep row 24.
Row 27: Ch 4, [tr in next ch-1 sp, tr in next tr] 6 times, [dc in next ch-1 sp, dc in next st] 6 times, [hdc in next ch-1 sp, hdc in next st] 6 times, sc in each of next 5 sts, [hdc in next ch-1 sp, hdc in next st] 6 times, [dc in next st, dc in next ch-1 sp] 6 times, tr in next st, [tr in next ch-1 sp, tr in next st] 6 times, turn. *(5 sc, 24 hdc, 24 dc, 26 tr)*
Row 28: Rep row 24.
Row 29: Rep row 25.
Row 30: Ch 3, [sk next st, hdc in next st] 10 times, [**sc dec** (see Stitch Guide) in next 2 sts] 8 times, sc in each of next 5 sts, [sc dec in next 2 sts] 8 times, [sk next st, hdc in next st] across, fasten off. *(21 sc, 22 hdc)*

First Strap

Row 1: Working around post of last sts of rows 25–30, join with sl st in row 25, ch 2, 2 hdc in same sp, 2 hdc in next row, [3 hdc in next row, 2 hdc in next row] twice, turn. *(15 hdc)*
Row 2: Ch 3, sk next st, hdc in next st, [ch 1, sk next st, hdc in next st] across, turn. *(8 hdc)*
Row 3: Ch 4, [tr in next ch-1 sp, tr in next st] across, turn. *(15 tr)*
Rows 4–9: [Rep rows 2 and 3 alternately] 3 times.
Row 10: Rep row 2, leaving a long length for sewing, fasten off.
Sew last row of this strap to last row of strap on Back.

2nd Strap

Row 1: Working around post of last sts of rows 25–30, join with sl st in row 30, ch 2, hdc in same sp, 2 hdc in next row, [3 hdc in next row, 2 hdc in next row] twice, turn. *(15 hdc)*
Rows 2–10: Rep rows 2–10 of First Strap.

Assembly

Matching row ends, stitch side seams attaching Front and Back Panels. With RS tog, center Front Panel with

170 JACKETS, WRAPS & MORE

Strips 1 and 2 in the middle of Front Panel, st seam tog attaching Front and Back Panels to Strips.

Armhole Trim

Rnd 1: With size C [D, E, F] hook, join with sc in first unworked st at underarm, sc in each of next 11 sts, working in row ends around opening, work 2 sc into each row end, join in beg sc. *(66 sc)*

Rnd 2: Ch 1, sc in same st, sk next 2 sts, 6 dc in next st, sk next 2 sts, [sc in next st, sk next 2 sts, 6 dc in next st, sk next 2 sts] around, join in beg sc, fasten off.
Rep on opposite armhole.

Neckline Trim

Rnd 1: Join with sc in first ch-1 sp of row 30 of Front Panel, sc in each of next 9 ch-1 sps, sc in each of next 2 sts, sc in each of next 10 ch-1 sps, working in row ends of Strap, work 2 sc into each row and 1 sc into seam, working in sts across back, [sc in each of next 4 sts, sc dec in next 2 sts] 4 times, [sc in next st, sc dec in next 2 sts] 3 times, [sc in each of next 4 sts, sc dec in next 2 sts] 3 times, sc in each of next 4 sts, working in row ends of 2nd Strap, work 2 sc into each row and 1 sc into seam, join in beg sc. *(168 sc)*

Rnd 2: Ch 3, 5 dc in same st, [sk next 2 sts, sc in next st, sk next 2 sts, 6 dc in next st] 5 times, [sk next 2 sts, sc in next st] twice, sk next st, sl st in next st, sk next st, sc in next st, [sk next 2 sts, 6 dc in next st, sk next 2 sts, sc in next st, sk next 2 sts] around, join in beg sc, fasten off. ■

SHORT & SEXY TANK CONTINUED FROM PAGE 131

For Sizes Large & X-Large Only
Row 58 [62]: Ch 1, sc dec in next 2 sc, sc in each of next 14 [19] sts, sc in back lps only of next 18 [18] sts, turn. *([33, 38] sts)*
Row 59 [63]: Ch 1, working in back lps only, sc in each of next 18 [18] sts, sc in each of next 15 [20] sts, turn. *([33, 38] sts)*

For Size Large Only
Rows 60–116: Rep rows 2–58. At the end of last rep, turn.

For Size X-Large Only
Row 64: Ch 1, sc dec in next 2 sc, sc in each of next 17 sts, working in back lps only, sc in each of next 18 sts, turn. *([36] sts)*
Row 65: Ch 1, working in back lps, sc in each of next 18 sts only, sc in each of next 18 sts, turn. *([36] sts)*
Rows 66–128: Rep rows 2–64. At the end of last rep, turn.

Joining

Loosely sl st last row of Tank to first row. Fasten off. Sl st shoulder seams closed. Fasten off after each shoulder.

JACKETS, WRAPS & MORE 171

& MORE continued

Armhole Border
Rnd 1 (RS): Attach 2 strands at underarm, ch 1, sc evenly spaced around opening, join in beg sc, fasten off. Rep on opposite armhole.

Neckline Border
Rnd 1 (RS): Attach 2 strands at shoulder seam, ch 1, sc evenly spaced around opening, working sc dec at corners to keep edges flat, join in beg sc, fasten off. ∎

WRAP-TIE TOP CONTINUED FROM PAGE 140

2nd Shoulder Shaping
Row 39 [43, 47, 51]: Sk next 15 sts of row 38 [42, 46, 50], attach yarn in next st, ch 2, work in Pattern Stitch across rem sts, turn. *(10 [12, 14, 16] sts)*
Row 40 [44, 48, 52]: Ch 2, work in Pattern Stitch across 10 [12, 14, 16] sts, fasten off.

Right Front
Row 25 [29, 33, 37]: Attach yarn in next unworked st of row 24 [28, 32, 36], ch 2, dc in same st as beg ch-2, Pattern Stitch across row to last 3 sts, sc in next st, hdc dec in next 2 sts, turn. *(15 [17, 19, 21] sts)*
Row 26 [30, 34, 38]: Work row 2 of Pattern Stitch.
Row 27 [31, 35, 39]: Work row 2 of Pattern Stitch across to last 2 sts, hdc dec in last 2 sts, turn. *(14 [16, 18, 20] sts)*
Row 28 [32, 36, 40]: Rep row 2 of Pattern Stitch.
Row 29 [33, 37, 41]: Rep row 27 [31, 35, 39]. *(13 [15, 17, 19] sts)*
Rows 30–35 [34–39, 38–43, 42–47]: [Rep rows 28 and 29 {32 and 33, 36 and 37, 40 and 41} alternately] 3 times. *(10 [12, 14, 16] sts)*
Rows 36–40 [40–44, 44–48, 48–52]: Rep row 2 of Pattern Stitch. At the end of last rep, fasten off.

Sleeve
Rnd 1: With RS facing, attach yarn at underarm, ch 2, work 34 [34, 36, 36] sc evenly spaced around, join in beg sc, turn. *(34 [34, 36, 36] sc)*
Rnd 2: Ch 1, [sc in next st, dc in next st] around, join in beg sc, turn.
Rnd 3: Ch 1, [sc in each dc, dc in each sc] around, join in beg sc, turn.
Rnds 4–7: Rep rnd 3. At the end of rnd 7, do not turn.
Rnd 8: Ch 1, sc in each sc and each dc around, join in beg sc, fasten off.
Rep on opposite underarm.

Border & Ties
Rnd 1: With RS facing, attach yarn on bottom edge in any st of Back, keeping st markers on each front edge,

172 JACKETS, WRAPS & MORE

ch 1, sc evenly spaced around outer edge, working 5 sc in center of each bottom corner, join in beg sc, do not turn.

Rnd 2: Ch 1, sc in each sc around, working 5 sc in center sc of each 5-sc group and working **sc dec** *(see Stitch Guide)* in each marked st on each side of Front, join in beg sc, do not turn.

Rnd 3: Ch 1, sc in each sc to first 5-sc corner, sc in each of next 2 sc, sl st in next sc, ch 81 *(approximately 30 inches long)*, sc in 2nd ch from hook, sc in each rem ch across, sl st in same sc as first sl st *(first Tie)*, sc in each rem st to st marker, working sc dec at each st marker to next 5-sc corner, sc in each of next 2 sc, sl st in next sc, ch 81, sc in 2nd ch from hook, sc in each rem ch across, sl st in same sc as first sl st *(2nd Tie)*, sc in each rem sc around, join in beg sc, do not turn.

Rnd 4: Ch 1, sc in each sc around to first Tie, *work 2 sc in st before the Tie, holding Tie to front and working behind Tie, work 2 sc in next sc after Tie*, sc in each sc to next Tie, rep between *, sc in each rem st around, join in beg sc, fasten off. ■

CANYON COLORS HAT & SCARF CONTINUED FROM PAGE 152

Rnds 7–9: Rep rnd 3. *(46 dc)*

Rnd 10: Fold elastic thread in 4 strands and tie tog at each end, while leaving an end, hold the 4 strands tog and working over elastic strands, rep rnd 3, fasten off. Weave rem ends of elastic into Hat.

Fur Trim

Rnd 1: With WS facing, attach 2 strands of champagne in any dc of rnd 10, ch 1, sc in same dc as beg ch-1, sc in each dc around, do not join, place marker to mark rnds as work progresses. *(46 sc)*

Rnd 2: Sc in each sc around.

Rnds 3–7: Rep rnd 2. At the end of rnd 7, sl st in next st, fasten off. ■

General Instructions

Please review the following information before working the projects in this book. Important details about the abbreviations and symbols used are included.

Hooks

Crochet hooks are sized for different weights of yarn and thread. For thread crochet, you will usually use a steel crochet hook. Steel crochet-hook sizes range from size 00 to 14. The higher the number of the hook, the smaller your stitches will be. For example, a size 1 steel crochet hook will give you much larger stitches than a size 9 steel crochet hook. Keep in mind that the sizes given with the pattern instructions were obtained by working with the size thread or yarn and hook given in the materials list. If you work with a smaller hook, depending on your gauge, your finished project size will be smaller; if you work with a larger hook, your finished project size will be larger.

Gauge

Gauge is determined by the tightness or looseness of your stitches, and affects the finished size of your project. If you are concerned about the finished size of the project matching the size given, take time to crochet a small section of the pattern and then check your gauge. For example, if the gauge called for is 10 dc = 1 inch, and your gauge is 12 dc to the inch, you should switch to a larger hook. On the other hand, if your gauge is only 8 dc to the inch, you should switch to a smaller hook.

If the gauge given in the pattern is for an entire motif, work one motif and then check your gauge.

Understanding Symbols

As you work through a pattern, you'll quickly notice several symbols in the instructions. These symbols are used to clarify the pattern for you: brackets [], curlicue braces {}, parentheses () and asterisks *.

Brackets [] are used to set off a group of instructions worked a specific number of times. For example, "[ch 3, sc in next ch-3 sp] 7 times" means to work the instructions inside the [] seven times.

Occasionally, a set of instructions inside a set of brackets needs to be repeated, too. In this case, the text within the brackets to be repeated will be set off with curlicue braces {}. For example, "[dc in each of next 3 sts, ch 1, {shell in next ch-1 sp} 3 times, ch 1] 4 times." In this case, in each of the four times you work the instructions included in the brackets, you will work the section included in the curlicue braces three times.

Parentheses () are used to set off a group of stitches to be worked all in one stitch, space or loop. For example, the parentheses () in this set of instructions, "Sk 3 sc, (3 dc, ch 1, 3 dc) in next st" indicate that after skipping 3 sc, you will work 3 dc, ch 1 and 3 more dc all in the next stitch.

Single asterisks * are also used when a group of instructions is repeated. For example, "*Sc in each of the next 5 sc, 2 sc in next sc, rep from * around, join with a sl st in beg sc" simply means you will work the instructions from the first * around the entire round.

Double asterisks ** are used to indicate when a partial set of repeat instructions are to be worked. For example, "*Ch 3, (sc, ch 3, sc) in next ch-2 sp, ch 3**, shell in next dc, rep from * 3 times, ending last rep at **" means that on the third repeat of the single asterisk instructions, you stop at the double asterisks.

Stitch Guide

ABBREVIATIONS

beg	begin/beginning
bpdc	back post double crochet
bpsc	back post single crochet
bptr	back post treble crochet
CC	contrasting color
ch	chain stitch
ch-	refers to chain or space previously made (i.e., ch-1 space)
ch sp	chain space
cl	cluster
cm	centimeter(s)
dc	double crochet
dec	decrease/decreases/decreasing
dtr	double treble crochet
fpdc	front post double crochet
fpsc	front post single crochet
fptr	front post treble crochet
g	gram(s)
hdc	half double crochet
inc	increase/increases/increasing
lp(s)	loop(s)
MC	main color
mm	millimeter(s)
oz	ounce(s)
pc	popcorn
rem	remain/remaining
rep	repeat(s)
rnd(s)	round(s)
RS	right side
sc	single crochet
sk	skip(ped)
sl st	slip stitch
sp(s)	space(s)
st(s)	stitch(es)
tog	together
tr	treble crochet
trtr	triple treble
WS	wrong side
yd(s)	yard(s)
yo	yarn over

Chain—ch: Yo, pull through lp on hook.

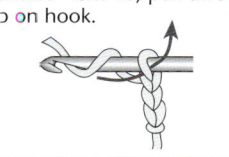

Slip stitch—sl st: Insert hook in st, yo, pull through both lps on hook.

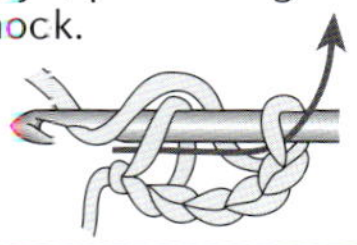

Single crochet—sc: Insert hook in st, yo, pull through st, yo, pull through both lps on hook.

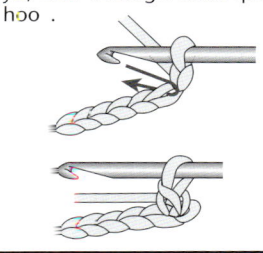

**Front loop—front lp
Back loop—back lp**

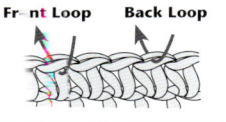

Front Loop   Back Loop

**Front post stitch—fp:
Back post stitch—bp:** When working post st, insert hook from right to left around post st on previous row.

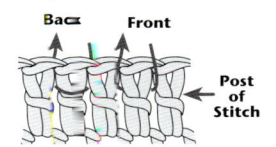

Back   Front
Post of Stitch

Half double crochet—hdc: Yo, insert hook in st, yo, pull through st, yo, pull through all 3 lps on hook.

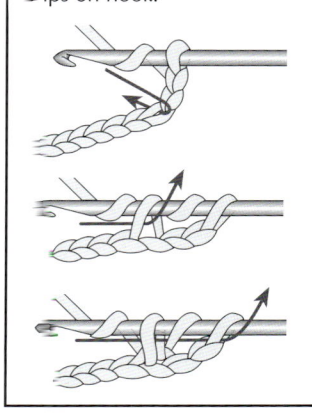

Double crochet—dc: Yo, insert hook in st, yo, pull through st, [yo, pull through 2 lps] twice.

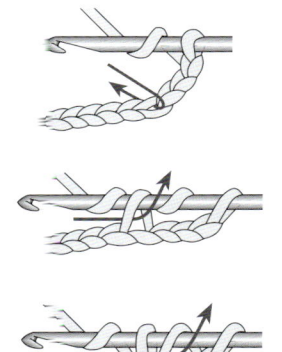

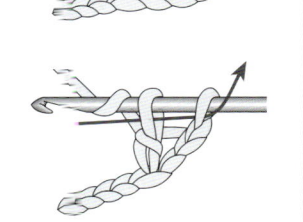

Change colors: Drop first color, with 2nd color, pull through last 2 lps of st.

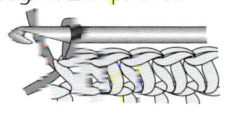

Treble crochet—tr: Yo 2 times, insert hook in st, yo, pull through st, [yo, pull through 2 lps] 3 times.

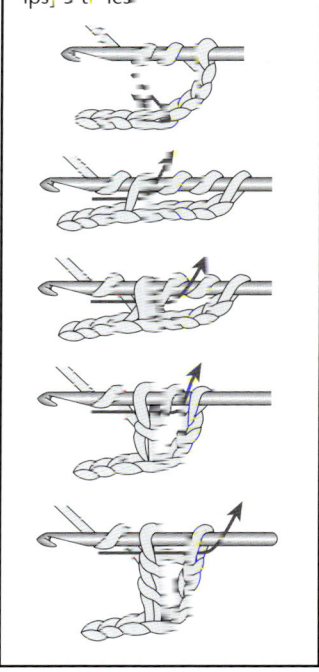

Double treble crochet—dtr: Yo 3 times, insert hook in st, yo, pull through st, [yo, pull through 2 lps] 4 times.

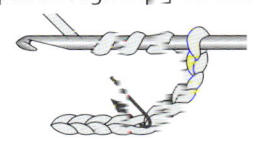

Single crochet decrease (sc dec): (Insert hook, yo, draw up a lp) in each of the sts indicated, yo, draw through all lps on hook.

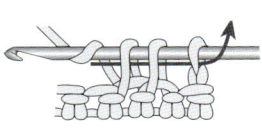

Example of 2-sc dec

Half double crochet decrease (hdc dec): (Yo, insert hook, yo, draw lp through) in each of the sts indicated, yo, draw through all lps on hook.

Example of 2-hdc dec

Double crochet decrease (dc dec): (Yo, insert hook, yo, draw lp through, yo, draw through 2 lps on hook) in each of the sts indicated, yo, draw through all lps on hook.

Example of 2-dc dec

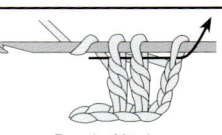

Treble crochet decrease (tr dec): Holding back last lp of each st, tr in each of the sts indicated, yo, pull through all lps on hook.

Example of 2-tr dec

US		UK
sl st (slip stitch)	=	sc (single crochet)
sc (single crochet)	=	dc (double crochet)
hdc (half double crochet)	=	htr (half treble crochet)
dc (double crochet)	=	tr (treble crochet)
tr (treble crochet)	=	dtr (double treble crochet)
dtr (double treble crochet)	=	ttr (triple treble crochet)
skip	=	miss

JACKETS, WRAPS & MORE

Special Thanks

Svetlana Avrakh
Cool Class Dress &
    Shoulder Cover

Colette Blair
Hot Summer Nights

Joyce Bragg
Clam Shell Purse
Hot Pants Set
Kiwi Vest & Headband
Ruffled Shoulder Wrap

Belinda "Bendy" Carter
Beaded Mesh Scarf

Sue Childress
Glam Gal Hat & Purse
Starlight Scarf
Very Victorian

Carolyn Christmas
Cowl-Neck Sweater

Terry Day
Ladybug & Victorian Boot Pins

DMC Corp.
Perfect in Plum Coat

JoHanna Dzikowski
Moonlight Magic

Katherine Eng
Ladder-Stitch Cloche

Nazanin Fard
Triangles Shawl

Laura Gebhardt
Enchanted Evening

Lisa Gonzalez
Confetti Cover-up
Cut-Away Cardi

Mary Jane Hall
Earth Child

Darla Hassell
Cowl-Neck Sweater

Lainie Hering
Gold Nugget Cocktail Cover-Up

Tammy Hildebrand
Granny Square Dress & Jacket
Lacy Pineapples Shell

Suede Fringed Vest

Jewdy Lambert
City Lights Vest
Cozy Café Au Lait Shrug
Peekaboo Poncho
Seaside Scallops Reversible Bag

Mary Layfield
Foiled Heart Necklace

Melissa Leapman
Shawl-Collared Cardigan

Zena Low
Earthy Glow Tunic Vest

Marty Miller
Granny Square Shrink Vest
Loopy Jacket
Short & Sexy Tank
Tabard Jacket
Wrap-Tie Top

Shirley Patterson
Classy Continental Hat

Mary Jane Protus
    for Coats & Clark
Sunset Poncho

Josie Rabier
Lilac Shawl

Darla Sims
Cropped Bomber Jacket
Fashion Flower Pins
Sleeveless Shorty Vest
Sweater For a Special Everning

Brenda Stratton
Hidden Treasures Scarf

Aline Suplinskas
Canyon Colors Hat & Scarf

Mary Beth Temple
Ruby Goes to Town

Julene Watson
Flower Purse

Kathryn White
Butterflies & Roses Filet Shawl

Glenda Winkleman
Bead-dazzling Purse

Buyer's Guide

Berroco Inc.
P. O. Box 367
14 Elmdale Road
Uxbridge, MA 01569-0367
(508) 278-2527
www.berroco.com

Classic Elite Yarns
122 Western Ave.
Lowell, MA 01851
(978) 453-2837
www.classiceliteyarns.com

Coats & Clark
(Red Heart, Moda Dea, Aunt Lydia's, TLC, J&P Coats)
Consumer Services
P.O. Box 12229
Greenville, SC 29612-0229
(800) 648-1479
www.coatsandclark.com
www.modadea.com

DMC Corp.
77 S. Hackensack Ave.
Port Kearny Building 10A
South Kearny, NJ 07032
(800) 275-4117
www.dmc.com

King Cole LTD
Merrie Mills
Elliott Street
Silsden, Keighly
West Yorkshire, BD20 ODE
UK
01535 650230
www.kingcole.co.uk

Knitting Fever Inc.
(On Line Yarns
Araucania Yarn)
P. O. Box 336
315 Bayview Ave.
Amityville, NY 11701
(516) 546-3600
www.knittingfever.com

Lion Brand Yarn
135 Kero Road
Carlstadt, NJ 07072
(800) 258-9276
www.lionbrand.com

Nova Yarn
(Grignasco Yarn)
155 Martin Ross, Unit 3
Toronto, ON M3J 2L9
CANADA
(416) 736-6111
www.novayarn.com

Plymouth Yarn Co., Inc.
P. O. Box 28
Bristol, PA 19007
(215) 788-0459
www.plymouthyarn.com

Sirdar Spinning Ltd
Flanshaw Lane
Wakefield
West Yorkshire
WF2 9ND
UK
+44(0) 1924 371501

Spinrite Yarns
(Bernat, Patons)
320 Livingstone Ave. South
Listowel, ON
Canada
N4W 3H3
(888) 368-8401
www.bernat.com
www.patonsyarns.com

S. R. Kertzer
c/o PMB 192
60 Industrial Parkway
Cheektowaga, NY 14227
(866) 444-1250
www.kertzer.com

Tahki-Stacy Charles, Inc.
70-30 80th St. Building 36
Ridgeway, NY 11385
(800) 388-9276
www.takistacycharles.com

SCIENCE SPOTLIGHT
STAGE AND SCREEN

Ian Graham

Evans

Evans Brothers Limited

Evans Brothers Limited
2A Portman Mansions
Chiltern Street
London W1M 1LE

© Evans Brothers Limited 1995

All rights reserved. No part of this publication may be reproduced, stored in a retrieval system or transmitted in any form or by any means, electronic, mechanical, photocopying, recording or otherwise, without prior permission of Evans Brothers Limited.

First published 1995

Printed in Hong Kong by Dah Hua Printing Co. Ltd

ISBN 0 237 51453 2

Editor: Su Swallow
Designer: Neil Sayer
Production: Jenny Mulvanny
Illustrations: Hardlines, Charlbury
　　　　　　　　Graeme Chambers

Acknowledgements

The author and publishers would like to thank the following people: Hibbert Ralph Animation, Dolby Laboratories Inc, IMAX Systems Corporation, The National Theatre, Theatretech Ltd., Sue Watts of the Really Useful Group Limited
Cover (top) Aquarius Picture Library, (bottom) Science Photo Library **Page 4** (top) Clive Barda, Performing Arts Library (bottom) Sue Hyman Associates Ltd, **page 5** (top) BBC Library and Archive, (bottom) Oscar Burriel, Latin Stock, Science Photo Library **page 6** (top) Martyn F Chillmaid, Robert Harding Picture Library, (bottom)NMPFT, Science and Society Picture Library **page 7** (left) British Museum, Robert Harding Picture Library, (right) Mary Evans Picture Library **page 8** (top) The Hulton-Deutsch Collection, (bottom left) Aquarius Library, (bottom right) NMPFT, Science and Society Picture Library **page 9** (top) The Ronald Grant Archive, (bottom left) The Hulton Deustch Collection, (bottom right) NMPFT, Science and Society Picture Library **page 10** (top) Jaime Villaseca, The Image Bank, (bottom) The Hulton Deutsch Collection **page 11** British Film Institute **page 12** IMAX **page 13** (top) IMAX, (bottom) Strand Lighting **page 14** (top) Dolby, (bottom) Aquarius Picture Library **page 15** (top) Dolby, (bottom) Aquarius Picture Library **page 16** (top and middle) The Ronald Grant Archive, (bottom) Hibbert Ralph Entertainment Ltd/BBC **page 17** Hibbert Ralph Entertainment Ltd/BBC **page 18** Nigel Francis **page 19** (top) The Ronald Grant Archive, (bottom) New Scientist **page 20** (top) Brtish Film Institute, (bottom) The Ronald Grant Archive **page 21** The Ronald Grant Archive **page 22** British Film Institute **page 23** (top) Aquarius Library, (bottom) British Film Institute **page 24** (top) British Film Institute, (bottom) Aquarius Library **page 25** North Parsons **page 26** The Ronald Grant Archive **page 27** Ronald Grant Archive **page 28** (top) Oscar Burriel, Latin Stock, Science Photo Library, (bottom) Francois Sauze, Science Photo Library **page 29** Strand Lighting **page 30** (middle and bottom left) Philippe Plailly, Science Photo Library, (bottom right) NMPFT, Science and Society Picture Library **page 31** (top) The Hutchison Library, (bottom) Adam Woolfitt, Robert Harding Picture Library **page 32** Peter Menzel, Science Photo Library **page 33** (top) Jerry Mason, Science Photo Library, (bottom) Claude Charlier, Science Photo Library **page 34** Peter Menzel, Science Photo Library **page 35** James King-Holmes, Science Photo Library **page 36** (top) Fritz Curzon, Performing Arts Library, (bottom) Clive Barda, Performing Arts Library **page 37** (top) Mark Douet, Performing Arts Library, (bottom) Strand Lighting **page 38** Strand Lighting **page 39** (top) Adam Woolfitt, Robert Harding Picture Library, (bottom) Simon Wilkinson, The Image Bank **pages 40 and 41** The Really Useful Group **page 42 and 43** Clive Barda, Performing Arts Library

Contents

Introduction 4
Moving pictures 6
Cinema today 10
Surround sound 14
Animation 16
Trick shots 20
Computer movies 26
Television 28
Virtual reality 34
Treading the boards 36
Glossary 44
Index 44

Introduction

STORYTELLERS, PUPPETEERS, ACTORS, dancers and singers have entertained people in their various ways all over the world for thousands of years. At the beginning of the twentieth century, scientific discoveries and advances in technology made new forms of entertainment possible, namely cinema and television, and brought traditional entertainments to a much wider audience. Lasers harvest high quality music from silver discs. Computers create colourful characters that dance across a screen as games players expertly operate their controls.

In a theatre auditorium, little can be seen of the hi-tech machinery needed for lighting, sound, scenery and special effects.

AS COMPUTERS HAVE BECOME MORE POWERFUL and less expensive, programmers have been able to create increasingly complex games. The ultimate computer trip must be virtual reality, in which the computer hijacks the games player's real world and creates a new one.

Every form of entertainment has been influenced by the computer's information storage and processing capacity – none more so than film and television special effects. 'Special effects' usually conjures up mental images of movie monsters, robots, spacecraft gliding past planets or death rays zapping space troopers. But special effects have been used in the theatre for hundreds of years before the first film was made. As soon as moving pictures were invented, film-makers began experimenting with the new freedom that film gave them, and that included photographic

In the musical *Starlight Express* a huge overhead ramp allows performers to skate off the stage and round the back of the audience.

special effects.

In recent years, computers have revolutionised special effects. Nowadays, pictures produced by computers are so lifelike and indistinguishable from photographs that film-makers can create almost any image they wish and mix the computer-generated images seamlessly with live action filmed in the normal way.

Stage & Screen reveals the science and technology used by the entertainment industry. **History Spotlight** features throughout the book focus on important people, discoveries and events in the history of stage and screen entertainment.

A television drama is filmed by a camera mounted on a dolly, a wheeled support which allows the camera to be moved round smoothly.

The first TV picture was produced in 1925.

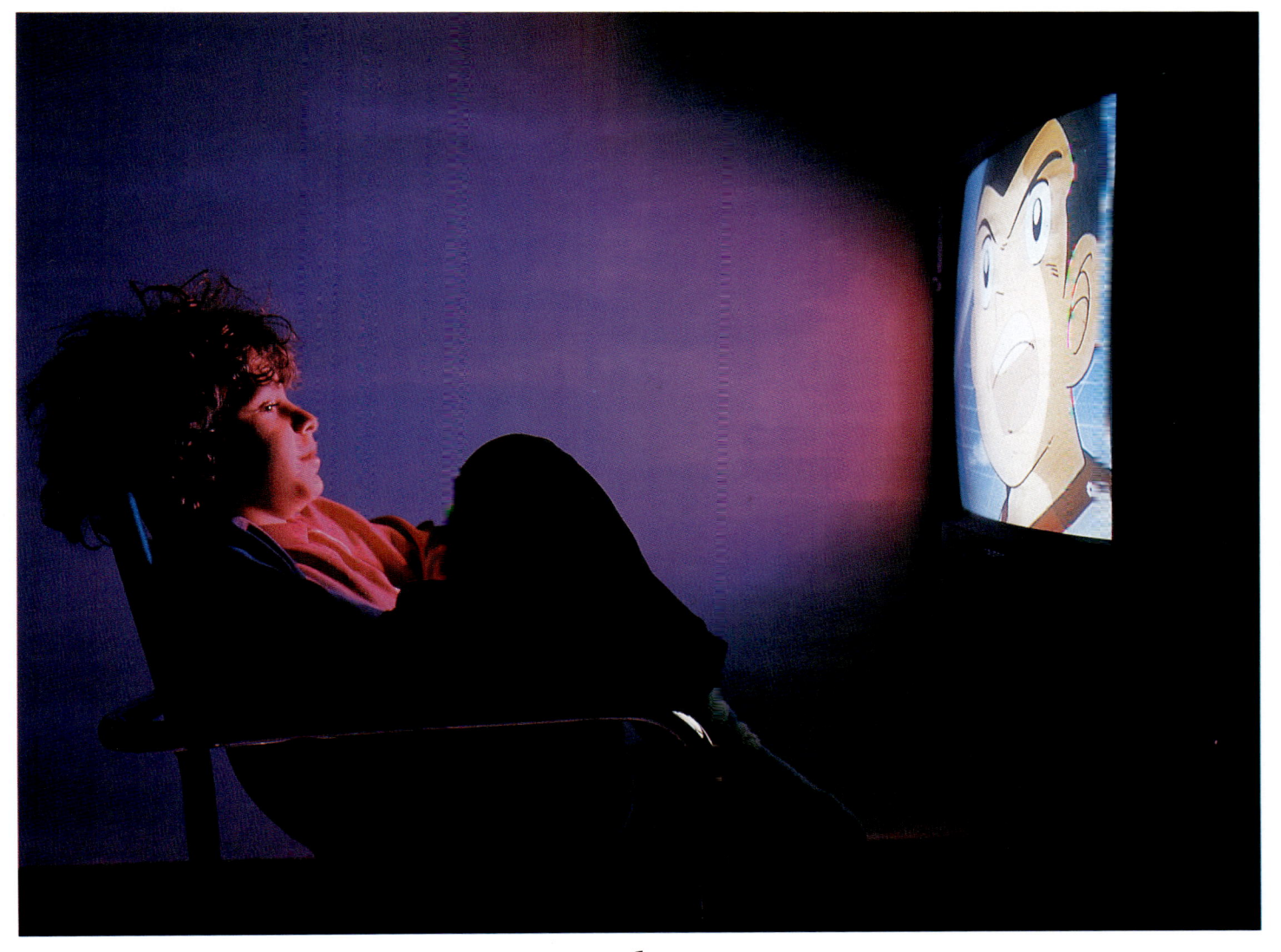

5

Moving pictures

THE SIMPLEST OBSERVATIONS or experiments have often led to dramatic developments in science and technology. In 1765 a Frenchman, Chevalier d'Arcy, tied a glowing coal to a wheel and started it spinning. He noted that the glowing coal left a trail of light as it whirled around. How did this simple observation lead to the first movies in little more than 100 years?

PEOPLE HAD KNOWN FOR THOUSANDS OF YEARS that when a glowing branch from a fire was whirled around, it seemed to have a short trail of light behind it. Chevalier d'Arcy applied a scientist's brain to this ancient observation and realised the reason for the glowing trail. It was that the brain retained the image of the glowing coal for a fraction of a second after the eye had registered it.

By the 1820s, scientists were investigating this phenomenon, which became known as persistence of vision. Toymakers used persistence of vision to make toys that created the illusion of movement where none existed. They came in all shapes and sizes and tended to have long complicated names, like the Praxinoscope or Phenakistoscope, but they all worked in the same way. A series of drawings or paintings was stuck to the edge of a disc or the inside of an open drum. Each picture showed a person or animal in a slightly different

Some of the earliest moving images on a screen were produced by shadow puppets. The puppets were operated behind a screen, and a light behind the puppets cast dark moving shadows.

Two 19th-century toys which produced moving images: a Praxinoscope (below) and a Zoetrope (right)

position from the preceding picture. When the disc or drum was spun around on an axle and the pictures were viewed through slits in the disc or drum, each picture was seen for a fraction of a second. The brain retained each picture for just long enough to bridge the gap until the next picture appeared and they all merged together to give the illusion of a single moving picture.

The first photograph

IN 1839, THE INVENTION OF PHOTOGRAPHY provided a way of replacing the pictures in these toys with photographs of actual people and animals. The early cameras recorded pictures on glass plates treated to make them sensitive to light. But they needed an exposure of at least several seconds to register a single picture. Everything in front of the camera had to remain absolutely stationary during this time or the photograph would be blurred.

By the 1870s faster film that could record an image in a fraction of a second was available. The eccentric English-born photography pioneer, Eadweard Muybridge, invented a way of taking a series of photographs in rapid succession. He built a short track with threads strung across it at intervals. As something moved along the track, a galloping horse for example, it broke the threads one after another. Each thread was linked to a different camera and as each thread broke, it operated the camera shutter and took a picture. The result was a series of pictures, each taken a fraction of a second apart. Muybridge's 'sequence photography' as it was called, revealed details of movement never seen before because it froze blindingly fast motion in a series of time-slices that could be studied at length.

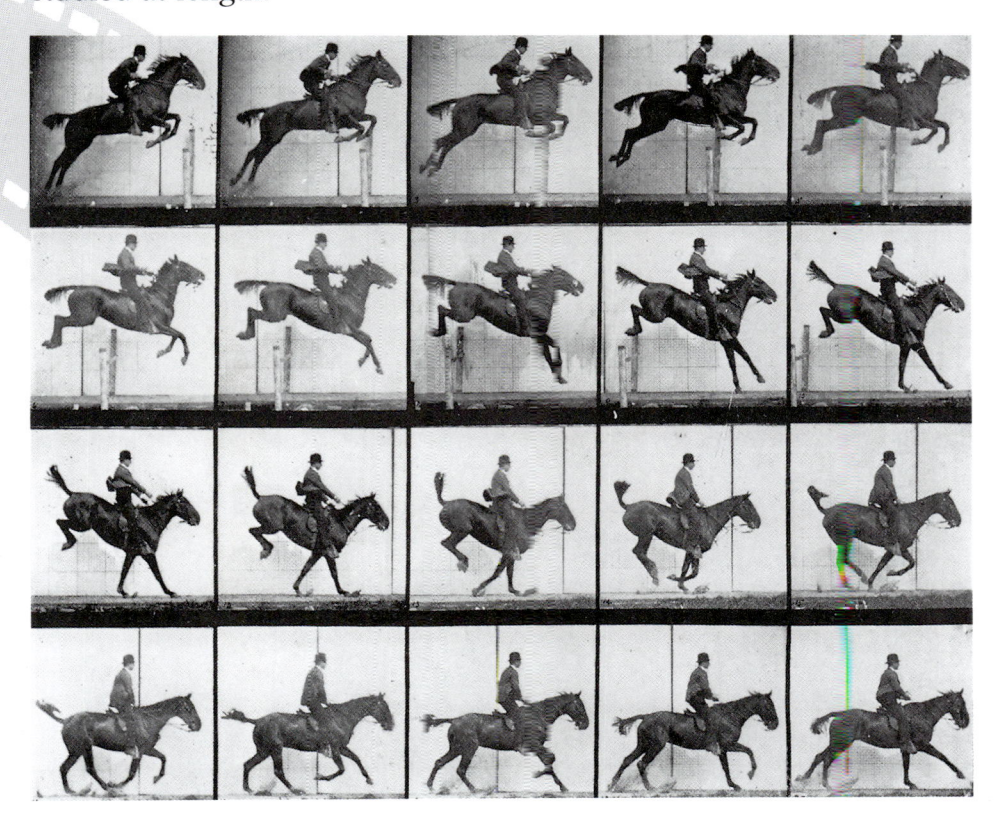

HISTORY SPOTLIGHT

MUYBRIDGE'S SEQUENCE photography settled a long-standing argument amongst horse-racing enthusiasts. Half of them thought that a trotting horse always had at least one foot on the ground. The other half were equally certain that at times all four of the horse's feet left the ground. The problem could only be resolved by Muybridge because the horse's trotting action was too fast to be seen clearly by the unaided eye. Leland Stanford, the former governor of California and President of the Central Pacific Railroad, asked Muybridge to photograph a horse in an attempt to settle the argument. In May 1872, Muybridge set up his equipment at the Union Park racecourse in Sacramento, California, and photographed a horse called Occident. The first attempt was unsuccessful because the photographic process was not sensitive enough to freeze the horse's leg action. In April 1873, a second attempt was successful. The photographs clearly showed that the horse lifted all four feet off the ground as it trotted along.

Eadweard Muybridge

A horse and rider in action, taken by Muybridge in 1887.

From stills to movies

INSPIRED BY THE WORK OF MUYBRIDGE and others, the American inventor Thomas Alva Edison made the first motion picture camera in 1891. He called it a Kinetograph. It used George Eastman's newly developed celluloid roll film (see page 11). Films made using it were viewed using a Kinetoscope. Only one person at a time could peer through Kinetoscope's eyepieces and see the film.

Meanwhile in France two brothers, Auguste and Louis Lumière, set about finding a way of showing films to larger audiences. They invented a device called a cinématographe that could be used as a camera to make a film and, when the film was developed, it could also be used as a projector to show the film on a screen. Its unique feature was a pair of claws that caught in holes along the edge of the film and pulled it through the mechanism one frame at a time. By showing their films to paying audiences, Auguste and Louis Lumière had invented the cinema.

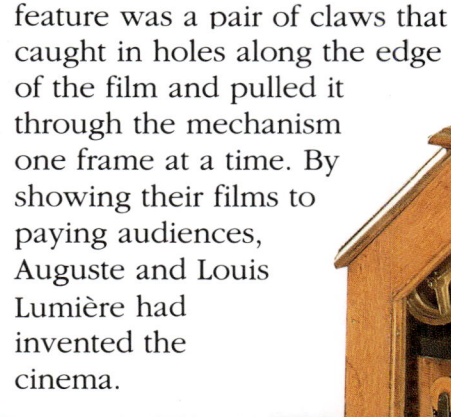

Thomas Edison, with his motion picture camera

Inside a Kinetoscope (above), showing the strip of film. (Left) Edison's Kinetoscope parlours opened in the USA in April 1894.

The talkies

EARLY FILMS WERE MADE WITHOUT SOUND. Each time an actor on the screen said something, his or her words would appear printed on the screen for a few moments. In the 1890s, film makers tried recording sound on a wax disc and playing it while the film was showing. It was not a great success. The speed of the disc and the speed of the film could not be controlled and matched accurately enough. How could words be synchronised with the actors' lip movements more closely?

Sound-on-film

THE ANSWER was to record the sound directly on to the film. Most films today have an optical soundtrack. Two thin clear strips down one side of the film carry all the information needed to recreate all the movie's speech, music and sound effects. As the film runs through the projector, a light shines through the clear strips on to two photocells, which convert the light into electricity. The varying width of the strips constantly changes the amount of light that gets through to the photocells and therefore varies the electrical signals they produce. When these are amplified, they reproduce the rich texture of sounds that accompany the pictures

The cinématographe was a camera and a projector.

HISTORY SPOTLIGHT

THE OLDEST SURVIVING FILM was made by the Frenchman Louis-Aimé-Augustin Le Prince in 1888. It shows traffic crossing a bridge in Leeds, England. Le Prince's first camera had 16 lenses arranged in a 4 x 4 square. Two rolls of light-sensitive paper were fixed behind the lenses. The first eight shutters were opened electrically one after another. Then, while that film was wound on until a new piece lay behind the lenses, the second group of eight lenses were opening one by one and exposing the second roll of film. When the paper was developed, the rolls were cut up into separate pictures which had to be fixed together in the right order before the film could be shown. Le Prince later developed a single lens camera which used just one roll of sensitized paper. On September 16th 1890, he boarded a train in Paris bound for Dijon, but he never arrived and was never seen again. No one has ever been able to explain what happened to him.

The oldest surviving film – traffic on a bridge in Leeds shot by Le Prince – and (right) Le Prince's single lens camera

9

Cinema today

A reel of 35mm motion picture film

THE FIRST PHOTOGRAPHIC ROLL FILM was 35mm wide. Most modern movies are still made on 35mm film, but dozens of other formats have been used. Some wide-screen formats simply used wider film or several films shown side by side, but others used technical trickery to squeeze wide-screen pictures on to normal film.

IN 1900, THE PARIS EXHIBITION featured a magical balloon ride that never left the ground! The balloon's 'passengers' looked out from their fake balloon basket at a screen that completely encircled them, while ten projectors underneath them recreated what they would have seen on a flight over Europe's great capital cities. Cinéorama, as it was called, was the world's first multi-screen system. In 1952 Cinerama was developed in the USA. Cinerama films were shot by three 35mm cameras side by side. The three separate films were shown side by side in the cinema by three projectors so that they joined together to form one wide picture on a huge screen more than 16 metres across and eight metres high.

A drawing showing the inside of Cinéorama. You can see the projectors and the images watched by the audience in the balloon's gondola.

CinemaScope trickery: an image is squashed on to 35mm film by a special lens (below) and a projector lens spreads the image out again to produce a wide-screen picture (right).

The wide screen

CINERAMA'S TECHNICAL COMPLEXITY meant that it never became very popular, but its big screen picture excited audiences and movie makers alike. Cinerama pictures were more than twice as wide as their height compared to a normal 35mm picture which is a third wider than its height. What movie makers and cinemas really wanted was a widescreen film format that could be shown in ordinary cinemas without having to use special projectors or specially shaped screens. In 1953, the film company Twentieth Century Fox introduced CinemaScope. This used optical trickery to squeeze a wide-screen picture on to normal 35mm film. A specially shaped camera lens called an anamorphic lens squashed a wider than normal image on to standard 35mm film. In the cinema, a projector lens designed to work in the opposite way to the camera lens spread the squashed-up image out again to produce a wide-screen picture almost two and a half times wider than it is high.

HISTORY SPOTLIGHT

THE PAPER, AND LATER CELLULOID, roll film that George Eastman invented at the end of the 19th century was 35mm wide. Why was it 35mm wide and not 30mm or 50mm? Before he made roll film, Eastman made glass photographic plates. He started with a sheet of window glass and repeatedly cut it in half until he had lots of small glass plates the size he wanted. When he started making roll film, he chose the same picture size as the glass plates. So, the width of the film used to make movies at the end of the 20th century is based on the size of window glass on sale in America more than 100 years ago!

George Eastman (left) with Thomas Edison

The BIG screen

THE BIGGEST CINEMA PICTURES are produced by the biggest film frame there has ever been. The IMAX format creates pictures as tall as a seven-storey building from 70mm-wide film! Other movie formats have used 70mm film before, but they ran it through the camera and projector vertically, creating pictures above one another. The width of each frame is therefore limited by the width of the film. IMAX runs the film through horizontally, so that the frames are side by side and there is no limit to the frame width. The IMAX frame is ten times the size of a standard 35mm film frame. The audience sits close to the screen in steeply inclined seating, so that the picture on the screen fills their field of view and they are not aware of the screen's edges. Each person in the audience is totally immersed in the image before him or her.

IMAX movies are specially filmed with IMAX cameras to be shown in specially constructed IMAX theatres. IMAX cameras have to be tough and reliable because they are used in more extreme conditions than most movie cameras. They have been blasted into space on-board a space shuttle, strapped to the tail of an aircraft, and plunged into the ocean to capture some of the most breathtaking images ever seen in the cinema.

IMAX projectors are the most powerful ever built. They use a unique way of moving the film through the mechanism. Instead of claws or toothed wheels pulling the film along by the sprocket holes along its edges, an IMAX film advances in a series of rolling loops in a smooth wave-like motion that resembles a caterpillar. As each frame passes behind the lens, it is sucked into position to produce a rock-steady picture on the screen.

In one version of IMAX, called OMNIMAX, the film is projected on to the inside of a

Inside an IMAX cinema in Ohio, USA. On screen, an image from the IMAX film *Titanica*.

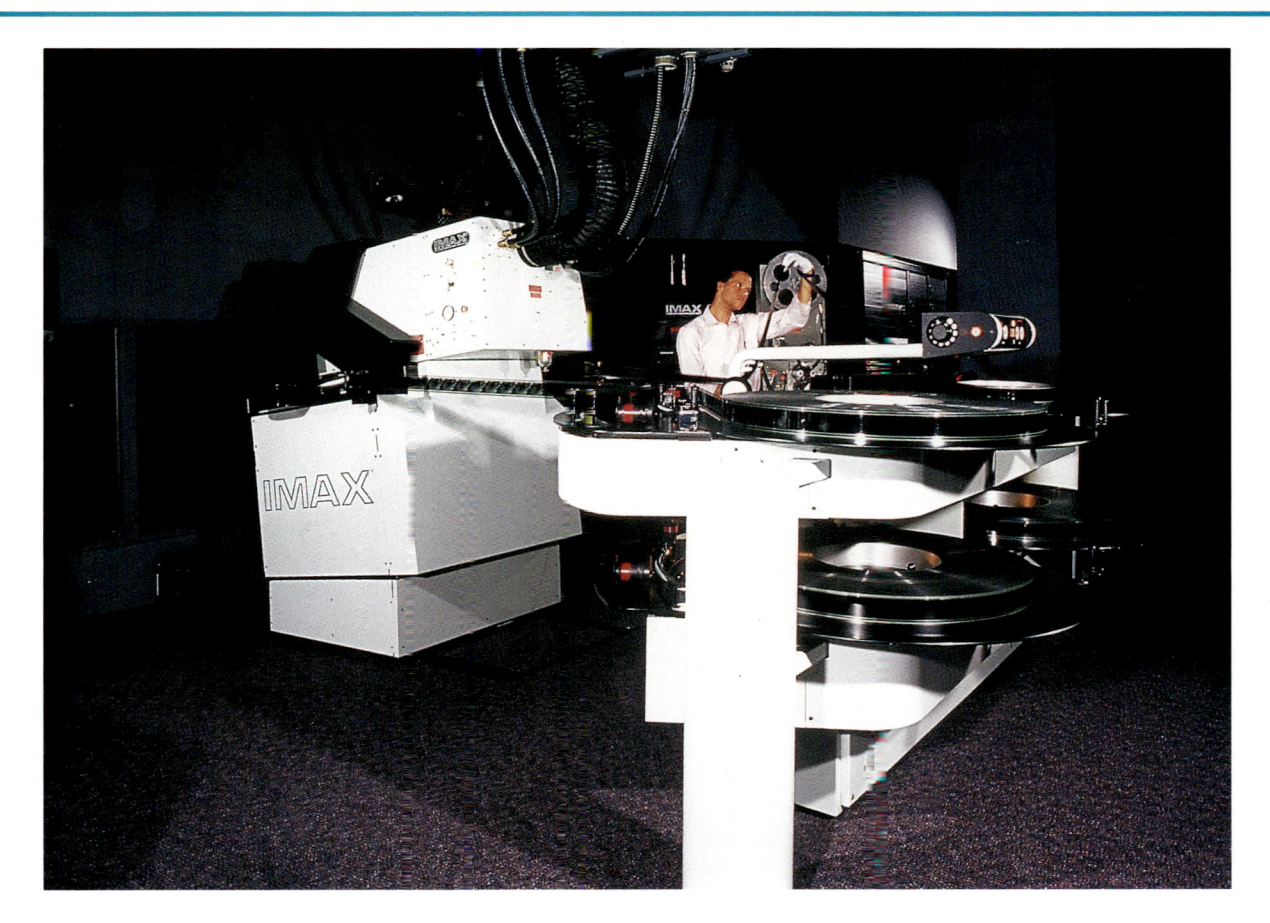

An operator checks a film on the powerful IMAX projector.

dome above the audience. The ideal position for the projector is in the middle of the audience, but the projector and the spools that supply it with film are enormous pieces of equipment. To avoid having to take out too many seats to accommodate them, the projection room is built underneath the theatre. Once the film is threaded through the equipment, the projector is raised up into a tiny housing in the middle of the seating, but the film spools stay down below in the projection room.

Films, plays and operas can be relayed to large crowds in the open air on huge mobile screens while a smaller audience is watching the same performance inside the theatre. Fans in Hollywood could watch the premiere of Arnold Schwarzenegger's *The Last Action Hero* outside while the press and invited audience enjoyed the film in the theatre.

13

Surround sound

The digital soundtrack for today's films is recorded in blocks between the sprocket holes.

MOVIE MAKERS TRY TO MAKE AUDIENCES BELIEVE they are part of the world in which a film is set. Big screens help to create that illusion, but sound has to play its part too. How can cinema sound possibly mimic the real world, where different sounds come at us from all directions?

IT IS EASY TO SURROUND an audience with sound. Loudspeakers placed all around the audience can play the soundtrack from every angle. But this isn't what happens in the real world and it doesn't fool the audience. We never hear precisely the same sounds from every direction – as sounds spread out, they are reflected by some objects and absorbed by others.

In the 1950s, some films were released with stereo soundtracks. Unlike stereo music at home, which has two channels (left and right), these 'stereo' film soundtracks had at least four separate sound channels. More than two were needed because of the width of the cinema screen. An ordinary stereo soundtrack would sound right only to people in the middle of the theatre. Anyone in seats at either side of the theatre would hear the sound from that side only. The extra sound channels filled in the space between the two sides and allowed more people to enjoy the sound as it was meant to be heard.

The sound was recorded on magnetic strips running down each side of the film. Many of these early stereo films had one additional sound channel that was intended to be played through loudspeakers at the back of the theatre. It was used occasionally for eerie effects to make the audience's spine tingle. Film makers gradually used this rear channel more and more to create a more natural soundtrack. It sounded more natural because the audience heard sounds coming from different directions, more like the real world.

HISTORY SPOTLIGHT

MULTICHANNEL SOUND IN THE CINEMA dates back to the 1940s. When Walt Disney was planning a new animated film to follow the hugely successful *Snow White and the Seven Dwarfs*, he wanted to produce the world's most exciting adventure in animation. When Disney heard a recording of some of the film's music, he felt that it did not recreate the rich texture of sounds produced by an orchestra, so he set about designing a new sound system. Disney's cartoon film *Fantasia*, released in 1941, was the first film with stereo sound to be shown to the public. The first film to use sound from rear speakers was a horror film called *House of Wax*, released in 1953.

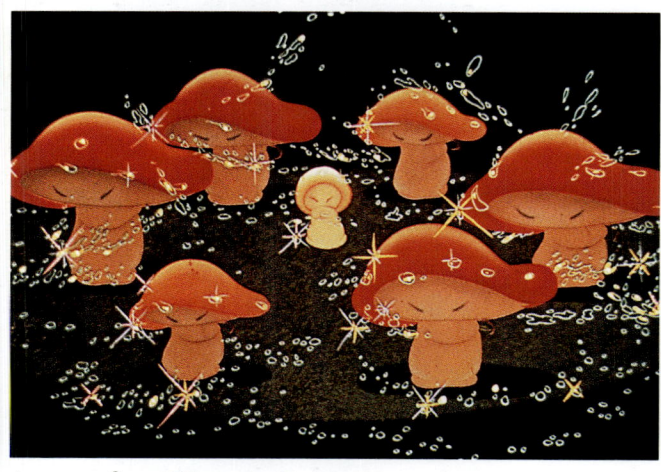

A scene from Disney's *Fantasia*

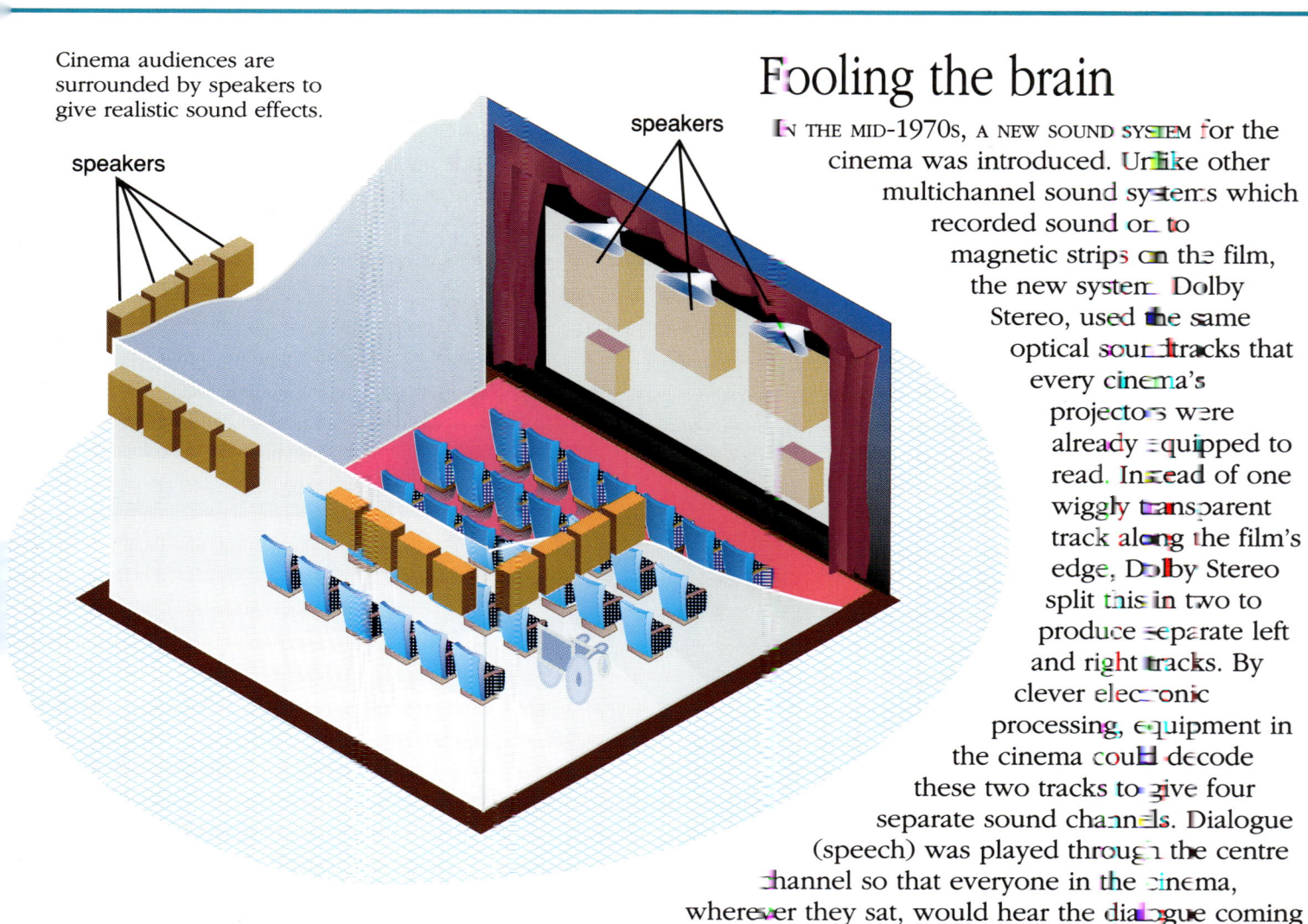

Cinema audiences are surrounded by speakers to give realistic sound effects.

speakers

speakers

Close Encounters of the Third Kind (below) and *Star Wars*, released in 1977, were the first blockbuster movies to have a Dolby Stereo soundtrack. They made such a big impression that every major film since then has been made in Dolby Stereo.

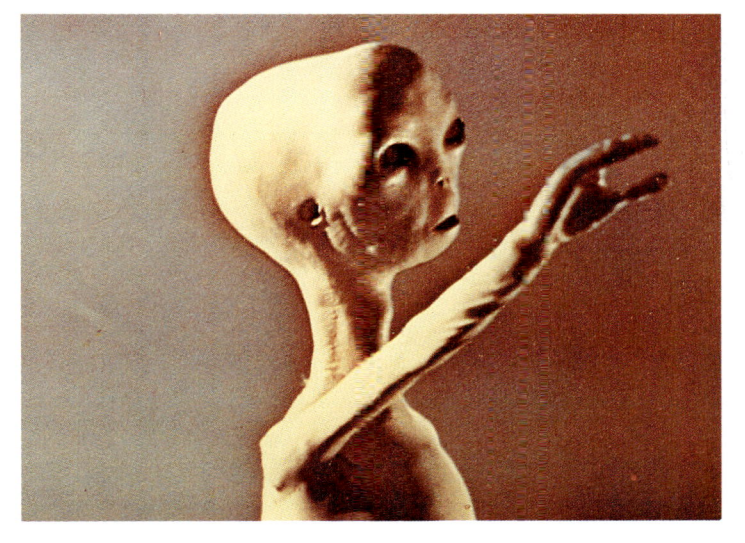

Fooling the brain

IN THE MID-1970S, A NEW SOUND SYSTEM for the cinema was introduced. Unlike other multichannel sound systems which recorded sound on to magnetic strips on the film, the new system, Dolby Stereo, used the same optical soundtracks that every cinema's projectors were already equipped to read. Instead of one wiggly transparent track along the film's edge, Dolby Stereo split this in two to produce separate left and right tracks. By clever electronic processing, equipment in the cinema could decode these two tracks to give four separate sound channels. Dialogue (speech) was played through the centre channel so that everyone in the cinema, wherever they sat, would hear the dialogue coming from the centre of the screen. Most of the music and background sounds were played through the left and right channels. The fourth channel played sound effects through loudspeakers at the back of the cinema.

The brain assumes that sounds come from whichever direction they are heard from first. Later reflections are ignored. This is called the Haas effect. Dolby Stereo decoders make use of this by inserting a time delay of 15-30 milliseconds between the front and rear speakers to ensure that any sounds from the front speakers that 'leak' into the rear speakers are not heard. If the delay is any longer than 20-30 milliseconds, the Haas effect doesn't work and the brain hears the delayed sound as an echo.

During the last 15 years, there has been another revolution in sound recording technology. Vinyl records have largely been replaced by Compact Discs (CDs) on which sound is recorded as millions of digital impulses instead of a groove in a disc. Dolby Stereo has moved on too. When *Batman Returns* was released in 1992, it was the first of many Hollywood films to have a digital soundtrack. The film contains an extra soundtrack printed between its sprocket holes.

Animation

FILM CAMERAS NORMALLY CHOP UP live action into thousands of frozen still frames. Animation turns this process on its head. Thousands of separate pictures, each slightly different from the one before, are photographed one by one in sequence to bring cartoon characters to life. New technology is now helping to speed up the process.

Daffy Duck made his first screen appearance in 1936.

PRODUCING A CARTOON FILM in the traditional way is a long, laborious process. The film has to be planned in meticulous detail to make sure that the story works well before artists paint every frame on a clear plastic sheet called a cel. As the finished film will be shown at 24 frames per second, a five-minute cartoon contains more than 7,000 frames and a feature-length cartoon film like Disney's *Beauty and the Beast*, 81 minutes long, is composed of more than 116,000 frames!

In a live action movie, like *Superman* or *Raiders of the Lost Ark*, the camera often moves as it films a scene. A moving camera makes the picture more interesting, leading the eye to different parts of the image, following the action from place to place. Some animated films involving puppets include scenes that look as if the camera was moving. In fact, the camera is stationary when each frame is photographed, but to simulate a moving camera, it is shifted a fraction after each frame is photographed. When the film is projected at normal speed, all the tiny movements of the camera between the frames add together.

Once a script is ready, the director works out a storyboard, a series of images showing the main stages in the story. This is the storyboard for Walt Disney's *Sleeping Beauty* (1959).

The camera used to photograph the cels that make up a cartoon film doesn't move either, but the artist can simulate a

Before the artists can get to work, the director works out character models – front, back and side views – for the artists to follow.

Once the characters have been worked out, the artists can prepare detailed pencil drawings (right), which can then be painted (below), backgrounds are painted (far right) and the characters placed over the backgrounds (bottom).

moving camera by changing the point of view of each painting. It's difficult to do, because the artist has to work out not only how the characters move from frame to frame, but also how their appearance should change if they were being filmed by a camera that is itself moving. Not only that, everything in the background has to be drawn from a slightly different angle in each frame. That's difficult to do, even for an experienced artist, but computers can help.

© Hibbert Ralph Entertainment

An animator drawing at his desk fitted with a lightbox. His outline will then be transferred to clear film (a cel) and painted.

In the paint and trace department, an artist paints an image on a cel. Sometimes one artist paints the backgrounds and another the characters.

Once all the cels have been painted they are shot in the right order to make the film. Here, an editor checks the film on screen.

The magic carpet in *Aladdin* was created by computer.

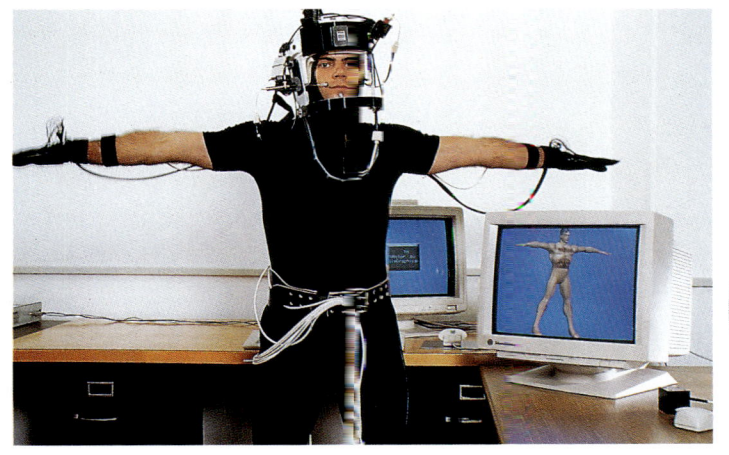

A character on the screen is animated by an actor who is linked to a computer by sensors.

Computer animation

THE COMPUTERS USED BY ENGINEERS, car designers and architects are very good at turning objects round on the computer's screen so that they can be seen from any angle – just what animators need to produce exciting cartoon animations. In Disney's *Aladdin*, Aladdin's magic carpet stood up and twisted and turned, behaving like a real character. Its complicated pattern would have been almost impossible for an artist to animate. Instead, a painting of the flat carpet was fed into a computer and the computer twisted the carpet and its complicated pattern into the required shapes.

Follow the leader

IT IS ALSO POSSIBLE FOR CHARACTERS to be animated 'in real time'. The person controlling the character can think of a movement or something to say and, without any panning or painting, the character instantly performs the movement or says the words.

The secret is that there is an actor sitting out of sight and wearing a special headset linked to a computer. Sensors attached to the actor's face pick up changes in facial expressions and send this information to a computer which animates the character on the screen so that it produces the same expressions.

Trick shots

SOME OF THE EARLY FILM MAKERS wanted to show their audiences something magical, something that seemed impossible. Over the years, they perfected the basic special effects techniques and continually improved them. How did these pioneers of film special effects make people gasp with amazement?

A scene from *L'Homme à la tête de caoutchouc*, showing one of the earliest trick shots in the cinema.

Death rays from a spaceship in *War of the Worlds*

WHEN THE FRENCH FILM-MAKER Georges Méliès was making a film in a Paris street in 1896 his camera jammed for a few seconds. When he watched the film, he was astounded to see people vanishing at the moment when the camera jammed. It gave him the idea of using the same effect to make actors seem to disappear or move from one side of the picture to the other in an instant. In 1901 he made a film called *L'Homme à la tête de caoutchouc* (meaning The Man with the Rubber Head). In it, a scientist played by Méliès makes a living copy of his own head, places it on a table and blows it up with a pump. First, he filmed himself as the scientist in his laboratory. Then he rewound the film and filmed his own head on the same piece of film. To make his head appear to grow larger, he simply moved closer to the camera. When the film was shown, Méliès as the scientist and Méliès as the disembodied head appear together.

Matte technique, as this is known, is still used in film-making today. A matte may be a metal mask cut out to cover part of the film or, as in Méliès' case, a blank space left in a film so that a new image can be added later.

War of the Worlds, made in 1953 by George Pal, included scenes of spaceships from Mars firing death rays at the Earth. The rays were painted straight on to each frame of the film. Three years later, *Forbidden Planet* featured an invisible monster terrorising astronauts who had landed on an alien planet. When the monster was required to appear, it was visualised by a technique called rotoscoping. The monster was drawn by an animator on cels (plastic sheets) laid over an enlarged copy of each frame. Finally, each frame of film-plus-cel was re-photographed so that the animated monster became part of the film

Travelling matte

THE MODERN EQUIVALENT of early matte techniques is the blue screen travelling matte process. In one of the *Back to the Future* films Doc Emmett Brown's time machine, a de Lorean car, takes off

Astronauts on the *Forbidden Planet* face the enemy – a monster created by early animation techniques.

HISTORY SPOTLIGHT

THE FIRST RECORDED USE of special effects in a film was in *The Execution of Mary Queen of Scots*, made in the United States in 1895. The queen, who was actually played by a man, laid her head on the executioner's block. The camera was then stopped and the actor was replaced by a dummy. When the camera was started again, the executioner chopped off the dummy's head with an axe. But the audience saw an uninterrupted film of Mary Queen of Scots walking up to the block, laying her head on it and then having it chopped off. Unaware of camera tricks, they were amazed.

Captain Kirk, in *Star Trek* 'flies' through the air suspended on two wires which are filmed in front of a blue screen so that they disappear in the final version.

from the road and flies into the distance. A model of the car was filmed in front of a blue screen. This was used to make a matte, or mask, consisting of the opaque silhouette of the car against a clear background. Next, the matte and a film of the background shot from a helicopter are printed on to another strip of film to produce a film of the background with a clear 'hole' the precise shape of the car. This is used to make a counter-matte, with an opaque background and a clear area the shape of the car. The counter-matte and the film of the car are printed together on to a new film to produce a film of the car without its blue background. Finally, this is printed into the hole left in the background shot. The result is a film of the car flying through the air.

Stop motion animation

ONE OF THE MOST FAMOUS special effects experts was Ray Harryhausen. He specialised in a technique called stop motion animation using models and puppets. In 1933, he worked on a film called *King Kong* about a giant ape which escaped from its cage in New York and made off with the film's star, Fay Wray. The ape was actually a 45cm-high model which Harryhausen photographed frame by frame, moving the model a fraction after each frame.

A new era in cinema special effects dawned in 1977 with the release of *Star Wars*. Dogfights between spacecraft and chases across the galaxy looked more realistic than ever before thanks to

King Kong towers above the skyscrapers of New York, yet he is only 45cm tall.

motion control. Each sequence was carefully choreographed so that the positions of every spacecraft in the shot is known at every instant. Their flight paths were modelled on World War II films of aerial combat between fighter planes to make them look authentic. Each spacecraft model was filmed by a camera on a moving platform controlled by a computer. When all the models had been filmed, the separate images were combined on a single piece of film.

Animatronics

MODERN MOVIE PUPPETS are often filmed 'in real time' - moving realistically in front of the camera at the same time as the actors. They are usually made from a flexible latex (rubber) skin fitted over a metal skeleton. Cables attached to the moving parts are operated by technicians to make the puppet move. Larger creatures are played by actors wearing creature suits. A mask over the actor's face is controlled by cables to make the eyes blink, eyebrows raise and mouth open and close. They are not controlled by the actor, who needs to keep both hands free. Instead, they are operated by a puppeteer by radio control.

Special effects space ships in *Close Encounters of the Third Kind*.

23

This technique is known as animatronics. One of the model aliens built for the film *ET* was controlled by animatronics. Another was an alien suit worn by a small person for scenes in which the alien had to be shown walking.

When the Teenage Mutant Ninja Turtles took on the bad guys on the movie screen, the actors playing the four wrong-righters wore animatronic turtle heads, each controlled by more than 20 motors operated by a puppeteer out of shot. Some of the dinosaurs that terrorised the characters in *Jurassic Park* were animatronic machines. Others were images created entirely by computers. In some scenes, where a dinosaur's head appeared, only the head was built with its animatronic control system and hoisted on a crane to make it move realistically.

One of the animatronic heads created for the film *Teenage Mutant Ninja Turtles*

A model used to make *Star Wars*

Model magic

MODELS ARE OFTEN USED in scenes that are too expensive or difficult to film for real. A well-made model filmed cleverly can look very realistic, but film-makers have to be extra careful when models are used with water or fire. Waves and flames have a certain scale of their own and if a model is too small, any waves or flames in the same shot will make it look false.

Films made in the 1940s and 1950s about World War II often included scenes showing warships at sea. It wasn't always possible to film real ships, so models floating in water tanks were used instead. To make them look more realistic, the

History Spotlight

THE FIRST MOTION CONTROL SYSTEM, used to control a motorised camera for filming models, was a US Army gunnery computer. It was designed to guide an anti-aircraft gun on to its target. Special effects designer John Whitney bought it at a war surplus sale and adapted it to control a movie camera. It wasn't a box full of electronics, as we think of a computer today. It was an armour-plated box full of gearwheels and motors — a device known as a mechanical analogue computer. Modern motion control systems use faster digital computers.

TV advertisements for electricity have used a series of models which appear to move freely. The models are moved a fraction of an inch at a time and photographed, and the photographs are run together to make a moving film.

film was run through the camera faster than normal, so that tiny ripples on the water's surface were slowed down when the film was shown to look more like large waves. Even so, some of the model sequences used in these old films look false because of the scale of the waves compared to the ships. Nowadays, models used in water are rarely smaller than a quarter the size of the real thing.

Fire in the movies isn't always what it seems. When a Mercury space capsule had to be filmed re-entering the Earth's atmosphere for *The Right Stuff* (1983), the special effects crew used a model of the capsule and a cylinder of nitrogen gas. The gas, released through the blunt end of the model capsule, would normally produce a white cloud, but illuminated by an orange light and blown along the model by fans, it looked as if the capsule was plunging into the atmosphere enveloped in fire as its heat shield burned away.

Computer Movies

How does a film-maker achieve this kind of special effect?

A COMPUTER'S ABILITY to take in information, process it and send it out again very quickly can be applied to pictures as well as text or numbers. Computer technology is advancing so rapidly that every year it can offer film-makers new ways of tricking the audience.

THE FILM *TERMINATOR 2: JUDGMENT DAY* (1991) featured a terrifying robot, the T-1000, that could change into any shape. It appeared to change from a real person into liquid metal which flowed into a new shape before the audience's eyes. In *Death Becomes Her* (1992), Meryl Streep twisted her head round till it pointed backwards and pulled her head up until her neck stretched to twice its normal length. Actors, even very experienced actors, need a little help from computers to achieve these spectacular effects!

Computers are used in three ways. They can create images, called computer-generated imaging (CGI), change live action, called digital manipulation, and combine several images on a single piece of film, called digital compositing or matting.

Morphing

CHANGING ONE PERSON or object into another in one smooth magical movement is a digital manipulation technique called morphing. Morphing is the secret of the T-1000 robot in *Terminator 2: Judgment Day*. The actor who played the T-1000 was filmed running along by two synchronised cameras. Marks drawn on his body were loaded into a computer and used to create a computerised skeleton that moved just like the actor. Finally, the skeleton was transformed into a lifelike character by adding a skin and clothes created by the computer – a process called rendering.

Some of the dinosaurs that starred in *Jurassic Park* were created by computers and combined with the filmed scenes in this way. Meryl Streep's extraordinary behaviour in *Death Becomes Her* was made possible by computers too. She was filmed wearing hoods to hide her head and filmed again with her body hidden. The separate shots of her head and body were then fed into a computer which could manipulate them separately to make it look as if her head was turning to face backwards.

HISTORY SPOTLIGHT

THE DISNEY FILM *TRON*, released in 1982, was the first major movie that explored the new world of computer graphics on the big screen. A computer games designer is sucked inside a video game where he has to fight for his life against his enemy. The actors played against backgrounds generated by computers.

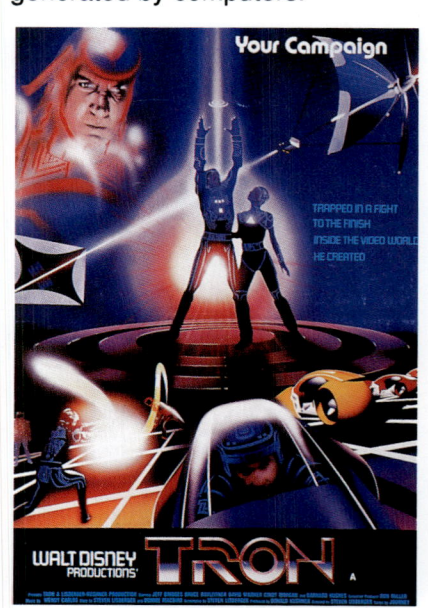

Computer-aided design in *Tron*

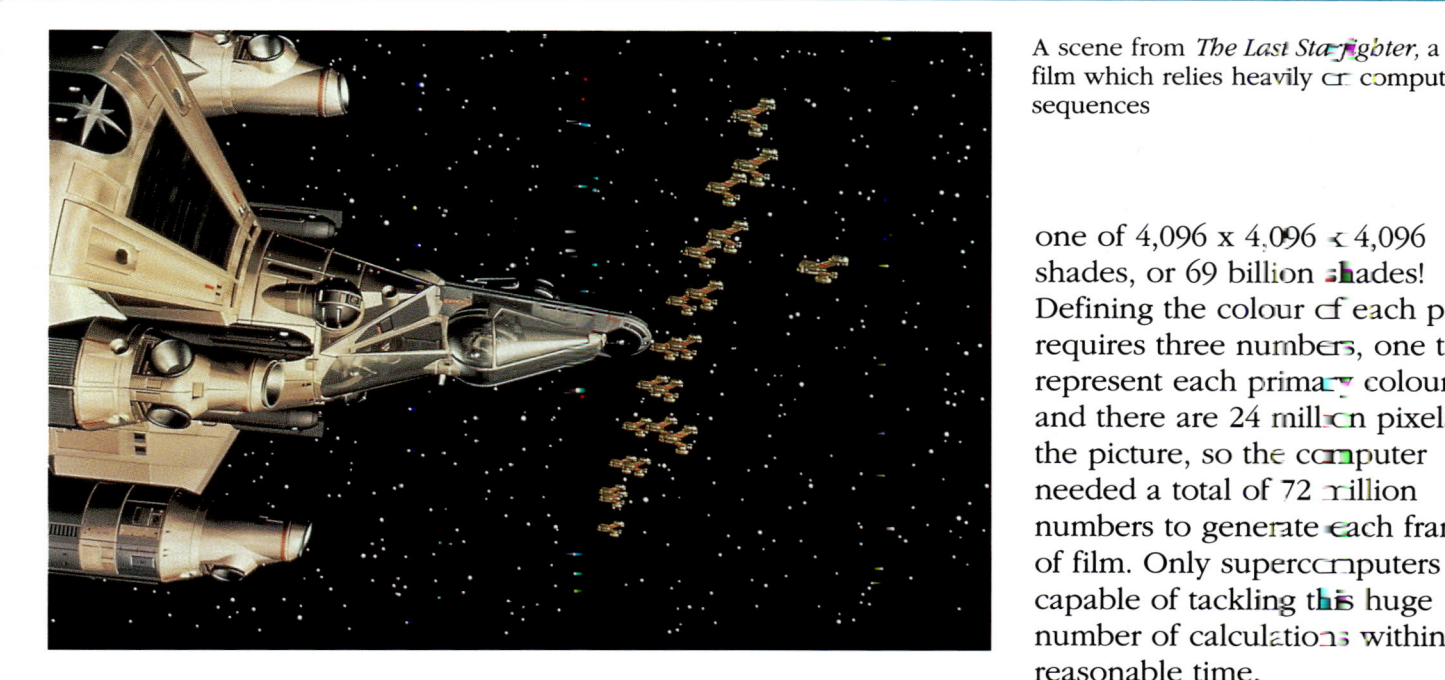

A scene from *The Last Starfighter*, a film which relies heavily on computer sequences

Making pictures

THE LAST STARFIGHTER, made in 1984, was the first feature film to include sequences that were entirely created by a computer. The picture was composed of 4,000 lines, each with 6,000 pixels (picture cells) across the screen. Each pixel was composed of a mixture of the three primary colours (red, green and blue) and each primary colour could be one of 4,096 intensity levels. So, each point on the screen could be one of 4,096 x 4,096 x 4,096 shades, or 69 billion shades! Defining the colour of each pixel requires three numbers, one to represent each primary colour, and there are 24 million pixels in the picture, so the computer needed a total of 72 million numbers to generate each frame of film. Only supercomputers are capable of tackling this huge number of calculations within a reasonable time.

In 1981, it took 40 minutes to build up each frame and display it on a computer screen. Today, it takes just 1/24th of a second.

Repairing images

COMPUTERS ARE NOT ONLY used to add images to films. They are also often used to take unwanted things out. Models or people required to fly through the air are often suspended on wires or rigid metal supports which must not appear in the film. They used to be painted out by hand on every frame. Now it can be done in a fraction of the time by computer. When Michael J. Fox sailed through the air on his anti-gravity skate-board in *Back to the Future II*, the 5cm pipe that actually supported the board was erased by computer.

The blue-screen travelling matte process used to combine two pictures in many special effects (see page 22) often produced pictures with black or blue lines around the separate images in the pictures. Computers eliminate these tell-tale outlines.

The skateboard in *Back to the Future II* seems to ride on air, thanks to the computer.

Television

TELEVISION TECHNOLOGY is advancing rapidly. New developments will give us bigger and better pictures, more channels and new services. The shape of the TV set itself will change too. The question is not whether these developments will be introduced, but when?

A TELEVISION PICTURE IS AN OPTICAL ILLUSION. It isn't a moving picture at all. You are actually watching a flying spot that starts at the top of the screen, traces out hundreds of horizontal lines across it and then snaps back to the top of the screen and starts all over again. It all happens so quickly that it fools the brain into seeing a moving picture.

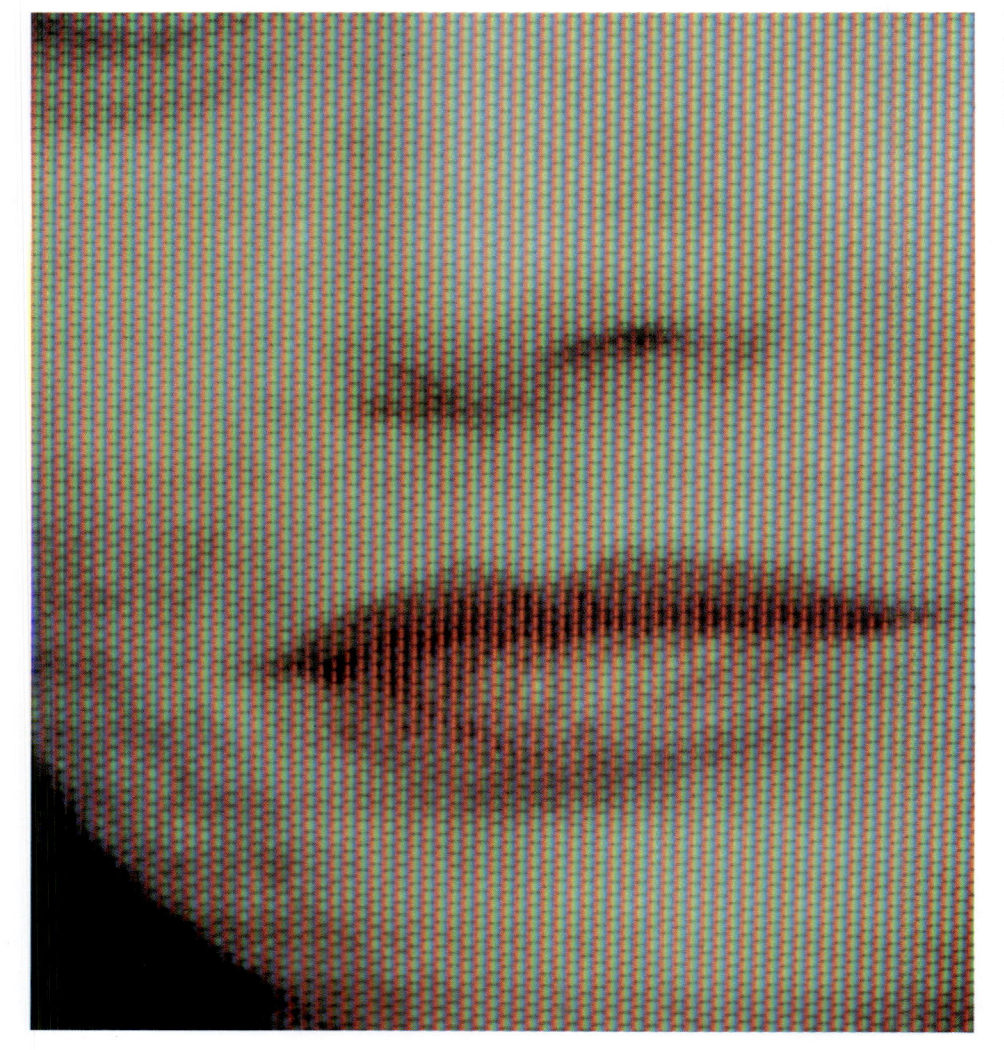

A trick shot of a television cameraman in a studio

A close-up of part of a television screen, showing the red, green and blue phosphor strips which make up the image.

(Opposite) A new TV studio in Cologne, Germany, fitted with several hundred lamps. The studio complex was designed with the help of CAD (computer-aided design).

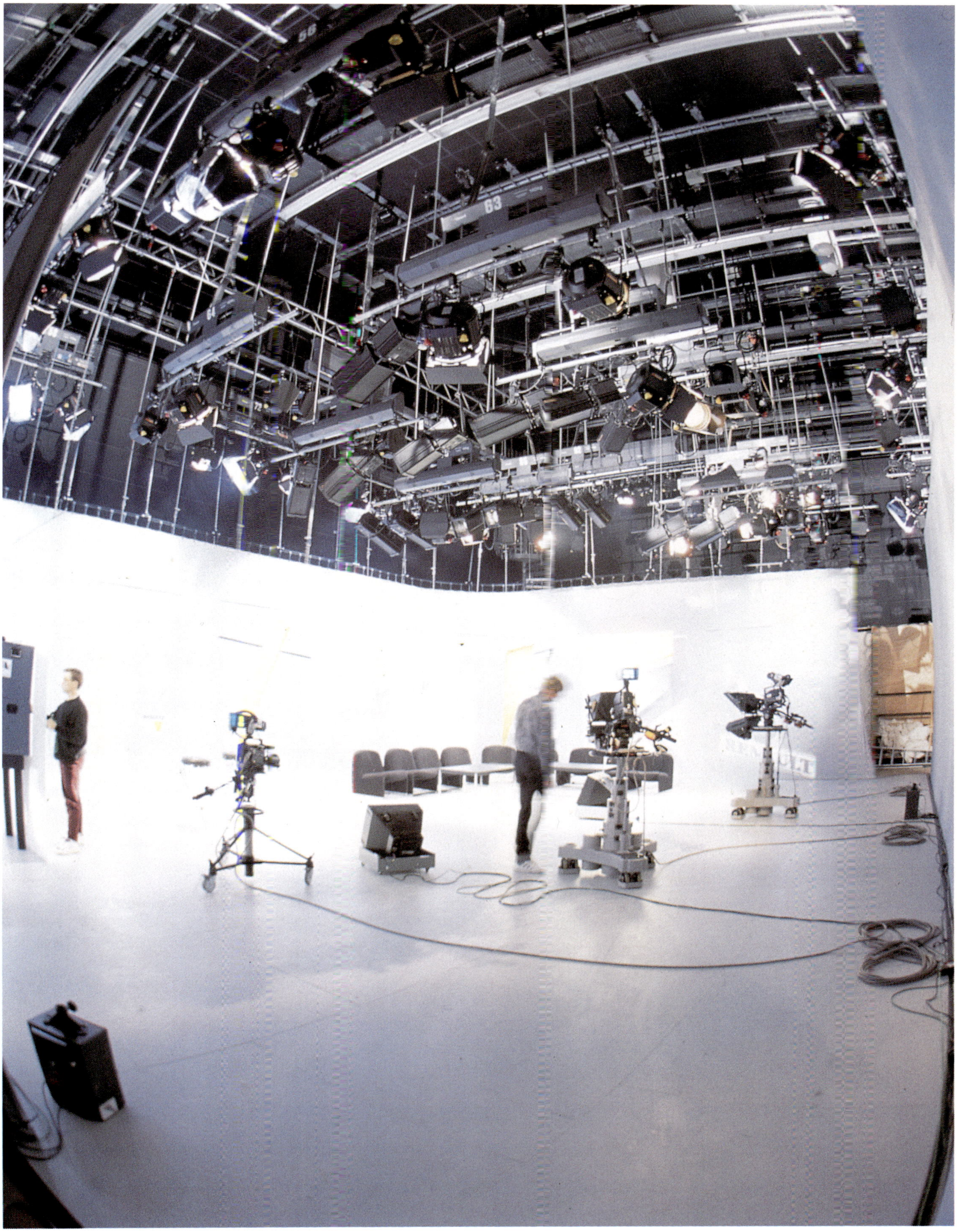

The spot traces out all the even numbered lines first and then all the odd numbered lines.

The bright spot is produced by a beam of electrons flying from the back of the set and landing on a material called a phosphor inside the screen. The phosphor glows when electrons crash into it. There are three different phosphors on the screen - one that glows red, one green and one blue - arranged in spots or stripes so that red, green and blue phosphors are always next to each other. By turning the three colours on in different proportions, any colour can be produced at any point on the screen. The flying spot scans the screen 50 or 60 times every second, producing 25 or 30 complete pictures every second, depending on where in the world you live. American and Japanese TV sets make 30 pictures of 525 lines every second, while European sets make 25 pictures of 625 lines every second. The technology to produce TV pictures containing double the existing number of lines is now available. It's called High Definition Television or HDTV. Doubling the number of lines produces a sharper picture, so HDTV screens can be much larger before the lines begin to show.

Until now television screens, whatever their size, have been four units wide by three units high. This 4:3 format is called the screen's aspect ratio. But our eyes actually see a wider view of the world. And cinema screens are wider too. In future, television screens will be wider to provide a more natural view and so that cinema films can be shown full-width on television. Future TV screens will have an aspect ratio of 16:9, 16 units wide by nine units high. The first 'widescreen' TV sets are already on sale.

The image produced by high-definition television (above) is much sharper than that produced by the ordinary TV system (below) in use today.

History Spotlight

As soon as Alexander Graham Bell succeeded in transmitting speech by electricity when he invented the telephone in 1876, scientists and inventors started searching for a way of transmitting pictures too. In October 1925 the Scottish electrical engineer John Logie Baird succeeded in transmitting an image of a face. It was the face of an office boy called William Taynton. Baird's TV picture was composed of 30 vertical lines and the pictures were transmitted at the rate of 12½ pictures per second. The picture was watched by looking through a spiral of holes in a spinning metal disc. There were experimental broadcasts of Baird's system by the BBC from 1929 to 1935. Meanwhile, the EMI company had developed an all-electronic television system (no spinning discs) which produced much sharper pictures than Baird's system. They were sharper because they were composed of 405 lines instead of only 30. Television today is a direct descendant of the EMI system.

Some of Baird's original television apparatus

A television camera crew filming in the Sahel region of the Sahara Desert

The personal video head set, worn here by its inventor, uses a liquid crystal display screen.

The end of the TV tube?

THE TELEVISION SCREEN is based on technology that is a century old. The screen is one end of a glass tube that extends from the back of the set to the front. TV sets are the large size they are because of the size of the tube. Some watches, computer games and pocket TV sets have screens that are just a few millimetres thick. They are made from two sheets of glass with a special liquid crystal material between them. Light normally shines through the liquid crystal, bounces off a mirror at the back and passes out through the liquid crystal again. But when an electric voltage is applied to the liquid crystal by means of transparent electrodes on the glass, microscopic crystals in the liquid turn and stop light from passing through.

That part of the display appears to turn black. A picture can be built up by turning lots of points in the display black. If the display is covered with thin red, blue and green stripes and the points are turned on or off rapidly enough, it can show a colour television picture. Shining a light through the screen from behind produces a brighter picture.

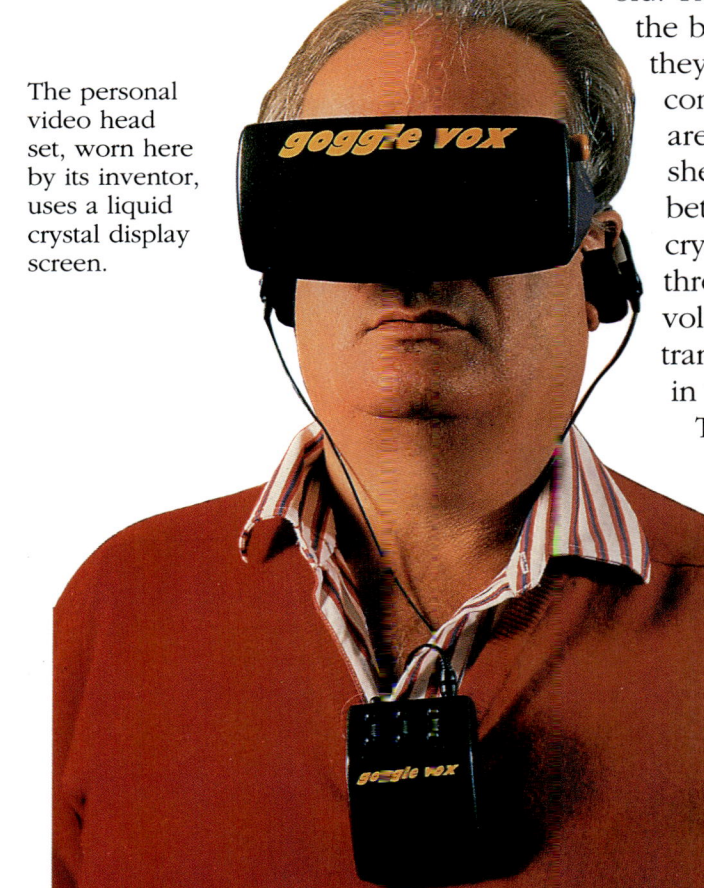

So, why do we not have super-thin TV screens that hang on the wall like a picture? The problem is that large liquid crystal displays (LCDs) are difficult and expensive to make. A large screen must be covered with thousands of transparent switches built into the screen itself to turn each pixel

(picture cell) on or off. If only one of the thousands of pixel switches fails to work, it is immediately noticeable on the picture and the whole screen must be thrown away. There are different ways of making thin screens that don't use such complex electronics on the screen itself. Gas plasma screens create a picture by making gas inside the thin screen glow like a fluorescent light in some places but not in others. Micro-cathode screens replace the single large tube with thousands of tiny tubes. One of these technologies or perhaps something completely new will provide the thin TV screen of the future.

Video

THE FIRST RECORDINGS of television programmes were made by placing a film camera in front of a television set and filming the picture on the screen, but the picture quality was very poor. Sound recording using magnetic tape had been perfected in Germany during World War II, but using it to record television pictures presented challenging problems.

If sound can be recorded on magnetic tape, then why is it not possible to record television pictures using an ordinary audio (sound) cassette recorder? Pictures contain much more information than sound. To record it all on a piece of magnetic tape, the tape has to travel past the recording head very quickly indeed. In fact, the tape speed is so great as to make it impractical to record TV pictures on a recorder that works in the same way as an audio recorder.

In the 1950s, a new type of video recorder appeared. Instead of recording tracks along the tape, these machines recorded video tracks at an angle across it. The shape of the tape as it threaded through the machine resembled a helix, so the system became known as helical scanning. Modern video cassette recorders still use helical scanning. The most popular format is VHS (Video Home System), introduced by the Japanese manufacturer JVC in 1975.

The future

THE NEXT LEAP IN HOME VIDEO TECHNOLOGY will be the digital video recorder. It will use the same helical scanning system as existing video recorders, but it will have to use more, smaller heads to record information on the tape fast enough. Existing VHS video tape is coated with relatively coarse magnetic particles that need an area of 25 square micrometres (thousandths of a millimetre) to record one digital bit of

At work in a large video editing studio in California, USA

Playing a computer game held on a CD-Rom disc

History Spotlight

THE FIRST VIDEO GAME was invented by Nolan Bushnell in the United States in 1972. It was a simple bat and ball game for two players called Pong. Each player used a hand controller to steer a bat up and down each side of the screen and tried to hit a ball that bounced across the screen – an electronic version of table tennis. As the electronics that controlled video games advanced, so the games became more complex.

information. A digital video recorder will have to be able to record one digital bit in less than one square micrometre of tape. It could be the end of the 1990s before such advanced video recorders are available.

Video history seems to be coming full circle. John Logie Baird, who invented television, experimented with recording television pictures on discs in 1927. All the video recording systems made since the 1950s have used magnetic tape, but now, with the popularity of CDs and CD-sized recordable video discs on the way, the days of the video tape could be numbered.

Video games

THE FIRST VIDEO GAMES were very simple, with very basic graphics (pictures), for two reasons. Their computers could not process information very quickly and their memories were too small to hold the computer code for complicated characters and backgrounds. Nowadays, computer games consoles and personal computers can create very detailed full colour pictures and animate them so that characters rush around the screen when the player operates a hand controller.

The hand controller or joystick isn't always the best way of communicating with a games machine. Games designers are constantly looking for new ways of doing it. One system enables someone to play a martial arts game by simply punching and kicking the air in front of the TV screen. Each punch or kick breaks a light beam shining up from the edge of a pad the player stands on and makes a character on the screen punch or kick his fighting opponent. There are three ways of feeding a game into a computer or games console - floppy discs, CDs and games cartridges. Computers usually take in information by 'reading' it off floppy discs – flimsy magnetic discs inside plastic cases – but CD-ROMs, small laser discs similar to CDs, are becoming popular too. Video games consoles usually receive their games programmed in a microchip inside a games cartridge, or cart. But CD-based games are also gaining popularity here too.

Each of them has its own advantages and disadvantages. A CD can hold up to six times as much information as a cart or a floppy disc. CDs are not damaged by static electricity or magnetic fields, and they're more difficult for games pirates to copy illegally than a floppy disc or a cart.

A video disc under test in Japan

Virtual reality

Doctors in the USA using a virtual reality system to study the anatomy of the human leg

COMPUTERS CAN CREATE REALISTIC PICTURES of imaginary places. They can mimic the sounds of the real world too. Could a computer create a simulation of the world, a 'virtual reality', so realistic that it might fool someone who experiences it? Is that the real world out there, or a computer simulation?

COMPUTERS NOW ROUTINELY CREATE stunningly realistic images of the world, real or imaginary, for television commercials and parts of feature films. If we see them on small screens and can see around the edges of the screen to the surrounding room or theatre, it's easy to see that they are pictures on a screen. But the larger a screen is and the more difficult it is to see its edges, the easier it is to forget that it is just a picture on a screen. Pilots training in a flight simulator experience the same effect. They are surrounded by a computer-generated moving image of an airport or the ground below as they 'fly' the simulator.

Some VR systems display their images on ordinary computer screens. For example, architects can use VR systems to help them design buildings. Once a design is programmed into the system, they can view the building from any angle, from any distance or even from inside by using a series of joystick type controls to move around or through the building on the screen. City planners can use VR systems to try out different road layouts and traffic systems. Astronauts can use them to learn how to manoeuvre spacecraft safely. VR systems can also be programmed with data from spacecraft circling other planets to simulate what it would be like to fly over the planet.

Other VR systems aim to blot out the user's view of the real world and replace it with the computer's imaginary world. The user straps on a helmet with video screens in front of the eyes. The computer creates an imaginary world with a landscape, buildings, vehicles and people. If the user's head moves, motion sensors on the helmet detect the movement and make the view inside the helmet move as if it were real. The VR user can move through the imaginary landscape, fly over it and even enter the buildings in it.

VR can be great fun for playing games. Players can pit their skills against the computer or against each other. VR systems designers are now creating systems that will enable players in different cities or countries to be linked inside the same computer-generated VR world by telephone line or satellite.

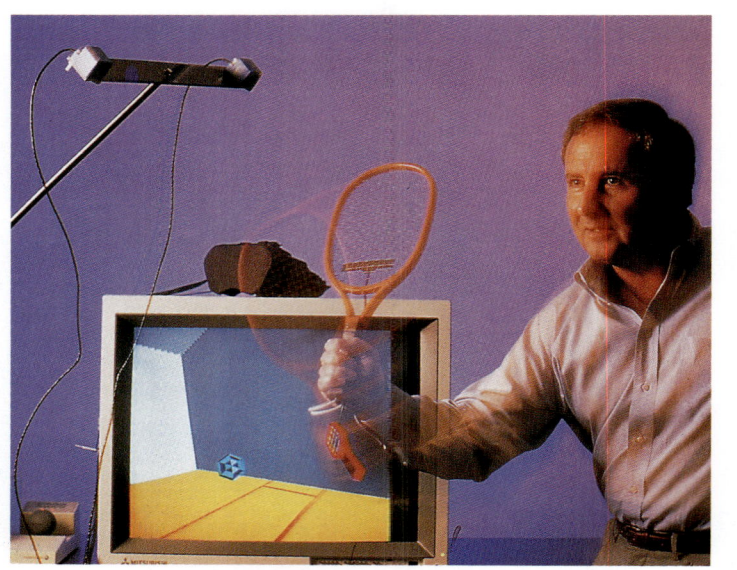

Once he is wearing a headset and a glove with sensors, this player will be able to play a 'real' game of racketball with the computer.

(Opposite) Stereo vision in the headset gives the player the impression of being in another world (which we can see on the TV screen).

34

35

Treading the boards

THEATRICAL PRODUCTIONS, especially musicals, often achieve a spectacular visual impact with the help of impressive sets. Lighting can play tricks on the audience too. Behind the scenes, how do theatrical science and technology add to the entertainment?

A stage set in *Sunset Boulevard*, Andrew Lloyd Webber's musical

IN PLAYS AND MUSICAL DRAMAS, the location of the action shifts to different places as the story unfolds. How can one stage represent more than one place? For hundreds of years, theatres have solved this problem by having intervals between the acts long enough to enable the scenery and props to be taken off the stage and replaced. Alternatively, sets can be 'flown' (hoisted) up into the fly tower, the space above the stage, while a new set is pushed into place from the rear or sides. Some theatres have computerised 'flying systems'. Once hoists have been positioned in the fly tower and the locations of various sets and scenery have been programmed into the computer, they can be flown on to and off the stage at the touch of a button.

When the Olivier Theatre in London was home to a production of *The Wind in the Willows*, it made full use of its ingenious stage design that incorporates a moving centre section. The Drum Revolve, as it is called, is a revolving stage 11 metres across that can rise, fall and rotate. The top of the platform represented ground level. When it was raised it revealed Rat's underground home. It could also rotate to show different sets on each side.

The revolving stage used in *The Wind in the Willows*, Kenneth Grahame's tale of Toad of Toad Hall, Rat, Mole, Badger and other animals of the field and riverbank.

Part of the barricades used in *Les Misérables*

A matter of gravity

SET DESIGNERS have to be careful not to exceed the weight limit of a stage. The barricades that featured prominently in the musical *Les Misérables* weighed six tonnes. The Olivier Theatre's Drum Revolve has a weight limit of only three tonnes. A greater weight limit would have allowed all the sets needed for *The Wind in the Willows* to be built into the Drum Revolve. But their combined weight would have exceeded the three tonne limit. The problem was solved by changing the scenery in the lower level of the Drum Revolve while it was out of sight below the stage. The stage crew could remove one set and install another one within 15 minutes.

In the limelight

SOMEONE WHO IS IN THE PUBLIC EYE is said to be in the limelight, because of a type of lighting that was used in the theatre. A cylinder full of lime (calcium oxide) was heated in an oxy-hydrogen flame (a burning mixture of oxygen and hydrogen). The lime glowed very brightly and lit up the stage. Nowadays, when a play is being planned, the lighting designer can use an array of different types of lights to create the right atmosphere for each scene. Floodlights illuminate large areas of the stage. Spotlights produce a narrow beam to light up a small area. There are two types of spotlight – the profile spot and the Fresnel spot. The profile spot is fitted with

A powerful Fresnel lamp

Special lighting effects have been used in this theatre production to make the action on stage as dramatic as possible.

shutters that can be adjusted to make the light beam broader or narrower.

These three lights – the flood, profile and Fresnel – are the most commonly used theatre lights. All of them have a reflector behind the bulb to throw the light forwards and a lens in front to focus it on the stage. For special lighting effects, they can be fitted with a mask, a sheet of metal with a shape cut out of it, that casts a shadow on the stage. For example masks can give the effect of light shining through a window or trees. Gels (sheets of translucent coloured plastic) fitted in front of the bulb add colour to the beam.

Computer control

THEATRE LIGHTS used to be controlled manually by technicians throwing switches and operating faders (to bring lights up to full intensity gradually) at the right points in a play. Nowadays, computers are taking over. A computerised lighting control board is programmed with all the different lighting arrangements for a play. A screen shows the lighting operator which lights are working at which settings at any time. At the touch of a button, one lighting set is faded out and the next set is brought up at just the right speed.

A lighting control desk for large theatres, concert halls and TV studios. The lighting director can operate 250 spots and more than 1500 dimmers.

38

Concert halls like this one were built before computers were available. Today, computer programmes allow designers to test the acoustics of a new building long before it is built.

History Spotlight

The Fresnel lens was invented by Augustin Jean Fresnel at the beginning of the 19th century for use in lighthouses. Before Fresnel invented his lens, lighthouses needed thick heavy glass lenses to bend the light from their lanterns into a narrow beam. Fresnel made his lens by slicing the heavy lens up and rearranging it into a series of concentric steps, so that each ring behaved like part of a thicker lens, but the Fresnel lens was thinner and lighter.

Sounds good

Most of the world's great concert halls were built before the science of acoustics, the study of sound, was well understood. Nowadays, new halls are designed with the help of computers that can generate the sound of a musical instrument in the hall and show how the sound will change if the hall design is changed. Designers can tell how a piece of music played on the stage will sound in the back row of seats before a single brick is laid. This is an impossible task without computers. Sounds have to be traced as they spread out from the stage and bounce off the floor, walls and ceiling. Millions of calculations are necessary. The latest systems generate a pure sound, as if it were made in the open air, and then allow the designer to bring in walls and ceilings, and hear how they change the sound. Designers can try different shapes of hall, different shapes and angles of walls and ceilings and different types of decoration. All of them absorb or reflect the sound differently.

Halls with the best sound quality seat 1,700 to 2,100 people and are rectangular in shape, 22-26 metres across. In smaller halls, a sound reinforcement system can be used to produce a big-hall sound. Microphones stationed around the hall pick up sound from the stage and pass it to computers, they analyse it and reinforce where necessary by amplifying certain frequencies (notes) and not others

Creating a Musical

THE FIRST PERFORMANCE OF *Joseph and the Amazing Technicolor Dreamcoat* was in 1968. It lasted 20 minutes. Since then a piece of music written for a school choir has developed into a full-length musical which has proved highly successful, playing to audiences in London and on Broadway in New York for 20 years or more. Behind the scenes, computer technology is used to control much of the lighting and to ensure the best sound quality. But as in any live theatre performance, the success of the show depends on a huge team of people, backstage and on the stage.

Stage designers draw plans and make small-scale models of sets and props before developing the full-size versions.

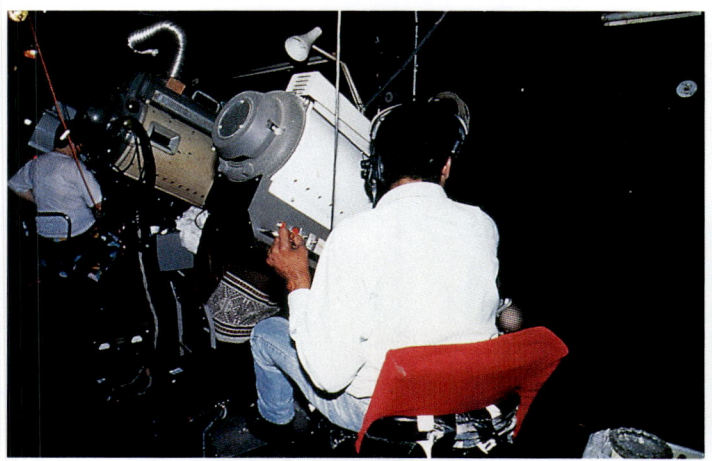

Computers control hundreds of lights above the stage, but special effects are created by lighting operators around the theatre.

The composer Andrew Lloyd Webber (above, right) discusses the musical production and the orchestra, seated in the 'pit' below the stage, rehearse (right). It is the conductor's job to synchronise their playing with the action on the stage.

The choreographer trains the cast in dance and movement.

The cast rehearse for weeks, sometimes months, to get the show ready for public performance.

Costumes are designed, made up and finally fitted, by a large team of people.

Making up

ACTORS DON'T OFTEN have to wear animatronic bodies or masks. Make-up alone can create very impressive effects. By using coloured powders, skin paints and false hair, an actor's face can be aged, rejuvenated or reshaped. Knife and bullet wounds, burns and skin diseases can also be simulated very realistically by make-up. For more dramatic changes in appearance, an actor's own features can be built up by sticking skin-like latex pieces over them to make a bigger nose, a more prominent chin or Spock's famous ears in *Star Trek*. The latex is poured on to a plaster cast of the actor's face, moulded and allowed to set. It can then be peeled off the cast and stuck to the actor's face.

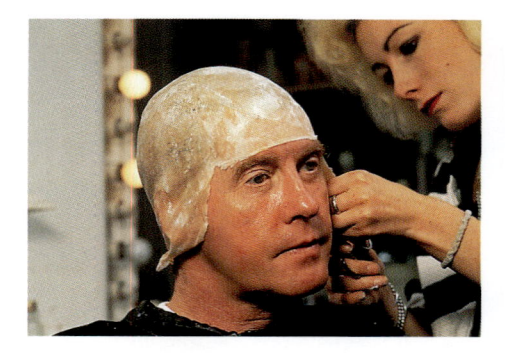

Making up as the Phantom of the Opera can take nearly as long as the performance itself. First a skull cap conceals the actor's hair.

Then latex pieces are stuck to the face.

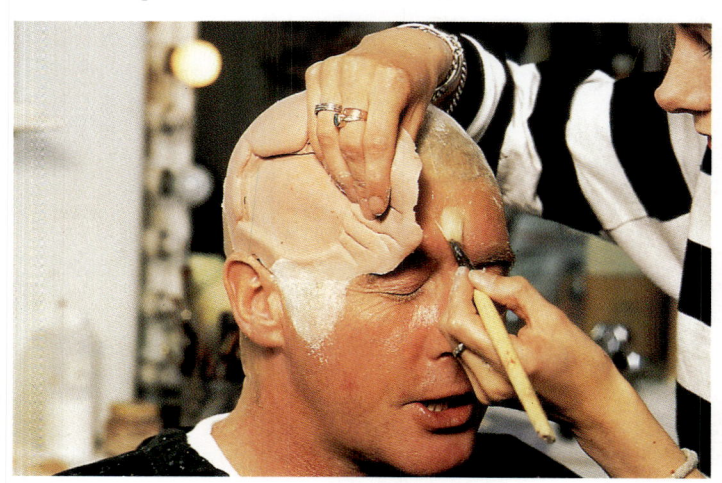

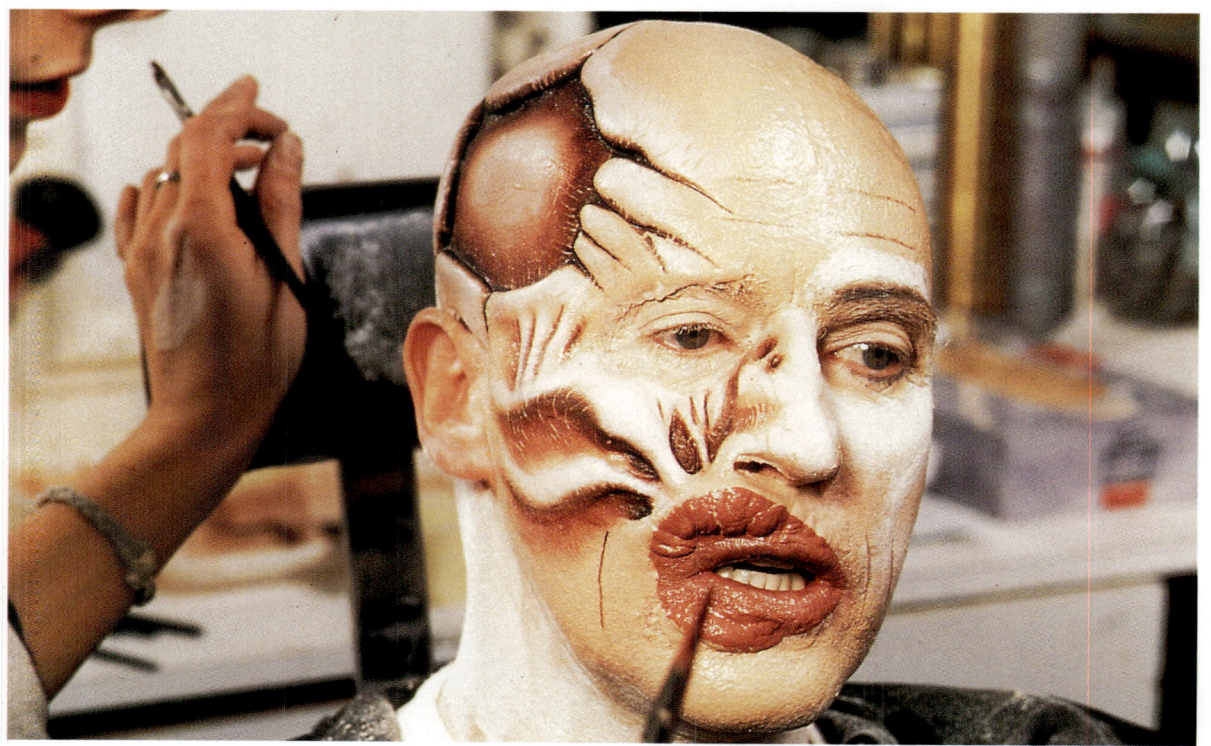

Coloured make-up is carefully painted on to create dramatic effects.

(Opposite) The full impact of the distorted face will only be revealed to the audience when the Phantom removes his mask.

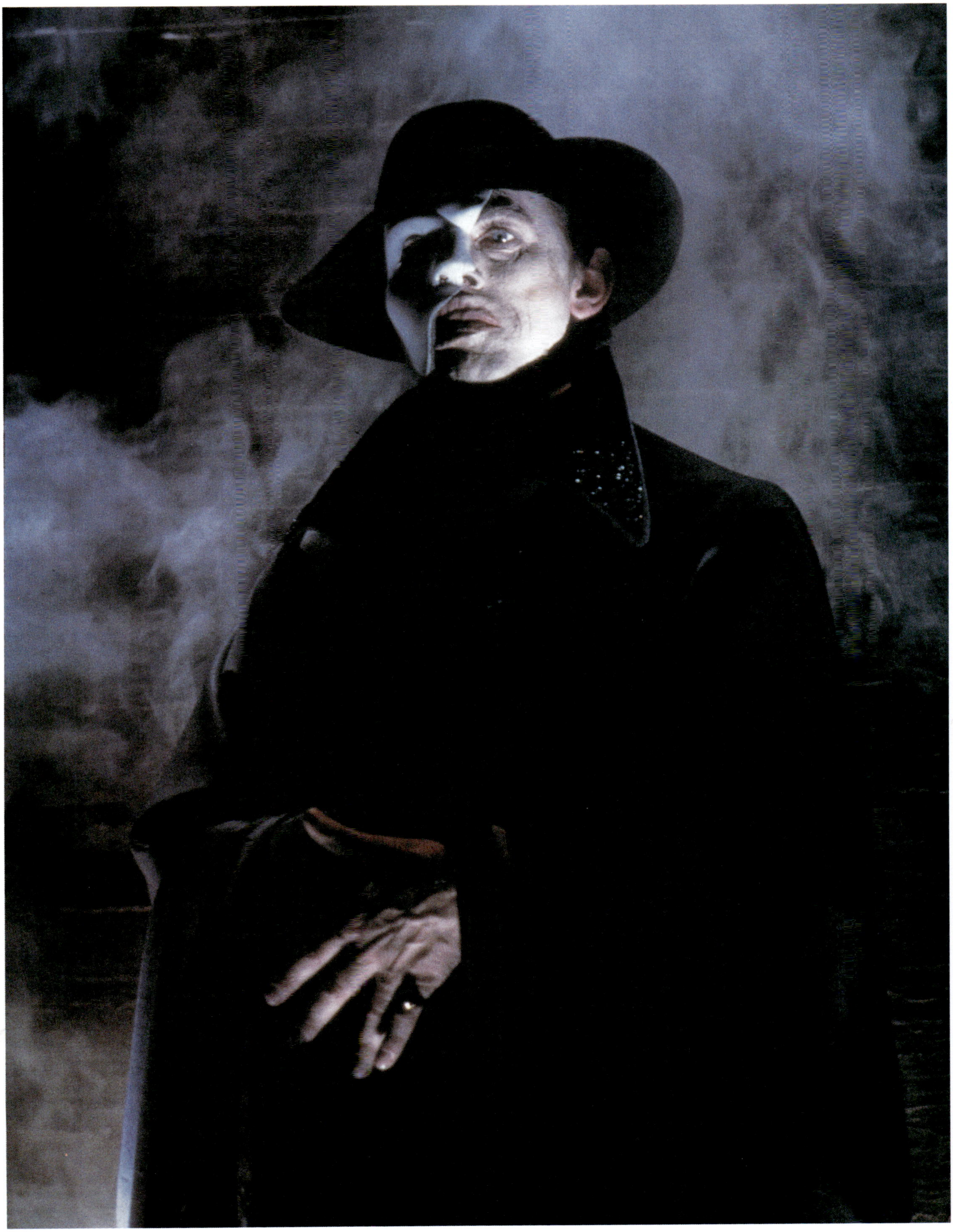

Glossary

Aspect ratio a measure of the width of a television screen or cinema screen compared to its height. A normal television screen has an aspect ration of 4:3 - four units wide and three high.
Cel a sheet of clear cellulose acetate film on which the moving parts of a cartoon film are painted so that the background can be seen through it.
Digitising changing sound or picture into the numbers (digits) that a computer can store and process.
Dolly a platform or frame on wheels on which a camera tripod can be mounted. The wheels allow the camera and tripod to be moved smoothly while the camera is recording.
Electron a tiny particle found in all atoms. When electrons escape and hop from atom to atom, the result is an electric current.
Field all the odd-numbered lines or all the even-numbered lines of a television picture - half the total number of lines that make up the picture.
Frame a single still television picture composed of two fields. Depending on which country you live in, 25 or 30 frames are transmitted every second. Each of the thousands of still pictures that make up a cartoon film is also called a frame.

Laser a device that produces an intense beam of light that can 'read' a compact disc (CD). A laser beam reflected from the disc into a photocell transfers information stored on the disc to a CD player's electronics.
Morphing using computers to make one picture change smoothly into a different picture.
Optical soundtrack the sound for a film, usually recorded as a clear line down one side of the film. Optical soundtracks work by shining a light through the clear film and using a photocell to pick up the light that passes through.
Persistence of vision the eye's ability to retain an image for a fraction of a second after it has disappeared.
Phosphor a substance that glows when it is struck by electrons. Phosphors coating the back of a television screen glow to create the picture.
Photocell a device that converts light into electricity, used in compact disc players to change a laser beam bounced off the disc into an electrical signal.
Pixel an abbreviation of picture element, the smallest part of a television picture.
Rendering in computer generated imaging (CGI), the process that adds the final lifelike appearance to a picture or an object in the picture.

Index

Acoustics 39
Anamorphic lens 11
Animation 16, 19, 22
Animatronics 23, 24

Baird, John Logie 30, 33
Blue screen travelling matte 21, 22, 27
Bushnell, Nolan 33

CD-ROM 33
Cinema 8, 14, 15, 20-27
Cinemascope 11
Cinématographe 8, 9
Cinéorama 10
Cinerama 10, 11
Compact disc (CD) 15, 33
Computer animation 19
Computer games 4, 33, 34
Computer graphics 19, 33
Computers 4, 5, 19, 23, 24, 26, 27, 33, 34, 36, 38-40
Concert halls 39

Digital manipulation 26

Digital sound 15
Disney 14
Dolby Stereo 15
Dolby Surround 15

Eastman, George 8, 11
Edison, Thomas Alva 8, 11

Fresnel, Augustin Jean 39
Fresnel lens 38, 39

Games cart 33
Gas plasma screen 32
Gels 38

Haas effect 15
Harryhausen, Ray 22
Helical scanning 32

L'Homme à la tête de caoutchouc 20

IMAX 12, 13

Kinetograph 8

Kinetoscope 8

Last Starfighter, The 27
Le Prince, Louis-Aimé-Augustin 9
Lighting 38
Liquid crystal screens 31
Lumière Brothers 8

Make-up 42
Matte 20, 21, 26
Méliés, Georges 20
Micro-cathode screens 32
Models 24, 25
Morphing 26
Motion control 23, 24
Musicals 40-43
Muybridge, Eadweard 7

Omnimax 12
Optical soundtracks 9

Phantom of the Opera 42
Phenakistoscope 6
Praxinoscope 6

Puppets 6

Rotoscoping 21

Sequence photography 7
Sound 9, 14, 32, 39
Special effects 4, 5, 20-26
Stage design 40
Stereo sound 14
Stop motion animation 22, 23

Talkies 9
Television 4, 5, 28-31
Terminator 2: Judgment Day 26
Theatre 36-38
Travelling matte 21
Tron 26

Video games 33
Video recording 32, 33
Virtual reality 4, 34

Wide screen formats 10, 11, 30

Real Progress in Reading

David Bessey, Clare Constant
and Emma Page
Series Editor: Alan Howe

The publisher would like to thank the following for permission to reproduce copyright material:

Acknowledgements: p.5: 'Best views in London', published in Metro, 5 March 2013, from http://www.tfl.gov.uk/corporate/media/newscentre/metro/27398.aspx; p.7: '6 Nations Country Guide' from Six Nations Magazine (February, 2013); p.9: Derren Brown, from Tricks of the Mind (Transworld, 2007), copyright © Objective 2007; p.9: National Geographic, from Your Brain: A User's Guide (100 Things You Never Knew (2012); p.10: Griff Rhys Jones, from Semi-Detached (Penguin Books, 2007); p.12: Mary-Ann Russon, 'Cosplay Photographers' Tips and Tricks', Neo Magazine (February, 2013); p.14: Kate Thompson, from The New Policeman (Random House, 2006); p.17: Robert Muchamore, from Cherub: Guardian Angel (Hachette Children's Books, 2013); p.20: Food Standards Agency, 'Protect yourself and your family in the battle against germs', leaflet (May, 2011), © Crown copyright; p.22: Food Standards Agency, 'Food allergen labelling' from http://www.food.gov.uk/policy-advice/allergyintol/label, © Crown copyright; p.22: Susan & Sam Stern, from Get Cooking (Walker Books, 2007), text © 2007 Susan and Sam Stern, reproduced by permission of Walker Books Ltd, London SE1 5HJ, www.walker.co.uk; p.25: 'Be a Tiger and Lion Keeper For The Day', webpage from http://www.chessington.com/xras/zoo-keeper-for-a-day/carnivore-keeper.aspx; p.27: 'We rescue, care for and rehabilitate injured primates in West Africa', leaflet from http://www.apeactionafrica.org, reproduced by permission of Ape Action Africa; p.28: Alice Jones, 'Adele's right, she needs life experience', from The Independent online (19 April, 2013), www.independent.co.uk, reproduced by permission of ESI Media; p.30: Barack Obama, Speech (28 September 2011) from http://www.whitehouse.gov/blog/2011/09/28/president-obama-back-school-set-your-sights-high; p.33: 'Someone At Sainsbury's Used Their Loaf. They Went To Iceland' from Daily Mail (20 April, 2013), reproduced by permission of Iceland Foods Limited; p.34: Chris Barez-Brown, from How to Have Kick-Ass Ideas (Harper Element, 2006); pp.35, 132: Suzanne Collins, from The Hunger Games, copyright © 2008 by Suzanne Collins, reprinted by permission of Scholastic Inc; p.37: George Monbiot, 'My search for a smartphone ends here' from http://www.guardian.co.uk/commentisfree/2013/apr/25/smartphone-samsung-tin-bangka-island (25 April, 2013), copyright Guardian News & Media Ltd 2013, reproduced by permission of the publisher; p.38: 'The Boss of Me', Radio Times, from http://www.radiotimes.com/news/2013-04-18/british-animal-honours-david-blunkett-on-why-his-new-guide-dog-isn't-a-hero-just-yet (Immediate Media Co.); p.39: The Guide Dogs for the Blind Association, 'Guide Dogs could change your life', leaflet from www.guidedogs.org.uk (2009); p.41: Michael Morpurgo, from Alone on a Wide, Wide Sea (HarperCollins, 2006); p.42: Janet Street Porter, 'Today is the day I dread...' from Daily Mail, http://www.dailymail.co.uk/femail/articles-2278358/Janet-Street-Porter-Valentines-Day-Its-just-smug-CREEPS.html#ixzz2SKfdRYnO (13 February, 2013); p.46: Michael Morpurgo, from War Horse (Egmont, 1982); p.47: Monk and Nigel Ashland, from Kaimira: The Sky Village (Walker Books, 2008); p.51: Wilfred Owen, 'Dulce et Decorum Est' from The Collected Poems of Wilfred Owen (Chatto & Windus, 1963), © The Executors of Harold Owen's Estate 1920, 1931, 1963; p.55: Michael Morpurgo, from Private Peaceful (HarperCollins, 2003) p.57: Memphis Barker, 'Young, Ambitious and broke...' (adapted) from The Independent, http://www.independent.co.uk/voices/comment/young-ambitious-and-broke-not-to-worry-on-upstart-you-can-find-a-21st-century-patron-8662185.html (17 June, 2013), reproduced by permission of ESI Media; p.59: Anthony Horowitz, from Scorpia Rising (Walker Books, 2011), text © 2011 Stormbreaker Productions Ltd, reproduced by permission of Walker Books, London, SE11 5HJ; p.66: Biography of Benjamin Zephaniah from www.poemhunter.com/benjamin-zephaniah/biography; pp. 68–69: Benjamin Zephaniah, 'Dis poetry' from City Psalms (Bloodaxe Books, 1992), reproduced by permission of the publisher; p.75: 'Swim Your Way To Fitness With Swimfit', leaflet from http://www.bracknell-forest.gov.uk/swim-your-way-to-fitness-leaflet.pdf (2012), reproduced by permission of Swimfit; p.76: Isabel Choat, 'Must like water slides' from http://www.theguardian.com/travel/2013/jan/08/slide-tester-swimming-pool-first-choice?INTCMP=SRCH (8 January, 2008), copyright Guardian News & Media Ltd 2013, reproduced by permission of the publisher; p.77: Roger Deakin and David Holmes, from Waterlog: A Swimmer's Journey Through Britain (Vintage, 2000); p.80: Doris Lessing, from 'Through the Tunnel' from To Room Nineteen: Collected Stories Volume 1 (Fourth Estate, 1989); p.87: Gary Soto, 'A Red Palm' from New and Selected Poems (Chronicle Books, 1995), copyright © 1995 by Gary Soto; p.91: 'Beasts of the Nile, from How It Works magazine, http://www.howitworksdaily.com/beasts-of-the-nile (24 March, 2013); pp.94–95: 'Running a poetry slam in school: a toolkit' from http://www.literacytrust.org.uk/assets/0001/6013/Write_On_poetry_slam_toolkit_v2.pdf; pp.98–99: Joshua Stamp-Simon, 'Trigger happy' from http://www.theguardian.com/lifeandstyle/2002/oct/02/familyandrelationships.com (2 October, 2002), copyright Guardian News & Media Ltd 2002, reproduced by permission of the publisher; pp.102–103: Web-pages from www.dubble.co.uk/fairtrade/fairtrade-chocolate and www.dubble.co.uk/fairtrade/shopping-can-change-world, reproduced by permission of Divine Chocolate Ltd; p.107: Michael Winerip, 'Harry Potter and the Sorcerer's Stone' from The New York Times, http://www.nytimes.com/1999/02/14/books/rowling-sorcerer.html; pp.110, 112: Michael Palin, from Around the World in 80 Days (BBC Books, 1989); pp.110, 114: Karl Pilkington, Ricky Gervais and Stephen Merchant, from An Idiot Abroad (Canongate Books, 2011); pp.121: Linda Hogan, from People of the Whale (W.W.Norton, 2008); p.123: 'The Story Behind Our Partnership', webpage from https://www.whiskas.co.uk/wwf/our-story.aspx; p.126–127: 'A cry for the tiger' from http://ngm.nationalgeographic.com/2011/12/tigers/alexander-text, reproduced by permission of the National Geographic Society; p.130: S.E. Hinton, from The Outsiders (Puffin Books, 1967); p.133: Description of Anne Frank from http://www.history.co.uk/biographies/anne-frank.html; p.136: Lloyd Jones, from Mister Pip (John Murray, 2008); p.138: Steve Backshall, from Looking for Adventure (Phoenix, 2012); pp.140–141: Berlie Doherty, from Requiem (Penguin Books, 1991); p.144: 'The Essentials for Traveling in Bear Country' from http://www.adfg.asalka.gov/index.cfm?adfg=livingwithbears.bearcountry; p.145: Bill Bryson, from A Walk in the Woods (Black Swan, 1998); p.146: Seamus Heaney, 'Digging' from New Selected Poems 1966–1987 (Faber & Faber, 1990); p.147: Vernon Scannell, 'Nettles' from New & Collected Poems 1950–1993 (Robson Books, 1993), reproduced by permission of the Estate of Vernon Scannell; Permission for re-use of © Crown copyright information is granted under the terms of the Open Government Licence (OGL).

Every effort has been made to trace and contact copyright holders. The publishers will be glad to rectify any errors or omissions at the earliest opportunity.

Photo credits: p.5tl © mark phillips / Alamy; p.5b © Getty Images/Hemera/Thinkstock; p.5tr © Getty Images/Brand X; p.7 © Allstar Picture Library / Alamy; p.10 ©Tony Kyriacou/Rex Features; p.12 ©Andrey Kiselev – Fotolia; p.14 © LOOK Die Bildagentur der Fotografen GmbH / Alamy; p.19 Front cover from Guardian Angel by Robert Muchamore, first published in the UK by Hodder Children's, an imprint of Hachette Children's Books, 338 Euston Road, London NW1 3BH; p.22 © michaeljung – Fotolia; p.25t © Hemera Technologies/Getty Images/Thinkstock; p.25b © Getty Images/iStockphoto/Thinkstock; p.28 © Jon Furniss/WireImage/Getty Images; p.30 © Mandel Ngan/AFP/Getty Images; p.31 © Mandel Ngan/AFP/Getty Images; p.37 © Beawiharta/X01068/Reuters/Corbis; p.38 ©Lucy Ray/Daily Mail/Rex Features; p.41 ©TopFoto; p.42 ©Steve Meddle/Rex Features; p.45 © Getty Images/moodboard RF/Thinkstock; p.46 ©Roger-Viollet / TopFoto; p.48 © Mary Evans Picture Library/Alamy; p.50 ©The Print Collector / HIP / TopFoto; p.53l © The Francis Frith Collection/Corbis; p.53r © ullsteinbild / TopFoto; p.55 © The Print Collector / HIP / TopFoto; p.59 ©.MGM/Everett/Rex Features; p.66 © PA Archive/Press Association Images; p.68 © JEP Celebrity Photos / Alamy; p.71 Getty Images/iStockphoto/Thinkstock; p.73 © krzych-34/iStockphoto/Getty Images/Thinkstock; p.76 © First Choice; p.80 © Orlando Florin Rosu – Fotolia; p.83 © Photos.com/Getty/Thinkstock; p.85 © Erica Guilane-Nachez – Fotolia; p.98 © Getty Images/Comstock Images/Thinkstock; p.105 Kuapa farmer Rose Birago with a bar of Divine. Photography by Kim Naylor; p.111 © stephenallen75 – Fotolia; pp.112–115 © Swisshippo/Getty Images/Thinkstock; p.123 © Getty Images/Purestock/Thinkstock; p.127 © Getty Images/iStockphoto/Thinkstock; p.128 Wikimedia Commons-http://commons.wikimedia.org/w/index.php?title=File:Austen_-_Pride_and_Prejudice,_third_edition,_1817.djvu&page=9; p.130 © Warner Brothers/courtesy Everett Collection/Rex Features; p.135 © Everett Collection/Rex Features.

Although every effort has been made to ensure that website addresses are correct at time of going to press, Hodder Education cannot be held responsible for the content of any website mentioned. It is sometimes possible to find a relocated web page by typing in the address of the home page for a website in the URL window of your browser.

Orders: please contact Bookpoint Ltd, 130 Milton Park, Abingdon, Oxon OX14 4SB. Telephone: (44) 01235 827720. Fax: (44) 01235 400454. Lines are open 9.00–17.00, Monday to Saturday, with a 24-hour message answering service. Visit our website at www.hoddereducation.co.uk

© David Belsey, Clare Constant and Emma Page, 2014
First published in 2014 by
Hodder Education
An Hachette UK Company
338 Euston Road
London NW1 3BH

Impression number   5 4 3 2 1
Year   2018 2017 2016 2015 2014

All rights reserved. Apart from any use permitted under UK copyright law, no part of this publication may be reproduced or transmitted in any form or by any means, electronic or mechanical, including photocopying and recording, or held within any information storage and retrieval system, without permission in writing from the publisher or under licence from the Copyright Licensing Agency Limited. Further details of such Licences (for reprographic reproduction) may be obtained from the Copyright Licensing Agency Limited, Saffron House, 6–10 Kirby Street, London EC1N 8TS.

Illustrations by Datapage (India) Pvt. Ltd.

Typeset in Helvetica Neue LT Std 10/14 by Datapage (India) Pvt. Ltd.

Printed in Italy

A catalogue record for this title is available from the British Library.

ISBN 978 1 444 168952

Contents

UNIT 1 Know how to read for comprehension 4
   1 Know how to skim 4
   2 Know how to scan 6
   3 Know how to understand unfamiliar vocabulary 8
   4 Know how to read in detail 10
   5 Know how to distinguish between fact and opinion 12
   6 Know how to make deductions 14
   7 Know how to make inferences 16

UNIT 2 Know how to understand purpose, audience and context 20

UNIT 3 Know how to analyse structural features 24
   1 Know how to understand the structure of a text 24
   2 Know how to analyse the structure of a whole text 26
   3 Know how to analyse paragraph structure 28
   4 Know how to respond to sentence order and construction 30

UNIT 4 Know how to refer to evidence in texts 32
   1 Know how to identify and select what is relevant 32
   2 Know how to summarise information and ideas in a text 34
   3 Know how to identify and track a line of argument in a text 36
   4 Know how to compare information across texts ... 38

UNIT 5 Know how to understand themes, ideas and point of view 40
   1 Know how to understand the writer's ideas and themes 40
   2 Know how to understand the writer's viewpoint 42
   3 Know how to understand bias 44
   4 Know how to understand narrative point of view 46

UNIT 6 Know how to comment on language and its impact 50
   1 Know how to respond to a writer's use of language 50
   2 Know how to respond to a writer's grammar and punctuation choices 56

UNIT 7 Know how to understand texts in context 62
   1 Know how to use historical contextual knowledge to interpret texts 62
   2 Know how to use cultural contextual knowledge to interpret texts 66
   3 Know how to understand language in texts from a different historical period 70
   4 Know how to comment on literary language in a text from a different historical period 72

UNIT 8 Know how to compare texts 74
   1 Know how to compare form, presentation, ideas and language in texts 74

UNIT 9 Know how to respond to texts 82
   1 Know how to interpret a text to prepare a dramatic reading aloud 82
   2 Know how to write a detailed analysis of a text 86

UNIT 10 Know how to read texts for different audiences and purposes 90
   1 Know how to read information texts 90
   2 Know how to read instruction texts 94
   3 Know how to read argument texts 98
   4 Know how to read contrasting argument texts ... 102
   5 Know how to read reviews and opinion texts 106
   6 Know how to read travel writing texts 110
   7 Know how to read heritage texts 116
   8 Know how to read fiction texts 120
   9 Know how to compare non-fiction texts 122
   10 Know how to compare old and new fiction 128

UNIT 11 Assess your progress in reading 132

UNIT 12 Track your progress in reading 148

GLOSSARY 181

UNIT 1
Know how to read for comprehension

1 Know how to skim

I am learning how to:
- skim to get an overview of a text
- sum up first thoughts on what a text is about.

You can skim a text to give you a general idea of what it is about.
- Run your eyes over a whole text without stopping to read every word. Just focus on understanding what the pictures, captions, main headings and first paragraph are telling you.
- The writer's main points will be in the heading, any subheadings and, usually, the first sentence of each paragraph of the main text. Read these and then decide what the text is about.

Key term
Skim – skim by running your eyes across the whole text. Notice pictures, captions, headings and main points. This will give you an overview of what the text is about. You will also then know where to find different pieces of information in the text.

Activity 1 — Skim the whole text to gain an overview

1 Skim the text on page 5. Let your eyes run over the whole text, pausing to read the headings. What are your first thoughts on what the article is about?
2 Next, look at the pictures.
   a) What do the three photographs show you?
   b) What is the link between them?
3 How does the main heading link to the pictures?
4 Skim the 'standfirst' – the first paragraph, printed in bold. Then sum up in one sentence what your skimming skills tell you the article is about, for example:

   This article tells readers… about…

Activity 2 — Skim the main points

1 Read the headings again. Which types of transport are named?
2 What kinds of transport might be suggested by these headings?

   'Take to the air'
   'Riverside views'

3 Read the first sentence of each paragraph. This is the topic sentence, which often says what the paragraph will be about. Why might readers take these different types of transport?

Activity 3 — Sum up what a text is about

1 Read the summary below, written by a student, of their first thoughts of what the text is about. What do you think of the summary?

   The article is about different ways of travelling by the Thames. It tells readers they can use a bike, train, bus or plane, and really enjoy seeing the cityscape.

2 Improve the summary. Check back to the text to make sure you are accurate in your overview and the detail of the main points.

Focus your effort
When you first meet a text, you can skim the whole text and sum it up. Then check the text again to make sure your summary is accurate and includes enough detail.

Unit 1 Know how to read for comprehension

Best views in London

The capital's public transport network isn't only about getting from A to B – it can also take you to and from the city's most stunning sights.

Take to the air

Opened in time for the 2012 Olympic Games, the Emirates Air Line offers fabulous views across the Thames and London. Running between North Greenwich and the Royal Docks, the UK's first urban cable car offers easy access to the O2 Arena and ExCeL Exhibition Centre.

Front row seats

Catch a Docklands Light Railway (DLR) train and head for Cutty Sark station for the Royal Observatory in Greenwich.

Views from the top are second-to-none – night and day.

Remember to sit at the front of the train if possible – a treat in itself.

Alternatively, get off at Limehouse for a waterside stroll. British Waterways cares for 100 miles of London's waterways, including the docks surrounding Canary Wharf, the Regent's Canal and the River Lea in east London.

If it's more of a cityscape you're looking for, the walk from Canary Riverside (at Westferry or Canary Wharf DLR) towards Tower Bridge (by Tower Gateway DLR or Tower Hill tube) is a must.

If you time it right you might even catch a glorious sunset.

Let the train take the strain

Board a train to Greenwich station and head to the top of Greenwich Park Hill for sweeping views across the Thames to St Paul's Cathedral and beyond.

Greenwich Park is the largest of the Royal Parks and boasts rose gardens, tennis courts, a boating lake and its very own herd of deer.

Hop on a bike

Have a go on a Barclays Cycle Hire bike.

There are heaps of routes to try, which could take you past canals, waterways and the open spaces of the Royal Parks.

For more information, visit tfl.gov.uk/cycling

Riverside views

Whether you're new to the capital or a local, there's always something to discover on a trip along the Thames.

London's river services offer fast routes for commuters, as well as more sedate tourist cruises for visitors wanting to stop off at, or just admire, London's landmarks.

On the buses

Hop on a bus to Primrose Hill for a stunning view of the city (routes C11, 31 and 274 are among those that stop nearby).

Its position north of Regent's Park gives you a fine view of London Zoo, as well as the City in the distance and Canary Wharf to the east.

2 Know how to scan

I am learning how to:
→ scan to find specific information in a text
→ comment on the information I find.

Key term
Scan – track the text to find specific facts or details in it. You know what you are searching for.

You can scan a text to find specific facts or details.
- Before you scan, decide what is likely to help you spot the information you need. For example, if you're looking for dates, look for numbers; if you're looking for names, look for capital letters.
- Use features such as headings and bold print to work out where the information you need is likely to be found in the text.
- Run a finger along each line to help your eyes track and search for specific details. Then read the whole sentence closely to make sure it is telling you the information that you need.

Activity 1 — Scan for specific details

Scan the text on page 7 opposite. Use the **kind** of text you are looking for to help you find these specific details:

1 When did England first win the Grand Slam? Search for a date.
2 Which team conceded most points to England in a match? Search for a name.
3 Which individual scored the most penalties in a match? Search for a number.

Activity 2 — Scan for a number of related details

Use the headings and organisation of the text to help you scan for related details.

1 How many records in total does Wilkinson hold?
2 When did England win the Championship, a Grand Slam and a Triple Crown in the same years?
3 Where and on what date did Alex Goode make his first appearance as a 6 Nations player?

Activity 3 — Scan for details so that you can compare them

To scan for details to compare them, break the task into stages. For example, to compare the achievements of individual England players in 2001 and 2003:

1 Find and list the achievements that the individual England players gained in 2001.
2 Find and list the achievements that the individual England players gained in 2003.
3 Compare the individual England players' achievements in 2001 and 2003. In which year did England players win the most individual awards?

Activity 4 — Comment on the information you find

When you scan a text and use the details in your writing, you should quote evidence from the text and comment on it.

1 Find evidence to prove that the England team was highly successful in both 2001 and 2003.
2 Write a short paragraph explaining your findings. Include details from Activities 1 to 4. Explain your ideas using phrases such as *because…* or *this shows that…*

Unit 1 Know how to read for comprehension

This article tells readers about some of the England rugby team's achievements while playing in the 6 Nations competition.

Championship records

Championship wins – 26: 1883, 1884, 1892, 1910, 1913, 1914, 1921, 1923, 1924, 1928, 1930, 1934, 1937, 1953, 1957, 1958, 1963, 1980, 1991, 1992, 1995, 1996, 2000, 2001, 2003, 2011

Grand Slams – 12: 1913, 1914, 1921, 1923, 1924, 1928, 1957, 1980, 1991, 1992, 1995, 2003

Triple Crowns – 23: 1883, 1884, 1892, 1913, 1914, 1921, 1923, 1924, 1925, 1934, 1937, 1954, 1957, 1960, 1980, 1991, 1992, 1995, 1996, 1997, 1998, 2002, 2003

Team

Most points in a season: 229 (2001)
Most tries in a season: 29 (2001)
Most points scored: 80 v Italy (2001)
Most points conceded: 43 v Ireland (2007)
Biggest winning margin: 57 v Italy (2001)
Biggest losing margin: 30 v Ireland (2007)

Individual

Most points: 546 J.P. Wilkinson (1998–2011)
Most points in a season: 89 Wilkinson (2001)
Most points in a match: 35 Wilkinson v Italy (2001)
Most tries: 18 C.N. Lowe (1913–1923), R. Underwood (1984–1996)
Most tries in a season: 8 Lowe (1914)
Most tries in a match: 4 R.W. Poulton v France (1914), C.J. Ashton v Italy (2011)
Most conversions: 89 Wilkinson
Most conversions in a season: 24 Wilkinson (2001)
Most conversions in a match: 9 Wilkinson v Italy (2001)
Most penalties: 105 Wilkinson
Most penalties in a season: 18 S.D. Hodgkinson (1991), Wilkinson (2001)
Most penalties in a match: 7 Hodgkinson v Wales (1991), C.R. Answer v Scotland (1995), Wilkinson v France (1999)
Most drop-goals: 11 Wilkinson
Most drop-goals in a season: 5 Wilkinson (2003)
Most drop-goals in a match: 2 R. Hiller v Ireland (1970), A.G.B. Old v France (1973), J.P. Horton v France (1980), P.J. Grayson v France (1996), Wilkinson v Wales and Ireland (2003)
Most appearances: 54 J. Leonard (1991–2004)

One to watch

Alex Goode

Position: Full-back
Date of birth: 7/5/88
Caps: 6

Made his debut as a substitute centre in the Johannesburg loss to South Africa, but selected at full-back in the next Test at Port Elizabeth and hasn't looked back since. His experience at fly-half for Saracens gives England an extra option in attack and he can also kick goals. His impressive form has led to recognised full-back Mike Brown being played on the wing and means Ben Foden will have a battle to regain his place.

Form in 2012

Tournament	Date	Match	Venue
Six Nations	Feb 4	Scotland 6 v ENG 13	Edinburgh
Six Nations	Feb 11	Italy 15 v ENG 19	Rome
Six Nations	Feb 25	ENG 12 v Wales 19	Twickenham
Six Nations	Mar 11	France 22 v ENG 24	Paris
Six Nations	Mar 17	ENG 30 v Ireland 9	Twickenham
Tour	Jun 9	S Africa 22 v ENG 17	Durban
Tour	Jun 16	S Africa 36 v ENG 27	Johannesburg
Tour	Jun 23	S Africa 14 v ENG 14	Port Elizabeth
Tour	Nov 10	ENG 54 v Fiji 12	Twickenham
Cook Cup	Nov 17	ENG 14 v Australia 20	Twickenham
Tour	Nov 24	ENG 15 v S Africa 16	Twickenham
Hillary Shield	Dec 1	ENG 38 v N Zealand 21	Twickenham

P 12, **W** 6, **D** 1, **L** 5, **Points For** 277, **Points Against** 212

3 Know how to understand unfamiliar vocabulary

I am learning how to:
- make sense of unfamiliar vocabulary
- increase my own vocabulary.

When you meet an unfamiliar word or phrase in a text, a dictionary can help you find the meaning, or you can use what you *do* know to help you work out what you don't know.

Activity 1 — Work out the meaning from the context

1 You can use the context of the sentence, phrase or paragraph to work out the meaning of unfamiliar words.
   Read the text at the top of page 9. Explain how the context helps you to understand the words below.
   a) Title and paragraph 1:
      i 'technique'
      ii 'visual link'
      iii 'criteria'
   b) Paragraph 2:
      i 'vivid'
      ii 'repulsive'

2 Read a phrase (group of words) and use both the context and the meaning of each word in the phrase to help you work out what the whole phrase means. Read the text at the bottom of page 9 and then focus on the first sentence. What does each of these phrases mean?
   a) 'motor memory'
   b) 'fine motor control'
   c) 'practised actions'

Activity 2 — Search for clues within the word

1 Check whether the main part of the word is similar to another word whose meaning you already know. Then work out what the rest of the word may suggest. Look at the example below. Then choose a word from the heading of the text at the bottom of page 9 and explain it.

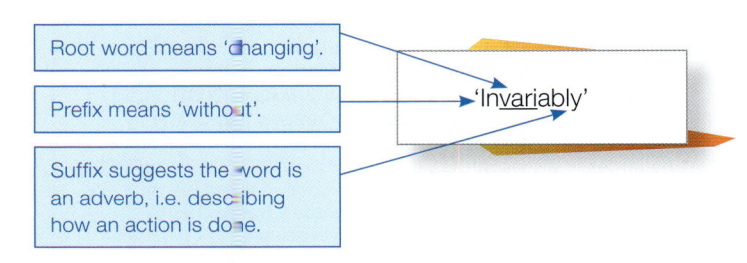

> Root word means 'changing'.
> Prefix means 'without'.
> Suffix suggests the word is an adverb, i.e. describing how an action is done.
> → 'Invariably'

2 Identify the root word, then work out what the word might mean by understanding the prefix. Use the word's context to guide your ideas. Try this with the words below.
   a) Text at top of page 9:
      i 'interact'
      ii 'interfacing'
   b) Text at bottom of page 9:
      i 'represent'
      ii 'refine'
      iii 'underlies'

3 Identify the root word, then work out what the word might mean by understanding the suffix. Use the word's context to guide your ideas. Try this with the words below.
   a) Text at top of page 9:
      i 'memorable'
      ii 'visualisation'
   b) Text at bottom of page 9:
      i 'memorised'
      ii 'additional'

Unit 1 Know how to read for comprehension

In the text below, famous magician Derren Brown explains a technique that will help you be able to recall a large number of objects.

How to memorise a list of words

Here's the technique in a nutshell: we're going to take each word and find a visual link with the word next to it. Not just any picture that happens to link them, but one that involves the following criteria.

1 The picture should be *vivid*. That means you need to take a moment to clearly see the picture in your head once you have decided on it. Also, let yourself engage emotionally with it for a moment. If the picture is amusing (many of them will be) look at it and find it funny. If it's disgusting, actually find it repulsive. Some people don't think that they can visualise anything but don't worry. There's no proper 'visualisation' involved. This is easy.

2 The elements of the picture should *interact*. Picturing A and B standing next to each other won't do the trick. It's much better if A could be made of B, or if A could be forced into B, or if A could smack or dance with B.

3 The picture should be *unusual*. If you have to link 'man' and 'cup', for example, you may be able to vividly imagine those two interfacing, but the picture may be too normal, such as 'a man drinking from a cup'. The picture will be more memorable if the man is trying to drink from a giant cup, or is sucking the cup into his face, or if there is a tiny man in a cup trying to get out before the tea gets poured in.

This text explains how your brain learns and remembers how to perform different actions.

Interdependent stages of motor memory

Motor memory provides fine motor control for practised actions. These include everything from the subtle controls over the vocal cords that produce speech, to the motor control that underlies the complicated act of walking without losing one's balance. Motor memory is tied to the learning of skills. Recent research suggests that motor memory's application to learning new skills takes place in two stages. The first stage recruits neural networks that best represent the motions required for the skill, such as eyes, ears and fingers for playing the piano. The second stage occurs after the basic motions are mastered and implicitly memorised, when the brain recruits additional neurons to refine the motions. That's the difference between the adequate performance of a weekend musician and the masterful performance of one who practises for a seat in a symphony orchestra.

Focus your effort

When you have learned a new word, make it part of your own vocabulary. You could memorise new words using the techniques described in the first text. Try to use the words in your speech and in your writing as soon as possible. Learn about prefixes and suffixes – for example:

- inter – means 'between'
- re – means 'again' or 'more'
- ical – means 'relating to'
- ious – means 'having the qualities of'.

9

4 Know how to read in detail

I am learning how to:
→ read a text closely so that I notice what the details tell me.

Read a text slowly and carefully to understand exactly what the detail tells you. Make sure you notice each new piece of information. You may need to read a text more than once to absorb all the information.

Like many teenagers, comedian and author Griff Rhys Jones' teeth needed straightening. Here he vividly remembers the orthodontic treatment he received.

> **Orthodontic** treatment seemed to be based on the most **rudimentary** of medical principles. Since my teeth were crooked they would be yanked into line. To make room, a couple of back teeth would be yanked out first. The straightforward physical effect was achieved through the most complex in-mouth engineering. The remaining teeth were encased in sheaths of metal and fixed with hooks and wires. I wore a plate made of the same startling shiny pink plastic as my grandfather's dentures, which slotted around my upper teeth and rested up against my **palate**, where it collected a gooey mat of whatever I ate. After meals I was supposed to take it out and wash it, but I was 12. If I could be bothered, or if the food was particularly suety or even tasty, I would lever the thing off the roof of my mouth and suck the residue off. Otherwise, it stayed in and hurt. It hurt because it was designed to force my teeth into new positions. I was given plastic bags of minute elastic bands. One end of the rubber band was attached to a hook on the back of my plate and the other around a projection sticking out of the front of my front teeth. These projections sometimes caught in the inner flesh of my cheeks, but were supposed to act as a grappling hook for a steady, **medieval rack**-like torture of the elastic, pulling the teeth into a new angle in their sockets.

Key term
Detail – an individual piece of information.

Expand your vocabulary
orthodontic – dental specialty of correcting crooked teeth using braces
rudimentary – in the earliest stages of development
palate – the roof of the mouth in mammals
medieval rack – an instrument of torture used in medieval times to stretch victims

Unit 1 Know how to read for comprehension

Activity 1 — Know how to be accurate

1 Read the account by Griff Rhys Jones in the text on page 10.
2 For each of the following questions check exactly **what** happens and **how** by reading the specific part of the text carefully. Make sure your answers are accurate and detailed.
   a) Which teeth are removed first?
   b) How are the teeth linked together by the braces?
   c) How does he clean his plate?
   d) Why do the projections hurt?
   e) How do the rubber bands help straighten his teeth?

Activity 2 — Know how to be thorough

1 Search carefully for details across the whole text to make a list of all the different parts of the brace worn by Griff Rhys Jones.
2 Use the detail to make a simple diagram of the brace and label it.
3 Notice details of how the writer uses language. Griff Rhys Jones does more than simply describe how his teeth were straightened. He chooses language to show his feelings. Pick out and explain words and phrases that show the reader:
   a) The painful, mechanical nature of the brace. For example, you might say:

   He uses the verb 'yanked' twice in the second and third sentences, which suggests a forceful, violent process.

   b) His sense of disgust as he remembers what the brace felt and looked like.

Activity 3 — Comment on the details in a text

Use your answers to Activities 1 and 2 to help you make a written response to this task:

1 How does Griff Rhys Jones' choice of details make his experience of wearing a brace vivid for the reader?
   • Group the different types of details you want to comment on in a paragraph – for example, the visual details, details that describe how the brace works, etc.
   • Pick out examples of each type of detail to comment on. Then work out what is the effect of those details.
   • The following words and phrases will help you:

   Using the word... suggests/hints/implies... or ...makes the reader picture/imagine...

11

5 Know how to distinguish between fact and opinion

I am learning how to:
→ recognise and tell the difference between fact and opinion.

Many texts include a mixture of facts and opinions. It is important to identify what is a fact that you can rely on and what is someone's point of view.

- A **fact** is knowledge or information that can be tested to prove that it is true or real. For example, *There are 260 students in Year 9.* You could count the number of students in Year 9.
- An **opinion** is someone's point of view. It may be expressed as a thought or feeling and can be agreed with or disagreed with by other people – for example, *Year 9 students are the nicest*.

Key terms
A **fact** – can be proved to be true.
An **opinion** – is someone's point of view.

Expand your vocabulary
cosplay – dressing up as a fictional character, e.g. from comics, anime, books

Cosplay photographers' tips and tricks

You've made a great costume, now it's time to capture the essence of the character.

As time goes by, **cosplay** is becoming an increasingly competitive game. It's no longer just about achieving roughly the right look; nowadays every detail of every fabric and prop counts. And once you've completed your costume you need to get good photographs that capture the spirit of the character you're portraying.

'To get a truly great shot is very difficult – almost impossible – at a cosplay event; one needs a location or studio, lights and make-up,' says Jason Moon, a photographer who specialises in a wide variety of styles including portraits, surrealism, fashion, art, music and festival photography. 'So, in essence, to get a great cosplay shot you have to approach it as you would a fashion shoot – it's no different. However, the important thing always to remember is that it's for fun!'

Photography graduate Jasmine Lilly feels that the teamwork between the photographer and cosplayer is important, as is the length of time of the shoot. 'Time is a key factor in getting a good picture,' she says. 'There is a certain point in a photo shoot where the model starts to feel more at ease in front of the cameras, and it really shows in their images. When everyone is enjoying themselves you get better images, but when you are pushed for time it is more down to luck whether you can get a good shot or not.'

According to photographer Eleanor Mayne (aka Eleae), cosplayers actually find it easier to produce good photographs than do other models. 'They know their character and can get into the role faster and easier,' she says. 'A lot of people don't use their face enough in photos, however, and need to watch their expressions. Don't simply smile – it's boring. Get some emotion in there and you're on to something.'

Unlike Jason, Eleanor prefers to shoot on location, rather than inside a studio. 'It's far cooler to give a cosplayer photos that actually look like they are the character in that setting, not just a person wearing a costume,' she told us.

12

Unit 1 Know how to read for comprehension

Activity 1 — Search for clues that show a detail is a fact

When you search for facts you look for precise information that can be checked to find out if it is true – for example, dates, statistics, names, qualifications, measurements, job titles.

1. Read the text on page 12.
2. What facts can you identify about the three photographers who were interviewed for the article?
   a) Jason Moon
   b) Jasmine Lilly
   c) Eleanor Mayne

Activity 2 — Search for clues that show a detail is an opinion

When searching for an opinion, the clues below can help you. You will still need to check whether it is an opinion or fact each time.

1. For each type of clue find an example of an opinion in the text.
   - Speech – scan for speech marks and then study what is said.
   - Feelings – look for words such as *enjoy, happy, sad, angry*; look for exclamation marks.
   - Approximate measurements – for example, *just about, perhaps, maybe, almost*.
   - Judgements – for example, *difficult, easier, simple, complicated, great, terrible, important, better*.
   - Verbs, such as *need, should, ought, feel, think*.

Activity 3 — Distinguish between facts and opinions

Which of these statements is a fact? Which is an opinion? What clues helped you decide?

- 'It's cooler to take photos that make cosplayers look like their character' (paragraph 6).
- 'It is very difficult to get a great shot' (paragraph 3).
- 'Jason Moon specialises in a wide variety of styles' (paragraph 3).
- 'Cosplayers actually find it easier to produce good photographs than do other models' (paragraph 5).

Focus your effort

You need to be able to recognise a writer's opinions even when they are subtly expressed. Then you can explain the writer's viewpoint or attitude. Practise noticing the different techniques writers use to express their opinions when you read other texts.

6 Know how to make deductions

I am learning how to:
→ read a text closely, searching for details
→ understand how details link together and decide what they tell me.

> **Key term**
> **Deduction** – when you deduce you search for relevant information in a text and then draw conclusions about what must definitely be true about the character, place, situation, and so on.

The example below shows how you can make a deduction. You can deduce that Garda (Officer) Treacy in the text below is probably in the driving seat of the police car, using the details in bold in this sentence:

> 'At the kerbside behind him his partner, Garda Treacy, leaned **across** the **empty passenger seat** of the **squad car** and tapped on the window.'

The main character in this extract from *The New Policeman* by Kate Thompson is discovering that there can be a big gap between what you expect a job to be like, and what it actually involves.

> The new policeman stood on the street outside Green's pub. On the other side of the bolted doors a gathering of musicians was at full throttle, the rich blend of their instruments cutting through the beehive buzz of a dozen conversations. Across the road the rising tide slopped against the walls of the tiny harbour. Beneath invisible clouds the water was **pewter**-grey with muddy bronze glints where it caught the street lights. Its surface was ragged. The breeze was getting up. There would be rain before long.
>
> Inside the pub there was a momentary hiccup in the music as one tune ended and another began. For a couple of bars a **solitary** flute carried the tune until the other musicians recognised it and pounced on it, lifting it to the rafters of the old pub. Out in the street, **Garda** O'Dwyer recognised the tune. Inside his **regulation** black brogues his cramped toes twitched to the beat. At the kerbside behind him his partner, Garda Treacy, leaned across the empty passenger seat of the squad car and tapped on the window.
>
> Larry O'Dwyer sighed and took a step towards the narrow double doors. He'd had a good reason for becoming a policeman but sometimes it was difficult to remember what it was. It wasn't this; he was sure of that much. He hadn't become a policeman to **curtail** the enjoyment of musicians and their audiences. A few miles away, in Galway city, violent crime was **escalating** dramatically. Street gangs were engaged in all kinds of thuggery and muggery. He would be of far more use to society there. But that, as far as he could remember, was not why he had become a policeman either. There were times, like now, when he suspected that the reason, whatever it was, might not have been a particularly good one.

> **Expand your vocabulary**
> **pewter** – a dark, grey-coloured metal
> **solitary** – the only one
> **Garda** – in the Republic of Ireland policemen are called Garda in the same way that British police are called Officer
> **regulation** – following the rules
> **curtail** – bring to an end
> **escalating** – increasing

14

Unit 1 Know how to read for comprehension

Activity 1 — Make deductions that are true

1 Read the text on page 14. Find and note down the information the writer gives you about Garda O'Dwyer. For example:

His toes are cramped.

2 Now decide five things the information shows are definitely true about Garda O'Dwyer. For example:

Detail	What the detail shows is true
Garda O'Dwyer's toes are cramped.	His shoes are too tight for his feet.

Activity 2 — Make deductions by linking or contrasting information

1 Link together the information you have listed in Activity 1 about Garda O'Dwyer to decide which of the statements below can be proved to be true.
   a) Garda O'Dwyer is a new policeman.
   b) Garda O'Dwyer does not want to stop the music in the pub.
   c) Garda O'Dwyer is following Garda Treacy's orders.
   d) Garda O'Dwyer would rather work in Galway.

2 Sometimes a writer points out that two people or places are very different from each other. Knowing what something is *not* like can help you deduce what it must *be* like. Use the information in the last paragraph to deduce what social problems are *not* happening in the Green's pub area, in contrast to Galway.

Activity 3 — Use your deductions to comment on the text

1 Use the information you have gathered and the deductions you have made to write a paragraph explaining what you have discovered about Garda O'Dwyer. Use direct (quotes) and indirect evidence from the text to support your explanation. These phrases will help you:

…shows the reader that…

…makes it clear that…

When the writer says… the reader knows…

15

7 Know how to make inferences

I am learning how to:
- use details in the text to form an opinion about what is likely to be true
- use my experience and general knowledge to work out what a writer is suggesting
- investigate and reach conclusions about a character using inference.

Key term

Inference – making an inference is where you work out from hints or clues in a text what is likely to be true about a character, place or situation.

Writers don't always state exactly what is happening, or what a character is thinking or feeling. Instead, they use words or details that help you work it out. For example, a writer might describe a character as secretly brushing away a tear. A reader might infer that the character is upset but doesn't want anyone to know.

In the extract opposite, from *Guardian Angel* by Robert Muchamore, three characters are on the deck of a ship late at night. One of them, Leon, is very hungry.

Activity 1 — Work out what words or phrases suggest

Read and sum up what the text is about before you focus on what the details suggest. Make sure that your inferences fit in with what the whole text is about.

1. Read the text opposite on page 17. Sum up what you think it is about.
2. Read the text again, noting the highlighted words. Then, using a table like the one below, decide what you think each word or phrase suggests to you about plot or character. Read the sentences the words are in particularly carefully, because they often provide a clue to work out what each word or phrase is hinting at!

Word	Relevant information	This suggests…
burrowed	**General knowledge:** an animal can burrow or dig for food or shelter. **Word as used in the text:** Leon burrowed into Ning's bag to search for food. **What we know from the text:** Leon is hungry and hasn't eaten for 18 hours. He secretly burrows into Ning's bag to search for biscuits. He is scared of Ning.	The writer might have chosen the word 'burrowed' to suggest that Leon needs to behave like an animal scavenging for food.

Activity 2 — Draw on your experience and general knowledge

Search for clues in the text and use your experience and general knowledge to work out your answers to these questions. Explain your ideas using tentative language such as 'might mean', 'could be that', 'maybe'.

1. Read the text again. Why doesn't Leon just ask Ning for a biscuit?
2. Read the last ten lines. Why does Leon give Daniel 'the bigger half' of the biscuit?
3. What might you infer about the person who opens the door, in the penultimate paragraph?

Unit 1 Know how to read for comprehension

Ning had hooked the straps of her backpack around her ankles to stop it getting washed away. As a mini wave swept the deck and sploshed through the **mound of ropes**, Leon reached towards the zip on Ning's pack.

It was a risky move: Ning was two years older and a champion boxer who could easily batter Leon. Despite the **throbs** of the trawler's propeller shaft and the sounds of wind and water, the click of each zip tooth **felt like a gun going off**.

Once he had an opening big enough for his hand, Leon felt blindly inside Ning's pack. He **burrowed** past underwear, which had been hand-washed but packed before it was fully dry. Grains of sand stuck to his arm as he went deeper, feeling the smooth handle of Ning's hunting knife, then at the very bottom pairs of shortcake biscuits in plastic wrapping.

As Leon pulled up the shortbread, his palm touched a larger packet. It was rectangular, with the biscuits sitting in a plastic tray and a spongy feel when he pushed down. It *had* to be jaffa cakes. Saliva flushed Leon's mouth as he anticipated the **tang** of orange and the chocolate melting against his tongue. As a small wave washed over the deck, he pulled out the little package and ripped it open with his teeth. Leon hadn't eaten in 18 hours and stifled a satisfied groan as he crammed a spongy biscuit into his mouth whole.

Soooo good!

He practically **inhaled** the second, but as the third jaffa cake neared Leon's mouth a hand touched his shoulder, making him jump.

'You gonna scoff them all yourself?' Leon's twin, Daniel, asked quietly.

Leon turned to face his brother and spoke in a whisper. 'You got dinner last night. I'm *starving*.'

'I'll tell Ning,' Daniel threatened, aiming his pointing finger at her back. 'She'll **crack you like an egg**.'

Leon knew his brother wouldn't really grass, but the knowledge also reminded him of his bond with his twin. He pulled the biscuit apart and gave Daniel the bigger half.

As Daniel made a quiet but appreciative *mmm*, the sliding door opened with a crash.

'Wipe your top lip,' Leon said anxiously, as he chewed fast and flicked chocolate flakes off his shirt. 'If he sees us eating we're dead.'

Expand your vocabulary

tang – a strong taste
inhaled – breathed in

17

7 Know how to make inferences

Activity 3 — Use inference to investigate character

1. Read the text on page 17 again. Find evidence of what Ning is like as a person, using the types of clues in the table below.
2. Then use your inference skills to work out what each clue tells you about Ning's character. Your inferences cannot contradict the evidence in the text and they must be realistic.

Type of clue about character	Evidence in the text	What can you infer from the evidence?
behaviour	Ning had hooked the straps of her backpack around her ankles to stop it getting washed away.	Ning is very practical. She plans ahead. She looks after her possessions.
belongings		
other characters' responses to them/ what other characters say about them		

Activity 4 — Use your inferences to comment on character

1. Sum up your overall impression of Ning.
2. Use your work on inferences to comment in detail on the character of Ning. Refer to evidence in the text and explain what it suggests about her. Use words and phrases that show you are making suggestions and thoughtful guesses about something the writer suggests rather than states. For example:

   This suggests that…
   This might/could show…
   One possible explanation might be…

Focus your effort

When you want to investigate a character you can search for these nine clues. All or some may be present in any text. Use inference to help you work out what they reveal about the character:

- appearance
- belongings
- speech
- thoughts and feelings
- behaviour
- what characters say about themselves
- what other characters say about them
- responses to events or other characters
- other characters' responses to them.

Unit 1 Know how to read for comprehension

UNIT 2
Know how to understand purpose, audience and context

1 Know how texts target audiences

I am learning how to:
- work out the audience for whom a text is meant
- recognise features that writers use to influence and appeal to different audiences
- comment on how a text is written for a particular audience.

Writers choose what to include and what to leave out so that their text will suit its specific audience and influence them. To do this they choose and use:

- **presentational features** – images, headings, colours, fonts
- **content** – information and ideas to appeal to particular interests
- **language** – for example, level of formality, choice of vocabulary.

This is a page from a leaflet advising readers how to prepare food safely.

Key term
Audience – the readers of texts. A text is written to influence and appeal to a particular group of people, for example, teenagers, older adults, children, families, parents, professionals, people on a high income, fans, special interest groups, and so on.

Protect yourself and your family in the battle against germs. When you're preparing food, remember the 4 Cs – cleaning, cooking, chilling and cross-contamination...

CLEANING

Right now, your hands could be carrying germs – thousands of them. They're invisible, and can easily spread on to food, making you and your loved ones ill.

Stop the invasion before it's too late! Keep yourself and your kitchen clean by washing and drying your hands thoroughly:

- before touching food
- after touching raw food, especially meat
- after going to the toilet.

Make sure you keep worktops, chopping boards and utensils clean. If they've been touched by raw meat, poultry or eggs, you'll need to wash them thoroughly.

Don't forget to wash dish cloths and tea towels regularly on a hot wash. They may look clean, but they're the perfect place for germs to breed.

ZAP!

GERM WATCH
KILLER FACT
Harmful germs spread more easily on damp hands. Keep yourself and your family safe by drying washed hands thoroughly.

Unit 2 Know how to understand purpose, audience and context

Activity 1 — Study the images and headings and decide who they influence

1 Writers choose images to appeal to their audience, and include the kind of people and contexts that are familiar to them. Look at the image in the leaflet on page 20.
   a) Exactly what does the image show?
   b) What impression do the details in the image create? For example, the white stars on her hands may be warning signs or they may show how sparkling clean her hands are.
   c) Which of the following groups do you think will most identify with the kind of person and context in the image?
      i   teenagers
      ii business people
      iii chefs
      iv adults.
2 Study the headings and the first paragraph. Find any clues that suggest who the audience may be.
3 What do the image and headings suggest about the audience of the text?

Activity 2 — Study fonts and colours and decide who they influence

Writers influence readers of a text by appealing to their emotions, values, desires and needs.

1 Describe the colours used in different aspects of the text. What impression do they create?
   a) headings
   b) writing
   c) images
   d) background, for example:

> Pale yellow background suggests clean, soft and warm, so it feels friendly.

2 Describe the fonts used in the text. What impression do they create? For example, large, black, bold font for headings creates an impression of strength and power.
3 Draw together all the clues in the images, headings, fonts and colours. Who is the target audience and why will the presentation influence and appeal to them?

Activity 3 — Study how presentation targets audience in two texts

1 Read the texts on page 22.
2 For each text, use the presentational features to work out what kind of audience each appeals to and influences. Remember to notice and comment on images, headings, colours and fonts.

1 Know how texts target audiences

This text is a webpage from the Food Standards Agency giving information about how food should be labelled so that people with allergies will know if it is safe for them to eat.

Food allergen labelling

People with food allergies have to be extremely careful about what they eat.
Food labelling is therefore very important to those with food allergies as there can be potentially serious consequences from eating food they are allergic to.

The current rules

Currently, the rules for pre-packed foods established a list of 14 allergens, which have to be indicated by reference to the source allergen whenever they, or ingredients made from them, are used at any level in pre-packed foods, including alcoholic drink. The list consists of cereals containing gluten, crustaceans, molluscs, egg, fish, peanuts, nuts, soybeans, milk, celery, mustard, sesame, lupin, and sulphur dioxide at levels above 10 mg/kg or 10 mg/litre, expressed as SO_2.

Some ingredients derived from the listed allergenic foods are so highly processed that they are no longer capable of triggering an adverse reaction. A list of products that were temporarily exempt from the labelling requirements of Directive 2003/89/EC was published in Commission Directive 2007/68EC in November 2007.

Do you enjoy cooking? Sam Stern loves it and tells you why below.

Why cook?

Hey, you're missing out if you don't do it. Every part of the process has got something cool going for it. First off – the shopping. Nope, it doesn't grow in carriers. Food shopping means you get to visit some great markets, shops, delis, farm shops – even the supermarket. Do it. Get out there. Talk to the people who've grown the stuff or who made it. You want to know as far as possible where your food has come from and how it has been produced. Keep it real. You want it to be good if you're going to swallow it. Cooking gives you power in loads of ways. It's a great way to be independent – chucking some good stuff together when you're just in or before you go out. Getting yourself ready for when you escape from home to work, college, gap year, uni, whatever. Cooking the right stuff can prop you up (after a night out), sort you out (when you're feeling lousy or exams loom), switch you on (head straight for chocolate or pudding), give you the energy you need just to get you through the day or the party, the game or another night of training.

Then there's the ultimate pleasure of the cooking itself. The hands-on and senses stuff– the smell and sight of chocolate melting down, separating an egg, kneading dough, curing salmon, making puffy Yorkshires, putting together a whole roast dinner, watching a mess of pudding mix transform itself through the cooking into something magnificent and so appetising.

Unit 2 Know how to understand purpose, audience and context

Activity 4 | Study the content and decide whom it influences

Writers only include content that will interest and influence the text's audience.

1 Read the text at the top of page 22 and consider the information it includes. Select which of the following audiences it intends to influence and appeal to:
   a) teenagers
   b) lawyers
   c) professional chefs
   d) business owners
   e) parents.

2 Read the text at the bottom of page 22 and consider the information it includes. Select which of the following audiences it intends to influence and appeal to:
   a) teenagers
   b) lawyers
   c) professional chefs
   d) business owners
   e) parents.

3 For each text, explain your decision. Refer to specific content and how it will appeal to a particular audience.

> **Focus your effort**
>
> When asked about the audience of a text, remember to comment on:
> - presentational features – images, headings, colours, fonts
> - content – information and ideas that appeal to particular interests
> - language – for example, level of formality, choice of vocabulary, simplicity.

Activity 5 | Study the language and decide whom it influences

Writers often use the same kind of language their readers use, to make the text familiar and appealing to them. For example, a text for a teenager might use informal vocabulary, slang and abbreviations, whereas a text for a professional might not.

1 Read the texts on page 22 again. For each text, select three examples of words, phrases or sentences the writer has used to suit their particular audience. Explain why your chosen words or phrases appeal to that audience.

2 Read the leaflet on page 20 again and search for words, phrases or sentences that reveal what kind of audience it is meant to appeal to. Explain your ideas using examples from the text.

Activity 6 | Comment on texts and the audiences they are aimed at

When you write about how the presentation, content and language suit different readers make sure you refer to specific details in the text.

1 Explain how the writer of each of the three texts on pages 20 and 22 targets the audience. Include specific details from each text. You could include the following phrases:

> The words... suit [name the audience] because...
>
> The image of... appeals to... because...
>
> This example also influences the reader by...

23

UNIT 3 Know how to analyse structural features

1 Know how to understand the structure of a text

I am learning how to:
- understand how different parts of a text work together
- understand how presentational features reinforce the structure of the text.

Key terms
Structure – the structure of a text is the way in which its different parts are organised.
Continuous prose – text that is written in sentences and paragraphs.
Non-continuous prose – text that is presented in formats such as lists, bullet points, diagrams, tables, etc.

The way a non-fiction text is organised helps the text reach its audience and achieve its purpose. It is useful to think of texts as having three main parts: the introduction, the main section, and the conclusion. Each of these does a different task:

- **The introduction** – this helps the reader engage with the text's purpose.
- **The main body of the text** – this is where the different pieces of information the reader needs to know are expressed.
- **The conclusion** – this closes the text and ensures its purpose has been achieved.

Presentational features may be used to emphasise differences between parts of the text while also helping to link them together.

Activity 1 Understand how the structure of the text helps express meaning

Read the text on page 25 and identify the different parts of it. Then work out how the structure helps express the meaning of the text by asking yourself: why has the writer put this information in this order?

1. Make a diagram showing where each of the parts of the text listed below is placed on the page. Then label what each part is and how it is presented – for example, *Heading in large bold print*.
   - heading
   - cost
   - introduction
   - how to book
   - image
   - first paragraph
   - conclusion
   - bullet points
   - continuous prose
   - non-continuous prose.

2. Sum up the different information readers are given by each part of the text listed above – for example, *The heading tells readers…*

3. Why is each piece of different information given in the order in which it is? (Remember, the audience reads the text from top to bottom.) For example, *The heading is at the top so the reader sees it first and understands… By placing the… after the heading next the reader will…*

Activity 2 Understand how presentation reinforces the text's structure

A presentational feature can help readers notice different types of information, guide readers through the text or present information with maximum impact. When readers see text or images in similar colours, fonts, etc., it helps link them in their mind.

1. Which of the presentational features are used to help readers notice different information? For example, *The bold print of the introduction contrasts with…*

2. Which of the presentational features are used to guide readers through the text? For example, *Listing…*

3. How does the writer ensure different information remains linked in readers' minds? For example, *The use of the same colour and font to…*

Unit 3 Know how to analyse structural features

Tiger & Lion Keeper For The Day (16+ Years)

Take a walk along Chessington's Trail of the Kings, where you'll get to work alongside our carnivores including Sumatran Tigers and Asiatic Lions. An awesome experience, which includes your entry tickets.

On arrival you'll meet up with one of our professional zoo keepers, who'll be your guide and buddy as they go about their daily tasks. He or she will introduce you to your chosen animals and get you involved with hands-on tasks like animal care and welfare, food preparation and keeping their enclosures spick and span.

- Cleaning the dens in which the carnivores are housed.
- Preparing the food and assisting with the public feed.
- Arranging and serving up the evening feed before closing up for the night.
- Five-hour experience for up to two people.
- Minimum adventurer age is 16 years.
- Meet and feed the carnivores, including the tigers, lions, otters, binturong and fossa.
- Spending time in the dens, meeting the animals up close and personal and asking any questions you may have.

A truly wonderful way to get up close and gain a real insight into some of the world's most fascinating animals. You'll go away with great memories, but don't take our word for it – read our reviews. Book your experience today or treat someone with a gift voucher.

£175 for one or £310 for two people.

BOOK NOW!

Bookings must be made 7 days in advance of experience.

Activity 3 — Writing about structure

Use the work you have already done to help you answer the question below.

1 How has the writer of the text structured the webpage 'Tiger & lion keeper for the day'?

You will need to be precise about where information is placed on the page and the order in which it is given. The following words and phrases will help you achieve this:

First the reader...	after that...	second...	above...
next...	below...	before...	finally...

The writer has linked these parts of the text by...

25

2 Know how to analyse the structure of a whole text

I am learning how to:
→ explain how the structure of the text helps it reach its audience and achieve its purpose.

A text is organised so that it achieves its purpose with its audience. To be able to analyse how it does this, read the text and work out its audience and purpose. Then examine its structure and ask yourself these questions:

- How does the opening introduce the main ideas and engage the audience?
- What order are points made in? How effective is this order?
- What links are made between different parts of the text?
- How does the conclusion ensure the text has achieved its purpose?

Activity 1 — Understand how organisation is integral to the text's meaning

1 Read the text on page 27.
   a) Draw a plan and label it to show how the text is organised.
   b) Make a flow chart showing the order of its ideas:

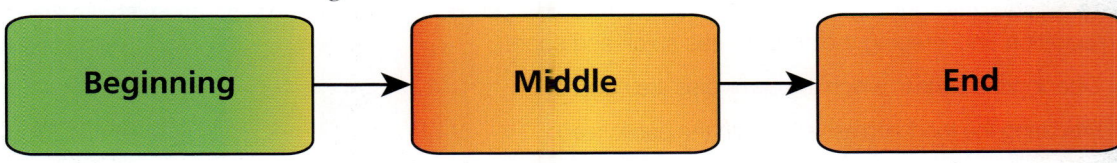

Beginning → Middle → End

2 Still looking at the text:
   a) Who is the text's audience?
   b) What is its purpose?

3 How does the order of the information in the text help engage the reader? Use the questions in the bulleted list above to help work out your ideas. These phrases might help you:

Starting with...makes the reader...

Then there is...

The text closes with...

4 How does the order of the information in the text help achieve its purpose? Use the questions in the bulleted list above to help work out your ideas. These phrases might help you:

The writer begins with...so that...

Next...

Then tells the reader...

The writer finishes with...

Activity 2 — Writing about the structure of a text

1 When you write about a text's structure you need to explain how each part of it helps achieve the text's purpose for its audience. You could include words such as *introduces, tells, reinforces, connects, builds, leaves*.

Use the information you have gathered to explain how the text's structure helps it suit its audience and achieve its purpose.

Unit 3 Know how to analyse structural features

we rescue, care for and rehabilitate injured primates in West Africa

Protecting primates

Working closely with the Cameroon government and local people, Ape Action Africa is working hard to protect apes and monkeys in Cameroon by:
- Helping in the rescue and naming of confiscated primates
- Encouraging children to take an interest in the environment through interactive education programmes
- Developing a reintroduction programme together with other ape sanctuaries

Photo by Max Hug-Williams

How can I help?

With more than 250 apes and monkeys to look after, money is always needed for food, medicine and for the wages for their dedicated carers. Chimps and gorillas can live for 40 to 50 years in captivity, so we have a long term commitment to care for them during their lifetime.

Adopt an Ape

By adopting one of the animals at our primate sanctuary, you can get directly involved in conservation and make a difference where it counts. We are a charity and rely entirely on donations. Your help is therefore vital to ensure that we can continue to fight for the survival of the great apes of Cameroon.

What you will receive

- The personal reward of investing in an individual animal's future
- Biography and colour photograph of your adopted ape
- Annual update about your adopted ape
- Regular Ape Action Africa newsletters and e-news

we work with local communities to ensure understanding of primates leading to their long-term protection

A gift with a difference

Why not give an adoption as a gift? Your friends and family will love our gift pack, and what's more they'll be giving something back by receiving one.
Adopt an ape and give a gift that cares.

www.apeactionafrica.org

3 Know how to analyse paragraph structure

I am learning how to:
- understand in what order information is given within paragraphs
- understand how organisation within a paragraph helps it suit its audience and achieve its purpose.

The way a paragraph is structured helps the text reach its audience and achieve its purpose.

To analyse paragraph structure, follow these steps:

> Read the paragraph, looking for the sentence which gives the main point or idea. This is the topic sentence. It is not always the first sentence.

> Read the rest of the paragraph. Decide how it develops the main point by asking:
> - Does it **explain it in more detail** (i.e. say the same thing but provide more detail)?
> - Does it give **evidence** that supports the main point (e.g. statistics, examples, facts)?
> - Does it make **comparisons** with the main point (e.g. *unlike…, similar to…*)?
> - Does it give **reasons** to support the main point (e.g. tell you why it's true)?

Key term
Paragraph structure – in non-fiction texts a paragraph usually has a topic sentence. The topic sentence gives the main point the paragraph is about. The rest of the paragraph develops the main point. For example, it might give more detail, reasons, evidence, or arguments for or against the point.

Adele's right, she needs life experience

Good old Adele. The soul singer has reportedly turned down a seven-figure deal from HarperCollins to write her autobiography. In her 24 years, she has accrued one Oscar, two mega-hit albums, four Brit Awards, nine Grammies, a personal fortune of £30 million, and 1.46 million clicks for 'Someone Like You', making it the most downloaded song ever. Nevertheless, she has said that she would like to gather a little more life experience before writing it all down.

She is quite right; 24 is far too young to start looking back. Although that hasn't stopped the likes of Katie Price (34, four autobiographies), Wayne Rooney (27, three volumes) and Justin Bieber (19, two down, many more to come). The world certainly doesn't need another stocking filler with an airbrushed glossy cover and a punny title (*Someone Like Me*, maybe?). And you might argue that Adele has already done her fair share of sharing on her two lovelorn albums, *19* and *21*.

There is also the small matter that last year, when she was essentially on maternity leave, Adele earned £41,000 a day in royalties, etc. So perhaps the usual motivation for putting pen to paper – turning a fast buck – doesn't apply.

Unit 3 Know how to analyse structural features

Activity 1 — Understand the text's audience and purpose

1 Read the text on page 28 which is an article published in a national newspaper.
2 Decide the audience(s) and purpose of the text from the list below. Give reasons for your answers.
   a) Audience:
      - children
      - teenagers
      - general adult
      - expert.
   b) Purpose:
      - explain
      - describe
      - inform
      - argue
      - advise.

Activity 2 — Understand what a sentence is contributing to a paragraph

To understand what a sentence contributes to a paragraph, ask yourself:
- Where is it in the paragraph? (*beginning, middle, end; after, before*)
- What it is doing for the reader? (*introducing the main point* (the topic sentence); *adding an opinion, description, facts, reasons*, etc.)

1 Find the sentence that expresses the main point in each paragraph in the text.
2 Decide how the other sentences develop the main point in each paragraph by asking: What does it do? For example, *it adds more detail, reasons, gives evidence, or makes a comparison.*

Activity 3 — Comment on paragraph structure

Use the work you have already done to help you write a response to the following questions:

1 How are the paragraphs in the text organised to help the text achieve its purpose and suit its audience?
2 Write a few sentences summing up what the text is about and explaining its purpose and audience.
3 Write about each paragraph in order. Explain how the way it is organised engages the reader and achieves the purpose.
   - What is the main point of the paragraph?
   - How does the main point engage the reader?
   - How does the rest of each paragraph support the main point?
   - How does this help achieve the text's purpose for its audience?
   For example:

   > First the reader is given the writer's opinion: 'Good old Adele'. This makes the reader wonder... Since the purpose of the text is... then this helps because... After... Then...

29

4 Know how to respond to sentence order and construction

I am learning how to:
- → recognise the order in which sentences are placed
- → understand how sentences are organised
- → understand the effect of the way in which sentences are organised.

When placed next to each other, sentences – and the different pieces of information within a sentence – can reinforce an idea, build an impression or contrast with each other. To understand the impact of the way a sentence or a sequence of sentences is constructed, ask yourself:

- What are the separate pieces of information I am being given?
- What order are these different pieces of information placed in?
- How do the different pieces of information link to each other? For example, does one explain the other further; do they reinforce, contrast or contradict each other?
- What effect does this order have on the reader? For example, does it surprise or convince the reader?
- How does this order help the text achieve its purpose?

Every year President Obama addresses all the students of the USA as they return to school in September. In the speech below he also spoke about the tireless work teachers do on behalf of students.

Key terms
Sentence – expresses a complete thought and makes sense on its own.
Clause – a chunk of meaning within the sentence. It has to contain a verb.
Main clause – a clause that makes sense on its own.
Subordinate clause – a clause that does *not* make sense on its own. It relies on the main clause of the sentence to make sense.

Teachers are the men and women who might be working harder than just about anybody these days. Whether you go to a big school or a small one, whether you attend a public or private or charter school – your teachers are giving up their weekends; they're waking up at dawn; they're cramming their days full of classes and extra-curricular activities. And then they're going home, eating some dinner, and then they've got to stay up, sometimes past midnight, grading your papers and correcting your grammar, and making sure you got that algebra formula properly.

And they don't do it for a fancy office. They don't. They sure don't do it for the big salary. They do it for you. They do it because nothing gives them more satisfaction than seeing you learn. They live for those moments when something clicks, when you amaze them with your intellect or your vocabulary, or they see what kind of person you're becoming. And they're proud of you. And they say, I had something to do with that, that wonderful young person who is going to succeed. They have confidence in you that you will be the citizens and leaders who take us into tomorrow. They know you're our future. So your teachers are pouring everything they've got into you, and they're not alone.

Unit 3 **Know how to analyse structural features**

| **Activity 1** | Understand how information is organised within a sentence |

Break longer sentences down into chunks of meaning and look at the order in which the writer gives information. The order will be helping to achieve the text's purpose.

1 Read the text on page 32.
   a) Sum up what it is about.
   b) What is its purpose?
   c) Who is its audience?
2 Read the second sentence in the first paragraph.
   a) What does the first half of the sentence (before the dash) tell you?
   b) What does the second half of the sentence tell you?
   c) How do these pieces of information link together?
   d) What effect does this order have on the reader?
   e) How does this order help the text achieve its purpose?
3 Read the third sentence in the first paragraph.
   a) How does it link to the sentence that went before?
   b) Describe the order in which information is given in the sentence, e.g. *First it tells you…*
   c) How do the pieces of information in the sentence link together?
   d) What effect does this order have on the reader?
4 How does the order information is given in across these sentences help the text achieve its purpose?

| **Activity 2** | Understand the effect of the order of sentences |

Look at the order in which the sentences are written and how they reinforce, expand on, contradict, contrast, and link with each other. The order of the sentences will be helping to achieve the text's purpose.

1 Read the first two lines of the second paragraph of the text.
   a) What idea is being expressed in these two lines?
   b) Look at each sentence in turn and work out how it links to the others. Does it:
   - introduce an idea?
   - reinforce an idea?
   - repeat an idea?
   - develop an idea?
   - contrast with an idea before/after?
   - contradict other sentences?
   c) Which words has the writer used to link these sentences together?
   d) How do the order of the sentences and the links between them help the writer achieve his purpose?
2 Read the remainder of the second paragraph.
   a) What idea is being expressed?
   b) Look at each sentence in turn and work out how it links to the others. Does it:
   - reinforce an idea?
   - contrast with an idea before/after?
   - develop an idea?
   - sum up?
   - express a new idea?
   c) What effect do these links have on the reader?
   d) How does the order of the sentences help the writer achieve his purpose?

31

UNIT 4
Know how to refer to evidence in texts

1 Know how to identify and select what is relevant

I am learning how to:
- recognise what is relevant (and what is not) in a text
- choose and use the best quotations to back up my ideas.

To work out what information is relevant in a text, first make sure you understand exactly what you need from it. Then read the text, selecting only the information needed for the task. Leave out anything that is not relevant.

Key term
Relevant evidence – information in a text is relevant only if it is exactly what you were asked to find.

Activity 1 Work out what is relevant in a text

Read the advertisement on page 33. Answer each of the questions below. Make sure you find **all** the relevant information in the text.

1. What did the Sainsbury's employee do?
2. Why is the chairman of Iceland impressed?
3. What is the chairman offering the Sainsbury's employee?
4. What jokes has the writer made about bread?

Focus your effort

Make sure you understand exactly what a task is asking you to do.
1. Read the task through twice and pick out the key words.
2. Work out what you need to do, using the key words.
3. Read the task again to check you are right.

Activity 2 Understand how to select and use the best quotations

Pick out the **fewest** words from the text that will make the point you want. Place them in quotation marks and copy the words from the text accurately, including the spelling and punctuation.

1. Pick out five quotations you could use to show how the writer gives a good impression of Iceland.
2. Make your quotation part of your sentence as you write your answer to the question below.
   How does the writer create a good impression of Iceland for readers?
   The following phrases will help you get started:

   When the writer says '…' it shows that…

   The words '…' suggest…

The following advertisement appeared in national newspapers after they ran a story with the headline that appears at the top.

SOMEONE AT SAINSBURY'S USED THEIR LOAF. THEY WENT TO ICELAND.

Iceland

Dear astute Sainsbury's employee,

Please forgive our attempts to butter you up in such a public forum but crumbs when we heard about your recent show of business acumen we thought 'here's an employee on the rise'. That's why we'd like to offer you a job at Britain's number one supermarket to work for.

We'd like to propose a toast to the initiative you showed in replenishing your store's stock of Warburtons bread with a much cheaper supplier (the Iceland store next door).

By making some healthy dough on the Sainsbury's mark-up, you demonstrated a nose for the best deals.

Feel free to contact me personally about this job offer, at Iceland we always knead high-rollers like you.

We trust you'll make the right choice. We genuinely think you're the best thing since… well, since frozen prawn rings.

Yours faithfully,

Malcolm Walker

Malcolm Walker
Chairman & Chief Executive, Iceland Foods Ltd.

Iceland

2 Know how to summarise information and ideas in a text

I am learning how to:
- identify main points and details in a text and sum them up
- find relevant information and ideas in a text.

A summary is an overview of the main information or ideas in a text. Read the text carefully to find and note down the main points. You do not need to include all the detail.

If the information you need to summarise is given through a lot of details then summarise what they say in a single sentence.

Do you think you are creative? The writer of the text below spends his life training people to become more creative in their work. This is what he believes.

Key terms
A **summary** – states only the main points being made about a topic.
A **main point** – a significant 'big picture' idea that a paragraph or text is expressing, such as, 'Teenagers across the world love eating pizza.'
A **detail** – tells you more about a main point, such as, 'In India teenagers' favourite pizza toppings are pickled ginger, minced mutton and paneer; whereas in Russia teenagers prefer mixed chopped fish and onions.' Details can be summarised, such as, 'The favourite toppings vary with each country.'

> You have some pretty amazing capabilities! As a human being you are naturally creative. And although our creative instincts tend to become **suppressed**, we have all the resources to change that around.
>
> As time goes on, we are taught there is a 'right' and a 'wrong' way of doing things. As a result, as adults our creativity often comes more through luck than application. The ice cream cone is a case in point. It was created by Ernest Hamwi in 1904 at the St Louis World's Fair. He was selling waffles and next door to him was an ice cream vendor who ran out of dishes. He rolled a waffle to put the ice cream in and the rest is history. Unfortunately these lucky instances are few and far between.

Expand your vocabulary
suppress – to put an end to something, to hold it back, or to hide it and prevent it from being known

Activity 1 | Summarise the main points in a non-fiction text

To summarise a text you need to find the main points.

1. Read the text above. It explains something important about humans, and gives some examples.
2. Note down the main points and ask 'what are the main points telling me?'
3. Use your notes to sum up in one sentence what the text tells you about humans.

Unit 4 Know how to refer to evidence in texts

Activity 2   Summarise the details in a non-fiction text

Search for all the relevant details in the text. Then decide what they tell you and sum this up in a single sentence.

1. Read the text on page 34 and note down all the details about how luck led to the invention of the ice cream cone.
2. Decide: when I put all the details together, what are they telling me?
3. Write a single sentence summing up how luck led to the invention of the ice cream cone.

What do you know about… the author?

Suzanne Collins has been writing for children's television since the early 1990s. Her name appears in the credits of many shows for young children. She then wrote a successful fantasy/war series of books set in an urban landscape, *The Underland Chronicles*. Her latest successful book series is *The Hunger Games Trilogy*.

The text below is taken from the novel *The Hunger Games* by author Suzanne Collins. Katniss has been taken from her home in one of the poorest parts of the country to the capital city to take part in a violent televised contest that entertains the country's rich rulers. The food she is given on her arrival amazes her.

> He presses a button on the side of the table. The top splits and from below rises a second tabletop that holds our lunch. Chicken and chunks of orange cooked in a creamy sauce, laid on a bed of pearly white grain, tiny green peas and onions, rolls shaped like flowers, and for desert, a pudding the colour of honey.
>
> I try to imagine assembling this meal myself back home. Chickens are too expensive, but I could make do with wild turkey. I'd need to shoot a second turkey to trade for an orange. Goat's milk would have to substitute for cream. We can grow peas in the garden. I would have to get wild onions from the woods. I don't recognise the grain; our ration cooks down to an unattractive brown mush. Fancy rolls would mean a trade with the baker, perhaps for two or three squirrels. As for the pudding, I can't even guess what's in it. Days of hunting and gathering for this one meal and even then it would be a poor substitute for the Capitol version.
>
> What must it be like, I wonder, to live in a world where food appears at the press of a button? How would I spend the hours I now commit to combing the woods for sustenance if it were so easy to come by?

Activity 3   Summarise the main points or ideas in a fiction text

Fiction writers show readers what is happening, so to sum up the main point or an idea in fiction you have to search for all the relevant information and deduce what the main point is from those details. You can then sum it up in a sentence.

1. Read the fiction text above. You are going to sum up the contrast between what Katniss is used to and what she is experiencing now.
   a) Search the text thoroughly and note down all the relevant details.
   b) Decide: when I put all the details together, what are they telling me?
2. Write a single sentence summing up the contrast Katniss experiences.

35

3 Know how to identify and track a line of argument in a text

Key terms

An **argument** – an attempt to convince the reader to agree with the writer. To do this writers make a series of points in favour of their view and support them with reasons and evidence.

A **line of argument** – means the order in which a writer makes the points, and how the argument builds up.

I am learning how to:
→ identify points that are part of an argument
→ follow the line of argument through a text
→ explain the line of argument in a text.

When writers express their views on a topic they create a logical argument and support it with reasons, statistics, examples, anecdotes, etc. To track the line of argument you need to recognise the main points and the order in which they are made. Look at the way an argument builds up from paragraph to paragraph. Each paragraph will either support the last point made, or add a new one.

The text on page 37 opposite is written by journalist George Monbiot and appeared in a national newspaper.

Activity 1 Find and follow the main points in an argument

The main points in an argument will be expressed in the topic sentences often towards the beginning of each paragraph. Find and note these down to work out the line of argument.

1. Read the text on page 37.
   a) Decide its purpose.
   b) Sum up the argument being put forward.
2. Read each paragraph, find its topic sentence and sum up the main point.
3. Paragraph 1 is a standfirst, appearing above the photo. Read the first sentence of each following paragraph 2–6. Look for words that show how each links to the previous point. Decide whether it adds a new point or develops one already made. Fill in a table like the one below.

Paragraph	Main point	Adds a new point	Develops a point
1	Author rejects Samsung smartphones because the tin comes from Bangka Island	✓	

4. Decide how the rest of each paragraph develops its main point – for example, by providing examples, expanding on the main point, giving reasons, statistics or a personal anecdote.

Activity 2 Explain a line of argument

Use the work you have already done to help you complete this task.

Explain how the writer develops his line of argument in the text.

- Write about the points in the same order as they appear in the text using words like:
  First the writer states that…
- Explain how each new point links to the last. For example:
  Then the next paragraph develops the previous point / adds a new point…
- Explain how each main point is developed. For example:
  The writer develops this point by giving reasons, such as…

Unit 4 Know how to refer to evidence in texts

My search for a smartphone ends here

Samsung's admission that its smartphones may contain tin from Bangka Island makes me think I'm better off without one after all.

At least we know now. Thanks to the campaign by Friends of the Earth, Samsung has at last discovered the source of the tin it uses to make its products – including smartphones. Despite years of campaigns about the human and environmental impacts of the metals used to make electronic goods, several of the biggest manufacturers have remained in a state of convenient ignorance about the sources of their raw materials.

Now, under intense public pressure, Samsung has traced some of the tin it uses to Bangka Island in Indonesia, whose mines are **notorious** for their great toll on human lives and ecosystems, and in particular for the fact that children work there in terrible conditions.

Obtaining information like this is often extremely hard, and it's a credit to Friends of the Earth's Make It Better campaign that we have acquired this fragment. Last month, when I tried to buy a smartphone that was not soaked in blood, I found myself stumbling around, blindfolded by the lack of information. As Nokia, which seems to have done more than any other such firm to investigate its own supply chain, told me, 'there has been no **credible** system in the electronics industry that allows a company to **determine** the source of their material'.

It seems amazing to me that our dependence on **sophisticated** electronics has progressed so far while these questions about their humanitarian impacts have progressed so little. Don't we want to know? Don't we even want the companies who manufacture them to know on our behalf?

After pursuing the issue of sourcing metals from the Democratic Republic of Congo…I decided not to buy a smartphone, unless FairPhone succeeds in manufacturing one. And perhaps not even then. Confronting this issue prompted me to ask another question altogether: do I really want one anyway, and might I not be happier without it? What about you?

Expand your vocabulary

notorious – famous for wrongdoing
credible – trustworthy, believable
determine – find out
sophisticated – elaborate, complicated

4 Know how to compare information across texts

I am learning how to:
→ find similar information in two texts
→ examine how texts use information on the same topic to achieve different purposes.

Texts may be about a similar topic but achieving a different purpose, or suiting a different audience. You need to work out each text's audience and purpose. Then look for similarities and differences between the information they contain. To compare the texts decide:

1 How is similar information expressed differently?
2 How does the different way similar information is expressed help the text achieve its purpose for its audience?
3 How does including different information help each text achieve its purpose for that audience?

Politician David Blunkett is blind and has had a number of guide dogs helping him over the years. Here he describes Cosby, his latest guide dog.

Key term
Comparing texts – identifying similarities and differences in texts' purpose or audience, and identifying how information in the texts helps the writer achieve this.

The boss of me

Fifteen months ago, I welcomed my sixth and latest guide dog, Cosby, a curly coat retriever/Labrador cross… Cosby took over from my previous faithful companion, Sadie, who sadly died last July. At nearly 43 kilos (95lb in old money) Cosby has just celebrated his third birthday, but at heart is still a puppy. Nothing suits him better than being thrown a ball. In fact he is prepared to go without his favourite biscuit while he carries the ball, which appears in all sorts of strange places – I wouldn't be at all surprised if one day I find his ball on the train between London and Sheffield.

After some effort, it has been possible to reduce one **element** of Cosby's behaviour – namely, **scavenging** from the kitchen – that can be a nightmare. When a dog is as tall as he is, there's no need for paws on the work surface, he literally just lifts off anything that takes his fancy from the breadboard, table or top of the fridge, so we have to be extremely careful.

Part of the problem, as dog owners will know, is actually catching them at it. As I understand it, there's no point in punishing a dog long afterwards for something that they will not actually remember having done. That said, quite often the dog ends up in his bed, in Cosby's case with his paws over his nose, when something untoward has happened, trying to pretend it has nothing to do with him.

Expand your vocabulary
element – a part of something
scavenge – search for materials worth saving, such as food

Activity 1 Identify the similarities and differences between the texts

1 Read the texts above and on page 39. Sum up what they are about.
2 What is each text's audience and purpose?
3 What is similar about the information in both texts?
4 What is different about the information contained in the two texts?

Unit 4 Know how to refer to evidence in texts

This leaflet about guide dogs is produced by the Guide Dogs charity.

Guide Dogs could change your life

Do you, or does someone you know, have sight loss that makes it difficult to get around independently or live life to the full? A guide dog could make a life-changing difference.

Did you know...?

- **A guide dog can offer a unique, safe and effective way of getting about independently and confidently.**
- **You don't need to have lost all your sight.** Most people who own a guide dog still have some vision. You don't have to be formally registered as blind or partially-sighted, either.
- **There's no upper age limit** – people of all ages can now apply for a guide dog. Young people through to people in their 70s, 80s and even 90s have become successful guide dog owners.
- **It costs just 50p to have a guide dog.** All essential equipment and training is provided by Guide Dogs, and we can also cover the cost of vet bills and dog food if people wish.
- **No previous experience of keeping or caring for a dog is necessary.** Providing you are committed and able enough to work with, support and care for a guide dog then our training will teach you all you need to know.
- **It's not just about improving your mobility.** A guide dog and its owner exist as a partnership, and the companionship, loyalty and fun that each partner brings to his relationship can be immensely rewarding.

Call us on: 0345 372 7499
Email us at: guidedogs@guidedogs.org.uk
Or visit: www.guidedogs.org.uk/enquiries

Guide Dogs

Activity 2 Compare the way information is used to achieve different purposes

First look at how similar information is expressed differently to help each text achieve its purpose. Then work out how having different information helps each text achieve its purpose.

1. Look at the similar information in the texts.
   a) How is it expressed in the text on page 38?
   b) How does this help the text achieve its purpose?
   c) How is it expressed in the text above?
   d) How does this help the text achieve its purpose?
2. Look at the differences in information included in each text.
   a) How does the different information in the text on page 38 help the text achieve its purpose?
   b) How does the different information in the text above help the text achieve its purpose?

UNIT 5 Know how to understand themes, ideas and point of view

1 Know how to understand the writer's ideas and themes

I am learning how to:
→ understand the ideas and themes in a text.

In non-fiction the writer might talk to you about themes directly. In fiction writers might show you their ideas about a theme through characters' experiences, setting, atmosphere and word choice. To work out the ideas or themes in a text first make sure you understand the information and events in it. Then ask yourself what big ideas or topics about people's experiences, feelings or values the writer is focusing on. Try to express your idea in a single word or short phrase. Once you have summed up the text's theme or idea search the text again for all the details that are relevant to that theme and decide what the details suggest about it.

Key term
An **idea** or **theme** – a topic to do with people or about life that the text focuses on. They are often to do with feelings, experiences or values. They are usually expressed in a single word or short phrase, e.g. *love, good and evil, suffering, prejudice*.

Activity 1 Work out the text's theme

Read the text on page 41.

1. Carefully read the text, then briefly sum up what it is about.
2. Think about the text as you answer these questions:
   a) List what the children experience on the farm.
   b) What feeling, experience or value is being explored? (Hint: complete this sentence in a single word or short phrase: *The children are experiencing…*)

Activity 2 Identify the ideas about the theme that the writer is expressing

Look closely at the details in the text that show something about the theme. What ideas do they reveal? What does the language used suggest about the writer's attitude to the theme?

1. Find all the details in the text that show the children are suffering. Look closely at the detail and the words used to express it. Work out what these suggest about the nature of their suffering.

Detail about suffering	What it suggests about the children's suffering
'We lived on soup and bread in that place.'	Suffering is created when the children eat the most basic food, 'soup and bread', day after day. It is boring, there is no variety, and it is not going to contain all the vitamins they need to be healthy. Children enjoy eating different meals but these children are deprived of that experience.

40

Unit 5 Know how to understand themes, ideas and point of view

At the end of the Second World War many orphans were sent to Australia to be taken in by families running farms and to begin a new life. In this extract from *Alone on a Wide, Wide Sea*, by Michael Morpurgo, the writer describes their experience on one of these farms.

This photograph shows child emigrants being shown the route to Australia on a map.

Lunch was soup and bread brought to our long trestle table in the dormitory and ladled out into our bowls by Mrs Bacon, who scarcely ever spoke to us. We lived on soup and bread in that place. Then in the afternoons we'd be set to clearing the paddocks of stones, or we'd be fetching and carrying water to the troughs, and blocks of salt, too. These buckets almost pulled my arms out of their sockets because they were so heavy. You had to fill them right up too, because if ever Piggy Bacon caught you carrying a half-empty bucket you were in big trouble, and trouble always meant the strap. So we filled them up to the brim every time. And when all the water-carrying was done, we'd be digging up weeds or filling in potholes in the tracks, or pulling out tree roots, all of us straining together on the ropes.

Our hands blistered, our feet blistered. Bites and sores festered. None of that mattered to Piggy Bacon. Once one job was done there was always another waiting. We worked hard because if we didn't he'd stop our food. We worked hard because if we didn't he'd strap us. We worked hard because if we didn't he'd cancel our evening playtime and make us work an hour extra at the end of the day. I so longed for that hour off – we all did – and we hated to miss it. That promise of an hour's playtime was what kept me going when every bone in my body ached with tiredness.

2 Know how to understand the writer's viewpoint

I am learning how to:
- identify and understand the writer's viewpoint.

To work out a writer's viewpoint, first decide what idea or theme is being written about. Find all the details to do with that topic and identify the writer's thoughts, feelings and opinions about it. Together these reveal the writer's point of view.

Read this article about Valentine's Day by Janet Street-Porter.

Key term
Viewpoint – the writer's point of view or attitude towards the idea or theme being written about.

Today is the day I dread. Valentine's Day is when the country is cruelly divided into winners and losers.

You can easily spot the winners – those **smug** creeps swanning around with a self-satisfied grin on their faces, like the cat that got the cream.

They're the ones who have had flowers delivered to their office, or who already know they have been invited out for a 'special treat' this evening. The ones who got a hand-delivered card or present posted through their letterbox at dawn.

The ones whose partner proposed to them on the train to work, or whose chap rented a billboard so the whole world could share in their undying love.

Or the ones who awoke to find a saucy e-card had plopped into their inbox overnight. YUCK!

The rest of us – the so-called losers in love – will spend today superficially behaving as normal, acting as if we've better things to do than drink Prosecco and eat oysters by candlelight (pretending we're going to our book clubs, have signed up for hot yoga or are meeting some friends for a pizza).

But deep down we'll be experiencing that mixture of jealousy and **impotent** rage that only comes on Valentine's Day – because we've been unfairly categorised as rejects, yet again.

Expand your vocabulary

smug – feeling great satisfaction about your situation or yourself, usually in a way that is offensive to others
impotent – unable to change anything, powerless

Unit 5 Know how to understand themes, ideas and point of view

Activity 1 — Work out what idea or theme the writer is writing about

Read the text on page 42 carefully then answer these questions. Use evidence from the text to support your answers.

1 What is the writer's situation?
2 Think of three words or phrases that sum up the writer's experience.
3 What idea is the writer expressing in this text? For example:

She is showing readers…

Activity 2 — Understand the writer's point of view

To understand the writer's point of view about a theme or idea, find details that reveal their thoughts, opinions and feelings towards it. Then sum up what the writer's views are.

1 Re-read the text. What points does the writer make about people's experience of Valentine's Day?
2 Search the text for words and phrases that reveal the writer's opinions and feelings about the idea they are writing about. Find three examples of each. These will be shown through their thoughts, comments and descriptions.

Opinions	Feelings
1 'Valentine's Day is when the country is cruelly divided into winners and losers.'	1 'dread'
2 'the winners – those smug creeps swanning around with a self-satisfied grin on their faces, like the cat that got the cream.'	2
3	3

3 Read through the information you have gathered. What is the writer's attitude toward the idea she is writing about? Your answer is the writer's viewpoint.

Activity 3 — Comment on the writer's viewpoint

When you comment on a writer's viewpoint you should explain what idea they are writing about and what their attitude is towards it. Include evidence from the text to support your ideas.

1 Use your work from the Activities above to answer this question.
What is Janet Street-Porter's viewpoint in this article?
You could use these phrases in your response:

…is expressing the idea that…
Her attitude towards… is…
She feels…
Her opinion of… is…
This is shown when she says…
Altogether her viewpoint is…

3 Know how to understand bias

I am learning how to:
→ identify the writer's point of view
→ recognise whether one side of an argument is put forward more strongly than another.

To decide whether a writer is biased or not, you need to work out what point of view is being put forward about a topic and whether alternative views are being given the same emphasis. You should also look for details that suggest the writer's feelings and opinions.

First decide what ideas or arguments are being expressed in a text. Then decide whether a balance of points of view is given or not.

> **Key term**
> **Bias** – preference is given to one point of view. It is put forward more strongly than other sides of an argument.

Activity 1 Identify whether a writer shows bias

1. Read the text on page 45. Sum up what it is about.
2. Read the text again and decide what point is made in each paragraph.
3. Review the points made – which of these statements is true?
    a) Only one point of view is given.
    b) More than one point of view is given.
    c) All the points of view are put forward with the same emphasis.
    d) One point of view is given more emphasis than others (the text is biased).

Activity 2 Understand how a writer creates bias

Search for words that reveal the writer's attitude towards each point that is made.

1. How does the writer describe people or ideas with which he:
    a) agrees?
    b) disagrees?
2. How does the way people are described position readers to value their comments?
3. Is the writer mostly positive towards people and points with which he agrees, and mostly negative towards people and points with which he disagrees?

Activity 3 Commenting on bias

1. Use the work you have already done to answer this question.
   How is the writer's bias revealed in the text?
   - Explain what the text is about.
   - Explain how the writer's bias is shown in the text.

Should schools insist students only carry a £1 mobile phone?

With the development of a mobile phone that costs only £1 and yet still sends texts and makes calls, headteachers are putting an end to the timewasting, stressful problems caused by students taking photos and video, listening to music and accessing the internet in school.

As Headteacher of the Year, Samuel Evans of Trustfell Academy wisely explains: 'So much time is wasted and unhappiness caused by mobile phones. Introducing a policy of "one phone for all" reduces bullying, makes children less vulnerable to mugging and helps them focus more on their learning.'

In September, Mr Evans introduced a school policy insisting that pupils can only bring to school an Alcatel One Touch 232, which costs £1. He also asks parents to buy each term only the minimum credit needed to get the phone up and running: £10. 'It has been an **unqualified** success,' he says. 'My staff and students are really seeing the benefits.

And parents are grateful that they are not under pressure to fork out for the latest gadget. Our policy has given parents a reason to say "No" and not give in to badgering.'

Of course, not all students at Trustfell Academy agree with their award-winning headteacher. When we talk to school truant Dan Riley, 14, who has an ASBO, he argues, 'What's the point of a phone if you can't play Angry Birds or update your Facebook status on it?'

Hard-working school governor Dot Oshun comments, 'The phone is excellent value for money as it features all the essentials a hard-working student could possibly want: an alarm clock, radio, calculator and a 3.8 cm (1.5 in) colour screen.'

Since the school introduced the 'one phone for all' policy in September there have been no recorded incidents in school of stolen phones, images of undesirable incidents being posted on the internet or pupils being bullied for not having the latest phone technology.

Parents are also delighted. As one said, 'I don't have to worry about what my son is getting up to on his phone at school, yet he can still text me if he is going to be late home. And he can't run up a massive phone bill sending photos to his friends. That's fantastic.'

Sixth former Alice Harman, who has been offered a place at Oxford University, said, 'When the "one phone for all" policy was introduced some people moaned, but I think it's quite freeing not to be judged by the quality of your phone.'

Not bad for only £1.

Expand your vocabulary

unqualified – no conditions or reservations

4 Know how to understand narrative point of view

I am learning how to:
- recognise the difference between first person and third person narrative
- understand the effect of different narrative choices.

Work out whether a text is told using the first person or third person by searching the narrative for pronouns. If the pronoun **I** is used then you are most probably reading first person narrative, but if only **she** or **he** is used then you are likely to be reading third person narrative. Writers choose which character's perspective to tell the story from and this affects the way the reader understands the story.

The text below is the opening of Michael Morpurgo's novel *War Horse*, which describes the experience of a horse used in the fighting in the First World War.

Key terms
Narrative – the part of the text that describes action, people, places.
Narrative point of view – the 'position' from which a writer tells a story. For example, a story might be told by a character (first person) or by the writer letting us know what one or more characters think or feel (third person).
Third person narrative – where the writer tells the story using *he/she*, *him/her*, *his/hers*.
First person narrative – where the writer chooses one character to tell the story. You see everything through that character's eyes only. The story is told by the character using *I/me/my/we*.
Dialogue – the words spoken in the text.

Expand your vocabulary
spindly – tall, thin and weak-looking
thoroughbred – a pure breed, often a racehorse

> My earliest memories are a confusion of hilly fields and dark, damp stables, and rats that scampered along the beams above my head. But I remember well enough the day of the horse sale. The terror of it stayed with me all my life.
>
> I was not yet six months old, a gangling, leggy colt who had never been further than a few feet from his mother. We were parted that day in the terrible hubbub of the auction ring and I was never to see her again. She was a fine working farm horse, getting on in years but with all the strength and stamina of an Irish draught horse quite evident in her fore and hind quarters. She was sold within minutes, and before I could follow her through the gates, she was whisked away out of the ring. But somehow I was more difficult to dispose of. Perhaps it was the wild look in my eye as I circled the ring in a desperate search for my mother, or perhaps it was that none of the farmers and gypsies there were looking for a **spindly**-looking half-**thoroughbred** colt. But whatever the reasons they were a long time haggling over how little I was worth before I heard the hammer go down and I was driven out through the gates and into a pen outside.

Unit 5 Know how to understand themes, ideas and point of view

Activity 1	Work out which narrative point of view is being used

Read the text on page 46 and search the narrative for the pronouns **I/me/my/we**. This will indicate that it is told in the first person. If only **his/her** are used it means the story is most likely being told in the third person.

1 Which narrative point of view is being used in the text?
2 Search for clues in the text that tell you about the character whose story is being told. This is the viewpoint character. What do you learn about the viewpoint character in this text?

Activity 2	Writing about narrative viewpoint in texts

Use the information you have already gathered as you answer this question.

1 What is the effect of the writer's choice of viewpoint in the text on page 46?
   - Explain what viewpoint is used.
   - Explain what it allows the writer to do.
   - Explain what effect this has on the reader.

The following phrases will help you:

The writer has used...

This makes sure the reader knows...

It makes the reader...

The text below is the opening of a story set in a grim future in which Mei, living in China, is about to leave her home because she has a vital role to play in overcoming the meks (intelligent but evil machines), which cause much suffering.

> Hundreds of hot air balloons bobbed in the wind, their baskets tied together with long stretches of rope. From the ground, the Sky Village looked like a giant net, poised to capture the clouds as it drifted far above. Mei strained her eyes to make out the figures painted on the two closest balloons – a dragon and a phoenix, both symbols of power.
>
> Mei had glimpsed the Sky Village only a few times in her life as it passed high over Luo Ye Village, like a parade of upside-down teardrops gliding across the sunrise. Now it was making a rare **descent**, on her account. But Mei did not want this special honour. She wished a sudden great gust of wind would blow the whole village high into the sky, far away from her and the home she wasn't ready to leave.
>
> She and her father stood on the peak of the highest mountain in the region, the lowest point to which the sky villagers were willing to descend. Mei's father squeezed her hand as he glanced nervously at the trees just beyond the clearing. Mei hadn't seen the meks chasing them, but she'd heard them clanking through the trees. She and her father had lost them by scrambling up a pass that was too steep for their metallic bodies.

Expand your vocabulary

descent – to travel downwards

47

4 Know how to understand narrative point of view

Activity 3 | Practise identifying the narrative viewpoint of a text

Remember to search the text carefully for pronouns. If only *she/he* is used and not *I* then the text could well be third person narrative.

1 Read the text on page 47. Which narrative point of view is being used?
2 Search for clues in the text that tell you about the character whose story is being told. This is the viewpoint character. What do you learn about the viewpoint character in this text?

In this extract from Charles Dickens' Victorian novel *Hard Times* he introduces Bounderby, a rich, successful businessman, who is the closest friend of the school master Mr Gradgrind.

…who was Mr Bounderby?

Why, Mr Bounderby was as near to being Mr Gradgrind's bosom friend, as a man **perfectly devoid of sentiment** can approach that spiritual relationship towards another man perfectly devoid of sentiment. So near was Mr Bounderby – or, if the reader should prefer it, so far off.

He was a rich man: banker, merchant, manufacturer, and what not. A big, loud man, with a stare and a metallic laugh. A man made out of a coarse material, which seemed to have been stretched to make so much of him. A man with a great puffed head and forehead, swelled veins in his temples, and such a strained skin to his face that it seemed to hold his eyes open and lift his eyebrows up. A man with a **pervading** appearance of being inflated like a balloon, and ready to start. A man who could never sufficiently **vaunt** himself a self-made man. A man who was always proclaiming, through that brassy **speaking trumpet** voice of his, his old ignorance and his old poverty. A man who was the Bully of **humility**.

A year or two younger than his eminently practical friend, Mr Bounderby looked older; his seven or eight and forty might have had the seven or eight added to it again, without surprising anyone. He had not much hair. One might have fancied he had talked it off; and that what was left, all standing up in disorder, was in that condition from being constantly blown about by his windy boastfulness.

Expand your vocabulary

perfectly devoid of sentiment – totally lacking in feelings
pervading – to be present throughout
vaunt – boast
speaking trumpet – an instrument shaped like a trumpet, which was used to make a speaker's voice louder to help a deaf person hear them
humility – the noun from the adjective 'humble' – to be modest, or to have a low opinion of yourself

48

Unit 5 **Know how to understand themes, ideas and point of view**

Activity 4 | Working out the effect of the writer's narrative viewpoint choices

Readers usually sympathise with the viewpoint character, as they see events from their perspective and know their thoughts and feelings. The writer can position the reader to take a particular view of events and themes by telling the story from a particular viewpoint.

1 Use what you have already learned about the viewpoint character of the text on page 46. Re-read the introduction to the text and study the image. What kind of things are going to happen to the horse?
2 How will having this narrative viewpoint help readers understand a horse's experience of war?
3 What are the advantages of choosing to tell this story from this character's viewpoint rather than that of a soldier?
4 Re-read the introduction to the text on page 47 and refer to what you have already discovered about the narrative viewpoint. What is Mei going to have to do?
5 What are the advantages of choosing to tell a story from the viewpoint of a 'good' character – who will solve the problems – instead of the point of view of one of the evil meks, who are the source of them?

Activity 5 | Understanding narrative viewpoint in an older text

In older texts writers often guide their readers' response to a character by expressing their opinions about them directly, and telling the reader how to interpret their behaviour.

1 Read the text on page 48. Is it told using first or third person narrative?
2 What facts are you told about Bounderby?
3 Find the words and phrases that reveal how the writer feels about Bounderby. What do they each suggest about him?
4 Re-read the last sentence in the first paragraph. What is the effect of referring to the reader here?
5 How has the writer made sure that the reader will dislike Bounderby?

Activity 6 | Writing about narrative viewpoint in older texts

Use the information you have already gathered as you answer this question.

1 What is the effect of the writer's choice of viewpoint in *Hard Times*?
   - Explain what viewpoint is used.
   - Explain how the writer uses it to express his views.
   - Explain what effect this has on the reader's view of characters.

The following phrases will help you:

> The writer has used...
>
> He tells the reader...
>
> This makes sure the reader notices...
>
> It makes the reader...

49

UNIT 6
Know how to comment on language and its impact

1 Know how to respond to a writer's use of language

I am learning how to:
- notice the writer's choice of vocabulary and literary techniques
- respond to the writer's choice of vocabulary and literary techniques.

To respond to a writer's choice of vocabulary or use of literary techniques make sure you first understand what the whole text is about. Then focus on how their language choices help to express their ideas effectively and contribute to the impact of the whole text.

The poem on page 51 was written by Wilfred Owen, a soldier in the First World War (1914–18). Men aged 16 and over had been persuaded to fight for the honour of their country out of a sense of duty and patriotism, believing their actions would be heroic. The reality of the terrible conditions and suffering they endured are expressed in this poem.

Key term
Literary techniques – the way that a writer creates meaning by using features such as imagery, rhyme, rhythm, sound patterns and choice of vocabulary.

Activity 1 — Gain an overview of the whole text

Before you study the details of a literary text, make sure you understand what it is about and, if necessary, have researched its context.

1 Read the poem on page 51 opposite several times, and the introductory context information above. Sum up the events that the poem describes.
2 Which of these themes is present in the poem? Give reasons for your answer.
- Dying out of patriotic duty is glorious.
- Dying in battle is not glorious.

Unit 6 Know how to comment on language and its impact

Dulce et Decorum Est

1 Bent double, like old beggars under sacks,
Knock-kneed, coughing like hags, we cursed through sludge,
Till on the haunting **flares** we turned our backs,
And towards our **distant rest** began to trudge.
5 Men marched asleep. Many had lost their boots
But limped on, blood-shod. All went lame, all blind;
Drunk with fatigue; deaf even to the **hoots**
Of gas-shells dropping softly behind.

Gas! GAS! Quick, boys! – An ecstasy of fumbling
10 Fitting the clumsy **helmets** just in time,
But someone still was yelling out and stumbling
And flound'ring like a man in fire or **lime**. –
Dim through the misty **panes** and thick green light,
As under a green sea, I saw him drowning.

15 In all my dreams before my helpless sight,
He plunges at me, **guttering**, choking, drowning.

If in some smothering dreams, you too could pace
Behind the wagon that we flung him in,
And watch the white eyes writhing in his face,
20 His hanging face, like a devil's sick of sin;
If you could hear, at every jolt, the blood
Come gargling from the froth-corrupted lungs,
Obscene as cancer, bitter as the cud
Of vile, incurable sores on innocent tongues, –
25 My friend, you would not tell with such high zest
To children ardent for some desperate glory,
The old Lie: **Dulce et decorum est**
Pro patria mori.

Expand your vocabulary

flares – these were rockets set off to give light so soldiers could see their targets
distant rest – a camp away from the front line where soldiers were sent to rest
hoots – the noise made by the bomb shells whizzing through the air
gas – a poisonous chlorine or phosgene gas used as a weapon – it filled soldiers' lungs as if they were drowning
helmets – gas masks
lime – a white chemical that burns skin and other living tissues
panes – the glass panel soldiers looked through in their gas masks
guttering – like a candle flame flickering out, or water draining down a gutter, or a sound half way between gurgling and stuttering
dulce et decorum est/pro patria mori – a Latin saying that was popular at the time and meant 'it is sweet and right to die for your country', i.e. it was a great honour to fight and die for England

1 Know how to respond to a writer's use of language

Activity 2 — Understand what words and phrases mean and suggest

To respond to a writer's vocabulary, think about whether one word is linked to another, what it means and suggests, how it builds ideas in the text, and what effect it has on the reader.

1 Work out what each of the words from the poem in the table below denotes and connotes in its position in the poem.

Word	Means	Suggests
'sludge'	Oozing mud	How wet and filthy the conditions are – slippery, too
'haunting flares'		
'trudge'		
'ecstasy'		
'clumsy helmets'		
'helpless sight'		
'smothering'		
'froth-corrupted lungs'		
'zest'		
'ardent'		

Activity 3 — Analyse the effect of a word image

To understand a word image, decide what is being compared within the image. Then consider what effect it has on the reader.

1 Below are five word images (a–e) from the poem. For each, work out what is being compared. Describe what it makes you think, see and feel.

　　a) 'coughing like hags' (line 2)　　d) 'like a devil's sick of sin' (line 20)
　　b) 'Drunk with fatigue' (line 7)　　e) 'bitter as the cud' (line 23)
　　c) 'As under a green sea' (line 14)

2 Decide what effect each of the word images above might have on the 'friend' (line 25) – a reader who believed fighting in the war was noble and a patriotic duty and may only have been soldiers in smart uniforms on parade.

3 How does each word image help to develop a key idea in the poem: the horror of war?

Unit 6 Know how to comment on language and its impact

These contrasting images show an idealised England, which soldiers were encouraged to think of, contrasted with the reality of war in the trenches.

4 For each of the five word images, write a paragraph explaining in full what the image suggests to you. Show how the image is linked to the ideas within the poem. When you write about the images, explain:
   • what is being compared/contrasted in the two images
   • the effect this has on the reader
   • how this contrast develops the ideas in the poem.

   These phrases will help you:

   > The image... compares...
   >
   > It makes the reader picture/imagine/contrast/notice...
   >
   > This adds to the idea that... because...

Activity 4 Understanding the effect of rhyme

Read the poem 'Dulce et Decorum Est' aloud. Focus on places where rhyme is used and decide how the use of rhyme links words and so reinforces the writer's ideas.

1 Find each place where the poet has used rhyme and ask yourself these questions:
   a) Where does the rhyme fall, and what word does it make you notice?
   b) Why does the poet want readers to notice that word especially?

1 Know how to respond to a writer's use of language

Activity 5 — Understanding the effect of rhythm

Read the poem on page 51 aloud and focus on places where rhythm patterns are used. Decide how they help express a mood or effect that helps to express the writer's ideas in that part of the poem.

1. While you read the poem out loud tap out the beat of each line. The poem does not have a regular rhythm. Think of the tired soldiers trudging. How does the rhythm echo this?
2. The punctuation in the poem interrupts the rhythm. How does this make it sound like the persona is speaking?
3. Focus on any lines or phrases where there is a noticeable rhythm, such as lines 5 and 6, and line 9, and decide:
   a) What words does the rhythm make the reader hear or notice?
   b) How is the rhythm created?
   c) What kind of mood or effect does the rhythm create?
   d) How does the mood or effect created by the rhythm suit the ideas expressed in that part of the poem?

Activity 6 — Understand the effect of sound effects

Notice any places where sound effects are created through the repetition of sounds, or where words are used whose sounds echo their sense. How does the sound express the ideas in those words?

1. Find any places where the writer has used each of these techniques:
   - alliteration
   - assonance
   - onomatopoeia.

   a) Decide what effect is created and which words are being emphasised.
   b) Decide how the sound effect reinforces the ideas those words suggest.

Activity 7 — Writing about sound techniques in a text

Use the work you have already done to respond to this task:

1. Explain how Wilfred Owen uses sound techniques to express the horror of war in 'Dulce et Decorum Est'.

   When you write about a sound technique:
   - name the technique used and quote the example
   - explain exactly how the effect is created
   - explain the effect of the sound effect and how it helps express the ideas contained in those words
   - explain how the effect in those words affects the reader.

   These words and phrases will help you:

   The writer creates… in the line… by…

   …makes the reader notice/imagine/hear…

   …emphasises/suggests/reinforces the idea of…

Unit 6 Know how to comment on language and its impact

Read this short extract from the novel *Private Peaceful* by Michael Morpurgo. It is a prose account of a gas attack during World War 1.

> The gas is only feet away now. In a moment it will be on me, around me, in me. I crouch down hiding my face between my knees, hands over my helmet, praying it will float over my head, over the top of the trench and seek out someone else. But it does not. It's all around me. I tell myself I will not breathe, I must not breathe. Through a yellow mist I see the trench filling up with it. It drifts into the dugouts, snaking into every nook and cranny, looking for me. It wants to seek us all out, to kill us all, every one of us. Still I do not breathe. I see men running, staggering, falling. I hear Pete shouting out for me. Then he's grabbing me and we run. I have to breathe now. I can't run without breathing. Half-blinded by my mask I trip and fall, crashing my head against the trench wall, knocking myself half-senseless. My gas mask has come off. I pull it down, but I have breathed in and know already it's too late. My eyes are stinging. My lungs are burning. I am coughing, retching, choking. I don't care where I am running as long as it's away from the gas.

What do you know about ...*Private Peaceful*?

Private Peaceful is a novel by Michael Morpurgo, first published in 2003. It is narrated by a boy called Thomas Peaceful. He tells the story of his life and his time in the trenches during World War I. This extract is about a gas attack that Thomas experiences.

Activity 8 — Apply your reading skills to a different text

Now **apply** your understanding of how to comment on the way a writer uses language to create an effect on the reader.

1. Re-read the extract, this time concentrating on the words, phrases and sentences that the writer has chosen to use to describe the event, and to show the narrator's feelings. Look back through your work on Activities 1-6 to remind yourself of aspects of language to notice and think about. You should consider:
   - Words and phrases that create the sense of the gas as a living creature.
   - The writer's choice of words to describe the effect of inhaling the gas on the narrator.
   - The effect of the writer choosing to use the present tense to describe the event.
   - The way that the writer uses repetition.
   - The use of short sentences.
2. Write a short 'appreciation' of the extract, in which you should comment on and explain, using examples, how the writer's use of language helps to bring the event to life for the reader.

2 Know how to respond to a writer's grammar and punctuation choices

I am learning how to:
- recognise different types of sentence construction
- recognise what grammatical choices have been made by a writer
- recognise how punctuation is used to clarify and signal meaning
- explain what effect sentence, grammar and punctuation choices have on the reader.

Punctuation makes the sentence's meaning clear for the reader, for example by showing it is a question or an exclamation, or showing how the chunks of meaning relate to each other. Writers choose and organise the way they express ideas in sentences to have an effect on the reader to achieve the purpose of their text.

In recent years it has become harder for young people to start up new businesses, go on courses or get jobs. In the newspaper article opposite the writer tells readers about a promising new development.

Key terms

Sentence types:

Single-clause – has one main clause. It expresses one idea and makes complete sense on its own.

Multi-clause: Coordinated – has at least two main clauses joined with one of these connectives: *and*, *or*, *but*.

Multi-clause: Subordinated – has one main clause and at least one subordinate clause (a subordinate clause does not make sense on its own). These clauses are joined using any connective except *and*, *or*, *but*.

Incomplete – acts like a simple sentence but lacks either a verb or a subject (or both). It might be only one word, e.g. '*No*'.

Sentence functions: There are four main functions of a sentence. It can be a statement, a command or instruction, a question, or an exclamation.

Activity 1 Understanding what kind of sentences are being used

1. Read the newspaper article on page 57.
    a) Sum up what it is about in a couple of sentences.
    b) What is the text's purpose?
2. Re-read the definitions of sentence types and functions in the Key terms box. Which type of sentence is each of these sentences from the text on page 57? Fill in a table like the one below with the type and function of each sentence. The first one has been done for you.

   a) sentence 1
   b) sentence 3
   c) sentence 6
   d) sentence 7
   e) sentence 8
   f) sentence 9
   g) sentence 11
   h) sentence 15
   i) sentence 17.

- single-clause
- multi-clause: coordinated
- multi-clause: subordinated
- incomplete
- question
- exclamation
- statement
- command

Focus your effort

Make sure you understand a text's purpose and content. Then look closely at the type of sentences the writer has used to express their ideas so that you can recognise the variety before considering their impact.

Sentence	Type of sentence	Function of sentence
a 'Oh, to have a patron.'	single-clause	statement

Unit 6 Know how to comment on language and its impact

Young, ambitious and broke?

Oh, to have a patron. Some bored and Platinum-carded soul ready to front up the cash for your MA in Garden Management, theatrical adaptation of *Infinite Jest* or ethical brassieres start-up. Wouldn't it be a dream? You – full of vigour, creativity and student debt. They – bamboozled by your promise and happy to pay for the privilege of seeing it realised.

Idle fantasy? Not quite. The role of **patron** appears to be swinging back in, if in a less generous form than its Roman original. Two thousand-plus years ago, patrons expected little more than a **sycophantic** line of verse in return for their denarii. Today's versions – connected to their recipient via the internet – have their eye on more commercial rewards.

A report in the *Economist* this week highlights the growth of a new type of **crowd-funding** in which wealthy backers offer a **start-up investment** to young people and their projects – in return for a percentage of what they earn in future.

Two new websites, Upstart and Pave, have dozens of members on either side of the funding divide. According to Upstart's founder, Dave Girouard, 50 candidates have attracted $1.4 million over the organisation's short history. These 'upstarts' – who advertise with headshots and dazzling credentials – receive enough money to pursue their visions without having to work graveyard shifts at a local pub to make ends meet. In time, of course, they must pay back the grant, and likely more – at a rate of up to 7 per cent of yearly earnings.

The more you think about this the more it starts to feel like a symbol of our times. Almost a quarter of the world's 15- to 24-year-olds are unemployed (some 290 million) and the **headwinds** against this generation gaining desirable work are stronger than they've been for decades.

Pre-crash, the British state served as a 'patron' to many: it paid for university fees, masters grants, even the odd creative fellowship. Many of these opportunities have either disappeared or are in the process of doing so. In March Westminster City Council cut the entirety of its arts budget, including youth theatre work in Soho. A spokesman said: 'We are literally choosing between arts projects or retaining gangs' workers on our estates.'

Engineers and their like can probably weather downturns like this. But what is left for the aspiring artist? Never a financially secure career path (the celebrated twentieth century director Luis Buñuel had his mother pay for early films), now it's sprinting towards being a flat-out **anachronism**.

So – despite their unnerving contractual basis – ventures like Upstart should be welcomed. They may be the only option left for the next Buñuel who finds herself with bills to pay and no rich parent to call on.

Activity 2 — Understanding the effect of different sentence choices

Writers can use different types of sentences to engage readers. For example, a question can set a reader wondering, or raise an objection in their mind to what is being said. An exclamation may surprise or challenge the reader's ideas.

1 In an introduction the writer wants to engage his audience's interest.
   a) What types of sentence are used in the first paragraph?
   b) How does using different types of sentence help engage the reader?

Activity 3 — Understanding the impact of where sentences are placed

Sentences placed next to each other can contrast, reinforce or develop each other, or they can act as a question and answer. Bear in mind also what part of the text they are being used in – for example, in the introduction to engage readers, in the main part of the text to develop ideas, or in the conclusion to sum up.

Expand your vocabulary

patron – a person who gives financial support to a person or organisation

sycophantic – attempting to win favour by flattering someone

crowd-funding – individuals pool their money, usually via the internet, to support a person or initiative

a **start-up investment** – investing in a business that is starting up

headwinds – winds blowing directly against the course of a ship or aircraft

anachronism – something that belongs to a different time

2 Know how to respond to a writer's grammar and punctuation choices

1 Which of these effects is used in the second paragraph?
2 How does the position of sentences in the second paragraph help make the explanation clear and interesting?
3 How does the position of sentences in the last two paragraphs help make the end of this explanation clear and engaging?

Activity 4 Understanding how punctuation expresses ideas

Punctuation signals to the reader what type of sentence they are reading (a question, exclamation, statement, etc.) and also how different pieces of information within a sentence link together – as an aside, a comment, explanation, list, or similar.

1 Read the sentences below. Explain how the highlighted punctuation shows readers what kind of sentence they are reading.

> a) 'Some bored and Platinum-carded soul ready to front up the cash for your MA in Garden Management**,** theatrical adaptation of *Infinite Jest***,** or ethical brassieres start-up.'
> b) 'Wouldn't it be a dream**?**'
> c) 'Pre-crash, the British state served as a "patron" to many**:** it paid for university fees, masters grants, even the odd creative fellowship.'
> d) 'A spokesman said**:** **"**We are literally choosing between arts projects or retaining gangs' workers on our estates.**"**'

2 Now read these sentences below, which are also taken from the article on page 57. Work out how the highlighted punctuation shows readers how the italic part of the sentence links to the remainder.

> a) 'You **–** *full of vigour, creativity and student debt*. They **–** *bamboozled by your promise and happy to pay for the privilege of seeing it realised*.'
> b) 'The role of patron appears to be swinging back in**,** *if in a less generous form than its Roman original*.'
> c) 'Today's versions **—** *connected to their recipient via the internet* **—** have their eye on more commercial rewards.'
> d) 'In time**,** *of course***,** they must pay back the grant, and likely more – at a rate of up to 7 per cent of yearly earnings.'
> e) 'Never a financially secure career path **(***the celebrated twentieth century director Luis Buñuel had his mother pay for early films***)**, now it's sprinting towards being a flat-out anachronism.'

3 Punctuation can also be used to signal subtle meanings to readers, such as signalling that words are not meant to be taken literally, perhaps because they are not quite correct or in order to create humour. What effect does the highlighted punctuation create in these sentences? (Hint: you will need to re-read the part of the text they are taken from.)

> a) 'These **"**upstarts**"** – who advertise with headshots and dazzling credentials – receive enough money to pursue their visions without having to work graveyard shifts at a local pub to make ends meet.'
> b) 'Pre-crash, the British state served as a **"**patron**"** to many: it paid for university fees, masters grants, even the odd creative fellowship.'

Unit 6 Know how to comment on language and its impact

In this extract from *Scorpia Rising* by Antony Horowitz, a helicopter has been hovering above teenage spy Alex Rider's school and the sniper on board has just taken a shot at him. Alex has given chase and is now on the roof of a building, watching as the helicopter is about to escape.

Somehow, incredibly, Alex remembered Mike Spencer in the classroom the moment after he had noticed the sniper. He had been using a bendy ruler to fire a rubber at another pupil. Could it possibly work? Yes! Why not? There was a TV aerial right on the edge of the roof and the fact that it was swaying meant that it surely had to bend. The aerial had four metal antennae that came together in the shape of a V. Alex ran over to it. He hoisted the fire extinguisher up so that it rested inside the V and then, using both hands, pulled it back. The whole thing bent towards him. Alex could feel the metal straining. If he let go now, he would launch the extinguisher halfway across the river. That was one advantage of being 15. He hadn't been this strong a year ago.

Suddenly the helicopter was level with him, filling his vision. He could feel the wind from the rotors beating at him, threatening to blow him off the roof, and the engine howled in his ears. His hair whipped around his eyes, half blinding him, but he had a clear view of the sniper through the back window. The man turned and saw him. His eyes widened in shock. He shouted something. The pilot seemed to have frozen too; the helicopter wasn't moving. It was just dangling there, a perfect target, right in front of him.

Alex let go of the fire extinguisher. The TV aerial whipped forward, propelling it like a medieval catapult. The red metal cylinder hit the cockpit, an oversized bullet that smashed into the glass, sending cracks in every direction. It wasn't enough to bring the helicopter down, but the pilot jerked back instinctively, losing control.

Alex threw himself to the ground as the tail of the helicopter swung round, scything through the air inches above where his head had just been. He felt another blast of air tearing at his shirt and jacket, trying to drag them off his shoulders. For a brief second he glimpsed the terrified face of the sniper, upside down – or at least that was how it seemed to him. The pilot was fighting for control and might have regained it, but then the tail rotor clipped the edge of the building and there was a dreadful grinding and snapping sound as part of the blade broke off. Lying flat on the roof, Alex covered his head with his hands, afraid that he was about to be torn to pieces. A slice of broken metal shot past him and shuddered into the brickwork.

And then the helicopter was gone, yanked into the air as if it were a fish on the end of an invisible line. It was completely directionless, spinning round and round. Alex dragged himself to his knees, gazing at his handiwork with a sense of disbelief. The helicopter was like a mad thing. He wondered what sort of nightmare the pilot and his passenger were experiencing inside. It was still moving fast.

Already it was a quarter of a mile away, mercifully flying upriver, away from Wandsworth Bridge. Alex stood up. The helicopter tried to right itself but it wasn't going anywhere. It hovered briefly, then crashed down into the river. There was a great explosion of white water and then nothing. Alex couldn't see any more.

2 Know how to respond to a writer's grammar and punctuation choices

Activity 5 — Respond to the writer's use of sentences and punctuation in fiction

Writers vary their sentence structures and use punctuation expressively when writing fiction, for example to reveal character or to create effects such as tension and suspense.

1. Read the extract on page 59 and sum up what it is about.
2. Re-read the first paragraph, which is written to show Alex's mind at work. Look carefully at the first five sentences.
   a) How does the writer vary them and use punctuation to create the impression of how fast Alex's brain is working things out?
   b) How does this help build tension?
3. Re-read the sentence below. How does the way the phrases are punctuated and organised help convey the effort it takes for Alex to bend the aerial back?

   'He hoisted the fire extinguisher up so that it rested inside the V and then, using both hands, pulled it back.'

4. Re-read the second paragraph. After the first sentence, it has two long multi-clause sentences and then a series of three short single-clause sentences.
   a) How does this help quicken the pace and increase tension?
   b) Why would the writer want to do this at this point in the story?
5. Re-read the sentence below. Why has the writer used the dash? How does it help convey what the writer is expressing in this sentence?

   'For a brief second he glimpsed the terrified face of the sniper, upside down – or at least that was how it seemed to him.'

Activity 6 — Responding to a writer's organisation of a sentence

Writers craft their sentences so that the information is placed within them in the best position to achieve the effect they want.

1. How does placing the two adverbs 'Somehow, incredibly,' at the beginning of the first sentence help the reader accept Alex suddenly remembering what Mike had done and coming up with his plan?
2. Look at the order of the three events in the sentence below.

   'He could feel the wind from the rotors beating at him, threatening to blow him off the roof, and the engine howled in his ears.'

   a) What impression of how Alex is feeling does this order create?
   b) Why is this effective at this point in the story?
3. Re-read the first sentence of the penultimate paragraph. How does beginning it with the connective 'And' emphasise the surprise of what happens next?

Unit 6 Know how to comment on language and its impact

Activity 7 | Respond to the writer's use of the passive and active voice

In a narrative the writer will use the active voice to focus on the character and make the action more immediate and exciting. In a report, however, you can use the passive voice to focus attention *away* from the person doing the action.

1 Find three examples of the active voice being used in the extract on page 59.
2 Writers can make the reader focus on different parts of a situation by using the passive or active voice. For example:
   - Active voice: Alex **fired** the fire extinguisher at the helicopter.
   - Passive voice: The helicopter **was hit by** a fire extinguisher.
   a) In which sentence above do you focus more on Alex's role? Why?
   b) In which sentence above do you focus more on the fire extinguisher? Why?
3 Now read the report below.
   a) How has the writer used the passive voice in the report to focus more on what happened to the helicopter and less on Alex's part in its destruction?
   b) How could you rewrite the last sentence in the report so that it is in the passive voice? (Hint: start your sentence with 'The River Thames…')
   c) Suggest some reasons why a writer might choose to use the passive voice in this formal report:

> **Key terms**
> **Passive voice** – the receiver of the action becomes the subject of the sentence.
> **Active voice** – whoever or whatever carries out the action is the subject of the sentence.

Report

The television aerial on the roof was bent back so that the fire extinguisher could be fired at the helicopter. When the helicopter's window was hit by the fire extinguisher it cracked. The shock made the helicopter pilot lose control. As it flew on, the helicopter drew nearer to the building that agent Alex Ryder was on, placing him in grave danger. Then the edge of the building was clipped by the tail rotor making it impossible for the pilot to regain control of the vehicle. After that, the helicopter spun out of control and landed in the River Thames.

UNIT 7

Know how to understand texts in context

1 Know how to use historical contextual knowledge to interpret texts

I am learning how to:
- use research to understand the historic context to interpret a text set in another time
- understand how the original readers might have responded to a text.

In older texts, the world that characters live in and their concerns may be unfamiliar. To understand a text better you will need to do some research into what influenced the writer, such as events that were happening at the time, their culture and ideas, people who influenced their writing, etc.

> **Key term**
> **Literary heritage** – many texts from different historical periods have been recognised for the quality of their writing. They continue to appeal because they carry important meanings for readers of any time. They are known as texts that are part of a literary heritage.

Activity 1 — Research the context and work out what might have shaped the text

To understand the historical context of a text, find out about the writer and what was important when they were writing. Use reliable books and websites from which the information can be trusted.

1. Read the information on the background to Macbeth on page 63. What do you learn about the following?
   - who could become a monarch
   - good and evil
   - Shakespeare's patron.
2. How could Shakespeare influence both the King's supporters and his enemies?
3. Bearing in mind what you know about the time when he is writing, if you were Shakespeare and writing to please your patron, what ideas might you include in a play?

Activity 2 — Read the text bearing in mind how the issues of the period have shaped it

Use what you know about the audience's beliefs at the time a text was written to help you work out how they might have responded to it. Bear in mind they might have reacted quite differently from you!

1. Read the extract from *Macbeth* on page 64. Bear in mind the ideas of good and evil at the time of writing, which would be in the minds of the audience. Then answer these questions:
   a) Which details in Banquo's description of the witches signal to the audience that they are evil?
   b) Macbeth is a soldier and Thane of Glamis, but he is not a blood relative of the King. What do the witches predict for Macbeth, that the audience know would be a disruption of the natural order and therefore an evil idea?

Unit 7 Know how to understand texts in context

2 Use what you have researched and noticed to work out the likely response of Shakespeare's audience as you answer these questions:
  a) How might Shakespeare's audience feel about the witches appearing on stage?
  b) How might Shakespeare's audience expect a good, loyal soldier to respond to the witches?
  c) What might Macbeth's reaction suggest about how he feels about the witches' predictions that he will rise to be first Thane of Cawdor and then King?

Background to *Macbeth*

The play *Macbeth* was written and performed roughly between 1603 and 1611, and was seen by large audiences at The Globe Theatre in London. Its writer, and chief actor, William Shakespeare led 'The King's Men', a theatre group funded and supported by the new King of England, Scotland and Ireland, James I.

While Shakespeare was writing his plays, England was experiencing turbulent times. There was a lot of conflict between **Protestants** and Catholics, and there had been great debate over who should **succeed** the Protestant, childless Queen Elizabeth I to the throne of England. In the end King James I, also a Protestant, who was already King of Scotland and Ireland, was crowned the King of England, too. In 1605, however, there was a shocking act of **treason**: the Gunpowder Plot, an attempt by English Catholics (including Guy Fawkes) to blow up the King and his political **allies** in the Houses of Parliament, London.

During Shakespeare's time people believed that God ruled the universe and had created an ordered world that must be sustained – i.e. the King was divinely appointed to be in charge of the country, and his people's duty was to support him loyally. An ordinary person could not rise to become King. The King had to belong to the highest class of people in the land. Men were powerful and meant to rule over women. They fought in battles and were fearless, while women stayed at home, and were expected to be gentle, to respect and serve their husbands, run the home and look after the children. People saw maintaining this Divine Order as good, and they greatly feared disruption of it because that would be evil.

King James I was a well-educated man, and wrote *Daemonologie*, a book arguing that all witches were working for the Devil and therefore a source of evil that could harm their country and so they should all be killed. During his reign, across Europe and America, numerous 'witches' were tried and put to death.

Expand your vocabulary

Protestant – a member of the English Church that had broken away from the control of Roman Catholicism during Henry VIII's reign
succeed to the throne – become the next ruler of England
treason – betrayal of the King
allies – people who co-operate with and help someone

63

1 Know how to use historical contextual knowledge to interpret texts

In this early scene from *Macbeth,* Macbeth and Banquo, noble, loyal soldiers, are returning from their victory in battle when they come upon some witches.

Banquo: What are these
So wither'd and so wild in their **attire**,
That look not like the inhabitants o' the earth,
And yet are on't? Live you? or are you aught
That man may question? You seem to understand me,
By each at once her **chappy** finger laying
Upon her skinny lips: you should be women,
And yet your beards forbid me to interpret
That you are so.

Macbeth: Speak, if you can: what are you?

First Witch: All hail, Macbeth! hail to thee, **Thane** of Glamis!

Second Witch: All hail, Macbeth, hail to thee, Thane of Cawdor!

Third Witch: All hail, Macbeth, thou shalt be king hereafter!

Banquo: Good sir, why do you start; and seem to fear
Things that do sound so fair? I' the name of truth,
Are ye fantastical, or that indeed
Which outwardly ye show? My noble partner
You greet with present grace and great prediction
Of noble having and of royal hope,
That he seems **rapt** withal: to me you speak not.
If you can look into the seeds of time,
And say which grain will grow and which will not,
Speak then to me, who neither beg nor fear
Your **favours** nor your hate.

First Witch: Hail!

Second Witch: Hail!

Third Witch: Hail!

First Witch: Lesser than Macbeth, and greater.

Second Witch: Not so happy, yet much happier.

Third Witch: Thou shalt get kings, though thou be none:
So all hail, Macbeth and Banquo!

First Witch: Banquo and Macbeth, all hail!

Expand your vocabulary

attire – clothes
chappy – rough
thane – a position in society similar to an earl or duke
rapt – amazed and speechless
favours – acts of kindness

Unit 7 Know how to understand texts in context

While King Duncan stays in Macbeth's home, Macbeth plots with his wife to murder Duncan so that Macbeth can become King. Macbeth has just carried out their plan and stabbed Duncan as he sleeps, but by mistake Macbeth has brought the knife with him rather than leaving it to be found as evidence that will place the blame on Duncan's servants.

Lady Macbeth: Go get some water
And wash this filthy witness from your hand.
Why did you bring these daggers from the place?
They must lie there. Go carry them, and smear
The sleepy grooms with blood.

Macbeth: I'll go no more:
I am afraid to think what I have done;
Look on't again I dare not.

Lady Macbeth: Infirm of purpose!
Give me the daggers. The sleeping and the dead
Are but pictures; 'tis the eyes of childhood
That fears a painted devil. If he do bleed,
I'll guild the faces of the grooms withal.
For it must seem their guilt. *[Exit]*

Activity 3 — Practise your skills in using context to interpret texts

Use what you know about the context of *Macbeth* and how the audience would have responded to the earlier scene (on page 64) as you read and respond to the extract from the scene above.

1 Read the extract above. How would an Elizabethan audience feel about what Macbeth has just done?
2 Re-read the context information on page 63.
   a) What would the audience expect a good wife to be like?
   b) To what extent does Lady Macbeth behave as she should?
   c) How would the audience judge her behaviour in the speech in the extract above?
3 How has Shakespeare made sure his audience would judge both Macbeth and Lady Macbeth to be evil?

2 Know how to use cultural contextual knowledge to interpret texts

I am learning how to:
- use research to help me understand the cultural context of a text
- interpret a text in the context of its culture.

Key term
Culture – the ideas, customs and behaviour of a particular society.

When a text is written in the context of a specific place and culture, it may be unfamiliar to you. Research the place, culture and what influenced the writer, to understand the text more fully.

Benjamin Obadiah Iqbal Zephaniah is a British Jamaican Rastafarian writer and dub poet. He is a well-known figure in contemporary English literature, and was included in *The Times*' 2008 list of Britain's top 50 post-war writers. Here is a short extract from a biography about him.

Life and work

Benjamin Zephaniah was born and raised in the Handsworth district of Birmingham, which he called the 'Jamaican capital of Europe'. He is the son of a Barbadian postman and a Jamaican nurse. A dyslexic, he attended an approved school but left aged 13 unable to read or write.

His poetry is strongly influenced by the music and poetry of Jamaica and what he calls 'street politics'. His first performance was in church when he was ten, and by the age of 15 his poetry was already known among Handsworth's Afro-Caribbean and Asian communities. He received a criminal record as a young man and served a prison sentence for burglary. Tired of the limitations of being a black poet communicating with black people only, he decided to expand his audience, and headed to London at the age of 22.

He became actively involved in a workers' co-operative in London, which led to the publication of his first book of poetry, called *Pen Rhythm*, published in 1980. Zephaniah has said that his mission is to fight the dead image of poetry in academia, and to 'take [it] everywhere' to people who do not read books, so he turned his poetry readings into concert-like performances.

His second collection of poetry, *The Dread Affair: Collected Poems* (1985) contained a number of poems attacking the British legal system. *Rasta Time in Palestine* (1990), an account of a visit to the Palestinian-occupied territories, contained poetry and travelogue.

His album *Rasta*, which featured The Wailers' first recording since the death of Bob Marley, as well as a tribute to Nelson Mandela, gained him international prestige and topped the Yugoslavian pop charts. It was because of this recording that he was introduced to the political prisoner and soon-to-be South African president Nelson Mandela. In 1996, Mandela requested that Zephaniah host the president's Two Nations Concert at the Royal Albert Hall, London. *We Are Britain!* (2002) is a collection of poems celebrating cultural diversity in Britain.

Benjamin Zephaniah is also a very successful children's poet, with his first book of poetry for children, *Talking Turkeys*, having to go into an emergency reprint after just six weeks. In 1999 he wrote an immensely successful novel for teenagers, *Face* – the first of four novels to date.

Unit 7 Know how to understand texts in context

Activity 1 — Research the culture of a writer and text

To understand the cultural context of a text, find out about the writer's background and culture. Use reliable books and websites that you can trust.

1 Read the text on page 66. It gives you some cultural context of the poet Benjamin Zephaniah.

a) Scan the text to find the information it gives you about Zephaniah's background. Identify and note three aspects of the culture and events that have shaped him and his writing.

b) During Zephaniah's lifetime different ethnic groups living in Britain have learned more about each other's cultures. Prejudice and racism have become unacceptable. What clues in the text suggest these changes have been significant in his life?

c) Compare the writer's culture with your own. What is similar and what is different? Make a list of questions that would help you understand Zephaniah's background and culture – for example, 'What is a Rastafarian?' Then research the answers to your questions.

d) Bear in mind what you have discovered about Zephaniah's culture and interests. What kind of ideas and references to his culture might you expect Zephaniah to include in his poetry?

Activity 2 — Understand and interpret a text in the context of its culture

Read the poem on pages 68–69 and use what you know about the writer's background and cultural context to help you understand the features and references.

1 Read the poem aloud, listening to its rhythm and repeated sounds.
2 The form of poetry used is rap. Make some comments and suggestions about how the choices of form and spelling reflect Zephaniah's culture.
3 Read the poem again and work out the main ideas.
   a) Make a list of what Zephaniah says his poetry is, and another list of what it is not.

What this poetry is	What this poetry is not
A rhythm that fires words	Party political
Meant to be chanted...	Like Shakespeare's poetry...

b) Read through the list you have just made. Then sum up what Zephaniah is claiming about his type of poetry.

c) How do Zephaniah's ideas about what poetry is and is not compare and contrast with your ideas about poetry?

d) Look back at what you found out about Zephaniah's culture and life. How does this poem reflect his experiences and concerns?

Dis Poetry

Dis poetry is like a riddim dat drops

De tongue fires a riddim dat shoots like shots

Dis poetry is designed fe rantin

Dance hall style, big mouth chanting,

Dis poetry nar put yu to sleep

Preaching follow me

Like yu is blind sheep,

Dis poetry is not Party Political

Not designed fe dose who are critical.

Dis poetry is wid me when I gu to me bed

It gets into me dreadlocks

It lingers around me head

Dis poetry goes wid me as I pedal me bike

I've tried Shakespeare, respect due dere

But dis is de stuff I like.

Dis poetry is not afraid of going in a book

Still dis poetry need ears fe hear an eyes fe hav a look

Dis poetry is Verbal Riddim, no big words involved

An if I hav a problem de riddim gets it solved,

I've tried to be more romantic, it does nu good for me

So I tek a Reggae Riddim an build me poetry,

I could try be more personal

But you've heard it all before,

Pages of written words not needed

Brain has many words in store,

Yu could call dis poetry Dub Ranting

De tongue plays a beat

De body starts skanking,

Unit 7 Know how to understand texts in context

Dis poetry is quick an childish

Dis poetry is fe dewise an foolish,

Anybody can do it fe free,

Dis poetry is fe yu an me,

Don't stretch yu imagination

Dis poetry is fe de good of de Nation,

Chant,

In de morning

I chant

In de night

I chant

In de darkness

An under de spotlight,

I pass thru University

I pass thru Sociology

An den I got a dread degree

In Dreadfull Ghetology.

Dis poetry stays wid me when I run or walk

An when I am talking to meself in poetry I talk,

Dis poetry is wid me,

Below me an above,

Dis poetry's from inside me

It goes to yu

WID LUV.

3 Know how to understand language in texts from a different historical period

I am learning how to:
- make sense of vocabulary in texts written before the twentieth century
- understand longer, subordinated sentence constructions in older texts.

The language in some older texts can be unfamiliar to today's reader. For example, vocabulary might be included that is not used today. Some older texts also include a lot of additional and descriptive detail by using long, multi-clause sentences. You need to work out the writer's use of language so you can understand the texts.

The text below is taken from *The Strange Case of Dr Jekyll and Mr Hyde*, by Robert Louis Stevenson. Its Victorian narrator is out walking through the streets of London with his friend when he recalls a strange event that happened in that area recently.

> **Key term**
> **Subordinate clause** – a clause in a sentence that does not make sense on its own and that adds further details. It relies on a main clause elsewhere in the sentence to make sense.

1 All at once, I saw two figures: one a little man who was stumping along eastward at a good walk, and the other a girl of maybe eight or ten who was running as hard as she was able down a cross street. Well, sir, the two ran into one another naturally enough at the corner; and
5 then came the horrible part of the thing; for the man trampled calmly over the child's body and left her screaming on the ground. It sounds nothing to hear, but it was hellish to see. It wasn't like a man; it was like some damned Juggernaut. I gave a view halloa, took to my heels, collared my gentleman, and brought him back to where there was
10 already quite a group about the screaming child.

He was perfectly cool and made no resistance, but gave me one look, so ugly that it brought out the sweat on me like running. The people who had turned out were the girl's own family; and pretty soon, the doctor, for whom she had been sent, put in his appearance. Well,
15 the child was not much the worse, more frightened, according to the Sawbones, and there you might have supposed would be an end to it. But there was one curious circumstance. I had taken a loathing to my gentleman at first sight. So had the child's family, which was only natural. But the doctor's case was what struck me. He was the usual
20 cut and dry **apothecary**, of no particular age and colour, with a strong Edinburgh accent and about as emotional as a bagpipe. Well, sir, he was like the rest of us; every time he looked at my prisoner, I saw that Sawbones turn sick and white with the desire to kill him. I knew what was in his mind, just as he knew what was in mine; and killing being
25 out of the question, we did the next best. We told the man we could and would make such a **scandal** out of this, as should make his name stink from one end of London to the other. If he had any friends or any credit, we undertook that he should lose them.

> **Expand your vocabulary**
> **apothecary** – a medical professional who made up medicines for doctors, surgeons, etc.
> **scandal** – pubic outrage at an event or behaviour regarded as very wrong

Unit 7 Know how to understand texts in context

Activity 1 Understanding vocabulary and references in older texts

Look up the meaning of an older word or expression in a dictionary or online, or use the context of the text to help you work it out.

1 Read the extract on page 70 and sum up what it is about.
2 Use the clues in the text to work out the meaning of these terms:
   a) 'stumping along' (line 1)
   b) 'a cross street' (line 3)
   c) a 'Juggernaut' (line 7)
   d) 'a view halloa' (line 7)
   e) 'credit' (last line).

Activity 2 Understanding longer sentences in older texts

Understanding how the punctuation and grammar works in older texts will help you understand the texts better.

1 Read the two longer sentences again in lines 1–5. Find the main clause(s) in each sentence. Sum up what each sentence is about.
2 The subordinate clauses in the first sentence add detail and description. Make a list of all the additional information that we gain.
3 Use the definitions in the Key terms box to help you understand what a main clause, colon and semi-colon can do. Where are they present in the first two sentences of the text?

Activity 3 Respond to the writer's use of language in older texts

1 Rewrite the account on page 70 in modern English, using the same point of view, i.e. that of a bystander who witnesses an unfortunate incident in the street.
2 Think about the type of sentences and vocabulary used within the text, which is supposedly spoken by a witness to the events being described. What do they suggest about his character?

Key terms
Main clause – can stand by itself; it makes sense by itself.
Colon – can be used to: introduce a list, a reason or an explanation in a sentence.
Semi-colon – may be used to separate items in a list that are described with a lot of words; link two sentences that are very close in meaning.

71

4 Know how to comment on literary language in a text from a different historical period

Key term
Literary language – literary language is used by writers to make the reader picture, imagine and notice by using word images, e.g. simile, metaphor, personification, alliteration, onomatopoeia.

I am learning how to:
→ understand and comment on literary language in a text from a different historical period.

When commenting on a poem from a different historical and cultural context, read the poem carefully, work out any unfamiliar vocabulary, and decide what idea each stanza is about. Then find the literary techniques that are familiar to you and work out how the poet is using them to make you picture, imagine or notice things to help you understand the poem more fully.

Activity 1 — Read the text and work out what it is about

The poem on page 73 was written by an eighteenth century poet, John Keats. He was part of the Romantic movement in which people valued nature above civilisation, and imagination and emotion above rational thought.

1. Read the poem carefully, at least twice, and decide what you think it is about overall.
2. Read each stanza and use a dictionary or the context to understand unfamiliar words. Decide what idea each stanza is about.

Activity 2 — Recognise literary techniques and comment on their effect

In older texts literary techniques are used in the same way as in modern texts. They are used to have an effect on the reader in order to express the writer's idea effectively.

1. Read the poem again and look at examples of each of the literary techniques below:
   - alliteration – words near each other beginning with the same sound, e.g. in line 6
   - sensory language – words that appeal to the senses of touch, taste, smell, hearing, etc., e.g. in line 8
   - adjectives – words that describe nouns, e.g. in line 11
   - personification – objects or ideas are given human characteristics, e.g. in the second stanza
   - verbs – a word that expresses experiencing a feeling, an action, a thought, e.g. in line 17
   - a simile – where a writer makes a comparison using the words *as* or *like*, e.g. in line 19
   - a metaphor – where a writer makes a more direct comparison using no comparing words – the object becomes the item it is being compared with, e.g. in line 27
   - onomatopoeia – a word whose meaning echoes its sense, e.g. in lines 30–33.

Find more examples of each technique, and explain:

a) how the technique is created in your example, for example:

The adjective 'mellow' is used to describe the fruitfulness of autumn.

b) what effect it has on the reader, for example:

Because the word 'mellow' carries several meanings it suggests the softness and laid-back nature of autumn as well as the way it grows.

c) how using it helps the writer express his ideas at that point in the poem, for example:

This adjective suits the way autumn is presented later in the poem as a relaxed, sleepy, gentle season that encourages growth.

Unit 7 Know how to understand texts in context

Ode to Autumn

1 Season of mists and mellow fruitfulness!
Close bosom-friend of the maturing sun;
Conspiring with him how to load and bless
With fruit the vines that round the thatch-eaves run;
5 To bend with apples the mossed cottage-trees,
And fill all fruit with ripeness to the core;
To swell the gourd, and plump the hazel shells
With a sweet kernel; to set budding more,
And still more, later flowers for the bees,
10 Until they think warm days will never cease,
For Summer has o'erbrimmed their clammy cells.

Who hath not seen thee oft amid thy store?
Sometimes whoever seeks abroad may find
Thee sitting careless on a granary floor,
15 Thy hair soft-lifted by the winnowing wind;
Or on a half-reaped furrow sound asleep,
Drowsed with the fume of poppies, while thy hook
Spares the next swath and all its twined flowers;
And sometimes like a **gleaner** thou dost keep
20 Steady thy laden head across a brook;
Or by a cider-press, with patient look,
Thou watchest the last oozings, hours by hours.

Where are the songs of Spring? Ay, where are they?
Think not of them, thou hast thy music too, –
25 While barred clouds bloom the soft-dying day
And touch the stubble-plains with rosy hue;
Then in a wailful choir the small gnats mourn
Among the river **sallows**, borne aloft
Or sinking as the light wind lives or dies;
30 And full-grown lambs loud bleat from hilly bourn;
Hedge-crickets sing, and now with treble soft
The redbreast whistles from a garden-croft;
And gathering swallows twitter in the skies.

Expand your vocabulary

gleaner – people who gather the grain left over after the crops have been harvested. Traditionally gleaners were poor and so given this opportunity out of charity by the rich farmers who owned the fields
Sallows – willow trees that grow close to the river

UNIT 8
Know how to compare texts

1 Know how to compare form, presentation, ideas and language in texts

I am learning how to:
→ compare different text ideas
→ compare the different perspectives in texts
→ compare the ways different texts present their ideas
→ compare the effect of the language techniques used in texts.

Texts that are about similar subjects may be presented in very different ways and use different language techniques to suit their audience and purpose. Writers may also write about the same subject expressing very different ideas and perspectives. Use the Activities below and on page 77 to help you examine the similarities and differences in texts that are about a common subject: swimming.

Key terms

Compare texts – consider and explain in detail the ways in which texts are similar, and where they differ from each other.

Form – the appearance of the text on the page; how the presentation features make it look.

Presentation features – layout techniques, e.g. headings, images, colour, fonts, space, bullet points, size and position of items on the page.

Activity 1 — Comparing texts' content, audience and purpose

1. Read the leaflet on page 75 and explain:
   a) what aspects of swimming it shows
   b) who is the likely audience
   c) what is its main purpose.

2. Read the article on page 76 and explain:
   a) what aspects of swimming it shows
   b) who is the likely audience
   c) what is its main purpose.

	Leaflet	Article
What it is about		
Audience		
Purpose		

Activity 2 — Compare how presentational features are used in different texts

A writer's text is written in a form that will suit their audience and achieve their purpose. Work out how the presentation features they use help them to do this.

1. Make a list of the different presentation features used in each text.
2. How do the presentation features in the leaflet on page 75:
   a) help it engage its audience?   b) achieve its purpose?
3. How do the presentation features in the article on page 76:
   a) help it engage its audience?   b) achieve its purpose?
4. Which presentation features are used in the same way in both texts?
5. Which presentation features are used in different ways?
6. Why are the presentation features you selected for Question 5 used differently?

Key terms

Idea or theme – can be the view that writers express about people and about life. In non-fiction the writer might talk to you about these directly. In fiction writers might use characters' experiences, setting, atmosphere and word choice to show their ideas.

Perspective – attitude to, or way of treating, the theme.

Language techniques – these are methods writers use, such as using descriptive verbs, making comments, asking questions, using humour, giving facts and opinions, making comparisons.

The champion of swims

For a swim fit for a champion, make Swimfit a part of your life and get active today!

The nation has witnessed the world's greatest sporting event right here on our doorstep. Now witness a world leading workout programme right here at your local pool.

If you're inspired to follow in the footsteps of Team GB, let Swimfit activate your fitness and motivate you to achieve it all in the pool.

From Tom Daley to Jess Ennis, each and every London 2012 athlete has been dedicated to achieving their goal. Achieve you goal with British Gas Swimfit and be part of the world's greatest innovation from the world of swimming.

Activate. Motivate. Dedicate.

Swimfit at your pool

Hit the lanes with Swimfit and you won't want to take a dip without it. Lane swimming has been transformed, with added structure to motivate you to go further in the pool.

Offering you expert poolside support, you can be assured to get the ultimate swim every time.

Join a Swimfit Activate group session delivered by a qualified instructor or pick up an Activate session card from poolside or reception and see for yourself why swimmers all over the country are choosing Swimfit.

1 Know how to compare form, presentation, ideas and language in texts

Must like water slides…

Tour operator First Choice is on the look-out for a slide-tester and general splasher-abouter to travel the world and 'test' its swimming pools.

A hard day's work … at a First Choice SplashWorld resort

Come January, many of us think about changing jobs; few of us imagine that a new job might involve one long holiday in the sun.

But that is effectively what First Choice is offering one candidate. The tour operator is looking for a 'slide-tester' to spend six months riding water slides and larking about in the pools at its SplashWorld resorts around the world.

In a job description that sounds like it was written by a child under the heading, 'What I'd like to do when I grow up', First Choice says, 'The successful candidate will get to ride and rate the slides based on the "biggest splash" and "adrenaline factor" as part of the role, as well as share their experiences with First Choice holidaymakers via Twitter and Facebook.'

But our favourite line in the job description is this: 'No two days will be the same!' Perhaps you wear a different swimming costume every day.

Your pay for spending six months splashing about in the pools of Mallorca, Turkey, Egypt and other sunny destinations? Ten thousand pounds, plus paid overseas travel expenses. At the end of the six-month contract you'll receive a seven-night holiday for two staying at one of the company's all-inclusive resorts … to relax by the pool after all that hard work.

First Choice plans to draw up a short-list of five candidates, who will then compete in a 'final challenge' at a SplashWorld resort. It's all starting to sound a bit like a bad reality TV show. Let's just hope the producers at ITV don't get wind of it – after the 'ratings success' of Tom Daley's debut show at the weekend, they may well be on the look-out for another water-based corker. Could *Celebrity Slide Tester* be this summer's *Splash!*?

Unit 8 Know how to compare texts

Activity 3 — Compare texts' presentation features

Follow these three steps when you compare texts' presentation features:

Step 1 First you should explain:
- what each text is about
- who is each text's likely audience
- the purpose of each text.

Step 2 Then explain in detail how each presentation feature that is similar is used to help the writer achieve his purpose and target his audience. For example:

> Both texts have a heading to engage the reader. In the leaflet the first green heading boasts that it is offering 'The champion of swims' and its second green heading includes the product's name, 'Swimfit at your pool', so readers know that the product will give them a great swimming experience and they can have it where they usually swim, which is appealing because they don't have to put in extra effort to have it.

Step 3 Then explain how any presentation features used in only one text help it to achieve its purpose and reach its audience. For example, 'Only the newspaper article has a standfirst.'

These phrases will help you:

> In the leaflet the writer uses… to… Similarly, in the article the writer…

> In the leaflet the writer uses… to… In the article, however, the writer…

1 Use the information you have gathered to write a comparison of how presentation features are used in the leaflet and article.

Worcestershire, 6 July

Fladbury is a village a few miles upstream of Evesham on the River Avon. Not the Bath Avon, or the Hampshire Avon, but the Avon that runs through Stratford-upon-Avon, Shakespeare's Avon. I followed my directions to walk down an alley beside a house on the village green, found myself on the banks of the river just above a weir, and recognised the old three-storey red brick mill house across the water. A handbell dangled from a willow. I rang it, as instructed by my hosts, and waited. Two children appeared on the opposite bank and began to approach laboriously on a **punt**, propelled by hauling on a cable slung from bank to bank. I jumped aboard, was ferried back, and welcomed by Judith, my host.

I had entered a swimmer's dream. People lolled half-submerged along the top of the **weir**, reading or sunbathing, while others paddled themselves about the river in **coracles**, swam, dived or just sat about in bathing costumes. It was a water rats' club straight from the pages of *The Wind in the Willows*. The mill sleeps 28, in an assortment of beds and bunks in more attics and bedrooms than I could count. The children showed me up and down little flights of stairs, in and out of a warren of rooms until I was dizzy.

The weather was perfect and the water tolerably warm, so throwing caution to the winds, Judith and I set out upriver. We dived off an old stone landing-stage into 16-foot-deep clear green water above the weir and recklessly breast-stroked a few hundred yards upstream as far as a bridge. Everyone likes to have a fixed point to swim to, even Channel swimmers.

Expand your vocabulary

punt – an open flat-bottomed boat only used in shallow waters; a long pole is used to move it along

weir – a low dam across a stream to hold back the water

coracles – a small rounded boat made of waterproof material stretched over a wicker frame

1 Know how to compare form, presentation, ideas and language in texts

Activity 4 — Identify the theme shared by two texts

To work out how two texts treat the same theme, read them both and sum up what aspects of the theme each shows.

1 Read the article on page 76. Sum up what it shows about swimming.
2 Read the text on page 77. Sum up what it shows about swimming.
3 Compare your summaries of the two texts. What ideas do they share?

Activity 5 — Identify different perspectives on the same theme

Writers exploring the same theme will have different ideas and views about it. Search each text to work out what the writer's attitude and ideas are about the theme, and how they differ.

1 What common theme do the texts on pages 76 and 77 share?
2 Read the article on page 76 and answer these questions.
   a) How is the theme explored?
   b) What is the writer's attitude towards the theme?
   c) Which words or phrases show you the writer's attitude?
3 Read the text on page 77 and answer these questions.
   a) How is the theme explored?
   b) What is the writer's attitude towards the theme?
   c) Which words or phrases show you the writer's attitude?

	Article (page 76)	Text (page 77)
How is the theme explored?	The theme of… is explored through…	The theme of… is explored through…
What is the writer's attitude towards the theme?	The writer's attitude is…	The writer's attitude is…
Which words or phrases show you the writer's attitude?	The writer's attitude is shown by the use of the words/phrases…	The writer's attitude is shown by the use of the words/phrases…

4 Compare the writers' attitudes and methods. In what ways are they similar or different?

Unit 8 Know how to compare texts

> **Activity 6** Understand how language techniques are used to express the writer's perspective

Identify the language techniques used to express ideas about the theme. Work out how each one helps the writer express their attitude and ideas about the theme.

1. Identify where these language techniques are used to express ideas about the theme in the article on page 76 and the text on page 77:
   - verbs
   - adjectives
   - comments
   - questions
   - humour
   - facts
   - opinions
   - comparisons.

2. For each language technique, carefully re-read the part of the text that uses it and work out:
   a) what the technique helps convey about the theme
   b) what effect using that technique has on the reader.

Technique	Example of technique	What it conveys about the theme	What effect it has on the reader
verbs			
adjectives			
comments			
questions			
humour			
facts			
opinions			
comparisons			

79

1 Know how to compare form, presentation, ideas and language in texts

In this text, from the short story *Through the Tunnel* by Doris Lessing, Jerry is on holiday and has been watching local, older boys swim through a tunnel in a rock that is deep underwater. He has set himself the difficult and frightening challenge of being able to swim through it, too. He reckons he needs to hold his breath for 115 seconds to achieve his goal. This is his final attempt and he is struggling.

He was in a small rockbound hole filled with yellowish-grey water. The water was pushing him up against the roof. The roof was sharp and pained his back. He pulled himself along with his hands – fast, fast – and used his legs as levers. His head knocked against something; a sharp pain dizzied him. Fifty, 51, 52 … He was without light, and the water seemed to press upon him with the weight of the rock. Seventy-one, 72 … There was no strain on his lungs. He felt like an inflated balloon, his lungs were so light and easy, but his head was pulsing.

He was being continually pressed against the sharp roof, which felt slimy as well as sharp. Again he thought of octopuses, and wondered if the tunnel might be filled with weed that could tangle him. He gave himself a panicky, convulsive kick forward, ducked his head, and swam. His feet and hands moved freely, as if on open water. The hole must have widened out. He thought he must be swimming fast, and he was frightened of banging his head if the tunnel narrowed.

A hundred, 101 … The water paled. Victory filled him. His lungs were beginning to hurt. A few more strokes and he would be out. He was counting wildly; he said 115, and then a long time later, 115 again. The water was jewel-green all around him. Then he saw, above his head, a crack running up through the rock. Sunlight was falling through it, showing the clean, dark rock of the tunnel, a single mussel shell, and darkness ahead.

He was at the end of what he could do. He looked up at the crack as if it were filled with air and not water, as if he could put his mouth to it to draw in air. A hundred and fifteen, he heard himself say inside his head – but he had said that long ago. He must go on into the blackness ahead, or he would drown. His head was swelling, his lungs cracking. A hundred and fifteen, 115, pounded through his head, and he feebly clutched at rocks in the dark, pulling himself forward, leaving the brief space of sunlit water behind. He felt he was dying. He was no longer conscious. He struggled on in the darkness between lapses into unconsciousness. An immense, swelling pain filled his head, and then the darkness cracked with an explosion of green light. His hands, groping forward, met nothing; and his feet, kicking back, propelled him out into the open sea.

Activity 7 — Practise comparing language and ideas in texts

The writer of the text above has used the structure of the text and language techniques as she tells a story about swimming in order to explore more subtle themes.

1 Read the text. What is the significance of the boy swimming through the hole in the rock?
2 Think about the text as you answer these questions.
   a) How has the writer organised the text to create suspense? (Hint: remember to consider the whole text, paragraphs and individual sentences.)
   b) How does creating suspense help the writer express the theme?

Unit 8 Know how to compare texts

3 Identify where any of these language techniques are used to express ideas about the theme:
- verbs
- adjectives
- sensory description
- similes
- metaphors.

4 For each language technique, carefully re-read the part of the text that uses it and work out:
   a) what the technique helps convey about the theme
   b) what effect using that technique has on the reader.

Technique	Example of technique	What it conveys about the theme	What effect it has on the reader
verbs			
adjectives			
sensory description			
similes			
metaphors			

5 Look back at the texts on page 77 and page 80.
   a) In what ways have the writers of the two texts treated swimming similarly?
   b) In what ways have the texts' writers treated swimming differently?
   c) Compare the ways the writers have used language techniques.

Activity 8 | Write to compare different writers' ideas

When you compare the way writers express their themes and ideas, you need to explain:
- how each writer or text approaches the theme – their similarities and differences
- what are their attitudes and ideas
- how the different language techniques they use help them express their attitudes and ideas.

These phrases will help you:

> The writer of the text on page 77 conveys his attitude by/through... He uses [technique] when he says... This conveys the idea/suggests/makes the reader think...

1 Use the information you have gathered in the Activities you have already done to answer the following questions:
   a) How do the writers of the article on page 76 and the text on page 77 explore the theme of the pleasure of swimming outdoors in different ways, using different language techniques?
   b) How do the writers of the texts on page 77 and page 80 treat the subject of swimming outdoors in different ways? You should consider:
      - what swimming outdoors represents
      - the writers' attitude towards swimming
      - the writers' use of language techniques.

UNIT 9
Know how to respond to texts

1 Know how to interpret a text to prepare a dramatic reading aloud

I am learning how to:
- develop an interpretation of a text
- use my understanding of a text to prepare to read it aloud.

Key term
Interpretation – examining a text in detail to understand its overall meaning.

You can share your response to a text by working out how to read it aloud, using expressions and gestures to express your understanding of the meaning and impact of the text.

Below and on page 83 opposite is an extract from *Oliver Twist* by Charles Dickens. The boys he describes are orphans who live in a workhouse, which is overseen by a committee of wealthy gentlemen. This committee has recently decided that the workhouses are attracting too many people and has also decided to ensure that people will only choose to live in them if they are truly desperate.

1 The room in which the boys were fed, was a large stone hall, with a **copper** at one end: out of which the master, dressed in an apron for the purpose, and assisted by one or two women, ladled the **gruel** at meal-times. Of this festive composition each boy had one porringer, and no more – except on occasions of great public rejoicing, when he had two ounces and a quarter of bread besides.
5 The bowls never wanted washing. The boys polished them with their spoons till they shone again; and when they had performed this operation (which never took very long, the spoons being nearly as large as the bowls), they would sit staring at the copper, with such eager eyes, as if they could have devoured the very bricks of which it was composed; employing themselves, meanwhile, in sucking their fingers most **assiduously**, with the view of catching up any stray splashes of gruel that might
10 have been cast thereon. Boys have generally excellent appetites. Oliver Twist and his companions suffered the tortures of slow starvation for three months; at last they got so **voracious** and wild with hunger, that one boy, who was tall for his age, and hadn't been used to that sort of thing, (for his father had kept a small cook's shop,) hinted darkly to his companions, that unless he had another basin of gruel **per diem**, he was afraid he might some night happen to eat the boy who slept
15 next him, who happened to be a weakly youth of tender age. He had a wild, hungry eye; and they implicitly believed him. A council was held; lots were cast who should walk up to the master after supper that evening, and ask for more, and it fell to Oliver Twist.

Expand your vocabulary

copper – a large pot made of copper heated by a fire, in which the gruel is made
gruel – a thin porridge made from water and cornmeal
assiduously – carefully
voracious – extremely hungry, almost starving
per diem – for each day

Unit 9 Know how to respond to texts

The evening arrived; the boys took their places. The master, in his cook's uniform, stationed himself at the copper; his pauper assistants ranged
20 themselves behind him; the gruel was served out; and a long grace was said over the short commons. The gruel disappeared; the boys whispered each other and winked at Oliver; while his next neighbours nudged him. Child as he was, he was desperate with hunger, and reckless with misery. He rose from the table and advancing to the master; basin and spoon in
25 hand, said, somewhat alarmed at his own **temerity** –

'Please sir, I want some more.'

The master was a fat, healthy man; but he turned very pale. He gazed in stupefied astonishment on the small rebel for some seconds; and then clung for support to the copper. The assistants were paralysed with
30 wonder; the boys with fear.

'What?' said the master at length, in a faint voice.

'Please, sir,' replied Oliver, 'I want some more.'

The master aimed a blow at Oliver's head with the ladle; **pinioned** him in his arms; and shrieked aloud for the **beadle**.

35 The board were sitting in a solemn conclave, when Mr Bumble rushed into the room in great excitement, and addressing the gentleman in the high chair, said.

'Mr Limbkins, I beg your pardon, sir! Oliver Twist has asked for more!'

There was a general start. Horror was depicted on every countenance.

40 'For *more*!' said Mr Limbkins. 'Compose yourself, Bumble, and answer me distinctly. Do I understand that he asked for more, after he had eaten the supper allotted by the dietary?'

'He did, sir,' replied Bumble.

'That boy will be hung,' said the gentleman in the white waistcoat, 'I
45 know that boy will be hung.'

Expand your vocabulary

temerity – his cheek or audacity in asking for more food
pinioned – trapped him with his arms
beadle – the manager of the workhouse

1 Know how to interpret a text to prepare a dramatic reading aloud

Activity 1 — Use inference to develop your understanding of a text

Read the extract on pages 82–83, searching for clues to help you work out what is happening, and how characters may feel about each other and the situation they face.

1 Read the passage carefully. Make a flow chart to show the sequence of events it describes.
2 Why are all the adults so horrified by Oliver's request?

Activity 2 — Build up your interpretation of the whole text

1 Understanding the **characters**. Find one example of each of the following aspects of character, and provide a quotation as evidence:
   - a timid boy
   - a cruel and violent adult
   - a desperate boy
   - an astonished, surprised official.
2 Understanding the **situation**. For each of the following descriptions, explain what it tells the reader about the situation that the boys are in:
   a) 'the master, dressed in an apron for the purpose, and assisted by one or two women, ladled the gruel at meal-times.' (lines 2–3, page 82)
   b) 'The bowls never wanted washing.' (lines 5–6, page 82)
   c) '…employing themselves, meanwhile, in sucking their fingers most assiduously'. (line 10, page 82)
   d) '…the boys whispered each other and winked at Oliver'. (line 24, page 83)
   e) 'He gazed in stupefied astonishment on the small rebel for some seconds; and then clung for support to the copper.' (lines 29–31, page 83)
   f) 'The master aimed a blow at Oliver's head with the ladle; pinioned him in his arms; and shrieked aloud for the beadle.' (lines 34–35, page 83)
   g) 'There was a general start. Horror was depicted on every countenance.' (line 39, page 83)

Activity 3 — Express your understanding and interpretation by reading the text aloud

Use the following steps to prepare a reading of the text that conveys how you have interpreted it.

1 Dickens wrote the novel *Oliver Twist* to be entertaining, but also to protest against the appalling treatment of people living in workhouses.
   a) Find sentences and phrases that are entertaining, and work out how to read them so that your audience will appreciate the humour of the situation.
   b) Find sentences and phrases that should be read seriously to emphasise the poor conditions in the workhouse. Practise reading them out aloud.

2 Practise reading your selected text aloud. Take care to:
- Read clearly. Project your voice so that all can hear every word.
- Pause, and emphasise words and phrases in response to the punctuation so that readers can understand the text. Practise with different length pauses.
- Focus on the key lines you identified earlier. Use a louder or softer voice, and speed up or slow down, to show whether you are emphasising the entertaining or serious side of the situation.
- Think carefully about the actual words spoken by the characters in the text. You should try to adopt a different tone of voice for:
  - Oliver
  - the master
  - Mr Bumble
  - the gentleman in the white waistcoat, Mr Limbkins.
- Identify any points in the text when you will use gestures or facial expressions to help your audience understand the text in the way that you want them to.

2 Know how to write a detailed analysis of a text

I am learning how to:
- write a critical essay about a text
- include detailed analysis of the text to support my ideas.

When you write an essay about a text you need to answer the question in a way that shows you have read and understood the text and can select relevant material to support your ideas. You must also:

- interpret the writer's ideas and perspectives
- explain how the writer has used different techniques to achieve effects and engage readers
- show that you understand the text's context.

The poem opposite on page 87 is written by American poet Gary Soto, who grew up in Fresno, California in the 1950s and 1960s. There he saw first-hand the hard lives of poor, badly educated people working long hours in the cotton fields and understood their longing for their children's lives to be better.

> **Key terms**
> **Quotation** – any words accurately copied from the text and used as evidence in your essay.
> **Quote** – the action of quoting.
> **Analysis** – examining the features of a text in detail, explaining how they are created and what effect they have in developing the text's meaning and in engaging readers.

Activity 1 Understand the text and the task

When you read a task or essay question, identify the key words such as *how, explain language features*, and so on.

1 Read this task:

> How does Gary Soto show the value of working hard in 'A Red Palm'? In your answer you should explore:
> - what the father does
> - what his motives are
> - the writer's use of language.

   a) What are the question's key words?
   b) Express the task in your own words, making it clear what you need to include in your essay.

2 What do you need to find out as you read and think about the text?

3 Read the poem on page 87 carefully. Then answer the questions below:
   a) Sum up what happens in the poem.
   b) Make a list of things the father does that show the value of hard work.
   c) Re-read lines 7–26. What do you learn about the father's motives for working hard? (Use evidence from the text to support your answer.)
   d) Look closely at lines 30–36. What does this suggest about the son's intelligence and the father's hopes for his future?
   e) Look at the features labelled on the poem and answer each question as fully as you can. Think about what the lines mean and how the technique used helps express the ideas in that part of the poem more effectively.

Unit 9 Know how to respond to texts

A Red Palm

You're in this dream of cotton plants.
You raise a hoe, swing, and the first weeds
Fall with a sigh. You take another step,
Chop, and the sigh comes again,
Until you yourself are breathing that way
With each step, a sigh that will follow you into town.

That's hours later. The sun is a red blister
Coming up in your palm. Your back is strong,
Young, not yet the broken chair
In an abandoned school of dry spiders.
Dust settles on your forehead, dirt
Smiles under each fingernail.
You chop, step, and by the end of the first row,
You can buy one splendid fish for wife
And three sons. Another row, another fish,
Until you have enough and move on to milk,
Bread, meat. Ten hours and the cupboards creak.
You can rest in the back yard under a tree.
Your hands twitch on your lap,
Not unlike the fish on a pier or the bottom
Of a boat. You drink iced tea. The minutes jerk
Like flies.

It's dusk, now night,
And the lights in your home are on.
That costs money, yellow light
In the kitchen. That's thirty steps,
You say to your hands,
Now shaped into binoculars.
You could raise them to your eyes:
You were a fool in school, now look at you.
You're a giant among cotton plants.
Now you see your oldest boy, also running.
Papa, he says, it's time to come in.
You pull him into your lap
And ask, What's forty times nine?
He knows as well as you, and you smile.
The wind makes peace with the trees,
The stars strike themselves in the dark.
You get up and walk with the sigh of cotton plants.
You go to sleep with a red sun on your palm,
The sore light you see when you first stir in bed.

---

1 Metaphor – how does this metaphor help describe the cotton plants fully?

2 Onomatopoeia – what makes the sound? What does it suggest?

3 Personification – what does the sigh represent and why will it 'follow' him?

4 Metaphor – how is the sun like a red blister on his hand? What is he doing that could cause a red blister on his hand?

5 Metaphor – in what way could his back look like a broken chair? How does this image of an abandoned school link to what we find out about his education later?

6 Personification – think about fingernails: a) How can the dirt look like a 'smile' under them? b) What does the word 'smile' suggest about his attitude to this work?

7 Alliteration and onomatopoeia – why would the cupboards be creaking after ten hours of him working in the cotton field?

8 Simile – picture his hands twitching like a fish flapping. Why are they twitching? What does this suggest about him?

9 Simile a) In what way do flies 'jerk'? b) What does this suggest about how he feels about the way time passes?

10 Metaphor – why are the person's hands shaped into binoculars?

11 Internal rhyme – 'fool' and 'school' together with the contrast of then and now: Why is the link between the man's past and his present important?

12 Symbolism – what does this suggest about the man's response to his son's ability to answer the Maths question correctly?

13 Metaphor – what does the red sun represent?

14 Metaphor – the blister is still red and sore in the morning, but what does calling it a 'light' suggest it means for the man?

2 Know how to write a detailed analysis of a text

Activity 2 — Plan the content of your essay

An essay should have an introduction, a series of paragraphs that each make a new point that builds your argument, and a conclusion. To achieve this takes careful planning, drafting and proofreading.

1. You are going to use the work you have already done on the poem on page 87. Re-read the essay question in Activity 1 on page 86.

   a) Turn each prompt into a question about the main essay title, for example:

   What does the father do that shows the value of hard work?

   b) Using the work you did earlier decide what points you will make that answer the questions you created in part a). For example:

   In stanzas… the father counts out what different parts of his work will earn.

Question based on essay prompt	Points that will answer it
What does the father do that shows the value of hard work?	• In stanzas 1 and 2 the father works very hard hoeing weeds to earn money. He counts out what each part of his work will earn.
	• The father's life has taught him what happens when you do not work hard at school and so he understands the value of working hard at school, which is why he checks that his son knows his times tables.

2. Next find the evidence in the text to support the points you want to make.

Point explaining how the value of working hard is expressed in 'A Red Palm'	Evidence
In stanzas 1 and 2 the father works very hard hoeing weeds to earn money. He counts out what each part of his work will earn.	'You chop, step, and by the end of the first row, You can buy one splendid fish for wife And three sons.'

Activity 3 — Write the introduction to your essay

1. Write the first paragraph of the introduction to your essay, telling your reader what issue you are exploring and how you will explore it. Make sure you include the name of the text and its author. Explain what the essay is asking you to do using the key words from the task and explaining the prompts in your own words - for example:

   In his poem 'A Red Palm', the poet Gary Soto explores the idea that working hard is a good thing. He does this through focusing on… as well as…

Unit 9 Know how to respond to texts

Activity 4 — Write the main body of the essay

Draft a series of paragraphs. Each paragraph should express one of the points you are making in response to the essay question.

1. Using the notes you made earlier, draft the opening of the paragraph.
    a) Begin with the point you are making.
    b) Then introduce the evidence that proves your point is sensible. For example:

    The poet shows the value of hard work in stanzas 1 and 2 where he describes the father working very hard hoeing weeds to earn money, saying:

    'You chop, step, and by the end of the first row,
    You can buy one splendid fish for wife
    And three sons.'

2. For the remainder of each paragraph explain how the evidence proves your point and anything else it suggests that is relevant to the essay question. Work out what to say by answering these five questions about the evidence you have quoted:

    a) What do the words in your quotation mean?
    Here the writer describes/says that…

    b) How are any literary effects in your quotation created?
    The [literary effect] in this quotation is created by…

    c) What effect does your quotation have on the reader?
    The words make the reader notice/ feel/wonder/imagine/hear/picture…

    d) How does what you have noticed prove your point?
    This suggests/hints/reinforces the idea…

    e) What more do the words suggest that is relevant to your task?
    In addition, this could also imply/ suggest/hint/convey the idea that…

Activity 5 — Write the conclusion to your essay

To write a good final conclusion to your essay, combine the conclusions you came to as you wrote each paragraph. Then sum up what all these say as your final answer to the essay question.

1. Each paragraph you wrote for your essay gives part of your total answer. Sum up the answer each paragraph gave. For example:

    Paragraph 1: Gary Soto shows the value of the father's hard work by having him count how much food each part of it buys for his family.

    Paragraph 2: He shows the value of hard work because the father says it means they can have electricity.

2. Write the final paragraph of your essay summarising all these part-answers so that you express your overall response to the essay task. For example:

    Gary Soto shows the value of hard work through the father's thoughts about what each part of his labour earns for his family.

Focus your effort

Include quotations in your essay:
- Begin quotations of four or more words on a new line.
- Copy them accurately from the text (including line endings, punctuation and spelling).
- Enclose the words you quote in a pair of inverted commas.
- Wherever possible make the quotation part of your sentence by introducing it with phrases such as 'when the writer says:…' or 'in the words:…'. For example:

When the poet says:

"You were a fool in school, now look at you.

You're a giant among cotton plants."

The word 'fool' makes the reader wonder whether the man was not very intelligent as a boy, or whether he wasted the opportunity to gain a good education by playing the fool.

89

UNIT 10 Know how to read texts for different audiences and purposes

1 Know how to read information texts

I am learning how to:
- find, understand and summarise information
- comment on how information is presented
- identify and explain effective use of language.

Read the article on page 91 from the magazine *How It Works*.

Activity 1 Scan the text to find specific information

Scan the text on page 91 and answer these questions.

1. Where can Nile crocodiles be found?
2. How tall is the grey heron?
3. Can you give two ways in which the dromedary camel is put to use?
4. In what kinds of environments do hippos live?

Key term
Scan – track the text to find specific facts or details in it. You know what you are searching to find. So, for example, if it's a date, search for numbers; if it's a name, search for capital letters. Use headings and bold print to narrow your search to the most likely parts of the text.

Activity 2 Visual and textual information

When you read a text, you can make use of visual as well as textual information to find your way around and make sense of a text.

1. Think back to the last Activity. Give three examples of where visual clues **within the text itself** helped you find the answers to the questions.

Visual clue	My example
numbers	
capital letters	
headings	

2. As well as using text, the information is given using pictures of the animals and a map of the Nile.
   a) How do the pictures add to the information in the text?
   b) How does the map add to our understanding of the text?

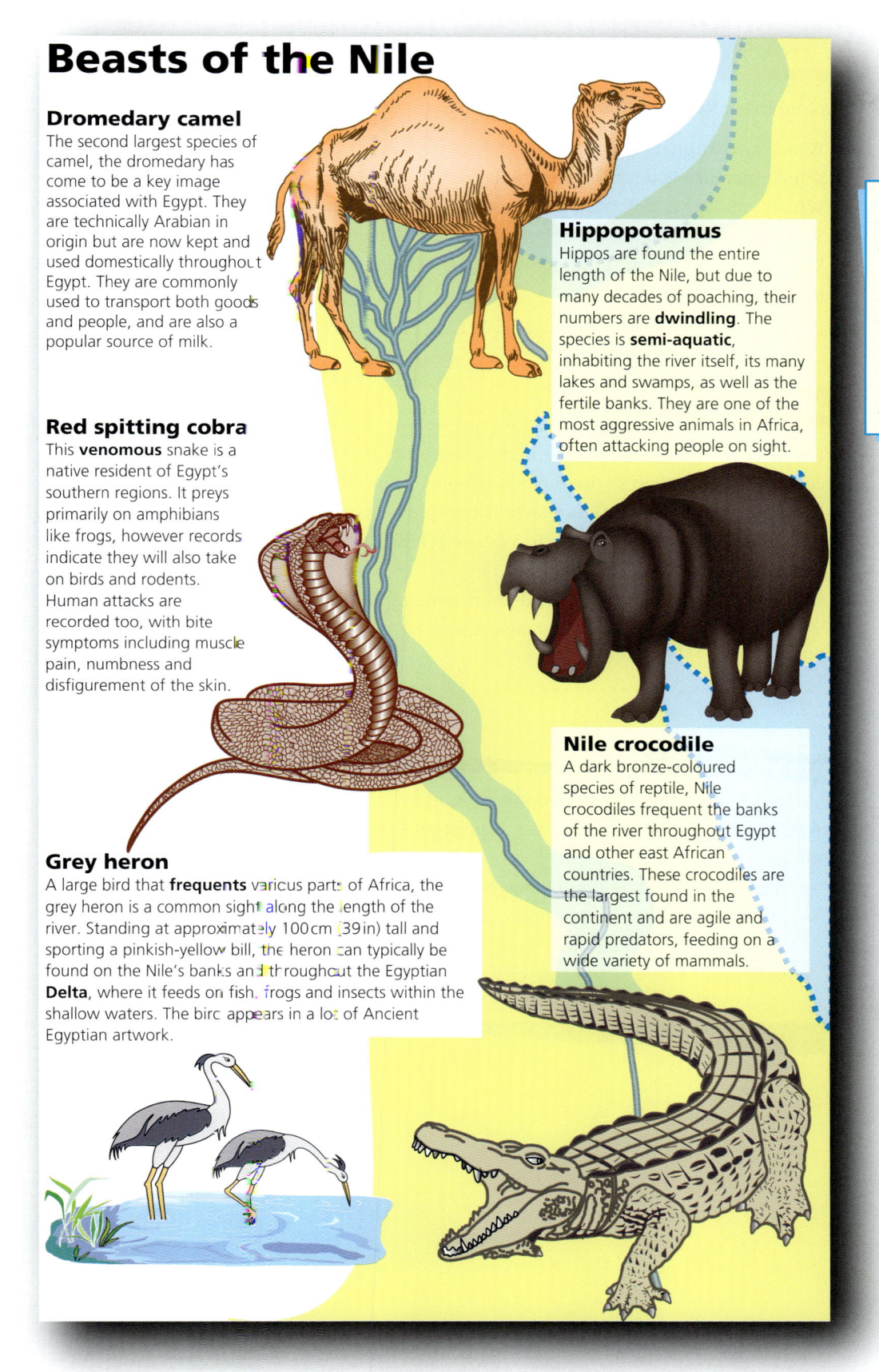

Unit 10 Know how to read texts for different audiences and purposes

Beasts of the Nile

Dromedary camel
The second largest species of camel, the dromedary has come to be a key image associated with Egypt. They are technically Arabian in origin but are now kept and used domestically throughout Egypt. They are commonly used to transport both goods and people, and are also a popular source of milk.

Red spitting cobra
This **venomous** snake is a native resident of Egypt's southern regions. It preys primarily on amphibians like frogs, however records indicate they will also take on birds and rodents. Human attacks are recorded too, with bite symptoms including muscle pain, numbness and disfigurement of the skin.

Grey heron
A large bird that **frequents** various parts of Africa, the grey heron is a common sight along the length of the river. Standing at approximately 100cm (39in) tall and sporting a pinkish-yellow bill, the heron can typically be found on the Nile's banks and throughout the Egyptian **Delta**, where it feeds on fish, frogs and insects within the shallow waters. The bird appears in a lot of Ancient Egyptian artwork.

Hippopotamus
Hippos are found the entire length of the Nile, but due to many decades of poaching, their numbers are **dwindling**. The species is **semi-aquatic**, inhabiting the river itself, its many lakes and swamps, as well as the fertile banks. They are one of the most aggressive animals in Africa, often attacking people on sight.

Nile crocodile
A dark bronze-coloured species of reptile, Nile crocodiles frequent the banks of the river throughout Egypt and other east African countries. These crocodiles are the largest found in the continent and are agile and rapid predators, feeding on a wide variety of mammals.

What do you know about… the River Nile?
The River Nile rises from south of the Equator in Uganda and travels through north-east Africa to the Mediterranean Sea. The last country it passes through is Egypt. The fertile Nile Delta region in northern Egypt is one of the world's largest river deltas.

Expand your vocabulary

venomous – able to inflict a poisonous bite or sting
frequent (verb) – to visit regularly
delta – a low area of land where a river divides before entering a large body of water
dwindling – becoming gradually less
semi-aquatic – adapted for living or growing in or near water; not entirely aquatic

1 Know how to read information texts

Activity 3 — Find related details

Explore the information further by finding and comparing related details.

1. Which two animals like to eat frogs?
2. Which creature is described as the largest of its kind?
3. Which creature is described as the second largest of its kind?
4. Which two animals are described as being a danger to humans?
5. Which animal do you think poses the greater danger to humans based on the information provided here?

Activity 4 — Summarise information

1. For three of the animals in the text, identify the three most important facts or comments, and express them in short bullet points.
2. Read the text carefully and answer these questions:
   a) Select the way in which each creature relates to humans (e.g. does a job, is used in art).
   b) Using this information, write a short paragraph explaining how the creatures connect with or relate to humans. Use your own words where possible.

Focus your effort

Taking notes from texts is a good technique for reading and research. Use it to understand a text better or answer a question that involves particular information. You can:

- make notes on key points, maybe using bullet points or a concept map
- arrange what you have found out under headings (e.g. appearance, habitat, eating habits) or in a table
- sum up in a few sentences what you have learned.

Unit 10 Know how to read texts for different audiences and purposes

Activity 5 | Comment on how information is presented

1 Use your work from the previous Activities. Plan a paragraph about how the writer has conveyed and presented information in this text.
   Ensure you include the following points:
   - the kinds of information included in the text
   - the different ways in which the information is presented
   - how clearly you feel the information is presented
   - who might read this text and find it useful
   - particular words that stand out (e.g. descriptive).

   You might find the terms below useful as you think about and comment on the text:
   - audience
   - bold
   - categories
   - colour
   - content
   - convey
   - heading
   - image
   - information
   - map
   - organisation
   - presentation
   - sub-heading
   - text
   - visual

2 Now write the paragraph. Pay attention to:
   - the suggested terms
   - using clear language
   - a definite sequence to your ideas and sentences.

2 Know how to read instruction texts

I am learning how to:
- identify audience and purpose in an instruction text
- comment on the effectiveness of a text's structure and organisation
- comment on effective use of language.

Read the following guidance taken from the downloadable resource 'Running a poetry slam in school: a toolkit' produced by the National Literacy Trust.

> **Key terms**
>
> The **purpose** of a text – what it is meant to achieve; what the writer intends, e.g. to inform, to guide or instruct, to entertain. Some texts might have more than one purpose.
>
> **Audiences** – the readers of texts. A text is written for a particular audience group, e.g. teenagers, older people, fans, special interest groups, and so on.

> **What do you know about… poetry slams?**
>
> A poetry slam is a competitive form of performance poetry in front of a live audience. It was invented by Chicago poet Marc Smith in 1984 and spread to New York in 1988. The idea was to invent a new and exciting way of enjoying and sharing poetry. Judges are often selected at random from the audience.

> **Expand your vocabulary**
>
> **hub** – busy centre of activity and interest
> **superfluous** – more than enough, unnecessary
> **impetus** – driving force, motivation

Preparing for and running your poetry slam

Deciding where to hold it

A great thing about the slam form is that it is adaptable.

Why not:

- turn your library into a literary **hub** by running a lunchtime slam – open to all!
- build a sense of community within your tutor group by running a slam during tutor time?
- fulfil National Curriculum goals for speaking and listening by having a slam in an English lesson?
- have your GCSE drama group organise a slam?
- raise the profile of poetry in your school by having a school-wide slam. Start by holding mini-slams within tutor groups, then get each tutor group champion to compete with the others from their year group. The winner from each year group can take part in an inter-year competition to decide the ultimate school poetry slam champion.

Pre-slam activities

1 Create

- The aim here is to get words on to paper. Believe me, it's harder than it sounds! Even for a professional writer the hardest part is getting started. Here are some ideas to get past the dreaded objection, 'I don't know what to write':
- The creative process should be divorced from the editing process. Encourage your students to write without worrying about spelling, grammar and punctuation. Tell them to focus only on telling their story.
- Challenge your students to 'free write' – to keep writing no matter what for a specific time period, even if it is gibberish. The goal is to generate material that can later be turned into a poem.
- Ask your students to write about a specific event – this is often easier than writing about something abstract. If they run into difficulties have them focus on clarifying the event in their imagination first and then the right words ought to come.
- Try the 'cut-up method': cut out words and have your students arrange them into a poem.

2 Edit

Slam is written for an audience, not exclusively for therapy or self-expression. Therefore, we need to edit our work with our audience in mind.

Questions to ask your students to help them edit their poem:

- Have you got rid of everything that is **superfluous** to your message?
- Is your message clear? Is it easy to understand your point?
- What rhetorical techniques can you use? Rhyme, rhythm, repetition, puns, wordplay, imagery, other techniques?
- What images have you come up with? Do they make sense? How can you make them clearer?

Why not set up an online group or message board where your students can post their poems and talk about ways they can improve?

3 Practise

It is preferable but not essential to learn a poem off by heart. Some videos of me discussing other performance techniques are available at www.literacytrust.org.uk/competitions/write_on

The event

You will need:
- performers
- a time-keeper
- an audience
- scorecards (numbered 1–10)
- three to five judges
- a prize for the winner.

Slams usually have an MC to host the event. You could choose a student or invite a teacher or ex-student to be the MC for your slam. Slams also often feature well-known poets, who perform a short set before and halfway through the slam competition. Why not invite a local poet to perform at your slam? Websites such as www.bookapoet.com and www.applesandsnakes.co.uk can help with this.

The rules
1. Each poet has three minutes to perform.
2. Scores out of 10 are given by the judges. Judges can be professional poets or just picked from the audience.
   a) Scores can be given using specific criteria, such as 'quality of writing', 'quality of performance' and 'audience reaction'.
   b) With five judges, for consistency sometimes the highest and lowest scores are discounted and the three remaining scores make up the final number.
3. The winner is the poet with the highest score.

Follow-up activities

Hopefully, through taking part in the slam, at the very least your students should have a positive experience with live poetry. They will have increased in confidence and perhaps some who normally struggle with writing will have done well on the strength of their performances.

The slam can be an **impetus** for class debate on the merits of slam as a form. Students could critique and discuss new media and its relationship to poetry; for example, performance poetry lends itself very well to YouTube, so videos have become a common way for performers to publicise their poems. What could this mean for the future of poetry?

Following on from this you could also use the students' experience of performing in the slam as a stimulus for discussion about ownership of their poems. How would they feel about other people performing their poem without permission, or using ideas from their poem without crediting them? It's a great opportunity to explore the world of copyright and creative ownership.

Other ideas

- Produce a book of your finalists' poems.
- Film the event for the school and use it to enter the Write On competition.
- Form a slam poetry club for your school.
- Hold an inter-school poetry slam with other schools in your local area.

2 Know how to read instruction texts

Activity 1 — Identify audience and purpose

Read the text on pages 94–95 again and answer the questions below. If you think the text has more than one audience and purpose, include these ideas in your answer.

1 Why do you think the text has been written (the purpose of the text)? Give reasons and evidence for your answer.
2 Whom do you think this text has been written for (the audience of the text)? Give evidence for your answer.
You can do this by identifying some words and phrases that indicate whom the audience is.

Activity 2 — Explore how the guidance has been structured and organised

The writer presents the detailed guidance in a step-by-step way, breaking it into chunks that can be managed. The writer also presents the guidance in the order it needs to be carried out (chronological order).

1 Identify two examples each of the following in the text:
- headings
- sub-headings
- sub-sub-headings
- bullet points
- clear use of chronological order
- explanations
- advice or suggestions
- other types of structural or organisational features.

You can do this by annotating (making notes around) a copy of the text.

Key term
Chronological order – organised in time periods, e.g. first event, second event, third event, etc.

[Heading] → **Preparing for and running your poetry slam**

[Sub-heading] → *Deciding where to hold it*

A great thing about the slam form is that it is adaptable.
Why not:

- turn your library into a literary **hub** by running a lunchtime slam – open to all!
- build a sense of community within your tutor group by running a slam during tutor time?
- fulfil National Curriculum goals for speaking and listening by having a slam in an English lesson?
- have your GCSE drama group organise a slam?
- raise the profile of poetry in your school by having a school-wide slam. Start by holding mini-slams within tutor groups, then get each tutor group champion to compete with the others from their year group. The winner from each year group can take part in an inter-year competition to decide the ultimate school poetry slam champion.

Unit 10 Know how to read texts for different audiences and purposes

Activity 3 — Investigate how the text uses language

The writer uses language effectively to communicate meaning clearly and purposefully to the reader.

1 Identify language features of the text that link to its purpose and audience:
   - particular words and phrases (small collections of words)
   - key sentences, including use of grammar or ways the sentences are expressed
   - use of punctuation.

   You could annotate a copy of the text, using different coloured highlighters for each of the above.

   To get you started, here is an example of each one:
   - Words: 'Turn', 'Build' (direct, imperatives, instructions).
   - Phrases: 'Believe me' (personal address to the reader).
   - Key sentences: 'What images have you come up with?' (Questions invite the reader to think and respond.)
   - Punctuation: colon (:) dash (–).

   Now find more examples.

   Explain how they are used and what effect they have.

Activity 4 — Comment on the effectiveness of this text

Use your work in the previous Activities to answer these questions.

1 How do the organisational and presentational features make this an effective and useful text?

   You could use these prompts to help you:

   > I think that the writer has chosen to use… because…
   > The writer makes the overall structure of the text clear for readers by…
   > The writer has organised each section of the text using… This is effective because…
   > I think the text's structure and organisation are suitable for its audience/purpose because…

2 What other features like language and punctuation, help make this text effective?

   You must find examples, but you could use these prompts to help you get started:

   > Using direct language such as imperative verbs helps the writer to…
   > Examples and explanations are often introduced by punctuation such as…
   > The writer sometimes uses more personal language to…
   > The language is often straightforward because…

97

3 Know how to read argument texts

I am learning how to:
- follow a writer's line of argument
- analyse structure and organisation – of the whole text and within each paragraph
- identify and comment on effective use of language.

Read the newspaper article below and opposite written by a 13-year-old boy, in which he defends computer games.

Activity 1 Follow the writer's line of argument

Read the introduction to Joshua Stamp-Simon's article again (first paragraph).

1. Who is the intended audience for this article, and how do you know?
2. What is the writer's purpose in writing this article, and how do you know?
3. What is his main claim about computer games?
4. What does he say about people who disagree with his main claim?

> **Key terms**
> The **purpose** of a text – what it is meant to achieve: what the writer intends, e.g. to inform, to argue or persuade, to entertain. Some texts might have more than one purpose.
> The **audience** – the readers of a text. A text is written for a particular audience group, e.g. teenagers, older people, fans, special interest groups, and so on.

> **Key terms**
> The **argument** – the main point of view, or the development of the main idea in the text. It will sometimes be closely connected to the purpose of the text. It is what the writer wants you to believe or agree with.
> A **counter-argument** – any view or developed idea that opposes the main argument.

Trigger happy

Whatever adults think, says Joshua Stamp-Simon, 13, computer games do not rot kids' brains.

I am obsessed with computer games. Of course, I am not alone in this. I am merely one of many who believe that the computer is the most worthwhile invention since the wheel. Despite the widespread extent of this obsession, many adults simply cannot comprehend how so many children can entertain themselves for hours on end by repeatedly clicking various buttons and staring at a small, brightly coloured screen. Well, help is at hand as I now take on the difficult task of explaining to all you confused parents why computer games are so great.

I'd like to straighten one thing out from the start. To most people, the term 'computer game' brings hazy images of mass destruction and mindless violence. This is true of only some games. Indeed, many games, such as The Sims, have no violence whatsoever. As for the rest, I wouldn't call it 'mindless' violence. Mind*ful* violence would be a better term.

Unit 10 Know how to read texts for different audiences and purposes

Computer games have always been viewed in a negative light. You'll hear parents boasting of their child's passion for reading, or how their child is a British chess champion. You would never dream of mentioning the hours your child spends on the computer. I always wonder why.

Silly argument no. 1: 'Computer games damage your eyes.' This is totally untrue. My eyes hurt far more after a long period reading a book than they do after playing on the computer. When you read a book, your eyes are constantly focused on it. When you play on the computer, your eyes are always darting around the screen, searching for enemies, treasure and so on.

Silly argument no. 2: 'Computer games are not educational.' Well, what do you expect your child to do after school – read an encyclopaedia? No, of course not. In fact, some computer games do turn out to be educational: for example, Civilisation II, in which you create a civilisation from scratch, building cities and discovering new technologies. Despite the large strategic element to the game, it also serves as a remarkably good history lesson. You start off with warriors and archers, then gradually, as you discover technologies, you move up the ages, and before you know it, you're defending your cities with riflemen and launching a spaceship to Alpha Centauri. Many other strategy games, such as Empire Earth, work the same way. Civilisation II's **predecessor**, Civilisation, was one of the main reasons I learned to read, as it was impossible to play without reading the various messages that popped up on the screen. All this from a no-good, eye-destroying computer game.

Silly argument no. 3: 'Computer games are anti-social.' Again, this is untrue. Many of my best friends play the same sorts of games I do, and that is one of the things that has brought us together.

Silly argument no. 4: 'Computer games encourage violent behaviour.' I play on the computer more than most, and I haven't become a psychotic axe murderer. At least, not yet.

I haven't mentioned my favourite type of computer game – the RPG. This stands for role-playing game, not rocket-propelled grenade or **rancid** poultry guts. As you may have guessed, in a role-playing game you take on the role of a character. Or several characters. RPGs are generally centred around violence. But even where enjoyment is **derived solely** from fighting, such as in Diablo II, there is a distinct difference between RPGs and the standard shoot-'em-up. The difference is that you make choices about the character you are playing, in terms of appearance, race, class, skills, and so on.

Being able to make these choices is the main reason that I like RPGs. If you are reading a book, you may understand a character. In RPGs, you *are* the character. Just for a few hours, you can be someone else. You can be evil and kill everything in sight, or not, if you wish. When you read a book, the author decides what happens next. You, the reader, are merely passively finding out. With computer games, *you* decide what happens.

Of course, the same is true with real life. You make the choices. But it is far easier to do it with someone else's life, especially if that someone is binary on a computer's hard disk. Choices in real life are either boringly simple, such as what to have for breakfast, or mind-bogglingly large, such as what career to pursue. You don't want to mess those up. That's what limits your choices in real life.

This doesn't apply to computer games – and that's why I like them.

What do you know about… computer games controversies?

Computer games have been popular since the 1980s. They are the subject of both controversy and research. Much research focuses on how the content of video games affects individuals the longer they play them. Some people are concerned that computer games can lead to aggression, violence and anti-social behaviour.

Expand your vocabulary

predecessor – a person or thing followed or replaced by another
rancid – nasty, unpleasant; having the smell or taste of something that is decomposing
derived – obtained, received
solely – entirely, completely

3 Know how to read argument texts

Activity 2 — Analyse whole text structure

Joshua doesn't just put forward his own argument in the article. He takes each 'silly argument' in turn and shows he understands the points of people who disagree with him (the counter-arguments). He then responds by putting forward his own arguments.

1 Fill in a table like the one below to show the counter-arguments Joshua uses in his article and the point or points he makes to attack these counter-arguments.

Counter-argument	Joshua's argument
'Computer games damage your eyes'	He says that reading hurts his eyes more than using computer games. He says that he thinks it's good that his eyes move around a lot when he's playing computer games rather than just focusing in one place.
'Computer games are not educational'	
'Computer games are anti-social'	
'Computer games encourage violent behaviour'	

2 Read the final four paragraphs of the article.
The first section shows the main arguments very clearly by organising them as 'Silly argument no….', then countering them. The arguments in the last four paragraphs are organised differently.
Write out or underline the four main sentences showing what the main argument is in each of the last four paragraphs (paragraphs 8, 9, 10 and 11). (Hint: you might not find them at the beginning of each paragraph.)

Activity 3 — Analyse how ideas are organised within paragraphs

1 In non-fiction texts a topic sentence often gives the main point of a paragraph. It is usually found at or near the start of the paragraph. Complete a table like the one below to note where the writer shows or says what his paragraph will be about.

Paragraph from main body of article	Main topic of the paragraph	Evidence from the paragraph	Where does this evidence appear? A = at the start of the paragraph B = near the start of the paragraph C = much later in the paragraph
2	Whether all computer games are violent.		
3	Negativity about computer games.	'Computer games have always been viewed in a negative light.'	
4	Whether computer games damage your eyes.		
5	Whether computer games can be educational.		

Unit 10 Know how to read texts for different audiences and purposes

6		'Silly argument number 3: computer games are anti-social'	
7			
8	Role-playing games		
9			

2 Now look closely at paragraphs 4, 5 and 8. Decide for each paragraph how the main point is developed in the rest of the paragraph. Use a table like the one below and put a tick in the appropriate column(s) for each paragraph.

Paragraph from main body of article	Does it explain the main point in more detail?	Does it give evidence to support the main point?	Does it make comparisons with the main point?	Does it give reasons to support the main point?
4				
5				
8				

Activity 4 — Investigate how the writer uses language effectively

1 Identify two further examples for each bullet point of how the writer uses language effectively to do the following:

- Be personal:
    → uses first person 'I'.
- Be conversational:
    → uses 'Well…'.
- Be humorous:
    → uses 'Silly argument no.…'.
- Tries to persuade you to think he is right:
    → uses 'Of course…'.
- Be assertive:
    → uses 'This is true of only some games'.
- Be direct and straightforward:
    → uses 'That's what limits your choices in real life'.

Activity 5 — Comment on a text that argues

1 Using the questions and answers to the previous Activities, write three or four paragraphs in which you comment on how effective the text is as an argument. You can use the prompts below:

- key points made
- ways in which the writer has organised them
- sentences and words used
- tone of voice (e.g. direct, conversational, assertive).

2 Do you think it would persuade the target audience of adults? If so, why? If you think it might not, explain why.

101

4 Know how to read contrasting argument texts

I am learning how to:
- analyse the use and impact of persuasive language and techniques.

Read the following text taken from the Dubble chocolate bar website.

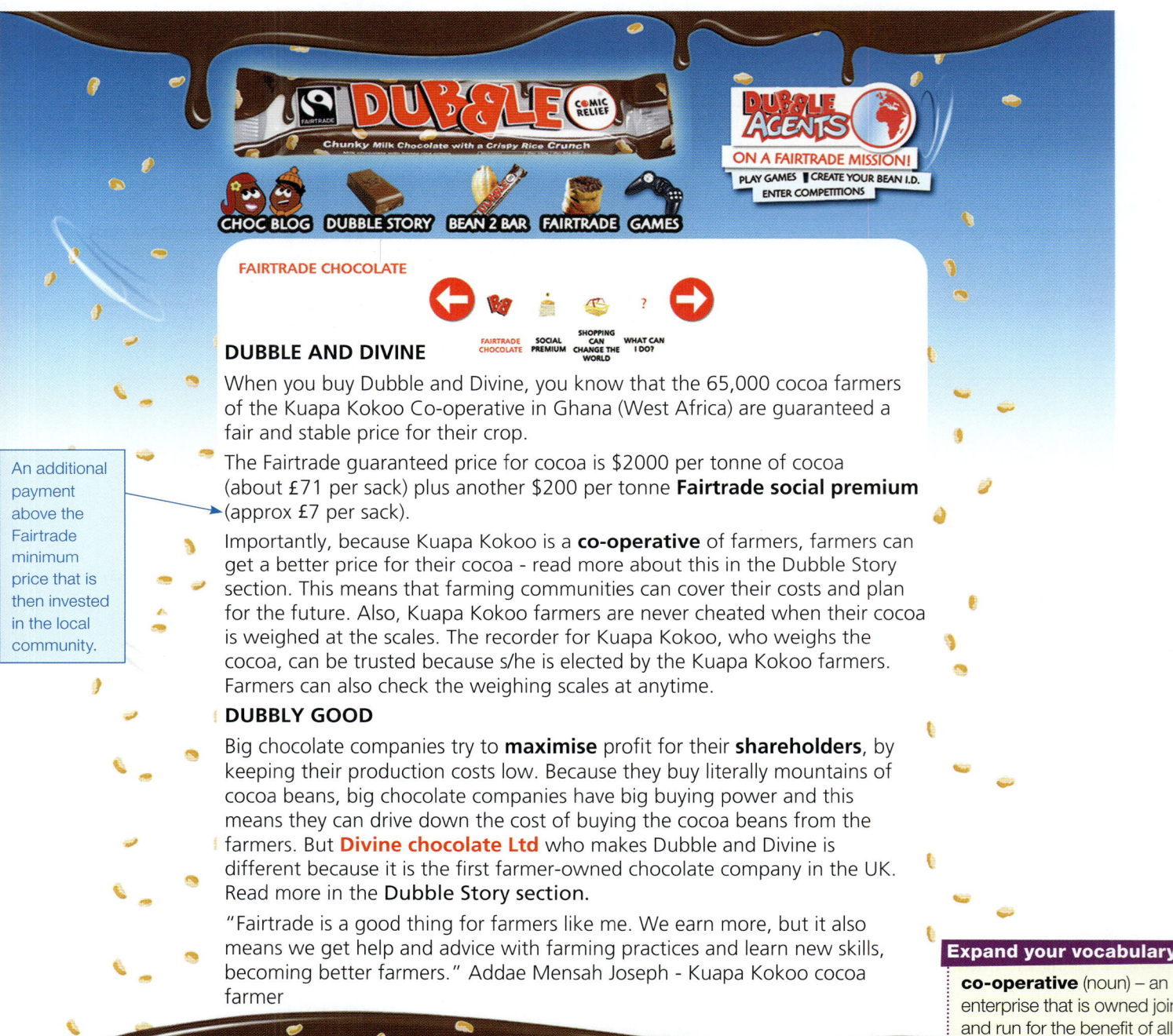

FAIRTRADE CHOCOLATE

DUBBLE AND DIVINE

When you buy Dubble and Divine, you know that the 65,000 cocoa farmers of the Kuapa Kokoo Co-operative in Ghana (West Africa) are guaranteed a fair and stable price for their crop.

The Fairtrade guaranteed price for cocoa is $2000 per tonne of cocoa (about £71 per sack) plus another $200 per tonne **Fairtrade social premium** (approx £7 per sack).

An additional payment above the Fairtrade minimum price that is then invested in the local community.

Importantly, because Kuapa Kokoo is a **co-operative** of farmers, farmers can get a better price for their cocoa - read more about this in the Dubble Story section. This means that farming communities can cover their costs and plan for the future. Also, Kuapa Kokoo farmers are never cheated when their cocoa is weighed at the scales. The recorder for Kuapa Kokoo, who weighs the cocoa, can be trusted because s/he is elected by the Kuapa Kokoo farmers. Farmers can also check the weighing scales at anytime.

DUBBLY GOOD

Big chocolate companies try to **maximise** profit for their **shareholders**, by keeping their production costs low. Because they buy literally mountains of cocoa beans, big chocolate companies have big buying power and this means they can drive down the cost of buying the cocoa beans from the farmers. But **Divine chocolate Ltd** who makes Dubble and Divine is different because it is the first farmer-owned chocolate company in the UK. Read more in the **Dubble Story section.**

"Fairtrade is a good thing for farmers like me. We earn more, but it also means we get help and advice with farming practices and learn new skills, becoming better farmers." Addae Mensah Joseph - Kuapa Kokoo cocoa farmer

Expand your vocabulary

co-operative (noun) – an enterprise that is owned jointly and run for the benefit of all its owners

maximise – make as big as possible

shareholders – the people who each own one or more shares in a company

Unit 10 Know how to read texts for different audiences and purposes

SHOPPING CAN CHANGE THE WORLD

Shopping connects us with millions of people across the world who produce the things we buy and use every day. But not everyone gets a fair deal. Many farmers in developing countries, who grow crops like cocoa, coffee, tea and bananas don't earn enough to pay for the things that we take for granted like access to clean water, medicines and a child's education.

FAIRTRADE MARK

When you spot this Mark on a product, you can be sure that farmers or workers in the developing world who helped to make the product were paid a fair price and worked in decent conditions. There are now over 3000 products on sale in the UK with the Fairtrade Mark from fruit to footballs, and of course your favourites Dubble and Divine. Find out more at www.fairtrade.org.uk

ADE ADEPITAN SAYS

"I have seen first-hand how buying Fairtrade chocolate has made a big difference to people's lives in Ghana".

Ade Adepitan, TV presenter and GB Paralympic basketball player

GLOBAL SHOPPING

Sometimes you have to pay a little bit extra for Fairtrade products, but it's worth it to know farmers are getting a fair deal. A little bit extra goes a long way.

DUBBLE AGENTS

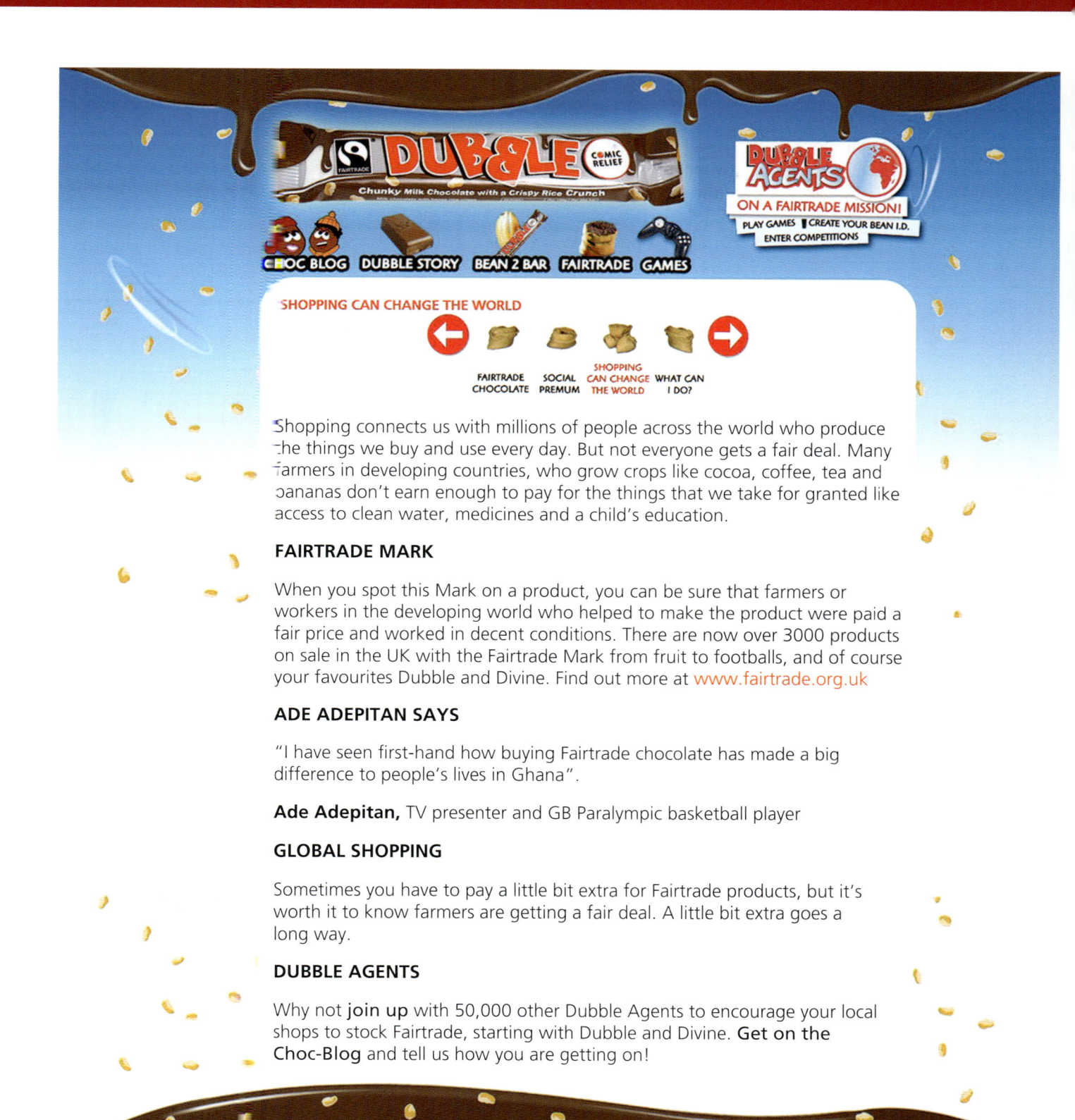

Why not **join up** with 50,000 other Dubble Agents to encourage your local shops to stock Fairtrade, starting with Dubble and Divine. **Get on the Choc-Blog** and tell us how you are getting on!

Changing the world chunk by chunk

About us
Contact us
Privacy Policy
Terms & Conditions
Help for parents

Stockists
Divine Chocolate Shop
Dubble Shop Map

Dubble Agents
Sign Up
Choc Blog

Teachers Resources

Comic Relief, registered charity 326568 (England & Wales); SC039730 (Scotland)

103

4 Know how to read contrasting argument texts

Activity 1 — Identify persuasive arguments

Read the texts on pages 102 and 103 again as you answer these questions.

1 The main purpose of these web pages is to persuade the reader to become a buyer of the chocolate. Who is the intended audience for these web pages?
2 Find five actions that this text is trying to persuade readers to take.
3 List each of the persuasive arguments used in the text to persuade readers to buy Dubble and Divine chocolate.

> **Key term**
> **Persuasive texts** – aim to persuade readers through the strength of their arguments. Writers use language techniques that affect the reader and make the message memorable. For example:
> - emotive language to appeal to the reader's emotions
> - addressing the reader direct
> - using persuasive language
> - asking rhetorical questions
> - including personal anecdotes or testimonials
> - using alliteration, lists of three, repetition and catchy slogans.

Activity 2 — Analyse persuasive language and techniques

1 Think about what the following words or sentences do to persuade the reader.
   - 'When you buy… you know that…'
   - 'Importantly…'
   - Repetition of 'big' to describe chocolate companies.
   - 'Why not join up…?'
2 Find and note examples of each of the persuasive techniques in the table below in the Dubble and Divine text.

Persuasive technique	Example
emotive language	'farmers are never cheated when their cocoa is weighed at the scales'
direct address to reader/listener	
persuasive language	
rhetorical questions	
personal anecdote or testimonial	
alliteration	
list of three	
repetition	
catchy slogan	

Unit 10 Know how to read texts for different audiences and purposes

Activity 3 — Comment on features that persuade

1 Look back at the examples you found in Activity 2. Explain how they are effective, by showing how they act to persuade the reader. Remember to identify the technique. For example:

> The writer uses an emotive word, 'cheated', to invite in the reader sympathy for farmers and moral indignation for producers. Also, the word 'never' stresses that the cheating must stop. Both words try to produce an emotional response in the reader.

Activity 4 — Comment on a text that persuades

1 Use your work from Activities 2 and 3 above. For each of the techniques and examples you have found, write a short paragraph to explain why it is effective in persuading the reader to take action.

Here is an example of a detailed response by a student to the first technique:

> An example of emotive language in this text is where it says that 'farmers are never cheated when their cocoa is weighed at the scales'. The word 'cheated' is a powerful choice that might make people feel angry that some other farmers are not being paid a fair price for their goods and the negative impact that this will have on them and their families. Readers will feel inspired to take action to help all farmers get a fair price for their cocoa.

5 Know how to read reviews and opinion texts

I am learning how to:
→ read and respond to texts that give personal opinions
→ interpret and comment on the author's viewpoint.

Read on page 107 opposite this first review of *Harry Potter and the Sorcerer's Stone* (the American edition of *Harry Potter and the Philosopher's Stone*) in *The New York Times*.

Activity 1 — Explore the context

Writers of book reviews often give an opinion (or viewpoint) based on their own personal knowledge and experience or what they have read before.

1 In the table below, pick out examples of references to other reading or experiences referred to in the review on page 107 oppposite.

Paragraph	Evidence
1	'So many of the beloved heroes and heroines'
3	
4	

Activity 2 — Explore the writer's structure

The way a text is organised into parts or sections is known as the **structure** of the text. There are seven paragraphs overall in the review.

1 Read through the text identifying in one sentence the main idea of each paragraph.

Paragraph	Main point
1	Children's books have heroes and heroines.
2	
3	
4	
5	
6	
7	This book is something quite special.

Unit 10 Know how to read texts for different audiences and purposes

Review of Harry Potter and the Sorcerer's Stone

So many of the beloved heroes and heroines of children's literature – from Cinderella and Snow White, to Oliver Twist and the Little Princess, to Matilda, Maniac Magee and the great Gilly Hopkins – begin their lives being raised by monstrously wicked, clueless adults, too stupid to see what we the readers know practically from page 1: this is a terrific person we'd love to have for a best friend.

And so it is with Harry Potter, the star of *Harry Potter and the Sorcerer's Stone*, by J.K. Rowling, a wonderful first novel from England that won major literary awards and has been at the top of the adult bestseller lists there and is having the same kind of success here, too. Poor Harry Potter is orphaned as a baby and is sent to live with his **odious** aunt and uncle, Petunia and Vernon Dursley, and their fat son, Dudley. While Fat Dudley Dursley has two bedrooms (one just for his **surplus** toys, like the television set he put his foot through when his favorite show was canceled), Harry is forced to sleep in a crawl space under the stairs, has never had a birthday party in his 11 years and must wear his cousin's way baggy hand-me-down clothes.

But Harry is destined for greatness, as we know from the lightning-shaped scar on his forehead, and one day he mysteriously receives a notice in the mail announcing that he has been chosen to attend Hogwarts, the nation's elite school for training wizards and witches, the Harvard of sorcery. Before he is done, Harry Potter will meet a dragon, make friends with a melancholy centaur and do battle with a three-headed dog; he will learn how to fly a broom and how to use a cloak that makes him invisible. Though all this hocus pocus is delightful, the magic in the book is not the real magic of the book. Much like Roald Dahl, J.K. Rowling has a gift for keeping the emotions, fears and triumphs of her characters on a human scale, even while the supernatural is popping out all over.

We feel Harry's fear when for the first time he is traveling to a faraway place, an 11-year-old boy arriving alone at King's Cross train station with a trunk bigger than he is, and no idea how to find Platform 9 ¾. This is a world where some people know from birth that they are wizards, and are raised by their sorcerer parents to attend fair old Hogwarts, while others, like Harry – raised in human, or what Rowling calls 'Muggle', families – don't find out that they have special powers until they receive their acceptance letters. As Harry worries that first day about whether he can compete with the privileged children of Hogwarts **alums**, I found myself thinking back 30 years to my first days at Harvard, wondering how, coming from a blue-collar shipyard town and a public high school, I could ever compete with **preppies** from Exeter and Andover.

> '"I bet I'm the worst in the class," says Harry. "You won't be," says a friend. "There's loads of people who come from Muggle families and they learn quick enough."'

The book is full of wonderful, sly humor. Exam period at Hogwarts means not just essay tests, but practical exams too.

> 'Professor Flitwick called them one by one into his class to see if they could make a pineapple tap-dance across a desk. Professor McGonagall watched them turn a mouse into a snuffbox – points were given for how pretty the snuffbox was, but taken away if it had whiskers.'

Throughout most of the book, the characters are impressively three-dimensional (occasionally four-dimensional!) and move along seamlessly through the narrative. A few times in the last four chapters, however, the storytelling begins to sputter, and there are twists I found irritating and **contrived**. To serve the plot, characters begin behaving out of character. Most noticeably, Hagrid, the gentle giant of a groundskeeper who has selflessly protected Harry over and over, suddenly turns so selfish he is willing to let Harry be punished for something that is Hagrid's fault. That's not the Hagrid I'd come to know.

These are minor criticisms. On the whole, *Harry Potter and the Sorcerer's Stone* is as funny, moving and impressive as the story behind its writing. J.K. Rowling, a teacher by training, was a 30-year-old single mother living on welfare in a cold one-bedroom flat in Edinburgh when she began writing the book in longhand during her baby daughter's nap times. But like Harry Potter, she had wizardry inside, and has soared beyond her modest Muggle surroundings to achieve something quite special.

Expand your vocabulary

- **odious** – hateful, arousing distaste or aversion
- **surplus** – more than what is needed
- **alums** – past students at a college or university (short term for alumni)
- **preppies** – students in a preparatory school
- **contrived** – obviously planned

5 Know how to read reviews and opinion texts

Key term
Style – the overall way in which a text is written. It includes all the key features, e.g. word choice, grammar, point of view.

Activity 3 — Explore language

1. The writer will use certain kinds of language in a book review. This is known as style. How it sounds can be known as tone. How would you describe the style and tone of this text? They might be different in different places in the text. Choose suitable words and phrases from the list below and add some of your own:

- accessible
- chatty
- complex
- descriptive
- detailed
- diary-like
- exploratory
- factual
- formal
- friendly
- impersonal
- informal
- personal
- reflective
- sensuous
- technical.

2. Now look more closely at the writer's vocabulary choices. For each word you chose for Question 1, draw a bubble and write that word in the middle. Then around it write some words or short phrases from the text that use that particular style or tone. Remember to put quotations inside speech marks.

'I'd come to know'

informal

'terrific person'

Activity 4 — Comment on the writer's opinions and viewpoint

1. The review is mainly positive. Pick out the three most positive things said about the book.
2. Now pick out three criticisms.
3. How do you know that the positive outweighs the negatives for the reviewer? Give evidence from the review.

Activity 5 — Comment on the use of quotation

The reviewer uses quotations or specific evidence from the Harry Potter book.

1. Identify four times where he does this: two should be direct quotations, two should be indirect reference (mentioning something that happens or that Rowling does in the book).
2. Then explain how these quotations and references are used. What do they show us?

Quote or reference	What does it tell us? How is it used?

Unit 10 Know how to read texts for different audiences and purposes

Activity 6 Comment on and explain the writer's use of language

The reviewer chooses certain words and phrases to have a desired effect on the reader. Below are some of these.

1 Explain why and how the writer uses them and the effect they have on the reader.

Language	Effect
'Though all this hocus pocus is delightful, the magic in the book is not the real magic of the book.'	
'We feel Harry's fear'	
'As Harry worries that first day about whether he can compete with the privileged children of Hogwarts alums, I found myself thinking back 30 years to my first days at Harvard'	
'wonderful, sly humor'	
'But like Harry Potter, she had wizardry inside'	

2 The first words of paragraphs seem to determine how the review is shaped. What can you say about this?

> So...
> And...
> But...
> We...
> The book...
> Throughout...
> These are...

Activity 7 Reviewing the review

1 Use the information and reflection from the previous Activities to write a short review of the book review. For example:

> It is a good review, not only good in what it says about Rowling's book but good in itself. We feel we know Rowling's book quite well by the end of it and we are likely to want to read it.

2 Now write three short paragraphs supporting your view of the review. Some prompts and starters are given below to help you.

> The book review is well structured. You can see this...
> The writer effectively uses quotations and references to Rowling's work...
> The tone of the review is...

- What do you think are the writer's intentions in this text?
- Analyse the kind of language used.
- How does the writer present his personal viewpoint over the course of the text and how is this reflected in the writing style?
- How effectively does he achieve his intentions?

109

6 Know how to read travel writing texts

I am learning how to:
- compare audience, purpose and tone
- compare vocabulary and other language choices.

Read the following two short extracts taken from different travel writing texts.

The writer helps us to imagine we are getting closer to the Pyramids alongside him.

Powerful choice of verb ('rise') and adjectives ('serene and powerful') reminds us that the Pyramids were the tombs of powerful rulers.

Extract 1:

'Closer now to the Pyramids and they are awesome. The blocks of sandstone at their base are twice as high as the small children playing around them. The structures rise serene and powerful above us, preserving an unmoving dignity, like great beasts surrounded by insects.'

The Pyramids inspire awe in the writer.

Descriptive detail helps us to understand the scale of the Pyramids, which adds to his and our sense of awe and wonder.

This simile sounds poetic and again reminds us of the size of the Pyramids. We get the impression that the writer feels dwarfed and humbled by what he has seen.

This phrase further adds to the tone of awe and reverence.

What do you know about… travel writing?

Travel writing ranges from guide books aimed at tourists to more literary writing that aims to describe particular places. Works of travel literature may trace a journey or be focused on one place. Well known travel writers include Bill Bryson, Bruce Chatwin, Ryszard Kapuscinski, Jan Morris, Rebecca Solnit and Paul Theroux.

Extract 2:

'I really can't believe what a state the Pyramids are in. I thought they had flat rendered sides, but when you get up close, you see how they are just giant boulders balanced on top of each other, like a massive game of Jenga that has got out of hand.'

Unit 10 Know how to read texts for different audiences and purposes

Activity 1 Compare first impressions

In both of these texts on page 110, each writer describes the world-famous Pyramids in Egypt.

1 Look at the comments that have been used to annotate Extract 1. They show some of the techniques used by the writer to convey what he sees, and his feelings about the experience.

2 Comment on Extract 2 in the same way, including:
  • the writer's reaction to what he sees
  • the tone of the extract
  • interesting language choices
  • the intended effect on the reader.

111

6 Know how to read travel writing texts

What do you know about… the author?

Extract 1 comes from *Around the World in 80 Days* by Michael Palin, published in 1989. *Around the World in 80 Days* was a BBC television travel series presented by comedian and actor Michael Palin. The show was inspired by Jules Verne's classic novel *Around the World in 80 Days*, in which a character named Phileas Fogg accepts a wager to circumnavigate the globe in 80 days or fewer. Palin was given the same deadline, and not allowed to use aircraft, which did not exist in Verne's time and would have made completing the journey far too easy. He followed Phileas Fogg's route as closely as possible. Along the way he commented on the sights and cultures he encountered. Following the trip Michael Palin wrote a book about the experience.

Now read this longer extract from Michael Palin's book in which he visits Cairo, the capital city of Egypt.

The Hotel Windsor, Cairo
Day 7: 1 October

I check in to the Hotel Windsor, which, like everything else in Cairo, is remarkable. I rather like its **surreal** atmosphere. The hotel was once under Swiss ownership and there are reindeer antlers and hunting trophies on the walls of the bar.

But the food is Egyptian. For dinner we have lentil soup, then a plateful of spring onions, cracked wheat, rice and fried onions, falafel (deep fried vegetable balls), a chilli and onion salad, and a thick and **treacherous** local wine, which is about the only thing that doesn't have onions in it.

Later, whilst Passepartout sorts out the film he's shot of this day's madness, I take a walk for a late-night look at the Nile. A brutal network of flyovers bars my way and I end up lost. A **courteous** Egyptian helps me out. He asks me where I'm from and what I think of the weather.

'A little hot for me.'

He laughs. 'This is very nice. It's the first time it has been below 95 for weeks.'

Back in my room, the bathtap produces only dreadful **bronchial** shudders and a thin trickle of water before sinking into total unconsciousness. There's a washbasin, but no plug, and the lavatory's unflushable. I work out an Emett-like temporary solution, however, involving twisting a coat hanger around the ball cock. Later, I discover it's my only coat hanger.

Frederick Rowland Emett (1906–90) was an English cartoonist and creator of eccentric artworks and machines.

Expand your vocabulary

surreal – oddly dreamlike
treacherous – not to be relied on, dangerous
courteous – polite and considerate
bronchial – relating to the bronchi (the tubes that connect to the lungs), looking and sounding like someone with a bronchial infection

Unit 10 Know how to read texts for different audiences and purposes

Activity 2 — Comment on audience, purpose and tone

1 How would you describe the intended audience for this book?
2 How would you describe the intended purpose?
3 The tone of the writing changes depending on what is being recounted or described. Find an example of where:
   a) the writer's tone is humorous and light-hearted
   b) the writer's tone is matter-of-fact and neutral
   c) the writer's tone is more serious
   d) one of these tones changes fairly quickly across a few sentences.

Activity 3 — Analyse vocabulary and other language choices

Look in more detail at Palin's language choices and their effects in the text on page 112. Support your answers with evidence of words and phrases from the text.

1 Which of his five senses does Palin use to convey his impressions of Cairo in this extract?
2 Is the text written in the past tense or the present tense? Why do you think the writer has chosen this tense?
3 The writer uses some rich descriptive language. For each of these, explain why this is an effective, well-chosen word or phrase, and what image it conveys to you:
   a) **'dreadful bronchial shudders'**
   b) **'treacherous local wine'**
   c) **'brutal network of flyovers'**.
4 Compare Michael Palin's description of staying at the Hotel Windsor in Cairo with Karl Pilkington's description on page 114 of the same hotel in his 2010 book *An Idiot Abroad*.

Key terms

Audiences – particular groups such as families, parents, teenagers, the elderly, professionals, people on a high income, fans, special interest groups, and so on.

Purpose – the purpose of a text is what it is meant to achieve; what the writer intends. Some texts might have more than one purpose. Every feature of the text is designed to help it achieve its purpose or purposes.

Tone – the tone of a text is the attitude that the writer conveys. For example, is the tone casual, formal, light-hearted, humorous, serious, passionate, etc.?

6 Know how to read travel writing texts

What do you know about… *An Idiot Abroad*?

An Idiot Abroad is a book based on a television series, created by Ricky Gervais and Stephen Merchant and starring Karl Pilkington. The theme of both the television series and the book is that Pilkington has no interest in global travel, so Merchant and Gervais make him travel while they stay in the United Kingdom and monitor his progress. In the book, Pilkington writes about the places he is sent to visit.

The Hotel Windsor, Cairo
Wednesday, 9 December

I was picked up at 4:30 a.m. and taken to the airport for our flight to Cairo. Six hours later we were on the road to our hotel. I hadn't been told anything about whom or what I'd be meeting, eating or seeing. Apparently that's the way each trip is going to work, which I know will annoy me as I don't really like surprises. Not big ones, anyway. Just having a pack of Revels holds enough surprise for me.

…It was a long journey to the hotel. As we drove, all the nice hotels seemed to disappear until we finally pulled up at a place called The Windsor… As well as being one of the oldest hotels, it had the staff to match. You wouldn't get people of this age working in hotels in England. An old fella brought my case from the coach. We were parked right outside the entrance, but it took the old fella the same amount of time it took me to fill out all the forms and collect my key…

Another man took me to my room. I was on the second floor, just where the cleaners **congregated**. I couldn't believe it. Not the fact that it's where they congregated, but the fact that the hotel had cleaners. It was also clearly a bit of a storage area, as there was a piano outside my door and five TV sets stacked on top of the wardrobe in my room.

I was given the full tour of the room: 'Telephone there. Bathroom here.' He said one or two other things, but I could not hear properly due to the creaking of the floorboards and the noise of the traffic outside. There were two beds separated by a fluorescent tube light on the wall that, once you switched it on, showed up all the damp stains on the walls in their full glory.

I wandered downstairs to meet with the crew and bumped into the owner outside my room. I don't know if he was waiting to meet me to check if everything was OK, or if he was about to have his piano lessons. He was in his late sixties and looked smart but tired. He was keen to tell me that Michael Palin had stayed here once. If these are the sorts of places Michael Palin stayed in, no wonder he went round the world in 80 days. He was obviously keen to get home as soon as poss.

Expand your vocabulary

congregated – gathered

Unit 10 Know how to read texts for different audiences and purposes

Activity 4 — Comment on audience, purpose and tone

1 How would you describe the intended audience for *An Idiot Abroad*?
2 How would you describe the intended purpose?
3 Pilkington's tone (who, like Michael Palin, is best known as a comedian) has been described as 'deadpan' (which is when humour is delivered in a casual, even monotone, way with no or little change in emotion).
Below is an example of Pilkington's deadpan style. Find, and comment on, another example from the text of this way of creating humour.

> 'I was on the second floor, just where the cleaners congregated. I couldn't believe it. Not the fact that it's where they congregated, but the fact that the hotel had cleaners.'

Activity 5 — Analyse vocabulary and other language choices

Look in more detail at Pilkington's language choices and their effects. Support your answers with evidence of words and phrases from the text.

1 Which of his five senses does Pilkington use to convey his impressions of Cairo in this extract?
2 The writer of this extract seems to avoid using rich descriptive language. Instead, he often chooses 'everyday' words and well-used phrases. For example:

> 'An old fella brought my case from the coach.'

  a) What do you notice about his use of language here?
  b) Find two more examples of Pilkington using 'everyday speech'.
  c) What is the effect of Pilkington choosing to write in this way?

Activity 6 — Compare the way both writers describe Cairo

Using the ideas and evidence you have gathered about the two texts, write a detailed answer to this question.

1 Compare the way both writers describe Cairo.
  Plan your answer by thinking about:
  - The different aspects each chooses to write about.
  - The differences in the tone of each piece.
  - The differences in the way that aspects of the visit are described.
  - Comment on the effectiveness of each extract. Which do you prefer and why?

Focus your effort
- Write in paragraphs that show you have organised your ideas.
- Support all your points with textual evidence.
- Relate your points to the audience and purpose of each text.

7 Know how to read heritage texts

I am learning how to:
- see how context helps me understand setting, plot and character
- work out the meaning of unfamiliar words, phrases and references.

Read the extract, on page 117 opposite, from near the beginning of the famous nineteenth century novel *Around the World in 80 Days* by Jules Verne.

Key term

Context – when reading a text, the context is the details of the time and place in which the text is set. Understanding the context in a novel can help you understand the characters, plot and setting – for example, way of life, how people behave, or their beliefs.

Activity 1 Clarify unfamiliar words or phrases

Some language in a novel from another time and context may be unfamiliar. Which techniques would you use to work out the meaning of the following words?

1 'trunk' and 'carpet-bag' (line 8).
2 'chary' (line 17).
3 'wardrobes' (line 19) – and how does this relate to how 'wardrobe' is used today?

Focus your effort

Knowing how to tackle unfamiliar words is an important technique. Here are three approaches you can use:

1 Read the sentence again. Use clues in the text to work out the meaning in context.
2 Think about whether an unfamiliar word links with words you already know.
3 If a word might have many meanings, think about which is most likely in this context.

Activity 2 Get the general idea of the plot

To help understand a text set in another time:

1 Read the text and, as you read, ask 'What is going on?' Summarise in a few sentences what is happening in this text.
2 Read the text again and find clues and evidence about what might be happening. Answer the questions in the table to start you off.

Questions	Answers and evidence
What do you find out about Passepartout?	Passepartout is Phileas Fogg's servant. Phileas Fogg is described as Passepartout's 'master'.
What do you find out about Phileas Fogg?	
What seems to have happened in the novel so far?	
What might happen next?	

Unit 10 Know how to read texts for different audiences and purposes

> **What do you know about... *Around the World in 80 Days*?**
> Jules Verne's classic adventure novel was first published in 1873 in French. In the novel, Phileas Fogg and his new employee Passepartout try to travel around the world in 80 days for a bet.

'Monsieur is going to leave home?'

'Yes,' returned Phileas Fogg. 'We are going round the world.'

Passepartout opened wide his eyes, raised his eyebrows, held up his hands, and seemed about to collapse, so overcome was he with **stupefied** astonishment.

'Round the world!' he murmured.

'In eighty days,' responded Mr Fogg. 'So we haven't a moment to lose.'

'But the trunks?' gasped Passepartout, unconsciously swaying his head from right to left.

'We'll have no trunks; only a carpet-bag, with two shirts and three pairs of stockings for me, and the same for you. We'll buy our clothes on the way. Bring down my mackintosh and travelling-cloak, and some stout shoes, though we shall do little walking. Make haste!'

Passepartout tried to reply, but could not. He went out, mounted to his own room, fell into a chair, and muttered: 'That's good, that is! And I, who wanted to remain quiet!'

He mechanically set about making the preparations for departure. Around the world in eighty days! Was his master a fool? No. Was this a joke, then? They were going to Dover; good! To Calais; good again! After all, Passepartout, who had been away from France five years, would not be sorry to set foot on his **native soil** again. Perhaps they would go as far as Paris, and it would do his eyes good to see Paris once more. But surely a gentleman so chary of his steps would stop there; no doubt – but, then, it was none the less true that he was going away, this so domestic person **hitherto**!

By eight o'clock Passepartout had packed the modest carpet-bag, containing the wardrobes of his master and himself; then, still troubled in mind, he carefully shut the door of his room, and descended to Mr Fogg.

Mr Fogg was quite ready. Under his arm might have been observed a red-bound copy of Bradshaw's *Continental Railway Steam Transit and General Guide*, with its timetables showing the arrival and departure of steamers and railways. He took the carpet-bag, opened it, and slipped into it a goodly roll of Bank of England notes, which would pass wherever he might go.

'You have forgotten nothing?' asked he.

'Nothing, monsieur.'

'My mackintosh and cloak?'

'Here they are.'

'Good! Take this carpet-bag,' handing it to Passepartout. 'Take good care of it, for there are twenty thousand pounds in it.'

Passepartout nearly dropped the bag, as if the twenty thousand pounds were in gold, and weighed him down.

> **Expand your vocabulary**
> **stupefied** – surprised, confused
> **native soil** – place where he was born
> **hitherto** – until this time

7 Know how to read heritage texts

Activity 3 — Understand the context and setting

This novel is an adventure story, written and set in the nineteenth century. It will help you understand and visualise the text if you understand more about the context.

1 What do you learn about:
   a) how men dressed then?
   b) how people travelled internationally then?
2 Passepartout is Phileas Fogg's servant. In fact he is what is called a 'manservant'. What do we learn about Passepartout's duties?
3 Use the contextual details you've found out to note down three challenges that Phileas Fogg and Passepartout might face in going round the world in 80 days.

Activity 4 — Understand character

One reader made this comment about *Around the World in 80 Days*:

'Jules Verne turned scientific discovery into adventure with the help of some great characters and a sense of humour.'

You can learn something about the author's humorous treatment of his two main characters from the short extract on page 117.

1 Focus on Passepartout.
   a) Find and comment on two examples from the text of what Passepartout *does*, which reveal what he thinks of the plans to travel around the world.
   b) Find two examples from the text of what Passepartout *says*, which indicate how he feels about the plans.
   c) Find two examples of *words* used to describe the *way* that Passepartout responds to his master, which indicate how he feels about the plans.
2 Focus on Phileas Fogg.

> '"Round the world!" he murmured.
> "In eighty days," responded Mr Fogg. "So we haven't a moment to lose."'

   a) What does this piece of dialogue reveal about Phileas Fogg's attitude to the plan to travel around the world? Think about how he might actually say these words.
   b) Find and comment on another piece of dialogue between Fogg and Passepartout that shows a similar difference between their two attitudes to travel.

Unit 10 Know how to read texts for different audiences and purposes

Activity 5 — Understand tone

1 Look at the definition of 'tone' in the Key term box. It is clear that the author means to be humorous and light-hearted. But which one of these is the dominant tone? Read the comments below from pupils in answer to the following question: How would you describe the author's tone in this extract?

> **Key term**
> **Tone** – the tone of a text is the attitude that the writer conveys. For example, the tone might be casual, formal, light-hearted, serious or humorous.

a. The author's tone is light-hearted. I feel like he is saying 'don't take this too seriously. It's just a bit of fun!'

b. The author's tone is comic and he is really trying to make the reader laugh. An example of this is when Passepartout nearly drops the bag.

2 Which of the comments do you agree/disagree with, and why? Give some evidence (a quote and an explanation) for your choice.

Activity 6 — Comment on the effectiveness of the text

1 Read the comments below from pupils in answer to the following question: Do you think this is a good way to start an adventure story?

a. I think that this is a really good way to start an adventure story. It's like Phileas Fogg can't wait to get started and nor can the reader!

b. I would have expected an adventure story to begin in a much more dramatic way.

2 Answer the following questions:
Which of the comments do you agree/disagree with, and why?
Add to your answer:
- evidence from the extract on page 117
- explanations of what has been said.

Now look at the answer with which you did *not* agree. Pretend you do agree with it and make a similar case for it. Add evidence and further explanation.

119

8 Know how to read fiction texts

I am learning how to:
- understand the context in which a novel is set
- use contextual knowledge to support a better understanding of novels
- identify and explain effective use of language.

Read the extract on page 121 opposite from the 2008 novel *People of the Whale* by Linda Hogan.

> **Key term**
> **Context** – when reading a text, context is the details of the time and place in which the text is set. Understanding the context in a novel can help you understand the characters, plot and setting – for example, way of life, how people behave, their beliefs.

Activity 1 Understand the context of a text

When you read any new text, you are given clues about the text's context, the time and place in which it is set.

1. Make a list of clues from the extract that help you understand the context of the novel. For example, 'a war has started'.
2. Read the wording below from the back cover of *People of the Whale*. Find more clues about the novel's setting. Add them to the list you started above.

> 'Raised in a remote seaside village, Thomas Witka Just marries Ruth, whom he has loved since infancy. But an ill-fated decision to fight in Vietnam changes his life forever. When he returns home a hero, he tries to reconcile his two lives, but finds his tribe in conflict over the decision to hunt a whale. With a keen sense of the environment, spirituality and the trauma of war, *People of the Whale* is a powerful novel from a writer who continues to take on the most difficult contemporary Native issues.'

Activity 2 Apply what you know about context to support your understanding

1. Now use the list you have to write a short paragraph describing the place and time in which this novel is set.

Activity 3 Explain how the writer uses language to convey feelings

1. Pick out words, phrases and sentences that describe:
   - Ruth's feelings about Thomas and what he has done
   - Thomas's feelings about Ruth and what he has done.

   For example:

   Ruth is surprised he has joined the army.

   'Don't you love me?' reveals that she questions his motives and loyalty.

Activity 4 Comment on characters' actions and attitudes

You now know more about the context and more about the characters and how they feel and act.

1. See if you can put these two aspects together. Comment on how you understand the characters' actions and attitudes. The following prompts can help you:
   - Why does Thomas join the army? (Note words like *together*, *patriotic*.)
   - What does Ruth feel about his decision?

Unit 10 Know how to read texts for different audiences and purposes

Still, the war finally came to the village. It was on a day Ruth was wearing sea-blue. For some reason, they would both remember that. She looked like a **mirage** to Thomas.

'What?' she was surprised. 'You have joined the army? You are going to boot camp and we've barely been married? Don't you love me?' she'd asked him when he **enlisted**. 'Why? We're just starting together!'

He loved her. He didn't know why he enlisted. 'We just all did it,' was his only reason. 'Together,' he said. They'd been drinking, 'the boys', as she called them. They believed in America. They did. They were **patriotic**. 'I'm not just an **Indian**. I'm an American, too.'

'You were drinking with them! That's why!'

She turned her back to him so he wouldn't see her cry. After a while she left the small bedroom in their rented place, the green walls and ceiling they'd once laughed about, that only paint they could find, which now seemed **pitiful**. And she put away dishes, quietly, carefully. He wished she would slam cupboards and silverware. Later he went to her, stood behind her and held her. She didn't forgive him, not then. Not really until years later when she realized how men were so influenced by their peers and governments. This was something Ruth, a woman who could stand alone in the world, would never understand.

Thomas was sent away before the others.

He argued with the recruiter. 'But the army promised us the buddy system. We'd go together. We were supposed to go together. We wanted to fight together for America.'

'The army promises a lot,' said the man at the recruiting station in the little shopping centre next to the police office. 'Don't worry. You'll all catch up with each other.' And maybe Thomas knew he lied, but it was too late. Now he was owned.

On the day Thomas left, Ruth was torn in half. The two of them, who'd always laughed together, floated in the water and talked together, who saw with the same eyes, were now separate. She wept when he left and she couldn't stop for days. Then she set her lips in tight **resignation**, more akin to sorrow, and went about her life of fishing.

What do you know about... the Vietnam War?

The Vietnam War lasted from 1955 until 1975. It was between North Vietnam and its communist allies and South Vietnam and its anti-communist allies, mainly the United States. Hundreds of thousands of lives were lost. The conflict resulted in victory for North Vietnam.

This extract, however, can be read as one that explores the emotions and conflicts that arise at any time in history when young men choose to go off to war, leaving their loved ones behind.

> He is referring to the fact that he is a Native American Indian.

Expand your vocabulary

mirage – something that can't be reached or isn't really there
enlisted – joined the armed forces
patriotic – feeling or expressing love for one's country
pitiful – deserving pity
resignation – acceptance that something can't be changed

Activity 5 Comment on ideas

1 Re-read the last paragraph. Explain what the writer is trying to convey in the following sentences:

'The two of them, who'd always laughed together, floated in the water and talked together, who saw with the same eyes, were now separate.'

'Then she set her lips in tight resignation, more akin to sorrow, and went about her life of fishing.'

2 Explain what the extract suggests to you about why men go to war, and how this affects those left behind, for example, wives and girlfriends.

9 Know how to compare non-fiction texts

I am learning how to:
➡ identify and compare purpose and audience in two different texts
➡ select and compare information from different texts.

Read the information on page 123 opposite taken from the Whiskas website.

Key terms
The **purpose** of a text – what it is meant to achieve, what the writer intends, e.g. to inform, to persuade, to entertain. Some texts might have more than one purpose.

Audiences – the readers of texts. A text is written for a particular audience group, e.g. teenagers, older people, fans, special interest groups, and so on.

Activity 1 — Identify audience and purpose

1 Read the Whiskas text opposite again.
   a Why do you think the text has been written?
   b For whom do you think this text has been written? There may be several possible audiences that the writer of the text had in mind.
   c What are your reasons for thinking that these are the text's main purpose and audiences?

The purpose of the text is…

I think that this text is aimed at… because…

2 An important purpose of this website is to inform readers about Whiskas' promotion of the campaign to save tigers. Texts often have more than one purpose. In addition to informing its readers about the Whiskas campaign, what else do you think this text aims to do? Look at the words in the table below. Which of these does it do? Give evidence (images, words, phrases or sentences from the text) for the ones that you think are appropriate.

Purpose	Evidence
advise	
argue	
comment	
describe	
explain	
instruct	
persuade or influence	
entertain	
recount	
report	

Unit 10 Know how to read texts for different audiences and purposes

The story behind the partnership

Just like the little cats who share our homes, tigers are graceful, independent spirits. Unlike our smaller feline friends, however, tigers are under threat. Over the last 100 years, populations of wild tigers have fallen by over 95 per cent and as few as 3200 remain.

As at Whiskas we care for all cats, big and small, we are helping to fund WWF's vital work to save tigers in the wild. This work encompasses everything from protecting habitats to combating threats such as poaching, illegal trade and conflict with humans.

Our work with WWF – the partnership ambition

Tigers face **unrelenting** pressure from **poaching**, **retaliatory** killings and **habitat** loss. They are forced to compete for space with dense and often growing human populations. Without urgent support, they could disappear from most of their range within a generation.

WWF aims to secure a future for this **iconic** animal by focusing on 12 global priority tiger landscapes, led by staff in Bhutan, Cambodia, China, India, Indonesia, Laos, Malaysia, Nepal, Russia, Thailand and Vietnam.

Together, Whiskas and WWF will provide increased protection in key habitats, working towards WWF's aim to double wild tiger numbers by 2022. We'll also focus on protecting Bengal tigers in the Terai Arc region of Nepal. It's one of the few remaining strongholds for this magnificent species, home to around 120 adult tigers.

Expand your vocabulary

unrelenting – not yielding, not giving up, determined
poaching – illegally hunting or catching animals
retaliatory – returning like for like, repaying in kind
habitat – place where something usually lives (e.g. a whale's habitat is the sea)
iconic – representing something important (e.g. Beckham is an icon of football)

9 Know how to compare non-fiction texts

Activity 2 — Explore the writer's use of fact and opinion

The Whiskas text on page 123 includes both factual information and opinions or points of view about tigers.

1 Identify some examples of facts and opinions given within the text.

Facts	Opinions
'3200 remain'	'Tigers are graceful'

2 Why do you think this text makes use of both facts and opinions in this way? Read these comments by students and then write your own ideas in response to the question.

> The information lets us know that Whiskas is supporting a campaign to save tigers. It supports the view that tigers are under threat.
>
> The fact that the website was created by Whiskas is an important one, because it tells us that one of the purposes is to promote and sell Whiskas cat food. The word 'Whiskas' is repeated twice. It is also linked with words like 'our' and 'together' to let us know there are strong links between the WWF's aims and Whiskas' campaign, even if one of the latter's purposes is to sell more cat food.
>
> The way the campaign is described is appealing. If it was all facts and figures it could be dry and boring but it also helps you think about the positive messages, the moral purpose and the need to support WWF as well as Whiskas.

Activity 3 — Explore sentences

1 Sentences are formed in certain ways to have a certain effect on the reader. Write an explanation of how the following sentences are written, including the language used.

> 'Just like the little cats who share our homes, tigers are graceful, independent spirits.'

> 'Without urgent support, they could disappear from most of their range within a generation.'

2 Now pick two other sentences that interest you, one from each of the last two paragraphs. Write about them in the same way.

Unit 10 Know how to read texts for different audiences and purposes

Activity 4 — Comment on the purpose or audience

The text on pages 126–7 is a short article that is part of a campaign, but it is not being used to promote or sell a product. It has a different purpose and audience.

1 Complete the same task as in Activity 1 Question 2, page 122. Concentrate on and give evidence for the following purposes:
   - inform
   - persuade.

2 The extract wants the reader to appreciate the tiger: what it looks like, how it behaves. Some sentences can even read as if it is part of a novel – for example,

   'Dawn, and mist holds the forest. Only a short stretch of red dirt track can be seen. Suddenly –'

   Select four examples from the opening paragraphs that are like this: examples of how the tiger is described – for example, 'a look of infinite and bored indifference'.
   Write a short explanation of how these are effective and comment on the language used.

3 Some of the text reads like a piece made to inform and persuade. Select four facts and four opinions to show this.

Activity 5 — Select and compare information from texts

1 To compare the way the writers of the texts give information, explore the similarities and the differences between the Whiskas text on page 123 and the article on pages 126–7.

	Similarities	Differences
Topic		
Type of text		
Intended audience		
Purpose(s)		

Activity 6 — Compare the texts using selected information

1 Read the texts on page 123 and pages 126–7 again. Compare the purposes and audiences for these texts. Use quotations to provide evidence to back up what you say. Explore the effects the writers are pursuing.
   Write about: language (words, phrases, sentences), key messages, the organisation of the writing.

> I think that... is aimed mainly at... because... whereas the...text is...
>
> Some of the purposes are similar. Both texts try to... We can see this in...
>
> There are distinct differences in purpose too, however. The...text is written to... You can see evidence for this by looking at...

9 Know how to compare non-fiction texts

Now read the following article. Get ready to compare it with the Whiskas text.

A cry for the tiger

We have the means to save the mightiest cat on Earth. But do we have the will?

Ranthambore National Park, India

Dawn, and mist holds the forest. Only a short stretch of red dirt track can be seen. Suddenly – emerging from the red-gold haze of dust and misted light – a tigress ambles into view. First she stops to rub her right-side whiskers against a roadside tree. Then she crosses the road and rubs her left-side whiskers. Then she turns to regard us with a look of infinite and bored **indifference**.

And then, as if relenting, she reaches up the tree to claw the bark, turning her profile to us, and with it the full impact of her tigerness – the improbable, the gorgeous, the **iconographic** and visibly powerful flanks.

The tiger, *Pantheratigris*, largest of all the big cats, to which even biological **terminology** defers with awed expressions like 'apex predator', 'charismatic megafauna', 'umbrella species'. One of the most formidable **carnivores** on the planet, and yet, amber-coated and patterned with black flames, one of the most beautiful of creatures.

Consider the tiger, how he is formed. With claws up to four inches long and retractable, like a domestic cat's, and carnassial teeth that shatter bone. While able to achieve bursts above 35 miles an hour, the tiger is built for strength, not sustained speed. Short, powerful legs propel his trademark lethal lunge and fabled leaps. Recently, a tiger was captured on video jumping – flying – from flat ground to 13 feet in the air to attack a ranger riding an elephant. The eye of the tiger is backlit by a membrane that reflects light through the retina, the secret of his famous night vision and glowing night eyes. The roar of the tiger – *Aaaaauuuunnnn!* – can carry more than a mile.

For weeks I had been travelling through some of the best tiger habitat in Asia, from remote forests to tropical woodlands and, on a previous trip, to mangrove swamps – but never before had I seen a tiger. Partly this was because of the animal's legendarily secretive nature. The tiger is powerful enough to kill and drag prey five times its weight, yet it can move through high grass, forest and even water in unnerving silence. The common refrain of those who

---

Expand your vocabulary

indifference – lack of interest or concern
iconographic – pictorial representation or illustration of a subject
terminology – vocabulary, language or terms used in a particular field or area of study
carnivore – meat eater
exacerbated – made worse

Unit 10 Know how to read texts for different audiences and purposes

have witnessed – or survived – an attack is that the tiger 'came from nowhere'.

But the other reason for the dearth of sightings is that the ideal tiger landscapes have very few tigers. The tiger has been a threatened species for most of my lifetime, and its rareness has come to be regarded matter-of-factly, as an intrinsic, defining attribute, like its dramatic colouring. The complacent view that the tiger will continue to be 'rare' or 'threatened' into the foreseeable future is no longer tenable. In the early twenty-first century, tigers in the wild face the black abyss of annihilation. 'This is about making decisions as if we're in an emergency room,' says Tom Kaplan, co-founder of Panthera, an organisation dedicated to big cats. 'This is it.'

The tiger's enemies are well-known: loss of habitat **exacerbated** by exploding human populations, poverty – which induces poaching of prey animals – and, looming over all, the dark threat of the brutal Chinese black market for tiger parts. Less acknowledged are botched conservation strategies that for decades have failed the tiger. The tiger population, dispersed among Asia's 13 tiger countries, is estimated at fewer than 4000 animals, though many conservationists believe there are hundreds less than that. To put this number in perspective: global alarm for the species was first sounded in 1969, and early in the '80s it was estimated that some 8000 tigers remained in the wild. So decades of vociferously expressed concern for tigers – not to mention millions of dollars donated by well-meaning individuals – has achieved the demise of perhaps half of the already imperiled population.

10 Know how to compare old and new fiction

I am learning how to:
- connect and compare themes, ideas and issues across texts
- compare and comment on how writers create a point of view.

Read the following extract from Jane Austen's *Pride and Prejudice*, written in the late eighteenth century. Two young women are talking about a man they have just met and what they think about him.

Key terms
Theme – a theme is a set of ideas about the same subject. For example, love, relationships, war, betrayal, family.
Point of view – a writer chooses a point of view when telling a story. For example, through one character's eyes alone (first person), or letting us know how all the characters think and feel (third person).

What do you know about… Jane Austen?
Jane Austen (16 December 1775 – 18 July 1817) was an English novelist whose works of romantic fiction, set among the landed gentry, have earned her a place as one of the most widely read writers in English literature. She is widely praised for her realism, biting irony and social commentary.

When Jane and Elizabeth were alone, the former, who had been cautious in her praise of Mr Bingley before, expressed to her sister how very much she admired him.

'He is just what a young man ought to be,' said she, 'sensible, good humoured, lively; and I never saw such happy manners! – so much **ease**, with such perfect good breeding!'

'He is also handsome,' replied Elizabeth, 'which a young man ought likewise to be, if he possibly can. His character is thereby complete.'

'I was very much **flattered** by his asking me to dance a second time. I did not expect such a **compliment**.'

'Did not you? I did for you. But that is one great difference between us. Compliments always take you by surprise, and me never. What could be more natural than his asking you again? He could not help seeing that you were about five times as pretty as every other woman in the room. No thanks to his **gallantry** for that. Well, he certainly is very **agreeable**, and I give you leave to like him. You have liked many a stupider person.'

'Dear Lizzy!'

'Oh! you are a great deal too **apt**, you know, to like people in general. You never see a fault in any body. All the world are good and agreeable in your eyes. I never heard you speak ill of a human being in my life.'

Expand your vocabulary
ease – freedom from worry, anxiety or pain; to lessen, release or pass smoothly
flattered – complimented a lot to be made to feel better or to win favour
compliment – an expression of praise or admiration, to praise or congratulate
gallantry – noble spirit or action, courage
agreeable – suitable, pleasing, liked by many
apt – likely, appropriate

Unit 10 Know how to read texts for different audiences and purposes

Activity 1 — Identify and comment on point of view

Austen's story is written in the third person, from the point of view of the writer, who sees both characters.

1 Read the extract again. Find three short quotations for each character (Elizabeth and Jane) where Austen reveals to the reader their thoughts and feelings.

Elizabeth	Jane
1 "Compliments always take you by surprise, and me never"	1 'had been cautious in her praise of Mr Bingley'
2	2
3	3

Activity 2 — Understand the writer's view

Notice how Elizabeth says more than Jane. Also, Elizabeth has more views on Bingley and Jane and relationships than Jane seems to express.

1 Identify three quotations that show how Elizabeth has definite views on things and is not worried about saying them, either.
2 Now look at the words that Jane says. Given that they are not so strong and opinionated, what does this tell us about Jane? Again, pick out a few quotations to provide evidence.
3 Now use this evidence to write a short paragraph exploring what you think the writer thinks about these two young women and how they are different. You can use the following prompts:

Jane seems to be a … person. You can see this when …

Elizabeth, her sister, however, has a different personality. She …

4 What do you think the writer thinks about these two sisters?
 - What does she like about them? How do you know?
 - Is she finding any small faults in them? How do you know?

Activity 3 — Understand themes

A theme is a main idea that a writer or text explores.

1 Find a quotation or some evidence from the extract for these themes or ideas:
 - People are different – they see things differently.
 - Love, relationships and marriage.

129

10 Know how to compare old and new fiction

What do you know about… the author?

Susan Eloise Hinton is an American writer best known for her young-adult novels set in Oklahoma. While still in her teens, Hinton became a household name as the author of *The Outsiders*, her first and most popular novel. She began writing it in 1965. The book was inspired by two rival gangs at her school, Will Rogers High School – the Greasers and the Socs – and her desire to show sympathy toward the Greasers by writing from their point of view. The book has sold more than 14 million copies and still sells more than 500,000 a year.

Now read the following extract from *The Outsiders* by S.E. Hinton, which was first published in 1967.

> When I stepped out into the bright sunlight from the darkness of the movie house, I had only two things on my mind: Paul Newman and a ride home. I was wishing I looked like Paul Newman – he looks tough and I don't – but I guess my own looks aren't so bad. I have light-brown, almost-red hair and greenish-grey eyes. I wish they were more grey, because I hate most guys that have green eyes, but I have to be content with what I have. My hair is longer than a lot of boys wear theirs, squared off in back and long at the front and sides, but I am a greaser and most of my neighbourhood rarely bothers to get a haircut. Besides, I look better with long hair.
>
> I had a long walk home and no company, but I usually lone it anyway, for no reason except that I like to watch movies undisturbed so I can get into them and live them with the actors. When I see a movie with someone it's kind of uncomfortable, like having someone read your book over your shoulder. I'm different that way. I mean, my second oldest brother, Soda, who is 16-going-on-17, never cracks a book at all, and my oldest brother, Darrel, who we call Darry, works too long and hard to be interested in a story or drawing a picture, so I'm not like them. And nobody in our gang digs movies and books the way I do. For a while there, I thought I was the only person in the world that did. So I loned it.

Activity 4 Comparing point of view

Hinton's story is told in the first person. So, it is told mainly from one point of view. Austen's is told from the third person: you see what both Elizabeth and Jane think, what they think of each other, and even what the writer might think of them. Hinton's story concerns what the young man thinks. The reader can find out what Hinton thinks of the young man, too, but it is not easy to see.

1. Read the extract above again. Notice that it is all told as if in the narrator's mind, using the first person pronoun *I*. Austen's was told through the sisters talking to each other. We read words said. With Hinton, we read words thought.
2. Pick out three moments where it is clear what the narrator is thinking and wondering, for example:

   'I have two things on my mind…'

Unit 10 Know how to read texts for different audiences and purposes

3 Pick out two moments where we are aware that what the narrator is thinking may not be the same as what others think, for example:

'Besides, I look better with long hair.'

4 Find three quotations from each paragraph in the extract where Hinton chooses to have the narrator think in a conversational (or colloquial) language.

Paragraph 1	Paragraph 2
1	1
2	2
3	3

Activity 5 Comparing themes and issues

1 Based on the extracts you have read, what can you say about how young people see themselves in these extracts? Think about some of the following:
- different from others
- confident or anxious
- looking for security or freedom
- young man or young woman
- different times (eighteenth and twentieth centuries).

2 For the themes or ideas you write about, select some quotes to back up what you say.

Activity 6 Analyse and compare the two texts

1 Use your understanding of the extracts to write a short essay of three or four paragraphs on **one** of the following:
- A writer's choice of narrator (first or third) affects how the reader feels about the characters and the events.
- It can seem difficult to know what a writer thinks about their characters, but you can explore it and work it out, whether first or third person narrative.

Plan your essay by thinking about:
- similarities and differences in the way that each writer shows us a character's point of view
- similarities and differences in the themes and ideas in each extract
- the qualities and impact of each extract on you as a reader. Which do you prefer? Give reasons, and use quotations to back up your views
- the language: how characters speak or think and how the writer writes.

UNIT 11 Assess your progress in reading

1 Fiction: *The Hunger Games*

> **What do you know about… the author?**
>
> Suzanne Collins has been writing for children's television since the early 1990s. Her name appears in the credits of many shows for young children. She then wrote a successful fantasy/war series of books set in an urban landscape, *The Underland Chronicles*. Her latest successful book series is *The Hunger Games Trilogy*.

When I wake up, the other side of the bed is cold. My fingers stretch out, seeking Prim's warmth but finding only the rough **canvas** cover of the mattress. She must have had bad dreams and climbed in with our mother. Of course she did. This is the day of the **reaping**.

I prop myself up on one elbow. There's enough light in the bedroom to see them. My little sister, Prim, curled up on her side, **cocooned** in my mother's body, their cheeks pressed together. In sleep, my mother looks younger, still worn but not so beaten-down. Prim's face is as fresh as a raindrop, as lovely as the primrose for which she was named. My mother was very beautiful once, too. Or so they tell me.

Sitting at Prim's knees, guarding her, is the world's ugliest cat. Mashed-in nose, half of one ear missing, eyes the colour of rotting **squash**. Prim named him Buttercup, insisting that his muddy yellow coat matched the bright flower. He hates me. Or at least distrusts me. Even though it was years ago, I think he still remembers how I tried to drown him in a bucket when Prim brought him home. Scrawny kitten, belly swollen with worms, crawling with fleas. The last thing I needed was another mouth to feed. But Prim begged so hard, cried even, I had to let him stay. It turned out OK. My mother got rid of the vermin and he's a born mouser. Even catches the occasional rat. Sometimes, when I clean a kill, I feed Buttercup the **entrails**. He has stopped hissing at me.

Entrails. No hissing. This is the closest we will ever come to love.

I swing my legs off the bed and slide into my hunting boots. Supple leather that has moulded to my feet. I pull on trousers, a shirt, tuck my long dark braid up into a cap, and grab my forage bag. On the table, under a wooden bowl to protect it from hungry rats and cats alike, sits a perfect little goat's cheese wrapped in basil leaves. Prim's gift to me on reaping day. I put the cheese carefully in my pocket as I slip outside.

Our part of District 12, nicknamed the Seam, is usually crawling with coal miners heading out to the morning shift at this hour. Men and women with hunched shoulders, swollen knuckles, many of whom have long since stopped trying to scrub the coal dust out of their broken nails and the lines of their sunken faces. But today the black **cinder** streets are empty. Shutters on the **squat** grey houses are closed. The reaping isn't until two. May as well sleep in. If you can.

Unit 11 Assess your progress in reading

Expand your vocabulary

canvas – heavy, rough cloth made of cotton, hemp or flax, usually used to make sails or tents
reap – cut, gather or harvest a crop
cocoon – protective case around insects (e.g. moths, butterflies); cover or wrap-round
squash – fleshy, edible fruit; pumpkin
entrails – a body's internal organs and parts
cinder – burned substance, reduced to ashes
squat – short and thickset

1. Identify some key facts that tell you about the world in which the characters are living.
   - How is the bed described?
   - How are the people outside in the street described? **(2 marks)**

2. As well as facts, there are many inferences used by Collins. Explain the following:
   - Why does the narrator think her sister climbed into bed with their mother?
   - Why has the cat stopped hissing at her? **(2 marks)**

3. The writer conveys a picture of the narrator being protective of her family. Find and explain evidence for this. **(4 marks)**

4. It seems as though life has been hard for the narrator and her family for some time. Find and explain at least four pieces of evidence from the text that show this. Comment on at least two of the following in your answer:
   - vocabulary choices
   - imagery
   - sentence construction and grammar choices
   - paragraphing
   - voice of the narrator. **(4 marks)**

Focus your effort

As you go about answering this question, look for where Collins has used the following techniques:
- words or phrases that suggest or infer
- references to time or how things have changed.

Remember to comment on the effectiveness of these techniques in order to fully answer the question.

➡ Now turn to page 148 to track your progress in reading.

2 Biography: *The Diary of Anne Frank*

Read this text about Anne Frank. As a biography, much of it is factual.

Anne Frank biography

The Diary of Anne Frank is one of the most widely read books in the world, but her time in hiding was just one part of this remarkable girl's short life.

Anne Frank is famous for the diary that she kept from 12 June 1942 to 4 August 1944.

She was born on 12 June 1929 in Frankfurt, Germany, and was the second daughter of Otto Frank and Edith Frank-Hollander. Her sister Margot was three years older. She enjoyed four happy years growing up in Frankfurt until the Nazis came to power.

Of German Jewish descent, she and her family moved to Holland in 1933, where her father set up a business. By 1934, Edith and the two girls were living in Amsterdam, where they both attended school. From a young age, Anne showed an **aptitude** for reading and writing, while her outspoken and energetic personality shone through. When Holland was occupied by the Nazis in 1940, their **heritage** put the family under threat.

The family were subjected to the same rules as German Jews, namely that Jewish children could only attend Jewish schools, they faced curfews, were not allowed to own a business and were forced to wear a yellow star. Otto transferred his shares in his company to a friend and resigned as director, leaving the family with enough income to survive.

On her 13th birthday, Otto gave Anne an autograph book bound with white and red checked cloth and closed with a small lock. She proceeded to use this as her diary, with the first entries detailing how her family were **segregated** and **discriminated against**. In July 1942, her sister Margot received a call-up notice from the Central Office of Jewish Emigration, ordering her to report for relocation to a work camp. This made the family move into hiding earlier than planned.

On 6 July 1942, Anne, her sister Margot and her parents went into hiding, along with four other families. Their hiding place, the annexe, was in a specially prepared space above the offices of their business.

Whilst in hiding, they were supported by a group of friends, who brought them food as well as anything else they needed.

Anne started each diary entry 'Dear Kitty' and what followed was an incredibly **candid** and **eloquent** account of her life in confinement. It expresses her fear, boredom and confusion at the situation in which she found herself.

As well as giving the reader an insight into what it was like to live under such extreme circumstances, it also shows Anne struggling with the universal problem of growing up.

Her diary ends in 1944 when the annexe was raided by the Nazi authorities. Anne and Margot were sent first to Auschwitz and then to Bergen-Belsen where they both died of typhoid in 1945.

She was survived only by her father Otto. Anne's diary was kept safe by the family friend, Miep Gies, who gave it to Otto when he returned to Holland. When Anne was still alive she had expressed interest in having her diary published as a record of her experience. After her death, her father edited it, and it was first published in 1947.

The Diary of Anne Frank is an exceptionally popular and well known piece of writing. It has been translated into 67 languages and is especially popular with young people.

Expand your vocabulary

aptitude – talent, ability
heritage – something passed down from preceding generations
segregated – separated or isolated from others
discriminated against – unfairly treated compared to others
candid – open, honest, free from bias
eloquent – persuasive, good with words

Unit 11 Assess your progress in reading

1. Find the following key facts in the text:
   - When and where she was born.
   - Where she moved to later with her family.
   - How old she was when she died and where she died. **(2 marks)**
2. There are some facts that suggest or imply other things.
   a) Why do you think the family moved from Germany to Holland?
   b) What qualities or abilities in Anne made it more likely that she might become a writer of a diary that others would want to read? **(2 marks)**
3. *The Diary of Anne Frank* is probably the most famous diary in the world. Using evidence from the text, give at least three reasons why so many people want to read it. **(4 marks)**
4. Explore and explain how effectively the writer uses two characteristics of this kind of short factual text. Give support for your answer from the text. Choose from the prompts below:
   - Structure or organisation.
   - Sentence construction and variety.
   - Language and choice of vocabulary. **(4 marks)**

Focus your effort

When you have located a relevant passage in the text, re-read it carefully to make sure you retrieve from the text all, rather than just some, of the answer.

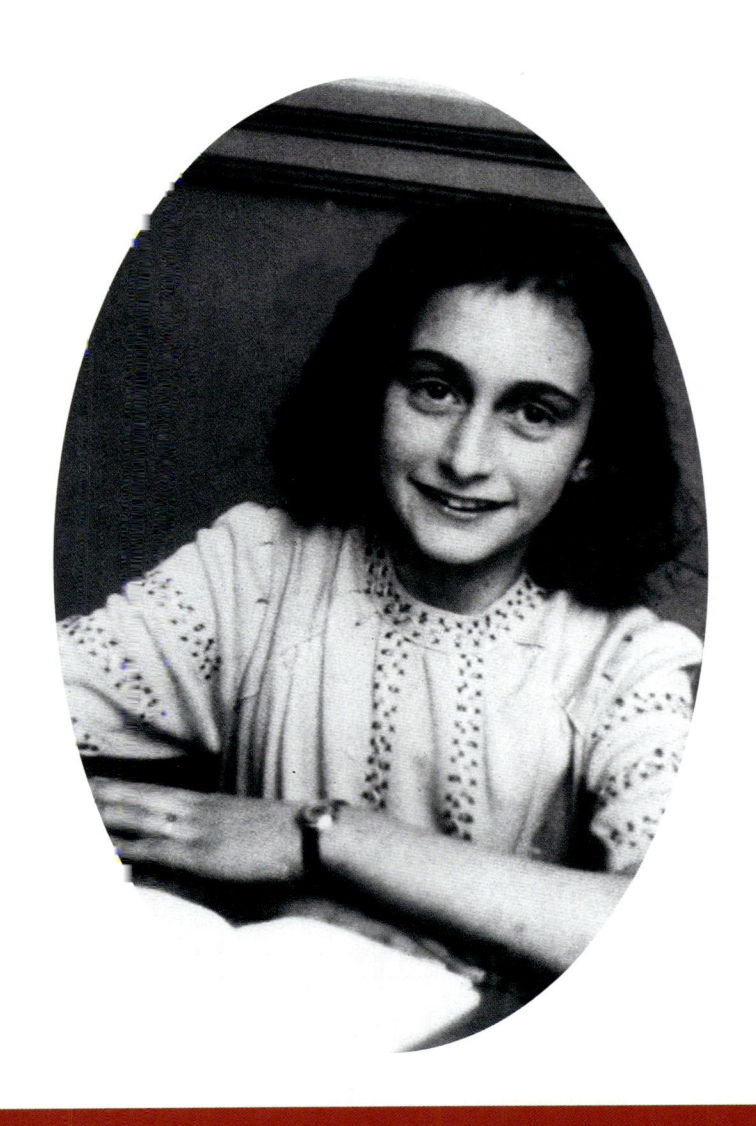

Now turn to page 151 to track your progress in reading.

3 Fiction: Mr and Mrs Pop Eye

Read the following text. It is the opening of the novel *Mister Pip* by Lloyd Jones, set on a Pacific island.

What do you know about… the author?

Lloyd Jones is a novelist from Wellington, New Zealand. *Mister Pip* was published in the UK in 2006 and was shortlisted for the prestigious Man Booker Prize in 2007. The book's title refers to the character of Pip from Charles Dickens' novel *Great Expectations*, which the children in the novel study with their teacher Mr Watts, who is also known as Pop Eye.

Expand your vocabulary

pawpaw – a tropical fruit (also known as papaya)
machetes – heavy cutting tools
penance – an act undertaken by someone to show they are sorry

---

1 Everyone called him Pop Eye. Even in those days when I was a skinny 13-year-old I thought he probably knew about his nickname but didn't care. His eyes were too interested in what lay up ahead to notice us barefoot kids.

5 He looked like someone who had seen or known great suffering and hadn't been able to forget it. His large eyes in his large head stuck out further than anyone else's – like they wanted to leave the surface of his face. They made you think of someone who can't get out of the house quickly enough.

10 Pop Eye wore the same white linen suit every day. His trousers snagged on to his bony knees in the sloppy heat. Some days he wore a clown's nose. His nose was already big. He didn't need that red light bulb. But for reasons we couldn't think of he wore the red nose on certain days that may have meant something to him.

15 We never saw him smile. And on those days he wore the clown's nose you found yourself looking away because you never saw such sadness.

He pulled a piece of rope attached to a trolley, on which Mrs Pop Eye stood. She looked like an ice queen. Nearly every woman on
20 our island had crinkled hair, but Grace had straightened hers. She wore it piled up, and in the absence of a crown her hair did the trick. She looked so proud, as if she had no idea of her own bare feet. You saw her huge bum and worried about the toilet seat. You thought of her mother and birth and that stuff.

25 At two-thirty in the afternoon the parrots sat in the shade of the trees and looked down at a human shadow one-third longer than any seen before. There were only two of them, Mr and Mrs Pop Eye, yet it felt like a procession.

The younger kids saw an opportunity and so fell in behind. Our
30 parents looked away. They would rather stare at a colony of ants moving over rotting **pawpaw**. Some stood by with their idle **machetes** waiting for the spectacle to pass. For the younger kids the sight consisted only of a white man towing a black woman. They saw what the parrots saw, and what the dogs saw while
35 sitting on their scrawny arses snapping their jaws at a passing mosquito. Us older kids sensed a bigger story. Sometimes we caught a snatch of conversation. Mrs Watts was as mad as a goose. Mr Watts was doing **penance** for an old crime. Or maybe it was the result of a bet. The sight represented a bit of uncertainty
40 in our world in which in every other way we knew only sameness.

Unit 11 Assess your progress in reading

1. What does the reader learn about Pop Eye's physical appearance in this text? Find six pieces of information. **(2 marks)**
2. Read paragraph 4. What do the descriptions 'looked like an ice queen' and 'in the absence of a crown' suggest to the reader about Mrs Pop Eye's appearance and character? **(2 marks)**
3. The narrator is very interested in Mr and Mrs Pop Eye. Give four reasons why.
   Support your points with quotations from the text, comments and explanations. **(4 marks)**
4. *Mister Pip* is written in the first person. How effectively does Lloyd Jones create a convincing and interesting narrator? Write two paragraphs in which you comment on:
   - What you learn about the narrator. **(2 marks)**
   - What the writer shows you about the narrator through vocabulary choices and the narrator's thoughts and feelings when using 'I' (paragraph 1), 'we' (paragraphs 3 and 6), 'us' (paragraphs 1 and 5). **(2 marks)**

Focus your effort

Sharpen your analysis of narrative voice and viewpoint.
- Whose point of view are you seeing events from?
- What do you know about that character?
- How might that affect how events are presented to you?
- How does the writer create a convincing narrative voice? Think about choice of language, what the character sees and knows, what the character might not know or fully understand.

➡ Now turn to page 155 to track your progress in reading.

4 Autobiography – *Looking for Adventure*

Read the following text, taken from *Looking for Adventure* by Steve Backshall, and answer the questions that follow.

> **What do you know about… the author?**
> Steve Backshall is a popular presenter of nature programmes, such as *Deadly 60*. In 2011 he published his autobiography, *Looking for Adventure*.

The next case down held a row of shrunken heads. Shrinking heads is a deeply **macabre** process. Having viciously killed the owner, the headhunter cuts the head open at the rear and removes the skull. He then sews the eyes and lips shut with palm threads, before boiling the head in tannins and cooking the now-leathery head in hot sand. The effect is deeply disturbing, as the head is still unmistakably human. The skin is tanned dark as a well-worn Chesterfield, the nose and other features are huge and distorted, and the hair is still long and **luxuriant** a hundred years on. But now the whole head is only the size of a grapefruit. (This bit might be my memory messing with me, as the process of shrinking heads is more common in the Amazon basin than in Melanesia, but I still see them grinning back at me in my memory's blurred etching.)

The last glass case was the one that really held my attention, and if I shut my eyes I can still envisage it most clearly now. It was full of pinned insects from the Papua forests. Until then, bugs to me had been just – well, bugs. Ugly yucky things that ruined your picnics and seemed designed purely to make life a bit more uncomfortable. This lot, though, were a whole different world of horror. There were **amethyst**, **amber** and **garnet**-inlaid beetles, yellow-and-black-striped spiders the size of my dad's mighty, meaty hand, and armoured scorpions whose sting must surely have meant instant death.

More scary than the scorpions, though, were the biggest, most monstrous insects I had ever seen: a foot long, and taking up half the case with their huge bulk. I know today that they were harmless stick insects, pinned with their spindly legs and colourful wings outspread to give them maximum effect, but at the time they were the most horrific things I had ever seen. Following the visit to the exhibition, I began to wake up at night, **tormented** by a nightmare that had me lying in the jungle leaf litter, wrapped up in a sleeping bag, with those vast stick insects crawling over my face looking for a place to begin feeding.

> **Expand your vocabulary**
> **macabre** – gruesome, connected with death
> **luxuriant** – has grown plentiful
> **amethyst**, **amber** and **garnet** – types of gemstone
> **tormented** – experiencing pain, anguish or torture

Unit 11 Assess your progress in reading

1. Steve Backshall describes how after the victim is killed there are several stages in the process of shrinking a human head. List the stages in the correct order. **(2 marks)**

2. Read the text again closely.
   a) Use your inference skills to decide which of the following statements about the writer is true:
      - He was scared by what he saw in the exhibition as a boy but is no longer afraid as an adult.
      - Looking back as an adult he finds the exhibits even more scary now than he did as a boy.
      - Even though he is now an adult he still remembers how afraid he was as a boy.
   b) For the statement you have chosen, select a short quotation (a phrase or a sentence) that is evidence for your conclusion, and explain why you have chosen it and how it supports the statement. **(2 marks)**

3. Identify the words and phrases the writer uses in his description in the second paragraph (see below) that create 'a whole different world of horror'. For each one, explain how the choice of words adds to the writer's sense of fear when he was a young boy. **(4 marks)**

   'This lot, though, were a whole different world of horror. There were amethyst, amber and garnet-inlaid beetles, yellow-and-black-striped spiders the size of my dad's mighty, meaty hand, and armoured scorpions whose sting must surely have meant instant death.'

4. How effectively does Steve Backshall use language to help the reader understand the deep impression made on him by what he saw that day? Comment on vocabulary choices and imagery. **(4 marks)**

> **Focus your effort**
>
> It can help you structure your answer if you start by making a quick plan. You could use a list or a spider diagram to brainstorm your points. List points about *both* the language Backshall uses about what he saw *and* the impression it made on him.

➡ Now turn to page 159 to track your progress in reading.

139

5 Fiction: *Requiem*

Read the following extract from Berlie Doherty's *Requiem* and then answer the questions that follow.

When we went in to choir practice that first time it was in the gym, and Mother Mary Rose, teacher of music, was playing a hymn on the piano. It made us march, and it made us laugh. I caught the eye of one of the girls, Veronica, and we smiled at each other. I was excited.

> **What do you know about… saints?**
> The word 'saint' is used in Christianity to describe an exceptionally holy and virtuous person. Common characteristics of saints include the rejection of worldly comforts, inspiring teachings, miracle-working and martyrdom.

We filed into the rows of chairs that had been set out for us and the playing stopped.

'Which of you girls is Cecilia Dearden?'

'Me, Mother,' I said.

'Who? Who? Who spoke?'

I put up my hand. I was in the middle of a row, somewhere near the back of the class. The nun made no effort to see me, but shouted, her old woman's voice ringing in the lofty gym.

'Who? Stand up. Stand up. Don't be such a goose, child. Stand up.'

I stood up, blushing fiercely as heads turned to look at me.

'Come out here to the front. I want to look at you. So.'

I stumbled over sandalled feet and out to the front. I knew my skirt was too long and that I wasn't wearing the uniform cardigan. It was nearly the same colour, but cheaper. My Aunt Bridget had knitted it for me. I knew that.

'So you're Cecilia.'

'Yes, Mother.'

The old nun stared at me, and I stared at her half-gloved fingers as they fidgeted like moths on the yellow keys.

'And do you know, child, whom it is you're called after?'

'I think it was my granny, Mother.'

There was a titter round the girls.

'Your granny, is it? Is that what you think?'

'Yes, Mother,' I whispered.

'She was a far greater lady than your granny is, or was, or will ever be, girl.'

'Remember that. You can tell your granny that Mother Mary Rose said that to you.'

'Yes, Mother.'

She slapped down the piano lid and sprang up from her chair. Her fingers grasped my arm as she turned me round to face the rest of the class.

'Well, who was she then? Who can tell me? November 22nd. Look in your **missals**, girls. Look in your missals. November 22nd is…?'

There was a fluttering of pages as girls rustled through their missals. I was holding mine but was too much of a fool to open it. She had made me stupid. There was no **redemption**.

Unit 11 Assess your progress in reading

'Please, Mother!'

'Yes?' Mother Rose pointed at one of the raised hands.

'Please, Mother. Saint Cecilia's day, Mother.'

'Good girl. What's your name, dear?'

'Veronica Murphy, Mother.'

'I believe I taught your dear mother. And who was Saint Cecilia, if she wasn't this girl's granny?'

The class **tittered** again. The missals had been closed and were reopened, pages shuffled in the fever of the race.

'Please, Mother!'

'Yes, Veronica.'

'Please, Mother. Martyr and Virgin, Mother.'

'…and…?'

'Please, Mother! Patron saint of music, Mother.'

'Yes, Veronica.'

The sigh was like the wind hushing through trees, as the girls sank back into their chairs. Mother Mary Rose let go my arm. 'Saint Cecilia, Martyr and Virgin, patron saint of music. Did you hear that, child?'

'Yes, Mother.'

'And are you worthy to be named after her?'

My head swam. 'I don't know, Mother.'

I could see the fine hairs on her pale cheeks, the fluff of **spittle** on her lips. 'It's yes or no, child. Yes or no? Do you love music? Yes or no?'

Do I love music! With my soul.

> **Expand your vocabulary**
>
> **missal** – a service book with prayers used by Catholics
> **redemption** – salvation, rescue from sin or evil
> **tittered** – laughed in a nervous or restrained way
> **spittle** – spit, saliva

1. This extract is written in the first person. Make a list of facts that we learn about Cecilia. **(2 marks)**
2. Use your inference skills to comment on what you learn about how Cecilia is feeling in the text below. Comment on how you have used clues in the text to come to your conclusions. **(2 marks)**

   'I stumbled over sandalled feet and out to the front. I knew my skirt was too long and that I wasn't wearing the uniform cardigan. It was nearly the same colour, but cheaper. My Aunt Bridget had knitted it for me. I knew that.'

3. In this extract, one theme or idea explored is that of power. Give two examples from the extract that show one person exerting power over another. For each, explain why you have chosen it and what it suggests about the characters' relationship. **(4 marks)**
4. Explain how Berlie Doherty creates a convincing picture of the music lesson through using first person narrative. **(4 marks)**

→ Now turn to page 164 to track your progress in reading.

141

6 Literary heritage: *Great Expectations*

Read this extract from Charles Dickens' novel *Great Expectations*. The main character and narrator is Pip, a young boy and an orphan. He is visiting the cemetery and his family's graves, which are surrounded by bleak, windswept and desolate marsh land. He thinks he is alone.

> **What do you know about… Charles Dickens and *Great Expectations*?**
> Charles Dickens is one of the great nineteenth century English writers. He wrote many powerful and comic novels, often about poverty, injustice and social wrongs. His novels have been adapted for cinema and television and are extremely popular. *Great Expectations* shows his interest in the influences that make children the adults they become. It is a story about growing up.

'Hold your noise!' cried a terrible voice, as a man started up from among the graves at the side of the church porch. 'Keep still, you little devil, or I'll cut your throat!'

A fearful man, all in coarse grey, with a great iron on his leg. A man with no hat, and with broken shoes, and with an old rag tied round his head. A man who had been soaked in water, and smothered in mud, and lamed by stones, and cut by **flints**, and stung by nettles, and torn by briars; who limped, and shivered, and glared and growled; and whose teeth chattered in his head as he seized me by the chin.

'O! Don't cut my throat, sir,' I pleaded in terror. 'Pray don't do it, sir.'

'Tell us your name!' said the man. 'Quick!'

'Pip, sir.'

'Once more,' said the man, staring at me. 'Give it mouth!'

'Pip. Pip, sir.'

'Show us where you live,' said the man. 'Point out the place!'

I pointed to where our village lay, on the flat in-shore among the alder-trees and pollards, a mile or more from the church.

The man, after looking at me for a moment, turned me upside down, and emptied my pockets. There was nothing in them but a piece of bread. When the church came to itself – for he was so sudden and strong that he made it go head over heels before me, and I saw the steeple under my feet – when the church came to itself, I say, I was seated on a high tombstone, trembling, while he ate the bread ravenously.

'You young dog,' said the man, licking his lips, 'what fat cheeks you ha' got.'

I believe they were fat, though I was at that time undersized for my years, and not strong.

'Darn me if I couldn't eat 'em,' said the man, with a threatening shake of his head, 'and if I han't half a mind to't!'

I earnestly expressed my hope that he wouldn't, and held tighter to the tombstone on which he had put me; partly, to keep myself upon it; partly, to keep myself from crying.

'Now lookee here!' said the man. 'Where's your mother?'

'There, sir!' said I.

He started, made a short run, and stopped and looked over his shoulder.

'There, sir!' I timidly explained. 'Also Georgiana. That's my mother.'

'Oh!' said he, coming back. 'And is that your father alonger your mother?'

'Yes, sir,' said I; 'him too; late of this parish.'

'Ha!' he muttered then, considering. 'Who d'ye live with – supposin' you're kindly let to live, which I han't made up my mind about?'

Unit 11 Assess your progress in reading

'My sister, sir – Mrs Joe Gargery – wife of Joe Gargery, the **blacksmith**, sir.'

'Blacksmith, eh?' said he. And looked down at his leg.

After darkly looking at his leg and me several times, he came closer to my tombstone, took me by both arms, and tilted me back as far as he could hold me; so that his eyes looked most powerfully down into mine, and mine looked most helplessly up into his.

'Now lookee here,' he said, 'the question being whether you're to be let to live. You know what a file is?'

'Yes, sir.'

'And you know what **wittles** is?'

'Yes, sir.'

After each question he tilted me over a little more, so as to give me a greater sense of helplessness and danger.

'You get me a file.' He tilted me again. 'And you get me wittles.' He tilted me again. 'You bring 'em both to me.' He tilted me again. 'Or I'll have your heart and liver out.' He tilted me again.

I was dreadfully frightened, and so giddy that I clung to him with both hands, and said, 'If you would kindly please to let me keep upright, sir, perhaps I shouldn't be sick, and perhaps I could attend more.'

He gave me a most tremendous dip and roll, so that the church jumped over its own weather-cock. Then, he held me by the arms, in an upright position on the top of the stone, and went on in these fearful terms:

'You bring me, to-morrow morning early, that file and them wittles. You bring the lot to me, at that old Battery over yonder. You do it, and you never dare to say a word or dare to make a sign concerning your having seen such a person as me, or any person sumever, and you shall be let to live. You fail, or you go from my words in any partickler, no matter how small it is, and your heart and your liver shall be tore out, roasted and ate.'

> **Expand your vocabulary**
> **flint** – a type of hard stone
> **blacksmith** – someone who smelts, forges and shapes metal, for such products as horseshoes, weapons and tools
> **wittles** – victuals, food

1. Pick out words and phrases from the text to show the following:
   - It is set in a graveyard.
   - The text contains language we do not use anymore.
   - The text contains language that captures the way a person speaks. **(2 marks)**
2. Find evidence for the following:
   - Despite the man being violent, he is scared.
   - Despite Pip being scared, he shows strength of character and courage. **(2 marks)**
3. The convict may be over-acting his threats to get the boy to obey. Show evidence from the text to support this view. **(4 marks)**
4. *Great Expectations* is written in the first person.
   How effectively does Dickens create a convincing and interesting narrator? Write a paragraph or two in which you comment on what you learn about the narrator. Use evidence of effective use of language from the text to support your answer. **(4 marks)**

> **Focus your effort**
> When answering evidence-based questions, use quotations from the text (words or phrases) and explain and explore their effect on the reader. Every word is the writer's choice and is there for a reason.

→ Now turn to page 167 to track your progress in reading.

7 Comparing non-fiction

You are about to read two texts which address in different ways meetings between humans and wild bears. Read the texts closely and answer the questions that follow.

Living with bears

Close encounters: what to do

If you see a bear, avoid it if you can. Give the bear every opportunity to avoid you. If you do encounter a bear at close distance, remain calm. Attacks are rare. Chances are, you are not in danger. Most bears are interested only in protecting food, cubs or their 'personal space'. Once the threat is removed, they will move on.

Remember the following:

Identify yourself

Let the bear know you are *human*. Talk to the bear in a normal voice. Wave your arms. Help the bear recognise you. If a bear cannot tell what you are, it may come closer or stand on its hind legs to get a better look or smell. A standing bear is usually curious, not threatening. You may try to back away slowly diagonally, but if the bear follows, *stop* and hold your ground.

Don't run

You can't outrun a bear. They have been clocked at speeds up to 35 mph, and like dogs, they will chase fleeing animals. Bears often make **bluff** charges, sometimes to within 10 feet of their **adversary**, without making contact. Continue waving your arms and talking to the bear. If the bear gets too close, raise your voice and be more aggressive. Bang pots and pans. Use noisemakers. Never imitate bear sounds or make a high-pitched squeal.

If attacked

If a bear actually makes contact, you have two choices: play dead or fight back. The best choice depends on whether the bear is reacting defensively or is seeking food. Play dead if you are attacked by a grizzly bear you have surprised or encountered on a **carcass**, or any female bear that seems to be protecting cubs. Lie flat on your stomach, or curl up in a ball with your hands behind your neck. Typically, a bear will break off its attack once it feels the threat has been **eliminated**. Remain motionless for as long as possible. If you move, and the bear sees or hears you, it may return and renew its attack. Rarely, lone black bears or grizzlies may perceive a person as potential food. Fight any bear that follows you or breaks into a tent or building. Fight any black bear regardless of circumstances.

Expand your vocabulary

bluff – pretending to be or do something, falsely confident
adversary – opponent
carcass – dead body of an animal
eliminate – to get rid of, to remove completely, to kill

Unit 11 Assess your progress in reading

A Walk in the Woods

We hiked till five and camped beside a **tranquil** spring in a small, grassy clearing in the trees just off the trail. Because it was our first day back on the trail, we were flush for food, including **perishables** like cheese and bread that had to be eaten before they went off or were shaken to bits in our packs, so we rather **gorged** ourselves, then sat around smoking and chatting idly until persistent and numerous midge-like creatures (no-see-ums, as they are universally known along the trail) drove us into our tents. It was perfect sleeping weather, cool enough to need a bag but warm enough that you could sleep in your underwear, and I was looking forward to a long night's snooze – indeed was enjoying a long night's snooze – when, at some **indeterminate** dark hour, there was a sound nearby that made my eyes fly open. Normally, I slept through everything – through thunderstorms, through Katz's snoring and noisy midnight pees – so something big enough or distinctive enough to wake me was unusual. There was a sound of undergrowth being disturbed – a click of breaking branches, a weighty pushing through low **foliage** – and then a kind of large, vaguely irritable snuffling noise.

Bear!

Expand your vocabulary

tranquil – free from disturbance, calm, peaceful
perishables – something, usually foodstuffs, that can decay
gorge – eat a lot greedily
indeterminate – not precisely determined or fixed
foliage – plant leaves and branches

1 What the text is about
   a) 'Living with bears' is organised into clear and separate sections by paragraphs. What is each paragraph about? **(2 marks)**
   b) In *A Walk in the Woods* the writer wants to make sure you know exactly where he is and what he is doing. Select four key facts that do this. For example, the first would be that they were 'hiking'. **(2 marks)**
2 The language used:
   a) Although the main purpose of 'Living with bears' is to explain and instruct, there are some moments when the writer wants you to feel what it is like to be there, facing a bear. – for example, 'Talk to the bear'. Pick out two more of these moments and comment on the language used. **(2 marks)**
   b) *A Walk in the Woods* uses language to invite the reader to feel what it is like to be there. Explain how Bryson makes the reader feel how relaxed and peaceful it is at first (use at least two references or quotes). **(2 marks)**
3 Compare the effectiveness of the following closing sentences from each text.
   • 'Fight any black bear regardless of circumstances.'
   • 'There was a sound of undergrowth being disturbed – a click of breaking branches, a weighty pushing through low foliage – and then a kind of large, vaguely irritable snuffling noise.
   'Bear!' **(4 marks)**
4 What are the different purposes of each text? Support your answer with at least one reference or quote from each text. **(4 marks)**

Focus your effort

As you re-read, look for hints and clues that give you an impression of what it feels or looks like to be facing a bear. You will need to look for words that appeal to the senses.

➡ Now turn to page 171 to track your progress in reading.

8 Comparing themes: Hopes and fears

What do you know about… the poet?
Seamus Heaney was an Irish poet, playwright, translator and lecturer who won the Nobel Prize for Literature in 1995, as well as a wide range of other awards. He has been called the 'greatest poet of our age'. He wrote mainly about Northern Ireland, its people, farms, cities and its complex history and culture. However, the poems are often universal in their meaning.

Toner's bog is a bog owned by Toner. Peat would be cut from the bog to provide fuel.

Expand your vocabulary
rasping – scraping or grating
sods – clumps of earth
curt – rudely short or abrupt

Digging

Between my finger and my thumb
The squat pen rests; snug as a gun.

Under my window, a clean **rasping** sound
When the spade sinks into gravelly ground:
My father, digging. I look down

Till his straining rump among the flowerbeds
Bends low, comes up twenty years away
Stooping in rhythm through potato drills
Where he was digging.

The coarse boot nestled on the lug, the shaft
Against the inside knee was levered firmly.
He rooted out tall tops, buried the bright edge deep
To scatter new potatoes that we picked,
Loving their cool hardness in our hands.

By God, the old man could handle a spade.
Just like his old man.

My grandfather cut more turf in a day
Than any other man on Toner's bog.

Once I carried him milk in a bottle
Corked sloppily with paper. He straightened up
To drink it, then fell to right away
Nicking and slicing neatly, heaving **sods**
Over his shoulder, going down and down
For the good turf. Digging.

The cold smell of potato mould, the squelch and slap
Of soggy peat, the **curt** cuts of an edge
Through living roots awaken in my head.
But I've no spade to follow men like them.

Between my finger and my thumb
The squat pen rests.
I'll dig with it.

Unit 11 Assess your progress in reading

Nettles

My son aged three fell in the nettle bed.
'Bed' seemed a curious name for those green spears,
That **regiment** of **spite** behind the shed:
It was no place for rest. With sobs and tears
The boy came seeking comfort and I saw
White blisters beaded on his tender skin.
We soothed him till his pain was not so raw.
At last he offered us a watery grin,
And then I took my **billhook**, **honed** the blade
And went outside and slashed in fury with it
Till not a nettle in that fierce parade
Stood upright any more. And then I lit
A funeral **pyre** to burn the fallen dead,
But in two weeks the busy sun and rain
Had called up tall recruits behind the shed:
My son would often feel sharp wounds again.

What do you know about… the poet?

Vernon Scannell was a British poet and writer. As a young man, his main passions were boxing and poetry. He enlisted in the army during the Second World War but deserted twice and was court-martialled and imprisoned as a result. He published many poetry books and wrote many poems about war, such as the collection *Walking Wounded*. He also wrote novels and a memoir, *The Tiger and the Rose*.

Expand your vocabulary

regiment – a military unit, a body of troops
spite – a desire to hurt, annoy or offend someone
billhook – a tool used for cutting shrubs and branches
honed – made sharper
pyre – a pile of wood (often for burning a dead body)

Focus your effort

As you re-read the two texts, highlight and annotate passages that you feel are relevant to the theme you have chosen, in this case the physical nature of the events the poets remember. Themes tend to be quite abstract ideas and they may not be directly mentioned within the text. Therefore it is a good idea when you write about themes to explain how your specific examples are connected to your chosen theme.

Poems can sometimes be quite dense and can look complicated. Try to concentrate on the theme and select two or three words or lines that illustrate it.

1. Read both poems carefully and answer these questions:
   a) In 'Digging' there are some facts given about the poet (the 'narrator' of the poem). Find four examples of these in the poem (words, phrases or lines). **(2 marks)**
   b) In 'Nettles' there are some facts given about the poet. Find three examples of these in the poem (words, phrases or lines). **(2 marks)**
2. Read both poems carefully and answer these questions:
   a) In 'Digging', identify and explain evidence from which you can infer that the poet has strong affection for his father and grandfather. **(2 marks)**
   b) In 'Nettles', identify and explain evidence from which you can infer that the poet has strong affection or love for his son. **(2 marks)**
3. Both poems explore a memory of an event from the past. Each poet finds this memory important for his own life. Identify from the text where the narrator says how important it is and explain why. **(4 marks)**
4. Explain and comment on the way both poets use language effectively to explore the physical nature of the events they remember. Focus on at least two examples in each poem. **(4 marks)**

→ Now turn to page 176 to track your progress in reading.

UNIT 12
Track your progress in reading

1 Fiction: *The Hunger Games*

When you have completed the questions on *The Hunger Games* on pages 132–33, check your responses against the answers below.

Question 1 Identify some key facts that tell you about the world in which the characters are living.
- How is the bed described?
- How are the people outside in the street described?

Marks:
- **1 mark** if you wrote about one of the bullet points.
- **2 marks** if you wrote about both.

Examples:
- *The bed is cold on one side; it has a rough canvas mattress cover.*
- *The people have 'hunched shoulders', 'swollen knuckles', 'broken nails' and 'sunken faces'.*

Question 1: marks out of 2 [_____]

Question 2 As well as facts, there are many inferences used by Collins. Explain the following:
- Why does the narrator think her sister climbed into bed with their mother?
- Why has the cat stopped hissing at her?

Marks:
- **1 mark** if you wrote about one bullet point.
- **2 marks** if you wrote about both.

Examples:
- *She climbed into bed with their mother because she had bad dreams. She may be afraid. The mention of 'the reaping' seems to suggest something to be afraid of.*
- *The narrator has fed the cat entrails. The way the word 'entrails' is followed by 'He has stopped hissing' suggests that the cat now relies on the narrator for food. Later, the narrator says, sadly but comically, this is about as close to love as their relationship gets.*

Question 2: marks out of 2 [_____]

Unit 12 Track your progress in reading

Question 3 The writer conveys a picture of the narrator being protective of her family. Find and explain evidence for this.

Marks:
- **2 marks** if you made up to two points.
- **3 marks** if you made up to four points with some comment, explanation, quotation.
- **4 marks** if you made up to four points with comment, explanation, quotation.

Examples:

- She is sharing a bed with her sister and her fingers 'stretch out' for her sister in what can be seen as a caring or checking gesture. She seems to care that her sister may have had bad dreams (paragraph 1).
- She looks at them from her bed with what seems like watchful or protective feelings. The language is loving: 'curled up on her side', 'cocooned in my mother's body', 'cheeks pressed together'. She cares about her mother looking worn and is sad that her beauty has gone. She enjoys her sister's 'fresh', 'primrose' look.
- She sees herself as the provider for the family: she hunts and uses the words 'mouth to feed' for the cat.
- The narrator looks after the gift from Prim (a cheese). She seems to value it not only as food but for the gift it is.
- She keeps coming back to the fact that it is the day of the reaping. She expresses fear or anxiety, but she also expresses protective feelings for herself and her family through this repetition.

Question 3: marks out of 4 [_____]

....

Question 4 It seems as though life has been hard for the narrator and her family for some time. Find and explain at least four pieces of evidence from the text that show this. Comment on at least two of the following in your answer:
- vocabulary choice
- imagery
- sentence construction and grammar choices
- paragraphing
- voice of the narrator

Marks:
- **2 marks** if you made up to two points.
- **3 marks** if you made up to four points with some comment, explanation, quotation.
- **4 marks** if you made up to four points with comment, explanation, quotation.

Examples:

- 'rough canvas cover of the mattress' and sisters sharing a bed. Both suggest poverty (paragraph 1).
- The 'scrawny' condition of the cat, the fact that they have vermin where they live, including rats, the narrator having to 'kill' animals and feed the entrails to the cat: all these point to some kind of tough life on the edge or outside the social comforts we might be used to (paragraph 2).

149

1 Fiction: *The Hunger Games*

- The hunting boots' leather is 'moulded' to the narrator's feet, so she has worn them for some time and has been hunting for some time. Hence she has a forage bag, too. They have to protect their food from 'hungry rats and cats'. It seems like food is in short supply: humans are competing with animals for the food there is (paragraph 3).

- They live in a district where people live a hard life. They mine coal, have 'hunched shoulders', 'swollen knuckles' and 'broken nails' from hard labour. The streets are not paved, they are rough and covered with 'cinders' (paragraph 4).

Question 4: marks out of 4 [_____]

Check your progress

For each question, note your mark for how well the following reading knowledge and skills have been used.

- **Q1** ➪ Find information and comment. (2 marks)
- **Q2** ➪ Understand what a writer infers. (2 marks)
- **Q3** ➪ Interpret the text. (4 marks)
- **Q4** ➪ Evaluate the effect of language and purpose. (4 marks)

Check your total out of 12

Overall, how successful was your response to this fiction text?

PARTIALLY 4 8 12 FULLY

Progress further

If you need to improve your reading, look again at what most needs to improve. You could then:
- look again at pages 46–49 (narrative viewpoint) and 50–62 (language)
- improve your responses to the questions and check your progress
- find out where you have improved and set further targets.

If your reading is high quality, congratulations! Now try this more challenging question:
- The writer uses a first person narrator. Explore how this engages the reader, particularly with moments where the narrator tells us her feelings.

2 Biography: *The Diary of Anne Frank*

When you have completed the questions on the biography of Anne Frank on pages 131–35, check your responses against the answers below.

Question 1 Read this text about Anne Frank. As a biography, much of it is factual. Find the following key facts:
- When and where she was born.
- Where she moved to later with her family.
- How old she was when she died and where she died.

Marks:
- **1 mark** if you included up to three facts.
- **2 marks** if you included all five facts.

Examples:
- Born 12 June 1929, in Frankfurt, Germany.
- Moved to Holland (in 1933).
- Died aged 15 in 1945, at Bergen-Belsen.

Question 1: marks out of 2 [_____]

Question 2 There are some facts that suggest or imply other things.
- a Why do you think the family moved from Germany to Holland?
- b What qualities or abilities in Anne made it more likely that she might become a writer of a diary that others would want to read?

Marks:
- **1 mark** if you made one point about each of the questions.
- **2 marks** if you made two points about each of the questions.

Examples of facts and what might be inferred or suggested:
- The family moved to Holland in 1933 after the Nazis came to power (paragraphs 1–2). This suggests that they felt they had to leave Germany as their lives were being made more difficult. We know from later in the text how these difficulties followed them and became more deadly.
- The writer asserts that Anne developed 'an aptitude for reading and writing', which would support her to write well and to have the required vocabulary and understanding to write a good diary. She also had an 'outspoken and energetic personality', which would be more likely to shine through in a diary and make the reader like or admire her.

Question 2: marks out of 2 [_____]

151

2 Biography: *The Diary of Anne Frank*

Question 3 *The Diary of Anne Frank* is probably the most famous diary in the world. Using evidence from the text, give at least three reasons why so many people want to read it.

Make up to four points from all or most of the paragraphs.

Support your points with quotations from the text, comments and explanations.

Marks:

- **2 marks** if you made up to two points.
- **3 marks** if you made up to three points with some comment, explanation, quotation.
- **4 marks** if you made up to four points with comment, explanation, quotation.

Examples of points, comments, explanations, quotations:

- She became a good writer, having 'an aptitude for reading and writing' that led to her being eloquent in her diary.
- She started and wrote the diary when she was so young, aged 13–16. People may be drawn by her youth, her 'outspoken and energetic personality', her 'candid' writing.
- The times in which she lived and her personal experience fascinate and horrify readers: they were dangerous times as their lives became more difficult, facing loss of employment, 'curfew', 'being segregated and discriminated against', going into hiding and eventually transported to a concentration camp at Auschwitz. Readers experience these extreme times through her eyes and feelings as she is struggling with 'growing up'.
- Readers are not only fascinated but probably haunted by the knowledge that she never did finally grow up but died in the concentration camp. It makes her diary even more poignant or telling.

Question 3: marks out of 4 [_____]

Unit 12 Track your progress in reading

Question 4 Explore and explain how effectively the writer uses two characteristics of this kind of short factual text. Give support for your answer from the text. Choose from the prompts below:
- Structure or organisation.
- Sentence construction and variety.
- Language and choice of vocabulary.

Marks:
- **1 mark** if you explained up to one characteristic not supported by the text.
- **2 marks** if you explained at least two characteristics not supported by the text.
- **3 marks** if you explained at least one characteristic supported by the text.
- **4 marks** if you explained at least two characteristics supported by the text.

Examples of structure and organisation:
- Use of paragraphs that are fairly short (opening and closing paragraphs) balanced with more expansive paragraphs (paragraphs 3 and 5).
- Sequential – telling the story briskly but with enough time and words given to ensure clarity. For example:

  'On 6 July 1942, Anne, her sister Margot and her parents went into hiding, along with four other families.'

- Developmental – we follow the story of Anne and her family but are reminded frequently of the context of their story. For example:

  'When Holland was occupied by the Nazis in 1940, their heritage put the family under threat.'

Examples of sentence construction and variety:
- Effective balance of short and longer sentences to help the reader access the information and explanation required (paragraph 2).
- Longer sentences are kept in check and contain only one or two subordinate clauses. This controls the flow of factual information and explanation that this kind of biographical text needs and ensures readers are not overloaded. For example:

  'Of German Jewish descent, she and her family moved to Holland in 1933, where her father set up a business.'

- Sentences have varied openings and endings to make even this short text engaging, so that facts are well expressed and meaning effectively pursued. For example:

  'Anne Frank is… Of German Jewish descent… On her 13th birthday… Whilst in hiding … Anne started…'

Examples of language and choice of vocabulary:
- Precise use of language appropriate to a text that is factual and explanatory. For example:

  'candid and eloquent account of her life in confinement.'

- Good balance of simple and complex vocabulary to engage the reader but also allow significant detail to be explored. For example:

  'Her diary ends in 1944 when the annexe was raided by the Nazi authorities.'

- Some use of more emotive language to express the urgency of the events and their significance in history and in personal lives. This kind of vocabulary appears more in the second half of the text as Anne's story develops (paragraph 8 'fear', 'confusion'; paragraph 9 'extreme', 'struggling'; paragraph 10 'raided', 'died').

Question 4: marks out of 4 [_____]

2 Biography: *The Diary of Anne Frank*

Check your progress

For each question, note your mark for how well the following reading knowledge and skills have been used.

Q1 ⇨ Find information and comment. (2 marks)

Q2 ⇨ Understand what a writer infers. (2 marks)

Q3 ⇨ Interpret the text for what makes it so popular. (4 marks)

Q4 ⇨ Evaluate how effectively information is expressed, focusing on language and purpose. (4 marks)

Check your total out of 12

Overall, how successful was your response to this literary non-fiction text?

PARTIALLY — 4 — 8 — 12 — FULLY

Progress further

If you need to improve your reading, look again at what most needs to improve. You could then:
- look again at pages 20–23 (purpose, audience) and 32–39 (evidence)
- improve your responses to the questions and check your progress
- find out where you have improved and set further targets.

If your reading is high quality, congratulations! Now try this more challenging question:
- Question 4 looks at sentence construction. Choose two longer paragraphs and analyse how the varied sentences work together to ensure an effective paragraph and reading experience.

3 Fiction: *Mr and Mrs Pop Eye*

When you have completed the questions on Mr and Mrs Pop Eye from the novel *Mister Pip* on pages 136–37, check your responses against the answers below.

Question 1 What does the reader learn about Pop Eye's physical appearance in this text? Find six pieces of information.

Marks:
- **1 mark** if you made up to three points.
- **2 marks** if you made four to six points.

Examples of Pop Eye's physical appearance:
- He had a large head.
- He had large, protruding eyes.
- He wore the same white linen suit every day.
- He had a large nose and some days he wore a clown's nose.
- He never smiled.
- He was white.

Question 1: marks out of 2 [_____]

....

Question 2 Read paragraph 4. What do the phrases 'looked like an ice queen' and 'in the absence of a crown' suggest to the reader about Mrs Pop Eye's appearance and character?

Marks:
- **1 mark** if you made up to two points.
- **2 marks** if you made up to four or more points.

Examples of what the phrases might suggest:
- As an 'ice queen' she might be a proud character, set apart from others.
- She might have a distant, cold, 'icy' character – she is 'ice' in contrast to the heat of the island.
- Perhaps she wants to act and look like a queen – she straightens her hair and piles it up because she wishes she had a crown.
- She has a queenly presence and usually a crown would set a queen apart, but in the absence of this her hair sets her apart as it is straightened, unlike the crinkly hair of most of the islanders.

Question 2: marks out of 2 [_____]

3 Fiction: *Mr and Mrs Pop Eye*

Question 3 The narrator is very interested in Mr and Mrs Pop Eye. Give four reasons why

Support your points with quotations from the text, comments and explanations.

Marks:
- **2 marks** if you made up to two points.
- **3 marks** if you made up to four points with some comment, explanation, quotation.
- **4 marks** if you made up to four points with comment, explanation, quotation.

Examples of points, comments, explanations, quotations:

- *The narrator is interested in whether Mr Pop Eye has suffered a lot. She observes that his 'large eyes pop out', they 'never saw him smile' and 'never saw such sadness'. It looks as if he has been through a lot in his life (paragraphs 2–3).*

- *The narrator is interested in why Mr and Mrs Pop Eye look odd. Mr Pop Eye sometimes 'wore a red nose' and Mrs Pop Eye looks like an 'ice queen' with straightened hair. She wants to know more about why they look this way (paragraphs 3–4).*

- *The narrator is interested in Mr and Mrs Pop Eye's unusual behaviour. The couple seems set apart from the islanders. Mr Pop Eye is 'white', unlike most of the people on the island, and he pulls his islander wife on a 'trolley'. They are different in a place where otherwise every day knew only 'sameness' (paragraphs 4–5).*

- *The narrator is interested in the mystery behind Mr and Mrs Pop Eye. The narrator is one of 'us older kids' who 'sense a bigger story'. They have heard 'snatches of conversation' that hint at a crime or bet and want to know what Mr and Mrs Pop Eye have done in the past (paragraph 6).*

Question 3: marks out of 4 [_____]

....

Question 4 *Mister Pip* is written in the first person. How effectively does Lloyd Jones create a convincing and interesting narrator? Write two paragraphs in which you comment on:
- What you learn about the narrator.
- What the writer shows you about the narrator through vocabulary choices, and the narrator's thoughts and feelings when using 'I' (paragraph 1), 'we' (paragraphs 3 and 6), 'us' (paragraphs 1 and 6).

Question 4a What you learn about the narrator.

Marks:
- **1 mark** if you made up to two points supported by the text.
- **2 marks** if you made at least four points supported by the text.

Examples of what you learn about the narrator:
- Thirteen years old (line 2).
- Skinny (line 2).
- Barefoot (line 4).
- Seems to have good friends – 'us older kids' (line 36).
- Wants to know about Mr and Mrs Pop Eye – interested in something different from the 'sameness' (line 40).
- Is very observant – more so than either the little kids or the adults (lines 3, 36, 40).

Question 4a: Total marks out of 2 [_____]

Question 4b What the writer shows you about the narrator through vocabulary choices, and the narrator's thoughts and feelings when using 'I' (paragraph 1), 'we' (paragraphs 3 and 6), 'us' (paragraphs 1 and 6).

Marks:
- **1 mark** if you made up to two points.
- **2 marks** if you made at least three points supported by the text.

Examples the writer shows you about the narrator:
- 'You saw her huge bum and worried about the toilet seat. You thought of her mother and birth and that stuff' (lines 23–24) – the writer shows that the narrator might be a teenager because of the choice of informal vocabulary a teenager might use.
- 'Even in those days when I was a skinny 13-year-old I thought he probably knew about his nickname but didn't care' (lines 1–3) – by using 'I was… I thought… probably…' the writer shows the narrator's observation of and insight in to other characters at the age of 13.
- 'But for reasons we couldn't think of he wore the red nose on certain days that may have meant something to him' (lines 13–14) – the writer shows that the narrator is aware that there are things she doesn't yet know or understand.
- 'Us older kids sensed a bigger story' – the writer shows the narrator is part of a group of kids who think there is a mystery behind Mr and Mrs Pop Eye and want to know more.

Question 4b: Total marks out of 2 [_____]

3 Fiction: Mr and Mrs Pop Eye

Check your progress

For each question, note your mark for how well the following reading knowledge and skills have been used.

- **Q1** ⇨ Find information and comment. (2 marks)
- **Q2** ⇨ Understand what a writer infers. (2 marks)
- **Q3** ⇨ Interpret the characters' relationship in the text. (4 marks)
- **Q4** ⇨ Evaluate the effect of language and purpose. (2 marks)
- **Q4b** ⇨ Evaluate the effect of language and purpose. (2 marks)

Check your total out of 12

Overall, how successful was your response to this literary fiction text?

PARTIALLY 4 ▶ 8 ▶ 12 FULLY

Progress further

If you need to improve your reading, look again at what most needs to improve. You could then:
- look again at pages 46–49 (narrative viewpoint) and 50–62 (language)
- improve your responses to the questions and check your progress
- find out where you have improved and set further targets.

If your reading is high quality, congratulations! Now try this more challenging question:
- The text ends with: 'The sight represented a bit of uncertainty in our world in which in every other way we knew only sameness.' Explore what you think the narrator means and how the rest of the text leads up to this.

4 Autobiography: *Looking for Adventure*

When you have completed the questions on *Looking for Adventure* on pages 138–39, check your responses against the answers below.

Question 1 Steve Backshall describes how after the victim is killed there are several stages in the process of shrinking a human head. List the stages in the correct order.

Marks:
- **1 mark** for up to three points.
- **2 marks** for four points in the correct order.

Examples of the stages:
- *The headhunter cuts the head open and removes the skull.*
- *He sews the eyes and lips shut with palm threads.*
- *The head is boiled in tannins.*
- *The now-leathery head is cooked in hot sand.*

Question 1: marks out of 2 [_____]

Question 2a Use your inference skills to decide which of the following statements about the writer is true:
- He was scared by what he saw in the exhibition as a boy but is no longer afraid as an adult.
- Looking back as an adult he finds the exhibits even more scary now than he did as a boy.
- Even though he is now an adult he still remembers how afraid he was as a boy.

Question 2b For the statement you have chosen, select a short quotation (a phrase or a sentence) that is evidence for your conclusion, and explain why you have chosen it and how it supports the statement.

Marks:
- **1 mark** for the correct statement about the writer.
- **2 marks** for a short quotation and explanation in evidence.

Example of correct choice of statement:

Even though he is now an adult he still remembers how afraid he was as a boy.

Examples of quotation and explanations:

Quotation *'this might be my memory messing with me…I still see them grinning back at me in my memory's blurred etching'*

Explanation *It is as though he cannot get the image of the grinning head out of his mind. Even though it is vague, it disturbs him.*

159

4 Autobiography: *Looking for Adventure*

Quotation 'I know today that they were harmless…but at the time…Following the visit to the exhibition, I began to wake up at night, tormented…'

Explanation *He acknowledges that what he saw in the exhibition will do him no harm. But he cannot get out of his mind, or his dreams, how afraid he was of these things in his childhood.*

Question 2: marks out of 2 [_____]

Question 3 Identify the words and phrases the writer uses in his description in the second paragraph (see below) that create 'a whole different world of horror'. For each one, explain how the choice of words adds to the writer's sense of fear when he was a young boy.

> 'This lot, though, were a whole different world of horror. There were amethyst, amber and garnet-inlaid beetles, yellow-and-black-striped spiders the size of my dad's mighty, meaty hand, and armoured scorpions whose sting must surely have meant instant death.'

Marks:
- **1 mark** if your answer was closest to a.
- **2 marks** if your answer was closest to b.
- **3 marks** if your answer was closest to c.
- **4 marks** if your answer was closest to d.

Examples:

a You've identified some words and phrases, for example:

  'world of horror…mighty, meaty hand'

b You've made brief comments on some language features, for example:

  uses the phrases 'a world of horror' and 'my dad's mighty, meaty hand', which make everything much bigger and more scary.

c You've explained the effect of language choices on the reader, for example:

  uses some words and phrases, such as 'world of horror' and 'mighty, meaty hand', that make the reader sense how the young boy was afraid because of the size of the insects, and describes how the spiders and beetles have beautiful colours but are really dangerous.

d You've commented on overall effect – for example, given a detailed explanation of how language is used and its effect on readers. For example:

  The writer creates a contrast by comparing the appearance of the beetles to gemstones (shiny and glittery), and the spiders, with their vivid colours, with their danger to humans. He uses a metaphor to describe the scorpions as 'armoured', comparing them to soldiers wearing armour, or an armoured vehicle, which creates the impression of them as dangerous fighters. He also uses the phrase 'instant death', which exaggerates their danger, as felt by the young boy looking at them.

Question 3: marks out of 4 [_____]

Unit 12 Track your progress in reading

Question 4 How effectively does Steve Backshall use language to help the reader understand the deep impression made on him by what he saw that day? Comment on vocabulary choices and imagery.

Marks:
- **1 mark** if your answer was closest to a.
- **2 marks** if your answer was closest to b.
- **3 marks** if your answer was closest to c.
- **4 marks** if your answer was closest to d.

Examples:

a You've noticed and commented on one language feature, for example:

He writes about the colours of the creatures ('yellow-and black-striped'). This helps the reader imagine what he saw.

b You've noticed and commented on at least two language features, for example:

The writer uses adjectives to describe how he feels, e.g. 'macabre', 'monstrous' and 'terrific', which tell us how he felt really scared as a young boy.

c You've commented on several features using supporting detail and quotations, for example:

He comments on the creatures' colours, shapes and sizes. For example, he describes a spider's yellow and black colours and stripy pattern and gives us an idea of its impression on him by comparing it with 'my dad's mighty, meaty hand'. This image helps us to understand the spider's size and perhaps also its strength and power.

4 Autobiography: *Looking for Adventure*

d You've commented on the overall effect of language on the reader – for example, given a detailed explanation of how language is used and its effect on readers. For example:

Interesting and stylish opening sentences showing good understanding of overall text.

Short, well-chosen quotations as evidence followed immediately by a thoughtful explanation.

Evidence to support point about the impact on the writer of what he saw that day (i.e. both halves of the question covered).

Good point about effect of grammar choice on reader.

Reference to elsewhere in the extract showing good understanding of how effects are built up throughout a text.

> The writer helps us see things through his eyes by taking us on the same journey he went on as a small boy. We can imagine him peering into the cases one by one and being more and more astounded by what he saw. He first of all sees the shrunken heads. Words like 'leathery', 'luxuriant' and 'the size of a grapefruit' help us picture the shrunken heads precisely, which is important as the reader might never have seen a shrunken head in real life. Words like 'macabre', 'viciously' and 'disturbing' help us understand not only the frightening appearance of the heads but also the violent way in which they were made, which has clearly had an effect on the boy. Indeed, he describes them as 'still ... grinning back at me', a reminder that they are real human heads. The use of the present tense makes it sound like he is haunted by what he saw, an idea backed up by the reference to a 'nightmare' in the third paragraph.

Question 4: marks out of 4 [_____]

Unit 12 Track your progress in reading

Check your progress

For each question, note your mark for how well the following reading knowledge and skills have been used.

Q1 ⇨ Find and comment on key facts or ideas in the text. (2 marks)
Q2 ⇨ Comment on the writer's inference in the text. (2 marks)
Q3 ⇨ Interpret the meaning of the text by looking at language. (4 marks)
Q4 ⇨ Evaluate the effectiveness and purpose of the text. (4 marks)

Check your total out of 12

Overall, how successful was your response to the literary non-fiction text?

PARTIALLY 4 — 8 — 12 FULLY

Progress further

If you need to improve your reading, look again at what most needs to improve. You could then:
- look again at pages 40–49 (ideas, themes) and 50–62 (language)
- improve your responses to the questions and check your progress
- find out where you have improved and set further targets.

If your reading is high quality, congratulations! Now try this more challenging question:
- 'Backshall conveys his excitement as well as his terror in this text.' To what extent do you agree with this statement?

5 Fiction: *Requiem*

When you have completed the questions on *Requiem* on pages 140–41, check your responses against the answers below.

Question 1 This extract is written in the first person. Make a list of facts that we learn about Cecilia.

Marks:
- **0 marks** if what you listed isn't stated in the text.
- **1 mark** if you listed up to two facts.
- **2 marks** if you listed four or more facts.

Examples of facts about Cecilia that we learn from the text:

- *Excited about music/marching/laughing.*
- *The march being played made her march/laugh.*
- *Wearing sandals.*
- *Not wearing a bought school uniform; wearing a too-long skirt and a cardigan knitted by Aunt Bridget.*
- *She thinks she was named Cecilia after her granny.*
- *She loves music.*

Question 1: marks out of 2 [_____]

Question 2 Use your inference skills to comment on what you learn about how Cecilia is feeling in the text below. Comment on how you have used clues in the text to come to your conclusions.

> 'I stumbled over sandalled feet and out to the front. I knew my skirt was too long and that I wasn't wearing the uniform cardigan. It was nearly the same colour, but cheaper. My Aunt Bridget had knitted it for me. I knew that.'

Marks:
- **1 mark** if your answer was closest to this example of a single short comment. For example:

  Cecilia might be blushing because she feels embarrassed.

- **2 marks** if your answer was closest to this example of a comment that shows fuller understanding. For example:

  Cecilia might be ashamed because it seems she is from a poorer family. We think this because her clothes are not regulation school uniform and have been made for her. The other girls might be wearing smart new uniforms that have been bought.

Question 2: marks out of 2 [_____]

Unit 12 Track your progress in reading

Question 3 In this extract, one idea or theme explored is that of 'power'.

Give two examples from the extract that show one person exerting their power over another. For each, explain why you have chosen it and what it suggests about the characters' relationship.

Marks:
- **1 mark** if your answer was closest to a.
- **2 marks** if your answer was closest to b.
- **3 marks** if your answer was closest to c.
- **4 marks** if your answer was closest to d.

Examples:

a Mother Mary Rose is powerful.

b Mother Mary Rose is powerful. This is shown by the way she speaks and acts, for example:

'The nun made no effort to see me, but shouted'

c Mother Mary Rose exerts her power by dominating the classroom, shouting commands, firing questions and selecting those who answer, as well as searching for right answers.

d An answer with the above but adding that the other girls also feel power over Cecilia by the way they 'titter' when she mentions her 'granny' and again when the teacher reminds her how wrong her answer was.

Question 3: marks out of 4 [_____]

Question 4 Explain how Berlie Doherty creates a convincing picture of the music lesson through using first person narrative.

Marks:
- **1 mark** if your answer was closest to a.
- **2 marks** if your answer was closest to b.
- **3 marks** if your answer was closest to c.
- **4 marks** if your answer was closest to d.

Examples:

a We can feel how she feels in this new classroom because the young girl tells the story.

b We can feel what she feels because she describes this through the words 'laughing', 'blushing', 'stumbling', 'whispered', 'stupid', 'swimming head'.

c Include an explanation of some of the above references, for example:

As the classroom atmosphere is made more stressful by the overpowering teacher, the narrator expresses a change from excitement, to embarrassment, to shame and fear.

d Include with the explanation of the references and quotes further explanation of the dialogue. Perhaps a mention of the last statement, which is happening in her mind, rather than the last words she speaks:

'I don't know, Mother.'

Question 4: marks out of 4 [_____]

165

5 Fiction: Requiem

Check your progress

For each question, note your mark for how well the following reading knowledge and skills have been used.

Q1 ⇨ Retrieve factual information. (2 marks)

Q2 ⇨ Understand inference and read between the lines. (2 marks)

Q3 ⇨ Interpret themes or ideas in the text. (4 marks)

Q4 ⇨ Evaluate effectiveness of the writing, including language. (4 marks)

Check your total out of 12

Overall, how successful was your response to this literary text?

PARTIALLY 4 ▸ 8 ▸ 12 FULLY

Progress further

If you need to improve your reading, look again at what most needs to improve. You could then:
- look again at pages 46–49 (narrative viewpoint) and 50–62 (language)
- improve your responses to the questions and check your progress
- find out where you have improved and set further targets.

If your reading is high quality, congratulations! Now try this more challenging question:
- Consider the mood the writer creates in this text.
  How does Doherty build an atmosphere of tension in her description of Cecilia's classroom experiences?
  Support your comments with evidence from the text.

6 Literary heritage: *Great Expectations*

When you have completed the questions on *Great Expectations* on pages 142–43, check your responses against the answers below.

Question 1 Pick out words and phrases from the text to show the following:
- It is set in a graveyard.
- The text contains language we do not use anymore.
- The text contains language that captures the way a person speaks.

Marks:
- **1 mark** if you found up to three quotations.
- **2 marks** if you found four to six quotations.

Examples that show it is set in a graveyard:

- 'the graves at the side of the church porch'
- 'I was seated on a high tombstone'
- 'held tighter to the tombstone'
- 'he came closer to my tombstone'

Examples that contain language we rarely use anymore:

- 'pray', meaning 'please'
- 'alonger'
- 'blacksmith'
- 'wittles'

Examples that contain language that captures the way a person speaks:

- 'give it mouth'
- 'and if I han't half a mind to't'
- 'lookee'
- 'wittles'
- 'bring 'em'
- 'sumever'
- 'partickler'

Question 1: marks out of 2 [_____]

6 Literary heritage: *Great Expectations*

Question 2 Find evidence for the following:
- Despite the man being violent, he is scared.
- Despite Pip being scared, he shows strength of character and courage.

Marks:
- **1 mark** if you provided at least two examples, one piece of evidence for each bullet point.
- **2 marks** if you provided at least four examples, with two pieces of evidence for each bullet point.

Examples of evidence that despite the man being violent, he is scared:

- *The description of the convict suggests he has had a hard time escaping and is vulnerable and fearful:*

  'soaked in water, and smothered in mud, and lamed by stones, and cut by flints, and stung by nettles, and torn by briars; who limped, and shivered'

- *The man overstates his threats to cut out parts of the boy and eat them, as though he is scared himself.*

- *When Pip points to his 'mother', the convict 'started, made a short run, and stopped and looked over his shoulder.' He has not realised Pip is referring to a gravestone and is scared that a real person is there. It is noticeable that he runs.*

- *The convict is keen not to be found. He says,*

  'ever dare to say a word or dare to make a sign concerning your having seen such a person as me.'

Examples of evidence that despite Pip being scared, he shows strength of character and courage:

- *Pip replies quickly and directly to all the man's questions, suggesting that he is keeping his wits about him: 'Pip, sir.'*

- *He shows respect easily despite the threats of violence: 'pray...', 'sir'.*

- *Pip holds 'tighter to the tombstone', 'partly, to keep myself upon it; partly, to keep myself from crying.' He does not want to cry, he is trying to be brave.*

- *He is 'dreadfully frightened' but still has enough awareness to say,*

  'If you would kindly please to let me keep upright, sir, perhaps I shouldn't be sick, and perhaps I could attend more.'

Question 2: marks out of 2 [_____]

....

Question 3 The convict may be over-acting his threats to get the boy to obey. Show evidence from the text to support this view.

Marks:
- **2 marks** if you made up to two points.
- **3 marks** if you made up to four points, with some comment, explanation, quotation.
- **4 marks** if you made up to four points, with comment, explanation, quotation.

Unit 12 Track your progress in reading

Examples of points, comments, explanations, quotations:

- The convict says he will 'cut' the boy's 'throat', but it seems he has no knife. He says it just after he says 'keep still', suggesting he is really just trying to scare the boy into submission.
- The convict quickly asks for the boy's name. This can be seen as an odd thing to do after threatening to cut his throat. Perhaps he is more interested in getting the attention of the boy and getting to know at least something about him.
- We find that once he has the boy's attention, he asks for 'wittles' and a 'file'. Even though he repeats his threats to 'have your heart and liver out', it is perhaps a further attempt to submit the boy to his will so that he will bring the goods, rather than an intention to kill him. The gruesome and bloody nature of the threat hides that he really just wants and needs food and a means of getting out of his chains.
- Even though he continues the gruesome threats in the last paragraph he shows he is secretly hoping that the boy will return with the food and file and will,

'never say a word or dare to make a sign'

Question 3: marks out of 4 [_____]

Question 4 *Great Expectations* is written in the first person.

How effectively does Dickens create a convincing and interesting narrator? Write a paragraph or two in which you comment on what you learn about the narrator. Use evidence of effective use of language from the text to support your answer.

Marks:
- **2 marks** if you made up to two points supported by evidence from the text.
- **3 marks** if you made up to three points supported by evidence from the text.
- **4 marks** if you made at least four points supported by the text.

Examples of what you learn about the narrator:

- Observant and has a good memory – he notices detail, such as 'all in coarse grey' and 'lamed by stones, and cut by flints, and stung by nettles, and torn by briars'. He produces a very detailed picture and memory of the convict.
- Courageous under pressure – he keeps his wits about him when the convict is threatening to kill him by saying,

  'If you would kindly please to let me keep upright, sir, perhaps I shouldn't be sick, and perhaps I could attend more.'

- Affectionate, as he is visiting his family's graves.
- Polite, as he repeats 'sir' so often, even under pressure, and uses words such as 'pray' when making a request.
- Direct and honest, as he answers all the convict's questions quickly and straightforwardly, even his family's names and where he comes from.
- He does not see himself as strong. He says he is,

  'at that time undersized for my years, and not strong'

Question 4: Total marks out of 4 [_____]

6 Literary heritage: *Great Expectations*

Check your progress

For each question, note your mark for how well the following reading knowledge and skills have been used.

Q1 ➯ Find factual information. (2 marks)

Q2 ➯ Understand what a writer infers. (2 marks)

Q3 ➯ Interpret the text. (4 marks)

Q4 ➯ Evaluate use of language in the first person narrator. (4 marks)

Check your total out of 12

Overall, how successful was your response to this literary fiction text?

PARTIALLY → 4 → 8 → 12 → FULLY

Progress further

If you need to improve your reading, look again at what most needs to improve. You could then:
- look again at pages 16–19 (inference) and 50–61 (language)
- improve your responses to the questions and check your progress
- find out where you have improved and set further targets.

If your reading is high quality, congratulations! Now try this more challenging question:
- The extract is mainly composed of dialogue. What does the descriptive detail add to the effectiveness of the writing? Focus on the wider landscape, the graveyard and church and the convict.

7 Comparing non-fiction

When you have completed the questions on comparing non-fiction on pages 144–45, check your responses against the answers below.

Question 1a 'Living with bears' is organised into clear and separate sections by paragraphs. What is each paragraph about?

Marks:
- **1 mark** if you wrote down the subtitles of the text.
- **2 marks** if you expanded a little to show what each paragraph is about.

Examples:
- Paragraph 1 outlines key actions you should take if you meet a bear.
- Paragraph 2 explores what you need to do to identify yourself to the bear.
- Paragraph 3 asserts you must not run and explains why.
- Paragraph 4 explains how you should respond if you are attacked by a bear.

Question 1a: marks out of 2 [_____]

Question 1b In *A Walk in the Woods* the writer wants to make sure you know exactly where he is and what he is doing. Select four key facts that do this. For example, the first would be that they were 'hiking'.

Marks:
- **1 mark** if you made up to two points.
- **2 marks** if you made four points.

Examples of key facts:
- 'camped beside a tranquil spring'
- 'camped…in a small, grassy clearing…just off the trail'
- Ate a lot – 'gorged'
- 'smoking and chatting'
- Driven into tents by midges
- Cool but still warm

Question 1b: marks out of 2 [_____]

7 Comparing non-fiction

Question 2a Although the main purpose of 'Living with bears' is to explain and instruct, there are some moments when the writer wants you to feel what it is like to be there, facing a bear – for example, 'Talk to the bear'. Pick out two more of these moments and comment on the language used.

Marks:
- **1 mark** if you identified and commented on one moment.
- **2 marks** if you identified and commented on two moments.

Examples of quotes and comment:

- 'Wave your arms' – this is simply an instruction or piece of advice. The simple language and imperative or active use of the verb 'wave' for a moment puts the reader right there in front of the bear. We can picture a person waving their arms.
- '…or stand on its hind legs to get a better look or smell' – for a moment, the reader is given a simple but detailed picture of the bear, described in the way it stands and what it might be doing (getting a 'better look or smell'). We carry this picture with us as we read on.
- 'Bang pots and pans' – this is almost comic, but still shows us ourselves in a dangerous situation trying to find things to do to get out of it. The alliterative sounds of 'b' and 'p' capture the sense of what it would be like: noisy, threatening, almost chaotic.
- There are lots of other moments where we are taken to the place and the moment. But they are always short and kept in check because the main purpose of the text is not to infer but to explain and persuade.

Question 2a: marks out of 2 [_____]

Question 2b *A Walk in the Woods* uses language to invite the reader to feel what it is like to be there. Explain how Bryson makes the reader feel how relaxed and peaceful it is at first (use at least two references or quotes).

Marks:
- **1 mark** if you used and commented on one quote or reference.
- **2 marks** if you used and commented on two quotes or references.

Examples of quotes and comment:

- 'tranquil spring' – 'tranquil' is more than just quiet, it also means peaceful and calm; 'spring' gives the feeling of newness and freshness, it is life-giving.
- 'grassy clearing' – 'grassy' is one of a number of words that help the reader sense how natural the place is; 'clearing' suggests a sense of there being little there other than nature.
- 'just off the trail' – 'trail' indicates that although humans go there, it is in small numbers and is fairly unspoilt and quiet; 'just off' indicates it is even more isolated.
- 'perfect sleeping weather' – 'sleeping' further supports a sense of calm; 'perfect' enhances this and can remind the reader of it all being natural.

Question 2b: marks out of 2 [_____]

Unit 12 Track your progress in reading

Question 3 Compare the effectiveness of the following closing sentences from each text.
- 'Fight any black bear regardless of circumstances.'
- 'There was a sound of undergrowth being disturbed – a click of breaking branches, a weight pushing through low foliage – and then a kind of large, vaguely irritable snuffling noise.
Bear!'

Marks:
- **1 mark** if you explained one sentence.
- **2 marks** if you explained each sentence with some comment on why or how it is effective.
- **3 marks** if you analysed each sentence, comparing how one is from a text that wants readers to see and feel the situation, and the other wants the reader to be informed and advised.
- **4 marks** if you analysed in detail each sentence, comparing purpose and audience and referring closely to language and its effect.

Example of a 4 mark answer:
- 'Fight any black bear regardless of circumstances.' The last sentence of the 'Living with bears' piece uses simple, direct language. It leaves the reader with an even more assertive comment. There is no 'if'; there is a simple command (an imperative) to 'fight', whatever the situation. Once a bear attacks, you need to fight back or you will simply die. This leaves the reader with no doubt, solely an instruction. The text tries to engage the reader but more to simply get across the key message: pay attention to the advice or you may die.
- 'The sound of undergrowth...' These sentences indicate a text that is looking to engage readers' emotions and help them picture and feel what it is like to be there. The word 'disturbed' is followed by a hyphen, which itself disturbs the sentence. Then follows descriptions appealing to the senses: 'click', 'break', 'push'. We stop and wait just like the narrator. It creates suspense. Finally, we hear the noise that really counts: the 'irritable snuffling noise'. It is still vague, in the same way that we do not yet know what it is. Soon the narrator and the reader will know. 'Bear!' This is separated on a new line and given an exclamation mark to emphasise the shock and danger and the sense of time standing still. The second text is non-fiction, but its purpose is to involve the reader almost like fiction would.

Question 3: Total marks out of 4 [_____]

....

Question 4 What are the different purposes of each text? Support your answer with at least one reference or quote from each text.

Marks:
- **1 mark** if you stated the purpose of one text.
- **2 marks** if you stated the purpose of both texts.
- **3 marks** if you stated the purpose of both texts and commented on one using evidence.

7 Comparing non-fiction

- **4 marks** if you stated the purpose of both texts and commented on both using evidence.

Example of a full 4 mark answer:

> The 'Living with bears' text is designed to explain, advise, instruct, persuade and warn readers about the dangers of bears and how to deal with them. In fact, how to survive meeting a bear. So it is not just about living with them but about living, rather than dying, after meeting them.
>
> 'If you see a bear, avoid it if you can.' The opening sentence sets the tone for the rest of the text. It is advice that is close to instruction. The purpose is to be clear and assertive. So the sentence is short, using simple, direct language that is almost monosyllabic (one syllable). It avoids inference because texts of this kind do not need inference: they do not want the reader to have to interpret what is being said. They want it clearly and quickly understood and even acted upon.
>
> 'You can't outrun a bear.' Again, the language used is simple and direct, mainly monosyllabic. It is even more emphatic. It tells the reader what to know and what to think. The purpose is to ensure the reader fully understands that there is only one thing to say about outrunning a bear: you can't! By using 'you' it seems to talk directly to the reader, almost personally.
>
> Some choice of vocabulary is designed to engage emotions or help the reader picture what it would be like to face a bear. This serves only to support the importance of the explanations and warning messages (see answer to Question 2 for examples of more emotive or descriptive language).
>
> The text from *A Walk in the Woods* is designed to involve the reader in the experience of the narrator, to describe what it was like to be there hiking peacefully only to have to face a bear, to create suspense and danger and excitement in the readers' minds.
>
> First person narrative helps make a non-fiction text feel more like a fictional text. 'So we rather gorged ourselves' makes us feel like the narrator at the time, happy, relaxed and almost complacent ('gorged' rather than 'ate').
>
> Descriptions of the incident express the build-up of threat or danger, the suspense that the narrator already knows and is trying to convey to us: 'at some indeterminate dark hour', 'made my eyes fly open'. We are drawn slowly into the moment when we and the narrator hear or see 'Bear!'

Unit 12 Track your progress in reading

Check your progress

For each question, note your mark for how well the following reading knowledge and skills have been used.

- **Q1a** ⇨ Find information and comment. (2 marks)
- **Q1b** ⇨ Find information and comment. (2 marks)
- **Q2a** ⇨ Understand what a writer infers. (2 marks)
- **Q2b** ⇨ Understand what a writer infers. (2 marks)
- **Q3** ⇨ Interpret the text. (4 marks)
- **Q4** ⇨ Evaluate the effect of language and purpose. (4 marks)

Check your total out of 12

Overall, how successful was your response to these non-fiction texts?

PARTIALLY — 4 — 10 — 16 — FULLY

Progress further

If you need to improve your reading, look again at what most needs to improve. You could then:
- look again at pages 74–81 (compare texts) and 90–131 (purpose)
- improve your responses to the questions and check your progress
- find out where you have improved and set further targets.

If your reading is high quality, congratulations! Now try this more challenging question:
- Develop your responses to Questions 3 and 4, explore and comment on the effect of one text being first person narrative, the other being more impersonal.

8 Comparing themes: *Hopes and fears*

When you have completed the questions on hopes and fears on pages 146–47, check your responses against the answers below.

Question 1a In 'Digging' there are some facts given about the poet (the 'narrator' of the poem). Find four examples of these in the poem (words, phrases or lines).

Marks:
- **1 mark** if you identified two to three facts.
- **2 marks** if you identified four facts.

Examples of facts about the narrator:
- The poet is sitting at his window, trying to write.
- He remembers his father digging 20 years ago.
- The poet remembers bringing a drink to the grandfather, 'milk in a bottle'.
- The poet does not have a spade.
- The poet is holding a pen (writing the poem with it).

Question 1a: marks out of 2 [_____]

Question 1b In 'Nettles' there are some facts given about the poet. Find three examples of these in the poem (words, phrases or lines).

Marks:
- **1 mark** if you identified up to two facts.
- **2 marks** if you identified three facts.

Examples of facts about the poet:
- He had a son.
- He saw 'white blisters' on the son's skin.
- He had a billhook.
- He used the billhook to 'slash' the nettles.
- He burned the nettles.

Question 1b: marks out of 2 [_____]

Question 2a In 'Digging' identify and explain evidence from which you can infer that the poet has strong affection for his father and grandfather.

Marks:
- **1 mark** if you identified evidence accurately.
- **2 marks** if you identified evidence and explained its meaning accurately.

Example of a full 2 mark answer:

> The affection he has for the two men shows in the middle of the poem:
>
> 'By God, the old man could handle a spade.
>
> Just like his old man.'
>
> The phrase 'By God' shows that the poet admires what the men were like and what they could do. It even affects how we read 'old man' with a respectful tone. It is followed by a statement that has pride in it. 'My grandfather cut more turf... Than any other man...' This pride is repeated in 'men like them'.

Question 2a: marks out of 2 [_____]

Question 2b In 'Nettles', identify and explain evidence from which you can infer that the poet has strong affection or love for his son.

Marks:
- **1 mark** if you identified evidence accurately.
- **2 marks** if you identified evidence and explained its meaning accurately.

Example of a 2 mark answer:

- The love he feels for his son is revealed in 'We soothed till his pain was not so raw'. He took action to take away the boy's hurt. The poet's next response, to slash the nettles and burn them, is expressed so violently ('slashed in fury') that it feels like he wants revenge for the hurt that has been done to his son. Towards the end of the poem he seems saddened that his son will 'feel sharp wounds again'. His love for the child can only go so far, he cannot protect the boy forever.

Question 2b: marks out of 2 [_____]

8 Comparing themes: *Hopes and fears*

Question 3 Both poems explore a memory of an event from the past. Each poet finds this memory important for his own life. Identify from the text where the narrator says how important it is and explain why.

Marks:
- **2 marks** if you described or quoted evidence from both poems.
- **3 marks** if you also explored the significance of the evidence in one poem.
- **4 marks** if you explored the significance of the evidence in both poems.

Example of a full 4 mark answer:

> In 'Digging', the poet remembers his father and grandfather digging the earth, working with their spades to dig the potatoes and the turf. At the opening of the poem the poet is revealed as a writer, with his 'squat pen' resting between his 'finger and thumb'. He is sitting at 'my window', perhaps trying to write but not yet succeeding, as the pen 'rests'. By the end of the poem, he decides that although he has not got a spade to dig, he does have a pen. He will 'dig with it', by which he implies that he too can work hard and seek truth in life by using his writing to explore the world. This is a positive message of hope, that he will continue the good work of his family.
>
> In 'Nettles', the poet remembers his son falling and hurting himself in a nettle bed. He soothes his son's hurt and 'in fury' takes revenge on the nettles by slashing and burning them in 'a funeral pyre'. This seems to stand for any time when a parent wants to protect their child against the world's dangers. The violence he metes out to the nettles is like the violence that waits to harm children. At the end of the poem, however, the 'busy sun and rain' have brought out more nettles, 'tall recruits behind the shed'. So the world's dangers will not simply go away: they grow again. The last line is one of sadness, of fear that he cannot and will not always be able to protect his son from harm:
>
> 'My son would often feel sharp wounds again'

Question 3: marks out of 4 [_____]

Unit 12 Track your progress in reading

Question 4 Explain and comment on the way both poets use language effectively to explore the physical nature of the events they remember. Focus on at least two examples in each poem

Marks:
- **2 marks** if you described or quoted evidence from both poems.
- **3 marks** if you also explored the significance of the evidence in one poem.
- **4 marks** if you explored the significance of the evidence in both poems.

Examples of effective use of language to explore the physical nature of events in 'Digging':

- We hear a 'clean rasping sound' as the spade 'sinks' into the 'gravelly' ground. This captures the sounds and actions of digging – 'rasping', 'gravelly' – through words that seem to reflect their meaning in their sound (onomatopoeia). It also reflects the effort: 'sinks'.
- The 'straining rump' of the father gives us a picture of his body moving in hard work.
- The boot 'nestled' on the spade, giving us a detailed image of how the boot fits snugly in the space designed for it. This is followed by a similar image of the handle of the spade being 'levered firmly', fitting inside the knee.
- Heaney uses a series of physical, active words to describe the actions of digging. The sounds of the words reflect the actions and sounds of digging: 'nicking', 'slicing', 'heaving'.
- Heaney also uses similar words to describe how things feel and look: 'squelch', 'slap'.

Examples of effective use of language to explore the physical nature of events in 'Nettles':

- With 'white blisters beaded on his tender skin' the poet describes how his son's skin looks ('white', blistered, 'beaded') and feels (blistered, 'beaded', and not smooth like a young child's skin anymore).
- The word 'raw' has a harsh quality to it. We can feel the hurt skin of the boy.
- The phrase 'watery grin' gives us a picture of a little boy's face wet with tears yet managing a grin.
- Words like 'slashed in fury' provide an image of the narrator's angry movements with the billhook. The word 'slashed' reflects the sound as the billhook is brought down on the nettles.

Question 4: marks out of 4 [_____]

8 Comparing themes: *Hopes and fears*

Check your progress

For each question, note your mark for how well the following reading knowledge and skills have been used.

Q1a ⇨ Find factual information. (2 marks)

Q1b ⇨ Find factual information. (2 marks)

Q2a ⇨ Understand what a writer implies through language. (2 marks)

Q2b ⇨ Understand what a writer implies through language. (2 marks)

Q3 ⇨ Interpret the meaning of events for the writer or reader. (4 marks)

Q4 ⇨ Evaluate the effect of language and purpose. (4 marks)

Check your total out of 16

Overall, how successful was your response to these poems?

PARTIALLY — 4 — 10 — 16 — FULLY

Progress further

If you need to improve your reading, look again at what most needs to improve. You could then:
- look again at pages 82–89 (respond to texts) and 50–61 (language)
- improve your responses to the questions and check your progress
- find out where you have improved and set further targets.

If your reading is high quality, congratulations! Now try this more challenging question:
- The events in both poems are remembered as significant by the narrator. Explore and explain how they have a 'universal' significance, in that the events tell us about important lessons in life.

Glossary

Active voice: Writing in the active voice means constructing sentences where the subject 'acts', e.g. 'I ate the sandwich.' Sentences in the active voice are direct and it is clear who is doing what.

Alliteration: The use of repeated consonant sounds, usually at the beginnings of words.

Analysis: Where you think carefully about some information, or about how a text has been written, breaking it down in order to understand it better.
- An **analysis essay** is where you write a careful argument to support your views, using evidence to back up what you conclude.

Annotate: Make brief notes on a text in order to highlight certain features.

Argument: In argumentative writing, the writer chooses which facts to present in order to present a case or argue for one point of view.

Assonance: The repetition of vowel sounds to create internal rhyming within phrases or sentences, for example:

'Somet**i**me too hot the **eye** of heaven sh**i**nes.'

Atmosphere: The mood, emotion or feeling that is conveyed by the setting in a story. A writer creates the sense of a particular place so that the reader can almost experience it for themselves.

Autobiography: A life story written in the first person.

Bias: A one-sided view of an issue, which doesn't present a balanced view of the topic.

Biography: A life story written in the third person, by someone who has access to a person's life.

Clause: A group of words that expresses a complete idea, usually consisting of a subject, verb and object.
- **Conditional subordinate clauses** begin with *if* or *unless*, for example:

  '**Unless** you leave now, I will call the police.'
- A **main clause** is a clause that can stand by itself (also known as a simple sentence). A main clause contains a subject and a predicate; it makes sense by itself.
- A **subordinate clause** is a clause that cannot stand on its own as a sentence.

Compare: Identify similarities and differences in two or more texts, and analyse the different ways in which each text achieves its purpose and effects.

Connotation: The idea or feeling that a word suggests in addition to its actual meaning.

Context: The situation in which a text is written, e.g. historical context, political context.

Culture: The shared language, traditions and beliefs of a group of people.

Deduce: Search for relevant information in a text and then draw conclusions about what must definitely be true about the character, place, situation, and so on.

Glossary

Denotation: The literal, actual meaning of a word in its context.

Emotive language: Emotive language aims to get an emotional response. It can be serious, as in charity appeals, or it can use a lighter approach to express a viewpoint.

Essay: A piece of writing that is usually written from the author's personal point of view.
- In an **expository essay**, you 'expose' your ideas and feelings and explain them interestingly.
- A **narrative essay** tells a true story, for example, an account of an experience.

Explanation: A text that explains usually presents some facts, but unlike a simple information text, it shows how they relate to each other. It is likely to do one of two things:
- enable the reader to understand an idea or concept
- present a process, showing a sequence of cause and effect.

Fact: Something that is clearly true, and can be proved to be so.

Fiction: Any work that deals, in part or in whole, with information or events that are not factual, but imaginary – invented by the author.

Formality: In writing, the use of formal expressions and standard written grammar. Formal writing tends to make more use of subordinated sentences, and uses more formal vocabulary, avoiding colloquial expressions.

Infer: Work out from hints or clues in a text what is likely to be true about a character, place or situation. This is called 'making an inference'.

Informality: Informal writing is closer to spoken language. It may include more colloquial expressions, such as slang, figures of speech, asides and so on. Informal writing takes a personal tone as if the writer were speaking directly to the audience (the reader).

Information texts: Information texts present facts and ideas in a clear and logical way. They are usually written in the present tense.

Instructions: An instructional text uses precise language and imperative verbs, and breaks information up into well-ordered steps. Instructional texts often combine words with pictures or diagrams.

Internal rhyme: Rhyming words occurring in the middle of a line rather than just at the end, for example:

'As if a r**ose** should cl**ose** and be a bud again.'

Interpret: To explain or tell the meaning of something that may not be immediately obvious. When you write an 'interpretation', you explain your views about a text and its meaning to you.

Literary heritage: 'Literary heritage' is a term for the literature from the best authors who wrote in the past, and which has 'lasting appeal'. These works have continued to be popular and valued long after the time when they were written.

Literary text: Any text that requires the reader to think and use their imagination, and which often leads to an emotional response. These are texts that are seen as having value because of what they have to say, and the quality of the way they are written and their ability to entertain (sometimes described as their 'artistic quality').

Metaphor: A word picture that brings something to life by describing it as if it is something else that is similar in at least one way but different in others. For example:

'You are a brick wall over which I must climb in order to succeed.'

Glossary

Narrative voice: Who is telling the story. This can be the writer, or a character in the story (*see* **Point of view**).
- A story written in the **first person** is told by one of the characters using *I, me, my*. This can make the story seem very vivid and immediate. As the narrator tells the story, they can express something of their own character.
- A story written in the **third person** is told by the writer, who can express what all the characters think and feel.

Non-fiction: Writing that deals with real events, issues and people. 'Literary non-fiction' does this in artistic and imaginative ways (*see* **Literary text**).

Non-literary text: Non-literary texts are informational writing, e.g. factual material, explanations, newspaper articles, textbooks, journal and diary entries. They are published in newspapers, magazines and current affairs journals, for example.

Onomatopoeia: The use of words that echo the sound they describe, e.g. *buzz, fizz, crash*.

Opinion: An author's view on a subject, backed up by reasons, examples and evidence.

Paragraph: A self-contained, coherent 'chunk' of meaning made up of several sentences dealing with a particular point, topic or idea.

Passive voice: Sentences where the subject is 'passive' – it is acted upon, rather than being the agent of action. e.g. 'Petrol prices were increased this year by 10 per cent.' The passive is used in more formal writing, or to 'hide' the 'agent' (who was doing the action).

Personification: Describes an abstract thing or idea as if it were a living thing. For example:

> 'The wolves of hunger howl outside the poor man's door.'

Perspective: In writing, 'perspective' is the view or outlook of a text or a writer on a particular issue or topic (*see* **Point of view**).

Persuasion: A persuasive text seeks to make the reader do or believe something. It employs a range of techniques to argue a particular point of view, or to make the reader want to act – these are often called 'persuasive devices'.

Point of view: A text can be written from one 'point of view' – in other words showing what happens from one perspective, which could be that of a character, or a narrator, or the writer (*see* **Narrative voice** *and* **Perspective**).

Quotation: A short extract, inside inverted commas, that is used as evidence when you are analysing a text.

Recount: A non-fiction text that tells the facts or the true story of something. Usually told using the past tense, and in chronological (time) sequence. Many newspaper reports are 'recounts'.

Resolution: In literature, this is the point in the story where a conflict or a plot line reaches its conclusion.

Rhetoric: The art and study of how to write and speak effectively and convincingly.
- Writers use a range of **rhetorical techniques** – such as repetition, making a point with three words or phrases, using lists – to drive home an argument or to convey their meaning with impact.

Rhyme: Repetition of similar sounds in two or more words, usually at the end of lines in poems or songs.

Glossary

Rhythm: A musical quality in writing made up of a series of repeated beats in words.

Scan: Search carefully for a specific piece of information, or a word or phrase, by running your eyes over the text, using features such as headings to help.

Sentence: One or more words that make sense on their own, and are linked together by their grammar. Most sentences contain a finite verb.
- **Single-clause sentences** contain one main clause. They are usually made up of a subject, verb and object.
- **Multi-clause sentences** contain two or more clauses linked by coordination or subordination.
- **Coordination: Sentences** with more than one main clause, usually joined by a coordinating conjunction, e.g. *and, but, or*.
- **Subordination: Sentences** with a main clause (a phrase that makes complete sense on its own) and one or more subordinate clauses (which depend on the main clause to make sense).
- **Cumulative sentences** are long sentences based on an independent clause, to which detail is added by several subordinate clauses or phrases, so that meaning accumulates.

Simile: A simile is a kind of word picture, also known as a figure of speech. It brings something to life by comparing it with something that is similar in at least one important way, but different in others. For example:

> 'A rugby player since childhood, Davies had **legs like oak trees**.'

Skim: Get the overall sense of what a text is about and what is in it (the 'gist') by running your eyes across the whole text.

Stanza: An alternative word for a 'verse' in a poem: a group of two or more lines that often have a set pattern of rhyme, rhythm, or number of lines.

Structure: The ways in which the different parts of a text are organised.
- **Continuous text** is written in sentences and paragraphs.
- **Non-continuous text** is presented in formats such as lists, bullet points, diagrams, tables, etc.

Style: 'Style' in writing refers to the overall way that a text is written, e.g. how a story is told or an argument presented. It includes all the key features of the writing, such as point of view, word choice, grammar, use of imagery.

Summary: A shortened version of a text containing the most important information.

Symbol: A word or group of words that stands for another idea. For example, the colour black can be said to symbolise death or evil, and white to symbolise purity or innocence, etc. Writers often use symbols to hint at or suggest another idea rather than stating it outright.

Synthesis: The pulling together of different ideas into a single explanation or account.

Tension: Meaning literally 'to pull something tight', in literature (or, for example, film) it refers to the way a story can build up gradually to a climax, so that the reader 'feels' tense as they read.

Theme: A subject or idea that a text is about.

Tone: The emotional quality of a piece of writing, e.g. angry, comic, sympathetic.